HUMAN RESOURCE MANAGEMENT

HUMAN RESOURCE MANAGEMENT

**DEREK TORRINGTON • LAURA HALL
STEPHEN TAYLOR • CAROL ATKINSON**

NINTH EDITION

Harlow, England • London • New York • Boston • San Francisco • Toronto • Sydney
Auckland • Singapore • Hong Kong • Tokyo • Seoul • Taipei • New Delhi
Cape Town • São Paulo • Mexico City • Madrid • Amsterdam • Munich • Paris • Milan

Pearson Education Limited
Edinburgh Gate
Harlow CM20 2JE
United Kingdom
Tel: +44 (0)1279 623623
Web: **www.pearson.com/uk**

First published in Great Britain under the Prentice Hall Europe imprint in 1987 (print)
Second edition published in 1991 (print)
Third edition published 1995 (print)
Fourth edition published 1998 (print)
Fifth edition published 2002 (print)
Sixth edition published 2005 (print)
Seventh edition published 2008 (print)
Eighth edition published 2011 (print)
Ninth edition published 2014 (print and electronic)

© Pearson Education Limited 2011 (print)
© Pearson Education Limited 2014 (print and electronic)

ISBN: 978-0-273-78663-4 (print)
       978-0-273-78668-9 (PDF)
       978-0-273-78664-1 (eText)

British Library Cataloguing-in-Publication Data
A catalogue record for the print edition is available from the British Library

Library of Congress Cataloging-in-Publication Data
A catalog record for the print edition is available from the Library of Congress

10 9 8 7 6 5 4 3
18 17 16 15

Print edition typeset in 10/12.5pt Sabon MT Std by 35
Print edition printed and bound by L.E.G.O. S.p.A. Italy

NOTE THAT ANY PAGE CROSS REFERENCES REFER TO THE PRINT EDITION

Brief contents

Contents

Contents

Guided tour

Learning Objectives work in conjunction with the chapter-ending Summary Propositions to quickly show you what you will learn about in the chapter and help you compare how well you have understood the learning you undertake.

Window on practice boxes provide you with examples of real organisational practice, survey results, anecdotes and quotations and court cases, helping you to build up your knowledge of real-World practice and prepare you for life after study.

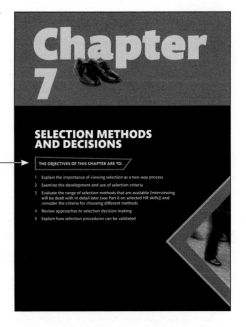

Chapter 7

SELECTION METHODS AND DECISIONS

THE OBJECTIVES OF THIS CHAPTER ARE TO:

1 Explain the importance of viewing selection as a two-way process
2 Examine the development and use of selection criteria
3 Evaluate the range of selection methods that are available (interviewing will be dealt with in detail later (see Part 8 on selected HR skills)) and consider the criteria for choosing different methods
4 Review approaches to selection decision making
5 Explain how selection procedures can be validated

Activity boxes encourage you to regularly review and critically apply your learning, either as an individual or within a group. These have been developed for both students with little or no business experience, as well as though with more practical knowledge.

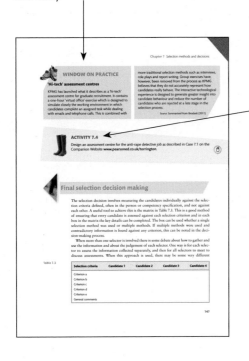

Regular **quotes** throughout help to enliven and contextualise the subject.

Summary Propositions provide a useful revision tool enabling you to recap and check your understanding of the chapter. In conjunction with the chapter-opening Learning Objectives, you can quickly determine whether you are prepared enough to move on, or need further study.

General Discussion Topics are useful both as a basis for group discussion within tutorials or study groups, as well as activities to help develop your better understanding of the topics covered within the chapter.

Theory into Practice case studies or learning activities that enable you to put your learning into practice within a realistic scenario. Improve your employability by answering the associated questions and developing a better understanding of business practice.

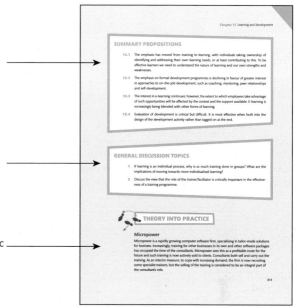

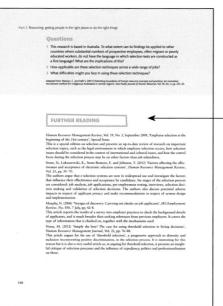

Further Reading sections provide guided access to some key readings in the area, help you to further develop your skills and learning.

Chapter 26 Health and well-being

WEB LINKS

www.ibm.com/ibm/responsibility/employee_well_being_management.shtml (IBM website, section on corporate social responsibility, accessed 24 March 2013).
www.ibm.com/ibm/responsibility/employees_global_wellness.shtml (IBM website, section on international wellness initiatives, accessed 24 March 2013).
www.investorsinpeople.co.uk (website of Investors in People, accessed 24 March 2013).
www.well-being.ac.uk (website of well-being funded by the HEFCE and the Scottish Funding Council to investigate and promote well-being in higher education, accessed 24 March 2013).
www.workandwell-being.com (website of Work and Well-being Ltd, a consultancy, accessed 24 March 2013).
www.dwp.gov.uk/health-work-and-well-being/about-us/ (accessed 24 March 2013).

REFERENCES

Allen, K., Shantz, A. and Truss, C. (2012) 'The link between perceived HRM practices, performance and well-being: The moderating effect of trust in the employer', *Human Resource Management Journal*, Vol. 22, pp. 409–27.
Atkinson, C. and Hall, L. (2011) 'Flexible working and happiness in the NHS', *Employee Relations*, Vol. 33, pp. 88–105.
CIPD (2007) *What's Happening with Wellbeing at Work?* London: CIPD.
CIPD (2008) *Smart Working: The impact of work organisation and job design*. London: CIPD.
CIPD (2012) *Building a Culture of Organisational Well-being*. London: CIPD.
CIPD (2013) *Health and Well-being at Work: Factsheet*. London: CIPD.
Cooney, R. (2004) 'Empowered self-management and the design of work teams', *Personnel Review*, Vol. 33, pp. 677–92.
Crush, P. (2009) 'Health and well-being: The science of employee well-being', *Human Resources*, 1 July.
De Woorde, K., Paauwe, J. and van Veldhoven, M. (2012) 'Employee well-being and the HRM–organisational performance relationship: A review of quantitative studies', *International Journal of Management Reviews*, Vol. 14, pp. 391–407.
DH (2004) *Choosing Health: Making healthy choices easier*, Cm 6374. London: The Stationery Office.
Greasley, K., Edwards, P., Baker-McClearn, D. and Dale, J. (2012) 'Why do organisations engage in HR initiatives? A test case of a health and well-being intervention', *Employee Relations*, Vol. 34, pp. 443–62.
Hall, L. and Atkinson, C. (2006) 'Improving working lives: Flexible working and the role of employee control', *Employee Relations*, Vol. 28, pp. 374–86.
Holman, D. (2002) 'Employer well-being in call centres', *Human Resource Management Journal*, Vol. 12, pp. 35–50.
HSE (2004) *Management Standards for Work-related Stress*. London: Health and Safety Executive.
HSE (2009) *How to Tackle Work-related Stress: A guide for employers on making the Management Standards work*. London: Health and Safety Executive.
Krazman, J. (2013) 'Putting feedback-seeking into "context": Job characteristics and feedback-seeking behaviour', *Personnel Review*, Vol. 42, pp. 50–66.
Marsden, D. and Moriconi, S. (2009) 'The value of rude health: Employees' well being, absence and workplace performance', *CEP Discussion Paper No. 919*. London: Centre for Economic Performance.

527

A detailed **Glossary** is included at the end of the book, for quick reference to key terms and definitions within each chapter.

Some chapters list relevant **Web Links** that can help expand your understanding of the topics covered within the chapter.

Detailed **References** provide quick and easy access to the research behind the chapter and additional sources of information to support your learning.

Glossary

The terms in this glossary have been taken selectively from the text. Rather than repeating definitions we have already given, we have chosen terms which are neologisms that may not appear in a dictionary, or are invented words, like presenteeism, which do not yet appear in a dictionary. We also include terms, like bureaucracy, which can benefit from more interpretation than we have provided in the text.

Absence/attendance. Until quite recently attendance at work was universally accepted as a duty and absence had to be justified by external verification, such as by a medical note or a call to undertake jury service. Without such independent evidence, some sort of punishment was usual. As social attitudes have changed and rights to time off have increased, so the managerial emphasis has changed, requiring managers to manage attendance, by paying attention to reasons for avoidable absence. This has a degree of altruistic concern for employee well-being, where some aspect of the work required from employees is a contributory cause of, for instance, an inability to return to work. There is also an emphasis on trying to minimise disruption to working patterns and persuading people not to be unreasonable. Stress has become a major absence factor since it has become more socially acceptable. Usually it is a perfectly valid feature of a person's working or personal life and can perhaps be alleviated by managerial initiatives. In some other situations it is manipulated by people who place their own interpretation on a right to sick leave. A recent visit to an engineering drawing office in March was surprising as more than half the

staff were missing. The drawing office manager explained that the absentees were 'getting in their sick leave' before the end of the leave year. A management attempt to make allowance for understandable sickness absence had been mismanaged in allowing it to become gradually accepted as an additional leave entitlement. In a different, current situation a school teacher has recently shown such unwillingness to implement new professional requirements that there is a risk of the school implementing capability procedure with the response, 'if they do that I will simply go off with stress'.

Apprenticeship. The typical idea of an apprentice is of a male who left school as soon as possible and then trained on the job in a manual trade like plumbing or as an electrician, possibly continuing education part time at a local college. Since a university degree has gradually become the must-have qualification for many fields of employment, the number of apprentices has dwindled: certainly not a prelude to a 'nice job'. Currently they are seeing a renaissance, as skills shortages are seen as an impediment to economic growth, but not necessarily for young males. In 2013 more than

half of those pursuing an apprenticeship were over 25.

Benchmarking. Originally a benchmark was a mark on a work bench that could be used to measure off a standard size. This idea of comparative measurement is used in HRM to describe the process of checking some aspect of work in one's own business against an external standard, like the average number of days lost through absence across the working population as a whole, or in a particular industry, by age, occupation, gender and so forth. It is slightly different from 'yardstick', which is literally a measuring stick a yard long. This is sometimes used as a rough-and-ready measure for some aspect of management effectiveness, but it lacks the dimension of external comparison.

Best fit/fit. In many fields of human endeavour there is an aim to find and implement the one best way, or the right way, of doing things. An alternative is to work out the best way of doing things in this or that situation. There is no single approach or method that is always right.

Bottom line. A term derived from accountancy, where it is the final

645

Preface

This book has been evolving through many changes since the very first edition of its predecessor *Personnel Management* in 1979. Our objective has always been to track the development of the personnel/ human resource (HR) function and its activities. Our preface to the eighth edition in 2011 opened by saying: 'Since the last edition the world has undergone a major recession, triggered by a banking crisis unprecedented in modern times. This has created great uncertainty about how human resource management (HRM) will be changed.' Then, many people still assumed that it would be like other recessions, followed by a steady recovery, renewed growth and we would all feel more secure. Three years on we can be more certain of some changes that will continue for the foreseeable future:

1 Rather than becoming more secure, for most people their *experience of employment will be less secure*. 'Jobs for life' had always been rare, but security of employment in terms of an open-ended contract that would be maintained in most cases for as long as the employee wished has slowly become less. Some businesses that experience sharp variations in demand for their products, like some in electronics, are employing certain categories of staff on fixed-term contracts via a consultancy in order to avoid the costs of making people redundant. This is just one example of subcontracting instead of directly employing people. Alongside this is the great change in pension provision. Outside the public sector, final salary schemes have dwindled to a handful and the contemporary substitutes are more likely to be owned by the employee, with a reduced level of dependence on the individual employer. Some companies rise and fall with breathtaking speed. In April 2012 Google bought a British IT company for $1 billion. The company had a single product, had been in existence for little over a year and employed only thirteen people. How can a company of that size be worth $1 billion? At the same time we see sudden failures, like HMV, Sea France, Comet and Hungarian Airlines.

2 The *shift towards the 'disaggregation' of employment in businesses* has increased. In 1984 John Atkinson published a short paper with a clever illustrative figure that identified a move towards businesses having a core workforce of vital people who were well paid and built into the businesses, surrounded by a peripheral workforce, with jobs requiring skills that were not specific to the business and might be directly employed or employed via an agency or as a sole trader. This attracted great interest and hundreds of HR lecturers reckoned that they could run at least three teaching sessions on the paper! Atkinson had described a process that had been going for some time and gave it a nudge. Subcontracting of staff in catering, office cleaning and security became commonplace and retail distribution is now normally subcontracted. The development of using the Internet for marketing has seen a great increase in the number of sole traders or very small businesses providing specialist services. In the UK in 2012, 74% of private-sector businesses were sole traders without employees and 3.8 million people were working from home. The general assumption that a business is a close-knit community of people who spend most of their time in one location with an organisational culture that generates morale and meets employees' needs to belong is no longer quite as universal as organisational studies have suggested.

3 *Levels of public-sector employment will remain depressed*. Together with most western economies, it has been an objective of the UK government to reduce the number of people in permanent employment in the public sector as part of an overall objective to rebalance the economy in favour

of the private sector. This has only partly succeeded, as much of the cost saving has been in reducing payments to arm's length organisations and charities providing services, rather than reducing the number on permanent contracts. Nonetheless growth of public-sector core employment seems unlikely after sustained growth over the last 60-70 years.

This is not to suggest that there has been a fundamental and complete change in employment practice; rather there is a change in the mix of factors to which HRM has to adapt and this will be a continuing feature in our approach to the subject in this edition. In preparing this edition we have analysed trends, reviewed the changes, examined all the novelties before discussing these among ourselves and taken account of the comments that many people using the book have suggested. This is to ensure that the book continues to reflect the reality of working life as it is evolving rather than how we would like it to be. We also have to ensure that the book makes sense to readers in different parts of the world, although the book remains the work of four Britons, whose work and understanding are inevitably informed by experience, research and scholarship mainly in the western world.

Apart from general updating, the main changes since the last edition are that we include a new pedagogical feature called 'Theory into practice' at the end of most chapters. These features are case studies or some other learning aid, as suggested by our publisher; we have removed the cases that previously closed each of the eight parts of the book. There are three fewer chapters overall through consolidation in some areas. Skills now include a section on job analysis, which had been unforgivably not featured in the last edition, despite its fundamental importance in so many aspects of HR practice.

As before, there is a range of assessment material and illustrations, as well as several design features to assist readers further in using and learning from the text, as follows:

(a) Integrated **Window on practice** boxes provide a range of illustrative material throughout the text, including examples of real company practice, survey results, anecdotes and quotations, and court cases.

(b) Integrated **Activity** boxes encourage readers to review and critically apply their understanding at regular intervals throughout the text, either by responding to a question or by undertaking a small practical assignment, individually or as part of a group. In recognising that this text is used on both professional and academic courses, most of the exercises reflect the fact that many students will have little or no business experience. Other exercises may appear to exclude students who are not in employment by asking readers to consider an aspect in their own organisation; however, the organisation could be a college or university, the students' union, a political body or sports team.

(c) **Discussion topics**: at the end of each chapter there are two or three short questions intended for general discussion in a tutorial or study group.

(d) **Theory into practice** features appear at the end of chapters to enable readers to review, link and apply their understanding of the previous chapters to a business scenario.

(e) **Web links** are given as appropriate at various points in the text. These are either to the text's Companion Website, where there is a great deal of further material, or to other websites containing useful information relating to the topics covered.

(f) **Further reading sections** for each chapter suggest further relevant readings, with guidance on their value.

(g) Each part of the text includes a brief introduction to its scope and purpose.

(h) **Chapter objectives** open and **Summary propositions** conclude each chapter to set up the readers' expectations and review their understanding progressively.

(i) **References** are given in full at the end of each chapter to aid further exploration of the chapter material, as required.

(j) The Companion Website, **www.pearsoned.co.uk/torrington**, has more material, including further case studies or exercises for each chapter and support for both tutor and student.

(k) **Glossary**: the book closes with a short glossary of terms taken selectively from the text.

Publisher's acknowledgements

Figures

Figure 3.2 from *Strategic human resource management* (Fombrun, C., Tichy, N.M. and Devanna, M.A. 1984) p. 41, John Wiley, New York, Reproduced with permission of John Wiley & Sons Inc.; Figure 3.3 from 'Front-line managers as agents in the HRM performance causal chain: theory, analysis and evidence', *Human Resource Management Journal*, Vol. 17, No. 1, pp. 3–20 (Purcell, J. and Hutchinson, S. 2007), p. 7, Figure 1, reproduced with permission of Wiley-Blackwell, Reproduced with permission of Wiley-Blackwell; Figure 3.4 adapted from Purcell, J., Kinnie, N., Hutchinson, S., Rayton, B. and Swart, J. (2003) Understanding the People Performance Link: Unlocking the black box. Research Report. London: CIPD, Model developed by Bath University for the CIPD. Reproduced with the permission of the publisher, the Chartered Institute of Personnel and Development, London (www.cipd.co.uk); Figure 3.5 from 'Human resources and sustained competitive advantage: a resource-based perspective', *International Journal of Human Resource Management*, Vol. 5, No. 2, p. 318 (Wright, P.M., McMaham, G.C., and A. McWilliams), reprinted with the permission of Taylor and Francis Ltd, www.tandf.co.uk/journals; Figure 4.5 adapted from 'The balanced scorecard: measures that drive performance', *Harvard Business Review*, January/February, pp. 71–9 (Kaplan, R. and Norton, D. 1992); Figure 5.1 from Smart Working: The impact of work organisation and job design, CIPD (2008), p. 11, Figure 2. With permission of the publisher, Chartered Institute of Personnel and Development, London (www.cipd.co.uk), Reproduced with the permission of the publisher, the Chartered Institute of Personnel and Development, London (www.cipd.co.uk); Figure 5.2 from 'Manpower strategies for flexible organisation', *Personnel Management*, August, 28–9 (Atkinson, J. 1984); Figure 13.1 from Binney, G. and Williams, C. (2005) 'The myth of managing change', in G. Salaman, J. Storey and J. Billsberry (eds), Strategic Human Resource Management: Theory and practice. A reader. London: Sage, Reprinted by permission of SAGE Publications www.sagepub.co.uk; Figure 17.1 from Marchington, M. and Cox, A. (2007) 'Employee involvement and participation', in: Storey, J. (ed.) Human Resource Management: A Critical Text. 3rd edn. London: Thomson Learning, Figure 10.1, p. 179, Copyright (2007) Thomson Learning. Reproduced by permission of Cengage Learning EMEA Ltd; Figure 26.1 from Chartered Institute of Personnel and Development (2008) Smart working: the impact of work organisation and job design, London: CIPD.

Tables

Table 3.1 from 'Linking competitive strategies with human resource management practices', No. 3, August (Schuler, R.S. and Jackson, S.E. 1987), reproduced with permission of the Academy of Management; Table 5.1 from 'Organisational learning and organisational design', *The Learning Organisation*, Vol. 13, No. 1, pp. 25–48 (Curado, C. 2006), The Learning Organisation, p. 38, © Emerald Group Publishing Limited all rights reserved; Table 6.1 from 'What is (or should be) the difference between competency modelling and traditional job analysis?' *Human Resource Management Review*, Vol. 19, No. 1, pp. 53–63 (Sanchez, J. and Levine, E. 2009); Table 6.2 from Table compiled from data in CIPD (2012) Resourcing and Talent Planning: Annual Survey Report 2012. London: CIPD, Reproduced with the permission of the publisher, the Chartered Institute of Personnel and Development, London (www.cipd.co.uk); Table 7.1 from Chartered Institute of Personnel and Development (2011) Resourcing and Talent Planning: Annual Survey Report 2011, Table 13. With permission of the publisher, the Chartered Institute of Personnel and Development, London (www.cipd.co.uk); Table 11.1 from *The Managerial Grid. Houston, Texas: Gulf Publishing* (Blake, R.R. and Mouton, J.S. 1964); Table 11.3 from 'Leadership that gets results', *Harvard Business Review*, March–April, pp. 80 & 82–3 (Goleman, D. 2000), reprinted by permission of by the Harvard Business School Publishing Corporation. All rights reserved; Table 15.1 after *Major learning trends and indicators for 2013 and beyond within the Asia Pacific Region*, Singapore: Cegos (Blain, J. 2013) Figure 18, p. 27; Table 15.2 adapted from 'Planned and emergent learning: a framework and a method', *Executive Development*, Vol. 7, No. 6, pp. 29–32 (Megginson, D. 1994), © Emerald Group Publishing Limited all rights reserved; Table 15.3 after *Major learning trends and indicators for 2013 and beyond within the Asia Pacific Region*, Singapore: Cegos (Blain, J. 2013) Figure 22, p. 32; Table 26.1 from From What's Happening with Wellbeing at Work? (CIPD, 2007), Table 2. With permission of the publisher, the Chartered Institute of Personnel and Development, London (www.cipd.co.uk), Reproduced with the permission of the publisher, the Chartered Institute of Personnel and Development, London (www.cipd.co.uk); Table 27.1 from *Culture's Consequences: International Differences in Work-Related Values*, 2nd, California: Sage Publications (Hofstede, G. 2001), Reproduced by permission of Geert Hofstede.

Text

Case Study on page 46 adapted from Build a better brand, *People Management*, Vol. 14, No. 15, pp. 24–5 (Chubb, L.), Reproduced with the permission of the publisher, the Chartered Institute of Personnel and Development, London (www.cipd.co.uk); Case Study on page 54 adapted from 'Human resource management strategies under uncertainty', *Cross Cultural Management: An International Journal*, Vol. 13, No. 2, pp. 171–86 (Fields, D., Chan, A., Aktar, S. and Blum, T. 2006), © Emerald Group Publishing Limited all rights reserved; Case Study on page 68 adapted from 'Who does workforce planning well?: Workforce Rapid Review Team Summary', *International Journal of Health Care Quality Assurance* Vol. 23, No. 1, pp. 110–19 (Curson, J., Dell, M., Wilson, R., Bosworth, D. and Baldauf, B. 2010), © Emerald Group Publishing Limited all rights reserved; Case Study on pages 81–82 after 'Human capital measurement: an approach that works', *Strategic HR Review*, Vol. 8, No. 6, pp. 5–11 (Robinson, D. 2009), © Emerald Group Publishing Limited all rights reserved; Case Study on pages 128–129 after 'Globalisation of HR at function level: 4 UK-based case studies of the international recruitment and selection process' *International Journal of Human Resource Management* Vol. 8, No. 5, pp. 845–867 (Sparrow, P. 2007), reprinted by permission of the publisher (Taylor & Francis Ltd, http://www.tandf.co.uk/journals); Case Study on page 223 after The Lizard Kings, *People Management*, Vol. 12(2), pp. 32–34 (Goffee, R. and Jones, G. 2006), Reproduced with the permission of the publisher, the Chartered Institute of Personnel and Development, London (www.cipd.co.uk); Case Study on page 226 adapted from Ford, J. and Harding, N. (2009) 'Telling an untold story: on being a follower rather than a leader'. Presented at the 25th EGOS Colloquium in Barcelona, Spain, July 2–4, 2009, By permission of Professor Jackie Ford and Professor Nancy Harding; Case Study on page 320 after 'Bright and Early', *People Management*, Vol. 14, No. 7, pp. 30–2 (Allen, A.), Reproduced with the permission of the publisher, the Chartered Institute of Personnel and Development, London (www.cipd.co.uk); Case Study on page 322 adapted from 'Hidden dragons' *People Management*, Vol. 14, No. 16, pp. 18–23 (Wilson, B.), Reproduced with the permission of the publisher, the Chartered Institute of Personnel and Development, London (www.cipd.co.uk); Extract on page 328 from 'On my agenda' *People Management*, August, pp. 28–31 (Smedley, T. 2012); Quote on page 329 from www.ernstandyoung.com; Box on page 346 adapted from Keeping the Commitment Model in the Air during Turbulent Times: Employee Involvement at Delta Air Lines Industrial Relations, *Industrial Relations*, 52, pp. 343–77 (Kaufman, B. 2013), © 2012 Regents of the University of California; Article on page 429 from Pandora's Pay Packet, *FT.com*, 14/05/2001 (Kellaway, L.), © The Financial Times Limited. All Rights Reserved; General Displayed Text on page 468 after *Reward Management: Annual Survey Report 2009*, London: Chartered Institute of Personnel and Development (CIPD 2009), Reproduced with the permission of the publisher, the Chartered Institute of Personnel and Development, London (www.cipd.co.uk); Extract on pages 474–475 from 'Four scenarios', *Journal of Medical Ethics*, Vol. 29(5), p. 267 (Gillon, R. 2003), Copyright 2003, with permission from BMJ Publishing Group Ltd; Case Study on page 520 adapted from 'Role redesign in the National Health Service: the effects on midwives' work and professional boundaries', *Work, Employment and Society*, Vol. 22, No. 4, pp. 695–712 (Prowse, J. and Prowse, P. 2008), copyright © 2008. Reprinted by Permission of SAGE; Box on page 614 adapted from CIPD (2012) Factsheet: Harassment and bullying at work., Reproduced with the permission of the publisher, the Chartered Institute of Personnel and Development, London (www.cipd.co.uk).

In some instances we have been unable to trace the owners of copyright material, and we would appreciate any information that would enable us to do so.

Part 1

HUMAN RESOURCE MANAGEMENT IN CHANGING TIMES

CHANGING TIMES

Human Resource
Management
Strategy
Planning
International
Skills

Human resource management (HRM) as a distinct function of the business has grown in stature and influence in recent years, particularly at the strategic level. For those entering the profession this book aims to demonstrate the interconnectedness of the discipline to which we are introducing you. We choose the metaphor of the honeycomb, a tight structure of contiguous cells of activity with a shared purpose, all connected both laterally and vertically. Training and development are not distinct activities separate from employee relations and performance management; reward is not to be considered separately from selection, retention, diversity and health and well-being. Strategy, policy, procedure and personal skill are not distinct specialisms but essential elements of every HR person's skill set.

Part 1 puts in place the totality of HRM in four ways. First comes the nature of HRM itself, a specialism which is every-where and in everything. Second, we review the global context within which it operates, as what you do in your small corner has to make sense in the global context of your business in your country and in all parts of the world and,

as everyone knows, the world is changing at a disconcerting pace. Third, we introduce two of the methods which HR uses and needs to understand in all of its dealings within the business of which it is a part. Strategy is not only setting the course of the business in the future, but also ensuring that the strategy is the right one from a mix of alternatives and then knowing when and how the strategy should be altered. Planning is the process of starting to implement the strategy by making the right things happen. Readers will remember the disastrous earthquake in Haiti at the beginning of 2010. For the first week afterwards there was intense interest and worldwide concern. Public donations poured in, rescue teams and equipment were mustered and there was a universal will to help, but there was no viable planning on the ground. Growing resources, personnel and motivation were mired in chaos. Only as a form of planning and coherent organisation was gradually developed did things begin to improve. HR people need to understand the differing nature of planning processes that are needed to make the right things happen.

Chapter 1

THE NATURE OF HUMAN RESOURCE MANAGEMENT

THE OBJECTIVES OF THIS CHAPTER ARE TO:

1 Define the term 'human resource management'

2 Explain the different ways in which the term 'human resource management' is used

3 Set out the main objectives of the human resource function

4 Review the historical evolution of the modern human resource function

5 Discuss links between human resource management activity and business performance

Human resource management (HRM) is the basis of all management activity, but it is not the basis of all business activity. A business may depend fundamentally on having a unique product, like the Dyson vacuum cleaner, or on obtaining the necessary funding, like the London bid to stage the Olympic Games, or on identifying a previously unnoticed market niche, like Saga Services. The basis of management is always the same: getting the people of the business to make things happen in a productive way, so that the business prospers and the people thrive.

All organisations have to draw on a range of resources to function and to achieve their objectives. They need access to capital to finance their operations, land and premises to operate from, energy, equipment and raw materials in order to manufacture a product or deliver a service. They also require access to some form of distribution network so that they can publicise, sell or dispense their goods and services. In addition, human resources are required in order to provide organisations with know-how, ideas and labour. In a competitive market economy the effectiveness and efficiency with which an organisation manages its relationship with the suppliers of all these kinds of resources determines its success. And the scarcer the resource and the more critical it is to a particular organisation's operations, the greater the skill, time and effort needed in order to manage the relationship.

There was a time when most people employed by organisations were required simply to provide manual labour. Relatively little skill, experience or intelligence was needed to do the jobs. The requisite training was cheap and speedy to provide, and payment methods unsophisticated. Finding people to do the work was rarely a problem and there were no restrictions of significance when it came to firing those who were not satisfactory or who displeased managers in some other way. This remains the situation in some industries and in some parts of the world, but in industrialised countries it is now increasingly rare. Instead we have a situation in which the majority of jobs require their holders to have mastered some form of specialised skill, or at the very least to possess attributes which others do not share to the same extent. The demand for higher-level skills has grown particularly quickly, there being a need for many more people to fill professional and managerial jobs than was the case twenty years ago. Moreover, almost all informed commentators believe that these established trends will accelerate in the future (UKCES 2012).

Just as the workforce has changed, so have the methods used to manage its members. The more specialised their roles, the harder it has become to find individuals with the right skills, qualifications, attributes and experience to undertake them. It has also become harder to keep people once they are employed because competitors are always keen to secure the services of the most talented people by offering them a better deal. Employing organisations have had to acquire a capacity for developing people effectively, together with increasingly sophisticated approaches to recruitment, selection, retention, employee relations and performance management. Further sophistication is required due to the substantial body of employment regulation that now governs the management of the employment relationship in most industrialised countries. The process becomes more complex still in the case of organisations that employ people in different countries. Not only do they have to grapple with a range of often diverse legislative and public policy regimes, but also they have to find ways of effectively managing people whose expectations vary significantly for cultural reasons.

These developments have led to the evolution of a more complex HRM function, charged with overseeing all aspects of managing the relationship between an organisation and its people in a professional and productive manner. The management of people, however, can never be a responsibility shouldered by specialists alone. It is an area of management activity that all managers must share if it is to be carried out effectively and contribute to the achievement of competitive advantage.

In this chapter we introduce HRM by setting out its purpose and showing how the effective management of people helps organisations to achieve their objectives. We go on to examine the historical development of HR work and speculate on how this may evolve further in the future. The final part of the chapter introduces thinking about the extent and nature of the link between HR activities and organisational effectiveness and performance.

WINDOW ON PRACTICE

In 2008, twenty-five years after it was first planned, Terminal 5 at Heathrow Airport in London finally opened its doors to passengers. The total cost of the building was £4.3 billion. The new terminal was exclusively for the use of British Airways, which had been planning for several years to move all its existing operations from the various other terminals at Heathrow into Terminal 5 and had gone so far as to contribute £330 million to its flamboyant interior design. The day before the opening an article in the *Financial Times* reported executives' concerns that the look of the place would raise expectations too high, but that it was 'beyond imagination to contemplate failure' (Blitz 2008). Yet spectacular failure was what followed.

In the first few days of operation over 300 flights scheduled to depart from Terminal 5 were cancelled, very long queues formed at check-in and transfer desks, while some 28,000 passengers found themselves separated from their luggage. The immediate cost to British Airways was £16 million, but the long-term direct costs were authoritatively estimated to be around £150 million (BBC 2008a), let alone vast further losses resulting from a deterioration in the airline's already poor brand image.

And why did this debacle happen? It appears that the major reason was simply extraordinarily poor management of people. The major immediate problem arose because the staff were not properly trained to use the equipment at Terminal 5 and were unprepared when it came to solving the technical 'glitches' that quickly appeared once the baggage handling machinery started operating. In addition long delays were caused on the first day as a result of staff being unable to find the staff car park or get through security screening on schedule. Later on, as flights began to arrive, staff simply failed to 'remove luggage quickly enough at the final unloading stage' (BBC 2008b).

Matters were not helped by the persistence over a long period of very poor employment relationships at British Airways. Done and Willman (2008) reported that the failure of the airline to solve this fundamental problem was the real underlying cause of the Terminal 5 debacle. An unnamed Heathrow executive said that they had all been expecting an outbreak of 'fuck'em disease' as the new terminal opened and some staff simply decided 'not to work very hard'. British Airways' staff were neither committed to the success of the operation nor to their employer. Goodwill was in short supply, leading staff to be intransigent and uncooperative when effort, positive enthusiasm and flexibility were what was required.

Defining HRM

The term 'human resource management' is not easy to define. This is because it is commonly used in two different ways. On the one hand it is used generically to describe the body of management activities covered in books such as this. Used in this way HRM is really no more than a more modern and supposedly imposing name for what used commonly to be labelled 'personnel management'. On the other hand, the term is equally widely used to denote a particular approach to the management of people which is clearly distinct from 'personnel management'. Used in this way 'HRM' signifies more than an updating of the label; it also suggests a distinctive philosophy towards carrying out people-orientated organisational activities: one which is held to serve the modern business more effectively than 'traditional' personnel management. We explore the substance of these two meanings of HRM in the following subsections, referring to the first as 'HRM mark 1' and the second as 'HRM mark 2'.

HRM mark 1: the generic term

The role of the HR functions is explained by identifying the key objectives to be achieved. Four objectives form the foundation of all HR activity.

Staffing objectives

HR managers are first concerned with ensuring that the business is appropriately staffed and thus able to draw on the human resources it needs. This involves designing organisation structures, identifying under what type of contract different groups of employees (or subcontractors) will work, before recruiting, selecting and developing the people required to fill the roles: the right people, with the right skills, to provide their services when needed. There is a need to compete effectively in the employment market by recruiting and retaining the best, affordable workforce that is available. This involves developing employment packages that are sufficiently attractive to maintain the required employee skill levels and, where necessary, disposing of those judged no longer to have a role to play in the organisation. The tighter a key employment market becomes, the harder it is to find and then hold on to the people an organisation needs in order to compete effectively. In such circumstances increased attention has to be given to developing competitive pay packages, to the provision of valued training and development opportunities and to ensuring that the experience of working in the organisation is, as far as is possible, rewarding and fulfilling. Recent years have seen organisations take a more strategic approach, at least in their rhetoric, towards the meeting of staffing objectives. They are, for example, increasingly seeking to differentiate and position themselves in their labour markets vis-à-vis competitors by managing their reputations as employers, by engaging in employer branding exercises and by seeking to be recognised as 'employers of choice'.

Performance objectives

Once the required workforce is in place, HR managers seek to ensure that people are well motivated and committed so as to maximise their performance in their different roles. Training and development have a role to play, as do reward systems to maximise effort and focus attention on performance targets. In many organisations, particularly where trade unions play a significant role, HR managers negotiate improved performance with the workforce. The achievement of performance objectives also requires HR specialists to assist in disciplining employees effectively and equitably where individual conduct and/or performance standards are unsatisfactory. Welfare functions can also assist performance by providing constructive assistance to people whose performance has fallen short of their potential because of illness or difficult personal circumstances. Last but not least, there is the range of employee involvement initiatives to raise levels of commitment and to engage employees in developing new ideas. It is increasingly recognised that a key determinant of superior competitive performance is a propensity on the part of an organisation's employees to demonstrate discretionary effort. Essentially this means that they choose to go further in the service of their employer than is strictly required in their contracts of employment, working longer hours perhaps, working with greater enthusiasm or taking the initiative to improve systems and relationships. Willingness to engage in such behaviour cannot be forced by managers. But they can help to create an environment in which it is more likely to occur. A term that is currently very fashionable in HR circles is 'employee engagement', an idea which encapsulates what is required if organisations are successfully to enhance individual performance. Engaged employees know what is expected of them, have a sense of ownership of their work, are satisfied (hopefully very satisfied) with their jobs and, as a result, are prepared to contribute positively both with their effort and their ideas.

Change-management objectives

A third set of core objectives in nearly every business relates to the role played by the HR function in effectively managing change. Frequently change does not come along in readily defined episodes precipitated by some external factor. Instead it is endemic and well-nigh continuous, generated as much by a continual need to innovate as from definable environmental pressures. Change comes in different forms. Sometimes it is merely structural, requiring reorganisation of activities or the introduction of new people into particular roles. At other times cultural change is sought in order to alter attitudes, philosophies or long-present organisational norms. In any of these scenarios the HR function can play a central role. Key activities include the recruitment and/or development of people with the necessary leadership skills to drive the change process, the employment of change agents to encourage acceptance of change and the construction of reward systems which underpin the change process. Timely and effective employee involvement is also crucial because 'people support what they help to create'. However, it must also be remembered that change, particularly when imposed without genuine employee involvement, is also a major potential source of conflict in organisations. This can be minimised if plenty of time is available, but a degree of conflict is inevitable where groups of staff lose out in some way as a result of change. The effective management of conflict and its avoidance through careful management of expectations and involvement in decision making are thus also significant features of an effective HR manager's role.

Administration objectives

The fourth type of objective is less directly related to achieving competitive advantage, but is focused on underpinning the achievement of the other forms of objective. In part it is simply carried out in order to facilitate an organisation's smooth running. Hence there is a need to maintain accurate and comprehensive data on individual employees, a record of their achievement in terms of performance, their attendance and training records, their terms and conditions of employment and their personal details. However, there is also a legal aspect to much administrative activity, meaning that it is done because the business is required by law to comply. Of particular significance is the requirement that payment is administered professionally and lawfully, with itemised monthly pay statements being provided for all employees. There is the need to make arrangements for the deduction of taxation and National Insurance, for the payment of pension fund contributions and to be on top of the complexities associated with Statutory Sick Pay and Statutory Maternity Pay, as well as maternity and paternity leave. Additional legal requirements relate to the monitoring of health and safety systems and the issuing of contracts to new employees. Accurate record keeping is also central to ensuring compliance with a variety of other legal obligations such as the National Minimum Wage and the Working Time Regulations. HR professionals often downgrade the significance of effective administration, seeking instead to gain for themselves a more glamorous (and usually more highly paid) role formulating policy and strategy. This is a short-sighted attitude. Achieving excellence (i.e. professionalism and cost-effectiveness) in the delivery of the basic administrative tasks is important as an aim in itself because it can provide a source of competitive advantage vis-à-vis other organisations who struggle administratively. Moreover, as Stevens (2005: 137) demonstrates, sound admin-istration in HR matters is important to achieve if 'potential legislative risks' are to be minimised. It also helps the HR function in an organisation to gain and maintain the credibility and respect that are required in order to influence other managers in the organisation. In this respect it can be persuasively argued that efficient administration is a prerequisite if the HR function is to make a really significant contribution in the three other areas outlined above.

ACTIVITY 1.1

Each of the four types of HR objective is important and necessary for organisations in different ways. However, at certain times one or more can assume greater importance than the others. Can you identify types of situation in which each could become the most significant or urgent?

HRM mark 2: a distinctive approach to the management of people

The second meaning commonly accorded to the term 'human resource management' denotes a particular way of carrying out the range of activities discussed above. Under this definition, a 'human resource management approach' is something qualitatively different from a 'personnel management approach'. Commentators disagree, however, about how fundamental a shift is signified by a movement from personnel management to human resource management. For some, particularly those whose focus of interest is on the management of collective relationships at work, the rise of HRM in the last two decades of the twentieth century represented something new and very different from the dominant personnel management approach in earlier years. A particular theme in their work is the contention that personnel management is essentially *workforce centred*, while HRM is *resource centred*. Personnel specialists direct their efforts mainly at the organisation's employees: finding and training them, arranging for them to be paid, explaining management's expectations, justifying management's actions, satisfying employees' work-related needs, dealing with their problems and seeking to modify management action that could produce an unwelcome employee response. The people who work in the organisation are the starting point, and they are a resource that is relatively inflexible in comparison with other resources, like cash and materials. Although indisputably a management function, personnel management is not totally identified with management interests. Just as sales representatives have to understand and articulate the aspirations of the customers, personnel managers seek to understand and articulate the aspirations and views of the workforce. There is always some degree of being in between management and the employees, mediating the needs of each to the other.

HRM, by contrast, is directed mainly at management needs for human resources (not necessarily employees) to be provided and deployed. Demand rather than supply is the focus of the activity. There is greater emphasis on planning, monitoring and control, rather than mediation. Problem solving is undertaken with other members of management on HR issues rather than directly with employees or their representatives. It is totally identified with management interests, being a general management activity, and is relatively distant from the workforce as a whole. Guest (1987) emphasised the differences between the two approaches in his model illustrating 'stereotypes of personnel management and human resource management' (see Table 1.1).

Table 1.1
Personnel versus
HRM

	Personnel management	**Human resource management**
Time and planning perspective	Short term, reactive, ad hoc, marginal	Long term, proactive, strategic, integrated
Psychological contract	Compliance	Commitment
Control systems	External controls	Self-control
Employee relations perspective	Pluralist, collective, low trust	Unitarist, individual, high trust
Preferred structures/ systems	Bureaucratic/mechanistic, centralised, formal defined roles	Organic, devolved, flexible roles
Roles	Specialist/professional	Largely integrated into line management
Evaluation criteria	Cost minimisation	Maximum utilisation (human asset accounting)

The evolution of modern HRM

Most large organisations have established a specialist HR function which is tasked with the efficient and effective management of the relationship that the organisation has with its employees. There is nothing at all new about the existence of such a function, managers specialising in people management having been employed at senior levels in organisations for centuries. Over time the nature of the role has evolved very significantly as have the labels that have conventionally been given to such managers, and the process of steady evolution continues today. However, this process has never totally seen the abandonment of earlier concerns. Instead, as time goes by and new issues have come to the fore, the HR function has tended to add further layers to its activities. Significant legacies from each stage in the evolution of modern HRM have remained in the function's bloodstream and hence retain some significance.

Theme 1: social justice

The origins of HRM lie in the nineteenth century, with the work of social reformers such as Lord Shaftesbury and Robert Owen. Their criticisms of the free enterprise system and the hardship created by the exploitation of workers by factory owners enabled the first personnel managers to be appointed and provided the first frame of reference in which they worked: to ameliorate the lot of the workers. Such concerns are not obsolete. There are still regular reports of employees being exploited by employers flouting the law, and the problem of organisational distance between decision makers and those putting decisions into practice remains a source of alienation from work.

In the late nineteenth and early twentieth centuries some of the larger employers with a paternalist outlook began to appoint welfare officers to manage a series of new initiatives designed to make life less harsh for their employees. Prominent examples were the progressive schemes of unemployment benefit, sick pay and subsidised housing provided by the Quaker family firms of Cadbury and Rowntree, and the Lever Brothers' soap business. While the motives were ostensibly charitable, there was and remains a business as well as an ethical case for paying serious attention to the welfare of employees. This is based on the contention that it improves commitment on the part of staff and leads potential employees to compare the organisation favourably with *competitors*. The result is higher productivity, a longer-serving workforce and a bigger pool of applicants for each job. It has also been argued that a commitment to welfare reduces the scope for the development of adversarial industrial relations. The more conspicuous welfare initiatives promoted by employers today include employee assistance schemes, childcare facilities and health-screening programmes.

Theme 2: humane bureaucracy

The second phase marked the beginnings of a move away from a sole focus on welfare towards the meeting of various other organisational objectives. Personnel managers began to gain responsibilities in the areas of staffing, training and organisation design. Influenced by social scientists such as F.W. Taylor (1856–1915) and Henri Fayol (1841–1925), personnel specialists started to look at management and administrative processes analytically, working out how organisational structures could be designed and labour deployed so as to maximise efficiency. The humane bureaucracy stage in the development of personnel thinking was also influenced by the Human Relations School, which sought to ameliorate the potential for industrial conflict and dehumanisation present in too rigid an application of these scientific management approaches. Following the ideas of thinkers such as Elton Mayo (1880–1949), the fostering of social relationships in the workplace and employee morale thus became equally important objectives for personnel professionals seeking to raise productivity levels.

Theme 3: negotiated consent

Personnel managers next added expertise in bargaining to their repertoire of skills. In the period of full employment following the Second World War, labour became a scarce resource. This led to a growth in trade union membership and to what Allan Flanders, the leading industrial relations analyst of the 1960s, called 'the challenge from below'. Personnel specialists managed the new collective institutions such as joint consultation committees, joint production committees and suggestion schemes set up in order to accommodate the new realities. In the industries that were nationalised in the 1940s, employers were placed under a statutory duty to negotiate with unions representing employees. To help achieve this, the government encouraged the appointment of personnel officers and set up the first specialist courses for them in the universities. A personnel management advisory service was also set up at the Ministry of Labour, which still survives as the first A in ACAS (the Advisory, Conciliation and Arbitration Service).

Theme 4: organisation

The late 1960s saw a switch in focus among personnel specialists, away from dealing principally with the rank-and-file employee on behalf of management, towards dealing with management itself and the integration of managerial activity. This phase was characterised by the development of career paths and of opportunities within organisations for personal growth. This too remains a concern of HR specialists today, with a significant portion of time and resources being devoted to the recruitment, development and retention of an elite core of people with specialist expertise on whom the business depends for its future. Personnel specialists developed techniques of labour or workforce planning. This is basically a quantitative activity, boosted by the advent of information technology, which involves forecasting an organisation's likely future skills needs and taking steps to ensure that they are met in practice.

Theme 5: HRM

The term 'human resources' was commonly used by social scientists in contrast to 'natural resources' for much of the twentieth century (see Ginzberg 1958), and a journal called *Human Resource Management* was launched at Michigan University in 1961. But the term 'HRM' only came to be used commonly in organisations in the 1980s when courses with that name began to be offered as part of MBA programmes at leading American business schools. Before long 'HRM' replaced 'personnel management' and is now almost universally used in organisations across the world. The change of label coincided with the decline of trade union influence in many organisations and, consequently, with the seizing by managers of the opportunities that this decline gave them. Previously, across most industrialised countries, industry-level collective bargaining systems had prevailed through which terms and conditions of employment were negotiated by trade unions and employer's associations on behalf of almost everyone in the country who worked in that industry. As a result pay, along with many other rules and management policies, were the same throughout a whole industry in each country, meaning that these were not issues about which local managers could make decisions. With the decentralisation of bargaining and the rise in many industries of non-union firms, managers in the private sector found themselves free and able to develop their own, local policies and practices.

Some chose to adopt a macho approach, particularly during recessionary periods when employees were in no position to resist the introduction of efficiency and cost-saving measures, leaner organisational structures and downsized workplaces. Others sought to enhance their profitability and competitiveness by seeking to gain employee commitment and by investing in their people. Either way, it was not long before organisations began to take an explicitly strategic approach to the management of human resources, setting objectives and seeking in a more proactive way to achieve these. As time went by the same kinds of approaches were increasingly used in the public sector too, so that by the turn of the millennium it was the norm for organisations to employ HR managers, officers and assistants whose aim was to add value by carrying out the four areas of activity we set out above in as efficient and effective a manner as possible. The objective, quite explicitly, was to make a major contribution to the achievement and maintenance of competitive advantage.

Theme 6: a 'new HR'?

Some writers and commentators have recently begun to argue that we are now witnessing the beginning of a new sixth stage in the evolution of personnel/HR work. While there is by no means a clear consensus about this point of view, it is notable that leading thinkers have identified a group of trends which they believe to be sufficiently dissimilar, as a bundle, from established practices to justify, at the very least, a distinct title. Bach (2005: 28–9), for example, used the term 'the new HR' to describe 'a different trajectory', which is now beginning to become discernible. Others have started using the term HR 2.0, likening recent developments to a new and improved edition of a software package. A number of themes are identified including a more global perspective, a tendency for issues relating to legal compliance to move up the HRM agenda and the rise of multi-employer networks which Bach calls 'permeable organisations'. Here, instead of employees having a single, readily defined employer, there may be a number of different employers, or at least more than one organisation which exercises a degree of authority over their work. Examples are found in public–private partnerships, joint ventures, franchises, situations where work is outsourced by one organisation to another, in the employment of agency workers and where strong supply chains are established consisting of smaller organisations which are wholly or very heavily reliant on the custom of a single large-client corporation.

Another apparently new trajectory can be summarised as an approach to the employment relationship which views employees and potential employees very much as individuals or at least small groups rather than as a single group and which seeks to engage them emotionally. It is associated with a move away from an expectation that staff will demonstrate commitment to a set of corporate values which are determined by senior management and towards a philosophy which is far more customer focused. Customers are defined explicitly as the ultimate employers and staff are empowered to act in such a way as to meet their requirements. This involves encouraging employees to empathise with customers, recruiting, selecting and appraising them according to their capacity to do so. In turn, and this is what seems to make 'the new HR' different from established HRM, managers are starting to refer to the staff and line managers whom they 'serve' as their 'internal customers', a client group which they aim to satisfy and which they survey regularly as a means of establishing how far this aim is in fact being achieved. Another term that is becoming very much more commonly used in HR is 'strategic business partner'. The image conjured up here is of the HR manager as internal consultant, assisting clients in the achievement of their objectives and expecting to be judged on results.

The practice of viewing staff as internal customers goes further still in some organisations with the use of HR practices that borrow explicitly from the toolkit of marketing specialists (see Edwards and Bach 2013). We see this in the widespread interest in employer branding exercises (see Chapter 7) where an organisation markets itself in quite sophisticated ways, not to customers and potential customers, but to employees and potential employees.

Gratton (2004) shows how highly successful companies such as Tesco go further still in categorising job applicants and existing staff into distinct categories which summarise their principal aspirations as far as their work is concerned, in much the same way that organisations seek to identify distinct market segments to use when developing, designing, packaging and marketing products and services. Such approaches aim to provide an 'employee value proposition' which it is hoped will attract the right candidates, allow the appointment of highly effective performers, motivate them to provide excellent levels of service and subsequently retain them for a longer period of time.

Lepak and Snell (2007) also note a move in HR away from 'the management of jobs' and towards 'the management of people', which includes the development of employment strategies that differ for different groups of employees. Importantly this approach recognises the capacity that most people have to become emotionally engaged in their work, with their customers, with their colleagues and hence (if to a lesser extent) with their organisations. The employment relationship is not just a transactional one in which money is earned in exchange for carrying out a set of duties competently, but also a relational one which involves emotional attachments. The 'new HR' understands this and seeks to manage people accordingly.

Cardy *et al.* (2007) are also keen to advocate the repositioning of the HR function as one which is focused on providing services to 'internal customers' who the aim is to satisfy. Like Gratton they argue in favour of a degree of segmentation. They also take the concept of 'customer equity' long used by marketing analysts and apply it to the employment relationship, developing the notion of 'employee equity'. The argument they advance is complex, but at base they advocate thinking about employment from the perspective of the employee and to take steps which serve to:

- increase the value employees perceive that they derive from the relationship (value equity);
- improve the reputation of the organisation as an employer (brand equity);
- establish and maintain high levels of loyalty with employees (retention equity).

Saunders and Hunter (2009) adopt the same philosophy, but focus on the practicalities of transforming a traditionally focused HR function into one which sees managers and employees at all levels as customers who the function needs to satisfy if it is to achieve its wider, longer-term objectives.

What we appear to be seeing here is a repositioning of HR thinking and activity. The aim is the same, that is to help the organisation achieve its objectives, but the means are different. Instead of simply devising and then operationalising HR strategies and policies which suit the short-term, current, financial needs of the organisation, there is an increased recognition that this cannot be done successfully over the longer term without the active engagement and support of people. In a world where many are employed because of their knowledge, in which skills that employers seek are often scarce and in which employees enjoy substantial protection from the law, there are major limits imposed on the extent of management's freedom to manage people at will. The most successful organisations are thus those which are best able to recruit good people, retain them and motivate them. This means looking after their interests and involving them as far as is possible in decision making – often using technologies that enable collaborative decision making. Hence we see the evolution of thinking based around internal customers, collaboration, partnership and employee engagement which are characteristic of the new HR trajectory.

ACTIVITY 1.2

Gratton (2004) reports that Tesco uses the following five 'identities' to categorise its staff. The way that they are managed and the reward packages that are available to them can thus be tailored so as to be more appropriate to the needs and aspirations of each individual:

- work–life balancers
- want it all
- pleasure seekers
- live to work
- work to live

Which of these categories best describes you as far as your present employment is concerned? What about friends and members of your family? Choose any two of the categories and think about in what ways it would make sense to manage people in each group differently from one another.

HRM and the achievement of organisational effectiveness

As Storey *et al.* (2009: 4) point out, unless HR activity can be shown to add value to an organisation, there is no point in devoting time and resources to it except insofar as is necessary 'to comply with prevailing employment laws or to meet minimum operational requirements in hiring, firing, labour deployment and the like'.

So for the past two decades the theme which has dominated the HR research agenda has been the study of links between HR practices and organisational effectiveness.

Two main types of research have been carried out extensively in this field:

1 The first involves establishing correlations between superior business performance as measured against a range of indicators and the presence of HR practices in thousands of organisations. Major examples of this kind of research are the studies carried out by Huselid (1995) in the USA and by Guest and his colleagues (2003) in the UK.

2 The second involves seeking to establish through interviews in successful case study organisations what factors have contributed to their growth, profitability, quality of service, etc. This type of work has been carried out by researchers such as Pfeffer (1994, 1998) in the USA and by John Purcell in the UK.

Both streams of research have produced strong, if by no means inconclusive, evidence to suggest that organisations which adopt appropriate, sophisticated, 'good-practice' HR practices are more likely to meet their business objectives over the long term than those which do not. What these business objectives are varies from organisation to organisation and industry to industry. For major private-sector corporations the aim is to gain and maintain sustained competitive advantage. For smaller organisations in the private and voluntary sectors growth or survival are key objectives. In the public sector organisational effectiveness and meeting government targets are the key objectives defined in terms of meeting a service need as cost-efficiently as possible and to the highest achievable standard of quality. In all these situations good HRM can be shown to correlate with the achievement of core business objectives, particularly when skills are in relatively short supply or where the potential contribution made by individual employees to the success of an organisation is substantial.

What is less clear is exactly through what processes HR makes this contribution. There are a number of possibilities, none of which are mutually exclusive:

- Good management and the establishment of a positive employment relations climate mean that an organisation is better able than its competitors to recruit, retain and motivate staff. Superior performance results because the best performers want to work for the organisation, because they are motivated to work hard and demonstrate commitment once employed, and because there is less resistance to change and a greater capacity to seize opportunities when they arise.

- Effective HRM alongside good management of other functions allows an organisation to develop and maintain a strong and positive corporate reputation. This enables it to raise money with relative ease when it is needed and also helps to ensure that managers of investment funds and financial advisers see it or its shares as a desirable place to put their clients' money. The maintenance of a positive reputation in the media is also an important objective as this helps to maintain and grow the customer base. A reputation for ethical management is increasingly important in this context.

- There is a big difference between the rhetoric of HRM, which is positive and people centred, and the experienced reality in many organisations. In the real world HRM is focused on reducing labour costs and extracting greater value for organisations from their human resources. This leads to the intensification of work and more efficient operations, and it is these which account for the apparent link between HRM and measures of corporate financial performance.

- The relationship between HR and business performance is in fact the other way around. The presence of a correlation does not mean that there is any causal relationship. Any HR contribution to the maintenance of superior business performance is limited. Having gained its competitive advantage, an employer has the resources to develop good HR practices.

Fleetwood and Hesketh (2010) rightly warn against uncritical acceptance of the findings of studies that link HR practices to business outcomes. Ultimately, they point out, it is the people who work in organisations who are generally responsible for the achievement of sustained superior business performance. At best all HR practices and policies can do is play 'an enabling role' in this process and in many organisations there is little evidence to suggest that the average employee's commitment or level of engagement is linked particularly closely to the formal 'architecture' of HRM.

Purcell *et al.* in 2003 and in subsequent publications also stress the inadequacy of thinking that assumes having in place a range of 'good-practice' HR policies and practices will lead inexorably to the achievement of sustained, superior business performance. Their research strongly suggests that this can help, but they argue that what really makes the difference in practice are sufficient numbers of line managers who are both willing and able to give life and meaning to the policies and practices. These are the people with whom employees interact on a day-to-day basis, and unless they buy in to the ideas that underpin progressive HRM and manage their teams accordingly, the chances that well-chosen HR policies will have any serious impact on organisational performance are very limited. Purcell *et al.* (2003) point out that poor implementation of policies and practices by line managers who have not bought into them is often worse for the organisation than not having any policies at all.

The central importance of the mediating role played by line managers in the delivery of HRM was further stressed by Purcell and Hutchinson (2007) in their identification of a 'people management–performance causal chain' and by Nishii and Wright (2008) in their 'process model of HRM' (see Den Hartog and Boon 2013). Both argue that an important distinction must be made between 'intended HR practices', how these are typically perceived by employees and what impact they actually have in practice. Without effective communication and, crucially, the active support of line managers in implementing the policies, there is little chance that the desired outcomes will ever materialise. It follows that all managers in an organisation must take a good deal of responsibility for the delivery of HRM practices if they are to add value in any meaningful way.

Increasingly, others play a role too as HRM in organisations is less and less shaped by generalist HR managers alone. In larger organisations there is scope to employ people to specialise in particular areas of HRM. Some, for example, employ employee relations specialists to look after the collective relationship between management and employees and to provide advice about legal developments. Further common areas of specialisation are training and development, recruitment, reward management and health and safety. In all these areas there is an increasing tendency for the term 'consultant' to be used instead of 'officer' or 'manager', indicating a shift towards a situation in which line managers determine the services *they* want rather than these being prescribed by a central HR function. Indeed, it is not at all uncommon nowadays for these aspects of HR work to be undertaken on behalf of organisations by subcontractors or independent consultants rather than by directly employed HR officers.

While responsibility for making sure that HRM really does add value for an organisation rests with all managers, it typically remains the role of HR managers with a generalist remit to shape the policies and practices that are ultimately implemented. Subsequently, their job is not merely to enable, but also actively to promote the effective implementation of these practices. It may be an enabling role, but it is nonetheless a crucial one. And on the question of which types of approaches are most likely to underpin superior business performance, the research that has been carried out over the last twenty years is fairly conclusive. The need, quite simply, is for organisations to achieve the core HR objectives described above more effectively than their competitors are able to. When this is achieved the result tends to be high levels of trust, a strong sense of shared purpose and an enhanced capacity for recruiting, retaining, motivating and engaging an excellent workforce that is both willing and able to adapt to changed circumstances when necessary. Purcell *et al.* (2003), like other researchers, stress the role that a bundle of progressive HR practices can play in bringing about these outcomes:

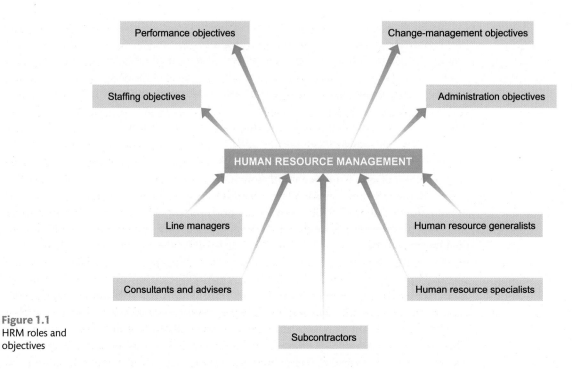

Figure 1.1
HRM roles and
objectives

- giving people career development opportunities;
- giving people influence over their own area of work;
- making jobs challenging and interesting;
- providing good training;
- appraising people regularly on their individual performance;
- teamworking;
- involving employees in decision making;
- providing a good work–life balance;
- employing line managers 'who are good at leadership and who show respect'.

A further potential contribution made by the HR function involves recognising the significance of the organisation's people as an effective barrier preventing would-be rivals from expanding their markets into territory that the organisation holds. The term 'human capital' is more and more used in this context to signify that the combined knowledge and experience of an organisation's staff are a highly significant source of competitive advantage, largely because these things are difficult for competitors to replicate easily. Attracting, engaging, rewarding, developing and retaining people effectively is thus vital. Failing to do so enables accumulated human capital to leak away into the hands of competitors, reducing the effectiveness of commercial defences and making it harder to maintain competitive advantage.

Fostering a positive reputation among would-be investors, financial advisers and financial journalists is also an aspect of organisational effectiveness to which the HR function makes a significant contribution. Key here is the need to reassure those whose job is to assess the long-term financial viability of the organisation that it is competently managed and well placed to meet the challenges that lie ahead in both the short and the longer term. The ability to attract and retain a strong management team is central to achieving this aspect of organisational effectiveness, as is the ability of the organisation to plan for the future by having in place effective succession planning arrangements and robust systems for the development of the skills and knowledge that will be key in the future. Above all, financial markets need to be assured that the organisation is stable and is thus a safe repository for investors' funds. The work of Stevens and his colleagues (2005) is helpful in this context. They conceive of the whole HR contribution in terms of the management of risk, the aim being to ensure that an organisation 'balances the maximisation of opportunities and the minimisation of risks.'

Finally, the HR function also plays a central role in building an organisation's reputation as an ethically or socially responsible organisation. This happens in two distinct ways. The first involves fostering an understanding of and commitment to ethical conduct on the part of managers and staff. It is achieved by paying attention to these objectives in recruitment campaigns, in the criteria adopted for the selection of new employees and the promotion of staff, in the methods used to develop people and in performance management processes. The second relates to the manner in which people are managed. A poor ethical reputation can be gained simply because an organisation becomes known for treating its staff poorly. In recent years well-known brands of fast food chains in the UK have suffered because of their use of zero hours contracts, while several large multinationals have had their reputations stained by stories in the media about the conditions under which their employees in developing countries are required to work.

SUMMARY PROPOSITIONS

1.1 It is possible to identify two distinct definitions of the term 'human resource management'. The first describes a body of management activities, while the second signifies a particular approach to carrying out those activities.

1.2 HR managers are concerned with meeting four distinct sets of organisational objectives: staffing, performance, change management and administration.

1.3 HRM activities are carried out in various ways through various forms of organisational structure. In some larger organisations HR generalists work alongside specialists in particular HR disciplines.

1.4 HRM can be characterised as one of the more recent in a series of incarnations that personnel practitioners have developed since the origins of the profession over 100 years ago.

1.5 The HRM function contributes to the achievement of different dimensions of organisational effectiveness. Prominent are the gaining and maintaining of competitive advantage, the fostering of a positive standing in financial markets and the development of a reputation for corporate social responsibility.

GENERAL DISCUSSION TOPICS

1 What are the major advantages and disadvantages associated with HR managers seeing employees as 'internal customers' who need to be satisfied?

2 How far do you agree with the view that an HR function which achieves administrative excellence adds value to an organisation just as much as one which focuses on improving its employees' performance.

3 To what extent is your organisation successful in translating its 'intended HR outcomes' into 'actual HR outcomes'? What could it do to make it more successful?

THEORY INTO PRACTICE

The following opinion piece by the very successful entrepreneur Luke Johnson was published a few years ago in the *Financial Times*. In it the author puts a case against HRM departments in organisations.

The truth about the HR department

By Luke Johnson

Human resources is a management term that should strike fear into the heart of every self-respecting entrepreneur.

The brilliant Avis boss Robert Townsend in his book 'Up the Organisation' suggests firing the entire personnel department. Indeed, I have radically downsized HR in several companies I have run, and business has gone all the better for it.

Tragically, we live in a time of overwhelming employment legislation, so getting legal procedures right can save time and heartache – that is the sort of task HR handles. It is probably the very definition of a necessary evil for a 21st Century business.

HR is like many parts of modern businesses: a simple expense, and a burden on the backs of the productive workers. Other divisions that can become the enemy include IT, legal and marketing. They don't sell or produce: they consume. They are the amorphous support services.

Often it makes sense to sub-contract these activities and reward the external provider based on performance. If they don't deliver, you don't pay and you can replace them. But managers too often think their company isn't grown-up unless it has all these important-sounding departments. It is a grave error to succumb to institutionalisation: good leaders care about results, not process. Too often I come across companies where staff in the field work not for customers but for HQ, which drains the company of cash and enthusiasm.

Typically an apparatus builds up around divisions such as HR to expand their role and cost more money. For example, compensation consultants are hired to come up with justifications for paying everyone more. Training advisers are employed to distract everyone from doing their job with pointless courses. Appraisal experts are contracted to critique staff relations. Experts are drafted in to devise an appropriate corporate social responsibility agenda – whatever that is. All this paraphernalia is accepted as essential good practice by modern-thinking corporate management. I think most of it is expensive, bureaucratic hogwash. But, clearly, it becomes a lucrative bandwagon for many to jump on – so they justify it all, come what may.

Of course, senior executives understand that HR is powerful – a bit like Mossad or the CIA. Those in personnel know everyone's salary and bonus and all their disciplinary records. Wily office politicians cultivate them, since they help decide who gets a pay rise and promotion, how contracts are drafted, how individuals are treated if there is a restructuring and so on. Meanwhile, headhunters spend their time cultivating the top talent and shuffling the deck, profiting at every turn.

Running organisations that employ lots of people is increasingly difficult. No wonder the Rich List is full of more property entrepreneurs than any other kind. Inanimate objects like buildings can't sue for unfair dismissal for discrimination over age, race, faith, gender, or sexual orientation – or demand flexible working or maternity rights.

Bosses who do a poor job can be as bad as workers: no one seems to accept blame for anything. Rose Gibb, chief executive of Maidstone and Tunbridge Wells Health Trust, received a £75,000 pay-off after at least 90 patients died from clostridium difficile in hospitals she ran. The message is: reward for catastrophic failure.

Companies should cut back on non-essential functions and ship expensive jobs abroad to cheap countries when they can. Legislators who have never met a payroll refuse to understand that when they gold-plate employment rights, they ultimately destroy jobs and prosperity. That is why unemployment is so high.

Companies should get fit now. As Albert Einstein said: 'Bureaucracy is the death of any achievement.' When it is a question of survival, there is no room for the non-essential. And the HR function is anything but essential.

Questions

1 What is the essence of Luke Johnson's case against HR departments and common HR practices?

2 The views about HRM expressed in this article are very commonly held by managers in organisations. Why do you think this?

3 What arguments could be deployed to counteract the major points Mr Johnson makes?

4 What steps should HR departments take in order to better justify their continued role in organisations?

Sources: Johnson, L. (2008) 'The truth about the HR department', *Financial Times*, 29 January.

FURTHER READING

Legge, K. (1995) *Human Resource Management: Rhetorics and realities*. London: Macmillan. This seminal book provides a rigorous discussion of the differences between personnel management and HRM, as well as introducing and considering a series of other debates about the nature of HRM and its purpose for organisations.

Withers, M., Williamson, M. and Reddington, M. (2010) *Transforming HR: Creating value through people*. Oxford: Butterworth–Heinemann/Elsevier.

A very accessible book which develops many of the themes we have introduced in this chapter, going on to explore the particular contribution the HR function can make in the contemporary business environment.

'Human resource management and performance' by Paul Boselie (2013), in *HRM & Performance: Achievements and challenges*, edited by Jaap Paauwe, David Guest and Patrick Wright.

Boselie's chapter sums up most effectively the current state of ongoing research into the extent and nature of the link between HRM activity and the achievement of superior business performance. Paauwe et al. examine the same issues at much greater length in their recent book.

REFERENCES

Bach, S. (2005) 'Personnel management in transition', in S. Bach (ed.), *Managing Human Resources: Personnel management in transition*, 4th edn. Oxford: Blackwell.

BBC (2008a) 'BA's terminal losses top £16 million', BBC News Website, 3 April.

BBC (2008b) 'What did go wrong at Terminal 5?', BBC News Website, 30 March.

Blitz, R. (2008) 'The trouble with great expectations', *Financial Times*, 26 March.

Boselie, P (2013) 'Human resource management and performance', in S. Bach and M. Edwards (eds), *Managing Human Resources*, 5th edn. Chichester: Wiley.

Cardy, R., Miller, J. and Ellis, A. (2007) 'Employee equity: Towards a person-based approach to HRM', *Human Resource Management Review*, Vol. 17, pp. 140–51.

Den Hartog, D. and Boon, C. (2013) 'HRM and leadership', in S. Bach and M. Edwards (eds), *Managing Human Resources*, 5th edn. Chichester: Wiley.

Done, K. and Willman, J. (2008) 'Goodwill of staff is often in short supply', *Financial Times*, 5 April.

Edwards, M. and Bach, S. (2013) 'Human resource management in transition', in S. Bach and M. Edwards (eds), *Managing Human Resources*, 5th edn. Chichester: Wiley.

Fleetwood, S. and Hesketh, A. (2010) *Explaining the Performance of Human Resource Management*. Cambridge: Cambridge University Press.

Ginzberg, E. (1958) *Human Resources: The wealth of a nation*. New York: Simon & Schuster.

Gratton, L. (2004) *The Democratic Enterprise: Liberating your business with freedom, flexibility and commitment*. Harlow: Pearson Education.

Guest, D.E. (1987) 'Human resource management and industrial relations', *Journal of Management Studies*, Vol. 24, No. 5, pp. 503–21.

Guest, D.E, Micie, J., Conway, N. and Sheehan, M. (2003) 'Human resource management and corporate performance in the UK', *British Journal of Industrial Relations*, Vol. 41, No. 2, pp. 291–314.

Huselid, M. (1995) 'The impact of human resource management practices on turnover, productivity and corporate financial performance', *Academy of Management Journal*, Vol. 38, No. 3, pp. 635–72.

Johnson, L. (2008) 'The truth about the HR department', *Financial Times*, 29 January.

Legge, K. (1995) *Human Resource Management: Rhetorics and realities*. London: Macmillan.

Lepak, D. and Snell, S.A. (2007) 'Employment sub-systems and the HR architecture', in P. Boxall *et al.* (eds), *The Oxford Handbook of Human Resource Management*. Oxford: Oxford University Press.

Nishii, L. and Wright, P. (2008) 'Variability within organisations: Implications for strategic human resource management', in D. Brent Smith (ed.), *The People Make the Place: Dynamic linkages between individuals and organisations*. New York: Taylor & Francis.

Paauwe, J., Guest, D. and Wright, P. (eds) (2013) *HRM & Performance: Achievements and challenges*. Chichester: Wiley.

Pfeffer, J. (1994) *Competitive Advantage Through People*. Boston, MA: Harvard Business School Press.

Pfeffer, J. (1998) *The Human Equation*. Boston, MA: Harvard University Press.

Purcell, J. and Hutchinson, S. (2007) 'Front-line managers as agents in the HRM–performance causal chain: Theory, analysis and evidence', *Human Resource Management Journal*, Vol. 17, No. 1, pp. 3–20.

Purcell, J., Kinnie, N., Hutchinson, S., Rayton, B. and Swart, J. (2003) *Understanding the People and Performance Link: Unlocking the black box*. London: CIPD.

Saunders, J. and Hunter, I. (2009) *Led Design: Planning the new HR function*. London: Gower.

Stevens, J. (ed.) (2005) *Managing Risk: The human resources contribution*. London: LexisNexis Butterworths.

Storey, J., Ulrich, D. and Wright, P. (2009) 'Introduction', in J. Storey et al. (eds), *The Routledge Companion to Strategic Human Resource Management*. London: Routledge.

UKCES (2012) *Working Futures 2010–2020: Evidence Report 41*. UK Commission for Employment and Skills.

Withers, M., Williamson, M. and Reddington, M. (2010) *Transforming HR: Creating value through people*, 2nd edn. Oxford: Butterworth–Heinemann/Elsevier.

Chapter 2

THE GLOBAL CONTEXT FOR HUMAN RESOURCE MANAGEMENT

THE OBJECTIVES OF THIS CHAPTER ARE TO:

1 Define and account for the development of globalisation

2 Set out the significance of globalisation for industry and the labour market

3 Examine the major consequences of globalisation for HRM

4 Explain why the global business environment is characterised by increasing uncertainty, volatility and unpredictability

In 2008 the UK economy, like those of most western industrialised countries, entered the sharpest and most prolonged downturn it has experienced since the 1930s. In an eighteen-month period the UK economy contracted by 6%, since when recovery has been slow and hesitant. At the time of writing (early 2013) the UK economy remains 3% smaller than it was before the recession commenced. While employment prospects are looking up and some sectors are seeing steady growth once again, there remains a serious lack of confidence in the business community which is hampering the start of a strong and steady period of recovery. Some countries have fared a lot better than the UK (e.g. Germany, Canada, Australia), while others (notably in Southern Europe) have suffered far worse drops in output and employment. Across the western world levels of personal and national debt are running at unsustainable levels and are having to be paid down in order to maintain an acceptable level of market confidence. Elsewhere in the world there has been a severe slowdown, but no recession. China and India, which between them account for over 40% of the world's population, have continued to see their economies grow strongly, albeit somewhat less strongly than was the case before 2008. Brazil, Russia, Poland and a number of African and Middle Eastern nations are also experiencing relatively high levels of growth as their economies expand and integrate further into a global financial, economic and trading system, but here too confidence is lower than it was five years ago, as are levels of growth. Immediate prospects for the world economy thus look uncertain and are likely to remain so until the US economy returns to steady growth and the Eurozone is able to find long-term solutions to its current difficulties.

Uncertainty and unpredictability are, however, nothing new. Long before the recent downturn they had long established themselves as dominant features of the evolving context in which organisations and their HR functions do business. And looking forward, even without the intervention of an unwelcome downturn in the fortunes of the world economy, it was always likely that the global business environment would become increasingly volatile for several decades to come. In this chapter our aim is to explain why this is the case and to set out what the key consequences are for the management of the HR function in organisations. At the same time we will introduce some other significant, long-term and well-established trends in the business environment – all linked to globalisation – which together are tending to make HR work more challenging.

Globalisation

The term 'globalisation' tends to be used in rather different ways by different people depending on their perspective (Scholte 2005). For some, it can be used interchangeably with the term 'internationalisation' to signify in general terms an increase in cross-border relations between peoples and governments. From this perspective the trend towards greater globalisation simply means the development of more international exchange and greater interdependence. Others see 'globalisation' as representing a more profound development. It is more than increased international activity, being used instead to signify a new development best described as 'international economic integration'. It is thus seen as representing a process of movement away from a world economic system which is dominated by national and regional economies for the most part trading internally, to one in which pretty well anyone based anywhere across the globe can sell things to anyone else. A third definition stresses universalism, by which is meant a dilution of national identity and separateness as people of all backgrounds increasingly share a similar global culture and set of aspirations, buy the same products and live under similar types of governmental and economic system. A fourth definition sees globalisation as Americanisation, sometimes conceived as the development of an American global empire. It thus focuses on the significance of capitalism, western-style representative government, liberalism, bureaucracy and rationalism in the establishment of a 'new world order'. The growing international power of US-based corporations is also often stressed by those who adopt this perspective. A fifth definition stresses a change in our perceptions of distance. Globalisation, according to this definition, is about the world becoming 'smaller' due to modern transportation and communications technologies which allow readier and much more affordable contact between people across national borders. For the purposes of thinking about the evolving global business environment it is helpful not to have any single definition of the term 'globalisation' in mind, but instead to accept that a variety of significant trends are observable and that they are having a differential impact on the lives of different people. 'Globalisation' is thus best conceived of as an umbrella term covering a variety of developments.

It is not possible to say when globalisation started because a degree of international economic exchange has been carried on for many centuries. Some argue that before the First World War economies such as the UK's were more globally integrated than they are in the modern era (Wes 1996: 5), but most agree that the process of globalisation that we observe today properly got going in the decades after 1945 as western countries recovered from the Second World War and steadily transformed into much more affluent, consumer-orientated societies. They started to trade more and more with one another and to welcome investment in their economies by overseas-based corporations. This period also saw the rapid rise of economies such as those of Japan, Taiwan, South Korea, Hong Kong and Singapore, expanding the number of consumers who were in a position to participate in international economic exchange. There was then a big acceleration after 1990 following the fall of the Berlin wall, the rise of capitalism in China, the adoption of a more western-orientated economic policy in India, the very rapid development of some economies in the Middle East, and the move towards liberal democratic forms of governance in South Africa and across much of South America. The full integration of these economies into the world trading system brought about its transformation – a process that is still very much ongoing (see Dicken (2011) for an excellent account of this process).

The practical consequences of these trends have been huge. First, since 1950 world output has increased six-fold, while world trade has increased over twenty-fold, meaning that the proportion of goods and services which are exported and consumed in countries other from that in which they originate has increased very markedly. Annual export growth across the world is now running at three to four times greater than the growth in world output. Second, we have seen unprecedented growth in levels of foreign direct investment (FDI) through which a corporation based in one country sets up operations overseas or acquires an existing overseas operation. FDI has grown even faster than international trade. This too is a long-term trend which saw great acceleration in the 1990s, since when FDI has grown annually at a faster rate than international trade and a much much faster rate than international output. Third, we are living through a period in which the amount of overseas travel, for both business and pleasure, has increased at unprecedented levels, making the travel industry by some margin the biggest and fastest-growing industry in the world. In 1954 the number of passengers going through UK airports was just 4 million. By 1974 it had reached 45 million, by 1984, 57 million and by 1994, 98 million.

In 2011 the total number of passengers using UK airports was over 220 million (Civil Aviation Authority 2012, **www.caa.co.uk**). Internationally the rate of growth has been more spectacular still. The number of air passengers has risen from just 9 million in 1945, to 88 million in 1972 and to 344 million in 1994. The International Air Transport Association now predicts that the total will top 3.3 billion in 2014 (IATA 2011).

Alongside increased international economic exchange, recent decades have also seen significant increases in migration across national boundaries. According to United Nations estimates, in 2010, there were 214 million people living long term in a country other than the one they were born in, compared with just 81.5 million in 1970. These figures probably represent a considerable underestimate because a great deal of cross-border migration is illegal in nature and so does not get recorded in the official statistics that governments collect, but the figures nonetheless demonstrate how much more likely people are now to move overseas than used to be the case, even when world population rises are taken into account (Goldin *et al.* 2011). The impact has been far greater in some regions than in others as migration is by no means spread evenly across the globe: 75% of all international migrants live in just 28 countries, over 20% of the total settling in the USA, while a further 30% live in European Union countries. This means that organisations are much more likely to employ multicultural teams of staff in some areas than in others. For example, while over 12% of the population of Western Europe originates overseas, this is true of less than 2% of the Eastern European population. The biggest immigrant populations are found in the Gulf countries where people born overseas make up a majority of the total population in some cases (Kuwait 63%, UAE 70% and Qatar 87%). As a proportion of the workforce in these countries, migrants account for even larger shares. In the UAE, in 2010, 90% of the workforce was born overseas. Elsewhere immigration levels are very much lower. In Indonesia, Vietnam and China, for example, only 0.1% of the population is made up by overseas immigrants, while in India it is just 0.4% (Betts 2011).

GLOBALISATION AND THE UK

The UK has been affected by globalisation more than most countries for a range of reasons. First, due to its history as a major imperial and maritime power, the UK has long established the habit of trading internationally and operating globally. UK industries have thus had to make less adjustment culturally in order to embrace some of the consequences of globalisation, such as competing on an equal footing with overseas-based corporations. Second, the UK (along with the Republic of Ireland) has benefited greatly from being for the most part English speaking at a time when English has firmly established itself as the language of international business, while also providing international investors with access to the European Single Market. This, combined with a relatively favourable tax regime, more limited business regulation and a preference for free trade arrangements, has helped to attract a great deal of FDI. Over 20% of all FDI coming into the European Union from overseas now comes into the UK (Ernst & Young 2012). UK-based companies are also among the biggest foreign investors in the world. They invest more in the USA than those of any other country as well as being the second-largest foreign investors globally after the USA. Overall, 8.2% of world FDI is carried out by UK companies (UNCTAD 2012). The UK has also long been a destination to which overseas migrants want to come. Net inward migration has topped 200,000 in almost all of the past twenty years, making parts of the country very diverse in terms of the population's cultural background. Over 25% of the babies now born in England each year have mothers who were themselves born overseas, while the figure for London reached 56% in 2011 (ONS 2012).

The causes of globalisation

One of the major debates about globalisation concerns its origins. Why did we start thinking and acting globally in the second half of the twentieth century and not earlier, and why, in particular, have we seen such an acceleration in the past two decades? While there is much disagreement about the significance of particular developments, it is generally agreed that different, interrelated factors have combined together to facilitate the change. Of these, two stand out as being particularly significant: technological developments and government policy.

Technology

There are two major areas of technological development that have made globalisation possible: transportation and information and communications technologies (ICTs), principally by bringing down very substantially both the costs associated with international communication and trade, and the time they take. Dicken (2011) notes that until the past 100 years, to all intents and purposes, communications and transportation technologies were one and the same. Their separation through telegraph, telephone, radio and now digital satellite thus represents one of the most extraordinary achievements of the twentieth century. Transportation was as slow 200 years ago as it was 2000 years ago. Since then a number of technological advances have transformed our ability to ship people, goods, raw materials and ideas around the world. The nineteenth century saw the development of steam power, enabling the development of trains and bigger, faster, ocean-going ships. These drove the development of international economic exchange in the years prior to the First World War. The early twentieth century then saw the development of the internal combustion engine, the development of the motor car and, in consequence, the speeding up of ships and trains. The late 1950s saw two major transport developments that have been major facilitators of globalisation:

1 The development of large commercial jet aircraft able to carry people and goods across the world at previously unimaginable speeds.
2 Containerisation (i.e. the use worldwide of standard-sized steel containers that can be easily and quickly shifted by crane from lorries to trains and on to ships).

ICTs, by contrast, have transformed our ability to transmit information in the years since then. The big breakthroughs here have been the evolution of satellite communications technology since the 1960s, of fibre-optic cables since the 1970s, and of course the World Wide Web and Internet technologies since the 1980s. Together these have given people, as well as organisations, the capacity to transmit very substantial quantities of information (now including video and sound as well as text) almost instantly to every corner of the world very affordably. Therefore, it is now possible not only for a consumer in the UK to find out about the existence of, say, a furniture manufacturer in Vietnam, but also to download detailed colour brochures, to order bespoke items and even to watch them being manufactured in real time. Moreover, the speed of container ships now permits delivery from Vietnam to the customer's home in less than a month after the original order was placed.

Government action

Commentators often point to deregulation as being the other major driver of globalisation alongside technology. They are referring here to the liberalisation of the world trading and economic system over recent years. However, as Dicken (2011) argues strongly, it is important to understand that globalisation has also been accelerated by a good degree of additional regulation in the form of cross-national standardisation in different fields (40 ft containers for transportation, customs documentation, air traffic control conventions, accounting standards, insurance rules, global patents, etc.). Moreover, the establishment of international property rights across most countries has hugely helped to promote FDI.

Nonetheless, it is unquestionably true that a major impetus for increased international trade has been the abandonment or relaxation in recent years of foreign exchange controls and by reductions in the strength and size of tariff regimes aimed at stifling global free trade. We have also seen a strong trend across much of the world away from forms of socialist and communist governance towards forms of liberal democracy. As far as economic policy is concerned, the result has been a great deal less direct state intervention in business activity, a tendency to privatise and to deregulate markets, and a preference on the part of governments across the world actively to encourage competition between businesses while also encouraging entrepreneurship.

The impact of globalisation

It is no exaggeration to claim that globalisation processes of the kind we have described above have utterly transformed the environment in which the vast majority of business is conducted. Moreover, it is unquestionably the case that further transformation will occur in the future, not least in the world's established geo-political balance as economic power steadily transfers from west to east. We only have space here to discuss some of the more apparent, direct effects of these profound developments, concentrating in particular on those which have the greatest implications for the management of people.

Competition

It is notoriously difficult to measure the extent of competition in an industry in any objective or satisfactory manner, and hence impossible accurately to track growth or decline in competitiveness over time. This is because industries vary so much in terms of their competitive structures. You might think that the number of firms in competition would be a good measure on the basis that the more players there are in the competition, the tougher it is to do well. This is, however, over-simplistic as some of the most cut-throat markets in the world are dominated by just two or three companies. We thus have a situation in which all informed opinion agrees that trading conditions in most economies have become hugely more competitive in recent years, but there is no way of measuring whether the change has doubled, tripled or increased twenty-fold over the past few decades. Instead economists use a series of different measures which each act, some more satisfactorily than others, as proxies for measures of competitive intensity. Examples are as follows:

- reductions in the length of time leading firms are able to maintain dominance of a market;
- increases in the extent of churn in 'industry membership';
- increases in the incidence of financial instability (among both established and newer entrants to a market);
- increases in the length of time that episodes of financial instability last;
- increases in the extent to which a market is open to overseas competitors;
- increases in the number of small businesses/start-ups, and increases in their growth rates;
- increases in concentration ratios (i.e. the extent to which the top five or top ten companies in an industry contribute to its total output);
- increases in the extent of 'discounting' (i.e. price reductions);
- decreases in 'perceived ability to increase prices' as measured in surveys of executives.

Against all these measures, while the extent of change varies greatly, the majority of industries both in the UK and across the world can be judged to have become very substantially more competitively intensive over the past thirty years, much of the increase being experienced in the most recent years (McNamara *et al.* 2003).

There is no question that globalisation has played a major role in creating more competitive commercial conditions simply by increasing several-fold the number of potential competitors any one organisation faces. Established organisations that once dominated national markets now find themselves to be relative small-fry in an expanding and much less predictable global market. Indeed, in recent years a number of academics and consultants have advanced the view that the competitive environment in some industries is not just reaching a new level of intensity, but developing in a qualitatively different direction than has been the case in the past. The term 'hyper-competition' is increasingly used in this context; another term that is sometimes used is 'high-velocity competition' (Adcroft *et al.* 2010, Chew and Osborne 2009). In conditions of hyper-competition turbulence and unpredictability are the norm, so that firms which gain competitive advantage find that it is rapidly eroded by the changing business environment. Competitive advantage thus becomes transitory in nature, requiring organisations that wish to grow to 'reinvent the wheel' continually or 'ride the wave of innovation'.

Hyper-competitiveness conditions are most readily observed in the finance, manufacturing, IT and biotechnology industries. But more generally, all organisations with any kind of exposure to international competition are finding it harder both to gain or sustain any kind of competitive advantage and to maintain a high level of profitability. In many cases survival has also become increasingly hard to guarantee.

Organisations thus have to develop strategies to cope effectively. For example, they have continually to seek ways of increasing the efficiency with which they conduct their operations, keeping a lid on costs while ensuring sufficient investment in value-producing activities. There is also an increased requirement to anticipate future environmental developments accurately as well as customer tastes and preferences in order to stay ahead of their competitors. Additional competition also requires companies to drive technological advances themselves through appropriate research and development (R&D) activity, to enter and exit markets with greater frequency and to participate in more merger and acquisition activity in order to generate economies of scale.

A number of the more significant contemporary issues and developments in the HR field derive directly from increased competitive intensity in product markets. Examples are the following, all of which we return to discuss at length later in the book:

1 The need to run the HR function in as efficient a manner as possible. The growth of the shared-services model, as well as HR outsourcing, is a result. The increased emphasis on measuring HR outcomes and progress against quantitative targets is another.

2 A capacity to recruit, retain and motivate high performers becomes increasingly significant the more competitive an industry becomes. The firms which gain and maintain exclusive access to the best brains are best placed to survive and thrive.

3 Increased competition tends to dampen wage demands, but in any event, produces a situation in which the capacity to increase pay is increasingly limited. Positive motivation, as well as the attraction and retention of staff, thus has to be achieved through different means. This is leading to an increased focus on the relational aspects of the employment experience and a reduced focus on transactional aspects.

4 Growing competitiveness means that it is more necessary to maintain high standards of quality and of customer service. This means meeting customer expectations, if possible surpassing them, and treating customers as individuals rather than as a mass. To achieve this it is necessary to treat employees in such a way as to elicit high levels of effort and performance. This requires more attention to be given to job satisfaction and to employee engagement so that employees feel both valued and committed.

Industrial restructuring

Over the past sixty years, the trend accelerating in more recent years, most economies in the world have restructured profoundly in response to globalisation. Put simply, agrarian economies have become industrial economies, while established industrial economies have largely become service based and knowledge based. This has rarely been a matter of choice. Instead, in order to maintain growth, economies have increasingly had to focus on industrial activities in which they have a particular competitive advantage of some kind. The UK is a good example of a country that has restructured profoundly in response to globalisation, experiencing what amounts to a second Industrial Revolution over the past three or four decades. The adjustment has often been very uncomfortable as its economy has moved in a generation from one which was largely based on manufacturing prowess to one which is now dominated by service industries.

The key long-term trends are shown in Figure 2.1. This shows how, during the period known as 'the Industrial Revolution', the proportion of UK output devoted to agriculture fell hugely as farming became more efficient, the population grew and became urbanised. Until the 1960s the manufacturing sector continued to grow and accounted for a very substantial proportion of the economy. Since then growth has been focused on the service sector, which now accounts for over 80% of both output and jobs.

The UK's shift in balance from manufacturing to services is typical of all the major western industrialised countries, although the process has been notably faster, and has gone further, in the UK than in most other EU member states and in the USA. The trend is almost entirely explained by the globalisation of the world economy. Quite simply it has become far cheaper to manufacture most products overseas in low-wage economies

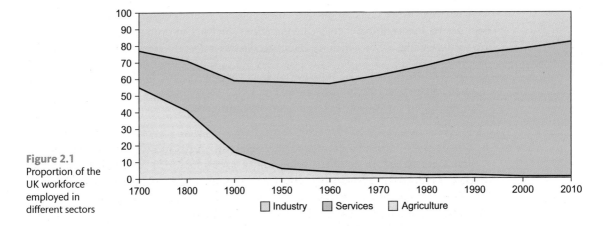

Figure 2.1
Proportion of the UK workforce employed in different sectors

and to ship them to the big consumer markets than it is to manufacture them close to the consumer. The same is true of mined goods and agricultural products. The manufacture of lower-cost goods is no longer profitable in the UK because the sources of raw materials are distant and because labour costs are relatively high here. It has also become cheaper for UK consumers to import much of their food from overseas rather than to grow it here.

In place of the mass production of manufactured goods, the UK economy like many others has had to adjust so that it specialises in the provision of services for which there is demand elsewhere in the world. Hence, in recent decades as traditional manufacturing and agriculture have become less significant, the following industries have grown:

- financial services
- business services
- creative and cultural industries
- higher education
- research/science
- tourism
- hi-tech manufacturing
- sports and leisure
- retailing
- restaurants/bars
- IT
- construction/engineering

Profound restructuring is also occurring across the developing world. Here we are seeing shifts of a similar nature to those experienced during the first Industrial Revolution in the UK. Agrarian economies in which most people worked on the land producing food are becoming industrial economies, manufacturing goods which are sold all over the world. The key difference this time is in the speed with which developing economies are transforming themselves. They are also, in many cases, fast moving beyond the manufacture of cheaper manufactured goods into hi-tech, high-value-added manufacturing and service provision. In the 1950s and 1960s Japan led the way, closely followed by other 'tiger economies' such as Hong Kong, South Korea, Singapore and Taiwan. These are now among the wealthiest nations in the world. We are currently seeing a similar transformation of the massive Chinese economy, which is truly now the centre of world manufacturing. Brazil, India and many other countries are following on close behind, with their vast populations and strong rates of economic growth. The beginnings of similar developments can also be observed in many African nations.

The impact of these changes on labour markets has been vast and continues to have a transformational effect. Quite simply they mean that the established stock of skills among a people becomes increasingly obsolete. We are all having to learn new ways of earning a living, and often having to relearn another set of skills later in life again. The process of industrial restructuring is thus a very painful one for many people, and indeed for whole communities. The skills that used to make people highly employable are increasingly not required. Established industries have less and less demand for people all the time as they decline and introduce labour-saving technologies, while newer industries often struggle to recruit people with the skills and experience that they need. We see this process happening across the world. It is creating in most countries a situation in which some skills are in over-supply, while others are in under-supply.

This has some deeply worrying social effects, as it leads inexorably to far greater levels of inequality. Goos and Manning (2007) and Goos *et al.* (2009) have argued in highly influential articles that labour markets in the UK and across Europe are increasingly assuming an hourglass shape as they become more polarised between higher and lower skills. In brief, they argue that the following is happening:

- Increasing numbers of people are being employed in relatively highly paid, secure, professional and managerial occupations in the finance, private services and some parts of the public sectors.

- Jobs in manufacturing along with many clerical and administrative roles are being 'exported' to countries in Eastern Europe, to China, India and other developing economies where cheaper labour is readily available.

- At the same time, the growing numbers of higher-paid people are using their disposable income to purchase services which cannot be provided from overseas – hence the simultaneous and rapid growth in demand for hairdressers, beauticians, restaurant workers, and people to work in the tourist and entertainment-orientated industries. These jobs tend to be lower paid.

The net impact is easy to appreciate. In the top half of the hourglass are people with skills that are in demand from the expanding industries. Here, over the long term there are more jobs available than there are people who are appropriately qualified to fill them. The result is a relatively tight labour market in which skills shortages are relatively common, leading to upwards pressure on wages and to desirable terms and conditions of employment. In short, employers have to pay well and to treat people well in order to attract and retain them. By contrast, in the bottom half of the hourglass things are very different. There are more people looking for jobs than there are jobs available. Wages are thus being pushed downwards, while employers get away with treating people poorly, employing them on terms which are undesirable. These trends can be traced back to the 1970s in the case of the UK and are clearly associated with the industrial restructuring that the economy has undergone in response to globalisation in the years since then. But the same processes are observable around the world as the new skills sought by economies are nearly always in shorter supply than those sought in the past. This is why, for example, there are major shortages of appropriately qualified managerial staff in China (Cooke 2005: 175), skilled factory workers in South Africa (Wood 2011: 308, 317), academics in India (Thankachan *et al.* 2010) and medical staff in a great many developing countries (Koser 2007: 52).

SKILLS SHORTAGES IN THE UK

Despite five years of recession, sluggish growth and relatively high unemployment, skills shortages remain common in the UK. The Chartered Institute of Personnel and Development's (CIPD) annual surveys on recruitment report that throughout the past ten years a good majority of respondents work in organisations that are facing 'recruitment difficulties due to skills shortages':

2002: 77%	2006: 82%	2010: 68%
2003: 93%	2007: 84%	2011: 75%
2004: 85%	2008: 86%	2012: 82%
2005: 85%	2009: 81%	

There is every reason to expect these trends to continue in the future, and if anything to worsen. This is for two main reasons:

1 The capacity of the UK's education and training system to furnish the workforce with the skills that the evolving economy requires is proving to be limited. All the growth as far as jobs are concerned is in the specialised, higher-level professional and managerial categories. Yet the UK still has a situation in which only a minority of young people go on to university courses after leaving school and in which vast numbers leave school either without any qualifications at all, or else with only very limited proficiency in science, maths and English. The Leitch Report (2006)

characterised the UK's performance on skills development as 'mediocre' by international standards, while projecting a situation in which over 40% of jobs will require either a degree or a further degree by 2020.

2 In the past fifty years the supply of skills has kept pace with increasing demand due chiefly to three key developments in the UK labour market: the entry into the workforce of many more women (female participation has risen from 42% in 1950 to over 75% today), the presence in the workforce of the unusually large 'baby-boom generation' consisting of people born between 1945 and 1965, and substantial net inward migration from overseas. All three of these sources of labour supply are now beginning to dry up somewhat. Female participation levels are now almost as high in the UK as they are anywhere in the world, reducing the prospects for further expansion. The baby-boom generation, meanwhile, has begun to retire, requiring employers to source skills from the far smaller Generation Y that is now being educated to provide them: 17.6 million people were born in the UK between 1945 and 1964, compared with just 14.8 million between 1985 and 2004. Finally of course we are seeing increasingly active attempts by government to curb the extent of net inward migration into the UK. The number of skilled and highly skilled entrants from outside the EU is now subject to a monthly cap, the aim being radically to reduce the numbers entering by tens of thousands each year.

The rise of multinational corporations

A multinational organisation is generally defined as one which is clearly based in a home country but which owns assets overseas. This is different from an organisation that operates internationally by exporting and importing products or services, but which does not own any overseas assets. Multinationals are also often distinguished from transnational corporations, which operate internationally but are not run from or necessarily originate in any one country. There are plenty of multinational corporations (MNCs). Vodaphone is an example of a major UK multinational. While based in the UK, the vast majority of its assets are overseas ($201,000 million out of a total of $219,000 million) as are its staff (69,000 of its 79,000 employees are based outside the UK).

As we explained above, FDI is the term that is used for a situation in which a company based in one country purchases assets in other countries. The United Nations Agency for Trade and Development (UNCTAD) publishes annual estimates of the total value of FDI across the world. UNCTAD has been using the same methodology since 1980, allowing us to track the huge extent of its growth over the past thirty years, including a rapid acceleration in more recent years. Once inflation is taken into account, UNCTAD calculates the total value of FDI stock to have been worth just over $700 billion in 1980. By 1990 the figure had tripled to $2.1 trillion and by 2000 had reached $7.4 trillion. Its last published estimates value the total value of world FDI at $20.4 trillion (UNCTAD 2012). This represents more than a twenty-five-fold increase over a period of thirty years.

These figures illustrate the sheer scale of the rise of multinational organisations in recent years. Many now have combined assets that are worth more than the gross domestic products of smaller countries. The company with the largest amount of foreign assets in the world at present is BNP Paribus, the French banking corporation. Its total assets are estimated by UNCTAD to be worth nearly $2.9 trillion. It operates in 61 countries and employs over 200,000 people. Other banks are not far behind, including the UK's largest banking group HSBC Holdings PLC with its $2.3 trillion of worldwide assets and 309,000 employees across 54 countries. Forbes, the American business journal, compiles a list of the biggest companies in the world as measured by an index which includes sales, profits, assets and overall market value. The top places are dominated by multinational banks and oil companies. But what is most interesting about the Forbes list is the way that it changes from year to year, allowing us to observe the key trends. In 2006, the top ten contained six American-owned companies, one Japanese company (Toyota), one from Germany (DaimlerChrysler), one from the UK (BP) and Royal Dutch Shell. Of these only Shell is still in the top ten today. Back then there were four car manufacturers in the top ten, but there are now only two – both German – in the top fifty. Another major recent trend is the rise up the list of the giant Chinese banking and oil corporations. They hardly featured in the upper echelons of the Forbes list ten years ago when there were only twelve listed in the top 500. There are now twenty-five Chinese companies in the top 500, including six in the top twenty-five. In the same period the number of Indian companies in the top 500 has grown from one to nine. In total, in 2006, out of the biggest 500, 430 were based in the USA, Europe or Japan. Five years later, 111 were based elsewhere in the world.

Giving these companies a single national designation is becoming less and less tenable over time as they expand internationally and are increasingly owned by shareholders based all over the globe. BP, for example, actively discourages the use of its full, original name (British Petroleum) on the grounds that it owns more assets in the USA than it does in the UK and employs as many people there too. Daimler Chrysler is labelled 'German' but was formed by the merging of two corporations, one German and the other American.

Firms internationalise their operations for a variety of reasons. For most the major motivation is growth and the wealth-generating possibilities that are associated with expansion into new markets. However, in some cases there is another aim: that is, the desire to reduce costs by locating operations where labour is cheaper or more productive and other resources are more readily available at a lower cost. Dicken (2011) distinguishes between these two approaches, naming the first a 'market orientation' approach to internationalisation, and the second, an 'asset orientation' approach. Other objectives also mentioned in books and articles on internationalisation are as follows:

1 To reduce risk associated with a domestic business cycle. When one country is in recession, another may be booming. It thus makes sense for a company to have a presence in several countries.

2 In response to foreign competition in the home market.

3 reduce costs by producing close to customers and suppliers.

4 To avoid tariffs by serving foreign markets from within. This is a key reason that many US-based and Japanese-based corporations invest in the UK as it allows them to produce goods and services within the tariff wall operated by the EU.

Expansion into overseas markets tends to occur through two main mechanisms. One approach involves an organisation establishing subsidiaries in overseas countries, often with the help of intermediaries such as banks and consultants who are familiar with markets and how they operate in those countries. The second approach, which is becoming more common, involves merging with or taking over companies based in the target markets. One or two organisations, according to Dicken (2011), have been 'born global', in the sense that they start out as joint ventures between entrepreneurs who are based in different countries. He gives the example of the Momenta Corporation, which was recently founded to exploit developments in 'pen-based computers'. Its founders come from four countries. Its initial operations were based in the USA, Germany and China, while its funding came from institutions based in several further countries.

In terms of its aims and objectives IHRM (i.e. HRM in an international or multinational organisation) is no different from HRM in an organisation based in one country. The purpose is to mobilise an appropriately qualified workforce, and subsequently to retain it, motivate it and develop it. IHRM, however, is more complex and necessarily has a rather different emphasis:

- IHRM involves working with an organisational structure that is more complex.
- There are a greater number of more diverse stakeholder groups to take account of.
- There is greater involvement in people's private/family lives because of the need to expatriate employees with their families.
- Diversity is necessary in terms of management style.
- There are greater numbers of external influences and risks to understand and manage.

IHRM is also generally harder to operationalise really well because of the communication difficulties that arise due to distance and language differences as well as cultural and institutional traditions and assumptions. This makes effective knowledge management and change management harder to achieve in particular. International HR managers thus need to have a somewhat different skill set from domestically focused HR managers and tend to develop careers exclusively in international organisations.

A particular issue of significance for international organisations concerns the design of internal structures and reporting lines. While these are complex issues at the best of times for large organisations, they are made a great deal more involved when geographically diverse workforces are included. Another significant way in which HR varies between nationally based and multinational organisations results from the presence of more multicultural teams, including senior management teams. While culturally diverse teams work well as generators of ideas and in their capacity to harness knowledge, they can operate in a dysfunctional fashion unless care is taken to manage them thoughtfully. Steers *et al.* (2010) set out what they describe as three 'coping strategies' to use and develop when managing culturally diverse teams:

- Avoiding cultural stereotypes (i.e. do not make assumptions about people based on a crude and limited understanding of their national cultures).

- See cultural differences in neutral terms (i.e. be fully aware of both the advantages and disadvantages that can come from the employment of diverse teams).

- Prepare for the unexpected (i.e. be aware of your own biases and cultural perspectives so that you can adapt quickly when dealing with those of others).

Volatility

The more competitive markets become, particularly as they internationalise, the more volatile and unpredictable the trading environment becomes for organisations. Economic stability of the kind that can exist and be promoted by government in a national market is much much harder to achieve internationally. Moreover, new technologies and applications are continually being developed all over the world and brought to market very rapidly. Insecurity, unpredictability and volatility are thus increasingly characterising many product markets, although the impact is far greater in some than it is in others. This inevitably makes it much harder than is the case in relatively stable business environments for organisations to be able to offer their staff long-term stable employment of a traditional kind.

More intense competition and greater volatility also provide the pretext for organisations to change heir structure more frequently. In some industries it has been observed that organisations are now engaged in 'permanent restructuring' as new opportunities present themselves and established businesses cease to generate the profits they once did.

Due in large part to globalisation we are thus faced with the evolution of a business environment which requires:

- more opportunistic approaches to business;
- maximum organisational agility;
- much more flexible working patterns;
- greater levels of functional flexibility;
- faster and more frequent change – both of a structural and cultural kind.

The result is a change in emphasis as far as HR is concerned. Different types of activity now top the HR agenda in organisations than used to in the past. There is, for example, a requirement to be much more actively involved in the promotion of effective change management. Organisations often handle the 'people side' of change very poorly. Decisions, even about major restructuring exercises, let alone mergers, acquisitions, downsizing and outsourcing initiatives, are frequently taken without consulting employees and, in many cases, without any genuine communication at all. This is partly due to poor management, partly due to wishes on the part of leaders to avoid conflict and resistance, and partly to the premium that must often be placed on commercial confidentiality in many situations (e.g. takeovers or sales of businesses).

Published research on the subject of change management is full of examples of situations in which change has been very poorly managed with negative consequences for organisations. Baxter and Macleod (2008), for example, undertook a major longitudinal research project involving change-management episodes in twenty diverse organisations. The aim, in each case, was to increase efficiency or quality. In practice all failed to meet their initial expectations due to poor management. Communication exercises were typically inadequate, while managers failed to take proper account of 'employees' feelings of insecurity and anger'. What was worse, though, according to this study, was that the senior managers who were responsible sometimes failed to accept that their initiatives had disappointed in practice. Great efforts were made to manipulate data so that the appearance of success could be proclaimed, even though the vast majority of employees knew this to be a fake. Further cynicism was then generated by the launch of newer initiatives aimed at achieving the same objectives, but with different names. According to Baxter and Macleod, it was only when employees were fully involved in planning and decision making that the same problems were subsequently avoided, making second attempts at introducing change more successful. This conclusion should come as no surprise. The well-known adage 'people support what they help to create' carries a great deal of truth, but is something that leaders in organisations often appear to ignore.

Conclusions

We can conclude this chapter by observing that globalisation is both deeply rooted and probably irreversible. Its impact on industry and the business context has been and continues to be transformational. As far as people management is concerned, globalisation has not, however, changed the core purpose of the HRM function. This remains as it always has been: to recruit, retain, develop, motivate and engage employees more effectively than competitors are able to in order to sustain superior levels of performance. Instead the major impact has been to complicate HR practice and in important ways to make it harder to accomplish the core purpose effectively. Globalisation requires us increasingly to manage in culturally diverse settings and to manage teams of staff from a wider variety of backgrounds. It requires us to manage people through more complex organisational structures and often to do so in a state of near-perpetual change. Increased competitive intensity requires us both to work harder at recruiting, retaining and motivating good performers, and at the same time to restrict the resources available to achieve these objectives as tighter cost control becomes increasingly necessary. We are tasked with making organisations much more flexible and responsive to change which inevitably reduces job security. Yet at the same time we are being urged to elicit loyalty and greater levels of discretionary effort from our staff. The need to keep a tight reign on costs is also creating a situation in which HR functions not only have to add value for their organisations, but also must be seen to be adding value, being required to justify their existence in raw financial terms. Above all, globalisation has brought much more uncertainty and unpredictability to our business environment. This makes longer-term HR planning less and less viable, its place in HR strategy gradually being replaced by the need to build a capacity for flexibility and organisational agility so that unforeseen opportunities can be seized and exploited more rapidly and effectively than can be achieved by competitor organisations.

SUMMARY PROPOSITIONS

2.1 Globalisation is the most significant contemporary development in the business environment. It has largely been brought about as a result of technological developments and the choices made by governments around the world.

2.2 Globalisation has had a major impact on businesses and the management of people. This will continue for the foreseeable future.

2.3 The major changes brought about by globalisation have been increased volatility in product markets, increased competitive intensity, wholesale industrial restructuring and the rise to prominence of multinational corporations.

2.4 The impact on HRM has largely been to make it more challenging and complex to achieve core people management objectives.

GENERAL DISCUSSION TOPICS

1 Would it be possible or desirable either to reverse the globalisation process or to slow it down considerably?

2 From a people management perspective, who are the biggest winners and who are the biggest losers from globalisation?

3 Why are the developments discussed in this chapter affecting some industries more profoundly than others?

 **THEORY INTO PRACTICE**

Dixon Ticonderoga

Until quite recently Dixon Ticonderoga was a dominant player in the US pencil market. Able to trace its origins back to the 1790s, throughout the twentieth century the company was a household name across the USA. For a hundred years the company managed to maintain a highly profitable 30–40% share of a growing US pencil market, its iconic 'Number 2' yellow and green pencils being used across the country by millions of children when sitting school tests and exams. By 1990, 4 billion pencils were being sold each year in the USA, a good chunk of them manufactured by Dixon at its plants in Florida. At this time four US manufacturers dominated the market, Dixon Ticonderoga being the second biggest, enjoying annual revenues of $90 to 95 million a year.

Things started to change rapidly after 1990 with the entry of Chinese manufactures into the US pencil market. By using cheaper labour and sourcing much cheaper raw materials of superior quality, Chinese pencils could be retailed at half the cost of those manufactured by Dixon. Moreover, in many consumers' eyes they not only looked the same, but functioned more effectively too. The result was a prolonged period in which pencils originating in Chinese factories steadily captured a greater share of the US market. In 1991 imported pencils accounted for just 16% of the total US pencil market, reaching 50% by the turn of the century. In 2004 imports accounted for 72% of the market and by 2010 for 87%. What is more, this level of penetration was achieved despite the US government applying big tariffs on imported pencils in order artificially to inflate their prices, $4 million being collected from Chinese pencil manufacturers in 2010.

Dixon Ticonderoga was slow to respond effectively to the challenge of overseas competition. Reluctant to downsize or close its US plants or to source materials from outside the USA, it held back from taking the radical strategic decisions necessary in order to secure its revenues and its future as an independent company. It was one of the companies that successfully lobbied for the imposition of tariffs on imported pencils in 1994.

Over time, though, changes were made. Dixon Ticonderoga started to ship wood from Indonesia and rubber for erasers from Korea. The company also experimented by making pencils out of recycled paper cases. But it was still unable to compete effectively with its Chinese competitors. Eventually the difficult decision had to be taken to stop manufacturing standard, mass-market pencils in the USA, so in 2000 production was shifted to a plant in Mexico and to a wholly owned subsidiary in China.

Today the Dixon Ticonderoga brand remains in existence, but its market share is tiny compared with that which it enjoyed twenty or thirty years ago. It focuses increasingly on niche stationery products at the luxury end of the market, and no longer manufactures pencils in the USA or uses raw materials sourced in the USA. Since 2005 Dixon Ticonderoga has been owned in its entirety by the Italian industrial conglomerate Fila-Fabricca Italiana.

Questions

1 How did Dixon Ticonderoga and the other US-based pencil manufacturers manage to hold on to such a dominant share of their market until 1990?

2 Why do you think managers at Dixon Ticonderoga were so slow to respond radically to the arrival of overseas competitors?

3 In retrospect what steps should they have taken in the 1990s to secure their future?

4 What would have been the likely HRM consequences had they taken these steps?

Sources: www.fundinguniverse.com/company-histories/dixon-ticonderoga-company-history; www.bloomberg.com/news

FURTHER READING

The book entitled *Global Shift* by Peter Dicken (2011), now in its sixth edition, offers a superb introduction to all aspects of globalisation including detailed case studies of the impact on particular industrial sectors.

Global HR: Challenges facing the function by Peter Reilly and Tony Williams (2012) provides a very readable, well-informed and up-to-date survey of the various different ways in which mostly UK companies are adjusting their HRM practices in the face of globalisation.

In *Contemporary Issues in Human Resource Management*, Stephen Taylor (2011) develops a number of the points made in this chapter, particularly those relating to competition and skills shortages at greater length and in more detail.

REFERENCES

Adcroft, A., Teckman, J. and Willis, R. (2010) 'Is Higher Education in the UK becoming more competitive?', *International Journal of Public Sector Management*, Vol. 23, No. 6, pp. 578–88.

Baxter, L. and Macleod, A. (2008) *Managing Performance Improvement*. London: Routledge.

Betts, A. (ed.) (2011) *Global Migration Governance*. Oxford: Oxford University Press.

Chew, C. and Osborne, S.P. (2009) 'Exploring strategic positioning in the UK charitable sector: Emerging evidence from charitable organisations that provide public services', *British Journal of Management*, Vol. 20, No. 1, pp. 90–105.

Cooke, F.L. (2005) *HRM, Work and Employment in China*. London: Routledge.

Dicken, P. (2011) *Global Shift: Mapping the changing contours of the world economy*, 6th edn. London: Sage.

Ernst & Young (2012) *UK Attractiveness Survey 2012*. London: Ernst & Young.

Goldin, G., Cameron, G. and Balarajan, M. (2011) *Exceptional People: How migration shaped our world and will define our future*. Princeton, NJ: Princeton University Press.

Goos, M. and Manning, A. (2007) 'Lousy and lovely jobs: The rising polarisation of work in Britain', *Review of Economics and Statistics*, Vol. 89, No. 1, pp. 118–33.

Goos, M., Manning, A. and Salomons, A. (2009) 'Job polarisation in Europe', *American Economic Review*, Vol. 99, No. 2, pp. 58–63.

IATA (2011) Press release 8. **www.iata.org**.

Koser, K. (2007) *International Migration: A very short introduction*. Oxford: Oxford University Press.

Leitch, S. (2006) 'Prosperity for all in the global economy – world class skills', *Final Report: The Leitch Review of Skills*. London: HM Treasury.

McNamara, G., Vaaler, P. and Devers, C. (2003) 'Same as it ever was: The search for evidence of increasing hypercompetition', *Strategic Management Journal*, Vol. 24, No. 1, pp. 261–78.

ONS (2012) *Births in England and Wales by Parents' Country of Birth, 2011*. Fareham: Office of National Statistics.

Reilly, P. and Williams, T. (2012) *Global HR: Challenges facing the function*. Farnham, Gower.

Scholte, J.A. (2005) *Globalisation: A critical introduction*, 2nd edn. Basingstoke: Palgrave.

Steers, R., Sanchez-Rubde, C. and Nardon, L. (2010) *Management Across Cultures: Challenges and strategies*. Cambridge: Cambridge University Press.

Taylor, S. (2011) *Contemporary Issues in Human Resource Management*. London: CIPD.

Thankachan, T., Sharma, P.B. and Singh, R.K. (2010) 'Managing the shortage of teaching faculty for technical education in India', *International Journal of Continuing Engineering Education and Life Long Learning*, Vol. 20, No. 3–5, pp. 365–80.

UNCTAD (2012) *World Investment Report 2012*. New York: United Nations Conference on Trade and Development.

Wes, M. (1996) *Globalisation: Winners and losers*. London. Institute for Public Policy Research.

Wood, G. (2011) 'Employment relations in South Africa and Mozambique', in M. Barry and A. Wilkinson (eds), *Research Handbook of Comparative Employment Relations*. Cheltenham: Edward Elgar.

Chapter 3

STRATEGIC HUMAN RESOURCE MANAGEMENT

THE OBJECTIVES OF THIS CHAPTER ARE TO:

1 Clarify the nature of strategic HRM

2 Investigate the relationship between business strategy and HR strategy

3 Explain the universalist and the contingency or fit perspectives of HR strategy, each proposing a different means of identifying which HR practices will lead to high performance

4 Explain *how* such practices may result in higher performance

5 Examine the resource-based view of HR strategy

6 Evaluate all three theoretical perspectives on the nature of HR strategy, each expressing a different view on how the contribution of people to the organisation might be understood and enhanced

Human resources are a critical, if not *the* source of, competitive advantage for the business, rather than, say, access to capital or use of technology (see e.g. Salaman *et al.* 2005). Thus attention needs to be paid, at a strategic level, to the nature of this resource and its management, as this will impact on the performance of the organisation, however defined. Batt and Banerjee (2012) found that, in an analysis of strategic HR research articles in British and American journals, the link between human resources and performance remains the dominant theme. Indeed Boxall and Purcell (2008: 55) argue that:

effective human resource strategy is a necessary, though not a sufficient condition, of firm viability.

On a more practical level, in the most recent Workplace Employment Relations Survey (WERS) it was found that 87% of workplaces with a strategic plan included some issues relating to employment relations (broadly defined) (Kersley *et al.* 2006). Directly comparable results for WERS6 (2011) were not available at the time of going to press.

Strategic HRM

Tyson's (1995) definition of HR strategy is a useful starting point, although somewhat limited, as will be seen from our later discussion:

the intentions of the corporation both explicit and covert, towards the management of its employees, expressed through philosophies, policies and practices.

Thus HR strategy need not be written on a piece of paper, and published, and may not be explicit, but reflects the way that management sees employee relations in a particular workplace. The Cranet Survey of International Strategic HR found that 39% of UK companies did not have a written HR strategy (Guthridge and Lawson 2008).

ACTIVITY 3.1

Using an organisation with which you are familiar:

1 Identify the explicit intentions of the organisation towards the management of its people in terms of overall philosophy, policies and practices.

2 Assess the extent to which you consider these intentions to be implemented in practice, giving evidence to support your judgement.

3 How can you explain any mismatch between explicit intentions and actual practice?

A strategy may be a physical document but a strategic approach can also be seen as an incremental process, affected by political influences and generating learning. Strategies are often neither finished, nor complete, but rather incremental and piecemeal. Much strategic HR tends to be issue based rather than the formulation of a complete and integrated strategy. Strategic thinking, strategic decision making and a strategic orientation are sometimes more realistic expectations, although increasingly some organisations do achieve a superficially more complete approach by the use of scorecards and dashboards, which we look at in the following chapter. In any event HR strategies need to be flexible and adaptable as circumstances change.

Much of the general strategy literature also views strategy as a process which is not necessarily rational and top down, but a political and evolutionary process. Mintzberg (1994), for example, argues that strategy is 'formed' rather than 'formulated' and that any intended strategy is changed by events, opportunities, the actions of employees and so on – so that the realised strategy is different from the initial vision. Strategy, Mintzberg argues, can only be identified in retrospect and, as Boxall and Purcell (2008) suggest, is best seen in the ultimate behaviour of the organisation. Indeed strategy is not necessarily determined by top management alone but can be influenced 'bottom up', as ideas are tried and tested in one part of the organisation and gradually adopted in a wholesale manner if they are seen to be applicable and successful. In tracing back strategy to its roots, Storey (2007) notes that there are likely to be instances of incremental learning and false leads.

Strategy is inevitably a process of change, as the organisation attempts to change from the state it is in to a strategically identified future state. The literature draws out the need to sense changes in the environment, develop a resultant strategy and turn this strategy into action. While the HR function has often found itself excluded from the business strategy formation process, HR strategy has more often been seen in terms of the implementation of organisational strategies. However, implementation of HR strategy has, at best, been weak. Among the qualities of the most successful organisations is the ability to turn strategy into action quickly (Ulrich 1998), in other words to implement the chosen strategy, and this continues to be a challenge according to Kaplan and Norton (2005) who found that 95% of employees did not know or did not understand their company's strategy. A lack of attention to the implementation of HR strategy has been identified, and Guest (2011) points out how this focuses attention on the role of the line manager and HR effectiveness. However, frameworks such as the HR scorecard (Becker *et al.* 2001), and others, are aimed, at least in part, at facilitating the management and implementation of HR strategy (see Chapter 4).

One organisation where the HR function has had a major role to play in the successful implementation of HR strategy is Kwik-Fit Financial Services. The overriding strategic purpose was to make the organisation 'a fantastic place to work' and this led to initiatives focusing on improving the working environment and encouraging employees to bring their whole selves to work (Griffiths 2006). The Window on practice below shows how one organisation implemented business and HR strategy and how it used a set of desired values as focus.

WINDOW ON PRACTICE

Implementing strategy at Fujitsu

Fujitsu Services, which designs, builds and operates IT systems and services, was formed in 2002 when the Japanese IT group acquired ICL. Three years after this a need was identified to ensure all employees were working towards the same goal and communicating clearly. To meet this strategic need a programme called 'Reputation' was designed with the aim of aligning all employees (senior managers, on-call engineers, service desk teleworkers) operating out of more than twenty countries, to the same values and customer brand so that customers received a consistent experience.

The Reputation model was introduced into small group sessions cascading through the organisation with 'Reputation champions' initially leading the programme. These champions trained 2,000 managers to deliver the programme to their teams.

The values chosen to reflect the company brand were: realism, straight-talking and tenacious. These were important as historically Fujitsu had been known for overpromising and underperforming. Both the HR and marketing functions promoted the programme aiming to ensure the internal (staff) and external (customers) coherence of the brand.

Staff were helped to understand how their behaviour affected colleagues, customers and the business overall, and a shared vocabulary has been developed. All staff were encouraged to regard themselves as key players, and always 'put their best face forward'. The sessions were also designed to open lines of communication and engage staff in debates about the business in groups with a mix of staff level and from a range of departments. This was intended to help people recognise that their goals were the same. Employee contributions were viewed as key and the programme intended to be interactive, not top down.

Fujitsu aimed to embed its values across the business: for example, when HR policies are designed these are tested against the values, with the idea of ensuring a consistent experience. Cohesive working is the ultimate aim of the programme.

Source: Adapted from 'Build a better brand', *People Management*, Vol. 14, No. 15, pp. 24–5 (Chubb, L.), Reproduced with the permission of the publisher, the Chartered Institute of Personnel and Development, London (**www.cipd.co.uk**).

The relationship between business strategy and HR strategy

The nature, desirability and feasibility of the link between business strategy and HR strategy is a consistent theme which runs through the strategy literature, although, as we shall discuss later, some theories suggest that implementing 'best practice' in HRM is even more important than this. Figure 3.1 is a simple model that is useful in visualising different ways in which this relationship may be played out and has relevance for the newer conceptions of strategy based on the resource-based view of the firm, as well as earlier conceptions.

In the *separation model* (A) there is no relationship at all, if indeed organisational and HR strategy *do* exist in an explicit form in the organisation. This is a typical picture of thirty years ago, but it still exists today, particularly in smaller organisations.

The *fit model* (B) represents a growing recognition of the importance of people in the achievement of organisational strategy. Employees are seen as key in the implementation of the declared organisational strategy, and HR strategy is designed to fit with this. Some

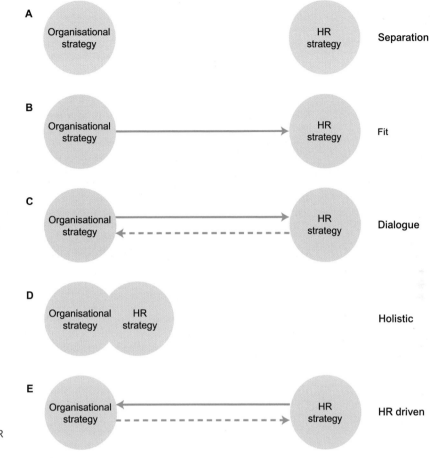

Figure 3.1
Potential
relationships
between
organisational
strategy and HR
strategy

of the early formal models of HR strategy, particularly that proposed by Fombrun *et al*. (1984), concentrate on how the HR strategy can be designed to ensure a close fit, and the same approach is used in the Schuler and Jackson example in Table 3.1 of this chapter.

This whole approach depends on a view of strategy formulation as a logical rational process, which remains a widely held view. The relationship in the fit model is exemplified by organisations which cascade their business objectives down from the senior management team through functions (including HR), through departments, through teams and so on, so that each can identify what they need to do to meet organisational demands.

The *dialogue model* (C) takes the relationship one step further, as it recognises the need for two-way communication and some debate. What is demanded in the organisation's strategy may not be viewed as feasible and alternative possibilities need to be reviewed. The debate, however, is often limited, as shown in the example in the Window on practice which follows.

Table 3.1
Business strategies, and associated employee role behaviour and HRM policies

Strategy	Employee role behaviour	HRM policies
1 Innovation	A high degree of creative behaviour	Jobs that require close interaction and coordination among groups of individuals
	Longer-term focus	Performance appraisals that are more likely to reflect longer-term and group-based achievements
	A relatively high level of cooperative, interdependent behaviour	Jobs that allow employees to develop skills that can be used in other positions in the firm
		Compensation systems that emphasise internal equity rather than external or market-based equity
	A moderate degree of concern for quality	Pay rates that tend to be low, but that allow employees to be stockholders and have more freedom to choose the mix of components that make up their pay package
	A moderate concern for quantity; an equal degree of concern for process and results	Broad career paths to reinforce the development of a broad range of skills
	A greater degree of risk taking; a higher tolerance of ambiguity and unpredictability	
2 Quality enhancement	Relatively repetitive and predictable behaviours	Relatively fixed and explicit job descriptions
	A more long-term or intermediate focus	High levels of employee participation in decisions relevant to immediate work conditions and the job itself
	A moderate amount of cooperative, interdependent behaviour	A mix of individual and group criteria for performance appraisal that is mostly short term and results orientated
	A high concern for quality	A relatively egalitarian treatment of employees and some guarantees of employment security
	A modest concern for quantity of output	Extensive and continuous training and development of employees
	High concern for process: low risk-taking activity; commitment to the goals of the organisation	
3 Cost reduction	Relatively repetitive and predictable behaviour	Relatively fixed and explicit job descriptions that allow little room for ambiguity
	A rather short-term focus	Narrowly designed jobs and narrowly defined career paths that encourage specialisation, expertise and efficiency
	Primarily autonomous or individual activity	Short-term results-orientated performance appraisals
	Moderate concern for quality	Close monitoring of market pay levels for use in making compensation decisions
	High concern for quantity of output	Minimal levels of employee training and development
	Primary concern for results; low risk-taking activity; relatively high degree of comfort with stability	

Source: R.S. Schuler and S.E. Jackson (1987) 'Linking competitive strategies with human resource management practices', *Academy of Management Executive*, Vol. 1, No. 3. Reproduced with permission of the Academy of Management.

The integrated/holistic model and the HR-driven model (D and E) show a much closer involvement between organisational and HR strategy.

The *integrated/holistic model* (D) represents the people of the organisation being recognised as the key to competitive advantage rather than just the way of implementing organisational strategy. In other words, HR strategy is not just the means for achieving business strategy (the ends), but an end in itself. HR strategy therefore becomes critical and, as Baird *et al*. (1983) argued, there can be no strategy without HR strategy. Boxall (1996) develops this idea in relation to the resource-based firm, and argues convincingly that business strategy can usefully be interpreted as broader than a competitive strategy (or positioning in the marketplace). In this case business strategy can encompass a variety of other strategies including HRM, and he describes these strategies as the pieces of a jigsaw. This suggests mutual development and some form of integration, rather than a slavish response to a predetermined business strategy, for example the integration of HR and marketing strategies so that the customer brand and the employer brand are aligned, and Simmons (2009) gives an example of this in relation to corporate social responsibility.

The *HR-driven model* (E) offers a more extreme form, which places HR strategy in prime position. The argument here is that if people are the key to competitive advantage, then we need to build on our people strengths. Logically, then, as the potential of our employees will undoubtedly affect the achievement of any planned strategy, it would be sensible to take account of this in developing our strategic direction. Butler (1988) identifies this model as a shift from HR as the implementers of strategy to HR as a driving force in the formulation of the strategy. Again this model is a reflection of a resource-based strategic HRM perspective, and sits well with the increasing attention being given to the notion of 'human capital' where it is the collective nature and quality of the people in the organisation which provide the potential for future competitive advantage (see e.g. Lengnick-Hall and Lengnick-Hall 2003).

ACTIVITY 3.2

1 Which of these approaches to HR strategy most closely fits your organisation? (If you are a full-time student read one or two relevant cases in *People Management* and interpret these as 'your organisation'.)

2 Why did you come to this conclusion?

3 What are the advantages and disadvantages of the approach used?

Theoretical perspectives of strategic HRM

Three theoretical approaches to strategic HRM can be identified. The first is founded on the concept that there is 'one best way' of managing human resources in order to improve business performance. The second focuses on the need to align employment policies and practice with the requirements of business strategy in order that the latter will be achieved and the business will be successful. This second approach is based on the assumption that different types of HR strategies will be suitable for different types of business strategies. The third approach is derived from the resource-based view of the firm, and the perceived value of human capital. This view focuses on the quality of the human resources available to the organisation and its ability to learn and adapt more quickly than its competitors. Supporters of this perspective challenge the need to secure a mechanistic fit with business strategy and focus instead on long-term sustainability and survival of the organisation via the pool of human capital.

Perspective 1: Universalist approach

The universalist approach is derived from the conception of HRM as 'best practice', as we discussed earlier (see Chapter 1). Researchers carried out large-scale statistical research projects to identify the HR practices which were linked to higher organisational performance. Attention was paid to sophisticated and innovative practices, and Huselid (1995), for example, evaluated the links between progressive HR practices and organisational performance using a sample of nearly 1,000 firms. His findings suggested clear statistical relationships between these practices and employee outcomes such as reduced labour turnover and productivity and long- and short-term firm measures of corporate financial performance. The focus was on identifying 'bundles' of practices which were mutually supporting in that the effect of combining a number of HR practices is greater than the effect of using them independently: combinations produce synergy, and this is known as the complimentarity thesis (Boxall and Macky 2009).

It is also generally agreed that grouping HR practices into 'bundles' in what has become known as a high-performance work system (HPWS; Boxall and Macky 2009) is performance enhancing. Such practices generally devolve a degree of control to employees, through, for example, involvement programmes, team-based work, enhanced training and development, and incorporate progressive methods of reward such as gain sharing. As Godard (2004: 349) points out, this 'high performance paradigm has been promoted as "best practice" both for employers, in that it yields higher performance than traditional employment relations practices, and employees in that it focuses on motivation and development'.

Pfeffer (2005), another well-known advocate of the best practice perspective, identifies a bundle of thirteen HR practices which will result in higher performance including: emphasising employment security; recruiting the right people; extensive use of self-managed teams; high wages; incentive pay; high spending on training; reducing status differentials; and sharing of information. He suggests that these practices applied in total will benefit all organisations. However, Lepak and Shaw (2008) point out that Pfeffer's elaboration is based more on interpretation than solid empirical evidence.

The universalist approach is thus based on the premise that one model of labour management – a high-commitment model (sometimes referred to as a high-involvement or high-performance model) – is related to high organisational performance in all contexts, irrespective of the particular competitive strategy of the organisation.

However, there are problems with this approach. For example, Guest *et al.* (2003) confirmed the association between HRM and performance but not that HRM *causes* higher performance. In other words, a high-performing organisation may result in the use of innovative HR practices as it has the funds to do so. This is an issue that continues to vex both academics and practitioners, and longitudinal studies may play a part in helping to resolve this.

There also remains some debate as to which particular bundle of HR practices will stimulate high commitment, as different researchers appear to have found different contradictory bundles. In addition there are problems with the reliability of how the HR practices were reported in the surveys – usually just one respondent at a higher level in the organisation – and no account is taken of line manager or employee views as to whether or how these practices were implemented.

The universalist approach is also unitarist, being based on the assumption that all managers have to do is to apply a certain set of practices and higher performance will result as workers will comply with whatever is required of them without questioning whether it is to their advantage to do so. These models provide some clarity which is attractive, but this is where the problems also lie, as managing people is far more complex than suggested in the model, and in most studies little account appears to be taken of context; the need for an organisation to manage different sections of the workforce in different ways; and the potential for this approach to create work intensification. For example, Truss *et al.* (2012) point to the difficulty of applying these practices in different cultures and countries with different employment laws. Because the prescriptive approach brings with it a set of values, it suggests that there is only one best way and this is it. Finally, Storey (2007) argues that such universalist approaches do not represent a *strategic choice*, being a representation of HRM in its generic sense, as a strategic choice is a differentiator. He argues that, in the early years of HRM, universalist approaches could be construed as strategic as few organisations had adopted them; however, as HRM has become mainstream it could be argued this no longer applies.

ACTIVITY 3.3

1 To what extent could or should an organisation apply best practice to some groups of employees and not others?

2 Use an organisation which you know well and identify whether this is happening, and evaluate the benefits and disadvantages of this approach.

Perspective 2: Fit or contingency approach

The fit or contingency approach is based on two critical forms of fit. The first is external fit (sometimes referred to as vertical integration) – that HR strategy fits with the demands of business strategy. The second is internal fit (sometimes referred to as horizontal integration) – that all HR policies and activities fit together so that they make a coherent whole, are mutually reinforcing and are applied consistently. While external fit is most commonly interpreted as fit with business strategy, Lepak and Shaw (2008) remind us that HR strategy must also fit with, for example, the technology and industry sector, and they consider fit with workforce trends and worker values as emerging factors in respect of fit. Indeed fit with cultural characteristics is becoming more important as international companies increasingly recognise that HR policies and practices cannot be, simply, exported in other cultural contexts. For example, western practices which emphasise individual appraisal and reward will sit awkwardly in a collectivist culture such as Japan.

One of the foundations of the fit approach is found in Fombrun *et al.* (1984), who proposed a basic framework for strategic HRM, demonstrating, within the firm, how HR management and organisation structure (which interact) are derived from the firm's mission and strategy management, with all in turn being influenced by political, economic and cultural forces in the external context. This exemplifies how the *fit model* (B) is used (see Figure 3.1). Figure 3.2 shows how activities *within* HR management can be unified and designed in order to support the organisation's strategy.

The strength of this model is that it provides a simple framework to show how selection, appraisal, development and reward can be mutually geared to produce the required type of employee performance. For example, if an organisation required cooperative team behaviour with mutual sharing of information and support, the broad implications for managing employees would be:

- **Selection**: successful experience of teamwork and sociable, cooperative personality; rather than an independent thinker who likes working alone.

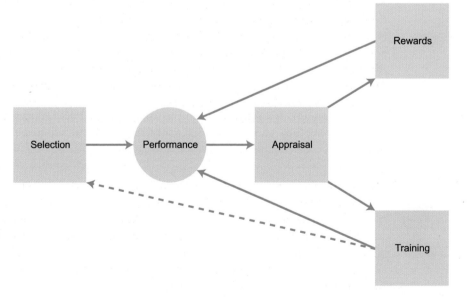

Figure 3.2
The HR cycle
Source: C. Fombrun, N.M. Tichy and M.A. Devanna (1984) *Strategic Human Resource Management.* p. 41. New York: John Wiley & Sons, Inc. © John Wiley & Sons, Inc. Reprinted with permission of John Wiley & Sons, Inc.

- **Appraisal**: based on contribution to the team, and support of others, rather than individual outstanding performance.
- **Reward**: based on team performance and contribution, rather than individual performance and individual effort.

Taking this model and the notion of fit one step further, HR strategy has been conceived in terms of generating specific employee behaviours. In the ideal form of this there would be analysis of the types of employee behaviour required to fulfil a predetermined business strategy, and then an identification of HR policies and practices which would bring about and reinforce this behaviour. In a step change from previous thinking, Schuler and Jackson (1987) produce an excellent example of this concept. They used the three generic business strategies defined by Porter (1980) and for each identified employee role behaviour and the HRM policies required. Their conclusions are shown in Table 3.1.

Similar analyses can be found for other approaches to business strategy, for example in relation to the Boston matrix (Purcell 1992) and the developmental stage of the organisation (Kochan and Barocci 1985). Some HR strategies describe the behaviour of all employees, but others have concentrated on the behaviour of chief executives and senior managers; Miles and Snow (1984), for example, align appropriate managerial characteristics to three generic strategies of prospector, defender and analyser. The types of strategies described above are generic, and there is currently more concentration on tailoring the approach more specifically to the strategic needs of the specific organisation via dashboards and scorecards (see Chapter 4).

Many HR strategies aim not just to target behaviour, but through behaviour change to effect a movement in the culture of the organisation. The target is, therefore, to change the common view of 'the way we do things around here' and to attempt to manipulate the beliefs and values of employees. There is much debate as to whether this is achievable.

There is little doubt that this type of internal fit is valuable. However, questions have been raised over the model's simplistic response to organisational strategy. The question 'what if it is not possible to produce a human resource response that enables the required employee behaviour and performance?' is never addressed. So, for example, the distance between now and future performance requirements, the strengths, weaknesses and potential of the workforce, the motivation of the workforce and employee relations issues are not considered. This model has been criticised because of its dependence on a rational strategy formulation rather than on an emergent strategy formation approach. It has also been criticised due to its unitarist assumptions, as no recognition is made of employees' interests and their choice of whether or not to change their behaviour.

Grundy (1998) claims that the idea of fit seems naive and simplistic. Ogbonna and Whipp (1999) argue that much literature assumes that fit can be targeted, observed and measured and there is an underlying assumption of stability. Given that most companies may have to change radically in response to the environment, any degree of fit previously achieved will be disturbed. Thus they contend that fit is a theoretical ideal which can rarely be achieved in practice. The aim for consistency is also a challenge, as it has been shown that firms use different strategies for different sections of their workforce.

However, in spite of the criticisms of this perspective, it is still employed in both the academic and practitioner literature, see, for example, Holbeche's (2008) book entitled *Aligning Human Resources and Business Strategy*.

A further form of fit which we have not mentioned so far is cultural fit, and the Window on practice below demonstrates this aspect, and shows how fit has to go far beyond a simple fit with business strategy.

WINDOW ON PRACTICE

The influence of national culture on HRM strategies

Fields and colleagues (2006) investigated whether, under similar conditions, organisations in different cultural contexts would strategically respond in a different manner. They compared US organisations with Hong Kong Chinese organisations and studied their strategic approach in conditions of uncertainty in the supply of qualified labour. They studied three aspects of HR relevant to this situation:

- training and development;
- monitoring and assessment of employee performance; and
- staffing through an internal labour market.

They found, as they expected, that in these conditions the Hong Kong Chinese companies increased their use of these three HRM strategies, but that the US companies decreased their use. They explain these different strategic approaches by reference to the cultural context.

You may wish to look ahead to the work of Hofstede, which we present later (see Chapter 6), before reading on.

Training and development (TD)

Fields *et al.* suggest that more TD would be positively viewed by the more collective Chinese culture as a symbol that the organisation is fulfilling its moral obligation to employees, as a way to increase the value of each individual to the collective organisation, and as a reward. Each of these would be valued by Chinese employees, and would encourage them to remain with the organisation. Alternatively, in the more individualistic US culture managers would be reluctant to invest in TD when labour supply is scarce as employees may take advantage of this and use it to find a better job elsewhere.

Emphasis on performance assessment (PA)

Fields *et al.* also suggest that in the Chinese culture, with greater power distance, greater PA may be viewed by employees as a positive symbol that managers are interested in them, and may act as a reminder of the employees' moral association with the organisation – thus encouraging employees to stay. Alternatively, in the US culture with lower power distance, more PA would be viewed negatively. It may be seen as emphasising the difference between managers and employees, and as a way of tightening up the employment relationship, both of which may lead employees to seek employment elsewhere.

Internal labour market (IL)

Greater use of the IL might be viewed in a collectivist culture by the Chinese employees as evidence that they are valued by the organisation and thus it may encourage retention. Alternatively, in an individualistic culture employees may view this unfavourably as evidence of a subjective rather than objective (based on merit) approach to promotion, and managers may view it as a means by which employees can barter for better rewards in a tight labour market.

Source: Adapted from Fields, D., Chan, A., Aktar, S. and Blum, T. (2006) 'Human resource management strategies under uncertainty', *Cross Cultural Management: An International Journal*, Vol. 13, No. 2, pp. 171–86.

Explaining the HRM practices–performance link

Both the universalist and contingency approaches seek to identify *which* HR practices best support high organisational performance; however, another strand of research seeks to explain *how* HR practices lead to enhanced performance. This has become known as unlocking the 'black box' of the HRM–performance link (Purcell *et al.* 2003). Purcell's

Figure 3.3
The people management–performance causal chain
Source: Purcell and Hutchinson (2007: 7), Fig. 1.

work has led to the argument that HR practices improve performance through the influence they have upon employee attitudes. HR practices are thus at the beginning of a causal chain which seeks to influence attitudes, behaviour and then outcomes such as performance (Figure 3.3).

In academic terms, employee attitudes are described as being the mediating variables between practice and improved performance, and determine whether an employee will engage in discretionary behaviour (going above and beyond the minimum they are required to contribute) and consequently achieve higher performance. Clearly if attitudes are the crux of how to influence performance, it is important to understand which employee attitudes HR practices should seek to influence. There is currently a great deal of debate around this and initial theorising focused on the concept of commitment, reflected in the widespread use of the terms 'high-commitment work practices' and 'high-commitment management' and their linkage with high performance. It was argued that such commitment from employees would lead to discretionary behaviour, and thus improve performance, and would also reduce labour turnover and absence costs.

In recent years, however, there has been a questioning of the dominance of commitment. It has been argued that other attitudes such as job satisfaction, motivation and trust are also important in encouraging employees to engage in discretionary behaviour (Macky and Boxall 2007). In our own work, we have argued that employee attitudes such as happiness are also important in affecting behaviour and performance. Happiness has long been neglected in HR literature following unsuccessful attempts to link happiness via job satisfaction to improved performance. It has re-emerged, however, in the positive psychology movement, which refocuses the attention of psychologists on what makes people happy as opposed to the historical trend of investigating what makes people unhappy. Conceptualising happiness as well-being, rather than job satisfaction, has led psychologists to argue once again for a link between this attitude and performance. This theorising is beginning to make its way into the HR literature, Peccei (2004), for example, investigating the extent to which HR practices influence well-being and potentially performance. Our own research (Atkinson and Hall 2011) certainly supports this line of argument and there is much work to be done in the area of employee attitudes and which HR practices influence them and to what extent.

It is only more recently that the importance of employee perceptions of HR practices and their impact on employee attitudes and performance have been recognised despite Kinnie *et al.* (2005: 11) arguing that:

the fulcrum of the HRM–performance causal chain is the employees' reactions to HR practices as experienced by them.

Furthermore, the critical role of the line manager is highlighted as such managers are responsible for the day-to-day implementation of HR practices.

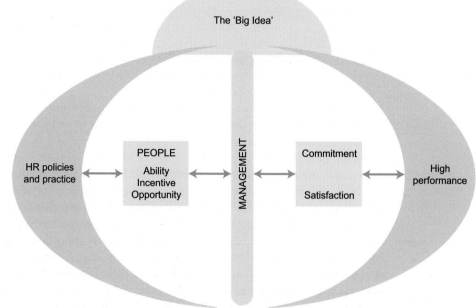

Figure 3.4
'High-performance' model of HR practices and business performance
Source: Adapted from Purcell, J., Kinnie, N., Hutchinson, S., Rayton, B. and Swart, J. (2003) *Understanding the People Performance Link: Unlocking the black box.* Research Report. London: CIPD, Model developed by Bath University for the CIPD. Reproduced with the permission of the publisher, the Chartered Institute of Personnel and Development, London (**www.cipd.co.uk**).

Perhaps the most well-used model of explaining the black box explaining how HR practices impact on employee performance is from Purcell *et al.* (2003). Their model exemplifies the importance of how HR practices are applied in that they will impact on the Ability and skills of employees, the Motivation and incentive provided to them and the Opportunity to participate in discretionary behaviour (which is why this is often referred to as the AMO model). In turn AMO impacts on employee attitudes, which they suggest as commitment, motivation and job satisfaction, which promote discretionary behaviour and better performance outcomes. The model also highlights the importance of the organisation having a 'big idea' which provides an appropriate focus around which people can pull together. A summary of the model is shown in Figure 3.4.

Perspective 3: Resource-based approach

The resource-based view of the firm (Barney 1991) has stimulated attempts to create a resource-based model of strategic HRM (Boxall 1996). The resource-based view of the firm is concerned with the relationships between internal resources (of which the human resource is one), strategy and firm performance. It focuses on the promotion of sustained competitive advantage through the development of human capital rather than merely aligning human resources to current strategic goals. Human resources can provide competitive advantage for the business, as long as they are unique and competing organisations cannot copy or substitute for them. The focus is not just on the behaviour of the human resources (as with the fit approach), but on the skills, knowledge, attitudes and competencies which underpin this, and which have a more sustained impact on long-term survival than current behaviour, although this is still regarded as important. Briggs and Keogh (1999) maintain that business excellence is not just about 'best practice' or 'leapfrogging the competition', but about the intellectual capital and business intelligence to anticipate the future, today.

Barney (1991) states that in order for a resource to result in sustained competitive advantage it must meet four criteria, and Wright et al. (1994) demonstrate how human resources meet these. First, the resource must be *valuable*. Wright and his colleagues argue that this is the case where demand for labour is heterogeneous, and where the supply of labour is also heterogeneous, in other words where different firms require different competencies from each other and for different roles in the organisation, and where the supply of potential labour comprises individuals with different competencies. On this basis value is created by matching an individual's competencies with the requirements of the firm and/or the job, as individuals will make a variable contribution, and one cannot be substituted easily for another.

The second criterion, *rarity*, is related to the first. This assumes that the most important competence for employees is cognitive ability due to future needs for adaptability and flexibility. On the basis that cognitive ability is normally distributed in the population, those with high levels of this ability will be rare. The talent pool is not unlimited and many employers continue to have difficulty finding the talent that they require, even with relatively high levels of unemployment in many countries as this is written.

Third, resources need to be *inimitable*. Wright et al. argue that this quality applies to the human resource as competitors will find it difficult to identify the exact source of competitive advantage from within the firm's HR pool. Also competitors will not be able to duplicate exactly the resource in question, as they will be unable to copy the unique historical conditions of the first firm. This history is important as it will affect the behaviour of the HR pool via the development of unique norms and cultures. Thus even if a competing firm recruited a group of individuals from a competitor it would still not be able to produce the same outcomes in the new firm as the context would be different.

Finally, resources need to be *non-substitutable*. Wright and his co-authors argue that although in the short term it may be possible to substitute human resources with others, for example technological ones, in the long term the human resource is different as it does not become obsolete (like technology) and can be transferred across other products, markets and technologies.

Although sometimes human capital is interpreted as the leaders in the organisation, who are easily identifiable, or other employees with skills critical to competitive advantage, it may also be viewed as the totality of human resources in the organisation. This sits well with the view of strategy as evolutionary and strategy being influenced from the bottom up as well as from the top down. Human capital may be expressed as intellectual capital, that is the knowledge skills and attributes of employees, and sometimes social capital, meaning the networks that employees have both internally and externally.

Whereas the universalist and fit models focus on the means of competitive advantage (HR practices) the resource-based view focuses on the source (the human capital). Wright et al. argue that, although the practices are important, they are not the source of competitive advantage as they can be replicated elsewhere, and they will produce different results in different places because of the differential human capital in different places. The relationship between human capital, HR practices and competitive advantage is shown in Figure 3.5.

Boxall (1996) argues that this theoretical perspective provides a conceptual base for asserting that human resources are a source of competitive advantage, and as such valued as generating strategic capability. Thus there is a case for viewing HR strategy as something more than a reactive matching process. Indeed Wright et al. argue that it provides the case for HR to be involved in the formulation of strategy rather than just its

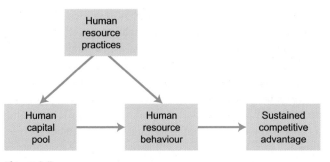

Figure 3.5

A model of human resources as a source of sustained competitive advantage

Source: P. Wright, G. McMahon and A. McWilliams (1994) 'Human resources and sustained competitive advantage: A resource-based perspective', *International Journal of Human Resource Management*, Vol. 5, No. 2, p. 318. Reproduced with the permission of Taylor & Francis Ltd. See **www.tandf.co.uk/journals**.

implementation. They suggest that it provides a grounding for asserting that not every strategy is universally implementable, and that alternatives may have to be sought or the human capital pool developed further, via HR practices, where this is possible.

The importance of this perspective is underlined by an increase in the emphasis on a firm's intangible assets. Numerous studies have shown that a firm's market value, expressed by the sum of the value of the shares, is not fully explained by its current financial results (see e.g. Ulrich and Smallwood 2002) or by its tangible assets and the focus has moved to a firm's intangible assets such as intellectual capital and customer relationships – all of which are derived from human capital. This emphasis has resulted in more attention being paid to the evaluation of human capital through measuring, for example, the aggregate of knowledge, skills and abilities in the firm, reporting it in the annual report, say, and managing it.

The perceived importance of people as an intangible asset is demonstrated in the action of Barclays Group, which on its Investor's Day was keen to demonstrate not only its financial results, but also its people strategies and improvements in staff satisfaction which it believed to have contributed to the results (Arkin and Allen 2002). However, the CIPD (2010), reporting a research study, found that investors' appetite for more information on human capital was variable, not changed much since 2007, and dependent on the importance of people in each type of business.

This approach has great advantages from an HR point of view. People in the organisation become the focus, their contribution is monitored and made more explicit, the way people are managed can be seen to add value and money spent on people can be seen as an investment rather than a cost. Some firms are using the balanced scorecard to demonstrate the contribution that human capital makes to firm performance, such as Aviva. However, there are inbuilt barriers in the language of the resource-based view. One is the reference to people as 'human capital', which some consider to be unnecessarily instrumental. Another is the focus on 'firms' and 'competitive advantage' which makes it harder to see the relevance of this perspective for organisations in the public sector. There is also the issue of what is being measured and who decides this. The risk is that too much time is spent measuring and that not everything that is measured is of critical value to the organisation. So far, such measures appear very varied, although different firms will, of course, need to measure different things. Measures often appear to be taken without a coherent framework (Scarborough and Elias 2002) and Ployhart and Moliterno (2011) warn us that more is not always better.

Human capital is loaned: 'human capital is not owned by the organisation, but secured through the employment relationship' (Scarborough 2003: 2) and because this is so, the strategy for the management of people is also critical. It also means, as Wright and McMahan (2011) point out, that we should be concerned with how individuals themselves 'make choices regarding investments in their human capital, such as the choice to receive training, gain a college education or begin a physical workout regimen' (p. 94). Individuals may not choose to exploit their capital to the full, and of course they may leave the organisation.

Why does the theory matter?

It is tempting to think of these theories of strategic HRM as competing with each other. In other words, one is right and the others are wrong. If this were the case HR managers/directors and board members would need only to work out which is the 'right' theory and apply that. This is, of course, a gross oversimplification, as each theory can be interpreted and applied in different ways, and each has advantages and disadvantages. It could be argued that different theories apply in different sectors or competitive contexts. For example, Guest (2001) suggests that there is the possibility that a 'high-performance/high-commitment' approach might always be most appropriate in manufacturing, whereas strategic choice (which could be interpreted as choice to fit with business strategy) might be more realistic in the services sector. This could be taken one step further to suggest that different theories apply to different groups in the workforce. Indeed Storey (2007), on the basis of work in the public and private sector, suggests that there is value in HR directors crafting their strategy via four simultaneous pathways: best practice; best fit; building on and exploiting the people resource base (the three theoretical approaches we have discussed); and responding to an analysis of trends and demographics.

Consequently, these three theories do not necessarily represent simple alternatives. It is also likely that some board directors and even HR managers are not familiar with any of these theories. In spite of that, organisations, through their culture, and individuals within organisations operate on the basis of a set of assumptions, and these assumptions are often implicit. Assumptions about the nature and role of HR strategy, whether explicit or implicit, will have an influence on what organisations actually do. Assumptions will limit what are seen as legitimate choices.

Understanding these theories enables HR managers, board members, consultants and the like to interpret the current position of HR strategy in the organisation, confront current assumptions and challenge current thinking and potentially open up a new range of possibilities.

The international challenge

The strategic theories we have explored have all been developed in the west and while there is evidence that this body of knowledge is used internationally (see e.g. Sharma and Khandekar 2006), it must be acknowledged that they are limited by western cultures and mindsets. Turning the theories into practice internationally is even more of a challenge. We have mentioned that the universalist approach, identifying best practices which result in high performance, is dependent on the prevailing culture, institutions and legislation and therefore is most difficult to apply internationally. The fit approach presents the same challenge, unless fit with culture, institutions and legislation is included so that HR practices can be localised, but of course other aspects of fit are then lost. Perhaps it is easier to see how the resource-based perspective might be more easily translated into practice across the globe, but again actual practices adopted will inevitably be influenced by local circumstances.

Much literature on international HRM strategy is based on the multinational corporation (MNC), with an HQ in the originating country rolling out an HR strategy to international locations with the focus on applying it to expatriates, frequent international commuters, cross-cultural team members and specialists involved in international knowledge transfer (Sparrow and Braun 2007). Reilly and Williams (2012) note that western MNCs have a tendency to go for this 'one-company approach', yet suggest that a mix between global and local strategies may be more appropriate. They note that the Asian model is more decentralised, so more local than global practices. They recognise, however, that this is probably due to the fact that such Asian MNCs are holding companies for a diverse range of subsidiaries engaged in different activities, so meeting the needs of the specific business may be more important than commonality. Taking us forwards, Sparrow and Braun (2007) maintain that *global* strategic HRM is different from *international* strategic HRM in that it requires 'managing SIHRM activities through the application of global rule sets which carry meaning across cultures' (p. 186). This is a very different challenge.

SUMMARY PROPOSITIONS

3.1   Strategic HRM encourages us to consider strategy as a process, strategic thinking and strategic orientation, rather than limit ourselves to a 'strategy' which is written down and exists as a physical entity.

3.2   The nature of the link between business strategy and HR strategy is critical and can be played out in a variety of ways.

3.3   Three theoretical perspectives on strategic HR management can be identified: universalist/best practice; contingency/fit; and the resource-based/human capital view. Each has advantages and disadvantages.

3.4   The black box research seeks to explain how HR practices impact on performance, and is associated with the universalist and contingency approaches.

3.5   Globalisation presents more challenges for understanding and implementing HR strategy.

GENERAL DISCUSSION TOPICS

1   Is it feasible to link business strategy with the management of people in organisations?

2   HR strategies can be stimulating to produce and satisfying to display, but how can we make sure that they are implemented?

THEORY INTO PRACTICE

ARM Holdings

ARM Holdings according to its website is 'a truly global company with offices spread around the world'. It was founded in 1990 in Cambridge, UK, which remains its global headquarters; in addition it now has a regional headquarters in Shanghai covering Chinese, Indian, Japanese, Korean and Taiwanese offices, and another in San Jose covering US offices over five states from the east to the west coast.

The company designs chips for small low-powered devices, such as mobile phones and tablets (including i-Pods and i-Pads). ARM's business strategy is one of partnership, working with a wide range of other companies. It licenses production to manufacturing companies and carries out research and development on behalf of its customers. Also in its partnership collaboration are technology companies which write software or produce products using ARM-designed microprocessors. Sales growth is excellent, and ARM Holdings is the world's leading semiconductor IP company, winning a number of awards as top employer.

Interviewed for *People Management*, Graham Budd, Chief Operating Officer commented that: 'The value of the company is fundamentally in its people and in the network of relationships that those people have both inside the company and externally' (Arkin 2011: 37). Much HR activity is about connecting people across the global company sites and external partners – across cultures and time zones. The HR strategy is designed to develop an innovative, collaborative environment and focuses on social capital. Bill Parsons, the HR Director, says it is about 'the individual being less important than the network, the network being selfless individuals sharing knowledge to achieve a common vision' (Arkin 2011: 38).

ARM Holdings as an intellectual property company knows its biggest asset is its people and aims to recruit the best intelligent, leading-edge thinkers and release their talent within the company. The culture is collaborative and dynamic and the company has identified seven core values: delivery of results which benefit HRM; teamwork and selflessness; constructive pro-activity; partner and customer focus; responsiveness; innovation; and personal development.

Questions

1   How does HR strategy at ARM Holdings reflect the three theoretical perspectives on HR strategy which we have discussed in this chapter? Justify your answer.

2 How would you design and implement HR practices so that they supported the business and HR strategies? Give examples and justify for each HR practice – include recruitment/selection, development and reward practices as a minimum, but add other relevant practices to these.

3 What special challenges does the global nature of ARM Holdings have in implementing your proposals?

Sources: Arkin, A. (2011) 'Cash in the chips', *People Management*, May, pp. 36–9; Cooper, R. and agencies (2012) 'ARM sales jump as outpaces peers', *Telegraph Media Group*, 25 July (accessed via the Internet at **www.telegraph.co.uk**); **www.arm.com**.

FURTHER READING

Millmore, M., Lewis, P., Saunders, M., Thornhill, A. and Morrow, T. (2007) *Strategic Human Resource Management: Contemporary issues.* London: Prentice Hall/Financial Times.
This text provides a good overview of different perspectives on HR strategy and chapters dedicated to strategic approaches in specific areas such as recruitment and selection, performance management, development, reward, diversity management and managing the employment relationship.

Salaman, G., Storey, J. and Billsberry, J. (2005) *Strategic Human Resource Management: Theory and practice. A reader.* London: The Open University in association with Sage.
This is an excellent source book bringing together a variety of perspectives and divided into four sections: strategic HRM and knowledge; strategic HRM and business performance; the emergence of new organisational forms and relationships; and strategic HRM in practice. Each chapter is an article previously published, and is either produced in full or summarised. This means that some work is older than others, but the choice of chapters means that key and influential strategic works (e.g. Wright *et al.* mentioned in this chapter) are grouped together.

Truss, C., Mankin, D. and Kelliher, C. (2012) *Strategic Human Resource Management.* Oxford: Oxford University Press.
This is a very readable yet thorough and wide-ranging text of strategic HR. Chapters 5, 6 and 8 are particularly relevant for our chapter here.

WEB LINK

www.cranet.org

REFERENCES

Arkin, A. (2011) 'Cash in the chips', *People Management*, May, pp. 36–9.
Arkin, A. and Allen, R. (2002) 'Satisfaction guaranteed', *People Management*, Vol. 8, No. 21, pp. 40–2.
Atkinson, C. and Hall, L. (2011) 'Flexible working and happiness in the NHS', *Employee Relations*, Vol. 33, No. 2, pp. 88–105.
Baird, L., Meshoulam, I. and DeGive, G. (1983) 'Meshing human resources planning with strategic business planning: A model approach', *Personnel*, Vol. 60, Part 5, pp. 14–25.

Barney, J. (1991) 'Firm resources and sustained competitive advantage', *Journal of Management*, Vol. 17, No. 1, pp. 99–120.

Batt, R. and Banerjee, M. (2012) 'The scope and trajectory of strategic HR research: Evidence from American and British journals', *International Journal of Human Resource Management*, Vol. 23, No. 9, pp. 1739–62.

Becker, B., Huselid, M. and Ulrich, D. (2001) *The HR Scorecard: Linking people, strategy and performance*. Boston, MA: Harvard Business School Press.

Boxall, P. and Macky, K. (2009) 'Research and theory on high-performance work systems: Progressing the high-involvement stream', *Human Resource Management Journal*, Vol. 19, No. 1, pp. 3–23.

Boxall, P. and Purcell, J. (2008) *Strategy and Human Resource Management*. Basingstoke: Palgrave Macmillan.

Boxall, P.F. (1996) 'The strategic HRM debate and the resource-based view of the firm', *Human Resource Management Journal*, Vol. 6, No. 3, pp. 59–75.

Briggs, S. and Keogh, W. (1999) 'Integrating human resource strategy and strategic planning to achieve business excellence', *Total Quality Management*, July, p. 447.

Butler, J. (1988) 'Human resource management as a driving force in business strategy', *Journal of General Management*, Vol. 13, No. 4, pp. 88–102.

Chubb, L. (2008) 'Build a better brand', *People Management*, Vol. 14, No. 15, pp. 24–5.

CIPD (2010) *Human Capital Reporting: What information counts in the City?*, Research Report. London: CIPD.

Fields, D., Chan, A., Aktar, S. and Blum, T. (2006) 'Human resource management strategies under uncertainty', *Cross Cultural Management: An International Journal*, Vol. 13, No. 2, pp. 171–86.

Fombrun, C., Tichy, N.M. and Devanna, M.A. (1984) *Strategic Human Resource Management*. New York: Wiley.

Godard, J. (2004) 'A critical assessment of the high-performance paradigm', *British Journal of Industrial Relations*, Vol. 42, No. 2, pp. 349–78.

Griffiths, J. (2006) 'Keep-fit scheme', *People Management*, Vol. 12, No. 7, pp. 18–19.

Grundy, T. (1998) 'How are corporate strategy and human resources strategy linked?', *Journal of General Management*, Vol. 23, No. 3, pp. 49–72.

Guest, D. (2001) 'Human resource management: When research confronts theory', *International Journal of Human Resource Management*, Vol. 12, No. 7, pp. 1092–106.

Guest, D. (2011) 'Human resource management and performance: Still searching for some answers', *Human Resource Management Journal*, Vol. 21, No. 1, pp. 3–13.

Guest, D., Michie, J., Conway, N. and Sheehan, M. (2003) 'Human resource management and corporate performance in the UK', *British Journal of Industrial Relations*, Vol. 41, pp. 291–314.

Guthridge, M. and Lawson, E. (2008) 'Divide and survive', *People Management*, Vol. 14, No. 19, pp. 40–4.

Holbeche, L. (2008) *Aligning Human Resources and Business Strategy*. Oxford: Butterworth–Heinemann.

Huselid, M. (1995) 'The impact of human resource management practices on turnover, productivity and corporate financial performance', *Academy of Management Journal*, Vol. 38, No. 3, pp. 635–73.

Kaplan, R. and Norton, D. (2005) 'The office of strategy management', *Harvard Business Review*, Vol. 83, No. 10, pp. 73–80.

Kersley, B., Alpin, C., Forth, J., Bryson, A., Bewley, H., Dix, G. and Oxenbridge, S. (2006) *Inside the Workplace: Findings from the 2004 Workplace Employment Relations Survey*. London: Routledge.

Kinnie, N., Hutchinson, S., Purcell, J., Rayton, B. and Swart, J. (2005) 'Satisfaction with HR practices and commitment to the organisation: Why one size does not fit all', *Human Resource Management Journal*, Vol. 15, No. 4, pp. 9–29.

Kochan, T.A. and Barocci, T.A. (1985) *Human Resource Management and Industrial Relations: Text, readings and cases*. Boston, MA: Little Brown.

Lengnick-Hall, M. and Lengnick-Hall, C. (2003) *Human Resource Management in the Knowledge Economy*. San Francisco, CA: Berrett-Koehler.

Lepak, D. and Shaw, J. (2008) 'Strategic HRM in North America: Looking to the future', *International Journal of Human Resource Management*, Vol. 19, No. 8, pp. 1486–99.

Macky, K. and Boxall, P. (2007) 'The relationship between "high performance work practices" and employee attitudes: An investigation of additive and interaction effects', *International Journal of Human Resource Management*, Vol. 18, No. 4, pp. 537–67.

Miles, R.E. and Snow, C.C. (1984) 'Organisation strategy, structure and process', *Academy of Management* Review, Vol. 2, pp. 546–62.

Millmore, M., Lewis, P., Saunders, M., Thornhill, A. and Morrow, T. (2007) *Strategic Human Resource Management: Contemporary issues*. London: Prentice Hall/Financial Times.

Mintzberg, H. (1994) 'The fall and rise of strategic planning', *Harvard Business Review*, January–February, pp. 107–14.

Ogbonna, E. and Whipp, R. (1999) 'Strategy, culture and HRM: Evidence from the UK food retailing sector', *Human Resource Management Journal*, Vol. 9, No. 4, pp. 75–90.

Peccei, R. (2004) 'Human resource management and the search for the happy workplace', Inaugural Address to the Erasmus Research Institute of Management, Erasmus University, Rotterdam, 15 January.

Pfeffer, J. (2005) 'Producing sustainable competitive advantage through the effective management of people', *Academy of Management Executive*, Vol. 19, No. 4, pp. 95–106.

Ployhart, R.E. and Moliterno, T.P. (2011) 'Emergence of the human capital resource: A multilevel model', *Academy of Management Review*, Vol. 36, No. 1, pp. 127–50.

Porter, M. (1980) *Competitive Strategy*. New York: Free Press.

Purcell, J. (1992) 'The impact of corporate strategy on human resource management', in G. Salaman *et al.* (eds), *Human Resource Strategies*. London: Sage.

Purcell, J. and Hutchinson, S. (2007) 'Front-line managers as agents in the HRM performance causal chain: Theory, analysis and evidence', *Human Resource Management Journal*, Vol. 17, No. 1, pp. 3–20.

Purcell, J., Kinnie, N., Hutchinson, S., Rayton, B. and Swart, J. (2003) *Understanding the People Performance Link: Unlocking the black box*, Research Report. London: CIPD.

Reilly, P. and Williams, T. (2012) *Global HR: Challenges facing the HR function*. Aldershot: Gower.

Salaman, G., Storey, J. and Billsberry, J. (2005) 'Strategic human resource management: Defining the field', in G. Salaman *et al.* (eds), *Strategic Human Resource Management: Theory and practice. A reader*. London: Sage/Open University.

Scarborough, H. (2003) *Human Capital: External reporting framework*. London: CIPD.

Scarborough, H. and Elias, J. (2002) *Evaluating Human Capital*, Research Report. London: CIPD.

Schuler, R.S. and Jackson, S.E. (1987) 'Linking competitive strategies with human resource management practices', *Academy of Management Executive*, Vol. 1, No. 3, pp. 207–19.

Sharma, A. and Khandekar, A. (2006) *Strategic Human Resource Management*. London: Sage.

Simmons, J. (2009) 'Both sides now: Aligning internal and external brands for a socially responsible era', *Marketing Intelligence and Planning*, Vol. 27, No. 5, pp. 38–41.

Sparrow, P. and Braun, W. (2007) 'Human resource strategy in international context', in R. Schular and S. Jackson, *Strategic Human Resource Management*, 2nd edn. Malden, MA: Blackwell.

Storey, J. (2007) 'What is strategic HRM?', in J. Storey (ed.), *Human Resource Management: A critical text*. London: Thompson Learning.

Truss, C., Mankin, D. and Kelliher, C. (2012) *Strategic Human Resource Management*. Oxford: Oxford University Press.

Tyson, S. (1995) *Human Resource Strategy*. London: Pitman.

Ulrich, D. (1998) 'A new mandate for human resources', *Harvard Business Review*, January–February, pp. 125–34.

Ulrich, D. and Smallwood, N. (2002) 'Seven up', *People Management*, Vol. 8, No. 10, pp. 42–4.

Wright, P. and McMahon, G. (2011) 'Exploring human capital: Putting human back into strategic human resource management', *Human Resource Management Journal*, Vol. 21, No. 2, pp. 93–104.

Wright, P., McMahon, G. and McWilliams, A. (1994) 'Human resources and sustained competitive advantage: A resource-based perspective', *International Journal of Human Resource Management*, Vol. 5, No. 2, pp. 301–26.

Chapter 4

WORKFORCE PLANNING AND METRICS

THE OBJECTIVES OF THIS CHAPTER ARE TO:

1   Discuss the contribution and feasibility of workforce planning
2   Explore the scope of workforce planning
3   Explain an integrated workforce planning framework
4   Investigate the contribution of workforce metrics and analytics

Workforce planning is experiencing a resurgence of interest in our era of rapid and discontinuous change:

> the need for strategic workforce planning and execution of workforce plans has never been greater as organisations . . . operate in more turbulent environments and confront the key challenges of competing for key skills and talents and of containing payroll costs. (Lavelle 2007: 371)

Rudge (2011: 12), Cabinet Minister for Equalities and Human Rights, Birmingham City Council, suggests that:

> workforce planning and intelligence will be ever more important in order to avoid 'knee-jerk' reactions and falls in service standards

and the CIPD (2012) suggests that planning is vital in an ever-changing economy in order to develop sufficient capacity to adapt as new trends and opportunities emerge. The resurgence of interest in planning is often connected to the disruption caused by the recession and the need to upskill organisations. Workforce planning may specifically be prompted by revisions in service delivery, the need for increased efficiency and financial restraint, consolidation of operations in a single location, expansion and changing customer demand (IDS 2011), yet, paradoxically, planning is often unappreciated and underused.

The contribution and feasibility of workforce planning

A useful starting point is to consider the different contributions that strategy and planning make to the organisation. A common view has been that they are virtually one and the same – hence the term 'strategic planning'. Mintzberg (1994: 108) distinguished between *strategic thinking*, which is about synthesis, intuition and creativity to produce a not too precisely articulated vision of direction, and *strategic planning*, which is about collecting the relevant information to stimulate the visioning process and also programming the vision into what needs to be done to get there. It is helpful to look at workforce planning in the same way, and this is demonstrated in Figure 4.1. In more detail he suggests:

- **Planning as strategic programming**: planning cannot generate strategies, but it can make them operational by clarifying them, working out the consequences of them, and identifying what must be done to achieve each strategy.

Figure 4.1
HR strategic visioning and strategic planning
Source: After Mintzberg (1984).

| **Strategic planning** Providing HR data, ideas Asking difficult questions | ⟷ | **Strategic visioning** Defining a vision of the future (organisational and HR) | ⟷ | **Strategic planning** Programme the vision – HR objectives, targets, action plans |

- **Planning as tools to communicate and control**: planning can ensure coordination and encourage everyone to pull in the same direction; planners can assist in finding successful experimental strategies which may be operating in just a small part of the organisation.
- **Planners as analysts**: planners need to analyse hard data, both external and internal, which managers can then use in the strategy development process.
- **Planners as catalysts**: that is, raising difficult questions and challenging the conventional wisdom which may stimulate managers into thinking in more creative ways.

Planning is a basic building block of a more strategic approach, and there are four specific ways in which HR planning is critical to strategy, as it can identify:

- *capability gaps* – lack of sufficient skills, people or knowledge in the business which will prevent the strategy being implemented successfully;
- *capability surpluses* – providing scope for efficiencies and new opportunities to capitalise on the skills, people and knowledge, currently underused, in order to influence strategy;
- *poor workforce utilisation* – suggesting inappropriate HR practices that need to be altered;
- *talent pool development* – to ensure a ready internal supply of employees capable of promotion, and especially a leadership pipeline.

These four aspects are crucial to sustaining competitive advantage through making the most of human resources, reflecting the resource-based view we explained in the previous chapter.

Our environment of rapid and discontinuous change makes any planning difficult, and workforce planning is especially difficult as people have free will, unlike other resources, such as finance or technology. Both short- and longer-term planning are important and yet quarterly business reporting, as is common in the UK, encourages businesses to focus only on short-term planning. By contrast some other countries, like Japan, have a longer-term horizon for assessing business performance. A survey by the Adecco Institute found acceptance of the need for long-term planning and yet the average planning horizon of HR specialists was 1.1 years (Chubb 2008). The contribution and implementation of workforce planning is enhanced if:

- plans are viewed as flexible and reviewed regularly, rather than being seen as an end point;
- stakeholders, including all levels of manager and employee, are involved in the process, through, for example, surveys, focus groups and line manager representatives on the HR planning team;
- planning is owned and driven by senior managers rather than HR specialists, who are facilitators;
- plans are linked to business and HR strategy;
- plans are user friendly and not overly complex;
- it is recognised that, while a comprehensive plan may be ideal, sometimes it may only be feasible to plan on an issue-by-issue basis, or by different workforce specialisms or segments (see Lavelle (2007) for a good example of segmentation).

The CIPD guide to workforce planning (2010) provides some very useful advice on implementation.

WINDOW ON PRACTICE

Workforce planning and the NHS in the UK

Workforce planning is considered to be a top priority for the NHS (National Health Service) as an appropriate and competent workforce is required to provide successful service delivery and quality, and to this end a rapid review of workforce planning was commissioned by the House of Commons Health Committee's Workforce Review Team to identify the nature of workforce planning; to provide examples of best practice; and to identify the current effectiveness of UK health sector workforce planning. The work was carried out by the Institute for Employment Research at Warwick University.

The review team found that:

- workforce planning is not a homogeneous activity and can be carried out at different levels, for example organisational or national;
- traditional healthcare workforce planning has focused on supply and demand for specific occupations – in other words, it is segmented;
- this approach can result in professional silos and an integrated approach, planning for the system as a whole, would add value, because covering all staff groups simultaneously is essential to address skill mix and substitution issues;
- data availability and lack of resources to build sophisticated models restrict planning activity;

- planning for internal labour markets, that is the movement between posts within the organisation, is also important;
- it is important to plan for demographic factors both in terms of healthcare need and in terms of workforce supply;
- given the importance of quality in a healthcare setting, productivity improvement can be expressed as higher quality from the same inputs (i.e. workforce);
- there is a general lack of published work on good practices in workforce planning, and no examples of fully integrated workforce planning models were found;
- workforce planning time horizons are generally longer in the public than the private sector and succession planning remains important in larger hierarchical public bodies;
- 'workforce planning requires accurate data, modelling, continuous and iterative planning, specialist skills, scenario building and stakeholder involvement' (p. 117);
- workforce planning is essential for the NHS as a long lead time is required for training; wage adjustments are influenced by market forces; patient needs must be met; and taxpayers' money should not be wasted by training too many staff.

Source: Curson, J., Dell, M., Wilson, R., Bosworth, D. and Baldauf, B. (2010) 'Who does workforce planning well? Workforce rapid review team summary', *International Journal of Health Care Quality Assurance*, Vol. 23, No. 1, pp. 110-19.

Although this example relates specifically to the NHS, it is also typical of other parts of the public sector such as social care.

The scope of workforce planning

Originally workforce planning was concerned with balancing the projected demand for and supply of labour, in order to have the right number of the right employees in the right place at the right time. The demand for people is influenced by corporate strategies and objectives, the environment and the way that staff are utilised within the business. The supply of people is projected from current employees (via calculations about expected leavers, retirements, promotions, etc.) and from the potential availability of required employees and skills in the relevant labour market. Anticipated demand and supply are then reconciled by considering a range of options, and plans to achieve a feasible balance are designed.

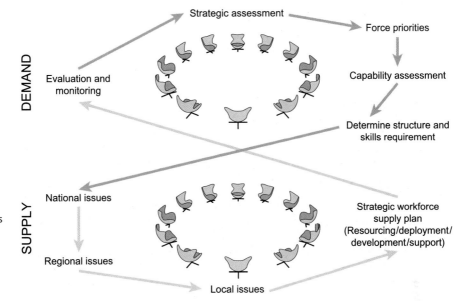

Figure 4.2
The workforce planning process at Dorset Police

Source: Workforce Planning: Right people, right time, right skills, Guide. CIPD (2010), London: CIPD.

Increasingly organisations now plan, not just for hard numbers, but for the *softer* issues of employee behaviour and organisational culture; organisation design and the make-up of individual jobs; and formal and informal systems. These aspects are all critical in terms of programming and achieving the vision or the strategic choice. Undoubtedly different organisations will place different emphases on each of these factors, and may well plan each separately or plan some and not others, but a good example is the workforce planning in the Dorset Police (CIPD 2010), shown in Figure 4.2.

The framework we shall use in this chapter attempts to bring *all* aspects of workforce planning together, incorporating the more traditional approach, but going beyond this to include behaviour, culture, systems and so on. Our framework identifies 'where we want to be', translated from responses to the strategic vision; 'where we are now'; and 'what we need to do to make the transition' – all operating within the organisation's environment. The framework is shown in diagrammatic form in Figure 4.3.

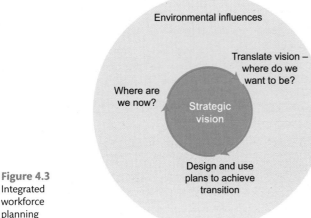

Figure 4.3
Integrated workforce planning framework

We shall now look in more depth at each of these four areas. The steps are presented in a logical sequence. In practice, however, they may run in parallel and/or in an informal fashion, and each area may well be revisited a number of times.

Analysing the environment

In this chapter we refer to the environment broadly as the context of the organisation, and this is clearly critical in the impact that it has on both organisational and HR strategy. Much strategy is based on a response to the environment – for example, what our customers now want or what competitors are now offering – or in anticipation of what customers will want or what they can be persuaded to want. In HR terms we need to identify, for example, how difficult or easy it will be to find employees with scarce skills and what these employees will expect from an employer so that we can attract them, and keep them. We shall be concerned with legislation which will limit or widen the conditions of employment that we offer, with what competitors are offering and with what training schemes are available, locally, nationally and internationally, depending on the nature of the organisation.

WINDOW ON PRACTICE

The global workforce challenge

Chinese wage increases

We have become accustomed to a world where global companies carry out their manufacturing in a low-wage country. However, some of these traditionally low-wage economies are now experiencing pressures for higher wages and better employment conditions. Jacob (2012) notes how 2012 has differed from previous years due to marked labour shortages in China. She highlights the case of David Liu, a handbag manufacturer who until recently would have queues of potential workers outside the factory gates, but now has to ask for help from employees to recruit new workers. There is a higher turnover of younger workers who switch jobs in search of better pay and conditions. She notes there have been double-digit wage increases over the past couple of years, and suggests that China is running out of workers.

Source: Jacob, R. (2012) 'Labour shortages: Double digit wage increases', **www.ft.com**, 11 December.

The impact on Japanese firms

Japanese businesses use Chinese operations for labour-intensive assembly, but have recently been moving to higher-value work requiring more skilled staff. At the same time the just-in-time production process leaves Japanese companies vulnerable to disruption. Decisions on pay are made centrally and not at plant level. This format has resulted in:

1 Higher pay in the Chinese plants (e.g. Honda upped wages by 24%).

2 Higher promotion levels for local managers (e.g. Komatsu aim to have Chinese managers leading all sixteen local subsidiaries).

3 More labour-intensive work is being moved to Vietnam, Thailand and Cambodia (e.g. Uniglo is reducing the proportion of garments made in China from 90% to 65% between 2013 and 2015).

Source: The impact on Japan is adapted from Brewster, C., Sparrow, P., Vernon, G. and Houldsworth, E. (2011) *International Human Resource Management*. London: CIPD, pp. 391–2.

In summary we need to collect data on social trends; demographics; political legislative and regulatory changes; industrial and technological changes; and current/new competitors. We need to assess the impact these will have on our ability to recruit, develop and keep the required employees with appropriate skills and behaviours. Planners need to identify the challenges that the changes pose, and work out how to meet these in order that the organisation can achieve its declared strategies and goals.

WINDOW ON PRACTICE

Analysing the environment at Queensland University of Technology Library in Australia

Stokker and Hallam (2009) identify change as the main driver for the Library's engagement with workforce planning. They believed environmental scanning was a key part of the process to explore trends impacting on libraries, the context, and trends within libraries. The scanning was carried out over twelve months and involved reading relevant documents and inviting guest specialist speakers to address library staff. All library staff were involved in the scanning process and five key areas were investigated, each led by a member of the senior library team:

- Higher education sector/government policy
- Teaching and learning
- Client service
- Research
- Information resources and scholarly information.

Initial findings were then developed in more detail. For example, several trends emerged that would impact on the faculty liaison service, such as the university's desire to gain a higher research profile by increasing the number of researchers and research students. This led to the development of three workforce planning strategies for the faculty liaison service: methods to allow librarians to specialise in research support or academic skills support; a review of the job classification scheme allowing librarians to progress further in recognition of their specialist work; and the design of a development programme to allow liaison librarians to acquire new skills and knowledge.

In addition to staff involvement in environmental scanning they were also represented in the workforce planning party and planning strategies were built using consultation. These methods were used to encourage staff ownership and engagement.

Source: Stokker, J. and Hallam, G. (2009) 'The right person, in the right job, with the right skills at the right time: A workforce-planning model that goes beyond metrics', *Library Management*, Vol. 15, No. 89, pp. 561–71.

ACTIVITY 4.1

Consider the external environment, for any organisation in which you are involved, for three to five years ahead. Individually, or as a group, identify all the important environmental influences and select the six most important ones. Identify the challenges these present to the organisation in achieving its goals and how the organisation could respond. Write a summary (one side of A4) of what you think your organisation's priorities should be in the people area over the next three to five years.

Forecasting future HR needs

Organisation, behaviour and culture

There is little specific literature on the methods used to translate the strategic objectives of the organisation and environmental influences into qualitative or soft HR goals. In general terms, they can be summed up as the use of managerial judgement. Brainstorming, combined with the use of structured checklists or matrices, can encourage a more thorough analysis. Organisation change literature and corporate planning literature are helpful as sources of ideas in this area. Three simple techniques are an HR implications checklist (see Table 4.1), a strategic brainstorming exercise (Figure 4.4). The use of *scenarios* may also be helpful (see e.g. Boxall and Purcell 2003; Turner 2002). Scenarios and contingency planning can be used to describe alternative organisational futures and prepare HR responses to these.

Table 4.1
The beginnings of an HR implications checklist

Corporate goal	HR implications	Methods of achieving this
	New tasks?	
	For whom?	
	What competencies needed?	
	Relative importance of team/individual behaviour	
	Deleted tasks?	
	How will managers need to manage?	

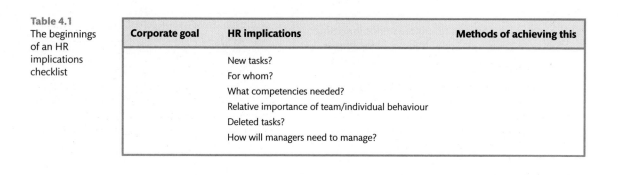

Figure 4.4
Strategic brainstorming exercise

Managers write a corporate goal in the centre and brainstorm changes that need to take place in each of the four areas, one area at a time

Employee numbers and skills (demand forecasting)

There is far more literature in the more traditional area of forecasting employee number demand based on the organisation's strategic objectives. Both objective and subjective approaches can be employed. Objective methods include statistical and work-study approaches.

Statistical models generally relate employee number demand to specific organisational circumstances and activities. Models can take account of determining factors, such as production, sales, passenger miles, level of service, finance available. Sophisticated models can take account of economies of scale, and other relevant factors such as employee utilisation, resulting from the introduction of new technology, or alternative organisational forms, such as high-performance teams, or simply expecting people to work harder and for longer hours.

The work-study method is based on a thorough analysis of the tasks to be done and the time each takes. From this the person-hours needed per unit of output can be calculated, and standards are developed for the numbers and levels of employees required. These are most useful in production work, but need to be checked regularly to make sure they are still appropriate. Work study is usually classified as an objective measure; however, it is often accepted that since the development of standards and the grouping of tasks is partly dependent on human judgement, it could be considered as a subjective method.

WINDOW ON PRACTICE

The postman's lot

Measuring workload has changed at Royal Mail. Roy Mayall, who has been a postman for many years, explains in his short book how volume of mail was previously measured by the weight of the grey boxes in which mail is delivered to the sorting offices. More recently he says it is done by averages, and it was agreed in consultation with the union that the average figure of letters in a box was estimated at 208. Subsequently Mayall (2009) reports that this estimate was changed to 150, and when a colleague did a one-man experiment counting the letters over a two-week period he found the average to be 267. Mayall recognises that this figure is neither representative nor scientific but the story does show how apparently objective figures can be subjective.

Source: Mayall, R. (2009) *Dear Granny Smith: A letter from your postman.* London: Short Books.

The most common subjective method of demand forecasting is managerial judgement (sometimes referred to as managerial opinion or the inductive method), and this can also include the judgements of other operational and technical staff, as well as all levels of managers, and relies on managers' estimates of workforce demand based on past experience. When this method is used it is difficult to cope with changes that are very different from past experiences. It is also less precise than statistical methods, but it is more comprehensive, and important, even when statistical methods are used.

The way that human resources are utilised will change the number of employees required and the necessary skills needed, and changes in utilisation are often prompted by the need to save money or the difficulty in recruiting. There are many ways to change how employees are used, and these are shown in Table 4.2. Some methods are interrelated or overlap and would therefore be used in combination.

Table 4.2
A range of
methods to
change employee
utilisation

- Introducing new materials or equipment, particularly new technology
- Introducing changes in work organisation, such as:
  - quality circles
  - job rotation
  - job enlargement
  - job enrichment
  - autonomous work groups
  - outsourcing
  - high-performance teams
  - participation
  - empowerment
- Organisation development
- Introducing changes in organisation structure, such as:
  - centralisation/decentralisation
  - new departmental boundaries
  - relocation of parts of the organisation
  - flexible project, matrix and network structures
- Introducing productivity schemes, bonus schemes or other incentive schemes
- Encouraging greater staff flexibility, multiskilling and work interchangeability
- Altering times and periods of work
- Training and appraisal of staff
- Developing managers and use of performance management

WINDOW ON PRACTICE

China's challenge

We introduced China's recruitment and higher-wages challenge as above. Jacob (2012) quotes Sunny Tan, Executive Director of Luen Thai Holdings: 'we want to change our model and work differently in China'. There is an emphasis on the need to provide more training to younger workers and raise productivity or risk going out of business. In a survey of 750 executives,

Neale O'Connor, from the University of Hong Kong, sought to find out how they were coping with the high-wage challenge. Rather than planning to introduce automation the emphasis was on changing the processes by which employees were managed, for example by introducing cross-functional teams and outsourcing some functions. Labour shortages were prompting efficiency improvements, more training and better people management.

Source: Jacob, R. (2012) 'Labour shortages: Double digit wage increases', **www.ft.com**, 11 December.

Analysing the current situation and projecting forward

Organisation, behaviour and culture

Possibilities here include the use of questionnaires to staff, interviews with staff and managerial judgement. Focus groups are an increasingly popular technique where, preferably, the chief executive meets with, say, twenty representative staff from each department to discuss their views of the strengths and weaknesses of the organisation, and what can be done to improve. These approaches can be used to provide information on, for example:

- Employee engagement.
- Motivation of employees.
- Job satisfaction.

- Organisational culture.
- The way that people are managed.
- Attitude to minority groups and equality of opportunity.
- Commitment to the organisation and reasons for this.
- Clarity of business objectives.
- Goal-focused and other behaviour.
- Organisational issues and problems.
- What can be done to improve.
- Organisational strengths to build on.

WINDOW ON PRACTICE

Jennifer Hadley is the Chief Executive of Dynamo Castings, a long-established organisation which had experienced rapid growth and healthy profits until the past five years. Around 800 staff were employed mostly in production, but significant numbers were also employed in marketing/sales and research/development. Poor performance over the last three years was largely the result of the competition who were able to deliver a quality product more quickly and at a competitive price. Dynamo retained the edge in developing new designs, but this consumed a high level of resources and was a lengthy process from research to eventual production. Most employees had been with the company for a large part of their working lives and the culture was still appropriate to the times of high profit where life had been fairly easy and laid back. Messages about difficult times, belt tightening and higher productivity with fewer people had been filtered down to employees, who did not change their behaviour but did feel threatened.

It was with some trepidation that Jennifer decided to meet personally with a cross-section of each department to talk through company and departmental issues. The first meeting was with research/development. As expected, the meeting began with a flood of concerns about job security. No promises could be given. However, the mid-point of the meeting was quite fruitful, and the following points, among others, became clear:

- Development time could be reduced from two years to one if some production staff were involved in the development process from the very beginning.
- Many development staff felt their career prospects were very limited and a number expressed the wish to be able to move into marketing. They felt this would also be an advantage when new products were marketed.
- Staff felt fairly paid and would be prepared to forgo salary rises for a year or two if this would mean job security; they liked working for Dynamo and did not want to move.
- Staff were aware of the difficult position the company was in but they really did not know what to do to make it any better.
- Development staff wanted to know why Dynamo did not collaborate with Castem Ltd on areas of mutual interest (Jennifer did not know the answer to this one).

The meeting gave Jennifer not only a better understanding of what employees felt, but also some good ideas to explore. Departmental staff knew their problems had not been wiped away, but did feel that Jennifer had at least taken the trouble to listen to them.

Turnover figures, absence data, performance data, recruitment and promotion trends and characteristics of employees may also shed some light on these issues.

Data relating to current formal and informal systems, together with data on the structure of the organisation, also need to be collected, and the effectiveness, efficiency and other implications of these need to be carefully considered. Most data will be collected from within the organisation, but data may also be collected from significant others, such as customers, who may be part of the environment.

Current and projected employee numbers and skills (employee supply)

Current employee supply can be analysed in both individual and overall statistical terms. To gain an overview of current supply the following factors may be analysed either singly or in combination: number of employees classified by function, department, occupation, job title, competencies, skills, qualifications, training, age, length of service, performance assessment results. This snapshot of the current workforce is essential when organisations face a sudden and/or major change, as it will allow them to respond more effectively.

Forecasting employee supply is concerned with predicting how the internal supply of employees will change, primarily how many will leave. Current levels of employee turnover are projected into the future to see what would happen if the same trends continued. Analyses can be segmented, for example by age group or job type or location. In countries where there is a legal pension age, this aspect of staff turnover can be predicted reasonably accurately. The impact of changing circumstances would also need to be taken into account when projecting turnover forward; for example, when job remits are substantially changed employee turnover often increases. Behavioural aspects are also important, such as investigating the reasons why employees leave. In larger and especially multinational organisations promotion and employee transfer trends may be analysed. Special attention is usually paid to the organisation's talent, however defined, and we discuss talent planning later (see Chapter 16).

Some sample statistics for projecting employee supply are included in the skills section.

ACTIVITY 4.2

1 Why do employees leave organisations?

2 What are the determinants of promotion in your organisation? Are they made explicit? Do staff understand what the determinants are?

3 What would be your criteria for promotion in your organisation?

Reconciliation, decisions and plans

We have already said that, in reality, there is a process of continuous feedback between the different stages of workforce planning activities, as they are all dynamic and interdependent. Key factors to take into account during reconciliation and deciding on action plans are the acceptability of the plans to both senior managers and other employees, the priority of each plan, key players who will need to be influenced and the factors that will encourage or be a barrier to successful implementation.

On the hard side, feasibility may centre on the situation where the supply forecast is less than the demand forecast. Here, the possibilities are to:

- alter the demand forecast by considering changes in the utilisation of employees (such as training, productivity deals, job redesign, multiskilling, high-performance teams and work intensification) by using different employees with higher skills, employing staff with insufficient skills and training them immediately, or outsourcing the work;

- alter the supply forecast by, say, reducing staff turnover, delaying retirement or widening the supply pool to potential employees from other countries (depending on immigration rules);

- change the company objectives, as lack of human resources will prevent them from being achieved in any case. Realistic objectives need to be based on the resources that are, and are forecast to be, available either internally or externally.

When the demand forecast is less than the internal supply forecast in some areas, the possibilities are to:

- consider and calculate the costs of overemployment over various timespans;

- consider the methods and cost of keeping staff but temporarily reducing their drain on company finances (e.g. by unpaid sabbaticals, reduced working hours), or losing staff;

- consider changes in utilisation: work out the feasibility and costs of retraining, redeployment and so on;

- consider whether it is possible for the company objectives to be changed. Could the company diversify, move into new markets, etc.?

Once all alternatives have been considered and feasible solutions decided, specific action plans can be designed covering all appropriate areas of HRM activity. Although these have been grouped in separate sections below, there is clearly potential overlap between the groups.

HR supply plans

Plans may need to be made concerning the timing and approach to recruitment or downsizing. For example, it may have been decided that in order to recruit sufficient staff, a public relations campaign is needed to promote the employer brand. Promotion, succession, transfer and redeployment and redundancy plans may be needed together with plans for the retention of those aged over 50 and flexible retirement plans. Further information on strategic and operational planning for downsizing can be found in Torrington *et al.* (2009).

WINDOW ON PRACTICE

A planned approach to downsizing

The recent recession has created a challenge in how to emerge in a healthy and strong position, unlike in the previous recession where unplanned and unthought-through downsizing meant that there was insufficient talent in many organisations to take advantage of the upturn. Evidence suggests that organisations are taking a more planful approach this time.

For example, the law firm Norton Rose has asked some of its graduate trainees who have been offered places but not yet started work if they would be prepared to defer their appointment until business picks up again. They were offered £10,000 if they accepted this option and used their time constructively such as doing voluntary work or learning a language.

They are also using a redundancy avoidance plan in order to retain key workers by asking them to voluntarily change their terms and conditions for a year giving Norton Rose the chance to agree unpaid sabbaticals and reduced working hours. (Phillips 2009)

KPMG has asked employees to voluntarily work a four day week, if required, or take a sabbatical at 30 per cent pay for between four and twelve weeks. It is proposed that these temporary changes to employment contracts last 18 months, that the maximum salary loss in any year be limited to 20 per cent and full benefits be paid throughout. (*People Management* 2009)

Source: Source: Phillips, L. (2009) '"Slash graduate recruitment at your peril": firms advised to plan for the future', *People Management*, p. 8, 9 April; *People Management* (2009) 'KPMG asks staff to accept temporary flexible contracts if the need arises', *People Management*, Vol. 15, No. 3, p. 8, 29 January.

Talent plans

There is an increasing need to focus on plans to attract, develop and retain a talent pool to draw on as required. For some organisations this will focus on leadership talent, for others it will focus on critical jobs and skills on which the organisation is particularly dependent. There is more on this later (see Chapter 16).

Organisation and structure plans

Organisation and structure plans may concern departmental existence, remit and structure and the relationships between departments. They may also be concerned with the layers of hierarchy within departments and the level at which tasks are done, and the organisational groups within which they are done. For more details of structural issues see the next chapter. Changes to organisation and structure will usually result in changes in employee utilisation.

Employee utilisation plans

Any changes in utilisation that affect HR demand will need to be planned. Some changes will result in a sudden difference in the tasks that employees do and the numbers needed, others will result in a gradual movement over time. Other plans may involve the distribution of hours worked, such as the use of annual hours contracts, or using functional flexibility where employees develop and use a wider range of skills. The people potentially affected will need to be consulted about the changes and be prepared and trained for what will happen.

Learning and development plans

There will be development implications from both the HR supply and the utilisation plans. The timing of development can be a critical aspect. For example, training for specific new technology skills loses most of its impact if it is done six months before the equipment arrives. If the organisation wishes to increase recruitment by promoting the excellent development that it provides for employees, then clear programmes of what will be offered need to be finalised and resourced so that these can then be used to entice candidates into the organisation. Decisions on whether to buy in talent and skills or develop them internally will affect the emphasis on and approach to development.

Performance management and engagement plans

These plans may include the development or renewal of a performance management system, and ensuring that employees are assessed on objectives or criteria that are key to organisational success, and which may then be linked to reward. The plans may also include setting performance and quality standards; culture change programmes aimed at encouraging specified behaviour and performance; or empowerment or career support to improve engagement and motivation.

Reward plans

It is often said that what gets rewarded gets done, and it is key that rewards reflect what the organisation sees as important. For example, if quantity of output is most important for production workers, bonuses may relate to number of items produced. If quality is most important, then bonuses may reflect reject rate, or customer complaint rate. If managers are only rewarded for meeting their individual objectives, there may be problems if the organisation is heavily dependent on teamwork. If individuals are rewarded for short-term gains rather than the achievement of objectives relating to longer-term sustainability, then, as evidence from the banking crisis demonstrates, individuals will work to achieve short-term gains at the expense of long-term sustainability.

Employee relations plans

These plans may involve unions, employee representatives or all employees. They would include any matters which need to be negotiated or areas where there is the opportunity for employee involvement and participation.

Communications plans

The way that planned changes are communicated to employees is critical. Plans need to include not only methods for informing employees about what managers expect of them, but also methods to enable employees to express their concerns and needs for successful implementation. Communications plans will also be important if, for example, managers wish to generate greater employee commitment by keeping employees better informed about the progress of the organisation.

Once the plans have been made and put into action, the planning process still continues. It is important that the plans are monitored to see if they are being achieved and if they are producing the expected results, and pick up any unanticipated consequences. Plans will also need to be reconsidered on a continuing basis in order to cope with changing circumstances.

Workforce metrics

There are two broad ways in which metrics, sometimes called analytics, can be used to support the organisation. The first focuses on ensuring high-quality information to support business decisions. The emphasis is on 'what do we need to know to about the workforce to run the company more effectively, and how can we turn that knowledge into action?' (Lesser 2010). To this end metrics can provide an in-depth picture of the current workforce and an expansion of the data that might be collected to assess current and future workforce supply and behaviour. So, for example, at a basic level, accidents, absence rates and so on may be measured in addition to turnover, and workforce profiles can be developed, for example against age, gender, skills and performance. With greater sophistication the measurement of attitudes and satisfaction can inform the development of people policies and potential antecedents to these can be tested, such as flexible working, coaching and mentoring to highlight and communicate the importance and effectiveness of these actions.

These metrics need interpretation from HR professionals who have a real and close understanding of the business, to develop insights. Such data can highlight the organisation's workforce challenges and enables the HR function to take a more proactive role in addressing them, for example the challenge of high absence levels in some departments, compared with others, or the characteristics of higher-performing managers. Metrics can be a means identifying the most productive and/or the speediest/or most cost-effective recruitment channels, or whether new skills would be best delivered over a shorter or longer timeframe. Given this depth of information, better decisions can be made to address these challenges. So in this first approach to metrics the emphasis is on improving the effectiveness of the organisation's human capital and the processes by which it is managed, and having more facts to support longer-term business decisions, and decisions made in crises.

ACTIVITY 4.3

Thinking of an organisation you know well, address the following questions, including justifications:

1 What people measures are routinely collected?
2 Why are these collected?
3 To what extent are the reasons widely understood?
4 How are the measures used?
5 What changes would you recommend and why?

The second approach to metrics is more obviously strategic and integrated. Through the use of a strategic framework or model the organisation can identify what drives the performance of employees in relation to the organisation's strategy. These drivers can then be expressed as a range of measures with indicators, and targets can be set at about

Figure 4.5
Kaplan and Norton's approach using the 'learning and growth' quadrant of the balanaced scorecard
Source: Adapted from Kaplan and Norton (1992).

'To achieve our vision/mission/strategic goals, how will we be able to sustain our ability to change and improve?'

What are the critical success factors?	What are the critical measurements?

the levels that need to be achieved. These targets are often cascaded down to employee level, and form the base for the 'hard' metrics approach to performance management as opposed to the softer 'good management' approach to HRM which we discuss later (see Chapter 10).

There are a variety of models that can be used; for more details see Matthewman and Matignon (2005) who identify six potential frameworks. Considerable attention has been given to the use of scorecards, such as the balanced scorecard (Kaplan and Norton 1992) and, later, the HR scorecard (Becker *et al*. 2001), in linking people, strategy and performance. Such scorecards utilise a range of HR measures which are viewed as critical to the achievement of the business strategy. Kaplan and Norton widened the perspective on the measurement of business performance by measuring more than financial performance. Their premise is that other factors which lead to financial performance need to be measured to give a more rounded view of how well the organisation is performing. This means that measures of business performance are based on measures of strategy implementation in a range of areas. Kaplan and Norton identify three other areas for measurement in addition to financial measures: customer measures; internal business process measures; and learning and growth measures. Figure 4.5 provides an example of Norton and Kaplan's approach.

In each of these areas critical elements need to be identified and then measures devised to identify current levels and to measure progress. Some organisations implementing this scorecard have developed the learning and growth area to include a wider range of HR measures. The next Window on practice shows the CAA's tailor-made balanced scorecard approach.

WINDOW ON PRACTICE

Civil Aviation Authority's (CAA) approach to human capital measurement (HCM)

As 60% of the CAA's costs are people costs, the CAA began an HCM process hoping that this would allow it to quantify the value of its staff and explore the relationship between staff performance and business outcomes. The CAA also anticipated that it would help in quantifying its objectives of continuous improvement, improved efficiency and cost-effectiveness. The

CAA developed a balanced scorecard approach to measuring human capital based on what constituted the 'bottom line', being a not-for-profit organisation. This bottom line comprised:

- External customer perception of CAA's performance
- Achievement of objectives
- Assessment of staff expertise.

In order to measure the value of their people, policies and practices, the CAA asked itself what it wanted to know about each of these in relation to the defined 'bottom line'.

What do we want to know?

Success of our policies & practices

- Are staff engaged?
- Are we retaining key employees?
- Are we recruiting strong candidates?
- Do our new recruits stay with the CAA?
- Are we managing attendance levels?
- Are our reward levels competitive?
- Do our managers have the necessary skills to manage their staff?

Value created by our people

- Are we continually raising the bar on performance?
- Are we developing our staff effectively?
- Are our 'customers' satisfied with our performance?

How can we measure that?

Success of our policies & practices

- Engagement index
- Quality of leaver
- Quality of hire
- Recent recruit turnover
- Absence rates/costs
- Pay benchmarks
- Manager competency framework & performance management process

Value created by our people

- Performance management index
- Training evaluation
- External customer survey

Figure 4.6
How the CAA defined measures to answer its human capital questions
Source: Robinson, D. (2009) 'Human capital measurement: An approach that works', *Strategic HR Review*, Vol. 8, No. 6, pp. 5–11, Figure 1.

Having decided the questions, the CAA then worked out where that information might be found and how it could be measured. The questions and measures are shown in Figure 4.6.

The CAA then ordered its measures in a four-level hierarchy and worked up the hierarchy starting with the basic measures at the base:

Level 4: Performance measures: link between input/output data and measures of CAA strategic performance.

Level 3: Outcome measures: for example, absence rates and costs, engagement data.

Level 2: Operational data: for example, number of training days.

Level 1: Workforce data: for example, headcount, demographics, equal opportunities data.

The fourth level, not surprisingly, was the hardest to define and measure, so the CAA are looking at correlations between input measures such as absence, turnover, training and length of service and outputs such as employee engagement.

Source: Summarised from Robinson, D. (2009) 'Human capital measurement: An approach that works', *Strategic HR Review*, Vol. 8, No. 6, pp. 5–11.

Metrics of whatever type are often presented in the form of dashboards and use sophisticated software (see e.g. Asselman 2012). While the value of metrics may be acknowledged, many organisations face barriers in implementation; Tootell and colleagues (2009) provide some excellent information on this in a New Zealand context.

SUMMARY PROPOSITIONS

4.1 Even in a context of rapid and discontinuous change, workforce planning still has a valuable contribution to make, but as HR planning deals with people, planners need to plan for what is acceptable as well as what is feasible.

4.2 The scope of workforce planning covers not only numbers of people and skills, but also structure, culture, systems and behaviour.

4.3 An integrated framework which attempts to cover all aspects of workforce planning involves:
- analysing the external environment and business strategy;
- analysing where we want to be (forecasting HR requirements);
- analysing where we are we now (defining the current HR position and projecting this forward);
- comparing the two and forming plans to bridge the gap.

4.4 Workforce planning is a continuous process rather than a one-off activity.

4.5 Metrics can assist in providing a clear picture of the current situation and can be used to monitor progress towards the desired state which will underpin the organisation's ability to achieve its goals.

GENERAL DISCUSSION TOPICS

1 Discuss the proposition that traditional (numbers) workforce planning is only of interest to organisations in periods of growth when unemployment levels are low.

2 'It is worthwhile planning even if you have no strategy.' For what reasons might you agree or disagree with this statement?

THEORY INTO PRACTICE

G4S and the London 2012 Olympics (August)

G4S, an international security firm, gained the contract to provide security at all Olympic locations. G4S contracted Wave, recruitment marketing specialists, to run the recruitment campaign. It was projected in 2010 that 2,000 security staff would be required, but by late 2011 this had risen to 10,400. Wave appeared to run a very thorough recruitment campaign (see e.g. CIPD 2012) and in May 2012 it appeared that everything was on track for the increased number of guards. However, suddenly in mid-July G4S admitted that it could not fulfil the whole contract and 3,500 soldiers were drafted in to cover the shortfall. Nick Buckles of G4S, interviewed on Radio 4, appeared to lack information about the detail of the recruitment/training/vetting processes, could not explain what had gone wrong and was unable even to confirm that all potential employees spoke fluent English.

G4S found there was a dropout of acceptable candidates when they realised the realities of the job, but even more importantly there was a shortage of licensed security guards and the company recognised that it would have to recruit inexperienced staff and train them up in order to meet the new target. Such candidates had to provide a lot of data about themselves and be vetted and screened, then trained for four days in order to acquire the necessary skills, and then meet the criteria for a Security Industry Licence before they could begin their employment. The sheer scale of this task defeated the organisation, and it accepted that it had underestimated the challenge.

Questions

1 In what ways might contingency planning have helped G4S?

2 The chief executive of G4S only found out that it could not fulfil the contract in mid-July, which was very close to the start of the games. How might communication have been improved within G4S, and between G4S and Wave, and how might this have helped the planning process?

3 In a similar situation, if you were tasked with recruiting 8,000 similar inexperienced staff, with less than a year to do this, how would you plan to ensure that all potential employees were vetted, screened, trained, licensed so they were qualified to begin work on time, and that the dropout rate was minimised?

Sources: Brockett, J. (2012) 'Olympian task', *People Management*, August, p. 9; Gabb, A. (2012) 'Safety in numbers', *PM Guide to Recruitment Marketing*, pp. 14–17; and general news media.

FURTHER READING

Day, G. and Schoemaker, P. (2005) 'Scanning the periphery', *Harvard Business Review*, November, pp. 135–48.

This article underlines the organisational importance of keeping a constant eye on peripheral features in an organisation's environment as well as its direct and close competitors. Examples are included of challenges that different organisations have faced and there are practical suggestions about how organisations could improve their scanning of the peripheral environment. Included is a self-assessment tool to identify the need for an organisation to have peripheral vision, and to assess its capability for peripheral vision. The capability part encompasses an assessment of leadership orientation, knowledge management systems, strategy-making processes, organisation structure and incentives, and culture (values, beliefs and behaviours).

McNeilly, M. (2002) 'Gathering information for strategic decisions', *Strategy and Leadership*, Vol. 30, No. 5, pp. 29–34.

This article focuses on information gathering, making strategic decisions and taking action, and provides some useful tools for each of these three stages. Some interesting suggestions for making strategic decisions include scenario planning and acting out scenarios in advance.

Turner, P. (2002) *Strategic Human Resource Forecasting*. London: CIPD.

An excellent and detailed text which covers issues involved in forecasting, strategy and planning and the HR role in these. Turner includes a wide range of HR aspects from employee numbers to employee relations and organisation design.

WEB LINKS

www.creatingpeopleadvantage.com
www.healthcareworkforce.nhs.uk
www.adeccoinstitute.com

REFERENCES

Asselman, S. (2012) 'Screen grabbers', *People Management*, June, pp. 43–6.

Becker, B., Huselid, M. and Ulrich, D. (2001) *The HR Scorecard: Linking people, strategy and performance*. Boston, MA: Harvard Business School Press.

Brewster, C., Sparrow, P., Vernon, G. and Houldsworth, E. (2011) *International Human Resource Management*. London: CIPD, pp. 391–2.

Boxall, P. and Purcell, J. (2003) *Strategy and Human Resource Management*. Basingstoke: Palgrave Macmillan.

Brockett, J. (2012) 'Olympian task', *People Management*, August, p. 9.

Chubb, L. (2008) 'Plan ahead to defuse the "demographic timebomb"', *People Management*, Vol. 14, No. 9, p. 7.

CIPD (2010) *Workforce Planning: Right people, right time, right skills*, Guide. London: CIPD.

CIPD (2012) *Strategic Human Resource Planning Factsheet*. London: CIPD.

Curson, J., Dell, M., Wilson, R., Bosworth, D. and Baldauf, B. (2010) 'Who does workforce planning well? Workforce rapid review team summary', *International Journal of Health Care Quality Assurance*, Vol. 23, No. 1, pp. 110–19.

Gabb, A. (2012) 'Safety in numbers', *PM Guide to Recruitment Marketing*, pp. 14–17.

IDS (2011) *HR Studies: Workforce Planning*. London: IDS.

Jacob, R. (2012) 'Labour shortages: Double digit wage increases', **www.ft.com**, 11 December.

Kaplan, R. and Norton, D. (1992) 'The balanced scorecard: Measures that drive performance', *Harvard Business Review*, January–February, pp. 71–9.

Lavelle, J. (2007) 'On workforce architecture, employment relationships and lifecycles: Expanding the purview of workforce planning and management', *Public Personnel Management*, Vol. 36, No. 4, pp. 371–84.

Lesser, E. (2010) 'Go figure', *People Management*, May, pp. 22–5.

Matthewman, J. and Matignon, F. (2005) *Human Capital Reporting: An internal perspective, a guide*. London: CIPD.

Mayall, R. (2009) *Dear Granny Smith: A letter from your postman*. London: Short Books.

Mintzberg, H. (1994) 'The fall and rise of strategic planning', *Harvard Business Review*, January–February, pp. 107–14.

People Management (2009) 'KPMG asks staff to accept temporary flexible contracts if the need arises', Vol. 15, No. 3, p. 8.

Phillips, L. (2009) '"Slash graduate recruitment at your peril": Firms advised to plan for the future', *People Management*, April, p. 8.

Robinson, D. (2009) 'Human capital measurement: An approach that works', *Strategic HR Review*, Vol. 8, No. 6, pp. 5–11.

Rudge, A. (2011) 'Workforce planning helps Birmingham to ride storms of change', *Human Resource Management International Digest*, Vol. 19, No. 1, pp. 12–14.

Stokker, J. and Hallam, G. (2009) 'The right person, in the right job, with the right skills at the right time: A workforce-planning model that goes beyond metrics', *Library Management*, Vol. 15, No. 89, pp. 561–71.

Tootell, B., Toulson, P. and Dewe, P. (2009) 'Metrics: HRM's Holy Grail?', *Human Resource Management Journal*, Vol. 19, No. 4, pp. 375–92.

Torrington, D., Hall, L., Taylor, S. and Atkinson, C. (2009) *Fundamentals of Human Resource Management*. Harlow: Pearson Education.

Turner, P. (2002) 'How to do HR forecasting and planning', *People Management*, Vol. 8, No. 6, pp. 48–9.

Part 2

RESOURCING: GETTING PEOPLE IN THE RIGHT PLACES TO DO THE RIGHT THINGS

CHAPTERS

CHANGING TIMES
RESOURCING

Strategy
Contracts
Recruitment
Selection
Retention
Ending the contract
Skills

In this part of the book, we deal with the resourcing aspects of HRM, how to design an organisation with a flexible workforce, how to get the right people in the right places and how to keep them. In particular circumstances, we may also need to understand how to end the contract legally and effectively. The first major activity of the HR specialist is to facilitate an effective organisation design, one that offers flexibility to both worker and organisation. Next is to find and bring in the people that the business needs for its success. These people may not be employees; they may be consultants or subcontractors. They may be temporary, full time, part time or occasional, and the working relationship between the business and its people is the contract, which sums up the features of that relationship so that both parties know where they stand. Nearly always there is a face-to-face meeting between the parties to agree terms before the relationship begins. The process of 'coming to terms' is one of mutual assessment. Many prospective employees reject a prospective employer by deciding not to apply for a post, or by discontinuing their application. Employers usually choose between many, and often feel there are too few applicants. Once recruited, people have to be retained within the business by a series of strategies that sustain their interest and motivation as well as keeping the focus of their activities within an evolving organisation and a changing business context. Contracts end as well as begin, and we have to be sure that the arrangements to end the contract are as sound as those for it to start.

The whole resourcing process is symbolised by the mutual assessment that takes place in the selection interview: 'Is this person right for us?' and 'Is this job and situation right for me?' The answers to those questions have major implications for both parties. The uncertainty about whether or not the right answers are found at the interview is why we have to examine resourcing so closely. At the end of each chapter you will find a case study which will help you to put these ideas into context and explore them more thoroughly.

Chapter 5

ORGANISATION DESIGN AND FLEXIBILITY

Organisation design

Organisational design relates to the shaping of an organisation to ensure efficient delivery of its activity. Activities focus on:

[ensuring] that the organisation is appropriately designed to deliver organisation objectives in the short and long-term and that structural change is effectively managed. (CIPD 2013)

Organisation design requires that choices made on a number of issues are consistent with contextual factors, such as the organisation's strategy and its environment (Burton and Obel 2004). Three key issues are **high** versus **low formality**, **differentiation** versus **integration**, and **decentralisation** versus **centralisation**.

High versus low formality refers to the design of organisational procedures. Typically small firms are relatively informal, low employee numbers meaning that face-to-face communication is usually possible in order to discuss and agree a way forward. As organisations grow, however, procedures are normally established which guide action to ensure consistency across a range of situations and people. It is important to ensure that procedures support and enable action, rather than constraining and disempowering, as can happen when organisations become very large and develop a plethora of inflexible and inconsistent procedures.

Differentiation requires specialisation of effort to ensure that an individual job or task is undertaken effectively, and integration is coordinating the output of the individual people so that the whole task is completed satisfactorily. Organising individual jobs varies according to the degree of predictability in what has to be done, so that organising manufacturing jobs or a call centre tends to emphasise strict obedience to the rules, clearly defined tasks and much specialisation. Jobs which have constantly fresh problems and unpredictable requirements, like marketing and social work, produce frequent redefinition of job boundaries, a tendency to flexible networks of working relationships rather than a clear hierarchy and a greater degree of individual autonomy. The integrating process will be influenced by the amount of differentiation. The greater the differentiation, the harder the task of coordination.

Centralisation/decentralisation refers to the extent to which certain aspects of authority and decision making are held at the centre of the organisation, as opposed to being devolved down to local level. Historically organisations have tended to favour centralisation, although the past couple of decades have seen greater decentralisation in the form, for example, of strategic business units. Here, the management of a particular unit is given an agreed budget and an agreed set of targets for the forthcoming period. Thereafter it has the freedom to manage itself as it sees fit provided that it first submits regular reports and, second, meets the targets and complies with the budget expectations. Decentralisation is thought to make decision making and responding to local needs and customers easier and quicker to achieve. Worren (2012) presents a detailed discussion of these design choices.

Using these three elements gives a range of design choices, often classified using systems metaphors (Eriksen 2005). Burns and Stalker (1961), for example, outline the

Table 5.1
Organisation
design choices

Mechanistic design	High formalisation	Extensive use of written procedures High degree of task specialisation Strict performance control
	Low integration	Little use of liaison processes Little use of liaison structures
	High centralisation	Little delegation of decision-making authority
Organic design	Low formalisation	Little use of written procedures Low degree of task specialisation Relaxed performance control
	High integration	Extensive use of liaison processes Extensive use of liaison structures
	Low centralisation	Extensive delegation of decision-making authority

Source: Curado (2006: 38).

classical distinction between organic and mechanistic designs. Organic systems are frequently described as loosely coupled systems where there is little formalisation, where complex integrating mechanisms are used, and decision making is delegated. In contrast, mechanistic organisations are highly formalised and centralised, and tend to use less complex integration mechanisms (Curado 2006). These design choices are presented in Table 5.1.

ACTIVITY 5.1

Thinking of an organisation with which you are familiar, how would you describe it in terms of the three key elements of organisation design:

1 To what extent are differentiation and integration evident?

2 Are procedures predominantly formal or informal?

3 What is the degree of centralisation versus decentralisation?

Different configurations of these choices have prevailed at various times across the history of organisation design. A CIPD (2008) report presents a timeline reflecting how thinking has developed (Figure 5.1).

The first attempts at organisation design were undertaken by F.W. Taylor and the scientific school of management. This approach was founded on the division of labour into simple jobs and rigid allocations of individuals to narrowly defined tasks. Concerns centred around efficiency, time and motion studies, for example, ensuring tasks were structured in a way that allowed workers to conduct them in the most efficient manner. This led to highly specialised jobs, workers at Ford's factories on assembly lines each carrying out, for example, very narrow specified elements of the construction of a motor car. Scientific management was premised upon the idea of 'man as machine': that is, rational, unemotional and focused upon economic concerns. Incentives, such as bonuses, were designed to meet the extrinsic motivations of employees. Jobs were, however, routine, repetitive and monotonous, leading to boredom and industrial unrest among workers.

Figure 5.1
Organisation
design timeline
(OD:
Organisational
Development;
ROI: Return On
Investment)

Source: From *Smart
Working: The impact
of work organisation
and job design*, CIPD
(2008): Figure 2.
With the permission
of the publisher, the
Chartered Institute
of Personnel and
Development,
London (**www.cipd.
co.uk**).

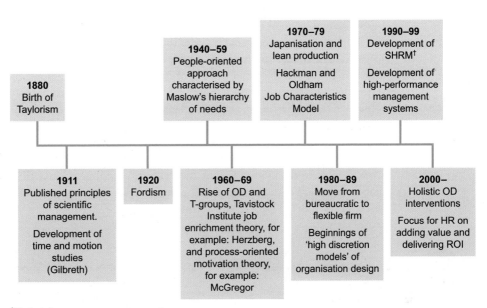

†Strategic human resource management

The recognition that workers had needs beyond economic ones led, from the 1940s on, to worker motivation being a key concern within organisation design. Maslow (1954), for example, suggested that there was a hierarchy of needs within workers and that design should meet a range of needs, such as social ones, rather than simply focusing on economic concerns. In recent decades, organisation design focused on worker motivation has continued but preoccupation with organisational efficiency is also once more prominent. So we see an emerging emphasis on job design (to be discussed further (see Chapter 26)), the flexible firm (see later in this chapter) and the role of strategic HRM within overall job design. We do not have the space here to provide a comprehensive review of these varying approaches to organisation and refer the reader to an organisational behaviour text for further information. Part 4 on organisation structures in Buchanan and Huczynski (2010) provides a detailed and helpful discussion of these issues.

While organisations have long reflected upon design choices, these have been made increasingly complex by contemporary concerns which have created demand for workforce flexibility. Indeed, CIPD (2008) suggests that delivering flexibility is the most important aspect of organisation design. Globalisation of markets has led to ever-greater product market competition and an increased need to gain competitive advantage. In striving for this, employers have provided less secure jobs, using 'flexible' workers in order to keep costs down and to retain or increase market share. Developments in technology enable a greater control of workflow, requiring flexible working hours to extend capital utilisation. The change in the economic base whereby there are more service industries with an emphasis on knowledge and knowledge workers has also influenced flexibility, as jobs in a knowledge-based economy tend to be more flexible than industrial jobs, with more varied working hours. Allied to this has been a perceived need for '24/7' service availability, leading to a dramatic move away from the standard working time model of 9–5 Monday to Friday and to employers demanding a far more flexible approach to work organisation.

The demand for flexibility, however, has not all been from employers. It has coincided with changes that have created a greater supply of labour at non-standard times. One of the primary drivers of this has been the increased labour force participation of women, particularly women in the childbearing years, which has led to a greater requirement for flexible working arrangements in order to accommodate childcare responsibilities. There has also been an increase in single-parent families and dual-career couples, meaning that a growing proportion of the workforce has to reconcile both work and non-work commitments. This augments the supply of labour at non-standard times, such as nights and weekends. A further demographic influence is the ageing population of western countries, with employees demanding flexibility to deal with both childcare and eldercare responsibilities. Pension concerns (see Chapter 23) may also force workers to remain in the workforce longer than previously anticipated and older workers frequently aspire to work flexibly in the later stages of their careers. Flexibility for both organisational and employee benefit is thus a significant contemporary issue in organisation design and we discuss this in detail later in this chapter.

WINDOW ON PRACTICE

The shape of things to come

The complexity of influences on organisation design which we discuss above means that many organisations frequently redesign themselves in order to be more efficient. They typically wish to improve customer responsiveness, gain market share or enhance internal efficiency. In many large organisations, this can happen as often as every three years. Redesign therefore needs to be a core organisational capability and address the increasing challenges of technology adoption and international operations. HR is central to organisation (re)design because of its impact on processes such as recruitment, reward and training. There is, however, often a lack of focus on people elements and neglect of redesign's impact on morale and retention. HR involvement is nevertheless very important. More than half of reorganisations involve involuntary redundancies, with significant numbers of voluntary redundancies, early retirements and other job moves. Many redesigns also involve substantial recruitment. Involving HR in redesign delivers more positive outcomes as it allows for an emphasis on leadership and culture together with changes in career and reward structures that otherwise receive relatively little attention.

Source: Adapted from Anon. (2002).

Organisation structures

There is no single ideal organisational form. Organisation structures reflect the decisions made by organisations about issues of formalisation, differentiation and centralisation (Table 5.1) and are based around hierarchy:

The hierarchy is the chain of command, the pyramid of authority that narrows at the top . . . if we eliminate all the paraphernalia of rank and authority in large organisations, we don't really know what we would end up with. There are no clear examples of large human organisations that operate without a formal hierarchy . . . some form of hierarchy is necessary for organising a complex set of people and resources. (Leavitt *et al.* 1973: 31–2)

Hierarchy creates a predictable system of roles and jobs. It enables us to understand how to get things done and how matters will be handled. Hierarchy also distributes power, rations power and ensures that people accept the power of others in the system. Holders of specified roles or jobs are empowered to make certain decisions and to control the behaviour of other people: power is distributed and rationed. Traditionally, large organisations have had *tall* hierarchies (i.e. many levels in them) with *narrow* spans of control (each person being responsible for the supervision of only a small number of people). Since the 1980s, however, there has been a trend to much *flatter* hierarchies with much *wider* spans of control. This trend has been termed 'delayering' and is the process of taking out layers of management in the hierarchy in order to speed response times and make the operation more efficient.

WINDOW ON PRACTICE

Delayering in large organisations

From the mid-1980s onwards many organisations which had traditionally had tall hierarchies set about the process of delayering. This was common practice in financial services organisations such as large banks (see e.g. Atkinson 2002) and in some newly privatised companies such as BT (see e.g. Newell and Dopson 1996). The logic behind this restructuring process was to make organisations more flexible and responsive to increasingly dynamic and competitive market conditions by devolving decision-making responsibilities to those closest to the customer. In removing layers of middle management which had come to be seen as blockages to change and

responsiveness, organisations sought to improve the efficiency and effectiveness of their operations.

While the theory behind delayering was sound, its implementation was in many instances problematic. As is often the case with change programmes, senior management gave insufficient consideration to the people aspects of delayering. There is a large body of research from this period which identifies the negative impact on the morale and motivation of those remaining in delayered organisations. Those left behind were said to suffer from 'survivor syndrome', characterised by mourning for lost colleagues, fearing for their own future job security and suffering work intensification as they struggled to cope with often increased workloads with fewer staff. In the face of these conditions, the hoped-for efficiency gains were rarely achieved.

While a huge variety of organisation structures is possible, most can be categorised into one of three broad types: entrepreneurial, bureaucratic and matrix.

The entrepreneurial form

The entrepreneurial form relies on central power and can be described as primarily organic. It is like a spider's web, with one person or group so dominant that all power stems from the centre, all decisions are made by the centre and all behaviour reflects expectations of the centre. There are few collective decisions, much reliance on individuals, and with actions requiring the approval of key figures. This form is frequently found in businesses where decisions must be made quickly and with flair and judgement rather than careful deliberation. Newspaper editing has an entrepreneurial form of organisation and most of the performing arts have strong centralised direction.

This is the form of most small and growing businesses as they owe their existence to the expertise or initiative of one or two people, and it is only by reflecting accurately this originality that the business can survive. As the business expands, this type of structure can become unwieldy because too many peripheral decisions cannot be made without approval from the centre, which then becomes overloaded. It is also difficult to maintain if the spider leaves the centre of the web, as a successor may not have the same degree of dominance. In some instances the problem of increasing size has been dealt with by maintaining entrepreneurial structure at the core of the enterprise and giving considerable independence to satellite organisations, provided that overall performance targets are met.

An extreme example is the organisation of the entourage surrounding a celebrity. An entertainer of international reputation may employ dozens or hundreds of people, but the sole purpose of their employment is to sustain and extend the reputation of the spider at the centre of their web. If that person dies the whole surrounding organisation rapidly unravels, having lost its reason for existence. Less unusual examples are in financial services, where a fund manager's team may collapse if that manager leaves, or in a school, where the tone of all that is done is largely determined by the head teacher.

The bureaucratic form

The bureaucratic form emphasises the distribution rather than centralisation of power and responsibility: it has a more extended and complex hierarchy and is primarily mechanistic in structure. It has been the conventional means of enabling an organisation to grow beyond the entrepreneurial form to establish an existence that is not dependent on a single person or group of founders. Disney is a classic example of a business, originally totally dependent on the flair of its founder, but then developed, expanded and diversified despite the demise of Walt Disney. Because the emphasis is on role rather than flair, operational processes become more predictable and consistent, with procedure and committee replacing individual judgement. Responsibility is devolved through the structure; this is a method of organisation well suited to stable situations, making possible economies of scale and the benefits of specialisation. There is seldom the flexibility to deal with a volatile environment which can be problematic and procedures can become an end in themselves, rather than a means to an end. Bureaucracy has been the standard form of structure for large organisations at least since the building of the Egyptian pyramids and remains the dominant form today. It has, however, come under criticism because of its inappropriateness in times of change and a tendency to frustrate personal initiative. 'Bureaucracy' is definitely a dirty word, so companies work hard at overcoming its drawbacks.

The matrix form

The matrix form emphasises the coordination of expertise into project-orientated groups of people with individual responsibility. It has been developed to counter some of the difficulties of the entrepreneurial and bureaucratic forms and tries to combine the strengths of both organic and mechanistic approaches. It was first developed in the USA during the 1960s as a means of satisfying the government on the progress of orders placed with contractors for the supply of defence materiel. Checking on progress proved very difficult with a bureaucracy, so it was made a condition of contracts that the contractor should appoint a project manager with responsibility for meeting the delivery commitments and keeping the project within budget. In this way the government was able to deal with a single representative rather than with a number of people with only partial responsibility. The contractors then had to realign their organisation so that the project manager could actually exercise the degree of control necessary to make the responsibility effective. They did this either by appointing a project manager with considerable status and power, or by creating product teams with specialists seconded from each functional area. The first method leaves the weight of authority with the functional hierarchy, while the project managers have a mainly coordinating, progress-chasing role as lone specialists. The second method shifts power towards the project managers, who then have their own teams of experts, with the functional areas being seen as a resource rather than the centre of action and decision.

The matrix form is the one that appeals to many managers because it is theoretically based on expertise and provides scope for people at relatively humble levels of the business to deploy their skills and carry responsibility. It has, however, recently lost favour because it can generate expensive support systems for project managers needing additional secretaries, assistants and all the panoply of office, as well as the unwieldy administration referred to above.

This three-fold classification is a means of analysis rather than a description of three distinct types of organisation with any undertaking being clearly one of the three. Bureaucracies will typically have matrix features at some points and few entrepreneurial structures are quite as 'pure' as implied here. Most large organisations could have one form dominant in one section of the business and another form dominant elsewhere. Large banks, for example, are bureaucratic in their retailing operations as consistency is of paramount importance and any changes need to be put into operation simultaneously by a large number of people as well as being comprehensible to a large number of customers. The same banks will, however, tend towards an entrepreneurial emphasis in their merchant banking activities and in currency dealings.

ACTIVITY 5.2

What experience have you, or someone you know, had of organisation restructuring? What happened? To what extent did the restructuring achieve its aims?

Organisational flexibility

As we have seen, a crucial aspect of organisation design is the extent to which it affords flexibility. Flexibility has increased significantly since the mid-1980s, with many employees experiencing substantial change in their traditional working patterns. Atkinson (1984), for example, suggested a 'flexible firm' model that explains employer behaviour in terms of work organisation and flexibility. However, tight labour markets in the period 1997–2007 placed increasing emphasis on employer efforts to accommodate employee demands for flexibility in order to recruit and retain scarce labour. It is often argued that employer and employee needs in flexible working practices are complementary and that

the practices adopted have benefits for both parties. There are tensions, however, between employer and employee needs. Practices presented as beneficial to employees are, in fact, often detrimental to them. For example, despite meeting the needs of some employees for flexibility, part-time work is often insecure and low paid. Nevertheless, there can be a coincidence of needs when an employee has access to a contract of choice. We present first flexible working practices that are typically considered to be demand led, adopting Atkinson's (1984) model of the flexible firm. While this model is much criticised, it remains one of the most comprehensive treatments of organisational flexibility. Second, we present flexible practices that are typically delivered for employee benefit.

Employer flexibility

Atkinson's (1984) model of the 'flexible firm' (Figure 5.2) is frequently adopted to describe how firms develop flexibility through numerical, temporal and functional means.

Numerical flexibility

Numerical flexibility allows the organisation to respond quickly to the environment in terms of the numbers of people employed. Some traditional full-time, permanent posts are replaced by short-term contract staff, staff with rolling contracts, outworkers and so on. This enables the organisation to reduce or expand the workforce quickly and cheaply.

Figure 5.2
Atkinson's model of the flexible firm
Source: J. Atkinson (1984) 'Manpower strategies for flexible organisations', *Personnel Management*, August. Used with the permission of the author.

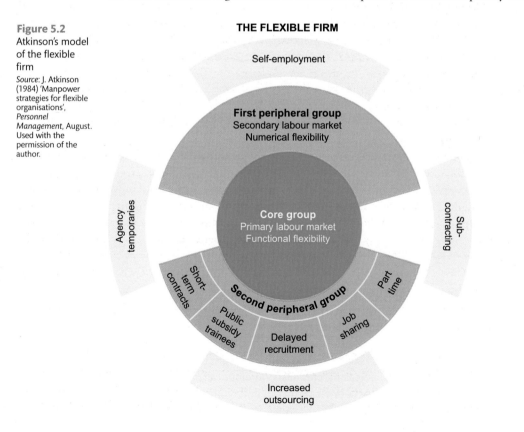

THE FLEXIBLE FIRM

Self-employment

First peripheral group
Secondary labour market
Numerical flexibility

Agency temporaries

Core group
Primary labour market
Functional flexibility

Sub-contracting

Second peripheral group

Short-term contracts

Public subsidy trainees

Delayed recruitment

Job sharing

Part time

Increased outsourcing

The flexible firm in this analysis has various ways of meeting the need for human resources. First, there are core employees, who form the primary labour market. They are highly regarded by the employer, well paid and involved in those activities that are unique to the firm or give it a distinctive character. These employees have improved career prospects and offer the type of flexibility to the employer that is so prized in the skilled professional with wide experience and adaptability.

There are then two peripheral groups: first, those who have skills that are needed but not specific to the particular firm, like typing and word processing. The strategy for these posts is to rely on the external labour market to a much greater extent, to specify a narrow range of tasks without career prospects, so that the employee has a job but not a career. Some employees may be able to transfer to core posts, but generally limited scope is likely to maintain a fairly high turnover, so that adjustments to the vagaries of the product market are eased.

The second peripheral group is made up of those enjoying even less security, as they have contracts of employment that are limited, either to a short-term or a part-time attachment. There may also be a few job sharers, although job sharing is not widely practised. An alternative or additional means towards this flexibility is to subcontract the work that has to be done, either by employing temporary personnel from agencies or by outsourcing the entire operation, adjusting the organisation boundary, redefining what is to be done in-house and what is to be subcontracted to various suppliers.

Temporal flexibility

Temporal flexibility concerns varying the pattern of hours worked in order to respond to business demands and employee needs. Moves away from the 9–5, five-day week include the use of annual hours contracts, increased use of part-time work, job sharing and flexible working hours. For example, an organisation subject to peaks and troughs of demand, such as an ice-cream manufacturer, could use annual hours contracts so that more employee hours are available at peak periods and fewer are used when business is slow. Flexible hours systems can benefit the employer by providing employee cover outside the 9–5 day and over lunchtimes, and can also provide employee benefits by allowing personal demands to be fitted more easily around work demands.

Research evidence suggests increasing use of temporal flexibility. Longer opening hours in retailing and the growth of the leisure sector mean that many more people now work in the evening and at night than used to be the case. The proportion of jobs that are part time also continues to rise, albeit at a slower rate than in the 1970s and 1980s, while the length of the working week for higher-paid full-time workers has increased by three hours on average during the past decade. There has also been some growth in the use of annual hours, but these arrangements have not become as widespread as was initially predicted a decade ago. Less than 10% of employers have chosen to adopt this approach for some of their staff (van Wanrooy *et al.* 2013).

Functional flexibility

The term 'functional flexibility' refers to a process in which employees gain the capacity to undertake a variety of tasks rather than specialising in just one area. Advocates of such approaches have been influenced by studies of Japanese employment practices as well as by criticisms of monotonous assembly-line work. Horizontal flexibility involves each individual employee becoming multiskilled so that he or she can be deployed as and where required at any time. Vertical flexibility entails gaining the capacity to undertake work previously carried out by colleagues higher up or lower down the organisational hierarchy.

The primary purpose of functional flexibility initiatives is to deploy human resources more efficiently. It should mean that employees are kept busy throughout their working day and that absence is more easily covered than in a workplace with rigidly defined demarcation between jobs. A further efficiency gain comes from employees being more stretched, fulfilled and thus productive than in a workplace with narrowly defined jobs. Despite its potential advantages, employers in the UK have been less successful than competitors elsewhere in Europe at developing functional flexibility, perhaps because of a reluctance to invest in the training necessary to support these new forms of working. Reilly (2001) also points to employee resistance and the increased likelihood of errors occurring when functional flexibility programmes are introduced. It could also simply be a reflection of increased specialisation as jobs become more technically complex, relying to a greater extent on specific expert knowledge.

ACTIVITY 5.3

1 What evidence do you see of numerical and functional flexibility in the organisation you work for, or one with which you are familiar?

2 To what extent do you think these forms of flexibility benefit:

- The employer?
- The employees?

Network organisations

As we noted above, Atkinson's model of the flexible firm is much criticised but has no clear successor. The network organisation (Powell 1990) has, however, received increasing interest in the debate on organisational flexibility in recent years. Network organisations describe long-term contractual arrangements between supplier and client organisations which involve a co-production process, for example the outsourcing of cleaning or IT operations to an external supplier. In this way, an organisation can gain numerical and functional flexibility by establishing relationships with other organisations, rather than through its own labour management strategies, as advocated in Atkinson's model of the flexible firm. Functional flexibility is achieved through agreements with specialist suppliers or producers, while numerical flexibility is delivered through outsourcing and the use of temporary agency labour. These inter-organisational relationships are often referred to as strategic alliances, joint ventures, partnerships or subcontracting. They are ongoing relationships which can lead to the blurring of organisational boundaries such that it can be difficult for the worker to know who he or she is working for.

Debates about flexibility

The growth in flexible working practices combined with their promotion by governments since the 1990s has led to the development of robust debates about their desirability and usage in practice. As much controversy has centred on the Atkinson model of the flexible firm as on the rather different elements that go to make it up. There has been a continuing debate, for example, about whether the model of core and periphery is a description of trends or a prescription for the future. Two streams of research have flowed from these interpretations. The first concerns the extent to which the model has been adopted in practice, the second focuses on the advantages and disadvantages of flexibility as a blueprint for the future organisation of work.

Evidence on the first of these questions is patchy. There is no question that rhetoric about flexibility and the language of flexibility is increasingly used. The flexible firm model appears to be something that managers aspire to adopt, but the extent to which they have actually adopted it is questionable. While some evidence suggests that there has been a steady increase in part-time work across Europe, findings from the 'Future of Work Programme' in the UK have challenged the degree of change that has actually occurred. Nolan and Wood (2003) have found that traditional working patterns, premised upon full-time permanent employment, remain dominant. Further, in many organisations the drive for economies of scale means that far from becoming more flexible, organisations are just as likely to introduce bureaucratic systems and standardised practices in response to competitive pressures. And yet we also have seen for a long period now increased use of part-time workers, consultants, subcontractors, agency workers and moves towards multiskilling. Legge's (1995) conclusion that flexibility is used in a pragmatic and opportunistic way rather than as a strategic HRM initiative thus seems to hold true today.

Turning to the second question, the desirability of flexibility is debatable. The theoretical advantage for organisations is that flexibility enables them to deploy employee time and effort more efficiently so that staff are only at work when they need to be and are wholly focused on achieving organisational objectives throughout that time. However, the extent to which this is achieved in practice is not clear. Many writers equate the term 'flexibility' with 'insecurity' and argue that the consequences for organisations in terms of staff commitment and willingness to work beyond contract are damaging, staff turnover is likely to increase and recruiting talented people will be harder too. It is questionable that the flexible firm model, at least as far as the 'peripheral' workforce is concerned, is compatible with best practice approaches to HRM which seek to increase employees' commitment. This is equally the case for the network organisation where terms and conditions for those providing numerical flexibility are still typically inferior to those providing functional flexibility. Another view, however, is that soft HRM adopting high-commitment HRM practices can adopt functional flexibility through practices such as flexible job design, cross-training, use of teams and work groups, and job rotation and enlargement. Lepak and Snell (1999) go further in arguing that soft and hard approaches may not be mutually exclusive and that the ability to manage different forms of flexibility may give an organisation sustainable competitive advantage, one that draws on robust HR policies.

WINDOW ON PRACTICE

Flexible working is not 'inferior'

Churchard challenges the view that flexible jobs are insecure and undesirable, creating a lack of commitment on the part of both the employer and worker. She reports her survey of over 11,000 workers and claims that flexibility does not negatively impact on job satisfaction, particularly for fixed-term contracts (one of the most common types of flexible contract). While there is some evidence that male workers dislike temporary agency work and that there is lower satisfaction with job security, overall she argues that flexible jobs are not inferior to full-time, permanent roles.

This could be an important message for HR practitioners, who may struggle to fill flexible jobs if the negative messages around them persist. Indeed, highly qualified workers may prefer the variety and (frequently) higher pay that accompany flexible jobs.

Source: Adapted from Churchard (2012).

More generally, however, flexibility is viewed as creating what is increasingly referred to as precarious work (Standing 2011): that is, it is insecure and (usually) low paid and low skilled. A number of authors (Appelbaum 2012; Kalleberg 2012) have argued that precarious work has become a central feature of work in both the USA and more widely. In Europe, a social partnership model of employment relations has led to a desire to address the problems associated with precarious work through 'flexicurity' which:

provides employers with the flexibility to adjust employment to meet the requirements of changing market conditions or technology and provides workers with the income security, training opportunities, and job search support to successfully weather the lack of job security without a deterioration in earnings. (Appelbaum 2012: 315)

Flexicurity thus denotes an attempt to address the tensions between labour market flexibility for employers and secure work for employees. It comprises three main elements: workers are provided with economic security to address the consequences of precarious work; the right to collective representation and bargaining power is guaranteed; and (re)training to equip workers to thrive in the labour market is offered. In return, employers have the right to implement flexible working practices that enhance business efficiency. While flexicurity is initially attractive, the high levels of unemployment in recent years have reduced its efficacy. Flexicurity policies have made it easy to dismiss workers but slack labour markets have rendered problematic transitions to alternative employment. There is a way to go yet to reconcile employer demands for flexibility with an acceptable deal for workers.

ACTIVITY 5.4

1 Do you agree with the view that flexible work is not inferior?

2 How effective do you think flexicurity is likely to be in reconciling employer and worker demands?

Employee flexibility (or work–life balance)

Now we consider employee flexibility or work–life balance (WLB), and the mechanisms by which this might be achieved. A number of high-profile organisations now seek to position themselves as 'employers of choice' by adopting WLB policies and it is often high up the agenda of many organisations, both in the UK and internationally. While provision of flexible working options initially increased over a number of years, this has now levelled off and the latest WERS survey (van Wanrooy *et al.* 2013) indicates no increase in provision between 2004 and 2011. While this may be because most organisations offer some form of flexible working (CIPD 2012), an increasing numbers of managers in the WERS survey (76%) indicated that it is an individual's responsibility to manage domestic and work responsibilities. Further, the availability of practices says little about their uptake and we outline below the 'rhetoric versus reality' of WLB in UK organisations.

WLB options focus on three different types of work flexibility: first, there is flexibility in terms of the number of hours worked; second, the exact timing of those hours; and, third, the location at which the work is carried out. Clearly some options may reflect all three types of flexibility. While UK legislation only addresses the need of parents and other carers (see Chapter 18), there is a strong lobby for flexible work options to be available for all employees and, despite some delays, legislation to support this seems likely to be implemented. There are many possible WLB options; clearly not all of these are appropriate for all jobs or employees, and employers will need to be convinced of their business benefits. In addition, flexibility will mean different things to different people, depending on their age, life circumstances, values, interests, personality and so on. Flexitime and reduced hours are the most commonly used options (van Wanrooy *et al.* 2013). At present flexible options which require reduction in hours, rather than rearrangement of hours, are predominantly taken up by women (Atkinson and Hall 2009). There are, however, a number of other possibilities, although their usage is low (CIPD 2012). We outline these in Table 5.2 and refer the reader to specific texts on WLB for further detail (e.g. Stredwick and Ellis 2005).

An interesting contribution is made by Strachan and Burgess (1998) who suggest that, in addition to the commonly accepted practices outlined in Table 5.2, employers should also provide practices to ensure both income and job security. These authors argue that employment that does not generate enough income to support a family cannot be described as 'family friendly' and casual employees, who often remain outside the organisation's internal labour market, may be denied WLB benefits. We return to this argument in the 'rhetoric versus reality' section below, noting for now the problems that may arise for employers providing WLB practices, while also seeking other forms of flexibility from employees.

Table 5.2
Options for achieving WLB

Part time	Term-time working	Unpaid leave
Flexitime	Job share	Unpaid sabbaticals
Compressed week	Self-rostering	Work from home
Annual hours	Shift swapping	Informal flexibility

Benefits of WLB

As we note later (see Chapter 18), there is limited regulation of WLB in the UK, the government adopting a 'business case' approach to it. This approach suggests that the benefits that flow from adopting WLB practices are greater than the costs associated with them, thus encouraging employers to offer such practices. We consider in this section the benefits that are said to accrue from WLB practices that underpin this 'business case'.

WLB practices have been shown in some instances to raise morale, increase levels of job satisfaction and reduce absence, especially unplanned absence (Atkinson and Hall 2011). IDS (2006) reported that flexible working has a positive impact on retention, recruitment and absenteeism, and both Beauregard and Henry (2009) and Avgar *et al.* (2011) link WLB to higher organisational performance. In our own research we found that informal flexibility was highly valued and associated with employee discretionary effort in terms of supporting colleagues, and patients where appropriate, and being available and flexible to cover emergencies (Hall and Atkinson 2006). Employees appreciated the flexibility they were given and therefore wanted to give something back, recognising the need for 'give and take'. CIPD (2012) also suggests a positive impact on motivation and well-being. Indeed Stevens (2010) argues that flexible working is more highly valued than bonuses.

WINDOW ON PRACTICE

Benefits experienced

Scott (2007) reports on the Britannia Building Society, which found that absence and employee turnover have both reduced as a result of its flexible working policy. Absence dropped from 3.06% in 2004 to 2.35% in 2006 and turnover from 18.94% in 2004 to 12.6% in 2006. While Britannia had adopted flexible working before 2004, it was ad hoc and inconsistent, so improvements were made by getting board commitment, engaging people across the business in focus groups and including the input of representatives into a new HR policy on flexible working. Britannia also claims that there is a direct link with customer satisfaction.

Phillips (2007) reports on Ellis Fairbank, Recruitment Consultants, who state that flexible working for all staff has increased productivity and helped to attract top talent. They also found lower absence, reduced employee turnover and raised morale. The consultancy specified the availability of flexible working in its advertising campaign to attract staff.

Such advertising is a surprisingly underused practice. The CIPD (2005) in their survey found that only 36% of respondent employers to its survey used flexible working in their recruitment advertising compared with 74% who communicate this information in staff handbooks.

Sources: Summarised from Scott, A. (2007) 'Flexible working cuts absence', *People Management*, Vol. 13, No. 6, p. 15, 22 March; and from Phillips, L. (2007) 'Add muscle with flexible work', *People Management*, Vol. 13, No. 5, p. 10, 8 March.

Take-up of WLB options

Initially the demand for flexible work options was much greater than the take-up, the 'take-up gap'. The desire to work different or more flexible hours has been identified as a significant determinant of employees moving jobs either within or between employers to achieve the flexibility they desire (Boheim and Taylor 2004). There are a number of reasons for this, which we discuss below, although the take-up gap has been narrowing in recent years.

Some WLB strategies cost the organisation money and financial limits are set for such practices to be viable. Further, operational difficulties can prevent the uptake of WLB options and are indeed the most common barrier (van Wanrooy *et al.* 2013). There is also evidence that some employers do not take a strategic approach to WLB. While organisations can sometimes easily provide reduced hours work for, say, administrative and sales staff, it is much more difficult to do this with professional staff. Anecdotal evidence suggests that many professionals moving from full- to part-time work find that they are really expected to do a full-time job in part-time hours and with part-time pay. Edwards and Robinson (2004) found that the lack of a strategic approach to WLB for nurses resulted in an unsatisfactory situation for both part-timers and full-timers alike.

There is some evidence that flexibility requests for childcare reasons are dealt with more favourably than requests on any other basis. The association that WLB practices have with women bringing up children creates two problems. The first is that WLB becomes a 'women's issue' (Atkinson and Hall 2009), as something done for women with children who are not interested in real careers. The second is that this causes alienation from the rest of the workforce who are not allowed these special privileges (van Wanrooy *et al.* 2013). In particular, working part time has been a popular option in combining work and other commitments, and yet there is considerable evidence that this limits career development (Smithson and Stokoe 2005). Miller (2013) presents an interesting example of a course that fathers can attend to learn how to work flexibly and still develop their careers in a sign that things are beginning, albeit very slowly, to change.

There is some evidence that the public sector makes much better provision for work–life integration than the private sector.

ACTIVITY 5.5

Discuss the following statement. To what extent do you agree or disagree with it, and why?
Employees should be equally entitled to WLB options, as long as business needs are met. It doesn't matter whether the reason is childcare, the desire to engage in sports activities, do extra gardening, or just loll around on the sofa watching television.

Managers are also a barrier to introducing and implementing work–life integration policies (CIPD 2012). While it is clear to those at a senior level in an organisation that WLB practices can be of value, it is line managers who have the unenviable task of reconciling performance and flexibility, especially where flexible working for some may mean higher workloads for others. There is a pressure on line managers to be fair and their decisions about who can work flexibly and in what way are under scrutiny and may result in a backlash. Managing workers who are not visible (working at home, for example) is a particular concern for line managers. Felstead *et al.* (2003) report the fear that working at home is a 'slacker's charter', but they also found that home-workers themselves had fears about not being able easily to demonstrate their honesty, reliability and productivity. Some managed this by working more hours than they should in order to demonstrate greater output. To counteract this fear, managers in Felstead *et al.*'s study introduced new surveillance devices, set output targets and brought management into the home via home visits. Managers also felt that home-working represented a potential threat to the integration of teams and the acceptance of corporate culture, and that it impeded the transmission of tacit knowledge. Overall, managing working time flexibility has emerged as a challenge in the past few years and line managers are likely to need much more support and encouragement in order to do this effectively.

Employee role and WLB

WLB is not available to most employees. Felstead *et al*. (2002) reveal that the option to work at home is usually the privilege of the highly educated and/or people at the top of the organisational hierarchy. People in these jobs, they suggest, have considerably more influence over the work processes they are engaged in. They also report that although more women than men work at home, there are more men who have the choice to work at home. Nolan and Wood (2003) also note that WLB is not for the lower paid. They report that 5% of such employees hold more than one job, and usually work in low-paid, low-status jobs in catering and personal services. Felstead *et al*. (2002) highlight an assumption in the WLB literature, which portrays working at home as always a 'good thing'. They argue that what is important is the *option* to work at home, as some people work at home doing low-paid unsatisfying jobs with no choice of work location, such conditions not necessarily being conducive to WLB. This reinforces the need outlined by Strachan and Burgess (1998), cited above, for policies of income and employment security to be included with WLB practices if more sophisticated policies are to be considered effective.

Rhetoric or reality?

Although a number of blue-chip organisations actively publicise their WLB practices, we suggest that problems of implementation, line manager resistance and the restriction of such practices to certain groups mean that WLB is still an aspiration rather than a reality for many employees. White *et al*. (2003), for example, argue that flexible working practices are enjoyed by only a small proportion of the workforce, and in any case only have a small effect. We suggest that work continues to be organised in a way that predominantly meets the needs of employers, the 'business case' for WLB often failing to initiate sufficient action to offer genuine WLB to the majority of employees.

SUMMARY PROPOSITIONS

5.1 Organisation design requires that choices are made in terms of formality, differentiation and centralisation of operations. Increasingly, flexibility is also central to organisation design.

5.2 While an infinite range of organisation structures is possible, most can be described as entrepreneurial, bureaucratic or matrix in form. In practice, many organisations combine all three types of structure to varying degrees.

5.3 Organisations increasingly require employees to be flexible in their working patterns. Models such as Atkinson's flexible firm and Powell's network organisation attempt to describe/prescribe mechanisms of organisational flexibility.

5.4 Tight labour markets in recent decades have required organisations to respond to employee demands for flexibility. A large number of work–life balance practices now exist, although in reality large numbers of employees may not have access to them.

GENERAL DISCUSSION TOPICS

1 Flatter organisation structures which decentralise decision making and empower employees will almost always be more efficient than highly centralised organisations with tall hierarchies. Discuss.

2 Flexibility in working time is nearly always for organisational benefit. In practice, few employees actually benefit from working time flexibility. Discuss.

THEORY INTO PRACTICE

Flex Co. is a large retail organisation that prides itself on its progressive approach to HRM. As a retailer, it recognises that its success depends on delivery of a 'fantastic' customer experience and invests heavily in the training and development of its store staff. Alongside this, it has a range of other progressive HR policies, including WLB options. The WLB policy allows for part-time working, term-time-only working, a compressed working week and shift swapping. For store employees, flexitime and working from home are not permissible, although these are offered to employees in head office and regional offices. A trial of self-rostering, where store workers pick their own shifts (within specified parameters), is also taking place within a small number of stores.

Flex Co. operates a decentralised structure in which each store is a profit centre and each store manager is responsible for the delivery of a certain level of sales and profits and for managing staff and other costs within the store. In common with many retail organisations, Flex Co. store managers use a range of employee contracts to ensure that high levels of staff are available at peak times, for example lunchtimes and weekends, but that a skeleton staff operate at quiet trading times. This means that, other than at store manager and assistant manager level, most contracts are part time and there is a high use of zero hours contracts. Managers argue that this is unproblematic as most employees are either women with childcare responsibilities or students. They are somewhat resistant to WLB policies that afford greater employee flexibility as this conflicts with their capacity to devise staff rosters that meet store requirements.

Flex Co. has just conducted a staff attitude survey and is disappointed with the results in relation to its WLB policy. Most store staff have indicated that the options within the policy are not readily available to them. Many wish to work term-time only for example but, as school holidays are typically busy trading periods, managers have been reluctant to agree these contracts. Those taking part in the self-rostering trial have also reported high levels of management interference in the determination of rosters and a sense that little autonomy has been gained. Finally, there is a sense of 'us and them' in respect of home-working and flexitime between those based in head and regional offices and those based in stores.

Questions

1 Flex Co. devises policies centrally at head office but devolves the responsibility for their implementation to store managers, whose priorities may conflict with the policy imperatives. To what extent will it ever be possible to ensure robust policy implementation in this organisation structure?

2 What tensions can you identify between flexibility that meets employer need and that which meets employee need? To what extent is it likely to be possible to reconcile these tensions? Which will take precedence?

3 What are the difficulties inherent in offering different WLB options to different groups of employees? Is it better to have a 'one size fits all' approach?

FURTHER READING

Worren, N. (2012) *Organisation Design*. Harlow: Pearson Education.
Worren presents a detailed and insightful discussion into both traditional mechanisms of organisation design and more contemporary approaches to designing flexible and adaptive organisations.

Kalleberg, A. (2001) 'Organising flexibility: The flexible firm in a new century', *British Journal of Industrial Relations*, Vol. 39, No. 4, pp. 479–504.
Kalleberg presents a thoughtful and comprehensive literature review on and critique of the flexible firm. Alternatives to this, including network organisations, are discussed.

Atkinson, C. and Hall, L. (2011) 'Flexible working and happiness in the NHS', *Employee Relations*, Vol. 33, pp. 88–105.
Here we consider the role of WLB as a high-performance work practice, demonstrating its impact on happiness (an important employee attitude) and how it positively influences outcomes such as absenteeism, retention and performance.

REFERENCES

Anon. (2002) 'The shape of things to come', *People Management*, **www.peoplemanagement.co.uk/pm/articles/2002/10/7622.htm.**

Appelbaum, E. (2012) 'Reducing inequality and insecurity', *Work and Occupations*, Vol. 39, pp. 311–20.

Atkinson, C. (2002) 'Career management and the changing psychological contract', *Career Development International*, Vol. 7, pp. 14–23.

Atkinson, C. and Hall, L. (2009) 'The role of gender in varying forms of flexible working', *Gender, Work and Organisation*, Vol. 16, pp. 650–66.

Atkinson, C. and Hall, L. (2011) 'Flexible working and happiness in the NHS', *Employee Relations*, Vol. 33, pp. 88–105.

Atkinson, J. (1984) 'Manpower strategies for flexible organisations', *Personnel Management*, August, p. 19.

Avgar, A., Givan, R. and Lui, M. (2011) 'A balancing act: Work–life balance and multiple stakeholder outcomes in hospitals', *British Journal of Industrial Relations*, Vol. 49, pp. 717–41.

Beauregard, A. and Henry, L. (2009) 'Making the link between work-life balance practices and organisational performance', *Human Resource Management Review*, Vol. 19, pp. 9–22.

Boheim, R. and Taylor, M. (2004) 'Actual and preferred working hours', *British Journal of Industrial Relations*, Vol. 42, pp. 149–66.

Buchanan, D. and Huczynski, A. (2010) *Organisational Behaviour*. Harlow: Pearson Education.

Burns, T. and Stalker, G. 1961. *The Management of Innovation*. London: Tavistock.

Burton, R. and Obel, B. (2004) *Strategic Organisational Diagnosis and Design: The dynamics of fit*. Dordrecht: Kluwer Academic.

Churchard, C. (2012) 'Pay and flexible work deal saves thousands of jobs at Vauxhall', *People Management*, www.peoplemanagement.co.uk/pm/articles/2012/05/pay-and-flexible-work-deal-saves-thousands-of-jobs-at-vauxhall.htm (accessed 29 May 2013).

CIPD (2005) *Flexible Working: Impact and implementation. An employer survey*. London: CIPD.

CIPD (2008) *Smart Working: The impact of work organisation and job design*. London: CIPD.

CIPD (2012) *Flexible Working: Provision and uptake*. London: CIPD.

CIPD (2013) *CIPD Professional Map* [Online]. London: CIPD (accessed 3 February 2013).

Curado, C. (2006) 'Organisational learning and organisational design', *The Learning Organisation*, Vol. 13, pp. 25–48.

Edwards, C. and Robinson, O. (2004) 'Evaluating the business case for part-time working amongst qualified nurses', *British Journal of Industrial Relations*, Vol. 42, pp. 167–83.

Eriksen, J. (2005) 'The influences of organisational design on strategy and performance: The case of exploration and exploitation', Workshop on Organisational Design EIASM, Brussels.

Felstead, A., Jewson, N., Phizacklea, A. and Walters, S. (2002) 'The option of working at home: Another privilege for the favoured few', *New Technology, Work and Employment*, Vol. 17, pp. 204–23.

Felstead, A., Jewson, N. and Walters, S. (2003) 'Managerial control of employees working at home', *British Journal of Industrial Relations*, Vol. 41, pp. 241–64.

Hall, L. and Atkinson, C. (2006) 'Improving working lives: Flexible working and the role of employee control', *Employee Relations*, Vol. 28, pp. 374–86.

IDS (2006) *Flexitime Schemes*, IDS Studies. London: IDS.

Kalleberg, A. (2012) 'Job quality and precarious work', *Work and Occupations*, Vol. 39, No. 4, pp. 427–48.

Leavitt, H., Dill, W. and Eyrig, H. (1973) *The Organisational World*. New York: Harcourt Brace Jovanovich.

Legge, K. (1995) *Human Resource Management: Rhetoric and realities*. Basingstoke: Macmillan.

Lepak, D. and Snell, S. (1999) 'The human resource architect: Towards a theory of human capital allocation and development', *Academy of Management Review*, Vol. 24, pp. 31–48.

Maslow, A. (1954) *Motivation and Personality*. New York: Harper & Row.

Miller, J. (2013) 'Can you teach dads how to work flexibly?', *People Management*, www.peoplemanagement.co.uk/pm/articles/2013/01/can-you-teach-dads-how-to-work-flexibly.htm.

Newell, H. and Dopson, S. (1996) 'Muddle in the middle: Organisation re-structuring and management careers', *Personnel Review*, Vol. 25, pp. 4–20.

Nolan, P. and Wood, S. (2003) 'Mapping the future of work', *British Journal of Industrial Relations*, Vol. 41, pp. 165–74.

Phillips, L. (2007) 'Add muscle with flexible work', *People Management*, Vol. 13, No. 5, p. 10.

Powell, W. (1990) 'Neither market nor hierarchy: Network forms of organisation', *Research in Organisational Behaviour*, Vol. 12, pp. 295–336.

Reilly, P. (2001) *Flexibility at Work*. Aldershot: Gower.

Scott, A. (2007) 'Flexible working cuts absence', *People Management*, Vol. 13, No. 6, p. 15.

Smithson, J. and Stokoe, E. (2005) 'Discourses of work–life balance: Negotiating 'genderblind' terms in organisations', *Gender, Work and Organisation*, Vol. 12, pp. 147–68.

Standing, G. (2011) *The Precariat*. New York: Bloomsbury.

Stevens, M. (2010) 'Flexible working "valued more than bonuses"', *People Management*, www.peoplemanagement.co.uk/pm/articles/2010/06/flexible-working-valued-more-than-bonuses.htm (accessed 29 May 2013).

Strachan, G. and Burgess, J. (1998) 'The "family-friendly" workplace', *International Journal of Manpower*, Vol. 19, pp. 250–65.

Stredwick, J. and Ellis, S. (2005) *Flexible Working*. London: CIPD.

Van Wanrooy, B., Bewley, H., Bryson, A., Forth, J., Freeth, S., Stokes, L. and Wood, S. (2013) *The 2011 Workplace Employment Relations Study: First findings*. London: BIS.

White, M., Hill, S., McGovern, P., Mills, C. and Smeaton, D. (2003) '"High performance" management practices, working hours and work–life balance', *British Journal of Industrial Relations*, Vol. 41, No. 2, June, pp. 175–95.

Worren, N. (2012) *Organisation Design*. Harlow: Pearson Education.

Chapter 6

RECUITMENT

RECRUITMENT

THE OBJECTIVES OF THIS CHAPTER ARE TO:

1 Discuss how to identify whether a vacancy exists and, if it does, explain how job and competency analysis support the determination of its requirements

2 Explain the role played by job descriptions and person specifications in the recruitment process

3 Analyse rational and processual approaches to recruitment and discuss the role of employer branding

4 Compare and contrast the major alternative recruitment methods

5 Assess developments in recruitment advertising and e-recruitment

6 Clarify the need for evaluation in recruitment

While the terms 'recruitment' and 'selection' are often used interchangeably, they are in fact quite distinct activities. In this chapter, we consider recruitment which 'includes those practices and activities carried out by the organisation with the primary purpose of identifying and attracting potential employees' (Breaugh and Starke 2000: 45). Selection refers to the methods used to decide which applicant to appoint to a vacancy and we discuss this later (see Chapter 7). Formal, structured recruitment methods are part of the best practice set of HR practices that is argued to be strategic and improve organisational performance. They build upon job or competency analysis which determines the requirements of the vacant role and employ person specifications and job descriptions to identify suitable candidates. Historically this 'rational' approach has dominated discussions of recruitment but there is increasing recognition of the benefits of a more processual approach to recruitment, one which recognises the applicant's role, and interest in the concept of employer branding has grown accordingly. We discuss all these aspects of recruitment in this chapter, together with recruitment advertising, which is central to communicating the employer brand, and e-recruitment, which has seen substantial growth over a number of years. Finally we consider the evaluation of recruitment activity. In the Theory into practice section, we consider how many of these issues are increasingly applied in an international context.

WINDOW ON PRACTICE

Over 3 million people are recruited by employers in the UK each year. It can be a costly and difficult process, with estimates of recruitment costs of £8,000 for senior managers and £3,000 for other staff (CIPD 2012a). Despite the economic climate, over 80% of employers in 2011 experienced difficulties recruiting in at least some areas of skills shortage, most in the context of reduced budgets. It is clear that effective recruitment remains a central HR objective whether labour markets are tight or slack.

In such circumstances the employer needs to 'sell' its jobs to potential employees so as to ensure that it can generate an adequate pool of applicants, but even then for some groups of staff it can be difficult to find people who are both willing and able to fill the vacancies that are available. That said, it is also important to avoid overselling a job in a bid to secure the services of talented applicants. Making out that the experience of working in a role is more interesting or exciting than it really is may be ultimately counter-productive because it raises unrealistic expectations which can damage the psychological contract established with the organisation. This can lead to demotivation and, perhaps, an early resignation. You will find further information and discussion exercises about realistic recruitment in Case 6.1 on the Companion Website **www.pearsoned.co.uk/torrington**.

Determining requirements

The first questions to be answered in recruitment are: Is there a vacancy? Is it to be filled by a newly recruited employee? Potential vacancies occur through someone leaving, as a result of expansion or from organisation change requiring new skills. These create no more than a prima facie case for filling the vacancy created. Recruiting a new employee may be the most obvious tactic but it is not necessarily the most appropriate and there may be other ways of filling the gap. Listed below are some of the options, several of which were discussed earlier (see Chapter 5):

- Reorganise the work.
- Use overtime.
- Mechanise the work.
- Stagger the hours.
- Make the job part time.
- Subcontract the work.
- Use an agency worker.

If your decision is that you are going to recruit, there are four questions to answer in determining the vacancy:

1 What does the job consist of?
2 In what way is it to be different from the job done by the previous incumbent?
3 What are the aspects of the job that specify the type of candidate?
4 What are the key aspects of the job that the ideal candidate wants to know before deciding to apply?

Job analysis is used to answer these questions. Job analysis comprises a series of techniques for collecting and analysing information about jobs. These include, among others, questionnaires, observations, interviews and critical incident techniques (Siddique 2004).

WINDOW ON PRACTICE

Searle (2004) outlines ten possible job analysis techniques:

1 Questionnaires and checklists: a structured questionnaire gathers information on a series of tasks.

2 Observation: information on tasks can be gathered by watching job holders undertake them.

3 Self-report by diaries and logs: role holders collect and log information about the tasks they undertake.

4 Participation: the analyst carries out the tasks him- or herself.

5 Hierarchical task analysis: a job is deconstructed into a series of tasks, sub-tasks and plans.

6 Interviews: job holders are questioned about the tasks they undertake.

7 Critical incident technique: job holders are asked to specify the most important tasks they undertake.

8 Repertory grid technique: an interview is used to elicit information on key aspects of the role using a grid construction technique.

9 Position analysis questionnaire: a verbal checklist of tasks is used to structure an interview.

10 Work-profiling system: an expert IT system is used to conduct structured job analysis.

The emphasis is on the work performed, not the person performing it. Job analysis is central to many HR activities and it is beyond the scope of this chapter to consider it beyond its influence on recruitment. Searle (2003) and Prien *et al.* (2009) provide a comprehensive coverage of job analysis techniques for those who require more detail.

In relation to recruitment, job analysis has traditionally sought to identify the key tasks and responsibilities which constitute a particular role and the knowledge, skills and abilities required to conduct those tasks and responsibilities. In more recent years, however, there has been a growth of interest in using job analysis to identify the competencies required to undertake a particular role. We discuss competencies in detail later

Table 6.1
Traditional
job analysis
compared with
competency-
based
approaches

Dimension	Traditional job analysis	Competency modelling
Purpose	Describe behaviour	Influence behaviour
View of the job	An external object to be described	A role to be enacted
Focus	Job	Organisation
Time orientation	Past	Future
Performance level	Typical	Maximum
Measurement approach	Latent trait	Clinical judgement

Source: After Sanchez and Levine (2009: 54).

(see Chapter 15). In brief they describe the behaviours required to undertake the role successfully, for example the ability to communicate well or work effectively as a member of a team.

Sanchez and Levine (2009) undertake an interesting comparison of traditional job analysis and competency-based approaches. They argue that these differ against six key dimensions (see Table 6.1).

Their review of existing research finds that competency-based approaches seek to influence employee behaviour in the role undertaken, rather than simply describe it, and have a future orientation that encourages the maximisation of organisational performance. This contrasts with job analysis, which is backwards looking and reflects typical, rather than maximum, levels of performance. Siddique (2004) presents an interesting study of competency-based analysis in the United Arab Emirates which supports the argument that it serves to improve organisational performance. In practice, the distinction between traditional job analysis and competency-based analysis is often blurred. Indeed Sanchez and Levine (2009) argue for the merging of the two approaches for maximum benefit, drawing on traditional job analysis to describe and measure tasks and responsibilities and competency-based approaches to strategically influence employee behaviour.

Whichever type of analysis is adopted, it forms the basis of the next stage in the recruitment process, the drawing up of job descriptions and person specifications (CIPD 2012b). Job descriptions involve recording the component parts and principal accountabilities of a role. An example is provided in Figure 6.1. Methods of doing this are well established and good accounts are provided by Martin (2010), Brannick and Levine (2002) and IRS (2003).

A person specification listing the key attributes and/or competencies required to undertake the role is then derived from the job description and used in recruiting the new person. You can see an example person specification at: **http://thedales.org.uk/person-specification-film-around-richmondshire/**.

As you can see, this combines attributes derived from job analysis, such as qualifications, knowledge, skills and experience, with competencies such as time management and planning and organisation. While this a common approach, the use of competencies has been criticised on the grounds that it tends to produce employees who are very similar to one another and who address problems with the same basic mindset (corporate clones, see e.g. Whiddett and Kandola 2000). This has also led to the suggestion that competency-based approaches can present a barrier to achieving an organisation's equality and diversity objectives (Kirton and Healy 2009). Where innovation and creativity are required, it is helpful to recruit people with more diverse characteristics, and the use of competencies may constrain this.

Job title: SENIOR SALES ASSISTANT

Context
The job is in one of the 13 high-technology shops owned by 'Computext'
Location: Leeds
Supervised by, and reports directly to, the Shop Manager
Responsible for one direct subordinate: Sales Assistant

Job summary
To assist and advise customers in the selection of computer hardware and software, and to arrange delivery and finance where appropriate.
Objective is to sell as much as possible, and to ensure that customers and potential customers see 'Computext' staff as helpful and efficient.

Job content
Most frequent duties in order of importance
1   Advise customers about hardware and software.
2   Demonstrate the equipment and software.
3   Organise delivery of equipment by liaising with distribution department.
4   Answer all after-sales queries from customers.
5   Contact customers two weeks after delivery to see if they need help.
6   Advise customers about the variety of payment methods.
7   Develop and keep up to date a computerised stock control system.

Occasional duties in order of importance
1   Arrange for faulty equipment to be replaced.
2   Monitor performance of junior sales assistant as defined in job description.
3   Advise and guide, train and assess junior sales assistant where necessary.

Working conditions
Pleasant, 'business-like' environment in new purpose-built shop premises in the city centre. There are two other members of staff and regular contact is also required with the Delivery Department and Head Office. Salary is £18,000 p.a. plus a twice yearly bonus, depending on sales. Five weeks' holiday per year plus statutory holidays. A six-day week is worked.

Other information
There is the eventual possibility of promotion to shop manager in another location depending on performance and opportunities.

Performance standards
There are two critically important areas:
1   Sales volume. Minimum sales to the value of £700,000 over each six-month accounting period.
2   Relations with customers:
    –   Customers' queries answered immediately.
    –   Customers always given a demonstration when they request one.
    –   Delivery times arranged to meet both customer's and delivery department's needs.
    –   Complaints investigated immediately.
    –   Customers assured that problem will be resolved as soon as possible.
    –   Customers never blamed.
    –   Problems that cannot be dealt with referred immediately to Manager.

Figure 6.1
Job description for a senior sales assistant

Job descriptions and person specifications underpin recruitment advertising, that is the communication of employer requirements to potential applicants. They also form the basis of selection activity, which we consider later (see Chapter 7).

ACTIVITY 6.1

How useful are competencies in determining requirements for a vacancy? To what extent do you think they should be combined with traditional job analysis in drawing up job descriptions and person specifications?

Rational versus processual approaches to recruitment

The recruitment process as we have described it so far is known as the 'rational approach' to recruitment. That is, it is a one-way process in which the employer determines the vacancy's requirements and communicates these to potential candidates in order to generate a pool of applications to support the selection process. Job analysis, job descriptions and person specifications are central to this as the job is fixed and the emphasis is upon finding the applicant who best fits this job. A dominant role for management is presumed and candidates are seen to hold relatively little power. Criticisms of this rational approach can be made on two grounds. First, there is no recognition of the power and politics that run through organisational life and subvert these supposedly rational processes. Van den Brink *et al.* (2012) present a fascinating account of recruitment processes which demonstrates how line managers resist what they perceive to be HR's bureaucratic procedures so that the 'best' person is often not appointed to the vacancy.

The second ground for criticism is that the rational approach ignores the role of the candidate. Increasingly recruitment is seen as a social process (Nickson *et al.* 2008) and there is recognition of the need to influence candidates to attract them to apply: a need to sell the organisation to potential employees. This approach often relies heavily upon competencies as the emphasis is upon identifying a candidate who fits well into the organisation, rather than a preoccupation with a restrictively defined role. Recruitment advertising is used to begin establishing the psychological contract, that is the expectations that the employer and employee have of each other. It communicates to potential employees what the experience of working for the organisation will be like. The recruitment process thus becomes two way, with candidates making decisions about prospective employers as well as vice versa, it being important to create a positive impression with potential employees.

The processual approach to recruitment has created considerable interest in employer branding, which advocates competing for staff by borrowing techniques long used in marketing goods and services to potential customers. In particular, many organisations have sought to position themselves as 'employers of choice' in their labour markets with a view to attracting stronger applications from potential employees. Those who have succeeded have often found that their recruitment costs fall as a result because they get so many more unsolicited applications. Central to this is the development over time of a positive 'brand image' of the organisation as an employer, so that potential employees come to regard working there as highly desirable. This approach has been used to positive effect by a number of public sector employers in the UK offering jobs that are presented as intrinsically rewarding rather than highly remunerated when recruiting, for example, teachers, social workers and police officers. It is also used in the voluntary sector to appeal to potential employees whose values match those of the organisation (Nickson *et al.* 2008). However, developing a good brand image is an easier task for larger companies with household names than for those which are smaller or highly specialised, but the possibility of developing and sustaining a reputation as a good employer is something from which all organisations stand to benefit.

A study of the Belgian Army confirmed the benefits of adopting a processual approach to recruitment premised on employer branding. Both instrumental (e.g. pay) and symbolic (e.g. defending one's country) aspects of the brand are important. The author recommends investigating the brand perceptions of both potential and current employees in order to compare and align these perceptions and develop a 'brand proposition' based upon them. He demonstrates that this has enhanced the recruitment process in the Belgian Army.

Source: Lievens (2007).

The key, as when branding consumer products, is to build on any aspect of the working experience that is different from that offered by other organisations competing in the same broad applicant pool. It may be relatively high pay or a generous benefits package, it may be flexible working, or a friendly and informal atmosphere, strong career development potential or job security. This is then developed as a 'unique selling proposition' and forms the basis of the employer branding exercise. The best way of finding out what is distinctive and positive about working in an organisation is to carry out some form of staff attitude survey. Employer branding exercises simply amount to a waste of time and money when they are not rooted in the actual lived experience of employees because people are attracted to the organisation on false premises. As with claims made for products that do not live up to their billing, the employees gained are not subsequently retained, and resources are wasted recruiting people who resign quickly after starting.

Once the unique selling propositions have been identified they can be used to inform all forms of communication that the organisation engages in with potential and actual applicants. The aim must be to repeat the message again and again in advertisements, in recruitment literature, on Internet sites and at careers fairs. CIPD (2007) presents the 'candidate journey' in diagrammatic form (Figure 5, p. 16) demonstrating how the employer brand should underpin recruitment (and later selection) activity. It is also important that existing employees are made aware of their employer's brand proposition, both as it forms the basis of their own psychological contract with the organisation and because so much recruitment is carried out informally through word of mouth. Provided the message is accurate and provided it is communicated effectively over time, the result will be a 'leveraging of the brand' as more and more people in the labour market begin to associate the message with the employer.

While branding emerged initially as a response to the difficulties of recruiting in tight labour markets, it has been suggested recently that it also has an important role to play during recessions when labour markets are slacker. We reflect some of the key messages from a recent People Management (2009) guide in the Window on practice that follows.

An employer brand that fails to live up to its messages will be found out quickly – particularly in a downturn when trust is at a premium. Difficult economic times can test a brand's values and responses such as dismissing employees by text or imposing pay cuts without consultation can destroy employer brand equity overnight. This is likely to have implications both for current employees and for the organisation's ability to recruit in the future. Companies need to maintain communications with potential employees even though they may not be in a position to recruit immediately, in order to maintain a positive image for when it is required. For example, KPMG, despite having filled all its graduate vacancies in 2009, took great pains to keep applicants up to date about posts to be filled and how the situation was

changing, and invited them to register on the website if they wanted to stay in touch with the firm about future vacancies. In this way, it hoped to stay ahead in the 'war for talent' in times of greater prosperity.

Source: People Management (2009).

Internal recruitment

Another important decision when filling a vacancy is whether to recruit internally or externally. Vacancies are often filled internally, creating what are referred to as 'internal labour markets'. Sometimes organisations advertise all vacancies publicly as a matter of course and consider internal candidates along with any external applicants. This approach is generally considered to constitute good practice, especially in respect of equality of opportunity and diversity, and is widely used in the UK public sector. However, many organisations prefer to invite applications from internal candidates *before* they look to external labour markets for new staff (Newell and Shackleton 2000; CIPD 2009). There are considerable advantages for the employer: it is much less expensive with no need for job advertisements or recruitment agencies. Instead a message can simply be placed in a company newsletter or posted on its intranet or staff noticeboards. Further cost savings and efficiency gains can be made because internal recruits are typically able to take up new posts much more quickly than people being brought in. Even if they have to work some notice in their current positions, they are often able to take on some of their new responsibilities or undergo relevant training at the same time. The other advantage stems from the fact that internal candidates, as a rule, are more knowledgeable than new starters coming in from other organisations about what exactly the job involves. They are also more familiar with the organisation's culture, rules and geography, and so take less time to settle into their new jobs and to begin working at full capacity.

Giving preference to internal recruits, particularly for promotions, has the great advantage of providing existing employees with an incentive to work hard, demonstrate their commitment and stay with the organisation when they might otherwise consider looking for alternative employment. The practice sends a strong signal from management that existing employees are valued and that attractive career development opportunities are available to them. Failing to recruit internally may thus serve to put off good candidates with potential from applying for the more junior positions in an organisation. Bayo-Mariones and Ortin-Angel (2006) present an interesting study of the benefits of internal labour markets in Spain.

The main disadvantage of only advertising posts internally is that a limited field of candidates are considered. While it may mean that someone who 'fits in well' is recruited, it may also mean that the best available candidate is not even considered. Over the long term the organisation can thus end up being less well served than it would have been had internal candidates been required to compete with outside people for their posts. For this reason internal recruitment sits uneasily with a commitment to equal opportunities and to the creation of a diverse workforce. Talented candidates from under-represented groups are not appointed because they never get to know about the vacancies that the organisation has.

It is also important to note that the management of internal recruitment practices is difficult to carry out effectively. Research carried out by the Institute of Employment Research (2006) shows that serious problems often occur when internal candidates fail to be selected. This is because they tend to enter the selection process with higher expectations of being offered the position than external candidates. Bitterness, antipathy and low morale are thus likely to follow. Moreover, failed internal candidates are considerably more likely to pursue claims of unfair discrimination following a selection process than external candidates. For these reasons it is essential that great care is taken when managing internal recruitment to ensure that the approach taken is both fair and seen to be fair. Giving honest, full, accurate and constructive feedback to non-appointed candidates is an essential part of the process.

External recruitment

Once an employer has decided that external recruitment is necessary, a cost-effective and appropriate method of recruitment must be selected. There are a number of distinct approaches to choose from, each of which is more or less appropriate in different circumstances. As a result most employers use a wide variety of different recruitment methods at different times. In many situations there is also a good case for using different methods in combination when looking to fill the same vacancy. Table 6.2 sets out the methods reported to be most effective by employers in a recent survey (CIPD 2012a).

A recruitment method must be chosen that will attract as many people as possible with the required skills and qualifications and to reach people who are either actively looking for a new job or thinking about doing so. The need is therefore to place the

Table 6.2
Most effective recruitment methods

Corporate website	61%
Recruitment agencies	53%
Employee referral scheme	35%
Commercial job boards	32%
Specialist journals and trade press	29%
Local newspaper advertisements	26%
Professional networking (e.g. LinkedIn)	22%
Speculative applications	20%
Search consultants	20%
Job Centre Plus	20%
Apprenticeships	17%
Education liaison	16%
Secondments	10%
National newspaper advertising	10%
Social networking (e.g. Facebook)	8%
Alumni (former employees)	7%

Source: Table compiled from data in CIPD (2012a) *Resourcing and Talent Planning: Annual Survey Report 2012*. London: CIPD. Reproduced with the permission of the publisher, the Chartered Institute of Personnel and Development, London (**www.cipd.co.uk**).

advertisement where job seekers who are qualified to take on the role are most likely to look. All the various methods of recruitment have benefits and drawbacks, and the choice of a method has to be made in relation to the particular vacancy and the type of labour market in which the job falls. For example, the most effective recruitment method for many organisations is now the corporate website. We discuss this in more detail in e-recruitment below (along with commercial job boards), but it is worth noting here that this method is more suitable to large organisations with many visitors to their websites than smaller organisations which typically generate much less website traffic. Recruitment agencies are cited as the second most effective method of recruitment by over half of organisations. This is a well-established recruitment method in which an organisation provides job descriptions and person specifications to an agent who both advertises the vacancy and trawls its own applicant databases to identify suitable candidates. In theory this creates access to a large potential applicant pool which is suitably qualified and reduces the administrative burden on the employer. In practice, candidates are often a poor match for organisational requirements and, even where this is not the case, the service is provided at a high cost which can average around 30% of the appointed candidate's salary.

Employee referral schemes, in which current employees recommend their contacts for employment in the organisation, have grown substantially in recent years, as evidenced by their being cited as the third most effective recruitment method. This is a low-cost method, as advertising costs are avoided, and those recommended are often suitable (as a current employee would not wish to recommend someone unsuitable) and a good organisational fit, as they know what to expect from their organisational contact. It does, however, limit the pool of candidates to those known by current employees and the best candidate for the job may never know that the vacancy exists. It can also create difficulties in relation to equality of opportunity and diversity in that recommendations are likely to perpetuate the make-up of the current workforce. Specialist journals and the trade press are also cited as fairly effective recruitment methods. This relates to the very targeted nature of these publications which are circulated to, for example, only solicitors or accountants. This means that the relevant population is accessed, although this can be very expensive. At one time, there could also be delays in recruitment advertising in using this method as publications tended to be less regular than other forms of press. Nowadays, however, they are usually supplemented by website advertising, which mitigates this problem.

It is also worth noting the falling popularity of national and local newspapers as effective recruitment methods. This is linked to the growth of e-recruitment, which has, to an extent, replaced traditional methods of recruitment advertising (see below for further discussion). Another factor is the substantial cost of such advertising, which can run to several thousand pounds and is increasingly unattractive given strained recruitment budgets for all but the most senior or difficult to fill vacancies. Another noteworthy point is the effectiveness of informal methods of recruitment. The use of professional or social networking sites such as LinkedIn and Facebook supports informal approaches to potential candidates. Responding to speculative applications is also effective for one-fifth of organisations in this survey (CIPD 2012a). This supports other reports of how people actually find their jobs in practice. These repeatedly show that informal methods (such as word of mouth and making unsolicited applications) are as, if not more, common than formal methods such as recruitment advertising, especially in sectors such as retail and hospitality (Warhurst and Nickson 2007). This is important to note and a point often overlooked in academic discussions of effective recruitment methods.

ACTIVITY 6.2

We have seen the significance of informal methods of recruitment whereby new employees come as a result of hearing about a vacancy from friends, or putting their names down for consideration when a vacancy occurs. What are the benefits and drawbacks of this type of arrangement? Why does it so often replace more sophisticated forms of recruitment?

Recruitment advertising

In order to assist in drafting advertisements and placing them in suitable media, many employers deal with a recruitment advertising agency. Such agencies provide expert advice on where to place advertisements and how they should be worded and will design them attractively to achieve maximum impact. This is important whether dealing with print copy or website-based advertisements. Large organisations often subcontract all their advertising work to an agency operating on the basis of a service-level agreement.

Recruitment advertising companies (as opposed to recruitment agencies) are often inexpensive because the agency derives much of its income from the commission paid by the journals on the value of the advertising space sold, the bigger agencies being able to negotiate substantial discounts because of the amount of business they place. A portion of this saving is then passed on to the employer so that it can easily be cheaper *and* a great deal more effective to work with an agent providing this kind of service. The important questions relate to the experience of the agency in dealing with recruitment, as compared with other types of advertising, the quality of the advice they can offer about media choice and the quality of response that their advertisements produce. Cyber-agencies now also play an important role in designing and placing website advertisements and we discuss this further in e-recruitment below.

The decision on what to include in a recruitment advertisement is important because of the high cost of space, where using hard copy publications, and the need to attract attention, whether hard or e-copy. Where agencies are used they will be able to advise on this, as they will on the way the advertisement should be worded, but the following is a short checklist of items that must be included:

- Name and brief details of employing organisation.
- Job role and duties.
- Training to be provided.
- Key points of the personnel specification or competency profile.
- Salary and benefits.
- Employment status (e.g. permanent or fixed-term contract).
- Instructions about how to apply.

Uggersley *et al.*'s (2012) study demonstrates the importance of communicating the characteristics of the job, organisation and recruitment process in recruitment advertising.

There are a number of other considerations when designing and placing a recruitment advertisement. For example, is the aim to deliver a high volume of applicants (graduate or call centre recruitment) or a smaller, highly selective group of applicants (senior manager recruitment, for example)? A balance also needs to be drawn between promoting the company and the job: one may be more attractive than the other, and this may reflect on whether the advertisement adopts a positive, selling approach or a more measured approach to what working in the organisation will be like. A final decision is how precise the information provided should be. A good example of this is in relation to salary. Many employers are reluctant to declare the salary that will accompany the advertised post. Sometimes this is reasonable as the salary scales are well known and inflexible. Elsewhere the reluctance is due either to the fact that the employer does not want to publicise the salary of a position to be filled for fear of dissatisfying holders of other posts, or to the fact that the employer does not know what to offer and is waiting to see 'what the mail brings'. All research evidence, however, suggests that a good indication of the salary is essential if the employer is to attract a useful number of appropriate replies. Recent research has also found that the use of photographs in recruitment advertising can increase the number of applications received. Crush (2012) reports on LV='s innovative approach using interactive recruitment posters featuring photographs of real staff.

WINDOW ON PRACTICE

Burt *et al.* (2010) report on three studies which investigated the use of photographs in recruitment advertisements in New Zealand. The first study demonstrated that around half of organisations used photographs of current employees as these were more positive in attracting applications than those not using photographs. The second study considered potential applicants' responses to the use of photographs in recruitment advertising. Applicants had more positive responses to photographs which showed teams of employees. The third study demonstrated that positive responses were higher when real teams of current employees, rather than models, were used in recruitment advertisements. The authors argue that more applicants are likely to be attracted by recruitment advertisements that use photographs and that the type of photograph used is important.

Source: Burt *et al.* (2010).

ACTIVITY 6.3

Table 6.3 contains phrases about the value in pay terms of twelve different jobs. Try putting them in rank order of actual cash value to the recipient. Then ask a friend to do the same thing and compare your lists.

Table 6.3
Phrases from
a quality
newspaper
about salary

1	c.£60,000 + bonus + car + benefits
2	from c.£35k
3	£30,000 – £40,000 + substantial bonus + car
4	You will already be on a basic annual salary of not less than £40,000
5	Six-figure remuneration + profit share + benefits
6	c.£60,000 package
7	Attractive package
8	Substantial package
9	£50,000 OTE, plus car and substantial benefits
10	£ excellent + benefits
11	£ Neg.
12	c.£60k package + banking benefits

E-recruitment

The use of the Internet for recruitment purposes, typically referred to as e-recruitment, is one of the most striking recent developments in the field, but its significance remains a question of debate. Initially, it was predicted that it would revolutionise the recruitment industry and that most of us would find our jobs online. It now appears that these predictions greatly overstated the influence of the Internet. A review of the use and success of e-recruitment in the UK (Parry and Tyson 2008) draws the conclusion that, while its use is now widespread in many organisations, it has not dominated the recruitment market in the way predicted. Indeed, its growth in usage has now levelled off and it is often used in combination with other methods of recruitment, for example newspaper advertising (Parry and Wilson 2009). Nevertheless, it is now a common recruitment method that warrants further discussion.

E-recruitment can draw on either corporate or commercial websites, the former being by far the more popular (see Table 6.2). Corporate websites, that is the employer's own website, advertise jobs alongside information about the products and services offered by the organisation. Larger organisations typically have part of their website dedicated to careers, or indeed even set up a website specifically for this purpose. Examples of this might be the BBC, Coca-Cola, McDonald's, Google and Microsoft. Commercial websites, provided by cyber-agencies, combine the roles traditionally played by both newspapers and recruitment agents. They advertise the job and undertake shortlisting before they send on a selection of suitable CVs to the employer.

For employers the principal attraction of e-recruitment is that it allows jobs to be advertised inexpensively to a potential audience of millions. According to Frankland (2000), the cost of setting up a good website is roughly equivalent to that associated with advertising a single high-profile job in a national newspaper. Huge savings can also be made by dispensing with the need to print glossy recruitment brochures and other documents to send to potential candidates. It is also a method that is easy for both candidates and employers to use. The other big advantage is speed. People can respond within seconds of reading about an opportunity by emailing their CV to the employer. Shortlisting can also be undertaken quickly with the use of CV-matching software or online application forms.

In principle online recruitment has a great deal to offer. In practice, however, there are major problems. A key drawback is the way that employers advertising jobs tend to be bombarded with hundreds of applications, many of which are unsuitable for the position advertised. This occurs because of the large number of people who read the advertisement and because it takes so little effort to email a copy of a CV to the employer. A further concern is the high number of applications received from candidates who do not have the necessary work permits. Additionally, e-recruitment may not target passive job seekers or reach a diverse population of job seekers and thus may fail to generate applications from potentially suitable candidates. Goldberg and Allen (2008) outline the difference in responses to recruitment websites between black and white applicants and similar difference have been observed in groups such as older workers or women returners.

Other problems concern fears about security and confidentiality: horror stories abound of candidates' CVs ending up on their employer's desktop (Weekes 2000: 35). There have also been criticisms of poor ethical standards on the part of cyber-agencies. As with conventional employment agents, there are a number who employ poor practice such as posting fictional vacancies and falsely inflating advertised pay rates in order to build up a bank of CVs which can be circulated to employers on an unsolicited basis. Some cyber-agencies also copy CVs from competitors' sites and send them on to employers without authorisation. Over time, as the industry grows, professional standards will be established and a regulatory regime established, but for the time being such problems remain.

The fact that there are so many drawbacks alongside the advantages explains why so many employers appear to use the Internet for recruitment while rating it relatively poorly in terms of its effectiveness. While employers rank the Internet highly vis-à-vis other methods in terms of its cost-effectiveness, they are much less convinced when asked about the quality of applicants and the ability of Web-based advertising to source the right candidates (IRS 2005: 45). While it is commonly used for graduates, knowledge workers and middle management jobs, it is often felt to be less appropriate for blue-collar and senior management jobs and for targeting groups such as older workers or women returners. Established approaches such as newspaper advertising are more likely to be combined with than replaced by e-recruitment.

WINDOW ON PRACTICE

In 2000 an unemployed 53-year-old electronics manager called David Hall took part in a project commissioned by Wynnwith, an established recruitment company. He spent three months unsuccessfully looking for a job using the services of twelve well-known cyber-agencies. He registered with each, giving full details of his background and skills. At the end of the period he concluded that 'these sites appear to offer little more than pretty coloured graphics and empty promises about job opportunities'. He was offered one interview during the twelve weeks, for a role that was unsuitable given his experience. Of the hundreds of job opportunities emailed to him, he reckoned that only 5% matched his capabilities. Among his criticisms were the following:

- the same jobs were advertised week after week;
- very little information was provided about most vacancies;
- salary levels were inflated to make jobs more appealing;
- he received no feedback on applications that failed;
- he was concerned that his CV was being circulated without his consent;
- his emails were often not acknowledged.

Source: 'Online Recruitment Study' at **www.wynnwith.com** (accessed February 2013).

Another emerging debate is around the use of technology in recruitment centres on 'surveillance' (Searle 2004) and the extent to which it is appropriate to use information gathered from, for example, social networking sites such as Facebook in recruitment and selection decisions. A benign perspective on the collection of candidate data through e-recruitment may lead to the suggestion that organisations can develop databases of candidates suitable for current and future vacancies and thus create a 'talent pool' (Parry and Tyson 2008). More critical analyses have, however, identified concerns around privacy and equity and the use of information in unintended ways (Searle 2004). There have been a number of well-publicised cases surrounding information made available on, for example, Facebook to influence recruitment decisions in a way detrimental to candidates. This is an area in which practice precedes research and in which there are doubtless still many debates to be had on technology and privacy.

The use of Web 2.0 technologies is another example where predictions of a revolution in recruitment have yet to be realised. As we have seen, professional networking sites, such as LinkedIn, are deemed effective for recruitment by 22% of employers and social networking sites by 8% (Table 6.2). Practice again runs ahead of research in the use of social media for recruitment, but both recruitment agents and candidates report high usage of LinkedIn for identifying and approaching potential candidates. Indeed, features have been developed on the site specifically for this purpose. Anecdotal reports are of substantial growth in the use of LinkedIn, particularly in respect of professional-level jobs. Relatively few employers, however, use platforms such as Twitter or Second Life for recruitment purposes (People Management 2009). There are examples of some firms holding virtual recruitment fairs in, for example, Second Life, in which candidates adopt an avatar to move through the fair and virtually discuss opportunities with employers. Facebook has also designed a recruitment campaign that runs on YouTube: **www.youtube. com/watch?v=7Rp-JAFVwNs.**

While these recruitment methods may be at their relatively early stages, it is likely that we will see them continue to grow in adoption and influence in the coming years. The Window on practice below demonstrates innovative uses of Web 2.0 technologies for recruitment purposes and their benefits in reaching international audiences.

WINDOW ON PRACTICE

L'Oreal has developed a virtual business game for use in its graduate recruitment that is available to anyone who visits its website. The online game allows students and graduates to problem-solve in a virtual L'Oreal environment and gives candidates personalised feedback and an interview for the best players who achieve the top results in the business game. Players adopt an avatar character to move through the business game and are assessed against what the company considers to the best solutions to the problems set. The business game is available in at least ten languages and is part of the firm's global graduate recruitment strategy, 15,000 students and graduates having logged on since its March 2010 launch. L'Oreal argues that it attracts candidates to L'Oreal as an employer and gives something, by way of detailed feedback, to participants.

Source: Adapted from Stevens, M. (2010) 'L'Oreal's recruitment gets a virtual makeover', **www.peoplemanagement.co.uk/pm/ articles/2010/05/loreal-uses-virtual-business- game-to-recruit.htm** (accessed 29 May 2013).

Evaluation of recruitment activity

The HR manager needs to monitor the effectiveness of recruitment methods, first, to ensure value for money and, second, to ensure that the pool of applicants produced by the various methods is suitable. As with many other HR activities, the evaluation of recruitment is typically poorly done by organisations. Breaugh and Starke (2000) outline a number of possible recruitment criteria against which recruitment activity can be measured and these include:

- the number, quality and diversity of applicants;
- cost per vacancy;
- speed of recruitment;
- number of vacancies filled;
- the ratio of offers to acceptances.

These are relatively short-term measures which are easy to quantify. For a deep understanding of recruitment effectiveness, Breaugh and Starke (2000) go on to argue that there should also be medium- to long-term measures of effectiveness such as job performance and retention rate and even softer measures such as staff attitudes. While an increasing number of organisations monitor short-term outcomes, attempts to link these to longer-term measures of success are much less common. This may result from a lack of robust processes for collecting relevant data. There is also a good case for monitoring effectiveness to ensure equality of opportunity is apparent across the recruitment process, in terms, for example, of gender, ethnic origin, reviewing those who are successful at each stage of the process and taking remedial action where an imbalance becomes apparent. Recent WERS data indicates that this is done by a small minority of UK organisations (van Wanrooy *et al.*, 2013).

There also needs to be information to get to the more intangible questions, such as 'Did the best candidate not even apply?' The most important source of information about the quality of the recruitment process is the people involved in it. Do telephonists and receptionists know how to handle the tentative employment enquiry? What did they hear from applicants in the original enquiries that showed the nature of their reaction to the advertisement? Is it made simple for enquirers to check key points by telephone or personal visit? Is there an unnecessary emphasis on written applications before anything at all can be done? Useful information can also be obtained from both successful and unsuccessful applicants. Those who have been successful will obviously believe that recruitment was well done, while the unsuccessful may have good reason to believe that it was flawed. However, those who are unsuccessful sometimes ask for feedback on the reasons. If a recruiter is able to give this, it is also a simple extension of this process to ask the applicant for comments on the recruitment process.

SUMMARY PROPOSITIONS

6.1 Alternatives to filling a vacancy include reorganising the work; using overtime; mechanising the work; staggering the hours; making the job part time; subcontracting the work; using an employment agency.

6.2 Job and competency analysis determine the requirements of a vacancy and support the drawing up of job descriptions and person specifications.

6.3 Rational approaches to recruitment have been increasingly criticised and a processual approach recognises a greater role for candidates and leads to an emphasis on employer branding. This involves actively selling the experience of working for an organisation by focusing on what makes the experience both positive and distinctive.

6.4 Effective recruitment methods are changing over time and traditional methods now combine with e-recruitment methods. Informal recruitment methods are also often highly effective.

6.5 Recruitment advertising draws on a range of methods to target suitable applicants. Well-designed advertisements are essential.

6.6 E-recruitment provides great potential advantages for employers but is still often used in conjunction with traditional methods.

6.7 Evaluation of recruitment effectiveness is essential but often poorly done.

GENERAL DISCUSSION TOPICS

1 What are the advantages and disadvantages of e-recruitment from an employer's point of view?

2 What steps could an organisation take to maintain its employer brand in times of recession when recruitment is limited?

3 What benefits are there to viewing recruitment as a social process as opposed to a rational process?

THEORY INTO PRACTICE

At one time, only HR practitioners responsible for recruiting and managing expatriates needed to consider the international dimension of recruitment. Globalisation now means that there are many types of staffing groups and international matters concern a great many recruiters. Examples of international staffing groups include workers on short-term overseas postings, international commuters, 'virtual' international workers on cross-country project teams, immigrants in national labour markets and workers based in one country but dealing with international customers and suppliers. The roles undertaken by these workers have also increased in variety and complexity and include: building new international markets, working on discrete projects, building social networks and facilitating knowledge exchange. Sparrow argues that this requires the internationalisation of all HR processes. In this adaptation of his paper, we concentrate on the internationalisation of recruitment.

The recruitment processes of four UK-based case studies are discussed and include:

- The BBC World Service: international recruitment focuses on the acquisition of specialist skills for the domestic labour market.
- Barclaycard International: international recruitment is focused on the setting up of operations in new countries as part of an expansion strategy.
- South East London Strategic Health Authority: international recruitment focuses on the acquisition of skills for the domestic labour market to tackle labour shortages.
- Save the Children: international recruitment is focused on the deployment of labour on overseas projects/operations.

The recruitment approaches adopted by these organisations are discussed in more detail below.

South East London Strategic Health Authority

South East London Strategic Health Authority (SHA) recruited in overseas markets to fill vacancies in specialist skill shortage areas, for example doctors and nurses. Global advertising campaigns were run using Web-based approaches which established and communicated a value proposition for international candidates. Part of this was the use of protocols to ensure that other (developing) countries were not damaged by recruitment of their specialist staff. The key matters to address included:

- Identifying professional expertise and technical support, for example HR networks and agencies.
- Balancing targeted recruitment campaigns with longer-term recruitment initiatives.
- Assessing the ethical and reputational issues linked to the campaigns.
- Developing an operational reputation as internationally competitive and attractive.

Three strategies flowed from this. First, active recruitment policies were established to target specific skills and countries. Arrangements with service providers were established and different media identified and tested. Second, passive recruitment policies simply tapped into the growing number of international employees in the domestic labour market. Finally, longer-term strategies ensured the continued attractiveness of the SHA in overseas markets.

BBC World Service

Here the emphasis was on the use of technology to recruit journalists/producers to work mainly in the UK but occasionally overseas. The BBC placed a heavy reliance on its employment brand in international recruitment and identified brand values including: international, trustworthy, award winning, accessible, impartial, educational and online. These values were used to inform all recruitment materials such as brochures and there was a particular emphasis on their use in the commercial website which advertised vacancies. This activity was undertaken largely by external providers as the BBC outsourced its HR delivery.

Barclaycard International

Barclaycard used its multicultural workforce to support its ambitious internationalisation strategy. Internally, vacancies were advertised on intranets. An international HR business partner was appointed to negotiate preferred supplier arrangements with headhunters and other institutions. An employee value proposition and employment brand was developed across countries and global versus local processes were evaluated and adjusted. Many recruitment processes were adopted across the whole (international) operation, while others had to be more flexible. Recruitment was undertaken in target markets ahead of entering those markets and research was undertaken into a wide range of geographical labour markets.

Save the Children

Save the Children operated across six geographical regions and recruited three types of international labour: long-term overseas development posts, emergency overseas posts and locally appointed posts. To support this, it launched a new employment brand and proposition and recruitment was devolved to local line managers. There were four main activities:

- Regional HR managers worked to identify internal talent at local level, employ local advertising media and build candidate networks and databases.
- Global protocols were developed to identify sources of applicants and ways to advertise roles.
- Collaborative arrangements with other agencies and charities were entered into.
- Recruitment relied on the overall brand image which informed all advertising.

Online recruitment was heavily relied upon and sold the benefits of working in a particular programme, country or region.

Questions

1 Why do you think that all four case study organisations relied so heavily on employer branding in their recruitment activity?

2 Why is e-recruitment so effective in international recruitment?

3 To what extent should consistent global recruitment processes be adopted? How might more local tailored processes be more effective?

Source: Adapted from Sparrow, P. (2007) 'Globalisation of HR at function level: Four UK-based case studies of the international recruitment and selection process', *International Journal of Human Resource Management*, Vol. 18, No. 5, pp. 845–67.

FURTHER READING

Edwards, M. (2010) 'An integrative review of employer branding and OB theory', *Personnel Review*, Vol. 39, No. 1, pp. 5–23.

Parry, E. and Tyson, S. (2008) 'An analysis of the use and success of online recruitment methods in the UK', *Human Resource Management Journal*, Vol. 18, No. 3, pp. 257–74.

Searle, R. (2003) *Selection and Recruitment: A critical text.* Milton Keynes: The Open University.

Taylor, S. and Collins, C. (2000) 'Organisational recruitment: Enhancing the intersection of research and practice', in C. Cooper and E. Locke (eds), *Industrial and Organisational Psychology.* Oxford: Blackwell.

Academic research on recruitment as opposed to selection processes is relatively undeveloped and there remain many central issues that have not been rigorously studied. Searle (2003) presents a detailed and critical text that begins to study some of these issues. Taylor and Collins (2000) provide a shorter treatment with an additional practical focus. Parry and Tyson (2008) present an in-depth review on the progress and limitations of e-recruitment in recent years in the UK and Edwards (2010) presents a synthesis of the rapidly increasing body of research on employer branding.

REFERENCES

Bayo-Mariones, A. and Ortin-Angel, P. (2006) 'Internal promotion versus external recruitment: Industrial plants in Spain', *Industrial and Labour Relations Review*, Vol. 59, No. 3, Article 7.

Brannick, M.T. and Levine, E.L. (2002) *Job Analysis: Methods, research and applications for human resource management in the new millennium.* Thousand Oaks, CA: Sage.

Breaugh, J. and Starke, M. (2000) 'Research on employee recruitment: So many studies, so many remaining questions', *Journal of Management*, Vol. 26, No. 3, pp. 405–34.

Burt, C., Halloumis, S., McIntyre, S. and Blackmore, H. (2010) 'Using colleague and team photographs in recruitment advertisements', *Asia Pacific Journal of Human Resources*, Vol. 48, pp. 233–50.

CIPD (2007) *Employer Branding: A no-nonsense approach.* London: CIPD.

CIPD (2009) *Recruitment, Retention and Turnover: Annual Survey Report 2009.* London: CIPD.

CIPD (2012a) *Resourcing and Talent Planning: Annual Survey Report 2012.* London: CIPD.

CIPD (2012b) 'Recruitment: An overview', Factsheet, **www.cipd.co.uk/hr-resources/factsheets/recruitment-overview.aspx.**

Crush, P. (2012) 'Tough love', *People Management*, 26 November, pp. 40–2.

Frankland, G. (2000) 'If you build it, they will come', *People Management*, 16 March, p. 45.

Goldberg, C. and Allen, D. (2008) 'Black white and read all over: Race differences in reactions to recruitment websites', *Human Resource Management*, Vol. 47, No. 2, pp. 217–36.

Institute for Employment Research (2006) *Working Futures 2004–2014: National Report.* Warwick: Institute for Employment Research.

IRS (2003) 'Job descriptions and person specifications', *IRS Employment Review*, No. 776, 23 May.

IRS (2005) 'Online recruitment in the UK: 10 years older and wiser', *IRS Employment Review*, No. 822, pp. 42–8.

Kirton, G. and Healy, G. (2009) 'Using competency-based assessment centres to select judges: Implications for equality and diversity', *Human Resource Management Journal*, Vol. 19, No. 3, pp. 302–18.

Lievens, F. (2007) 'Employer branding in the Belgian army', *Human Resource Management*, Vol. 46, No. 1, pp. 51–69.

Martin, C. (2010) *Perfect Phrases for Writing Job Descriptions*. New York: McGraw-Hill.

Newell, S. and Shackleton, V. (2000) 'Recruitment and selection', in S. Bach and K. Sisson (eds), *Personnel Management: A comprehensive guide to theory and practice*. Oxford: Blackwell.

Nickson, D., Warhurst, C., Dutton, E. and Hurrell, S. (2008) 'A job to believe in: Recruitment in the Scottish voluntary sector', *Human Resource Management Journal*, Vol. 18, No. 1, pp. 20–35.

Parry, E. and Tyson, S. (2008) 'An analysis of the use and success of online recruitment methods in the UK', *Human Resource Management Journal*, Vol. 18, No. 3, pp. 257–74.

Parry, E. and Wilson, H. (2009) 'Factors influencing the adoption of online recruitment', *Personnel Review*, Vol. 38, No. 6, pp. 655–73.

People Management (2009) *PM Guide . . . to recruitment marketing*. London: People Management.

Prien, E., Goodstein, L., Goodstein, J. and Gamble, L. (2009) *A Practical Guide to Job Analysis*. San Francisco, CA: Pfeiffer.

Sanchez, J. and Levine, E. (2009) 'What is (or should be) the difference between competency modelling and traditional job analysis?', *Human Resource Management Review*, Vol. 19, No. 1, pp. 53–63.

Searle, R. (2003) *Selection and Recruitment: A critical text*. Milton Keynes: The Open University.

Searle, R. (2004) 'New technology: The potential impact of surveillance techniques in recruitment practices', *Personnel Review*, Vol. 35, No. 3, pp. 336–51.

Siddique, C. (2004) 'Job analysis: A strategic human resource management practice', *International Journal of Human Resource Management*, Vol. 15, No. 1, pp. 219–44.

Sparrow, P. (2007) 'Globalisation of HR at function level: Four UK-based case studies of the international recruitment and selection process', *International Journal of Human Resource Management*, Vol. 18, No. 5, pp. 845–67.

Stevens, M. (2010) 'L'Oreal's recruitment gets a virtual makeover', **www.peoplemanagement.co.uk/pm/articles/2010/05/loreal-uses-virtual-business-game-to-recruit.htm** (accessed 29 May 2013).

Uggersley, K., Fassina, N. and Kraichy, D. (2012) 'Recruiting through the stages', *Personnel Psychology*, Vol. 65, pp. 597–660.

Van den Brink, M., Fruytier, B. and Thunnissen, M. (2012) 'Talent management in academia: Performance systems and HRM policies', *Human Resource Management Journal*, doi: 10.1111/j.1748-8583.2012.00196.x.

Van Wanrooy, B., Bewley, H., Bryson, A., Forth, J., Freeth, S., Stokes, L. and Wood, S. (2013) *The 2011 Workplace Employment Relations Study: First findings*. London: BIS.

Warhurst, C. and Nickson, D. (2007) 'Employee experience of aesthetic labour in retail and hospitality', *Work, Employment and Society*, Vol. 21, No. 103, pp. 103–20.

Weekes, S. (2000) 'Hire on the wire', *Personnel Today*, 2 May, pp. 31–5.

Whiddett, S. and Kandola, B. (2000) 'Fit for the job?', *People Management*, 25 May, pp. 30–4.

Chapter 7

SELECTION METHODS AND DECISIONS

THE OBJECTIVES OF THIS CHAPTER ARE TO:

1 Explain the importance of viewing selection as a two-way process

2 Examine the development and use of selection criteria

3 Evaluate the range of selection methods that are available (interviewing will be dealt with in detail later (see Part 8 on selected HR skills)) and consider the criteria for choosing different methods

4 Review approaches to selection decision making

5 Explain how selection procedures can be validated

Selection is the process of choosing which applicant should be appointed to a vacancy. As we saw earlier, sophisticated selection processes form part of a strategic bundle of HR practices which contribute to improved organisational performance (see Chapter 3). Selection is also important as more attention is paid to the costs of poor selection, including poor performance, additional training, demotivation of others, high levels of absence and so on. Effective selection is thus critical to organisational effectiveness but is nevertheless recognised to be problematic. HR and line managers use a variety of imperfect methods to aid the task of predicting which applicant will be most successful in meeting the demands of the job, and/or be the best fit with the work group and culture of the organisation. Attention is also required to the applicant's perspective and the increasingly international nature of selection. In addition, equal opportunities legislation has underlined the importance of using well-validated selection procedures, so that the selection process discriminates fairly, and not unfairly, between applicants. Issues of equality of opportunity are dealt with later (see Chapter 19).

WINDOW ON PRACTICE

Pellizzari (2011) investigates the selection of unskilled workers in low-productivity jobs. While employers typically invest heavily in the selection of senior-level and/or skilled jobs, unskilled jobs comprise the bulk of vacancies in many countries. Pellizzari demonstrates that employers typically make limited investment in unskilled worker selection and that the resultant poor job/person matching leads to higher labour turnover with all its associated organisational costs, such as reduced productivity and worsening worker morale. More intensive selection leads to better matches that last longer and create higher employer satisfaction. This research suggests to us that organisations are well advised to adopt robust selection processes of the type discussed in this chapter.

Source: Summarised from Pellizzari, M. (2011) 'Employers' search and the efficiency of matching', *British Journal of Industrial Relations*, Vol. 49, pp. 29–53.

Rational versus processual approaches to selection

We discussed the role of candidate perceptions in the recruitment process in detail in the previous chapter. These perceptions are equally influential in selection processes, where the various stages provide information for decisions by both the employer and the potential employee. Lockyer and Scholarios (2007) describe this well in what they describe as the 'rain dance' of selection. Applicants choose between organisations by evaluating the developing relationship between themselves and the prospective employer. This takes place in the correspondence from potential employers; in their experience of the selection methods used by the employer; and in the information they gain at interview. Applicants will decide not to pursue some applications. Either they will have accepted another offer, or they will find something in their dealings with the organisation that discourages them and they withdraw. When large numbers of candidates withdraw it may be because the information provided by the organisation was sufficiently detailed, accurate and realistic for them to be able to make a wise decision that they were not suited to the organisation and that time would be wasted by continuing. On the other hand, it might be that potentially admirable recruits were lost because of the way in which information was presented, lack of information, or the interpretation that was put on the 'flavour' of the correspondence. The frame of reference for the applicant is so different from that of the manager in the organisation that the difference is frequently forgotten. The majority of applicants vest a significant amount of time and energy in the submission of an application. The psychological contract of a potential employee begins to be formed at this stage and this fact should not be overlooked: timely responses are the first element of this process. Indeed CIPD (2012) reports that up to one-third of organisations lose candidates due to the length of the recruitment and selection process.

Some of the points that seem to be useful about interacting with the candidate are:

1 Reply, meaningfully and quickly. Web-based selection can speed things up considerably, and we look e-shortlisting later in the chapter.

2 Conduct correspondence in terms of what the applicants want to know. How long will they have to wait for an answer? If you ask them in for interview or assessment centre, how long will it take, what will it involve, do you defray expenses, can they park their car, how do you find you, etc.?

3 Interviewers should be trained to ensure that they have not only full knowledge of the relevant information, but also the skills to manage the interaction effectively.

Selection criteria

Selection criteria need to be explicitly defined in order to choose the most appropriate selection methods, make credible selection decisions and validate the selection process (Searle 2003). Selection criteria are typically presented in the form of a person specification or competency profile representing the ideal candidate (see the previous chapter for further detail). Three perspectives can be used to determine selection criteria: job fit, team/functional fit (see e.g. Werbel and Johnson 2001) and organisational fit. Job fit emphasises the requirements of the person specification and identifies a candidate who can conduct that job, essentially selecting a 'square peg to fit a square hole'. Team and organisational fit approaches are less concerned with the job requirements and more concerned with how well a candidate will slot in. There has recently been an increasing emphasis on team and organisational fit, which has been supported by greater use of competencies in selection (Branine 2008). Competency profiles, often expressed in terms of personality, attitudes, flexibility, commitment and goals, are adopted as a means of setting the criteria against which to select, rather than the ability to do the specific job for which the person is being recruited. In many organisations, for example call centres, such selection approaches have led to a much greater emphasis on these competencies than on the education or experience typically demanded by the use of person specifications. Such organisational criteria are also important where jobs are ill defined and constantly changing. There is growing interest in how to select to ensure a good team fit, see for example Burch and Anderson's (2008) New Zealand study of a Team Selection Inventory. Whiddett and Hollyforde (2003) also provide a useful practical source of information on how to use competencies in the selection process.

The aim of compentencies is to promote objective selection criteria which are explicit and transparent, although Kirton and Healey (2009) warn that these still require human interpretations so may be less objective than suggested. Other critiques of selection based on competency have also included the danger of 'cloning', that is selecting very similar types of people for an organisation and thus limiting diversity, and that competencies are backward looking, focusing on what has previously made the organisation successful rather than the competencies that it may need for future success. Use of both person specifications and competency profiles to inform selection criteria is criticised and the search continues for criteria that will improve the process of selecting potential employees.

ACTIVITY 7.1

Write a person specification for your job (or one with which you are familiar). Now write a list of the competencies required to undertake the same role. Which do you think will be more helpful in the selection process and why?

Shortlisting

Robust selection criteria are essential to the whole selection process. In the first stage, shortlisting, they are used to reduce applications to those that are suitable for the later stages of selection. Shortlisting of candidates can be difficult in some instances because of small numbers of applicants and in other instances because of extremely large numbers of applicants. Such difficulties can arise unintentionally when there is inadequate specification of the criteria required or intentionally in large-scale recruitment exercises such as those associated with an annual intake of graduates. A fair and objective shortlisting system is essential to produce the best group of candidates to move forward to the next stage. This can be achieved in one of three basic ways – which can be used separately or in combination. The first involves using a panel of managers to undertake shortlisting, reducing the likelihood that individual prejudices will influence the process. A number of distinct stages can be identified:

Stage 1: Panel members agree essential criteria for those to be placed on the shortlist.

Stage 2: Using those criteria, selectors individually produce personal lists of, say, ten candidates. An operating principle throughout is to concentrate on who can be included rather than who can be excluded, so that the process is positive, looking for strengths rather than shortcomings.

Stage 3: Selectors reveal their lists and find their consensus. If stages 1 and 2 have been done properly the degree of consensus should be quite high and probably sufficient to constitute a shortlist for interview. If it is still not clear, they continue to the next stage.

Stage 4: Discuss those candidates preferred by some but not all in order to clarify and reduce the areas of disagreement. A possible tactic is to classify candidates as 'strong', 'possible' or 'maverick'.

Stage 5: Selectors produce a final shortlist by discussion, guarding against including compromise candidates: not strong, but offensive to no one.

The second approach involves employing a scoring system. As with the panel method, the key shortlisting criteria are defined at the start of the process (e.g. a degree in a certain discipline, certain types of job experience, evidence of particular competencies, etc.). The shortlister then scores each CV or application form received against these criteria, awarding an A grade (or high mark) where clear evidence is provided that the candidate matches the criteria, a B grade where there is some evidence or where the candidate partially meets the criteria and a C grade where no convincing evidence is provided. Where a structured application form has been completed by the candidates, this process can be undertaken quickly (two or three minutes per application) because a candidate can be screened out whenever, for example, more than one C grade has been awarded.

The third approach involves making use of the software systems on the market which shortlist candidates electronically. Such technologies, however, are not wholly satisfactory. Some that search for key words in CVs inevitably have a 'hit and miss' character and can be criticised for being inherently unfair. Good candidates may be rejected simply because they did not use a particular word or phrase. The same doubt exists about online application systems which include a handful of 'killer' questions designed to sift out unsuitable candidates at a very early stage. People with an unconventional career background may be automatically disregarded despite perhaps having the required talent or potential to do an excellent job. Caution is thus required. Despite these problems, such systems can be useful where the criteria are very clearly and tightly defined, and where an online application form is completed which makes use of multiple choice answers (for alternative ways in which this may be carried out see Mohamed *et al.* 2001). Such forms can be scored speedily and objectively, the candidates being given feedback on whether or not they have been successful, but there are questions about the legality of this method when used alone. Only those who make the 'right' choices when completing the online questionnaire are then invited to participate in the next stage of the selection process which may comprise various selection methods.

Selection methods

We present below recent CIPD research which outlines the most frequently used selection methods (Table 7.1). We discuss these methods in detail below.

It is interesting to note that interviews, particularly competency-based ones, are the most frequently used selection method in this survey. Other common selection methods include various types of tests and around a third of respondents use assessment centres. Typically, a combination of two or more of these methods is generally used, and the choice of these is dependent upon a number of factors:

1 **Selection criteria for the post to be filled.** For example, group selection methods and assessment centre activities would be most useful for certain types of jobs, such as managerial, professional, supervisory and those who will be part of self-managing teams.

2 **Acceptability and appropriateness of the methods.** These are for the candidates involved, or likely to be involved, in the selection. The use, for example, of intelligence tests may be seen as insulting to applicants already occupying senior posts.

3 **Abilities of the staff involved in the selection process.** This applies particularly in the use of tests and assessment centres. Only those staff who are appropriately qualified

Table 7.1
Methods used to
select applicants
(%)

Competency-based interviews	70
Interviews following contents of a CV/application form (i.e. biographical)	63
Structured interviews (panel)	56
Tests for specific job-related skills	49
Telephone interviews	43
Literacy and/or numeracy tests	38
Personality/aptitude questionnaires/psychometric tests	35
Assessment centres	35
Pre-application elimination/progression questions	25
General ability tests	23
Group exercises (e.g. role playing)	21
Pre-interview referencing	9
Other	3
Base: 605	

Source: From Chartered Institute of Personnel and Development (2011) *Resourcing and Talent Planning: Annual Survey Report 2011*, Table 13. With the permission of the publisher, the Chartered Institute of Personnel and Development, London (**www.cipd.co.uk**).

by academic qualification and/or attendance on a recognised course may administer psychological tests.

4 **Administrative ease.** For administrative purposes it may be much simpler, say, to arrange one or two individual interviews for a prospective candidate than to organise a panel consisting of four members, all needing to make themselves available at the same time. Web-based testing may save much administrative time, particularly when there are large numbers of candidates.

5 **Time factors.** Sometimes a position needs to be filled very quickly, and time may be saved by using telephone or video-based interviews, or organising individual interviews rather than group selection methods, which would mean waiting for a day when all candidates are available.

6 **Cost.** Tests may cost a lot to set up but once the initial outlay has been made they are reasonably cheap to administer. Assessment centres involve an even greater outlay and continue to be fairly expensive to administer. Interviews, on the other hand, cost only a moderate amount to set up in terms of interviewer training and are fairly cheap to administer. For the costlier methods great care needs to be taken in deciding whether the improvement in selection decision making justifies such costs.

7 **Accuracy.** In selection, this is usually referred to as validity and is the extent to which a selection method can predict subsequent job performance. If selection decisions relate highly to future performance, however defined, then the method is a good predictor. Validity is usually expressed as a correlation coefficient (r): if $r = 1$, then the selection method perfectly predicts performance; if $r = 0$, then there is no relationship between the selection method and performance. In practice, r will fall between 0 and 1, with different methods having varying levels of validity. A range of studies (see e.g. Schmidt and Hunter 1998) have shown that assessment centres have a correlation coefficient of around 0.6, structured interviews 0.5, work sampling 0.4, personality tests 0.3, unstructured interviews 0.1 and references 0. Validity in selection generally increases in relation to the number of appropriate selection methods used (see e.g. IRS 2002).

Choice of selection method is determined by all these factors. For example, while assessment centres may have the highest levels of validity ($r = 0.6$) they are also expensive, time consuming and difficult to administer. This explains why they are used only by around one-third of organisations (CIPD 2012), despite their capacity to predict job performance relatively effectively.

The 'classic trio', namely application forms, interviews and references, are traditional methods of selection. We consider these first, other than for face-to-face interviews which we consider in depth later (see Part 8). We then move on to consider more advanced methods of selection, such as testing, group methods and assessment centres.

The classic trio

Application forms

Application forms are generally used as a straightforward way of giving a standardised synopsis of the applicant's history. This helps applicants present their case by providing them with a predetermined structure, it speeds the sorting and shortlisting or sifting of applications either by hand or electronically and it guides the interviewers, with each piece of information on the form being taken and developed in the interview, as well as providing the starting point for employee records. While there is heavy use of CVs for managerial and professional posts, many organisations, especially in the public sector, require both – off-putting to the applicant but helpful to the organisation in eliciting comparable data from all applicants.

Application forms can also be used to collect biodata which describes personal information collected about a candidate (Breaugh 2009). Biodata is perhaps of most use for large organisations filling fairly large numbers of posts for which they receive substantial numbers of applications. This method is an attempt to relate the characteristics of applicants to the characteristics of a large sample of successful job holders. The obvious drawbacks of this procedure are, first, the time that is involved and the size of sample needed, so that it is only feasible where there are many job holders in a particular type of position. Second, it lacks face validity for applicants who might find it difficult to believe that success in a position correlates with being, for example, the first born in one's family. Despite this, Breaugh (2009) presents a review of biodata research and suggests that, as a selection method, it is one of the best predictors of employee performance and turnover and argues for its increased usage.

Despite the widespread adoption of application forms and CVs, there remain concerns about their reliability.

Telephone interviewing

Telephone interviews can be used if speed is particularly important, and if geographical distance is an issue, as interviews with appropriate candidates can be arranged immediately. CIPD (2012) reports that 43% of organisations use this method of selection, often as one of a combination of screening tools, as well as a test of telephone manner, where required. Telephone interviews are best used as a part of a structured selection procedure, generally in terms of pre-selection for a face-to-face interview. However, they may also have an important role when selecting for jobs in which telephone manner is critical, such as call centre staff. There may be problems such as lack of non-verbal information, and difficulties getting hold of the applicant. However, positive aspects have been reported, such as concentration on content rather than the person. From an applicant perspective telephone interviews can be daunting, if applicants have no experience of them, and Murphy (2005) refers to and replicates checklists for organisations and candidates in the most effective use of such interviews.

References

One way of informing the judgement of managers who have to make employment offers to selected individuals is the use of references. Candidates provide the names of previous employers or others with appropriate credentials and then prospective employers request them to provide information. There are two types: the factual check and the character reference. The factual check is fairly straightforward as it is no more than a confirmation of facts that the candidate has presented. It will normally follow the employment interview and decision to offer a post. The knowledge that such a check may be made will help focus the mind of candidates so that they resist the temptation to embroider their story. The character reference is a very different matter. Here the prospective employer asks for an opinion about the candidate before the interview so that the information gained can be used in the decision-making phases. The logic of this strategy is impeccable: who knows the working performance of the candidate better than the previous employer? The wisdom of the strategy is less sound, as it depends on the writers of references being excellent judges of working performance, faultless communicators and – most difficult of all – disinterested. Employers are increasingly nervous about providing character references, however, particularly where the comments to be made are not wholly positive. We outline some of the concerns employers face in providing references in the Window on practice below.

WINDOW ON PRACTICE

References: what employers should do and what they should avoid

May (2012) discusses the frequent concern among employers that providing a poor reference may lead to their being sued and cites a case where a former employer sued for libel over a statement contained in a reference. Although the case did not succeed, as employers are protected against libel claims providing that any inaccurate statements have not been made maliciously, it does serve to reinforce employer concerns. May provides the following checklist for employers to follow when providing references:

- Ensure there is an organisational policy on who can provide references, in what format and what its contents should be.
- Ensure that the policy is consistently applied to all current and former employees.

- Retain written notes of verbal references.
- If references confirm only employment dates and roles held, then this should be explicit.
- Ensure that genuine reasons for dismissal are provided.
- Ensure that refusal to provide a reference is not discriminatory and that disability is not a factor in any judgements made on performance or attendance.
- All statements should be clear and accurate.
- Ensure that the employee is aware of any concerns referred to in the reference.
- The reference does not need to be detailed: exercise caution when commenting on suitability for the new post.
- Mark the reference private and confidential and for the attention of the addressee only.

Source: Summarised from May (2012).

Advanced methods of selection

We turn now to consider more advanced methods of selection and issues surrounding their usage. Advanced methods comprise various forms of testing (including aptitude, attainment, personality and work sampling tests), group methods and assessment centres.

Testing

The use of tests in selection is surrounded by strong feelings for and against. Those in favour of testing in general point to the unreliability of the interview as a predictor of performance and the greater potential accuracy and objectivity of test data. Tests can be seen as giving credibility to selection decisions. Those against them either dislike the objectivity that testing implies or have difficulty in incorporating test evidence into the rest of the evidence that is collected. Questions have been raised as to the relevance of the tests to the job applied for and the possibility of unfair discrimination and bias. Also, some candidates feel that they can improve their prospects by a good interview performance and that the degree to which they are in control of their own destiny is being reduced by a dispassionate routine. CIPD (2012) found that 23% of organisations use general ability tests, 38% of organisations use literacy/numeracy tests and 35% use personality tests. Testing is more likely to be used for management, professional and graduate jobs – although as Web-based testing on the Internet becomes more common it is likely to be used for a wider range of jobs.

Types of test

Aptitude tests

People differ in their performance of tasks, and tests of aptitude (or ability) measure an individual's potential to develop in either specific or general terms. This is in contrast to attainment tests, which measure the skills an individual has already acquired. When considering the results from aptitude tests it is important to remember that a simple relationship does not exist between a high level of aptitude and a high level of job performance, as other factors, such as motivation, also contribute to job performance.

Aptitude tests can be grouped into two categories: those measuring general mental ability or general intelligence and those measuring specific abilities or aptitudes.

General intelligence tests

Intelligence tests, sometimes called mental ability tests, are designed to give an indication of overall mental capacity. A variety of questions are included in such tests, including vocabulary, analogies, similarities, opposites, arithmetic, number extension and general information. Ability to score highly on such tests correlates with the capacity to retain new knowledge, to pass examinations and to succeed at work. However, the intelligence test used would still need to be carefully validated in terms of the job for which the candidate was applying. Examples of general intelligence tests are found in IDS (2004).

Special aptitude tests

There are special tests that measure specific abilities or aptitudes, such as spatial abilities, perceptual abilities, verbal ability, numerical ability, motor ability (manual dexterity) and so on. An example of a special abilities test is the Critical Reasoning Test developed by Smith and Whetton (see IDS 2004).

Attainment tests

Whereas aptitude tests measure an individual's potential, attainment or achievement tests measure skills that have already been acquired, for example keyboard skills or the ability to use Word, PowerPoint or Excel software. There is much less resistance to such tests of skills as candidates are sufficiently confident of their skills to welcome the opportunity to display them and are in control, whereas they feel that the tester is in control of intelligence and personality tests as the candidates do not understand the evaluation rationale. Attainment tests are often devised by the employer.

Personality tests

Debate rages about the importance of personality for success in some jobs and organisations. The need for personality assessment may be high but there is even more resistance to tests of personality than to tests of aptitude, partly because of the reluctance to see personality as in any way measurable. There is much evidence to suggest that personality is also context dependent and may change over time. Personality tests are mainly used for management, professional and graduate jobs, although there is evidence of their use when high-performance teams are developed.

Theories of human personality vary as much as theories of human intelligence. Jung, Eysenck and Cattell, among others, have all proposed different sets of factors/traits which can be assessed to describe personality. Based on research to date, Robertson (2001) argues that it is now possible to state that there are five basic building blocks of personality: extroversion/introversion; emotional stability; agreeableness; conscientiousness; and openness to new experiences – and many tests are based around these traits. However, it is dangerous to assume that there is a standard profile of 'the ideal employee' (although this may fit nicely with theories of culture change) or the ideal personality for a particular job, as the same objectives may be satisfactorily achieved in different ways by different people. Another problem with the use of personality tests is that they rely on an individual's willingness to be honest, as the socially acceptable answer or the one best in terms of the job is seemingly easy to pick out, although 'lie detector' questions are usually built in. Ipsative tests (as opposed to normative tests)* seek to avoid the social desirability problem by using a different test structure – but other problems arise from this approach. Heggestad *et al.* (2006) suggest that in their pure form ipsative tests are

---

* Ipsative tests require the candidate to make a *choice*, usually between two statements or adjectives, rather than allowing the candidate to answer, for example, 'true' or 'false' or give a rating of 'to what extent' they agree an item applies to themselves, as in a normative test.

inappropriate for selection and that in their partial form they might be just as susceptible to faking as normative tests. Dalen *et al.* (2001) show that tests are indeed manipulable but not sufficiently for the candidate to match an ideal profile, and that such manipulation would be exposed by detection measures within the test. There is a further problem that some traits measured by the test will not be relevant in terms of performance on the job. Currently there is an increasing interest in aesthetic issues in selection, for example the attitudes and appearance of potential employees (Warhurst and Nickson 2007), and it is difficult to see how tests will be used to measure these attributes.

Online testing

Tests remain heavily used, and the key issue debated currently is the extent to which tests should be administered over the Web, particularly aptitude and psychometric tests. We outline the pros and cons in the Window on practice below.

WINDOW ON PRACTICE

Online testing: the case for and against

Tests can be used in one of three different ways:

1 uncontrolled – anyone can register to use them on the open Internet;

2 controlled – candidates need first to be registered by the organisation using the test, and their identity must be checked;

3 supervised – as above, and a qualified tester from the organisation also logs on and ensures that time limits and other requirements are met.

For:

- Cheaper in the long run.
- Immediate analysis.
- Immediate feedback to candidate.

- Can be used for wider range of (lower-paid) jobs.
- Speeds processes and helps to retain potential candidates.
- Good for company image.
- Can use a wider range of different tests – for example, video scenarios, followed by 'what would you do next?'.
- Can be convenient for applicants.

Against:

- Worries over confidentiality and security of personal data.
- Appears cold and impersonal.
- Open to misuse – who is actually completing the test?
- Can encourage the rapid development of new tests which are not properly validated.

Work sampling tests

Work sampling of potential candidates for permanent jobs can take place by assessing candidates' work in temporary posts or on government training schemes in the same organisation. For some jobs, such as photographers and artists, a sample of work in the form of a portfolio is expected to be presented at the time of interview. It has been suggested that managers and professionals should also be developing portfolios of their work experiences and achievements as one way of enhancing their employability. A relatively new development is to require candidates to undertake work experience as part of the selection process. We outline Pret A Manger's approach to this in the Window on practice below.

WINDOW ON PRACTICE

Job experience day at Pret A Manger

Pret A Manger has reduced staff turnover from 130% (not high for the industry) to 98%. The company puts this down to the use of a job experience day, which candidates have to do after an initial interview, but before they are granted a further competency-based interview.

Applicants do a day's work for which they are paid and they receive guidance and mentoring from an existing team member who is assigned to them for the day. But the aim is to enable applicants to work across a wide range of tasks with a wide range of team members. During the day the candidate also has an interview with the shop manager.

Team members who would be the applicant's future colleagues assess the applicant on competencies relevant to the job and then vote at the end of the day as to whether they would employ the applicant. The manager does not get a vote but can lobby for or against any candidate.

The success rate for the day is around 50%. Pret A Manger has found this a good way of sifting large numbers of applicants and at the same time developing team commitment to new recruits.

Source: Summarised from Carrington, L. (2002) 'At the cutting edge', *People Management*, Vol. 8, No. 10, 16 May, pp. 30–1.

Critical features of test use

Validity

Tests are chosen on the basis that test scores relate to, or correlate with, subsequent job performance, so that a high test score would predict high job performance and a low test score would predict low job performance (see above on choice of selection methods). The use of tests may vary by type of role. Lockyer and Scholarios (2004), for example, suggest that ability tests and work sample tests have high predictive validity for manual workers.

Reliability

The reliability of a test is the degree to which the test measures consistently whatever it measures. If a test is highly reliable, then it is possible to put greater weight on the scores that individuals receive on the test. However, a highly reliable test is of no value in the employment situation unless it also has high validity.

Use and interpretation

Tests need to be used and interpreted by trained or qualified testers. Test results, especially personality tests, require very careful interpretation as some aspects of personality will be measured that are irrelevant to the job. The British Psychological Society (BPS) provides a certificate of competence for occupational testing at levels A and B. Both the BPS and CIPD have produced codes of practice for occupational test use. It is recommended that tests are not used in a judgemental, final way, but to stimulate discussion with the candidate based on the test results and that feedback is given to candidates. In addition it is recommended that test data alone should not be used to make a selection decision (which could contravene the 1998 Data Protection Act), but should always be used as part of a wider process where inferences from test results can be backed up by information from other sources.

Problems with using tests

A number of problems can be incurred when using tests:

1 A correlation coefficient of $r = 0.4$ is comparatively good in the testing world and this level of relationship between test scores and performance is generally seen as acceptable. Tests are, therefore, not outstanding predictors of future performance.

2 Validation procedures are very time consuming, but are essential to the effective use of tests. There are concerns that with the growth of Web testing, new types of tests, such as emotional intelligence tests, are being developed without sufficient validation (Tulip 2002).

3 The criteria that are used to define good job performance in developing the test are often inadequate. They are subjective and may account to some extent for the mediocre correlations between test results and job performance.

4 Tests are often job specific. If the job for which the test is used changes, then the test can no longer be assumed to relate to job performance in the same way. Also, personality tests only measure how individuals see themselves at a certain time and cannot therefore be reliably reused at a later time.

5 Tests may not be fair as there may be a social, sexual or racial bias in the questions and scoring system. People from some cultures may, for example, be unused to 'working against the clock'. Tests also require a high facility with the language in which they are constructed. With many countries experiencing increasing levels of migrant workers, this may be problematic. In the Theory into practice section, we consider alternative types of test which may address this problem.

ACTIVITY 7.2

In what ways could you measure job performance for the following?

- A data input clerk.
- A mobile plumber.
- A call centre operator.
- A supervisor.

Group selection methods and assessment centres

Group methods

The use of group tasks is to provide evidence about the candidates' ability to:

- get on with others;
- influence others and the way they do this;
- express themselves verbally;
- think clearly and logically;
- argue from past experience and apply themselves to a new problem;
- identify the type of role they play in group situations.

These features are difficult on the whole to identify using other selection methods and one of the particular advantages of group selection methods is that they provide the selector with examples of behaviour on which to select. When future job performance is being considered it is behaviour in the job that is critical, and so selection using group methods can provide direct information on which to select rather than indirect verbal information or test results. The use of competencies and behavioural indicators, as a way to specify selection criteria, ties in well with the use of group methods.

There is a range of group exercises that can be used including informal discussion of a given topic, role plays and groups who must organise themselves to solve a problem within time limits which may take the form of a competitive business game, case study or physical activity.

Group selection methods are most suitable for management, graduate and sometimes supervisory posts. One of the difficulties with group selection methods is that it can be difficult to assess an individual's contribution, and some people may be unwilling to take part.

ACTIVITY 7.3

To what extent does a person's behaviour on these group selection tasks accurately reflect behaviour on the job? Why?

Assessment centres

Assessment centres incorporate multiple selection techniques, and the group selection methods outlined above form a major element, together with other work-simulation exercises such as in-basket tasks, psychological tests, a variety of interviews and presentations. Assessment centres are used to assess, in depth, a group of broadly similar applicants, using a set of competencies required for the post on offer and a series of behavioural statements which indicate how these competencies are played out in practice. Even assuming that the competencies for the job in question have already been identified, assessment centres require a lengthy design process to select the appropriate activities so that every competency will be measured via more than one task. Assessment centres have been proven to be one of the most effective ways of selecting candidates. This is probably due, as Suff (2005) notes, to the use of multiple measures, multiple assessors and predetermined assessment criteria. Thornton and Gibbons (2009) present a detailed evaluation of the validity of assessment centres in selection.

A matrix is usually developed to show how the required competencies and the activities link together. In terms of running the centre, sufficient well-trained assessors will be needed, usually based on the ratio of one assessor for two candidates to ensure that the assessor can observe each candidate sufficiently carefully. Lists of competencies and associated behaviours will need to be drawn up as checklists and a careful plan will need to be made of how each candidate will move around the different activities – an example of which is given in Table 7.2. Clearly candidates will need to be very well briefed both before and at the start of the centre.

Table 7.2
An example of the scheduling of events based on an assessment centre for a professional post (central government)

Day 1 Times	Activity	Who is involved
9.30–10.00	Introduction to centre	All
10.00–10.45	General discussion – given topics	All
10.45–11.15	Coffee	
11.15–12.00	General intelligence test	All
12.00–12.30	One-to-one interviews (30 min each)	Candidates A, B, C
12.30–1.30	Lunch	
1.30–2.00	One-to-one interviews (30 min each)	Candidates B, E, C
2.00–2.45	Spatial reasoning test	All
2.45–3.15	Coffee	
3.15–4.00	Personality test	All
4.00–4.30	One-to-one interviews (30 min each)	Candidates C, F, D

Day 2 Times	Activity	Who is involved
9.30–10.15	Verbal reasoning test	All
10.15–10.45	One-to-one interviews (30 min each)	Candidates D, A, F
10.45–11.15	Coffee	
11.15–12.00	Critical thinking test	All
12.00–12.30	One-to-one interviews (30 min each)	Candidates E, B, A
12.30–1.30	Lunch	
1.30–3.00	In-tray exercise	All
3.00–3.30	Coffee	
3.30–4.00	One-to-one interviews (30 min each)	Candidates F, D, E

Note: Based on six candidates (A, B, C, D, E, F) and three assessors.

At the end of the procedure the assessors have to come to an agreement on a cumulative rating for each individual, related to job requirements, taking into account all the selection activities. The procedure as a whole can then be validated against job performance rather than each separate activity. The predictive validities from such procedures are not very consistent, but there is a high 'face validity' – a feeling that this is a fairer way of selecting people. Reliability can also be improved by the quality of assessor training, careful briefing of assessors and a predetermined structured approach to marking. The chief disadvantage of these selection methods is that they are a costly and time-consuming procedure, for both the organisation and the candidates. The time commitment is extended by the need to give some feedback to candidates who have been through such a long procedure which involves psychological assessment – although feedback is still not always provided for candidates. Despite this, there is evidence of increasing use of assessment centres. A helpful text relating competency profiles and assessment centre activities is Woodruffe (2000), and IDS (2005) provides examples of different company experiences. Spray (2010) outlines 'how to run an assessment centre'.

As with all other aspects of selection, technology can now play a larger role in assessment centres, as we demonstrate in the Window on practice below.

WINDOW ON PRACTICE

'Hi-tech' assessment centres

KPMG has launched what it describes as a 'hi-tech' assessment centre for graduate recruitment. It contains a one-hour 'virtual office' exercise which is designed to simulate closely the working environment in which candidates complete an assigned task while dealing with emails and telephone calls. This is combined with

more traditional selection methods such as interviews, role plays and report writing. Group exercises have, however, been removed from the process as KPMG believes that they do not accurately represent how candidates really behave. The interactive technological experience is designed to generate greater insight into candidate behaviour and reduce the number of candidates who are rejected at a late stage in the selection process.

Source: Summarised from Brockett (2011).

ACTIVITY 7.4

Design an assessment centre for the anti-rape detective job as described in Case 7.1 on the Companion Website **www.pearsoned.co.uk/torrington**.

Final selection decision making

The selection decision involves measuring the candidates individually against the selection criteria defined, often in the person or competency specification, and not against each other. A useful tool to achieve this is the matrix in Table 7.3. This is a good method of ensuring that every candidate is assessed against each selection criterion and in each box in the matrix the key details can be completed. The box can be used whether a single selection method was used or multiple methods. If multiple methods were used and contradictory information is found against any criterion, this can be noted in the decision-making process.

When more than one selector is involved there is some debate about how to gather and use the information and about the judgement of each selector. One way is for each selector to assess the information collected separately, and then for all selectors to meet to discuss assessments. When this approach is used, there may be some very different

Table 7.3

Selection criteria	Candidate 1	Candidate 2	Candidate 3	Candidate 4
Criterion a				
Criterion b				
Criterion c				
Criterion d				
Criterion e				
General comments				

assessments, especially if the interview was the only selection method used. Much heated and time-consuming debate can be generated, but the most useful aspect of this process is sharing the information in everyone's matrix to understand how judgements have been formed. This approach is also helpful in training interviewers.

An alternative approach is to fill in only one matrix, with all selectors contributing. This may be quicker, but the drawback is that the quietest member may be the one who has all the critical pieces of information. There is a risk that not all the information available may be contributed to the debate in progress. Iles (1992), referring to assessment centre decisions, suggests that the debate itself may not add to the quality of the decision, and that taking the results from each selector and combining them is just as effective.

Validation of selection procedures

We have already mentioned how test scores may be validated against eventual job performance for each individual in order to discover whether the test score is a good predictor of success in the job. In this way we can decide whether the test should be used as part of the selection procedure in future. The same idea can be applied to the use of other individual or combined selection methods. Yet, despite the cost involved in selecting potential employees, few firms formally evaluate the success of their selection methods. Clifford (2008) presents a detailed methodology for evaluating selection methods and many organisations would benefit from its use.

SUMMARY PROPOSITIONS

7.1 Selection is a two-way process. The potential employer and the potential employee both make selection decisions.

7.2 Selection criteria are derived from person specifications and competency profiles and are essential to a structured and effective shortlisting process. Technology is increasingly used in shortlisting but can be problematic.

7.3 A combination of selection methods is usually chosen, based upon the job, appropriateness, acceptability, time, administrative ease, cost, accuracy and the abilities of the selection staff.

7.4 The most well-used selection methods are application forms, interviews (including those conducted by video and telephone), tests, group selection procedures, assessment centres and references. The increasing use of online selection methods is now levelling off.

7.5 A procedure for selection decision making needs to be agreed which can integrate all the selection information available.

7.6 Selection methods should be validated.

GENERAL DISCUSSION TOPICS

1   It could be argued that the selection process identifies candidates who are competent in the selection process rather than candidates who are most competent to perform the job on offer. Discuss this in relation to all forms of selection.

2   'It is unethical and bad for business to make candidates undergo a selection assessment centre without providing detailed feedback and support.' Discuss.

THEORY INTO PRACTICE

Pearson and Daff (2011) report on a fascinating study of selection methods that are not reliant upon work experience or high levels of formal education, particularly in relation to tests requiring a high facility with a country's dominant language. They argue for a particular type of personality test that is not language dependent to support the employment of Australian Indigenous people in Australia.

The Discovery Session is a selection test designed to be free of cultural bias that has been used in Australia, New Zealand and other countries in the region. It uses coloured beads, tiles and shapes and requires the candidate to construct forms or recall patterns. This does not require the candidate to have English-language competence and can be delivered in any language. Across six activities, it tests eighteen types of aptitude which have been identified as predictive of good job performance. One activity, for example, involves a computer screen which displays seven lily pads and six frogs. The objective is to change the position of the frogs, as per a defined set of instructions. The activity requires seventeen precise moves and a total of three minutes is allowed to complete it. Assessment of the aptitudes of motivation, coordination and knowledge building is undertaken.

The test is easy to administer, cannot be distributed to other candidates and has the potential to predict high job performance. Most candidates have also responded positively to its use and found the exercises demanding but enjoyable. The authors argue that its popularity relates to its lack of invasiveness, a difficulty often experienced by non-English-language speakers in other tests. As a selection method, it has wider application to societies experiencing problems with drawing marginalised populations into the mainstream workforce. Often these workers are disadvantaged as they lack competency in the dominant language and are typically screened out during a selection process. Administration of the Discovery Session is oral and is acultural, allowing candidates to demonstrate their capacity to learn and potential job performance. Research is at an early stage but it may have a substantial contribution to make to effective selection.

Questions

1 This research is based in Australia. To what extent can its findings be applied to other countries where substantial numbers of prospective employees, often migrant or poorly educated workers, do not have the language in which selection tests are constructed as a first language? What are the implications of this?

2 How applicable are these selection techniques across a wide range of jobs?

3 What difficulties might you face in using these selection techniques?

Adapted from: Pearson, C. and Daff, S. (2011) 'Extending boundaries of human resource concepts and practices: An innovative recruitment method for Indigenous Australians in remote regions', *Asia Pacific Journal of Human Resources*, Vol. 49, No. 3, pp. 325–43.

FURTHER READING

Human Resource Management Review, Vol. 19, No. 3, September 2009, 'Employee selection at the beginning of the 21st century', Special Issue.

This is a special edition on selection and presents an up-to-date review of research on important selection topics, such as the legal environment in which employee selection occurs, how selection issues should be considered in the context of international and cultural issues, and how the central focus during the selection process may be on other factors than job relatedness.

Stone, D., Lukaszewski, K., Stone-Romero, E. and Johnson, T. (2012) 'Factors affecting the effectiveness and acceptance of electronic selection systems', *Human Resource Management Review*, Vol. 23, pp. 50–70.

The authors argue that e-selection systems are now in widespread use and investigate the factors that influence their effectiveness and acceptance by candidates. Six stages of the selection process are considered: job analysis, job applications, pre-employment testing, interviews, selection decision making and validation of selection decisions. The authors also discuss potential adverse impacts in respect of applicant privacy and make recommendations in respect of system design and implementation.

Murphy, N. (2006) 'Voyages of discovery: Carrying out checks on job applicants', *IRS Employment Review*, No. 850, 7 July, pp. 42–8.

This article reports the results of a survey into employer practices to check the background details of applicants, and is much broader than seeking references from previous employers. It covers the type of information that is checked on, together with the mechanisms used.

Noon, M. (2012) 'Simply the best? The case for using threshold selection in hiring decisions', *Human Resource Management Journal*, Vol. 22, pp. 76–88.

This article argues for the use of 'threshold selection', a progressive approach to diversity and inclusion incorporating positive discrimination, in the selection process. It is interesting for this reason but it is also a very useful article as, in arguing for threshold selection, it presents an insightful critique of selection processes and the influence of expediency, politics and professionalisation on these.

REFERENCES

Branine, M. (2008) 'Graduate recruitment and selection in the UK', *Career Development International*, Vol. 13, pp. 497–513.

Breaugh, J. (2009) 'The use of biodata for employee selection: Past research and future directions', *Human Resource Management Review*, Vol. 19, pp. 219–31.

Brockett, J. (2011) 'KPMG launches "immersive" graduate assessment centre', *People Management*, **www.peoplemanagement.co.uk/pm/articles/2011/10/kpmg-launches-immersive-graduate-assessment-centre.htm** (accessed 29 May 2013).

Burch, G. and Anderson, N. (2008) 'The team selection inventory: Empirical data from a New Zealand sample', *Asia Pacific Journal of Human Resources*, Vol. 46, pp. 241–52.

Carrington, L. (2002) 'At the cutting edge', *People Management*, Vol. 8, No. 10, pp. 30–1.

CIPD (2012) *Resourcing and Talent Planning: Annual survey report*. London: CIPD.

Clifford, B. (2008) 'How to . . . evaluate your selection process', *People Management*, **www.peoplemanagement.co.uk/pm/articles/2008/01/howtoevaluateyourselectionprocess.htm** (accessed 29 May 2013).

Dalen, L., Stanton, N. and Roberts, A. (2001) 'Faking personality questionnaires in selection', *Journal of Management Development*, Vol. 20, pp. 729–41.

Heggestad, E., Morrison, M., Reeve, C. and McCloy, R. (2006) 'Forced-choice assessments of personality for selection: Evaluating issues of normative assessment and faking resistance', *Journal of Applied Psychology*, Vol. 91, pp. 9–24.

IDS (2004) 'IDS Study Plus: Psychological tests', *IDS Study 770*. London: IDS.

IDS (2005) 'Assessment centres', *IDS Study 800*. London: IDS.

Iles, P. (1992) 'Centres of excellence? Assessment and development centres, managerial competence and human resource strategies', *British Journal of Industrial Management*, Vol. 3, No. 2, pp. 79–90.

IRS (2002) 'Psychometrics: The next generation', *Employment Review*. London: IRS.

Kirton, G. and Healey, G. (2009) 'Using competency-based assessment centres to select judges: Implications for diversity and equality', *Human Resource Management Journal*, Vol. 19, pp. 302–18.

Lockyer, C. and Scholarios, D. (2004) 'Selecting hotel staff: Why best practice does not always work', *International Journal of Contemporary Hospitality Management*, Vol. 16, pp. 125–35.

Lockyer, C. and Scholarios, D. (2007) 'The "rain dance" of selection in construction: rationality as ritual and the logic of informality', *Personnel Review*, Vol. 36, pp. 528–48.

May, L. (2012) 'References', *People Management*, **www.peoplemanagement.co.uk/pm/articles/2012/07/references.htm** (accessed 29 May 2013).

Mohamed, A., Orife, J. and Wibowo, K. (2001) 'The legality of a key word search as a personnel selection tool', *Personnel Review*, Vol. 24, pp. 516–22.

Murphy, N. (2005) 'Got your number: Using telephone interviewing', *IRS Employment Review*, Vol. 832, pp. 43–5.

Noon, M. (2012) 'Simply the best? The case for using threshold selection in hiring decisions', *Human Resource Management Journal*, Vol. 22, pp. 76–88.

Pearson, C. and Daff, S. (2011) 'Extending boundaries of human resource concepts and practices: An innovative recruitment method for Indigenous Australians in remote regions', *Asia Pacific Journal of Human Resources*, Vol. 49, No. 3, pp. 325–43.

Pellizzari, M. (2011) 'Employers' search and the efficiency of matching', *British Journal of Industrial Relations*, Vol. 49, pp. 29–53.

Robertson, I. (2001) 'Undue diligence', *People Management*, Vol. 7, pp. 42–3.

Schmidt, F. and Hunter, J. (1998) 'The validity and utility of selection methods in personnel psychology: Practical and theoretical implications of 85 years of research findings', *Psychological Bulletin*, Vol. 124, pp. 262–74.

Searle, R. (2003) *Selection and Recruitment: A critical text*. Milton Keynes: The Open University.

Spray, J. (2010) 'How to . . . run an assessment centre', *People Management*, **www.peoplemanagement.co.uk/pm/articles/2010/01/how-to-run-an-assessment-centre.htm** (accessed 29 May 2013).

Suff, R. (2005) *Centres of Attention*. London: IRS Employment Review.

Thornton, G. and Gibbons, A. (2009) 'Validity of assessment centres for personnel selection', *Human Resource Management Review*, Vol. 19, pp. 169–87.

Tulip, S. (2002) 'Personality trait secrets', *People Management*, Vol. 8, pp. 34–8.

Warhurst, C. and Nickson, D. (2007) 'Employee experience of aesthetic labour in retail and hospitality', *Work, Employment and Society*, Vol. 21, pp. 103–20.

Werbel, J. and Johnson, D. (2001) 'The use of person–group fit for employment selection: A missing link in person–environment fit', *Human Resource Management*, Vol. 40, pp. 227–40.

Whiddett, S. and Hollyforde, S. (2003) *The Practical Guide to Competencies*. London: CIPD.

Woodruffe, C. (2000) *Development and Assessment Centres: Identifying and assessing competence*. London: Institute of Personnel and Development.

Chapter 8

ENGAGING AND RETAINING PEOPLE

THE OBJECTIVES OF THIS CHAPTER ARE TO:

1   Debate the meaning of the term 'engagement' in the context of work and employment

2   Discuss the benefits associated with engaging people

3   Identify concerns about engagement

4   Outline the main reasons for voluntary resignations

5   Assess the arguments for and against investing resources in staff turnover reduction programmes

6   Explore approaches which can improve engagement and retention

The previous two chapters focused on the processes used to mobilise a workforce, activities which are often expensive and time consuming. It is estimated that the costs associated with recruiting and training a new employee average between half and one and a half times the annual salary for the post in question, depending on the approaches used (Branham 2005: 3). In this chapter we consider the most important ways in which HR managers seek to maximise the return on this investment, that is by seeking to maximise levels of employee engagement and to minimise levels of voluntary staff turnover.

While use of the term 'engagement' in the context of the worlds of work and employment has often been imprecise and nebulous, most would agree that a workforce which is 'engaged' or, better still, 'actively engaged' is much more likely to be productive and to meet its objectives than one which is either 'disengaged' or 'actively disengaged'. It follows that enhancing levels of engagement, for all the confusion about what precisely this means, must be a major aim of any professionally managed HRM function.

Similarly, while arguments about the wisdom of investing extensively in initiatives aimed at maximising employee retention rates can sometimes be finely balanced, it is clear that for most organisations, most of the time, the loss of talent in which investment has been made is damaging. It follows that HR managers are right to view levels of voluntary staff turnover as a means of judging the success of people management in an organisation and are right to be concerned when the number of voluntary resignations rises higher than that of their major competitors.

Engagement and retention are different types of objectives, but are nonetheless linked closely together in important respects. First, it is clear from published research that relatively high levels of engagement tend to correlate quite strongly with relatively high employee retention rates. In other words, engaged employees are a good deal less likely to resign and seek alternative employment than disengaged employees. Indeed it is often disengagement that leads to resignations. Second, it is apparent from research into both areas that there is a good deal of similarity between the types of HR intervention that are commonly associated with high levels of engagement and low levels of unwanted turnover. It follows that implementing the same broad suite of initiatives is likely to have a positive effect on both turnover rates and the extent to which people in an organisation are positively engaged.

ACTIVITY 8.1

Employee retention becomes an important item on the HRM agenda when organisations are faced with skills shortages. When labour is in reasonably good supply leavers can easily be replaced by new starters. Aside from working harder at retaining staff, what alternative approaches could be adopted to help staff an organisation when the skills it requires are in short supply?

Defining engagement

The term 'employee engagement' has become very widely used in HRM circles in recent years. This is because 'engagement' seems to capture concepts that other commonly used terms such as 'motivation', 'satisfaction' and 'commitment' do not quite manage to so well.

Credit for inventing the term 'employee engagement' is often given to the American psychologist W.A. Kahn (1990) who conceived of its being made up of two distinct elements:

- **emotional engagement**: a situation in which employees have strong emotional ties to their managers, feel their opinions count and feel that their managers have an interest in their development;
- **cognitive engagement**: a situation in which employees know what is expected of them, understand their purpose or mission, are given opportunities to excel and grow, and are given information about how to improve their progress.

Subsequent researchers have taken up these ideas and have carried out many significant studies, refining their definitions of the term along the way. It remains the case, however, that we lack any kind of clear, precise, concise and widely agreed definition. Part of the problem is the sheer number of different ways in which the verb 'to engage' is defined in dictionaries and commonly used in everyday speech:

- we like people who are engaging company;
- in the context of war, we talk about engaging the enemy;
- we make engagements to meet with other people;
- we talk about engaging on a mission or a journey or a programme of study;
- we use the term to signify a betrothal leading to marriage.

The term 'employee engagement' does not seem to equate well to any of these usages. Instead it draws on another use of the term 'engage', namely the act of 'engaging' someone's interest in an idea, or 'engaging' gear when driving a car. The metaphor of engaging a car's gear is particularly useful in the context of 'employee engagement' because it implies the need to make a conscious choice in selecting the right gear for the right circumstances. It is also useful because drivers disengage gears as well as engaging them. Similarly, just as employees can become engaged, they can become disengaged just as easily.

Beyond this, however, the lack of any agreed definition is a very real hindrance for researchers trying to reach a better understanding of how employee engagement can be measured, for example, or improved through management interventions. As matters stand, well nigh every study that is published starts with its own definitions, some of which are more complex and multi-faceted than others. Here are some examples:

Work engagement is a positive, fulfilling, affective-motivational state of work-related well-being that can be seen as the antipode of job burnout. Engaged employees have high levels of energy and are enthusiastically involved in their work. Leiter and Bakker (2010: 1–2)

The extent to which employees thrive at work, are committed to their employer, and are motivated to do their best for the benefit of themselves and their organisation. Stairs and Gilpin (2010: 158)

A combination of commitment to the organisation and its values and a willingness to help out colleagues (organisational citizenship). It goes beyond job satisfaction and is not simply motivation. Engagement is something the employee has to offer; it can not be 'required' as part of the employment contract. Daniels (2010)

Peccei (2013) points out that, as yet, when it comes to defining 'employee engagement' we do not really even have agreement on the fundamentals. For example, he asks, when we use the term are we referring to engagement with our work or to engagement with our organisations? Moreover, is 'engagement' a long-term state, some being more engaged than others, or is it a state that we can move in and out of depending on our mood or the tasks we are working on at a particular time? More fundamentally still, he asks, is employee engagement properly conceived of as a state at all? Guest (see Macleod and Clarke 2009: 8) is blunter still in his assessment, expressing confusion about whether 'employee engagement' is 'an attitude, a behaviour, an outcome, or indeed all three', going on to argue that we should abandon the term altogether unless these very basic definitional questions can be answered.

As matters stand, however, we are far from abandoning the term. Instead its usage continues to grow and looks likely to do so for many years to come. The definitional problems have not prevented the publication of numerous articles on the subject and of some major scholarly works. In truth it is now seen as one of the key aims of HRM and people management more generally in organisations. The absence of a clear definition is not perhaps perceived as being problematic because, as several interviewees who contributed to the government-commissioned Macleod Report (Macleod and Clarke 2009) said, an 'engaged workforce is something that you know when you see it'.

There is also a sufficient degree of common ground between the various definitions to make the concept of 'employee engagement' useful from a practical management point of view. There is, for example, a shared understanding that 'engagement' represents a step beyond 'job satisfaction' and 'commitment' or even 'motivation'. Engaged employees have an emotional attachment to their work and/or their organisations which leads them to expend greater energy. There is thus a link to other widely used terms in HRM such as 'organisational citizenship', 'going the extra mile', 'working beyond contract' and 'discretionary effort'. Second, there is general agreement that being a positively engaged employee is beneficial both to the organisation and to the individual concerned. Engaged staff do not demonstrate enthusiasm and effort because they are forced to, but because they want to. We are not therefore talking here about responses to efforts on the part of managers to intensify work, squeezing more for less out of a reluctant workforce. Finally, it is abundantly clear that 'employee engagement' can only be usefully defined as a multi-dimensional concept that encompasses a variety of different elements. Indeed, it is quite likely that the antecedents of employee engagement vary from person to person, let alone workplace to workplace.

ACTIVITY 8.2

Looking back over your own working life to date, identify the time when you felt most actively engaged with your work or with the organisation you were working for. Then identify the time when you were least engaged or most disengaged with your work and with your employer.

1 In each case explain how your level of engagement affected your work. What difference did it make from the perspective of your employer?

2 What key factors can explain your positive engagement, lack of engagement or disengagement? Reflecting on the time that you were least engaged at work, explain what steps your employer could have taken to improve your level of engagement.

The benefits of employee engagement

To date by far the biggest and most cited research studies on employee engagement and its impact are those that have been carried out by the Gallup Organisation. These draw on data collected internationally using a simple twelve-question instrument which by 2002 had been administered to 198,514 people in 7,939 business units operating in all manner of industries over a thirty-year period. The twelve questions simply comprise statements such as:

I know what is expected of me at work.
In the last seven days, I have received recognition or praise for doing good work.

Respondents are asked to say whether they strongly agree, agree, disagree, strongly disagree or neither agree nor disagree, and scores then generated for a business unit employee's level of engagement (Harter *et al.* 2002). The sheer size of this dataset gives the analysis a strong measure of credibility. Furthermore, it enables statistically significant correlations to be sought between the extent of employees' emotional and cognitive engagement and other variables such as profitability, productivity, customer satisfaction and, importantly for our purposes in this chapter, employee turnover rates. Some of the key findings are as follows:

1 There is greater variation in terms of the level of employee engagement between different business units within the same organisation than there is between organisations. This is significant because it implies that the variability in levels is not related to the type of industry or characteristics of employees – it is in most cases due to the quality of management.

2 Impressive correlations were found to exist between relative levels of employee engagement in a business unit and the success of business units.

   Business units with the highest rates of employee engagement are twice as successful as those with the lowest when measured against indicators such as productivity, customer responses and profitability.

3 A particularly strong relationship was found between levels of employee involvement and rates of staff turnover. The size of the dataset allows separate analysis of high-turnover industries and low-turnover industries. In high-turnover business units (above 60% turnover rate), staff turnover was, on average, 29% lower in units which scored in the upper quartile for employee engagement than in the lower one. The variation, however, ranged between 14 to 51 percentage points. In low-turnover units the average difference was 10% (ranging from 4 to 19 percentage points) between upper and lower quartiles.

Other key headline findings from the Gallup Studies demonstrate the potential advantages of employee engagement from the perspective of employees:

- 86% of engaged employees 'very often feel happy at work' compared with only 11% who are disengaged;

- 45% of engaged employees 'get a great deal of their life happiness from work' compared with only 8% of people who are disengaged;
- 54% of actively disengaged staff state that 'work stress has caused them to behave poorly with friends or family in the past three months' compared with only 17% of engaged staff;
- 54% of actively disengaged staff report that their work lives 'are having a negative effect on their physical health' compared with just 12% of engaged staff.

The CIPD has also published research evidence (Truss *et al.* 2006) suggesting that people who are cognitively engaged with their work are three times as likely to exhibit 'six key positive emotions' at work – enthusiasm, cheerfulness, optimism, contentment, feeling calm and relaxed – than they are to experience negative emotions such as depression, gloominess and tension.

This research, like that of other researchers (e.g. Seligman 2003; Waddell and Burton 2006; Black 2008; Stairs and Gilpin 2010), links engagement to employee well-being and hence to heath and lower absence rates.

Another significant study that provides evidence of the positive business benefits associated with improving levels of employee engagement was that carried out by Towers Perrin–ISR (2006). Like the Gallup Studies this research was global in its scale, the data being gathered from questionnaires completed by 664,000 people working for fifty different corporations. Here too statistically significant links were found to exist between the level of engagement among a workforce and measures of business success, notably rises in operating income, net income and earnings per share. The highest-performing companies in terms of measures of employee engagement saw an average improvement in their operating income during the twelve-month period prior to the study of 19.2%. This compared with average falls of 32.7% in the operating income of companies with low levels of employee engagement. Furthermore, average net income was found to have grown by 13.7% in the companies with high employee engagement scores, but to have declined by an average of 3.8% in those with low levels of engagement.

WINDOW ON PRACTICE

Macleod and Clarke (2009: 37–59) summarise the results of several smaller-scale studies looking for evidence linking relatively high levels of employee engagement with superior business performance. Because they tend to define the term 'employee engagement' rather differently and measure 'business success' in a variety of ways, we must be cautious in reaching general conclusions, but all provide at least some evidence to suggest strong links between high levels of engagement and positive business outcomes.

The most interesting and compelling evidence is found in studies that compare different business units in the same company, each of which provides the same range of services using the same operational procedures. Boots, the Standard Chartered Bank and the Nationwide Building Society all carried out research of this kind, and in all three cases found good evidence of business outcomes being positively associated with high levels of engagement. Nationwide found that its 'high-engagement' branches achieved 14% higher sales of banking products and 34% higher sales of insurance than branches with low-engagement scores. There were similar findings on measures of customer service, staff turnover and absence. Standard Chartered and Boots also identified significant differences between high- and low-engagement branches on measures of profitability.

The impact of staff turnover

There is some debate about the level which staff turnover rates have to reach in order to inflict measurable damage on an employer. The answer varies from organisation to organisation. In some industries it is possible to sustain highly successful businesses with turnover rates that would make it impossible to function in other sectors. Some chains of fast food restaurants, for example, are widely reported as managing with turnover rates in excess of 300%. This means that the average tenure for each employee is only four months (Ritzer 1996: 130; Cappelli 2000: 106). Yet the companies concerned are some of the most successful in the world. By contrast, in a professional services organisation, where the personal relationships established between employees and clients are central to ongoing success, a turnover rate in excess of 10% is likely to cause damage to the business.

There are sound arguments that can be made in favour of a certain amount of staff turnover. First, it is fair to say that organisations need to be rejuvenated with 'fresh blood' from time to time if they are to avoid becoming stale and stunted. This is particularly true at senior levels, where new leadership is often required periodically to drive change forward. More generally, however, new faces bring new ideas and experiences which help make organisations more dynamic. Second, it is possible to argue that a degree of turnover helps managers to keep firmer control over labour costs than would otherwise be the case. This is particularly true of organisations which are subject to regular and unpredictable changes in business levels. When income falls it is possible to hold back from replacing leavers until such time as it begins to pick up again. In this way organisations are able to minimise staffing budgets while maintaining profit levels during leaner periods. Redundancy bills are also lower in organisations with relatively high staff turnover because they are able to use natural wastage as the main means of reducing their workforce before compulsory lay-offs are needed. Third, it can be plausibly argued that some employee turnover is 'functional' rather than 'dysfunctional' because it results in the loss of poor performers and their replacement with more effective employees.

The arguments against staff turnover are equally persuasive. First, there are the sheer costs associated with replacing people who have left, ranging from the cost of placing a recruitment advertisement, through the time spent administering and conducting the selection process, to expenses required in inducting and training new employees. On top of these there are less easily measurable losses sustained as a result of poorer performance on the part of less experienced employees. For larger organisations employing specialist recruiters these costs can add up to millions of pounds a year, with substantial dividends to be claimed from a reduction in staff turnover levels by a few percentage points. The second major argument in favour of improving staff retention results from a straightforward recognition that people who leave represent a lost resource in whom the organisation has invested time and money. The damage is all the greater when good people, trained and developed at the organisation's expense, subsequently choose to work for competitors. Finally, it is argued that high turnover rates are symptomatic of a poorly managed organisation. They suggest that people are dissatisfied with their jobs or with their employer and would prefer to work elsewhere. It thus sends a negative message to customers and helps create a poor image in the labour market, making it progressively harder to recruit good performers in the future.

159

We may thus conclude that the case for seeking to reduce staff turnover varies from organisation to organisation. Where replacement employees are in plentiful supply, where new starters can be trained quickly and where business levels are subject to regular fluctuation it is possible to manage effectively with a relatively high level of turnover. Indeed, it may make good business sense to do so if the expenditure required to increase employee retention is greater than the savings that would be gained as a result. In other situations the case for taking action on turnover rates is persuasive, particularly where substantial investment in training is required before new starters are able to operate at maximum effectiveness. Companies which achieve turnover rates below their industry average are thus likely to enjoy greater competitive advantage than those whose rates are relatively high.

WINDOW ON PRACTICE

The length of time that employees remain in their jobs, or at least with the same employers, varies considerably from country to country. Auer *et al.* (2004) analysed the proportion of staff who had less than a year's service in the OECD countries and the proportion who had completed more than ten years' service. The country with the most

shorter-term employees is the USA, where 24.5% have less than a year's service, while only 26.2% have been with their employers for more than ten years. At the other end of the scale is Greece, where only 9.8% have less than a year's service and as many as 52% have over ten years' service. High rates of job stability are also common in Italy, Belgium and Portugal. By contrast relatively low stability rates are found in the UK, Denmark and Ireland.

ACTIVITY 8.3

Why do you think staff turnover rates are so much higher in some industries than others? Make a list of the different factors that you consider may account for variations.

Analysing staff turnover

There is little that an organisation can do to manage turnover unless there is an understanding of the reasons for it. Information about these reasons is notoriously difficult to collect. Most commentators recommend exit interviews (i.e. interviews with leavers about their reasons for resigning), but the problem here is whether the individual will feel able to tell the truth, and this will depend on the culture of the organisation, the specific reasons for leaving and support that the individual will need from the organisation in the future in the form of references. Despite their disadvantages, exit interviews may be helpful if handled sensitively and confidentially – perhaps by the HR department rather than the line manager. In addition, analyses of turnover rates between different departments and different job groups may well shed some light on causes of turnover. Attitude surveys can also provide relevant information.

People leave jobs for a variety of different reasons, many of which are wholly outside the power of the organisation to influence. One very common reason for leaving, for example, is retirement. It can be brought forward or pushed back for a few years, but ultimately it affects everyone. In many cases people leave for a mixture of reasons, certain factors weighing more highly in their minds than others. The following is one approach to categorising the main reasons that people have for voluntarily leaving a job, each requiring a different kind of response from the organisation.

Outside factors

Outside factors relate to situations in which someone leaves for reasons that are largely unrelated to their work. The most common instances involve people moving away when a spouse or partner is relocated. Others include the wish to fulfil a long-term ambition to travel, pressures associated with juggling the needs of work and family and illness. To an extent such turnover is unavoidable, although it is possible to reduce it somewhat through the provision of career breaks, forms of flexible working and/or childcare facilities.

Functional turnover

The functional turnover category includes all resignations which are welcomed by both employer and employee alike. The major examples are those which stem from an individual's poor work performance or failure to fit in comfortably with an organisational or departmental culture. While such resignations are less damaging than others from an organisation's point of view, they should still be regarded as lost opportunities and as an unnecessary cost. The main solution to the reduction of functional turnover lies in improving recruitment and selection procedures so that fewer people in the category are appointed in the first place. However, some poorly engineered change-management schemes are also sometimes to blame, especially where they result in new work pressures or workplace ethics.

Push factors

With push factors the problem is dissatisfaction with work or the organisation, leading to unwanted turnover. A wide range of issues can be cited to explain such resignations. Insufficient development opportunities, boredom, ineffective supervision, poor levels of employee involvement and straightforward personality clashes are the most common precipitating factors. Organisations can readily address all of these issues. The main reason that so many fail to do so is the absence of mechanisms for picking up signs of dissatisfaction. If there is no opportunity to voice concerns, employees who are unhappy will inevitably start looking elsewhere.

Pull factors

The opposite side of the coin is the attraction of rival employers. Salary levels are often a factor here, employees leaving in order to improve their living standards. In addition there are broader notions of career development, the wish to move into new areas of work for which there are better opportunities elsewhere, the chance to work with particular people, and more practical questions such as commuting time. For the employer losing people as a result of such factors, there are two main lines of attack. First, there is a need to be aware of what other employers are offering and to ensure that as far as possible this is matched – or at least that a broadly comparable package of pay and opportunities is offered. The second requirement involves trying to ensure that employees appreciate what they are currently being given. The emphasis here is on effective communication of any 'unique selling points' and of the extent to which opportunities comparable with those offered elsewhere are given.

What are the most common reasons?

UK-based studies focusing on people's reasons for leaving organisations are few and far between, but those that have been published tend to emphasise that a mix of different factors applies and that these vary from industry to industry (e.g. DiPietro *et al.* 2007; Carroll *et al.* 2008). Taylor and his colleagues (2002) interviewed 200 people who had changed employers about why they left their last jobs. They found a mix of factors at work in most cases but concluded that push factors were a great deal more prevalent than pull factors as causes of voluntary resignations. Very few people appear to leave jobs in which they are broadly happy in search of something even better. Instead the picture is overwhelmingly one in which dissatisfied employees seek alternatives because they no longer enjoy working for their current employer.

Interestingly this study found relatively few examples of people leaving for financial reasons. Indeed more of the interviewees took pay cuts in order to move from one job to another than said that a pay rise was their principal reason for switching employers.

Other factors played a much bigger role:

- Dissatisfaction with the conditions of work, especially hours.
- A perception that they were not being given sufficient career development opportunities.
- A bad relationship with their immediate supervisor.

This third factor was by far the one most commonly mentioned in the interviews, lending support to the often stated point that people leave their managers and not their organisations.

Branham (2005), drawing on research undertaken by the Saratoga Institute, reached similar conclusions. His seven 'hidden reasons employees leave' are as follows:

- the job or workplace not living up to expectations;
- a mismatch between the person and the job;
- too little coaching and feedback;
- too few growth and advancement opportunities;
- feeling devalued and unrecognised;
- stress from overwork and work–life imbalance;
- loss of trust and confidence in senior leaders.

Samuel and Chipunza (2009) looked at why long-serving staff had remained in their jobs, rather than focusing on why leavers had left. Their study took place in four large South African organisations, two in the private sector and two in the public sector.

They found that the four key factors that served to retain staff were:

- training and development;
- challenging and interesting work;
- freedom for innovative thinking;
- job security.

It would follow logically that organisations that do not provide these to their people will lose staff to competitors who can.

ACTIVITY 8.4

Think about jobs that you or members of your family have left in recent years. What were the key factors that led to the decision to leave? Was there one major factor or did several act together in combination?

Engagement and retention strategies

The straightforward answer to the question of how best to retain staff is to provide them with a better deal, in the broadest sense, than they perceive they could get by working for alternative employers. This will also help to engage them. But it is much more than a question of getting the terms and conditions of employment right. There is also a need to provide jobs which are genuinely satisfying, along with career development opportunities, as much autonomy and involvement as is practicable and, above all, competent line management. Indeed, it can be argued that most of the practices of effective HRM described in this book can play a part in enhancing engagement and reducing staff turnover. Below we look at five interventions that can be shown to have a positive effect.

Pay

There is some debate in the literature about the extent to which raising pay levels either reduces staff turnover or improves job satisfaction to any significant degree. On the one hand, there is evidence to show that, on average, employers who offer the most attractive reward packages have lower attrition rates than those who pay poorly (Gerhart 2009: 215–16), an assumption which leads many organisations to use pay rates as their prime weapon in retaining staff (White 2009: 35–9). On the other, there is evidence which suggests that pay is a good deal less important than other factors in a decision to quit one's job (Bevan *et al*. 1997; Taylor 2002). The consensus among researchers is that pay has a role to play as a satisfier, but that it will not usually have an effect when other factors are pushing an individual towards quitting. Raising pay levels may thus result in greater job satisfaction, and hence employee engagement, where people are already happy with their work, but it will neither deter unhappy employees from leaving, nor re-engage many disengaged employees. Sturges and Guest (1999), in their study of leaving decisions in the field of graduate employment, summed up their findings as follows:

> As far as they are concerned, while challenging work will compensate for pay, pay will never compensate for having to do boring, unstimulating work. (Sturges and Guest 1999: 19)

Recent research findings thus appear to confirm the views expressed by Herzberg (1966) that pay is a 'hygiene factor' rather than a motivator. This means that it can be a cause of dissatisfaction at work, but not of positive job satisfaction. An employer who pays badly or is perceived to pay people inequitably will be unlikely to benefit from a highly engaged workforce. But higher pay will not generally lift levels of engagement if other factors such as the quality of the work or the management are poor. Similarly, people may be motivated to leave an employer who is perceived as paying badly, but once they are satisfied with their pay, additional increases tend to have little effect on turnover intentions.

While pay rates and benefit packages may play a relatively marginal role in the engagement and retention of good people, reward in the broader sense plays a more significant role. If employees do not find their work to be 'rewarding' in the broadest sense of the word, they will be much more likely to start looking for alternative jobs. This is a good deal harder for managers to achieve because different people find different aspects of their work to be rewarding. There is thus a need to understand what makes people tick and to manage them as individuals accordingly. It is far harder for would-be competitors to imitate the effective motivation of an individual than it is for them to increase the salary that a person is paid.

ACTIVITY 8.5

The case for arguing that pay rates have a relatively minor role to play in explaining individual resignations rests partly on the assumption that other elements of the employment relationship are more important. It is argued that people will 'trade in' high pay in order to secure other perceived benefits and that consequently low-paying employers can retain staff effectively.

1 What other factors do you think employees consider to be more important than pay?

2 What role can the HRM function play in helping to develop these?

Managing expectations

For some years research evidence has strongly suggested that employers benefit from ensuring that potential employees gain a 'realistic job preview' before they take up a job offer. The purpose is to make sure that new staff enter an organisation with their eyes wide open and do not find that the job fails to meet their expectations. A major cause of job dissatisfaction, and hence of high staff turnover and low levels of employee engagement, is the experience of having one's high hopes of new employment dashed by the realisation that it is not going to be as enjoyable or stimulating as anticipated.

Several researchers have drawn attention to the importance of these processes in reducing high turnover during the early months of employment (e.g. Wanous 1992: 53–87; Breaugh 2008: 105–8). The need is to strike a balance at the recruitment stage between sending out messages which are entirely positive and sending out those which are realistic. In other words, it is important not to mislead candidates about the nature of the work that they will be doing.

We also know from extensive research carried out into the nature of 'psychological contracts' that failing to meet expectations, and hence managing them effectively, can have serious de-motivational effects. The establishment of the concept of the 'psychological contract' is one of the most significant recent developments in the study of HRM (see Rousseau 1989; Conway and Briner 2005). The core idea is that employers and employees have a relationship that is much more complex and sophisticated than is set out in formal contracts of employment. The legal contract sets out the expectations and obligations each side has towards the other in respect of pay and terms and conditions of employment, but the reality of the relationship consists of much more than this. The 'psychological contract' can thus be defined as comprising expectations and obligations that the two sides have of one another and their relationship above and beyond what is formally agreed in any legal contract.

When an employer breaches the legal contract of employment there are legal consequences. For example, if pay is cut or the work location changed without contractual authorisation the employees who are affected can go to court to get injunctions or to sue for damages. If an employee breaches the legal contract (e.g. by going on strike), the employer responds by cutting wages. By contrast, when the psychological contract is breached the consequences are psychological – reduced commitment and loyalty, lower levels of motivation and reduced levels of trust both individually and collectively. The result is reduced employee engagement and higher levels of unwanted staff turnover.

Induction processes play an important role in establishing expectations at the start of the employment relationship. It follows that a timely and well-designed induction programme can play an important part in enhancing employee retention and engagement. It is very easy to overlook the importance of induction in the rush to get people into key posts quickly and it is often carried out badly. But it is essential, particularly if avoidable early turnover is to be kept to a minimum. Gregg and Wadsworth (1999: 111) show in their analysis of 870,000 workers starting new jobs in 1992 that as many as 17% had left within three months and 42% within twelve months. No doubt a good number of these departures were due either to poorly managed expectations or to ineffective inductions.

Induction has a number of distinct purposes, all of which are concerned with preparing new employees to work as effectively as possible and as soon as is possible in their new jobs. First, it plays an important part in helping new starters to adjust emotionally to the new workplace. It gives an opportunity to ensure that they understand where things are, who to ask when unsure about what to do and how their role fits into the organisation generally. Second, induction provides a forum in which basic information about the organisation can be transmitted. This may include material about the organisation's purpose, its mission statement and the key issues it faces. More generally a corporate induction provides a suitable occasion to talk about health and safety regulations, fire evacuation procedures and organisational policies concerning matters like the use of telephones for private purposes. Third, induction processes can be used to convey to new starters important cultural messages about what the organisation expects and what employees can expect in return. It thus potentially forms an important stage in the establishment of the psychological contract, leaving new employees clear about what they need to do to advance their own prospects in the organisation. All these matters will be picked up by new starters anyway in their first months of employment, but incorporating them into a formal induction programme ensures that they are brought up to speed a good deal quicker, and that they are less likely to leave at an early date.

Family-friendly HR practices

Labour Force Survey statistics show that between 5% and 10% of employees leave their jobs for 'family or personal reasons' (IRS 1999: 6), while Hom and Griffeth (1995: 252) quote American research indicating that 33% of women quit jobs to devote more time to their families – a response given by only 1% of men. UK employers believe that 21% of their leavers resign 'to have children or look after them', a further 7% leaving to look after other family members (CIPD 2009: 31). Official statistics also show that average job tenure among women with children in the UK is over a year shorter than that of women without children and almost two years shorter than that of men. Taken together these statistics suggest that one of the more significant reasons for voluntary resignations from jobs is the inability to juggle the demands of a job with those of the family. They indicate that there is a good business case, particularly where staff retention is high on the agenda, for considering ways in which employment can be made more family friendly. Research into the antecedents of employee engagement also strongly suggests that the ability of people successfully to combine work and home responsibilities is one of the most significant factors in explaining high levels of engagement (Peccei 2013: 346–9).

As a result of legislation, UK employers, like those in many countries, are now obliged by law to provide their employees with a range of family-friendly rights (see Chapter 18). Many, however, have decided to go a good deal further down this road than is required by law. The most common example is the provision of more paid maternity leave and the right, where possible, for mothers to return to work on a part-time or job-share basis if they so wish. Crèche provision is common in larger workplaces, while others offer childcare vouchers instead. Career breaks are offered by many public sector employers, allowing people to take a few months off without pay and subsequently to return to a similar job with the same organisation. Flexitime systems are also useful to people with families and there is also growing interest in 'eldercare' arrangements aimed specifically at providing assistance to those seeking to combine work with responsibility for the care of elderly relatives.

Providing flexible working opportunities of these kinds is a very good way of retaining and engaging staff, particularly when organisations do more than their competitors. This is because juggling family and work responsibilities is a big issue in many employees' lives and because evidence suggests that it is thus hugely appreciated by them (DiPietro *et al.* 2007).

Training and development

There are two widely expressed, but wholly opposed, perspectives on the link between training interventions and employee turnover. On the one hand, there is the argument that training opportunities enhance commitment to an employer on the part of individual employees, making them less likely to leave voluntarily than they would if no training were offered. On the other, the alternative view holds that training makes people more employable and hence more likely to leave in order to develop their careers elsewhere. The view is thus put that money spent on training is money wasted because it ultimately benefits other employers.

Green *et al.* (2000: 267–72) report research on perceptions of 1,539 employees on different kinds of training. The authors found that the overall effect is neutral, 19% of employees saying that training was 'more likely to make them actively look for another job' and 18% saying it was less likely to do so. However, they also found the type of training and the source of sponsorship to be a significant variable. Training which is paid for by the employer is a good deal less likely to raise job mobility than that paid for by the employee or the government. Firm-specific training is also shown in the study to be associated with lower turnover than training which leads to the acquisition of transferable skills. The point is made, however, that whatever the form of training, an employer can develop a workforce which is both 'capable and committed' by combining training interventions with other forms of retention initiative.

The evidence linking training and career development opportunities to employee engagement is much less unambiguous. Meta-analyses investigating the antecedents of relatively high levels of employee engagement place 'opportunities for development' close to the top of the list of factors that have a positive influence (Peccei 2013: 348). This is unsurprising because, in financing courses and training events, employers are sending a very clear signal to the employees concerned that their contribution is valued sufficiently for money to be invested in their personal development and potential career advancement.

Improving the quality of line management

If it is the case that many, if not most, voluntary resignations are explained by dissatisfaction on the part of employees with their supervisors, it follows that the most effective means of reducing staff turnover in organisations is to improve the performance of line managers. Investing in improving the quality of line management can also be shown to improve the chances that staff will be more engaged with their work, 'leader–member exchange' being a significant factor in determining how engaged any individual employee is likely to be (Peccei 2013: 348).

Too often, it appears, people are promoted into supervisory positions without adequate experience or training. Organisations seem to assume that their managers are capable supervisors, without recognising that the role is difficult and does not usually come naturally to people. Hence it is common to find managers who are 'quick to criticise but slow to praise', who are too tied up in their own work to show an interest in their subordinates and who prefer to impose their own solutions without first taking account of their staff's views. The solution is to take action on various fronts to improve the effectiveness of supervisors:

- select people for line management roles following an assessment of their supervisory capabilities;
- ensure that all newly appointed line managers are trained in the art of effective supervision;
- regularly appraise line managers on their supervisory skills.

This really amounts to little more than common sense, but such approaches are the exception to the rule in most UK organisations.

Of particular importance in promoting both employee retention and engagement is the need for line managers to involve people in decision making, and particularly, to allow them as much autonomy as possible in terms of how they perform their own role. Line managers thus need to be encouraged to stand back as much as possible to avoid supervising people more closely than is necessary. It is also important for line managers to ensure, at least as far as is possible given operational constraints, that working life is as interesting and varied as can be achieved.

SUMMARY PROPOSITIONS

8.1 Despite the lack of a clear and generally accepted definition, the term 'employee engagement' is increasingly used, while the concept is increasingly perceived as being managerially significant.

8.2 An engaged employee is someone who willingly works with greater enthusiasm and effort than is strictly required under the terms of his or her contract.

8.3 Considerable research evidence is now being amassed which links high levels of employee engagement to superior business performance.

8.4 Although there are arguments that can be deployed in favour of modest staff turnover, it is generally agreed that too great a rate is damaging for an organisation.

8.5 In planning retention initiatives it is important to analyse the causes of turnover among different groups of employees.

8.6 HR initiatives which lead to improved employee engagement and retention include better induction, the effective management of expectations, family-friendly initiatives, training opportunities, employee involvement and the improvement of line management in organisations.

GENERAL DISCUSSION TOPICS

1 Staff turnover is generally low during recessions, but it increases substantially in firms which get into financial difficulty. What factors account for this phenomenon?

2 Why has interest in employee engagement as an idea increased so much in recent years?

THEORY INTO PRACTICE

McDonald's UK

During the 1990s negative impressions about employment at the McDonald's restaurant chain were fuelled in the UK, as elsewhere, by the growth in usage of the term 'McJob' as a generic label for low-status occupations. The term first appeared in 1991 in the bestselling novel *Generation X* written by the Canadian writer Douglas Coupland, where it is defined as 'a low-pay, low-dignity, low-benefit, no-future job in the service sector'. In 2003, much to the irritation of the company, the term 'McJob' appeared in the *Oxford English Dictionary* for the first time, defined as 'an unstimulating, low-paid job with few prospects, especially one created by the expansion of the service sector'.

The McDonald's UK operation tended to suffer from negative connotations about its employment practices more than was the case in most of the other countries where the company operates. This is partly because food service work in general tends to be accorded less prestige in the UK than is the case elsewhere in the world and partly because of the extraordinary growth that McDonald's enjoyed in the country during the 1980s and 1990s when the company opened between 50 and 100 new restaurants each year. This mass expansion was accompanied by limited central direction as far as employment practices were concerned. Local managers and franchisees were given responsibility for staffing up their restaurants, leading to the adoption of inconsistent approaches. They often struggled to recruit and retain effective employees, and were not always particularly choosey when deciding who to hire. This led to the development of the widely held view that anybody could get a job 'flipping burgers' at their local McDonald's just by turning up and asking for a job.

McDonald's UK responded by carrying out a staff attitude survey which found that the popular characterisation of its jobs was by no means accurate. In 2004, 74% of the company's employees reported being satisfied with their jobs and happy to 'recommend working at McDonald's to a friend', 77% stated that they were committed to their work, while 86% were happy with the training and skills development opportunities they were given. Staff were particularly positive about the flexibility that their jobs gave them to juggle work and home responsibilities, the career paths that were provided for them to follow and the enjoyment they got from working as a member of a team. The definition accorded to the term 'McJob' was not therefore a fair or correct reflection of the lived reality for a good majority of people working in the company's 1,200 UK restaurants.

However, the survey also revealed that staff were generally dissatisfied with their pay and that only 60% agreed with the statement 'I am proud to work at McDonald's'. Staff turnover was also running at very high levels in 2004. The annual rate had reached over 80%, while the ninety-day turnover rate (i.e. the proportion of new starters leaving before they have completed three months' service) was running at 24.5%. It appeared that poor hiring decisions were being made too often and that the company was not effectively managing the expectations of new starters about exactly what their jobs would involve on a day-to-day basis. The 2004 staff attitude survey thus showed that, although the company had plenty of scope to improve its HR operations, its poor reputation as an employer in the UK was by no means at all justified. The definition of the term 'McJob' was a thoroughly unfair characterisation of the experience of working in the company's UK outlets.

The company addressed these issues in a variety of ways, investing substantial sums in initiatives that were designed to improve retention and engagement, while also radically altering the company's reputation as an employer:

- A state-of-the art corporate development centre was established offering highly flexible training programmes and the opportunity for staff to gain a range of qualifications up to degree level. Management development was the major priority.

- A discount scheme was set up which could save employees many hundreds of pounds on a range of retailed products, on holidays and driving lessons.

- More flexible working initiatives were launched including family and friends contracts which allowed groups of people to decide for themselves who would work which shift.

- A range of employee involvement initiatives was introduced enabling, for example, staff to play a role in determining uniform styles.

- Additional investment was put into the organisation of social events for staff, often revolving around raising money for charities.

Managers at McDonald's in the UK are generally very happy with the impact that their initiatives have had. Between 2004 and 2010 the percentage of staff stating in surveys that they were committed to the company increased from 77% to 88%, while the percentage of those stating that they are proud to work for McDonald's went up from 60% to 84%. Increased staff satisfaction was also reflected in the figures for employee turnover. The crude annual rate for staff working in McDonald's restaurants declined from 80.2% in 2004 to 37.9% in 2010. The ninety-day turnover rate, a measure of the number of new staff leaving within the first three months, stood at 24.5% in 2004, reflecting the tendency for people to have false expectations about what their jobs would involve and the number of unsuitable people that managers were hiring. By 2010 this had fallen to just 2.4%.

Questions

1 What other factors, aside from the introduction of these HR initiatives, might explain the striking reduction in staff turnover levels that McDonald's achieved between 2004 and 2010?

2 What other sorts of initiative might the company consider introducing in the future to further increase levels of employee engagement and retention?

3 What wider business advantages might accrue to the company as a result of its success in improving its reputation as an employer?

FURTHER READING

Despite being nearly twenty years old now, *Employee Turnover*, by Peter Hom and Rodger Griffeth (1995), remains by far the best source of information about academic research on turnover and staff retention issues. It is now out of print, but the same authors' more recent book, *Retaining Valued Employees* (2001), is available.

Resourcing and Talent Management by Stephen Taylor (2010) contains two chapters covering the practicalities of managing turnover and retention. There are detailed sections on measurement, costing, analysing the reasons for turnover and on the major steps that employers can take to reduce turnover levels. Key debates in the field are also covered.

Riccardo Peccei (2013) provides an excellent summary of the state of academic research into employee engagement, discussing in particular the ongoing thorny issue of defining the term adequately. Simon Albrecht's (2010) book of articles provides a much lengthier and more thorough treatment of the subject.

The McLeod Report (McLeod and Clark 2009) provides an excellent introduction to employee engagement, its potential benefits and how to achieve these in practice.

REFERENCES

Albrecht, S. (ed.) (2010) *Handbook of Employee Engagement: Perspectives, issues, research and practice*. Cheltenham: Edward Elgar.

Auer, P., Berg, J. and Coulibaly, I. (2004) *Is a Stable Workforce Good for the Economy? Insights into the tenure–productivity–employment relationship*. Geneva: International Labour Organization.

Bevan, S., Barber, L. and Robinson, D. (1997) *Keeping the Best: A practical guide to retaining key employees*. Brighton: Institute for Employment Research.

Black, C. (2008) *Working for a Healthier Tomorrow: Review of the health of Britain's working age population*. London: The Stationery Office.

Branham, L. (2005) *The Seven Hidden Reasons Employees Leave*. New York: The American Management Association.

Breaugh, J.A. (2008) 'Employee recruitment: Current knowledge and important areas for future research', *Human Resource Management Review*, Vol. 18, No. 3, pp. 103–18.

Cappelli, P. (2000) 'A market-driven approach to retaining talent', *Harvard Business Review*, January/February, pp. 103–11.

Carroll, M., Smith, M., Oliver, G. and Sung, S. (2008) 'Recruitment and retention in front-line services: The case of childcare', *Human Resource Management Journal*, Vol. 19, No. 1, pp. 59–74.

CIPD (2009) *Recruitment, Retention and Turnover: Annual survey report 2009*. London: Chartered Institute of Personnel and Development.

Conway, N. and Briner, R. (2005) *Understanding Psychological Contracts at Work: A critical evaluation of theory and research*. Oxford: Oxford University Press.

Daniels, K. (2010) 'Employee engagement', CIPD Factsheet, **www.cipd.co.uk**.

DiPietro, R., Thozhur, S. and Milman, A. (2007) 'Hourly employee retention factors in the United Kingdom quick service restaurant industry', *Journal of Foodservice Business Research*, Vol. 10, No. 4, pp. 39–61.

Gerhart, B. (2009) 'Compensation', in A. Wilkinson et al. (eds), *The Sage Handbook of Human Resource Management*. London: Sage.

Green, F., Felstead, A., Mayhew, K. and Pick, A. (2000) 'The impact of training on labour mobility: Individual and firm-level evidence from Britain', *British Journal of Industrial Relations*, Vol. 38, No. 2, pp. 261–75.

Gregg, P. and Wadsworth, J. (1999) 'Job tenure, 1975–98', in P. Gregg and J. Wadsworth (eds), *The State of Working Britain*. Manchester: Manchester University Press.

Griffeth, R.W. and Hom, P.W. (2001) *Retaining Valued Empolyees*. Thousand Oaks, CA: Sage.

Harter, J., Schmitdt, F.L. and Hayes, T.L. (2002) 'Business-unit-level relationship between employee satisfaction, employee engagement and business outcomes: A meta-analysis', *Journal of Applied Psychology*, Vol. 87, No. 2, pp. 268–79.

Herzberg, F. (1966) *Work and the Nature of Man*. Cleveland, OH: World Publishing.

Hom, P. and Griffeth, R. (1995) *Employee Turnover*. Cincinnati, OH: South Western College Publishing.

IRS (1999) 'Benchmarking labour turnover: Annual guide', *Employee Development Bulletin*, No. 118, October.

Kahn, W. (1990) 'Psychological conditions of personal engagement and disengagement at work', *Academy of Management Journal*, Vol. 33, pp. 692–724.

Leiter, M. and Bakker, A. (2010) 'Work engagement: Introduction', in A. Bakker and M. Leiter (eds), *Work Engagement: A handbook of essential theory and research*. New York: The Psychology Press.

MacLeod, D. and Clarke, N. (2009) *Engaging for Success: Enhancing performance through employee engagement. A report to government*. London: Department for Business, Innovation and Skills.

Peccei, R. (2013) 'Employee engagement: An evidence-based review', in S. Bach and M. Edwards (eds), *Managing Human Resources*, 5th edn. Chichester: Wiley.

Ritzer, G. (1996) *The McDonaldization of Society: An investigation into the changing character of contemporary social life*, rev. edn. Thousand Oaks, CA: Pine Forge.

Rousseau, D.M. (1989) 'Psychological and implied contracts in organizations', *Employee Responsibility and Rights Journal*, Vol. 2, pp. 121–39.

Samuel, M. and Chipunza, C. (2009) 'Employee retention and turnover: Using motivational variables as a panacea', *African Journal of Business and Management*, Vol. 3, No. 8, pp. 410–15.

Seligman, M. (2003) *Authentic Happiness: Using the new positive psychology to realise your potential for lasting fulfilment*. London: Nicholas Brealey.

Stairs, M. and Gilpin, M. (2010) 'Positive Engagement: From employee engagement to workplace happiness', in A. Linley *et al.*, *Oxford Handbook of Positive Psychology and Work*. Oxford: Oxford University Press.

Sturges, J. and Guest, D. (1999) *Shall I Stay or Should I Go?* Warwick: Association of Graduate Recruiters.

Taylor, S. (2002) *The Employee Retention Handbook*. London: CIPD.

Taylor, S. (2010) *Resourcing and Talent Management*. London: CIPD.

Towers Perrin–ISR (2006) *The ISR Employee Engagement Report*. London: Towers Perrin.

Truss, C., Soane, E., Edwards, C., Wisdom, K., Croll, A. and Burnett, J. (2006) *Working Life: Employee attitudes and engagement 2006*. London: CIPD.

Waddell, G. and Burton, A. (2006) *Is Work Good for Your Health and Well Being?* London: The Stationery Office.

Wanous, J.P. (1992) *Organizational Entry*. Reading, MA: Addison-Wesley.

White, G. (2009) 'Determining pay', in G. White and J. Druker (eds), *Reward Management: A critical text*, 2nd edn. London: Routledge.

Chapter 9

ENDING THE CONTRACT

THE OBJECTIVES OF THIS CHAPTER ARE TO:

1 Outline the framework in which the law of unfair dismissal operates in the UK

2 Set out the major reasons for which an employer can and cannot lawfully dismiss employees

3 Explain the concept of 'reasonableness' in unfair dismissal cases and its significance

4 Review the law on dismissals on grounds of capability, misconduct and redundancy

5 Describe the operation of the law of constructive dismissal and the law of wrongful dismissal

In the previous chapter we looked at situations in which employees decide to end their contracts of employment by giving their employers notice. Here we focus on circumstances when the contract is brought to an end by the employer through a dismissal of one kind or another, something that close to half a million employees experience in the UK each year (DBIS 2012: 23). In some cases employees are happy to leave (or at least not unhappy) such as when they are retiring or when they are due to receive a large redundancy payment. In others their dismissal is neither unexpected nor even necessarily unwelcomed, such as when a fixed-term contract comes to an end. A good proportion of dismissals are thus entirely uncontentious. However, when people who have been dismissed are unhappy and perceive either that the manner of the dismissal or that the reason for it were unlawful, they can take their case to an employment tribunal. In practice, around one in seven of all dismissed workers who qualify do bring such claims (Knight and Latreille 2000), leaving the Employment Tribunal Service to deal with 40,000–50,000 cases each year (Employment Tribunal Service 2012). If someone wins their case they may ask to be reinstated, but will usually settle for a compensation payment. The size of such awards is not generally substantial (around £9,000 on average), but occasionally people are awarded larger sums. Whatever the final outcome, there are often additional legal costs for the employer to bear, not to mention the loss of a great deal of management time. An organisation's reputation as a good employer can also be damaged by adverse publicity arising from such cases. Employers generally take careful account of the requirements of the law when dismissing employees. The alternative is to run the risk of being summoned to an employment tribunal and possibly losing the case or being required to reach a financial settlement with the ex-employee that is large enough to deter further legal action. To a great extent the law therefore effectively determines practice in the field of dismissal.

In the UK there are three forms of dismissal claim that can be brought to a tribunal. Rights associated with the law of wrongful dismissal are the longest established. A person who claims wrongful dismissal complains that the way they were dismissed breached the terms of their contract of employment. Constructive dismissal occurs when someone feels forced to resign as a direct result of their employer's actions. In this area the law aims to deter employers from seeking to avoid dismissing people by pushing them into resignation. The third category, unfair dismissal, is by far the most common. It is best defined as a dismissal which falls short of the expectations of the law as laid down in the Employment Rights Act 1996.

Unfair dismissal

The law of unfair dismissal dates from 1971, since when it has been amended a number of times. Although new additions and the outcomes of leading cases have made it more complex than it was originally, the basic principles have stood the test of time and remain in place. In most circumstances the right to bring a claim of unfair dismissal applies to employees who have completed a year's continuous service with their employer on the date their contract was terminated. However, due to a recent amendment in the law, people whose employment started after 6 April 2012 have to wait for two years before they gain unfair dismissal rights. These probation periods allow employers a period of time to assess whether or not an individual employee is suitable before the freedom to dismiss is restricted. The restrictions on qualification apply except where the reason for the dismissal is one of those listed below, which are classed as 'automatically unfair' or 'inadmissible'. A further requirement is that the claim form is lodged at the tribunal office before three months have elapsed from the date of dismissal. Unless there are circumstances justifying the failure to submit a claim before the deadline, claims received after three months are ruled out of time.

Before a case comes to a tribunal, officers of the Advisory, Conciliation and Arbitration Service (ACAS) will often try to help the parties reach a settlement. The papers of all cases lodged with the employment tribunal's offices are sent to ACAS with a view to conciliation taking place ahead of a tribunal hearing. In part as a result of ACAS conciliation, a majority of cases either get settled or are withdrawn without the need for the parties to attend a full tribunal hearing. ACAS also offers an alternative arbitration method of resolving unfair dismissal claims. Where both sides agree, they can opt to have their case heard outside of the judicial system by ACAS officials whose aim is to conciliate a mutually acceptable settlement. If none can be agreed the arbitrator makes a binding judgment, but only after trying hard to settle the case satisfactorily. This alternative system has not been taken up by many. Employers and employees, so it seems, prefer to have their cases settled in court by a panel led by an employment judge.

When faced with a claim of unfair dismissal, and where it is not disputed that a dismissal took place, an employment tribunal asks two separate questions:

1 Was the reason for the dismissal one which is classed by the law as legitimate?

2 Did the employer act reasonably in carrying out the dismissal?

Where the answer to the first question is 'no', there is no need to ask the second because the dismissed employee will already have won his or her case. Interestingly the burden of proof shifts as the tribunal moves from considering the first to the second question. It is for the employer to satisfy the tribunal that it dismissed the employee for a legitimate reason. The burden of proof then becomes neutral when the question of reasonableness is addressed.

ACTIVITY 9.1

Consider the working activities of some of your colleagues (and perhaps your own working activities). What examples are there of behaviour that you feel justify dismissal? Make a list of your ideas and check them when you have finished this chapter and see how many might be classified by a tribunal as unfair dismissals.

Automatically unfair reasons

Certain reasons for dismissal are declared in law to be inadmissible or automatically unfair. Where the tribunal finds that one of these was the principal reason for the dismissal, it will find in favour of the claimant (i.e. the ex-employee) whatever the circumstances of the case. In practice, therefore, there is no defence that an employer can make to explain its actions that will be acceptable to the tribunal. Moreover, the one year/two years' service requirement does not apply, so all employees can bring cases from the first day of employment. Some of the automatically unfair reasons relate to other areas of employment law such as non-discrimination, working time and the minimum wage, which we discuss in more detail later (see Chapter 18). In 2013 the list of automatically unfair reasons for dismissal was as follows:

- Dismissal for a reason relating to pregnancy or maternity.
- Dismissal for a health and safety reason (e.g. refusing to work in unsafe conditions).
- Dismissal because of a spent conviction.
- Dismissal for refusing to work on a Sunday (retail and betting workers only).
- Dismissal for a trade union reason.
- Dismissal for taking official industrial action (during the first twelve weeks of the action).
- Dismissal in contravention of the part-time workers' or fixed-term employees' regulations.
- Dismissal for undertaking duties as an occupational pension fund trustee, employee representative, member of a European Works Council or in connection with jury service.
- Dismissal for asserting a statutory right (including rights exercised under the Employment Rights Act, as well as those connected with the Working Time Regulations, the National Minimum Wage Regulations, the Public Interest Disclosure Act and the Information and Consultation of Employees Regulations; the right to request flexible working, the right to time off for dependants, the right to adoptive, parental or paternity leave, the right to be accompanied at disciplinary and grievance hearings and the claiming of working tax credits).

Potentially fair reasons

From an employer's perspective it is important to be able to satisfy the tribunal that the true reason for the dismissal was one of those reasons classed as potentially fair in unfair dismissal law. Only once this has been achieved can the second question (the issue of reasonableness) be addressed. The potentially fair grounds for dismissal are as follows:

- Lack of capability or qualifications: if an employee lacks the skill, aptitude or physical health to carry out the job, then there is a potentially fair ground for dismissal.
- Misconduct: this category covers the range of behaviours that we examine in considering the grievance and discipline processes: disobedience, absence, insubordination and criminal acts. It can also include taking industrial action.
- Redundancy: where an employee's job ceases to exist, it is potentially fair to dismiss the employee for redundancy.
- Statutory bar: when employees cannot continue to discharge their duties without breaking the law, they can be fairly dismissed. Most cases of this kind follow disqualification of drivers following convictions for speeding, drunk or dangerous driving. Other common cases involve foreign nationals whose work permits have been terminated.
- Some other substantial reason: this most intangible category is introduced in order to cater for genuinely fair dismissals for reasons so diverse that they could not realistically be listed. Examples have been security of commercial information (where an employee's husband set up a rival company) or employee refusal to accept altered working conditions.
- Dismissals arising from official industrial action after twelve weeks have passed.
- Dismissals that occur on the transfer of an undertaking where a valid ETO (Economic, Technological or Organisational) reason applies.

Determining reasonableness

Having decided that potentially fair grounds for the dismissal exist, the tribunal then proceeds to consider whether the dismissal is fair in the circumstances. The test used by the tribunal in reaching decisions about the fairness of a dismissal is that of the reasonable employer. Tribunal members are not required to judge cases on the basis of what they would have done in the circumstances or what the best employers would have done. Instead they have to ask themselves whether what the employer did in the circumstances of the time fell within a possible band of reasonable responses. In practice this means that the employer wins the case if it can show that the decision to dismiss was one that a reasonable employer *might* conceivably have taken.

In assessing reasonableness tribunals always take a particular interest in the procedure that was used. They are also keen to satisfy themselves that the employer has acted broadly consistently in its treatment of different employees and that it has taken into account any mitigating circumstances that might have explained a deterioration in an employee's conduct or performance. In addition, they are required to have regard to the size and resources of the employer concerned. Higher standards are thus expected of a large PLC or a public sector body with a well-staffed HR department than of a small owner-managed business employing a handful of people. The former, for example, might be expected to wait for several months before dismissing someone on grounds of ill health, while a small business could justify dismissing after a few weeks because of the operational difficulties the absence was causing.

The significance attached to procedure has varied over the years. At present the judgment of the House of Lords in the case of *Polkey* v. *AE Dayton Services* (1987) applies. Since then, with the exception of a brief period between 2004 and 2009, tribunals have been obliged to find dismissals unfair where the employer had not completed a proper procedure before making the final decision to dismiss. Any major procedural deficiency thus renders a dismissal unfair in law, whatever the outcome might have been had these procedures been followed. Employers are therefore obliged to follow any procedures they have themselves devised in addition to the minimum standard set out by ACAS in its code of practice.

In this book we have separated the consideration of discipline from the consideration of dismissal in order to concentrate on the practical aspects of discipline (putting things right) rather than the negative aspects (getting rid of the problem). The two cannot, however, be separated in practice and the question of dismissal needs to be reviewed in light of the material to be presented later (see Chapter 20).

WINDOW ON PRACTICE

In recent years the Employment Appeals Tribunal (EAT), the court that hears appeals of cases decided in employment tribunals, has made a number of controversial judgments in dismissal cases which remind us of how employer friendly unfair dismissal law is, provided procedures are followed correctly before a dismissal takes place.

In *Weston Recovery Services* v. *Fisher* (2010) a tribunal found that a claimant should not have been dismissed on grounds of gross misconduct when he had failed properly to secure some seats in a minibus after he had borrowed it to drive to France on holiday.

In *Look Ahead Housing & Care Ltd* v. *Rudder* (2010) an employee was overheard by a client making a discriminatory remark. There had been no consideration by the employer of whether an alternative sanction short of dismissal might have been more appropriate. Managers had simply dismissed on grounds of gross misconduct following a disciplinary hearing. So the tribunal found the dismissal to be unfair.

In *Quadrant Catering* v. *Smith* (2011) the claimant had sworn in the presence of a manager, there being some doubt about whether her words had been directed at the manager. Here the tribunal ruled that dismissal on grounds of gross misconduct was too harsh a sanction in the circumstances and stated that it should be a last resort and not a first resort.

In *Wincanton Group* v. *Stone* (2011) a driver was dismissed on grounds of misconduct. According to the employer, the dismissal was justified despite his breach of the rules being relatively minor because he had already been given a formal warning following another unrelated incident. The first warning was at the time of his dismissal the subject of an ongoing appeal. The EAT found the dismissal unfair, mainly because

it considered the incidents to be too trivial to justify dismissal.

In all these cases the EAT said that the tribunals had misapplied the law by substituting their own views as to what it would have been reasonable for the employer to have done. That is not the job of an employment tribunal. If the facts are clear, a proper procedure has been carried out, and it is the genuine belief of the employer that the employee is guilty of misconduct, the employer has the right to dismiss. It may be harsh, but if the decision to dismiss falls into the band of possible reasonable responses, then the dismissal should be found to have been fair in law.

Lack of capability

A common reason for dismissal is poor performance on the part of an employee. The law permits dismissals for this reason. It also allows employers to determine for themselves what constitutes an acceptable level of performance in a job, provided of course that a broadly consistent approach is followed between different employees. However, such dismissals are only considered to be reasonable (and hence fair in law) if the employee concerned has both been formally warned about his or her poor performance at least once and given a reasonable opportunity to improve. Formality in this context means that a formal hearing has been held at which the employee has been entitled to be represented and after which there has been a right of appeal to a more senior manager.

The employer will always need to demonstrate the employee's unsuitability to the satisfaction of the tribunal by producing evidence of that unsuitability. This evidence must not be undermined by, for instance, giving the employee a glowing testimonial at the time of dismissal or by the presence of positive appraisal reports on the individual's personal file. Lack of skill or aptitude is a fair ground when the lack can be demonstrated and where the employer has not contributed to it by, for instance, ignoring it for a long period. Redeployment to a more suitable job is also an option that employers are expected to consider before taking the decision to dismiss.

The requirement on employers to warn an employee formally that his or her performance is unsatisfactory at a meeting at which the employee has the opportunity to answer back, and the subsequent requirement to give the employee concerned support during a reasonable period in which he or she has an opportunity to improve, mean that dismissals on grounds of poor performance can take several weeks or months to carry through. Moreover, during this time relationships can become very strained because formal action has been taken and a formal warning given. For these reasons managers often seek to avoid dismissing in line with the expectations of the law, instead seeking to dress up poor performance dismissals as redundancies or cases of gross misconduct. However, employment tribunals are very aware of this tendency and always find dismissals that occur in such circumstances to be unfair.

Another aspect of employee capability is health. It is potentially fair to dismiss someone on the grounds of ill health which renders the employee incapable of discharging the contract of employment. Even the most distressing dismissal can be legally admissible, provided that it is not too hasty and that there is consideration of alternative employment.

Employers are expected, however, to take account of any medical advice available to them before dismissing someone on the grounds of ill health. Companies with occupational health services are well placed to obtain detailed medical reports to help in such judgements but the decision to terminate someone's employment is ultimately for the manager to take and, if necessary, to justify at a tribunal. Medical evidence will be sought and has to be carefully considered, but dismissal remains an employer's decision taken on managerial grounds, not a medical decision.

Normally, absences through sickness have to be frequent or prolonged in order for dismissal on the grounds of such absence to be judged fair, although absence which seriously interferes with the running of a business may be judged fair even if it is neither frequent nor prolonged. In all cases the employee must be consulted and effectively warned before being dismissed. In the leading case of *Egg Stores* v. *Leibovici* (1977) the EAT set out nine questions that have to be asked to determine the potential fairness of dismissing someone after long-term sickness:

(a) how long has the employment lasted; (b) how long had it been expected the employment would continue; (c) what is the nature of the job; (d) what was the nature, effect and length of the illness; (e) what is the need of the employer for the work to be done, and to engage a replacement to do it; (f) if the employer takes no action, will he incur obligations in respect of redundancy payments or compensation for unfair dismissal; (g) are wages continuing to be paid; (h) why has the employer dismissed (or failed to do so); and (i) in all the circumstances, could a reasonable employer have been expected to wait any longer?

A different situation is where an employee is frequently absent for short spells. Here too it is potentially reasonable to dismiss, but only after proper consideration of the illnesses and after warning the employee of the consequences if his or her attendance record does not improve. Each case has to be decided on its own merits. Medical evidence must be sought and a judgement reached about how likely it is that high levels of absence will continue in the future. The fact that an employee is wholly fit at the time of his or her dismissal does not mean that it is necessarily unfair. What matters is the overall attendance record and its impact on the organisation.

In another leading case, that of *International Sports Ltd* v. *Thomson* (1980), the employer dismissed an employee who had been frequently absent with a series of minor ailments ranging from althrugia of one knee, anxiety and nerves to bronchitis, cystitis, dizzy spells, dyspepsia and flatulence. All of these were covered by medical notes. (While pondering the medical note for flatulence, you will be interested to know that althrugia is water on the knee.) The employer issued a series of warnings and the company dismissed the employee after consulting its medical adviser, who saw no reason to examine the employee as the illnesses had no connecting medical theme and were not chronic. The EAT held that this dismissal was fair because proper warning had been given and because the attendance record was deemed so poor as not to be acceptable to a reasonable employer. This position was confirmed by the Court of Appeal in *Wilson* v. *The Post Office* (2000) where it was held to be quite acceptable, in principle, for an employer to dismiss someone simply because of a poor absence record.

The law on ill-health dismissals was affected in important ways by the passing of the Disability Discrimination Act 1995 (now part of the Equality Act 2010). We will look at this important area of legislation in detail later (see Chapter 18). Here it is simply necessary to state that dismissing someone who is disabled according to the definition given in the Equality Act, without first considering whether adjustments to working practices or the working environment would allow them to continue working, is unlawful. Reasonable adjustments might well include tolerance of a relatively high level of absence, especially where the employer is large enough to be able to cope perfectly well in the circumstances. Employers are well advised to pay particular attention to disability discrimination issues when dismissing people on the grounds of ill health because the level of compensation that can be awarded by tribunals in such cases is considerably higher than it is for unfair dismissal. In practice we now have a situation in which two bodies of law (unfair dismissal and disability discrimination) cover ill-health dismissals. Care needs to be taken to adhere to the requirements of both.

ACTIVITY 9.2

Some American companies evaluate the individual performance of all their employees each year and use the scores to rank everyone in a particular department or division. They then fire the bottom 10% as a matter of policy. The approach is known as 'stack ranking'. Can you explain why such an approach would be unlawful in the UK? Should it be made lawful or remain unlawful?

Misconduct

The law expects employers to make a distinction between two classes of misconduct when dismissing employees or considering doing so. Misconduct is defined as a breach of the employers' rules:

1 **Gross misconduct.** This occurs when an employee commits an offence which is sufficiently serious to justify summary dismissal. To qualify, the employee must have acted in such a way as to have breached either an express term of his or her contract or one of the common law duties owed by an employee to an employer (see Chapter 18). In practice this means that the employee's actions must be 'intolerable' for any reasonable employer to put up with.

2 **Ordinary misconduct.** This involves lesser transgressions, such as minor breaches of rules and relatively insignificant acts of disobedience, insubordination, lateness, forgetfulness or rudeness. In such cases the employer is deemed by the courts to be acting unreasonably if it dismisses as a result of a first offence. The dismissal would only be fair if, having been formally warned at least once, the employee failed to improve his or her conduct.

Employers have a wide degree of discretion when it comes to deciding what exactly does and does not constitute gross misconduct, and this will vary from workplace to workplace. For example, a distinction can be made between uttering an obscene swearword in front of colleagues (ordinary misconduct) and swearing obscenely at a customer (gross misconduct). While much depends on the circumstances, the tribunals also look carefully at an employer's established policies on matters of conduct.

Where the disciplinary rules spell out clearly the type of conduct that will warrant dismissal then a dismissal for this reason may be fair. Conversely, if the rules are silent or ambiguous as to whether particular conduct warrants dismissal, a dismissal for a first offence may be unfair. It is important, therefore, for employers to set out in writing what standards of conduct they expect, to make clear what will be regarded as 'sackable misconduct', and to ensure that everyone is aware of these rules.

The second key principle in misconduct cases concerns procedure. Whether the individual is dismissed summarily for gross misconduct or after a number of warnings for ordinary misconduct, the tribunals look to see if a reasonable procedure has been used and satisfy themselves that the employer has followed any of its own procedures which go beyond the minimum standard set out in the ACAS code of practice. They thus ask questions such as the following:

- Was the accusation thoroughly, promptly and properly investigated by managers before the decision was made to dismiss or issue a formal warning?
- Was a formal hearing held at which the accused employee was given the opportunity to state his or her case and challenge evidence brought forward by managers?
- Was the employee concerned permitted to be represented at the hearing by a colleague or trade union representative?
- Was the employee treated consistently when compared with other employees who had committed similar acts of misconduct in the past?

Only if the answers to all these questions are 'yes' will a tribunal find a dismissal fair. Tribunals do not, however, expect employers to adhere to very high standards of evidence gathering such as those employed by the police in criminal investigations. Here, as throughout employment law, the requirement is for the employer to act reasonably in all the circumstances, conforming to the principles of natural justice and doing what it thought to be right at the time, given the available facts.

WINDOW ON PRACTICE

In recent years employment tribunals have had to come to grips with a new type of dismissal case: situations in which people are dismissed for downloading and storing pornographic images from the Internet. Tribunals have had to consider whether or not such actions constitute gross misconduct (leading to summary dismissal without notice), or whether they should be considered as ordinary misconduct, in which case summary dismissal for a first offence would be regarded as being unfair.

Cases have been decided in different ways depending on the clarity of established rules and procedural matters. In *Parr* v. *Derwentside District Council* (1998), Mr Parr was summarily dismissed having been caught by his employers accessing pornography from his computer while at work. He claimed that he had visited the site concerned by accident, had got himself stuck in it and had subsequently 'revisited it only because he was disturbed by the prospect that entry could easily be made by children'. His claim for unfair dismissal failed because the employers had used a fair procedure and because they were able to show that Mr Parr had broken established codes of conduct.

By contrast, in *Dunn* v. *IBM UK Ltd* (1998), a summary dismissal occurring in similar circumstances was found to fall outside the 'band of reasonable responses'. In this case the employers were found not to have investigated the matter properly and not to have convened a fair disciplinary hearing, the whole matter having been handled far too hastily. Moreover, there was no company policy on Internet usage for Mr Dunn to have broken and he was unaware that he had done anything that would be construed as gross misconduct. He won his case, but had his compensation reduced by 50% on the grounds that he was partly responsible for his own dismissal.

In a third case, *Humphries* v. *VH Barnett & Co* (1998), a tribunal stated that in normal circumstances the act of accessing pornography from the Internet while at work should not be construed as gross misconduct unless such a policy was made clear to employees and established as a workplace rule. However, in this case, the tribunal decided that the pictures downloaded were so obscene that Mr Humphries could be legitimately treated as having committed an act of gross misconduct.

Source: IDS (1999) 'Downloading pornography', *IDS Brief 637*, May.

Redundancy

Dismissal for redundancy is protected by compensation for unfair redundancy, compensation for genuine redundancy and the right to consultation before the redundancy takes place:

An employee who is dismissed shall be taken to be dismissed by reason of redundancy if the dismissal is attributable wholly or mainly to:

the fact that his employer has ceased, or intends to cease, to carry on the business for the purposes of which the employee was employed by him, or has ceased, or intends to cease, to carry on that business in the place where the employee was so employed,

or

the fact that the requirements of that business for employees to carry out work of a particular kind, or for employees to carry out work of a particular kind in the place where he was so employed, have ceased or are expected to cease or diminish. (Employment Rights Act 1996, s. 139(1))

Apart from certain specialised groups of employees, anyone who has been continuously employed for two years or more is guaranteed a compensation payment from an employer, if dismissed for redundancy. The compensation is assessed on a sliding scale relating to length of service, age and rate of pay per week. If the employer wishes to escape the obligation to compensate, then it is necessary to show that the reason for dismissal was something other than redundancy. The inclusion of age in the criteria for calculating redundancy payments has remained, despite the introduction of age discrimination law in 2006.

Although the legal rights relating to redundancy have not altered for almost forty years, there have been persistent problems of interpretation, different courts reaching different decisions when faced with similar sets of circumstances (see IRS 2000). In 1999 the House of Lords provided some long-needed clarification of key issues in the cases of *Murray et al.* v. *Foyle Meats Ltd*, where it was decided that tribunals should look at the actual facts of someone's working situation rather than at their written contractual terms when deciding whether or not their jobs were redundant. In so doing it confirmed that the practice of 'bumping', where the employer dismisses a person whose job is remaining to retain the services of another employee whose job is disappearing, is acceptable under the statutory definition. The questions laid out by the EAT in *Safeway* v. *Burrell* (1997) are thus now confirmed as those that tribunals should ask when considering these cases:

- Has the employee been dismissed?
- Has there been an actual or prospective cessation or diminution in the requirements for employees to carry out work of a particular kind?
- Is the dismissal wholly or mainly attributable to the state of affairs?

The employer has to consult with the individual employee before dismissal takes place, but there is also a separate legal obligation to consult with recognised trade unions or some other body of employee representatives where no union is recognised. If twenty or more employees are to be made redundant, then the employer must give written notice of intention to any recognised unions concerned and the Department of Business,

Innovation and Science (DBIS) at least thirty days before the first dismissal. Having done this, the employer has a legal duty to consult on the redundancies. There is no obligation to negotiate with employees, merely to explain, listen to comments and reply with reasons. Employees also have the right to reasonable time off with pay during their redundancy notice so that they can seek other work.

One of the most difficult aspects of redundancy for the employer is the selection of who should go. The traditional approach provides that people should leave on a last-in–first-out basis, or LIFO, as this provides a rough-and-ready justice with which it is difficult to argue from the point of view of consistency. It frees the employer from any obligation to choose on grounds of merit and is also inexpensive as the people who leave are those entitled to the least compensation. It is, however, questionable whether a pure LIFO-based system could be justified under age discrimination law as the approach is clearly detrimental to younger staff. In *Rolls Royce* v. *Unite* (2009) the High Court ruled that a system which included length of service alongside other factors was justifiable in law when it had been agreed with a recognised trade union, but as yet (i.e. March 2013) there has been no definitive ruling on the general question of whether or not a system that is based entirely on the LIFO principle can be justified.

In any event employers have tended to prefer other selection schemes in recent years. The preference nowadays is for one of two alternative types of approach:

- A matrix-type system in which a mix of criteria is used to score employees. Typically these include factors such as performance, qualifications, competency, future potential and attendance records.

- A selection-based system in which a new post-redundancy organisation structure is drawn up. Employees are then invited to apply for the jobs that will remain.

Increasingly, employers are trying to avoid enforced redundancy by a range of strategies, such as not replacing people who leave, early retirement and voluntary redundancy. It is also much more common than was the case in the past for employees to agree to work shorter hours or to take pay cuts as part of a deal to minimise redundancies or even avoid them altogether. Employers are also tending to make the management of redundancy more palatable by appointing specialist redundancy counsellors or outplacement consultants to advise people who are at risk of redundancy about how to secure new jobs or access training. Contrary to some popular perception, there is no legal requirement to offer such services or to ask for volunteers before carrying through a programme of compulsory redundancies.

WINDOW ON PRACTICE

Packman Lucas Associates v. *Fauchon* (2012) [IRLR 721]

This case was about whether or not a reduction in hours in the absence of any accompanying reduction in headcount represents a 'diminution of work' as defined in redundancy law and can thus give rise to a redundancy situation. According to the EAT the answer is yes.

Mrs Fauchon was asked to work reduced hours and refused. She was therefore dismissed. She argued that while there had been no reduction in the number of employees at Packman, there had nonetheless been a redundancy situation because there was 'a reduced need for employees to carry out work of a particular kind'. In dismissing her for this reason her employers had therefore made her redundant and she was entitled to a redundancy payment. The EAT agreed with her.

Some other substantial reason

As the law of unfair dismissal has evolved since 1971 one of the most controversial areas has been the category of potentially fair dismissals known as 'some other substantial reason'. Many commentators see this as a catch-all or dustbin category which enables employers to dismiss virtually anyone provided a satisfactory business case can be made. All manner of cases have been successfully defended under this heading including the following: dismissals resulting from personality clashes, pressure to dismiss from subordinates or customers, disclosure of damaging information, the dismissal of a man whose wife worked for a rival firm, and the dismissal of a landlord's wife following her husband's dismissal on grounds of capability.

The majority of cases brought under this heading, however, result from business reorganisations where there is no redundancy. These often occur when the employer seeks to alter terms and conditions of employment and cannot secure the employee's agreement. Such circumstances can result in the dismissal of the employee together with an offer of re-employment on new contractual terms. Such dismissals are judged fair provided a sound business reason exists to justify the changes envisaged. It will usually be necessary to consult prior to the reorganisation but the tribunal will not base its judgment on whether the employee acted reasonably in refusing new terms and conditions. The test laid down in *Hollister v. The National Farmers' Union* (1979) by the Court of Appeal merely requires the employer to demonstrate that the change would bring clear organisational advantage.

Written statement of reasons

The Employment Rights Act 1996 (s. 92) gives employees the right to obtain from their employer a written statement of the reasons for their dismissal if they are dismissed after completing a year's continuous service. If asked, the employer must provide the statement within fourteen days. If it is not provided, the employee can complain to an employment tribunal that the statement has been refused and the tribunal will award the employee two weeks' pay if it finds the complaint justified. The same right applies where a fixed-term contract of more than a year's duration is not renewed after having expired. The employee can also complain, and receive the same award, if the employer's reasons are untrue or inadequate, provided that the tribunal agrees.

Such an award is in addition to anything the tribunal may decide about the unfairness of the dismissal, if the employee complains about that. The main purpose of this provision is to enable the employee to test whether there is a reasonable case for an unfair dismissal complaint or not. Although the statement is admissible as evidence in tribunal proceedings, the tribunal will not necessarily be bound by what the statement contains. If the tribunal members were to decide that the reasons for dismissal were other than stated, then the management case would be jeopardised.

Constructive dismissal

When the conduct of the employer causes an employee to resign, the ex-employee may still be able to claim dismissal on the grounds that the behaviour of the employer constituted a repudiation of the contract, leaving the employee with no alternative but to resign. The employee may then be able to claim that the dismissal was unfair. It is not sufficient for the employer simply to be awkward or whimsical; the employer's conduct must amount to a significant breach, going to the root of the contract, such as physical assault, demotion, reduction in pay, change in location of work or significant change in duties. The breach must, however, be significant, so that a slight lateness in paying wages would not involve a breach, neither would a temporary change in place of work.

Some of the more interesting constructive dismissal cases concern claims that implied terms of contract have been breached, such as the employer's duty to maintain safe systems of working or a relationship of mutual trust and confidence.

WINDOW ON PRACTICE

A former manager of an off-licence called Mrs Gullyes won a case of constructive dismissal. She argued successfully that her employer had breached an implied term of her contract and that this had led directly to her resignation.

At the time of her resignation, Mrs Gullyes had been employed as a branch manager for four years – a job she carried out with conspicuous success. As a result she had been promoted into a manager's role in a larger branch with severe staffing problems. She accepted the new post with some reluctance after agreeing with the company that she could transfer again if things did not work out.

She found the new job hard from the start, finding herself working seventy-six hours a week and gaining insufficient help from other members of staff. After a few months she went away on holiday, returning to find that two of her staff had been transferred to other branches in her absence. At this point she requested a transfer herself and was refused. She resigned and brought a claim of constructive dismissal.

Mrs Gullyes won her case by arguing that the company had breached its common law duty to provide adequate support to her in the new job. The case was appealed to the EAT, where she won again.

Whitbread PLC/Thresher v. Gullyes (1994).

Constructive dismissal, like unfair dismissal, dates from 1971. It too only applies to employees who have completed a year's continuous service. The cases are harder for employees to win and easier for employers to defend because of the need to establish that a dismissal has taken place, before issues of reasonableness in the circumstances are addressed. The burden of proof is on the employee to show that he or she was forced into resigning as a result of a repudiatory breach on the part of the employer.

Compensation for dismissal

Having found in favour of the applicant in cases of unfair or constructive dismissal, the tribunal can make two types of decision: either it can order that the ex-employee be re-employed or it can award some financial compensation from the ex-employer for the loss that the employee has suffered. Originally it was intended that re-employment should be the main remedy, although this was not previously available under earlier legislation. In practice, however, the vast majority of ex-employees (over 98%) want compensation.

Tribunals will not order re-employment unless the dismissed employee wants it and it is considered reasonable for the employer to take the individual back. Tribunals can choose between reinstatement or re-engagement. In reinstatement the old job is given back to the employee under the same terms and conditions, plus any increments, etc., to which the individual would have become entitled had the dismissal not occurred, plus any arrears of payment that would have been received. The situation is just as it would have been, including all rights deriving from length of service, if the dismissal had not taken place. The alternative of re-engagement will be that the employee is employed afresh in a job comparable with the last one (usually in a different department), but without continuity of employment. Ultimately, though, no employer can ever be required to reinstate or re-engage. Even if a tribunal considers that it would be practicable and just in a particular case, the employer can refuse and opt instead to pay a higher level of compensation. In practice it is increasingly rare for re-employment orders to be made, compensation being awarded instead in the vast majority of cases.

Tribunals currently calculate the level of awards under three headings. First, there is the basic award which is based on the employee's age and length of service. It is calculated in the same way as statutory redundancy payments, and like them has not been changed following the introduction of age discrimination law:

- half a week's pay for every year of service below the age of 22;
- one week's pay for every year of service between the ages of 22 and 41;
- one and a half weeks' pay for every year of service over the age of 41.

The basic award is limited, however, because tribunals can only take into account a maximum of twenty years' service when calculating the figure to be awarded. A maximum weekly salary figure is also imposed by the Treasury. This was £450 in 2013. The maximum basic award that can be ordered is therefore £13,500. In many cases, of course, where the employee has only a few years' service the figure will be far lower. In addition a tribunal can also order compensation under the following headings:

- Compensatory awards take account of loss of earnings, pension rights, future earnings loss, etc. The maximum level in 2013 was £74,200.
- Additional awards are used when an employer fails to comply with an order of reinstatement or re-engagement. The maximum award is fifty-two weeks' pay, but also subject to a cap of £450 per week.

A tribunal can reduce the total level of compensation if it judges the individual concerned to have contributed to his or her own dismissal. For example, a dismissal on grounds of poor work performance may be found unfair because no procedure was followed and consequently no warnings given. This does not automatically entitle the ex-employee concerned to compensation based on the above formulae. If the tribunal judges the employee to have been 60% responsible for his or her own dismissal, the compensation will be reduced by 60%. Reductions are also made when the employer has failed to follow procedures fully, but in which the outcome would not have differed had the employer done so. If the tribunal concludes that the employee would have been made redundant or dismissed in any event, it reduces compensation accordingly. Further reductions are made if an ex-employee is judged not to have taken reasonable steps to mitigate his or her loss by applying for new jobs while waiting for the case to come to court.

ACTIVITY 9.3

In what circumstances do you think a dismissed employee might welcome reinstatement or re-engagement, and in what circumstances might the employer welcome it?

Wrongful dismissal

In addition to the body of legislation defining unfair and constructive dismissal, there is a long-standing common law right to damages for an employee who has been dismissed wrongfully.

Cases of wrongful dismissal are taken to employment tribunals where the claim is for less than £25,000; otherwise, they are taken to the County Court. These cases are concerned solely with alleged breaches of contract. Employees can thus only bring cases of wrongful dismissal against their employers when they believe their dismissal to have been unlawful according to the terms of their contract of employment. Wrongful dismissal can, therefore, be used when the employer has not given proper notice or if the dismissal is in breach of any clause or agreement incorporated into the contract. This remains a form of remedy that very few people use, but it could be useful to employees who do not have sufficient length of service to claim unfair dismissal and whose contracts include the right to a full disciplinary procedure. There may also be cases where a very highly paid employee might get higher damages in an ordinary court than the maximum that the tribunal can award.

WINDOW ON PRACTICE

In order to bring a claim of unfair dismissal ex-employees must have been employed continuously for at least twelve months by the organisation concerned when they are dismissed (twenty-four months if employed after 6 April 2012). As a result it is common for employers to dismiss people after eleven months' service (now twenty-three months') in the belief that they will never have to justify their actions in court. However, such approaches can backfire, as was shown in the case of *Raspin* v. *United News* (1999). Here the applicant brought a case of wrongful dismissal, basing the claim on the presence in the contract of employment of a disciplinary procedure. The EAT decided that had the employer fulfilled its contractual duties and dismissed the employee using the procedure, the date of the dismissal would have occurred after twelve months' service had been completed. In assessing compensation the matter was thus treated as if it was an unfair dismissal claim.

Notice

An employee qualifies for notice of dismissal on completion of four weeks of employment with an employer. At that time the employee is entitled to receive one week's notice. This remains constant until the employee has completed two years' service, after which it increases to two weeks' notice, thereafter increasing on the basis of one week's notice per additional year of service up to a maximum of twelve weeks for twelve years' unbroken service with that employer. These are minimum statutory periods. If the employer includes longer periods of notice in the contract, which is quite common with senior employees, then they are bound by the longer period.

The employee is required to give one week's notice after completing four weeks' service and this period does not increase as a statutory obligation. If an employee accepts a contract in which the period of notice to be given is longer, then that is binding, but the employer may have problems of enforcement if an employee is not willing to continue in employment for the longer period.

Neither party can withdraw notice unilaterally. The withdrawal will be effective only if the other party agrees. Therefore, if an employer gives notice to an employee and wishes later to withdraw it, this can be done only if the employee agrees to the contract of employment remaining in existence. Equally, employees cannot change their minds about resigning unless the employer agrees. Notice exists when a date has been specified. The statement 'We're going to wind up the business, so you will have to find another job' is not notice: it is a warning of intention.

SUMMARY PROPOSITIONS

9.1 Of the many dismissals that take place in a year, a minority are reported to tribunals and a small minority are found in favour of the ex-employee.

9.2 The main grounds on which an employee can be dismissed without the likelihood of an unfair dismissal claim are lack of capability, misconduct, redundancy, statutory bar and some other substantial reason.

9.3 If an employee is dismissed on one of the above grounds, the dismissal must still be procedurally acceptable and fair in the circumstances.

9.4 An employee who resigns as a result of unreasonable behaviour by the employer can claim constructive dismissal and, if successful, have the case treated as if he or she had in fact been dismissed.

9.5 Minimum notice periods, in most cases amounting to a week for every year of service, must be given when terminating employees' contracts.

GENERAL DISCUSSION TOPICS

1 If you were dismissed in circumstances that you regarded as legally unfair, would you prefer to seek satisfaction through ACAS conciliation or through a tribunal hearing? Why?

2 In some countries a dismissal cannot be made until *after* a tribunal hearing, so that its 'fairness' is decided before it takes effect. What do you see as the benefits and drawbacks of that system?

3 What changes would you make in the criteria for dismissal on the grounds of misconduct?

THEORY INTO PRACTICE

In some countries it is more common for organisations to dismiss people than in others and this is linked to the ease with which it is possible to terminate a contract legally. In a majority of jurisdictions, employees enjoy some protection against unfair dismissal along similar lines to the UK law. The principle of just cause applies, meaning that unless an employer has a good, genuine reason for dismissing someone, it is unlawful to terminate their contracts. However, compensation levels are rather lower in the UK than elsewhere in the world and nowhere else does a two-year waiting period apply before a claim of unfair dismissal can be brought.

In some countries, notably the USA, Canada, Switzerland and Denmark, it is easier and much less costly for an employer to dismiss employees. In the USA the principle of 'employment at will' applies, although it is often modified by the terms of individual contracts. This means that employees can be summarily fired quite lawfully 'for a good reason, a bad reason or no reason at all', however long their length of service and however unjust such a dismissal might be. Underpinning this approach is the idea that employers should be able to terminate a contract of employment in just the same way that an employee can. There is no need to give reasons and no need to pay any compensation beyond that which is set out in individual contracts.

More restrictive regimes than that of the UK apply in most western, industrialised countries. The most restrictive of all seems to be the long-established Dutch system that reserves major powers for the UWV-Werkbedriff. These are locally based officials who police employment regulations, and from whom permission must be sought before a contract of employment can legally be terminated. The process takes six weeks or so, during which time the employee must be paid. Dismissals that happen without permission are regarded in law as being void.

In the United Arab Emirates a very different dismissal regime has been set up. Here, most employees are foreign nationals or guest workers who have been imported on a temporary basis to work in the UAE's booming economy. The law treats UAE nationals wholly differently from overseas workers. The latter have relatively few employment rights and can be dismissed without a great deal of difficulty. By contrast there is a much greater range of restrictions placed on an employer's right to sack a UAE national. Furthermore, it is unlawful to dismiss a UAE national in most circumstances when someone from overseas is employed in a similar role by the same employer. As a result, when redundancies occur, employers are effectively obliged to fire their overseas workers first.

Source: Global Legal Group (2011).

Questions

1 What advantages might a government see in maintaining a regime in which employers can readily terminate contracts freely without needing to pay compensation?

2 What would be the main advantages and disadvantages in the UK if the Dutch, American or UAE approaches were to be adopted in place of existing unfair dismissal law?

3 How long should a new employee have to wait before he or she is entitled to bring a claim of unfair dismissal? Justify your answer.

FURTHER READING

Collins, H. (2004) *Nine Proposals for the Reform of the Law on Unfair Dismissal*. London: Institute of Employment Rights.

Davies, A.C.L. (2009) *Perspectives on Employment Law*, 2nd edn. Cambridge: Cambridge University Press.

Dickens, L., Jones, M., Weekes, B. and Hant, M. (1985) *Dismissed: A study of unfair dismissal and the industrial tribunal system*. Oxford: Blackwell.
These three publications provide thought-provoking introductions to the major debates about the law of unfair dismissal and how it might be reformed.

Blanpain, R. *et al.* (eds) (2012) *The Global Workplace: International and comparative employment labour law*. New York: Wolters Kluwer.
This is the best guide to the ways in which employment law varies across the world. It includes extensive material on dismissal law.

IDS (2010) *Unfair Dismissal*. London: Incomes Data Services.

Yew, J. (2005) *Dismissals, Law and Practice*. London: The Law Society.
These are the two most comprehensive, practical guides to the law of unfair dismissal. Both review the leading cases and deal with all the practical aspects of dismissing people lawfully.

REFERENCES

DBIS (2012) *Dealing with Dismissal and Compensated No Fault Dismissal for Micro Businesses: Call for evidence*. London: Department for Business, Innovation and Science.

Employment Tribunal Service (2012) *Annual Report*. London: The Stationery Office.

Global Legal Group (2011) *The International Comparative Legal Guide to Employment and Labour Law*. London: GLG.

IDS (1999) 'Downloading pornography', *IDS Brief 637*, May.

IDS (2010) *Unfair Dismissal*. London: Incomes Data Services.

IRS (2000) 'The (re)definition of redundancy', *Industrial Relations Law Bulletin*, No. 633, January.

Knight, K.G. and Latreille, P.L. (2000) 'Discipline, dismissals and complaints to employment tribunals', *British Journal of Industrial Relations*, Vol. 38, No. 4, p. 533.

LEGAL CASES

Dunn v. *IBM UK Ltd* (1998) *IDS Brief 637*, May 1999.
Egg Stores v. *Leibovici* [1977] ICR 260.
Hollister v. *The National Farmers' Union* [1979] ICR 542.
Humphries v. *VH Barnett & Co* (1998) *IDS Brief 637*, May 1999.
International Sports Ltd v. *Thomson* [1980] IRLR 340.
Look Ahead Housing & Care Ltd v. *Rudder* [2010] UKEAT/0163/10/JOJ.
Murray et al. v. *Foyle Meats Ltd* [1999] IRLR 562.
Packman Lucas Associates v. *Fauchon* [2012] IRLR 721.
Parr v. *Derwentside District Council* (1998) *IDS Brief 637*, May 1999.
Polkey v. *AE Dayton Services* [1987] ICR 142.
Quadrant Catering v. *Smith* [2010] UKEAT/0362/10/RN.
Raspin v. *United News* [1999] IRLR 9.
Rolls Royce v. *Unite* [2009] IRLR 49.
Safeway v. *Burrell* [1997] IRLR 200.
Weston Recovery Services v. *Fisher* [2010] UKEAT/0062/10/ZT.
Whitbread PLC/Thresher v. *Gullyes* [1994] EAT 478/92.
Wilson v. *The Post Office* [2000] IRLR 834.
Wincanton Group v. *Stone* [2011] UKEAT/0011/12.

Part 3

PERFORMANCE: SUCCESS THROUGH INDIVIDUAL AND COLLECTIVE ACHIEVEMENT

CHAPTERS

10 Employee performance management

11 Leadership

12 Managing attendance and absence

CHANGING TIMES
RESOURCING
PERFORMANCE

Strategy
Organisational
performance
Employee
performance
Leadership and
change
Absence/
attendance
Skills

It is no good having all the right people all in the right places if they are not delivering the goods. This part of the book starts with consideration of how to manage individual employee performance. It has been suggested that there has been a general change of emphasis in attitude to the contract between the parties, away from a contract *of employment* towards a contract *for performance*. We all have to perform effectively. A large part of achieving effective performance is getting the organisational processes right, but within the organisational framework there are the teams, groups and individuals who do the work. Also within that framework we have to understand what it is that motivates people to perform and deploy leadership skills that match those motivations. A key feature is the nature of leadership and how it is carried out effectively, especially in situations requiring change.

Performance management is an idea that has been developed to coordinate several features, especially targets, training, appraisal and payment, in order to deliver effectiveness. Also included here is the management of absence or of attendance. What is needed is not just managing processes which encourage people to attend, but also dealing with the problem of people being absent. These are separate issues, not simply alternative ways of wording the problem. At the end of each chapter, you will find a case study which will help you to put these ideas into context and explore them more thoroughly.

Chapter 10

EMPLOYEE PERFORMANCE MANAGEMENT

THE OBJECTIVES OF THIS CHAPTER ARE TO:

1 Clarify the nature and purpose of performance management and performance appraisal

2 Outline the characteristics of performance management systems

3 Explain the stages of a typical performance management system

4 Evaluate the impact of varying national contexts on performance management

5 Evaluate the effectiveness of performance management systems in improving individual and organisational performance

Managing individual performance in organisations has traditionally centred on assessing performance and allocating reward, with effective performance seen as the result of the interaction between individual ability and motivation. Increasingly, it is recognised that planning and enabling performance have a critical effect on individual performance, with performance goals and standards, appropriate resources, guidance and support from the individual's manager all being central. The words 'performance management' are sometimes used to imply organisational targets, frameworks like the balanced scorecard, measurements and metrics, with individual measures derived from these. This meaning of performance management has been described by Houldsworth (2004) as a harder 'performance improvement' approach compared with the softer developmental and motivational approaches to aligning the individual and the organisation, which she suggests equates to good management practice. We adopt this as a very helpful distinction and in this chapter focus on the softer approach to employees, covering aspects of the organisational measurement approach later (see Chapter 25). We begin by comparing and contrasting performance appraisal and performance management systems, before outlining the characteristics of a typical performance management system. We then consider in detail the component parts of performance management, drawing out their likely effectiveness in a range of national contexts. Finally we evaluate the effectiveness of performance management systems in improving individual and thus organisational performance.

Performance management or performance appraisal?

Performance appraisal systems have operated in many organisations since the 1950s and are distinct from performance management systems, which have changed (and broadened) the nature of performance appraisal (Fletcher 2001). Here we compare and contrast performance management and performance appraisal. Detailed definitions of each can be found in Aguinis and Pierce (2008) and Decramer *et al.* (2012).

Performance appraisal

Traditionally performance appraisal systems have provided a formalised process to review employee performance. They are centrally designed, usually by the HR function, and require each line manager to appraise the performance of staff, often in just one performance review meeting a year. Elaborate forms are completed as a record of the process, but these are not living documents. They are generally stored in the archives of the HR department, and the issue of performance is often then neglected until the next round of performance review meetings. In a survey (IRS 2005a), 146 of the 154 respondents used appraisal, and of the 146 respondents, of mixed size, but mainly large companies, 91% appraised all employees. But while performance appraisal has gradually been applied to wider groups of employees, beyond managers and professionals, there are concerns that appraisal systems are treated as an administrative exercise, are ineffective and do little to improve the future performance of employees.

Performance management systems

While many appraisal systems are still in existence and continue to be updated, performance management systems are increasingly seen as the way to manage employee performance. An appraisal/review process is incorporated into this but is distinct from a traditional appraisal system. We consider the performance appraisal interview later in the context of either an appraisal or a performance management system (see Part 8).

Aguinis and Pierce (2008: 139) provide a useful definition of performance management, stating that its essence is:

a continuous process of identifying, measuring, and developing the performance of individuals and teams and aligning performance with the strategic goals of the organisation.

A strategic approach is thus adopted in which there is an attempt to ensure that employee efforts are directed to the achievement of organisational goals. Attention is paid to both task *and* contextual performance. Contextual performance is often addressed via the use of competencies (Fletcher 2001) so that *how* something is achieved is as important as the results themselves. In this way, organisations seek to ensure long-term sustainable performance rather than quick wins which may damage ongoing business relationships. Employee development also becomes recognised as a key element of performance management and the emphasis is on an ongoing cycle of performance development. The system is line manager driven.

Many organisations now claim to operate performance management systems. CIPD (2005) reports that 87% of the organisations it surveyed operated a formal process to measure and manage performance. Of these 37% were new systems, demonstrating the increasing focus on the issue of performance. Originally a private-sector phenomenon, performance management has now spread to the public sector in many countries (Tuytens and Devos 2012; Decramer *et al.* 2012) in support of neo-liberal agendas which seek to operate sectors such as health and education using business principles. It is also a global phenomenon. Aguinis and Pierce (2008), for example, suggest that over 90% of the multinational companies surveyed across fifteen countries implemented a performance management system and that this figure also reflects practice in Australian companies. Emerging economies, such as India (Gupta and Kumar 2013), are also recognising its importance. Almost all research into performance management emanates, however, from a western context (Briscoe and Claus 2008) and there is limited understanding of how effective these systems might be in other national contexts. We consider the implications of this throughout the chapter.

WINDOW ON PRACTICE

Merrill Lynch moved away from its traditional performance appraisal system to implement a performance management system. Rather than a once-a-year conversation about performance, an ongoing dialogue between manager and employee was developed which was based around managers coaching their subordinates. Employees received regular feedback on progress against goals and personal development plans were established to support improved performance. The end-of-year review was changed to include feedback from a number of sources (360-degree feedback) and to emphasise a developmental focus. Feedback was also provided on the contribution that employee performance made to the achievement of organisational goals. Managers were trained in how to set objectives, coach and carry out appraisals. They are also supported by an intranet that provides information on the performance management system. The aim is to ensure that all employees knows what is expected of them, what development they will receive and how their performance will be judged and rewarded.

Source: Adapted from Aguinis and Pierce (2008).

Characteristics of performance management systems

A view is emerging of performance management which centres on 'dialogue', 'shared understanding', 'agreement' and 'mutual commitment', rather than rating for pay purposes. To this end organisations are increasingly suggesting that employees take more ownership of performance management (see Scott (2006) for a good example) and become involved in collecting self-assessment evidence throughout the year (IDS 2005). Many organisations do, however, try to achieve both development and reward outcomes, which may undermine the motivational outcomes of development-focused approaches that encourage time spent with the line manager and two-way communication. See the CIPD Factsheet (2012) for further information. Alternatively, where there is a measurement focus, performance management is seen as judgemental, a chance to assess and get rid of employees, emphasises control and getting more out of staff, raises false expectations and is a way to manage the salaries bill. (See Table 10.1.)

Table 10.1
Characteristics of performance management systems

- Top-down link between business objectives and individual objectives (compared with performance appraisal where there may be no objectives, or objectives not explicitly linked to business objectives)
- Line manager driven and owned (rather than being owned by the HR function, as typically with performance appraisal)
- A living document where performance and development plans, support and ongoing review are documented as work progresses, and prior to annual review (rather than an archived document retrieved at appraisal time to compare achievement with intentions)
- Performance is rewarded and reinforced

ACTIVITY 10.1

Think of the performance appraisal or performance management system at your place of work.

1 To what extent does it focus on development and to what extent does it focus on reward?

2 How, and how well, are each of these purposes achieved? Explain why this is.

3 What would you do to improve the system, and what impacts would these actions have?

In summary, performance management, as opposed to performance appraisal, provides strategic links to organisational objectives, provides ongoing feedback to improve performance and is a continuous process driven by management, rather than an annual event owned by HR (Aguinis and Pierce 2008). In this chapter, we discuss performance management systems. We use the term 'performance appraisal' to denote the review of performance comprised within these systems, *not* to describe traditional performance appraisal systems.

Theoretical bases of performance management

The conceptual foundation of performance management relies on a view that performance is more than ability and motivation. It is argued that clarity of goals is key in enabling the employee to understand what is expected and the order of priorities. In addition goals themselves are seen to provide motivation. This is based on goal-setting theory originally developed by Locke (1968) and further developed with practical applicability (Locke and Latham 1990). Research to date suggests that for goals to be motivating they must be sufficiently specific, challenging but not impossible, and set participatively. Also the person appraised needs feedback on future progress.

Another theoretical base of performance management is expectancy theory, which states that individuals will be motivated to act provided they expect to be able to achieve the goals set, believe that achieving the goals will lead to other rewards and believe that the rewards on offer are valued (Vroom 1964). Some performance management systems are development driven and some are reward driven, although Hendry *et al.* (2000) use expectancy theory to demonstrate the difficulties of reward-based systems. CIPD (2005) found that 35% of survey respondents reported a link with financial reward, although more recent research suggests that this is becoming less common (CIPD 2009).

A final theoretical perspective that is emerging strongly in relation to performance management and appraisal is that of organisational justice. In recent years there has been a stream of papers that reinforce this (see e.g. Byrne *et al.* 2012; Dewettinck and van Dijk 2012; Gupta and Kumar 2013). The three facets of organisational justice can be clearly linked to performance management:

- Procedural justice: this relates to the extent to which procedures are perceived to be fair and requires performance management procedures to be transparent and robust.
- Distributive justice: this relates to the perceived fairness of the allocation of outcomes. This is particularly important where performance management is linked to pay but is also relevant in relation to training, promotion and other similar outcomes of a performance management system.
- Interactional justice: this relates to the perceived quality of interpersonal treatment received and relates to performance appraisal but also to other interactions such as coaching and feedback.

The growing weight of evidence is persuasive that these forms of justice need to be demonstrated in order for performance management systems to achieve their potential in improving performance at both individual and organisational levels.

Performance management across national contexts

As we noted above, almost all research into performance management has been conducted in a western context and the implications for its effectiveness in other national contexts are not well understood (Briscoe and Claus 2008). Hofstede's work on the dimensions of national culture has informed early attempts to explore these issues (see e.g. Fletcher and Perry 2001; Milliman *et al.* 2002; Mendonca and Kanungo 1996) but there is little or no exploration of matters such as religion on performance management systems. We have written elsewhere, for example, about the tensions between Buddhist beliefs and providing negative feedback. It seems to be widely accepted, however, that national context will influence the operation of all aspects of these systems from the content or aim of the appraisal through objective setting to the review/appraisal stage, as well as influencing who provides the feedback and the process or style used. We consider this in more detail in each of the stages of the performance management process outlined below, providing an early indication of contextual implications for performance review in the next Window on practice.

WINDOW ON PRACTICE

Applicability of review/appraisal in different cultural settings

The way that an appraisal process is used may be affected by the cultural context in which it takes place. For example, Varma *et al.* (2005) compare the use of performance appraisal in manufacturing organisations in the USA and India using statistical analysis. They found that interpersonal affect (the like–dislike relationship between supervisor and subordinate) appeared to have no impact in performance appraisal rating given in the USA, but that in India supervisors inflated the rating of low performers. Varma *et al.* suggest that this may be due to local cultural norms and a collectivist Indian culture as opposed to an individualistic US culture, and a greater concern in India for positive relationships.

Another example is an event experienced by one of this book's authors when running a course on performance appraisal in the Czech Republic sometime after the Velvet Revolution. Managers on the course said that the use of performance appraisal would be entirely unacceptable at that time as workers would associate it with what had gone before under the communist regime. Apparently every year a list of workers was published in order of the highest to the lowest performer. Although this list was claimed to represent work performance, the managers said that in reality it represented degrees of allegiance to the Communist Party and was nothing to do with work performance.

Stages in a performance management system

Figure 10.1 shows a typical performance management system. The system is cyclical: it starts by defining the organisation/work group objectives and then moves to translate these into individual-level objectives and to specify the development required to achieve these. Performance is then delivered by the individual and monitored by the manager: this is the most important stage of the continuous cycle of performance management in which coaching may take place and ongoing feedback is provided. Finally there is an assessment of performance and (where appropriate) a link to reward before the cycle begins again. The main stages of the cycle are discussed in more detail below.

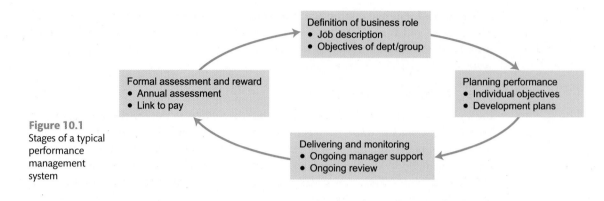

Figure 10.1
Stages of a typical performance management system

Business mission, values, objectives and competencies

There is an assumption that before it is able to plan and manage individual performance, the organisation will have made significant steps in identifying the performance required of the organisation as a whole. In most cases this will involve a mission statement so that performance is seen within the context of an overriding theme. In addition many organisations will identify the strategic business objectives that are required within the current business context to be competitive and that align with the organisation's mission statement.

Many organisations will also identify core values of the business and the key competencies required. Each of these has a potential role in managing individual performance. Organisational objectives are particularly important, as it is common for such objectives to be cascaded down the organisation in order to ensure that individual objectives contribute to their achievement (for an example of an objective-setting cascade, see Figure 10.2).

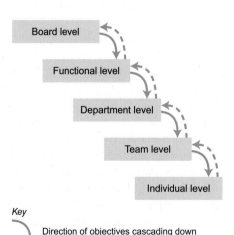

Figure 10.2
An objective-setting cascade

The cascade of strategic objectives is often, however, weak (Decramer *et al.* 2012). This may relate in part to the emergent, rather than rational, nature of organisational strategy.

Planning performance: a shared view of expected performance

Individual objectives derived from team objectives and an agreed job description can be jointly devised by manager and employee. These objectives are outcome/results orientated rather than task orientated, are tightly defined and include measures to be assessed. The objectives are designed to stretch the individual, and offer potential development as well as meeting business needs. It is helpful to both the organisation and the individual if objectives are prioritised. Many organisations use the 'SMART' acronym for describing individual objectives or targets:

- Specific
- Measurable
- Appropriate
- Relevant
- Timebound.

It is clearly easier for some parts of the organisation than others to set targets. There is often a tendency for those in technical jobs, such as computer systems development, to identify purely technical targets, reflecting the heavy task emphasis they see in their jobs. Moving staff to a different view of how their personal objectives contribute to team and organisational objectives is an important part of the performance management process. An objective for a team leader in systems development could be:

To complete development interviews with all team members by end of July 2014 (written March 2014).

Clearly, the timescale for each objective will need to reflect the content of the objective and not timescales set into the performance management system. As objectives are met, managers and their staff need to have a brief review meeting to look at progress in all objectives and decide what other objectives should be added, changed or deleted. Five or six ongoing objectives are generally sufficient for one individual to work on at any time. A mix of objectives about new developments and changes as well as routine aspects of the job is generally considered to be appropriate.

Difficulties have, however, been experienced with purely results-focused objectives (the 'what') as there may be appropriate and inappropriate ways of achieving an objective. For example, a manager with an objective to ensure that another department agrees to a plan of action could achieve this in different ways. The manager may pressure susceptible members of the other department and force agreement through without listening to the other department's perspective. This may alienate the other department and damage future good relations. For this reason, it is recommended that organisations also set behavioural objectives, usually in the form of competencies, as to 'how' results are to be achieved (Aguinis and Pierce 2008). The requirement to display teamwork in achieving results might, for example, prevent the inappropriate behaviour described in the previous example. The use of competencies also supports a softer, developmental approach to performance management as opposed to a harder, target-driven approach. Further, it allows employees to achieve goals, even where they have relatively little influence over results (Williams 2002) and emphasising these developmental aspects has been shown to be effective in improving employee performance (Tuytens and Devos 2012). However, CIPD (2005) research demonstrating that only around a third of organisations actually use competencies in their performance management systems might suggest that many systems are not as developmentally focused as claimed. Dewettinck and van Dijk (2012) also argue that results are typically emphasised over development.

WINDOW ON PRACTICE

Leadership competencies in performance management

People managers at Microsoft are scored in a 'leadership league' to underline the drive for performance management, according to one of the company's HR business partners. As the software industry has become more complex and competitive, the company decided to develop its culture and leadership competency is a very important part of the evolved culture. A spokesperson said:

If a manager does not achieve excellence goals and good employee feedback, even if their business results are exceptional, they will not receive 'execution excellence'. This is part of Microsoft's performance review and is tied to salary increases and bonuses, so it's a real driver.

The league rating is partly based on the employee survey, which asked staff to rate how their manager interacted with the rest of business. League scores are based on the competencies in Microsoft's People Scorecard, which gives a performance snapshot and includes the employee feedback.

Source: People Management, 18 November 2009.

Objectives may also be set at the team rather than individual level (Aguinis and Pierce 2008). However, despite the claimed importance of teamworking, only 6% of organisations in a recent survey operated a team system (CIPD 2005). Supporting team and individual performance is a critical balancing act as there can be conflicts built into performance management activity causing employees' pursuit of individual objectives to damage the performance of the team they are in, and vice versa. Team objectives, however, might experience difficulties in the form of peer pressure and social loafing (see e.g. Clark 2005). Peer pressure can be experienced by an individual, such as, for example, the pressure not to take time off work when feeling ill, as this may damage the achievement of objectives; or pressure to work faster, make fewer mistakes and so on. Social loafing occurs in a situation where one or more team members rely on the others to put in extra effort to achieve objectives, to cover for their own lack of effort. It works when some members are known to be conscientious or competitive or to care deeply about the rewards available, and there are others who are likely to be less concerned and who know the conscientious team members will make sure by their own efforts that the objectives are achieved. Van Vijfeijken *et al.* (2006) provide a helpful discussion of managing the performance of teams.

Whether at team or individual level, establishing a *shared* view of performance is essential: handing out a job description or list of objectives/competencies to the employee is not adequate. Performance expectations need to be understood and, where possible, to involve a contribution from the employee. For example, although key accountabilities may be fixed by the manager, they will need to be discussed and the competencies required to achieve them identified. Planning the support, development (usually in the form of a personal development plan) and resources necessary for employees to achieve their objectives is imperative. A key benefit of performance management is that it directs training and development resources efficiently (Aguinis and Pierce 2008). Without this support it is unlikely that even the most determined employees will achieve the performance required.

Objective setting is not, however, a straightforward process. SMART targets can be problematic if they are not constantly reviewed and updated, although this is a time-consuming process. Pre-set objectives can be a constraining factor in such a rapidly changing business context, and they remind us of the trap of setting measurable targets, precisely because they are measurable and satisfy the system, rather than because they are most important to the organisation. A further concern with SMART targets is that they inevitably have a short-term focus, yet what is most important to the organisation is developments which are complex and longer term, which are very difficult to pin down to short-term targets. In this context systems which also focus on the development of competencies will add greater value in the longer term. There is, however, a long way to go to describe performance adequately and define what is really required for organisational success.

National context may also create challenges for the use of objectives and competencies. For example, we have argued that objective setting should be a joint activity between supervisor and employee. This notion of participation is, however, a western concept that does not translate well into countries where supervisors are expected to direct employees what to do and to assign them goals (Fenwick 2004). This respect for hierarchy is typically found in China where goals have to be both assigned and easily attainable, to avoid loss of face if not achieved (Lindholm *et al.* 1999). Chinese firms have also been shown to evaluate moral and ideological behaviour, rather than task achievement (Shen 2004), and in Indian workplaces personalised relationships are often privileged over the accomplishment of job objectives (Mendonca and Kanungo 1996). Much fuller understanding of the implications of these contexts for performance management is required.

Delivering and monitoring performance

While the employee is working to achieve the performance agreed, the manager retains a key enabling role. Organising the resources and off-job training is clearly essential. So too is being accessible. There may well be unforeseen barriers to the agreed performance which the manager needs to deal with, and sometimes the situation will demand that the expected performance needs to be revised. The employee may want to sound out possible courses of action with the manager before proceeding, or may require further information. Sharing 'inside' information that will affect the employee's performance is often a key need, although it is also something that managers find difficult, especially with sensitive information. Managers can identify information sources and other people who may be helpful.

Ongoing **coaching** during the task is especially important as managers guide employees through discussion and by constructive feedback. Managers can refer to practical job experiences to develop the critical skills and competencies that the employee needs, and can provide job-related opportunities for practice. Managers can identify potential role models to employees, help to explain how high achievers perform so well, and oil the organisational wheels. Coaching is an opportunity to both seek and deliver feedback – essential as feedback has been demonstrated to improve job performance, increase job satisfaction and discretionary behaviour and reduce intention to quit (Krasman 2013).

ACTIVITY 10.2

Think of any organisation in which you have had some involvement:

1 How has individual performance been supported?

2 How effective was/is this?

3 How would you improve the way in which performance was/is supported?

Employees carry out ongoing reviews to plan their work and priorities and also to advise the manager well in advance if the agreed performance will not be delivered by the agreed dates. Joint employee/manager review ensures that information is shared. For example, a manager needs to be kept up to date on employee progress, while the employee needs to be kept up to date on organisation changes that have an impact on the agreed objectives. Both need to share perceptions of how the other is doing in their role, and what they could do that would be more helpful.

These reviews are normally informal, although a few notes may be taken of progress made and actions agreed. They need not be part of any formal system and therefore can take place when the job or the individuals involved demand, and not according to a pre-set schedule. The review is to facilitate future employee performance, providing an opportunity for the manager to confirm that the employee is 'on the right track', redirecting him or her if necessary. The review thus provides a forum for employee reward in terms of recognition of progress. A 'well done' or an objective signed off as completed can enhance the motivation to perform well in the future. During this period evidence collection is also important. In the Scottish Prison Service (IDS 2003) line managers maintain a performance monitoring log of their team members' positive and negative behaviours in order to provide regular feedback and to embed the practice of ongoing assessment. Employees are expected to build up a portfolio of evidence of their performance over the period to increase the objectivity of reviews and to provide an audit trail to back up any assessment ratings. It is also during this part of the cycle that employees in many organisations can collect 360-degree feedback to be used developmentally and as part of an evidence base. This developmental approach may be problematic, however, in some national contexts. In countries such as China and Russia, for example, development through feedback may not be successful as managers are more likely to be reluctant to engage in two-way communication and the offer of direct feedback is not culturally acceptable (Fletcher and Perry 2001).

Formal performance review/appraisal

Regular formal reviews (perhaps once or twice each year) are required. A well-designed system will measure the extent to which set (ideally agreed) objectives have been met. When a competency profile has been identified for a particular job, it is also possible to use this in the appraisal of performance. Many systems combine competency assessment with assessment against objectives or job accountabilities. IRS (2005b) reports that 89% of its respondents that used appraisals measured employees against objectives or goals, with 56% measuring against competencies and 53% measuring against pre-set performance standards, as might be used in a harder approach to performance improvement. In many organisations, for example Microsoft and AstraZeneca, employees are now invited to assess their own performance and prepare an initial draft of their achievements (IDS 2003). Performance measures may be either quantitative or qualitative. Qualitative appraisal is often an unstructured narrative on the general performance of the appraisee, although some guidance might be given about the areas on which the appraiser should comment. The problem with qualitative appraisals is that they may leave important areas un-appraised, and that they are not suitable for comparison purposes. When using quantitative measures, it is common to use a Likert scale to rate performance with either numbers or letters. Some organisations continue to have overall assessment ratings which have to conform to a forced distribution, requiring each team/department to have, say, 10% of employees on the top point, 20% on the next point, and so on, so that each individual is assessed relative to others rather than being given an absolute rating. These systems are not popular: Chattopadhayay and Ghosh (2012) present a detailed review of their problems, suggesting that they create employee dissatisfaction and lead to high labour turnover. These authors propose using an employee's relative position within his or her work group to improve the effectiveness of forced distribution systems. Other approaches include behaviourally anchored rating scales (BARS) and behavioural observation scales (BOS), which are specific methods of linking ratings with behaviour at work, although evidence suggests that these are not widely used (Williams 2002). Lastly, performance may be appraised by collecting primary data via various forms of electronic surveillance system. There are increasing examples of how activity rates of computer operators can be recorded and analysed, and how the calls made by telephone sales staff can be overheard and analysed. On another level some companies test the performance of their sales staff by sending in assessors acting in the role of customer, often termed 'mystery shoppers'. Other organisations encourage employees to give upwards feedback to their managers at this point in the cycle. Further details of this stage in the process will be presented later (see Part 8).

One particular form of review/appraisal is 360-degree feedback, which is a very specific term used to refer to multi-rater feedback. It is increasingly being used within performance management systems and as a separate development activity. This approach to feedback refers to the use of the whole range of sources from which feedback can be collected about any individual. Thus feedback is collected from every angle on the way that the individual carries out his or her job: from immediate line manager, peers, subordinates, more senior managers, internal customers, external customers and from individuals themselves. It is argued that this breadth provides better feedback than relying on the line manager alone, who will only be able to observe the individual in a limited range of situations. It also provides a better way to capture the complexities of performance and individuals will find feedback from peers and subordinates compelling and more valid (Atwater *et al.* 2002). Space here precludes a detailed discussion of 360-degree feedback and you can find this in Torrington *et al.* (2008).

Performance review/appraisal attracts perhaps most criticism of any aspect of a performance management system. Its effectiveness hinges on a range of different factors. Research by the Institute for Employment Studies (IRS 2001) found that review was only seen as fair if the targets set were seen as reasonable, managers were seen to be objective and judgements were consistent across the organisation. Longenecker (1997) identified the three most common reasons for failure of an appraisal system as: unclear performance criteria or an ineffective rating instrument (83%); poor working relationships with the boss (79%); and that the appraiser lacked information on the manager's actual performance (75%). Other problems were a lack of ongoing performance feedback (67%) and a lack of focus on management development/improvement (50%). Smaller numbers identified problems with the process, such as lack of appraisal skills (33%) and the review process lacking structure or substance (29%). See also Davis (2011) for common problems with appraisal. Aguinis and Pierce (2008) have also found that many employees are dissatisfied with the level of feedback and frequency of performance review. Informal reviews that are more frequent may thus be more effective (Dewettinck and van Dijk 2012). Fairness and trust in supervisors are thus essential to an effective appraisal (Byrne *et al.* 2012) and to fostering employee participation (Dewettinck and van Dijk 2012). Subjectivity is, however, hard to avoid and may explain managers' reluctance to undertake appraisals (Neu Moren 2013).

National context again has substantial implications for performance review. The emphasis on relationships in India, for example, leads managers to rate all employees at a similar standard and direct criticism is unacceptable in cultures such as China where importance is attached to saving face (Lindholm *et al.* 1999). Milliman *et al.*'s (2002) study of performance appraisal in ten countries across the Pacific Rim found that cultural difference impacted on its purpose. Some used it primarily for development while others emphasised its judgemental/reward functions. Shen (2004) supports this, arguing that Chinese firms use performance review to drive pay, whereas western firms tend to focus on its developmental aspects.

WINDOW ON PRACTICE

Performance management at EE

To meet a very competitive environment and the convergence of a number of businesses, EE (then Orange) recognised that it needed to make its performance management process more robust. There were a number of concerns with the existing system including the five-point ratings scale, executives feeling that HR owned the process, employees feeling that objective setting often did not support the business, and some feelings of lack of support and direction.

The new system has five core principles:

- one clear cascade process for objectives;
- reward should stay linked to performance;
- a balance between 'what' and 'how' objectives;
- process needs to be owned by the business;
- performance should be clearly and consistently differentiated across the ratings.

The design of the system was led by senior representatives of the core businesses and a decision was made to keep the best parts of the current system and incorporate 'snippets of good stuff' from elsewhere, rather than looking for a 'best practice' model used elsewhere to implement.

The five-point ratings scale was kept but the labels attached to each point were changed to demonstrate that the mid-point was a good place to be (which was used previously when employees had met their objectives and were doing a good job, and which had caused disagreements). The new scale ranged from 'unacceptable' (1); 'getting there' (2); 'great stuff' (3, the mid-point); '4' (four) to 'exceptional' (5). The distribution curve used to ensure consistent ratings was abandoned in favour of 'calibration', which takes place at various levels and involves managers sharing the ratings they have given to those who report directly to them with other managers at their level, providing justification for their ratings and being prepared to explore and discuss their views. Objective setting is now linked to the balanced scorecard approach EE has adopted, with vice presidents' objectives being set at the same time (and published on the intranet) and cascaded down the organisation. Objectives are weighted to ensure prioritisation, and staff must have two or three behavioural ('how' or input) objectives. Orange has a profit-sharing scheme for non-managers called 'success share', and now performance ratings are used to determine the proportion received by each individual. For managers the bonus scheme has altered, giving senior managers more flexibility to allocate rewards for each point on the five-point scale, without having to manipulate ratings.

Source: Summarised from Johnson, R. (2006) 'Orange blossoms', *People Management*, Vol. 12, No. 21, pp. 56–60.

ACTIVITY 10.3

Think of any organisation in which you have had some involvement:

1 How has individual performance been measured and rated?
2 What impact has this had?
3 Would you recommend qualitative or quantitative descriptions of performance?

Reward

Performance management systems, and performance review/appraisal in particular, can be used to allocate reward. This can be both financial and non-financial reward, although much of the debate centres around financial reward. It is not difficult to understand why. Performance management systems are effective and relatively uncontentious in supporting non-financial rewards such as training and development, quality of working life and strong supervisor/employee relationships. The allocation of financial reward is much more contentious (Aguinis and Pierce 2008). Many performance management systems still include a link with pay, although this is reducing in popularity (CIPD 2009), and staff almost universally dislike the link (Armstrong and Baron 1998). Clark (2005) provides a good discussion of the problems with the pay link and we include a detailed discussion of performance-related pay later (see Chapter 21).

National cultures again impact on the performance management/reward link, particularly in relation to pay. Milliman *et al.* (2002) argue that performance/pay links are common in individualistic countries such as the USA, Canada and Australia but less common in cultures which place a high value on harmony, face and teamwork. Here importance is placed on not disturbing group harmony through differentiation of employees in performance review. In contrast, Snape *et al.* (1998) argue that monetary rewards are emerging as being of prime importance to workers in Hong Kong as Asian cultures are more materialistic than their western counterparts. Again further research is needed to develop better understanding of these issues.

Performance management: does it improve performance?

Although the practitioner literature somewhat uncritically accepts that effective performance management systems improve individual and organisational performance (see e.g. CIPD 2009), the findings of academic research have been more mixed. This might, in part, derive from the failure of many organisations to evaluate their performance management systems (Armstrong and Baron 2005). For example, CIPD (2005) reports that 61% of organisations surveyed regarded their systems as effective to some degree and Houldsworth (2004) reports that 68% of organisations rated their performance management effectiveness as excellent, yet it is not clear how effectiveness was measured. The early findings from more rigorous academic research were unpromising. However, more recent research has been more positive about the impact of performance management systems. Research on the HR/performance link (see e.g. Purcell *et al.* 2003, West *et al.* 2002) has included performance management in the bundle of HR practices that are associated with improved organisational performance. Studies on performance management itself have been similarly promising. For example, it has been demonstrated that over half of organisations with formal performance management systems have better financial outcomes than those without and over 40% have better outcomes in respect of customer satisfaction and employee retention (Aguinis and Pierce 2008). Decramer *et al.* (2013) have also reported positive outcomes within higher-education systems. To achieve these benefits, robust systems that are well implemented are required. We consider below some of the key requirements, together with some of the criticisms of performance management systems.

Performance management needs to be line rather than HR driven. The incorporation of line managers alongside HR managers in a working party to develop the system is important as it not only takes account of the needs of the line in the system design, but also demonstrates that the system is line led. CIPD (2005) reports that 75% of managers suggest that they own and operate the performance management process. Training in the introduction and use of the system is also ideally line led. However, some researchers have found that line managers are the weak link in the system (Tuytens and Devos 2012). Difficulties can arise in many forms. Redman *et al.* (2000) found incomplete take-up of performance management, with some aspects being adopted and not others. They noted that there was a general lack of integration of activities. This is rather unfortunate as one of the key advantages of performance management is the capacity for integration of activities concerned with the management of individual performance. There remains confusion both over the nature of performance management and what an integrated approach means. Ownership of the system is also important. If it is designed and imposed by the HR function, there may be little ownership of the system by line managers. Similarly, if paperwork has to be returned to the HR function it may well be seen as a form-filling exercise for someone else's benefit and with no practical value to performance within the job. Performance management also seems to suffer from the same problems as traditional appraisal systems. Armstrong and Baron (2005) report, for example, that employees feel that managers give their best ratings to people that they like and many managers feel they do not receive sufficient training in performance management processes. A further problem with performance management systems is the lack of clarity of purpose and they may be expected to deliver in too many areas. Systems may focus on development, identifying future potential, reward, identifying poor performers, or motivation. Many systems try to encompass both developmental and judgemental approaches; for example, in the IRS survey (IRS 2005b) 92% companies used appraisal to determine training and development needs (mainly formally), and 65% used the system either formally or informally to determine pay, with 43% using it formally or informally to determine bonuses. However, as these approaches conflict, the results are typically unsatisfactory. Although it is recommended that a primarily developmental approach is adopted, many managers still predominantly perceive the primary purpose of the performance management process to be performance evaluation and control (Dewettinck and van Dijk 2012). An emerging issue given demographic changes in many countries is managing performance across different generations within the workforce. A recent report for example has claimed that a younger generation of workers, the so-called 'generation Y', needs a very different type of approach to performance management than their older colleagues (Churchard 2012). More research is required into these intergenerational differences and, as we note at various points above, the impact of national context on performance management processes.

More fundamentally some argue that the problems are not simply related to poor design or implementation of performance management systems, but rooted deeply in the basic reaction of organisational members to performance management. In the critical literature, debates on the role and theory of appraisal centre on the underlying reasons for appraisal (see e.g. Barlow 1989; Townley 1993; Newton and Findlay 1996). These are radical critiques which posit that performance management systems are an abuse of power and create exploitation and work intensification. These are powerful criticisms which have been recently built upon by Neu Moren (2013) in her challenge to the basis of performance appraisal and the need to view it as a social practice.

SUMMARY PROPOSITIONS

10.1 Employee performance management systems incorporate appraisal activity, but include other aspects such as a link to organisational objectives and competency frameworks, an emphasis on ongoing review, motivation, coaching and support, and reinforcement/reward for performance achieved.

10.2 There is a conflict in many appraisal and performance management systems as managers frequently have a dual role as assessor and developer.

10.3 Current trends in sophisticated performance management activity include greater employee ownership, emphasis on the 'how' as well as the 'what', emphasis on evidence collection from both manager and employee, and upwards feedback to the line manager as well as downwards feedback to the employee.

10.4 Most employee performance management systems focus on the individual, but there is a need to ensure that team contributions are not neglected and more importantly that team and individual goals do not conflict.

10.5 Performance management systems are generally believed to improve performance but research evidence is mixed.

10.6 The impact of national context on performance management processes is poorly understood and further research is required.

GENERAL DISCUSSION TOPICS

1   In what ways is the concept of performance management different from the way in which appraisal has been traditionally practised? What are the advantages and disadvantages for employees and employers?

2   Critics argue that, rather than being focused on development and improvement, performance management systems are a form of employee control that create work intensification. How would you respond to this criticism?

THEORY INTO PRACTICE

Steel Co. is a small manufacturing company, run by an owner manager and employing around sixty-five people, mainly male, full-time, permanent, unskilled or semi-skilled workers. The firm has been established for approximately thirty years, many of the employees having long periods of service, and has, in this time, had mixed performance. In recent years, however, in the face of increased competition and difficult trading conditions, financial performance has been poor and little profit has been made. This situation has meant that the owner manager has imposed a pay freeze for the last three years. Employees have expressed discontent with the pay freeze and suggest that, in general, the firm is a poor employer.

The firm is divided into two main sections, the sales team ('Sales'), which comprises around eight employees, and the manufacturing operation (the 'Works'), which comprises the remainder of the employees, other than for a small number of employees who work in administrative or quality assurance roles. Historically, the owner manager has managed the whole firm, but about twelve months ago, appointed a Divisional Director who is now responsible for managing the Works. In line with his autocratic approach, the owner manager has always adopted a command and control style of management, viewing employees as a cost to the business and investing little in them. This is evident in his management of the sales team, who have sales targets to hit and are closely monitored by the owner manager in respect of achieving these targets but receive little other support from him. The Divisional Director, however, has a more participative style of management and understands the need to view employees as assets through which the firm can develop and sustain high performance.

The historical management style meant that, on his arrival, the Divisional Director was faced with a group of employees who lacked commitment to the firm and were focused purely on working their shift and earning their pay, making the minimum possible contribution to the firm. The Divisional Director has thus undertaken a number of initiatives in order to improve both individual and firm performance, including the implementation of a performance management system. The system revolves around production targets which have been devised by the Divisional Director, based on the firm's overall requirements, and are posted on the noticeboard at the beginning of each week, together with a report indicating performance against the previous week's targets. Production data is available at both the team and individual level and the Works Manager regularly discusses poor performance with individuals where appropriate. It is common for those employees regularly not meeting their targets to be disciplined. An annual performance review is held for employees at which their performance is rated unsatisfactory, satisfactory or good.

In an attempt to overcome the dissatisfaction created by the pay freeze, the Divisional Director then introduced a bonus scheme where payment is triggered by individual and team achievement of production targets. Employees support management's disciplinary approach as they perceive that those who are underperforming are likely prevent payment of team bonuses. Team leaders are nominally responsible for coordinating team efforts, although the role is a new one, which has not been formally defined, and the employees appointed to these roles have been given no training and do not understand their responsibilities. Indeed, little training, other than on health and safety issues, takes place at any level in the Works.

A year after implementing the changes, the Divisional Director undertook a review of performance and was disappointed to discover that neither productivity nor quality have improved in the Works. In discussions with the Works Manager, the Divisional Director has formed the view that the attitude of the employees has changed little and motivation is still weak, despite most earning bonuses in seven of the twelve months.

Questions

Advise on why this might be the case with particular reference to:

1 The methods used to set targets/objectives.

2 The failure to manage behaviours or competencies.

3 A discipline- rather than a development-focused approach to managing performance.

4 The linking of financial reward to performance.

FURTHER READING

CIPD (2009) *Performance Management in Action: Current trends and practice*. London: CIPD. A recent report that provides up-to-date information on this topic, reflecting organisational practice at a time of economic recession. Discusses the changing context both economically and in relation to issues such as the role of line managers and the need to consider online systems.

Rao, A. (2007) 'Effectiveness of performance management systems: An empirical study in Indian companies', *International Journal of Human Resource Management*, Vol. 18, No. 10, pp. 1812–40. Considers the effectiveness of such systems, integrating consideration of cultural issues within the Indian context.

Kuvaas, B. (2006) 'Performance appraisal satisfaction and employee outcomes: Mediating and moderating roles of work motivation', *International Journal of Human Resource Management*, Vol. 17, No. 3, pp. 504–22.
This article reflects a stream of research looking at the outcomes of appraisal from the employee perspective, in particular focusing on job satisfaction, intention to quit and commitment.

Byrne, Z. *et al*. (2012). 'Trusting the fair supervisor: The role of supervisory support in performance appraisals', *Human Resource Management Journal*, Vol. 22, pp. 129–47.
This article is part of the fast-increasing literature which emphasises the vital role of organisational justice in effective performance management systems.

211

REFERENCES

Aguinis, H. and Pierce, C. (2008) 'Enhancing the relevance of organisational behaviour by embracing performance management research', *Journal of Organisational Behaviour*, Vol. 29, pp. 139–45.

Armstrong, M. and Baron, A. (1998) *Performance Management: The new realities.* London: CIPD.

Armstrong, M. and Baron, A. (2005) *Managing Performance: Performance management in action.* London: CIPD.

Atwater, L., Waldman, D. and Brett, J. (2002) 'Understanding and optimising multi-source feedback', *Human Resource Management*, Vol. 41, pp. 193–208.

Barlow, G. (1989) 'Deficiencies and the perpetuation of power: Latent functions in management appraisal', *Journal of Management Studies*, Vol. 26, pp. 499–518.

Briscoe, D. and Claus, L. (2008) 'Employee performance management: Policies and practices in multinational enterprises', in P. Budwar and A. Denisi (eds), *Performance Management Systems: A global perspective.* Abingdon: Routledge.

Byrne, Z., Pitts, V., Wilson, C. and Steiner, Z. (2012) 'Trusting the fair supervisor: The role of supervisory support in performance appraisals', *Human Resource Management Journal*, Vol. 22, pp. 129–47.

Chattopadhayay, R. and Ghosh, A. (2012) 'Performance appraisal based on a forced distribution system: Its drawbacks and remedies', *International Journal of Productivity and Performance Management*, Vol. 61, pp. 881–96.

Churchard, C. (2012) 'Gen Y "demands improved performance management"', *People Management*, **www.peoplemanagement.co.uk/pm/articles/2012/05/gen-y-demands-improved-performance-management.htm**.

CIPD (2005) *Performance Management.* London: CIPD.

CIPD (2009) *Performance Management: Discussion paper.* London: CIPD.

CIPD (2012) *Factsheet: Performance Management* [Online]. London: CIPD.

Clark, G. (2005) 'Performance management strategies', in G. Salaman *et al.* (eds), *Strategic Human Resource Management: Theory and practice.* London: The Open University/Sage.

Davis, P. (2011) 'Seven biggest problems with performance appraisals: And seven development approaches to rectify them', *Development and Learning in Organisations*, Vol. 26, pp. 11–14.

Decramer, A., Smoulders, C., Vanderstraeten, A., Christiaens, J. and Desmidt, S. (2012) 'External pressures affecting the adoption of employee performance management in higher education institutions', *Personnel Review*, Vol. 41, pp. 686–704.

Decramer, A., Smoulders, C. and Vanderstraeten, A. (2013) 'Employee performance management culture and system features in higher education: Relationship with employee performance management satisfaction', *International Journal of Human Resource Management*, Vol. 24, pp. 352–71.

Dewettinck, K. and van Dijk, H. (2012) 'Linking Belgian employee performance management system characteristics with performance management system effectiveness: Exploring the mediating role of fairness', *International Journal of Human Resource Management*, Vol. 24, pp. 806–25.

Fenwick, M. (2004) 'International compensation and performance management', in A. Harzing and J. Ruysseveldt (eds), *International Human Resource Management*, 2nd edn. London: Sage.

Fletcher, C. (2001) 'Performance appraisal and management: The developing research agenda', *Journal of Organisational and Occupational Psychology*, Vol. 74, pp. 473–87.

Fletcher, C. and Perry, E. (2001) 'Performance appraisal and feedback: A consideration of national culture and a review of contemporary and future trends', in N. Anderson *et al.* (eds), *International Handbook of Industrial, Work and Organizational Psychology.* Beverley Hills, CA: Sage.

Gupta, V. and Kumar, S. (2013) 'Impact of performance appraisal justice on employee engagement: A study of Indian professionals', *Employee Relations*, Vol. 35, pp. 61–78.

Hendry, C., Woodward, S., Bradley, P. and Perkins, S. (2000) 'Performance and rewards: Cleaning out the stables', *Human Resource Management Journal*, Vol. 10, pp. 42–62.

Houldsworth, E. (2004) 'Managing performance', in D. Rees (ed.), *People Management: Challenges and opportunities.* Basingstoke: Macmillan.

IDS (2003) *IDS Studies: Performance Management*. London: IDS.

IDS (2005) *IDS Studies: Performance Management*. London: IDS.

IRS (2001) 'Performance appraisal must try harder', *IRS Employment Trends*. London: IRS.

IRS (2005a) 'Appraisals (1): Not living up to expectations', *IRS Employment Review*. London: IRS.

IRS (2005b) 'Appraisals (2): Learning from practice and experience', *IRS Employment Review*. London: IRS.

Johnson, R. (2006) 'Orange blossoms', *People Management*, Vol. 12, No. 21, pp. 56–60.

Krasman, J. (2013) 'Putting feedback-seeking into "context": Job characteristics and feedback-seeking behaviour', *Personnel Review*, Vol. 42, pp. 50–66.

Lindholm, N., Tahvanainen, M. and Borkman, I. (1999) 'Performance appraisal of host country employees: Western MNE's in China', in C. Brewster and H. Harris (eds), *International HRM: Contemporary issues in Europe*. London: Routledge.

Locke, E. (1968) 'Towards a theory of task performance and incentives', *Organisational Behaviour and Human Performance*, Vol. 3, pp. 157–89.

Locke, E. and Latham, G. (1990) *A Theory of Goal Setting and Task Performance*. Englewood Cliffs, NJ: Prentice Hall.

Longenecker, C. (1997) 'Why managerial performance appraisals are ineffective: Causes and lessons', *Career Development International*, Vol. 2, pp. 212–18.

Mendonca, M. and Kanungo, R. (1996) 'Impact of culture on performance management in developing countries', *International Journal of Manpower*, Vol. 17, pp. 65–75.

Milliman, J., Nason, S., Zhu, C. and de Ciere, H. (2002) 'An exploratory assessment of the purposes of performance appraisals in North and Central America and the Pacific Rim', *Human Resource Management*, Vol. 41, pp. 87–102.

Neu Moren, E. (2013) 'The negotiated character of performance appraisal: How interrelations between managers matters', *International Journal of Human Resource Management*, Vol. 24, pp. 853–70.

Newton, T. and Findlay, P. (1996) 'Playing God? The performance of appraisal', *Human Resource Management Journal*, Vol. 6, pp. 42–58.

Purcell, J., Kinnie, N., Hutchinson, S., Rayton, B. and Swart, J. (2003) *Understanding the People Performance Link: Unlocking the black box*. London: CIPD.

Redman, T., Snape, E., Thompson, D. and Ka-Ching Yan, F. (2000) 'Performance appraisal in the National Health Service: A Trust Hospital study', *Human Resource Management Journal*, Vol. 10, pp. 1–16.

Scott, A. (2006) 'Intensive care', *People Management*, Vol. 12, pp. 14–15.

Shen, J. (2004) 'International performance appraisals: Policies, practices and determinants in the case of Chinese multinational companies', *International Journal of Manpower*, Vol. 25, pp. 547–63.

Snape, E., Thompson, D., Ka-Ching Yan, F. and Redman, T. (1998) 'Performance appraisal and culture: Practice and attitudes in Hong Kong and Great Britain', *International Journal of Human Resource Management*, Vol. 9, pp. 841–61.

Torrington, D., Hall, L., Taylor, S. and Atkinson, C. (2008) *Fundamentals of Human Resource Management*. Harlow: Pearson Education.

Townley, B. (1993) 'Performance appraisal and the emergence of management', *Journal of Management Studies*, Vol. 30, pp. 27–44.

Tuytens, M. and Devos, G. (2012) 'Importance of system and leadership in appraisal', *Personnel Review*, Vol. 41, pp. 756–66.

Van Vijfeijken, H., Kleingeld, A., Van Tuijl, H. and Algera, J. (2006) 'Interdependence and fit in team performance management', *Personnel Review*, Vol. 35, pp. 98–117.

Varma, A., Pichler, S. and Srinivas, E. (2005) 'The role of interpersonal affect in performance appraisal: Evidence from two samples – the US and India', *International Journal of Human Resource Management*, Vol. 16, pp. 2029–44.

Vroom, V. (1964) *Work and Motivation*. Chichester: Wiley.

West, M., Borrill, C., Dawson, J., Carter, M. and Waring, J. (2002) 'The link between the management of employees and patient mortality in acute hospitals', *International Journal of Human Resource Management*, Vol. 13, pp. 1299–310.

Williams, R. (2002) *Managing Employee Performance*. London: Thomson Learning.

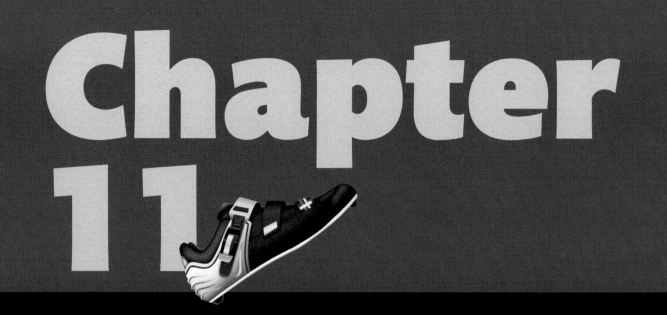

Chapter 11

LEADERSHIP

Leadership is one of the most loaded and misunderstood words in management. Individual managers are often seduced by concepts of leadership that show them to be knights in shining armour with superhuman qualities and (this is the really dangerous bit) adoring followers. The followers rarely have that view of their managers. We must not, however, underestimate the importance of leadership. There are indeed sometimes needs for individual leaders with outstanding qualities who achieve extra-ordinary change in their business. There are, however, infinitely more roles which call on different, more subtle and modest leadership skills, which can be learnt and which are equally important, even if they lack the 'heroism' associated with some forms of leadership.

Understanding of leadership developed greatly in the second half of the twentieth century and this is the basis of our understanding and analysis today. Major develop-ments in recent years have included: an appreciation of the impact of the changing circumstances of contemporary business; the role of women in leadership; the neglect of followers in leadership theory; and the need to recognise the influence of national con-text. All of the twentieth-century studies and theories were based on two complementary assumptions: first, the business norm was of large, stable organisations steadily getting bigger; second, management was almost exclusively a male activity, with male norms conducted in a western (predominantly American) context. This led to explanations and suggestions based on those two givens. We now see a weakening of these assumptions. Effective businesses are not necessarily large, growing organisations and there are many more women in the workforce and in management positions within it. Although charismatic leaders (a predominantly male concept) are still needed in some situations, empowering leaders are increasingly required. The applicability of American leadership theory to a variety of contexts has also been subject to increasing scrutiny and we have seen an increasing interest in the concept of followership and its impact on leadership effectiveness. We chart the development of leadership theories and their implications throughout this chapter.

WINDOW ON PRACTICE

Much of the leadership research considered in this chapter has emerged from the USA and has been unproblematically applied across the world. In their internationally recognised GLOBE study, however, House *et al.* (2004) demonstrate how effective leadership is influenced by national context. Differences are apparent even in the western context. Tavanti (2012), for example, demonstrates how cultural dimensions in Italy affect approaches to leadership. In non-western contexts, stark differences are beginning to emerge as understanding of leadership develops. Yooyanyong and Muenjohn (2010), for example, demonstrate these differences in Japan and Bolden

and Kirk (2009) introduce the idea of the 'African renaissance' and call for a re-engagement with indigenous knowledge and practices. This is part of a stream of research that explores the notion of Ubuntu (a social philosophy that highlights good social and familial relations, and encourages collectivism and kinship among indigenous peoples) and its role in African leadership. Eyong (2012), for example, presents one typology of African leadership based upon Ubuntu that is premised on the promotion of respect and dignity of followers, teamwork and group solidarity, service to others, and valuing harmony and interdependence. Religion may also have a role to play in understanding leadership; for example, El Garah *et al.* (2012) explore Islam and leadership.

Leadership and management

Northouse (2006) suggests that there are four components that characterise leadership: leadership is a process; it involves influence; it occurs within a group context; and it involves goal attainment. This corresponds with Shackleton's (1995: 2) definition, which we shall use as a working definition for the remainder of the chapter:

leadership is the process in which an individual influences other group members towards the attainment of group or organisational goals.

This definition is useful as it leaves open the question of whether leadership is exercised in a commanding or a facilitative manner. It does suggest, however, that the leader in some way motivates others to act in such a way as to achieve group goals.

The definition also makes no assumptions about who the leader is; it may or may not be the nominal head of the group. Managers, therefore, may or may not be leaders, and leaders may or may not be managers. Some authors distinguish very clearly between the nature of management and the nature of leadership, but this draws on a particular perspective, that of the transformational leader, and we will consider this in the section on whether the organisation needs heroes. This is a school of thought that concentrates on the one leader at the top of the organisation, which is very different from organisations and individuals who use the terms 'manager' and 'leader' interchangeably with nothing more than a vague notion that managers should be leaders. Indeed, any individual may act as a manager one day and a leader the next, depending on the situation. In addition we should not assume that leadership is always a downwards process, as sometimes employees and managers lead upwards (Hollington 2006).

The flow of articles on leadership continues unabated, but it would be a mistake to think that there is an ultimate truth to be discovered; rather, there is a range of perspectives from which we can try to make sense of leadership and motivation. Grint (1997: 3) comments insightfully that

What counts as leadership appears to change quite radically across time and space.

In the following three sections we will look at three questions which underlie virtually all the work on leadership. First, what are the traits of a leader, or an effective leader? Second, what is the 'best' leadership style or behaviour? Third, if different styles are appropriate at different times, what factors influence the desired style?

What are the traits of (effective) leaders?

Trait approaches, which were the earliest to be employed, seek to identify the traits of leaders – in other words, what characterises leaders as opposed to those who are not leaders. These approaches rest on the assumption that some people are born to lead due to their personal qualities, while others are not. It suggests that leadership is only available to the chosen few. These approaches have been discredited for this reason and because there has been little consistency in the lists of traits that research has uncovered. However, this perspective is frequently resurrected (see e.g. Fache 2009).

Kilpatrick and Locke (1991), in a meta-analysis, did seem to find some consistency around the following traits: drive to achieve; the motivation to lead; honesty and integrity; self-confidence, including the ability to withstand setbacks, standing firm and being emotionally resilient; cognitive ability; and knowledge of the business. They also note the importance of managing the perceptions of others in relation to these characteristics. Northouse (2006) provides a useful historical comparison of the lists of traits uncovered in other studies. Perhaps the most well-known expression of the trait approach is the work relating to charismatic leadership. House (1976), for example, describes charismatic leaders as being dominant, having a strong desire to influence, being self-confident and having a strong sense of their own moral values. We will pick up on this concept in a later section.

In a slightly different vein Goleman (1998) has argued that leadership competencies comprise technical, cognitive and emotional competencies, and that emotional competencies 'proved to be twice as important as the others'. He goes on to describe five components of emotional intelligence:

- **Self-awareness**: this he defines as a deep understanding of one's strengths, weaknesses, needs, values and goals. Self-aware managers are aware of their own limitations.
- **Self-regulation**: the control of feelings, the ability to channel them in constructive ways; the ability to feel comfortable with ambiguity and not panic.
- **Motivation**: the desire to achieve beyond expectations, being driven by internal rather than external factors, and to be involved in a continuous striving for improvement.
- **Empathy**: considering employees' feelings alongside other factors when making decisions.
- **Social skill**: friendliness with a purpose, being good at finding common ground and building rapport. Individuals with this competency are good persuaders, collaborative managers and natural networkers.

Goleman refers to competencies which include a combination of traits *and* abilities. He maintains that the five aspects of emotional intelligence can be learnt, although we feel that this is still a matter for debate, and as many of the terms used by Goleman are similar to those of the previous trait models of leadership, we have categorised his model as an extension of the trait perspective. To some extent his work sits between the trait approach and the style approach which follows. It is interesting that a number of researchers and writers are recognising that there is some value in considering a mix of personality characteristics and behaviours, and in particular Higgs (2003) links this approach to emotional intelligence.

ACTIVITY 11.1

Think of different leaders you have encountered – in particular those that were especially effective or ineffective:

1 What differences can you identify in terms of their traits (personal characteristics)?
2 What differences can you identify in terms of their behaviour?
3 Are the trait and behaviour lists connected in any way? If so how?
4 Which of these two approaches – trait or behaviour – do you find more useful in helping you to understand the nature of effective leadership?

What is the 'best way to lead'? Leadership styles and behaviours

Dissatisfaction with research that saw leadership as a set of permanent personal characteristics led to further studies that emphasised the nature of the leadership process, the interaction between leader and follower, aiming to understand how the leaders *behave* rather than what they *are*. The first such studies sought to find the 'best' leadership style; from this perspective leadership comprises an ideal set of behaviours that can be learnt. Fullop *et al*. (1999) suggest that McGregor's (1960) work, *The Human Side of Enterprise*, can be understood from this perspective. McGregor argued that American corporations managed their employees as if they were work-shy, and needed constant direction, monitoring and control (theory 'x'), rather than as if they were responsible individuals who were willing and able to take on responsibility and organise their own work (theory 'y'). McGregor argued that the underlying assumptions of the manager determined the way he or she managed the employees and this in turn determined how the employees would react. Thus if employees were managed as if they operated on theory 'x' then they would act in a theory 'x' manner; conversely, if employees were managed as if they operated on theory 'y' then they would respond as theory 'y' employees would respond. The message was that management style should reinforce theory 'y' and thus employees would take on responsibility, be motivated by what they were doing and work hard. Although the original book was written fifty years ago, this approach has been revisited in more recent years (see e.g. Heil *et al*. 2000) and it fits well with the empowering or post-heroic approach to leadership that we discuss later. Another style approach is reflected in Blake and Mouton's (1964) famous 'Managerial Grid'. The grid is based on two aspects of leadership behaviour: concern for production, that is task-orientated behaviours such as clarifying roles, scheduling work, measuring outputs; and concern for people, that is people-centred behaviour such as building trust, camaraderie, a friendly atmosphere. These two dimensions are at the heart of many models of leadership and have been more recently explored by Cowsgill and Grint (2008) who seek to develop the task/relationship dichotomy by suggesting that senior managers who seek to satisfy the demands of both their superiors and subordinates will be the most successful leaders.

Blake and Mouton proposed that individual leaders could be measured on a nine-point scale in each of these two aspects, and by combining them in grid form they identified the four leadership styles presented in Table 11.1.

Table 11.1
Blake and Mouton's four leadership styles

High concern for people Low concern for production **Country Club management**	High concern for people High concern for production **Team management**
Low concern for people Low concern for production **Impoverished management**	Low concern for people High concern for production **Authority-compliance management**

Source: Adapted from R.R. Blake and J.S. Mouton (1964) *The Managerial Grid*. Houston, TX: Gulf Publishing.

Such studies suggest that leadership is accessible for all people and is a matter of learning leadership behaviour. Many leadership development courses have therefore been based around this model. However, as Northouse (2006) argues, there is an assumption in the model that the team management style (high concern for people and high concern for production; sometimes termed 9,9 management) is the ideal style, yet this claim is not substantiated by the research. This approach also fails to take account of the characteristics of the situation and the nature of the followers.

WINDOW ON PRACTICE

A large organisation adopted the 'Managerial Grid' as the framework for its leadership development programme. The programme was generally well accepted and successful application of the team management style was seen to be connected to future promotions. Most managers, on leaving the programme, set out to display 9,9 leadership behaviours. However, this had unexpected and undesirable consequences. Not only were team members daunted by their managers suddenly displaying a different style, but sometimes the 9,9 style was not appropriate in the circumstances in which it was used. The organisation eventually discontinued the programme due to the damage that it was causing.

Much of the recent work on the notion of transformational/heroic leadership, and post-heroic leadership, similarly assumes that what is being discussed is the one best way for a leader to lead, and we return later to this leadership debate.

Do leaders need different styles for different situations?

WINDOW ON PRACTICE

Goffee and Jones (2006) highlight the situational nature of leadership by using examples of key figures. They identify how Winston Churchill was an inspirational wartime leader but when this time and place were gone his 'bulldog' style was not well suited to leading the reconstruction of post-war Britain. As an alternative they name Nelson Mandela as someone who could offer leadership across a wide range of contexts, adjusting from leading while in a prison cell on Robben Island to leading from Union House in Pretoria when he was released and was elected President of South Africa.

Source: Goffee, R. and Jones, G. (2006) 'The Lizard Kings', *People Management*, Vol. 12, No. 2, 26 January, pp. 32–4.

A variety of models, sometimes termed contingency models, have been developed to address the importance of context in terms of the leadership process, and as a consequence these models are complex. Many retain the concepts of production-centred and people-centred behaviour as ways of describing leadership behaviour, but use them in a different way. Hersey (1988) developed the Situational Leadership® model which identified that the appropriate leadership style in a situation should be dependent on the model's diagnosis of the follower's 'readiness' to perform a task. The model works on the premise that leaders can 'adapt their leadership style to meet the demands of their environment' (Hersey and Blanchard 1988: 169). Readiness of followers is defined in terms of ability and willingness. Level of ability includes the experience, knowledge and skills that an individual possesses in relation to the particular task at hand; and level of willingness encompasses the extent to which the individual has the motivation and commitment, or the self-confidence, to carry out the task. Having diagnosed the Performance Readiness® level of the followers, Hersey suggests that the leader then adapts his or her behaviour to fit. Hersey identifies two dimensions of leader behaviour: task behaviour, which is sometimes termed 'directive'; and relationship behaviour, which is sometimes termed 'supportive'. Task behaviour refers to the extent to which leaders spell out what has to be done. On the other hand, relationship behaviour is defined by the extent to which the leader engages in two-way or multi-way communication. The behaviours include listening, facilitating and supporting behaviours. The extent to which the leader emphasises each of these two types of behaviour results in the usual two-by-two matrix. The four resulting styles are identified as shown in Table 11.2.

Hersey and Blanchard produced questionnaires to help managers diagnose the readiness of their followers.

Other well-known contingency models include Fiedler's (1967) contingency model where leadership behaviour is matched to three factors in the situation: the nature of the relationship between the leader and members; the extent to which tasks are highly structured; and the position power of the leader. The appropriate leader behaviour (i.e. whether it should be task orientated or relationship orientated) depends on the combination of these three aspects in any situation. Fiedler's model is considered to be well supported by the evidence. The research was based on the relationship between style and performance in existing organisations in different contexts. For a very useful comparison of contingency models see Fullop *et al.* (1999).

Goleman (2000) makes a further contribution to the leadership debate in identifying six leadership styles, which are shown in Table 11.3, and argues that 'leaders with the best results do not rely on only one leadership style' (p. 78).

Goleman goes on to consider the appropriate context and impact of each style, and argues that the more styles the leader uses, the better. We have already reported Goleman's work on emotional intelligence, and he links this with the six styles by

High relationship behaviour Low task behaviour Followers are able, but unwilling or insecure **Supportive (participating) style (3)**	High relationship behaviour High task behaviour Followers are unable, but willing or confident **Coaching (selling) style (2)**
Low relationship behaviour Low task behaviour Followers are both able and willing or confident **Delegation style (4)**	Low relationship behaviour High task behaviour Followers are unable and unwilling or insecure **Directing (telling) style (1)**

Table 11.2 Hersey and Blanchard's four styles of leadership

Source: Adapted from P. Hersey and K.H. Blanchard (1988) *Management of Organizational Behavior: Utilizing human resources,* 5th edn. Englewood Cliffs, NJ: Prentice Hall International. © Copyright material, adapted and reprinted with the permission of Center for Leadership Studies, Escondido, CA 92025.

Table 11.3
Six leadership
styles reported by
Goleman

Coercive style	Leader demands immediate compliance
Authoritative style	Leader mobilises people towards a vision
Affiliative style	Leader creates emotional bonds and harmony
Democratic style	Leader uses participation to build consensus
Pacesetting style	Leader expects excellence and self-direction from followers
Coaching style	Leader develops people for the future

Source: Reprinted by permission of *Harvard Business Review*. Adapted from 'Leadership that gets results', by D. Goleman, March–April, pp. 80 and 82–3. Copyright © 2000 by the Harvard Business School Publishing Corporation; all rights reserved.

suggesting that leaders need to understand how the styles relate back to the different competencies of emotional intelligence so that they can identify where they need to focus their leadership development.

ACTIVITY 11.2

For each of Goleman's six styles think of a leader with whom you have worked, or who you know. For each of these individuals write a list of the behaviours that they use. Then consider the impact that these behaviours have on followers.
Do the behaviours have the same impact on all followers? If not, why not?

In a less mechanistic vein Goffee and Jones (2006) suggest that what works for one leader will not necessarily work for another. While adaptability of styles to suit different contexts is key, aspiring leaders need to discover what it is about themselves that they can mobilise in a leadership situation. Given this perspective, leadership appears very personal and is influenced by psychosocial perspectives and our sense of self (see Ford (2010) for an interesting discussion of this).

One of the differences between the contingency models we have just discussed and the 'best' style models is the implications for development. The Blake and Mouton model suggests leaders can be developed to lead in the one best way. The Hersey and Blanchard model, and most other contingency models, stress the flexibility of the leader – to learn to lead differently with different employees depending on their needs; hence, leaders should learn many styles and learn to diagnose the needs of their employees. Fielder's model, however, emphasises matching the leader to the context (a selection decision), rather than developing leaders in the context. An interesting contribution to this field comes from Hannah *et al.* (2009) who acknowledge its high degree of complexity and present an overarching model which seeks to integrate a substantial number of the factors discussed above.

Transformational leadership: do we really need heroes?

A different approach to understanding leadership is transformational (or heroic) leadership, which focuses on the leader's role at a strategic level, so there is a concentration on the one leader at the top of the organisation. There is a wide range of literature in this vein, most of it written in the 1980s. Since that time the academic literature may have moved on but the image of the transformational leader still remains widely attractive. Transformational leadership shows elements of the trait approach, as leaders are seen to 'have' charisma, which sets them apart as extraordinary and exceptional, and they are also seen to use a set of 'ideal' behaviours, with the assumption in many studies that this is the 'best' approach. A recent analysis of leadership advertisements demonstrates the extent to which notions of transformational leadership now dominate conceptualisations of leadership (den Hartog *et al.*, 2007)

Leaders are usually characterised as heroes and appear to know exactly what they are doing and how to 'save' the organisation from its present predicament (and consequently such leadership is found more often when organisations are in trouble). Leaders involve followers by generating a high level of commitment, partly due to such leaders focusing on the needs of followers and expressing their vision in such a way that it satisfies these needs. They communicate high expectations to followers and also the firm belief that followers will be able to achieve these goals. In this way the leaders promote self-confidence in the followers and they are motivated to achieve more than they ordinarily expect to achieve. In terms of behaviours, perhaps the most important is the vision of the future that the leaders offer and that they communicate this to the followers. Such leaders are able to help the followers make sense of what is going on and what needs to be done in the future as well as why. It is from this perspective that the distinction between management and leadership is often made. Bennis and Nanus (1985), for example, suggest that leadership is path finding while management is path following, and that leadership is about doing the right thing whereas management is about doing things right. Kotter (1990) identifies leaders as establishing a direction (whereas managers plan and budget); leaders align people with the vision (whereas managers organise things); leaders motivate and inspire (whereas managers control and solve problems); and leaders encourage change (whereas managers encourage order and predictability).

The approach does have a great strength in taking followers' needs into account and seeking to promote their self-confidence and potential, and the idea of the knight in shining armour is very attractive and potentially exciting. However, in spite of the emphasis on process there is also an emphasis on leadership characteristics which harks back to the trait approach to leadership, which has been characterised as elitist. Further, Fullop *et al.* (1999) identify factors in a rapidly changing turbulent environment which by the 1990s diluted the appropriateness of concentrating on the one leader at the top of the organisation. These factors include: globalisation making centralisation more difficult; technology enabling better sharing of information; and change being seen as a responsibility of all levels of the organisation – not just the top. They also note a dissatisfaction with corporate failures, identify few transformational leaders as positive role models, suggest that such a model of male authoritarian leadership is less relevant, and in particular that the macho leader with all the answers does not necessarily fit well with the encouragement of creativity and innovation. In addition they suggest that increasing teamwork and an increasing emphasis on knowledge workers mean that employees will be less responsive now to a transformational leader. Collinson (2012) has also termed this approach 'prozac leadership' in that the all-powerful leader is persuaded to believe in his or her own rhetoric and success and followers are unable to raise problems or acknowledge mistakes.

Maybe we should ask whether organisations really require such leaders or, indeed, whether such transcendental, all-powerful leaders can really exist (Ford 2010). Different conceptions of leadership, encompassed in the term 'post-heroic leadership', are now offered as alternatives, partly a reaction to the previous approach and partly a response to a changing environment. These could be described as the currently favoured ideal way to lead.

Post-heroic leadership

The focus in leadership research has moved away from understanding the traits and style of the one leader at the top of the organisation who knows how to solve all the organisation's problems, to how post-heroic leaders can facilitate many members of the organisation in taking on leadership roles. In this context Appelbaum *et al.* (2003) comment that female leadership styles are more effective in today's team-based, consensually driven organisations. Many commentators speak of leaders with integrity and humility, the ability to select good people and to remove barriers so they can fulfil their potential and perform (see e.g. Alimo-Metcalfe and Alban-Metcalfe 2002). There are a number of streams within post-heroic leadership research including distributed leadership, servant-leadership, authentic and ethical leadership (Gardner *et al.* 2010).

Distributed leadership presents a challenge to heroic models: it is not just the what of leadership, but the how and why, and it encourages a focus on leadership practice rather than roles (Spillane 2006). Leadership can emerge anywhere and is growing in importance as a result of increasingly virtual or distributed teams (Al-Ani *et al.* 2011). See Bennett *et al.* (2003) for a detailed review.

WINDOW ON PRACTICE

Goffee and Jones (2006) provide an excellent example of leadership by someone lower down in the organisation. They met Marcia, who was a cleaning supervisor in a large New York office block. She had the ability to read people from different cultures, and although often brash she was able to use humour to great effect, not tolerating slovenly cleaning. She managed in unpromising circumstances to forge a high-performing team as members knew she demanded that the job be done well but at the same time she cared about them.

Source: After 'The Lizard Kings', *People Management*, Vol. 12(2), pp. 32–34 (Goffee, R. and Jones, G. 2006), Reproduced with the permission of the publisher, the Chartered Institute of Personnel and Development, London (**www.cipd.co.uk**).

According to servant-leadership theory, the leader becomes a developer who can help others identify problems as opportunities for learning, and who can harness the collective intelligence of the organisation. Leaders should *design* the organisation in terms of vision, purpose, core values and the structures by which these ideas can be translated into business decisions and involve people at all levels in this design task. It is the role of the leader not to identify the right strategy, but to encourage strategic thinking in the organisation, and to design effective learning processes to make this happen. The leader should coach, guide and facilitate, and act as a servant in taking responsibility for the impact of his or her leadership on others, and in the sense that he or she overrides his or her own self-interest by personal commitment to the organisation's larger mission. This involves actively seeking others' views, experimenting, encouraging enquiry and distinguishing 'the way things are done' from 'the way we think things are done'.

WINDOW ON PRACTICE

'Servant-leadership', an idea dreamt up forty years ago by the American management development guru Robert Greenleaf, was based on a much older tradition of service and promotes leadership that is not motivated by self-interest and the pursuit of power. Great leaders are motivated by the desire to serve others and the best test of the servant-leader is whether those who are served grow as people. Do they, while being served, become healthier, wiser, freer, more autonomous, more likely themselves to become servants? There are ten characteristics of a servant leader:

1 Listening: seeks to identify the will of a group and helps to clarify that will.

2 Empathy: strives to understand and empathise with others.

3 Healing: has the potential for healing, or helping to 'make whole', oneself and others.

4 Awareness: understands issues involving ethics and values; can view most situations from a more integrated, holistic position.

5 Persuasion: seeks to convince others, rather than to coerce compliance. This aspect offers one of the clearest distinctions between the traditional authoritarian model and that of servant-leadership.

6 Conceptualisation: demonstrates the ability to look at a problem (or an organisation) from a conceptualising perspective, meaning that he or she must think beyond day-to-day realities.

7 Foresight: displays the ability to predict the likely outcome of a situation.

8 Stewardship: Greenleaf's view of all institutions was one in which chief executives, staff and trustees all played significant roles in holding their institutions in trust for the greater good of society.

9 Commitment to the growth of people: is deeply committed to the growth of each individual within his or her institution.

10 Building community: seeks to identify some means for building a community among those who work within a given institution.

Arkin (2009) argues that leaders adopting these characteristics might be what is required to lead organisations out of troubled times.

Source: Adapted from: Arkin, A. (2009) 'Back seat drivers', *People Management*, 7 May, p. 26.

While servant-leadership is an interesting development, it may be over-simplistic and again ignores the importance of national context (on servant-leadership in Italy see e.g. Bobbio *et al.* 2012).

There is also an increasing interest in **authentic leadership.** Wong and Cummings (2009) argue that authentic leadership is at the heart of effective leadership because of its emphasis on honesty, integrity and high ethical standards. Other conceptions focus on self-awareness and being true to oneself, which may have some resonance with trait theory and an emphasis on personal charisma (Lawler and Ashman 2012). Authentic leadership focuses on relationship building with followers and in this way raises the profile of followership, an emergent theme with leadership theory which we discuss below. This focus on authenticity is perhaps an outcome of the economic uncertainties starting in 2007 in which trust in those leading in government and institutions was severely damaged:

Upheavals in society have energised a tremendous demand for authentic leadership.

The destruction on 9/11, corporate scandals at companies like WorldCom and Enron and massive failures in the banking industry have all created fear and uncertainty. People feel apprehensive and insecure . . . they long for bona fide leadership they can trust and for leaders who are honest and good. People's demand for leadership makes the study of authentic leadership timely and worthwhile. (Northouse 2010: 205, cited in Lawler and Ashman 2012)

Authenticity certainly became a widely used term in the late 2000s to describe the behaviour required of politicians and leaders: followers want leaders who mean what they say and live what they believe (Deegan 2009).

Aligned to authentic leadership, the notion of **ethical leadership** is also becoming popular. Neubert *et al.* (2009) suggest that leaders can become 'agents of virtue', positively influencing the ethical climate within an organisation. They suggest that this can have positive outcomes such as increased job satisfaction and improved organisational commitment. In this way, positive ethical leadership behaviours can have desirable impacts on organisational performance. Ethical leadership also makes prominent the role of followers and **respectful leadership** follows in this vein (Quaquebeke and Eckloff 2010). Claudel and Casse (2012) outline two aspects to ethical leadership. The first is business leadership, which considers which stakeholder interests should be privileged, for example whether to pay or avoid corporation tax, an issue prominent in the UK in 2012. The second is team leadership, the key elements of which they outline as:

- reinforcing the team's purpose and mission
- not taking personal credit for the team's success
- encouraging team spirit and co-operation
- aligning individual and team interests
- treating all team members objectively, equally and fairly
- not abusing authority for personal advantage

(p. 34)

Ethical leadership also provides increasing recognition of the influence of religion on leadership. Ben-Hur and Jonsen (2012) explore Judaism and the role of Moses' teachings in respect of the visionary, teacher, servant, shepherd in leadership. Similarly Beekun (2012) considers leadership from an Islamic perspective

Both authentic and ethical leaders allow employees to identify and solve problems themselves and learn to take responsibility. The role of the leader is to develop collective self-confidence. As Grint (1997: 13) puts it, 'the apparent devolvement (or desertion – depending on your perspective) of responsibility has become the new standard in contemporary models of leadership'.

These visions of leadership are very attractive but they do require a dramatic change in thinking for both leaders and followers. For leaders there is the risk of giving away power, learning to trust employees, developing new skills, developing a different perspective of their role and overriding self-interest. Followers have the challenge of taking responsibility – which some may welcome, but others shun. Yet, if sustained competitive advantage is based on human capital and collective intelligence, these perspectives would seem to have much to offer.

Although empowering/authentic/ethical leaders have been shown to fit with the current climate, we may sometimes need heroic leaders. Kets de Vries (2003) makes the point that heroic leadership will never die as change makes people anxious and we need heroic leaders to calm them down, but since no one can live up to the expectations of heroic leaders, they will eventually become a disappointment. We conclude with the thought that there is no one best way – different leaders and different leader behaviours are needed at different times.

Followership

Much of the research on leadership takes a rather managerialist approach: that is, it assumes that leadership is a 'good thing' if only the right way of doing it can be found. Increasingly, however, more critical perspectives on leadership can be found which question the whole premise of leadership (for an example of this trend see Ford *et al.* 2008). One aspect of critical perspectives is to suggest that followers are important, but largely neglected, in treatments of leadership. Followers are clearly critical if leaders are to lead, but little thought has been given to them other than as a recipient of the leader's actions. There are a number of studies which have started to develop thinking in terms of followership, for example Rigio *et al.* (2008) have presented an edited collection of papers from a 1996 conference on followership. Jackson and Parry's (2008) work suggests ways of thinking that will support the examination of followers, for example social identity theories. Further, Smothers *et al.* (2012) argue that followers want equity rather than personalised treatment. These are early days for the study of followers but those who are engaging in this research have gone so far as to suggest that including the study of followers in leadership theory may call into question much of the existing theory. We give an example of this in the Window on practice that follows, which explores followership using a metaphor from Greek mythology – that of Odysseus leading his followers home from war.

WINDOW ON (MYTHICAL) PRACTICE

The story starts at the end of the Trojan War, when Odysseus sets out to return to his home in Ithaca. He leads several ships of soldiers who, we may presume, are similarly keen to return home. They are not to know that it is only Odysseus who will set foot once again on Ithaca, for the many adventures they will meet along the way will result in their decimation. For example, many men are lost in a battle at their first port of call, the island of the Cicones, and more are eaten by Polyphemus, a one-eyed giant, on the island of the Cyclops. And so it continues along the journey. Homer tells us of Odysseus's cleverness, in saving himself and (some of) his crew in many dangerous situations yet his crew are denied the pleasures of food and wine enjoyed by Odysseus and, ultimately, all perish.

Leadership contains, in this earliest recounting, a promise to followers of only horror, failure, betrayal, disappointment and denial. We are told that followers are incapable of agency unless organised by a leader,

but is it not the case that without his crew Odysseus literally could not have sailed between the Greek islands? Without his crew Odysseus is revealed to be incapable. We can imagine one of his crew telling his story:

The crew had waited interminably for Odysseus to continue the journey home to Ithaca, but Odysseus was bewitched on this enchanted island until one day we saw our chance. Circe was away. The lads begged me to go to Odysseus and to tempt him with thoughts of his home, his wife and son, so that he would agree we could leave that fated island and return to Ithaca. He eventually gave in, but blow me down if he did not find another reason for delay, and another, and another. And all along the way he was enjoying himself, while our number of men dwindled until only a few of us now remain. I have a foreboding about the future. I fear none of us will return to Ithaca.

Adapted from Ford, J. and Harding, N. (2009) 'Telling an untold story: On being a follower rather than a leader', EGOS Colloquium, Barcelona.

This alternative telling of Odysseus's tale presents a very different perspective from the heroic one that has been perpetuated across the centuries. This may have resonance for many who, since 2007, have lost their jobs in, for example, the banking sector and faced economic hardship, while those leading them into that position have benefited from large pay-offs and enormous pensions. It may now be that the time is right for a more detailed examination of the flipside of leadership: followership.

ACTIVITY 11.3

Thinking of your own experiences of being led (at work, school or other settings), what consideration was there of the role of followers? How could including their perspective have changed events?

SUMMARY PROPOSITIONS

11.1   Leadership is a process where one person influences a group of others to achieve group or organisational goals – leadership is thus about motivation.

11.2   The trait model of leadership, although often discredited, continues to play a part in our understanding of leadership.

11.3   Behavioural models are more helpful than earlier models as they concentrate on what leaders do rather than on what they are.

11.4   Some behavioural models offer a 'one best way' of leadership, but more sophisticated models take account of contingency factors such as maturity of followers and the nature of the task.

11.5   Models of transformational leadership treat the leader as a hero who can (single-handedly) turn the organisation around and deliver it from a crisis, whereas empowering and post-heroic leadership models conceptualise the leader as teacher and facilitator, who involves many in the leadership task.

11.6   There is an increasing interest in authentic and ethical leadership as an appropriate response to leading in turbulent economic times.

11.7   Critical perspectives on leadership argue for the surfacing of the role of followers and suggest that this may call into question much current leadership theory.

GENERAL DISCUSSION TOPICS

1 Do we need leaders at all? Discuss what alternatives there might be.

2 How likely is it that post-heroic forms of leadership will replace heroic leadership approaches?

3 In what way do you think that including the perspective of followers in the study of leadership will contribute to theory?

THEORY INTO PRACTICE

We have argued in this chapter that leadership models developed from American research may not be effective in other contexts, even other western contexts such as Europe and certainly not in Asia and Africa. Here we go further to consider whether integration of leadership concepts from elsewhere may in fact improve current leadership models. We draw on Bertsch's (2012) work on the African philosophy of Ubuntu and his application of this to American leadership models to explore this in some detail.

Our (widely adopted) definition of leadership centred on influencing people towards organisational ends. Globalisation and growing international operations have increased both the need to lead and influence across national and cultural boundaries and the recognition that what works in one country may not work in another. Yet multinational corporations have been slow to recognise this despite a substantial evidence base of the role of national context on leadership. Bertsch illustrates this through comparing the African philosophy of Ubuntu with heroic leadership models. Despite much criticism, these models of heroic leadership, centred on influencing, motivating and empowering, dominate American leadership thinking and Bertsch demonstrates that Americans tend to prefer charismatic and participative leadership styles. Ubuntu, however, is a philosophy of humaneness that rejects this notion of influence.

Bertsch defines Ubuntu as humaneness and explains it thus: 'a person is a person because of other persons [and requires] the capacity to express compassion, reciprocity, dignity, humanity, and mutuality in the interest of building and maintaining communities with justice and mutual caring' (p. 83). A person can only then function effectively as a human (and leader) when they acknowledge and appreciate the roles played by others. The five key elements of this philosophy comprise: survival; solidarity with others (missing in individual-centric American approaches); compassion; respect; and dignity. Bertsch argues that words such as harmony, connectedness, compassion, respect, human dignity and unity describe Ubuntu.

Ubuntu is thus at odds with American heroic leadership styles: it emphasises participation and agreement in decision making and presents a mechanism to ensure that decisions are ethical and that colleagues treat each other in appropriate ways. This arises from the fact that individuals are interconnected and must respect each other. Indeed, within this philosophy the ego and self-centredness often associated with heroic leaders is detrimental to good leadership. Leaders should be available and supportive of subordinates: a leadership position can only be retained if leaders act with civility, trust and respect and put the team's interests above their own. Self-awareness and self-assurance are essential. Leaders must promote the work and contribution of the team, which is again contrary to heroic leaders who seek recognition and glory.

Bertsch uses his analysis to argue that traits such as self-sacrificial, sincere, trustworthy, honest, group-focused and non-elitist are missing in contemporary American leadership practices. Further, that a move towards encouragement, compassion, solidarity would substantially alter these leadership practices and could address the ethical dilemmas facing many American-based corporations.

Questions

1 Do you agree that many of the aspects associated with Ubuntu are missing from heroic leadership models?

2 What similarities can you see between Ubuntu and emerging leadership models such as servant-leadership and authentic and ethical leadership models?

3 To what extent do you agree that the Ubuntu philosophy could improve American leadership models?

FURTHER READING

Goffee, R. and Jones, G. (2006) *Why Should Anyone be Led by You?* Boston, MA: Harvard Business School Press.

Goffee, R. and Jones, G. (2006) 'This time it's personal', *People Management*, Vol. 12, No. 21, pp. 28–33. Goffee and Jones combine sound concepts and practical advice on leadership in this thought-promoting book and article. They recognise that leadership, as well as being non-hierarchical, is situational and relational. In meeting the leadership challenge, they suggest, leaders need to know themselves and show who they are to a sufficient extent; they need to be prepared to take personal risks; they need to be sensitive to context and rewrite this; they need to be authentic, but conform sufficiently; and they need to manage the social distance between themselves and their followers.

Rigio, R., Chaleff, I. and Lipman-Blumen, J. (eds) (2008) *The Art of Followership: How great followers create great leaders and organisations*. San Francisco, CA: Jossey-Bass.
This book developed out of a series of papers presented at a conference on followership. The editors argue that a new subfield within leadership, that of followership, is emerging. The book seeks to define followership, set out what constitutes effective followership and consider the drawbacks and pitfalls of followership. It also discusses future research and practice in followership. It is a comprehensive treatment of this recent stream of research.

Avolio, B.J. and Gardner, W.L. (2005) 'Authentic leadership development: Getting to the root of positive forms of leadership', *Leadership Quarterly*, Vol. 16, pp. 315–38.
This editorial introduces a special issue on authentic leadership. It considers the environmental and organisational forces that have created interest in authentic leadership and the emerging questions and concerns that relate to it. Authentic leadership is also compared with other forms of leadership such as transformational and servant.

Gardner, W. *et al*. (2010) 'Scholarly leadership of the study of leadership: A review of The Leadership Quarterly's second decade, 2000–2009', *Leadership Quarterly*, Vol. 21, pp. 922–58.
This article presents a detailed analysis of published leadership research and how trends are developing. It demonstrates increased focus on post-heroic leadership research, but also that transformational leadership is still prominent.

REFERENCES

Al-Ani, B., Horspool, A. and Bligh, M. (2011) 'Collaborating with "virtual strangers": Towards developing a framework for leadership in distributed teams', *Leadership*, Vol. 7, pp. 219–49.

Alimo-Metcalfe, B. and Alban-Metcalfe, J. (2002) 'The great and the good', *People Management*, Vol. 8, pp. 32–4.

Appelbaum, S., Audet, L. and Miller, J. (2003) 'Gender and leadership? Leadership and gender? A journey through the landscape of theories', *Leadership and Organisation*, Vol. 24, pp. 43–51.

Arkin, A. (2009) 'Back seat drivers', *People Management*, 7 May, p. 26.

Beekun, R. (2012) 'Character centred leadership: Muhammad (p) as an ethical role model for CEOs', *Journal of Management Development*, Vol. 31, pp. 1003–20.

Ben-Hur, S. and Jonsen, K. (2012) 'Ethical leadership: Lessons from Moses', *Journal of Management Development*, Vol. 31, pp. 962–73.

Bennett, N., Wise, C., Woods, P. and Harvey, J. (2003) 'Distributed leadership: A review of the literature', *National College for School Leadership*. Milton Keynes: The Open University.

Bennis, W. and Nanus, B. (1985) *Leaders: The strategies for taking charge.* New York: Harper & Row.

Bertsch, A. (2012) 'Updating American leadership practices by exploring the African philosophy of Ubuntu', *Journal of Leadership, Accountability and Ethics*, Vol. 9, pp. 81–97.

Blake, R. and Mouton, J. (1964) *The Managerial Grid.* Houston, TX: Gulf Publishing.

Bobbio, A., Van Dierendonck, D. and Manganelli, A. (2012) 'Servant leadership in Italy and its relation to organisational variables', *Leadership*, Vol. 8, pp. 229–43.

Bolden, R. and Kirk, P. (2009) 'African leadership: Surfacing new understandings through leadership development', *International Journal of Cross Cultural Management*, Vol. 9, pp. 69–86.

Claudel, P. and Casse, P. (2012) 'The ethical leader', **www.trainingjournal.com**, August, pp. 32–5.

Collinson, D. (2012) 'Prozac leadership and the limits of positive thinking', *Leadership*, Vol. 8, pp. 87–107.

Cowsgill, R. and Grint, K. (2008) 'Leadership, task and relationship: Orpheus, Prometheus and Janus', *Human Resource Management Journal*, Vol. 18, pp. 188–95.

Deegan, D. (2009) 'The changing face of leadership: Past, present and future', **www.trainingjournal.com**, December.

Den Hartog, D., Caley, C. and Dewe, P. (2007) 'Recruiting leaders: An analysis of leadership advertisements', *Human Resource Management Journal*, Vol. 17, pp. 58–75.

El Garah, W., Beekun, R., Habisch, A., Lenssen, G. and Adaui, C. (2012) 'Practical wisdom for management from the Islamic tradition', *Journal of Management Development*, Vol. 31, pp. 991–1000.

Eyong, J. (2012) 'Leadership re-construction in sub-Sahara Africa (SSA): Interpretation from an ancient indigenous organisation', The EKPE 4th Developing Leadership Capacity Conference, University of Exeter.

Fache, D. (2009) 'Are great leaders born or are they made?', *Frontiers of Health Service Management*, Vol. 26, pp. 27–30.

Fiedler, F. (1967) *A Theory of Leadership Effectiveness.* New York: McGraw-Hill.

Ford, J. (2010) 'Studying leadership critically: A psychosocial lens on leadership identities', *Leadership*, Vol. 6, pp. 1–19.

Ford, J. and Harding, N. (2009) 'Telling an untold story: On being a follower rather than a leader', EGOS Colloquium, Barcelona.

Ford, J., Harding, N. and Learmonth, M. (2008) *Leadership as Identity: Constructions and deconstructions.* London: Palgrave Macmillan.

Fullop, L., Linstead, S. and Dunford, R. (1999) 'Leading and managing', in L. Fullop and S. Linstead (eds), *Management: A critical text.* South Yarra: Macmillan.

Gardner, W., Lowe, K., Moss, T., Mahoney, K. and Cogliser, C. (2010) 'Scholarly leadership of the study of leadership: A review of The Leadership Quarterly's second decade, 2000–2009', *Leadership Quarterly*, Vol. 21, pp. 922–58.

Goffee, R. and Jones, G. (2006) 'The Lizard Kings', *People Management*, Vol. 12, pp. 32–4.

Goleman, D. (1998) 'What makes . . . a leader?', *Harvard Business Review*, November–December, pp. 93–102.

Goleman, D. (2000) 'Leadership that gets results', *Harvard Business Review*, March–April, pp. 78–90.

Grint, K. (1997) *Leadership*. Oxford: Oxford University Press.

Hannah, S., Woodfolk, R. and Lord, R. (2009) 'Leadership self-structure: A framework for positive leadership', *Journal of Organisational Behaviour*, Vol. 30, pp. 269–90.

Heil, G., Bennis, W. and Stephens, D. (2000) *Douglas McGregor, Revisited: Managing the human side of the enterprise*. New York: Wiley.

Hersey, P. and Blanchard, K. (1988) *Management of Organizational Behavior: Utilizing human resources*, 5th edn. Englewood Cliffs, NJ: Prentice Hall International.

Higgs, M. (2003) 'How can we make sense of leadership in the 21st century?', *Leadership and Organisational Development Journal*, Vol. 24, pp. 273–84.

Hollington, S. (2006) 'How to lead your boss', *People Management*, Vol. 12, pp. 44–5.

House, R. (1976) 'A 1976 theory of charismatic leadership', in L. Hunt and L. Larson (eds), *Leadership: The Cutting Edge*. Carbondale: Southern Illinois University Press.

House, R., Hanges, P., Javidan, M., Dorfman, P. and Gupta, V. (2004) *Culture, Leadership and Organisations: The GLOBE study of 62 societies*. Thousand Oaks, CA: Sage.

Jackson, B. and Parry, K. (2008) *A Very Short, Fairly Interesting and Reasonably Cheap Book about Studying Leadership*. London: Sage.

Kets De Vries, M. (2003) 'The dark side of leadership', *Business Strategy Review*, Vol. 14, pp. 25–8.

Kilpatrick, S. and Locke, E. (1991) 'Leadership: Do traits matter?', *Academy of Management Executive*, Vol. 5, pp. 48–60.

Kotter, J. (1990) *A Force for Change: How leadership differs from management*. New York: Free Press.

Lawler, J. and Ashman, I. (2012) 'Theorising leadership authenticity: A Sartrean perspective', *Leadership*, Vol. 8, pp. 327–44.

McGregor, D. (1960) *The Human Side of the Enterprise*. New York: McGraw-Hill.

Neubert, N., Carlson, D., Kacmar, K., Roberts, J. and Chonko, L. (2009) 'The virtuous influence of ethical leadership behaviour: Evidence from the field', *Journal of Business Ethics*, Vol. 90, pp. 157–70.

Northouse, P. (2006) *Leadership: Theory and practice*. Thousand Oaks, CA: Sage.

Quaquebeke, N. and Eckloff, T. (2010) 'Defining respectful leadership: What it is, how it can be measured, and another glimpse at what it is related to', *Journal of Business Ethics*, Vol. 91, pp. 343–58.

Rigio, R., Chaleff, I. and Lipman-Blumen, J. (2008) *The Art of Followership: How great followers create great leaders and organisations*. San Francisco, CA: Jossey-Bass.

Shackleton, V. (1995) *Business Leadership*. London: Routledge.

Smothers, J., Absher, K. and White, D. (2012) 'In the eye of the beholder: A configurational analysis of followers' conceptualizations of the ideal academic department leader at private universities', *Leadership*, Vol. 8, pp. 397–419.

Spillane, J. (2006) *Distributed Leadership*. San Francisco, CA: Jossey-Bass.

Tavanti, M. (2012) 'The cultural dimensions of Italian leadership: Power distance, uncertainty avoidance and masculinity from an American perspective', *Leadership*, Vol. 8, pp. 287–301.

Wong, C. and Cummings, G. (2009) 'The influence of authentic leadership behaviours on trust and work outcomes of health care staff', *Journal of Leadership Studies*, Vol. 3, pp. 6–23.

Yooyanyong, P. and Muenjohn, N. (2010) 'Leadership styles of expatriate managers: A comparison between American and Japanese expatriates', *Journal of American Academy of Business*, Vol. 15, pp. 161–7.

Chapter 12

MANAGING ATTENDANCE AND ABSENCE

THE OBJECTIVES OF THIS CHAPTER ARE TO:

1   Review the national context on employee absence

2   Identify the impact of absence on the organisation

3   Explore the process of absence from work and absence causation

4   Discuss methods by which long- and short-term absence can be minimised

Our understanding of the importance of attendance at the workplace and the problem of absence is linked to the changes in working practices over the past 200 years:

industrial revolutions which transformed the economies of nations that had hitherto known only agriculture and handicrafts, aided by simple machines, brought new dangers and difficulties into society. (Neal and Robertson 1968: 9)

Note the phrase 'dangers and difficulties into society': the social impact was considerable and much quicker than any previous such change. Instead of fields and individual workshops, the standard workplace became the factory, with the central discipline of machinery powered from a single source, first water and later other forms of energy, and for reasons connected to supply of fuel, raw materials and transport. The underlying principle was that work had to be centralised to be efficient, and that principle has continued, regardless of the nature of the work being done. The modern 'factory' may be a bank in London, a restaurant in Paris, an automobile plant in Chicago, a hospital in Cape Town, or a hotel in Bangkok, but the workers have to be there, usually in large numbers. There may be moves towards home-working, decentralisation and subcontracting, but the traditional reasons of power, raw materials and transport have been replaced by specialisation and the concomitant need for intense communication, social interaction and proximity to the supply chain, facilities and resources. If employees need to be brought together for these newer reasons, they obviously need to be there at roughly the same time. People have to attend work in a specific place and at a specified time for a specified period. Attendance is key; absence is a problem.

Attendance and absence are relatively easy to monitor in the sense of a common culture and rules, deviation from which is obvious and manageable. Absence has always been a matter of concern to all employers, and methods for reducing it have frequently focused on disciplinary or punitive measures. Recently absence has been framed in a more positive discourse, and the focus is now on what can be done to promote attendance, as well as the rehabilitation of employees with long-term absence.

The national context

Absence may be short-term or long-term, authorised or unauthorised, due to sickness, holiday, maternity/paternity, parenting, the performance of public duty, company business, public holiday and so on. The CIPD carries out an annual survey of the level of absence omitting holidays and company business. In 2012 it found an average of 6.8 days absence per employee per year, down from 8.0 in 2009 (CIPD 2009) and 7.4 in 2008 (CIPD 2012). The average level of absence varies according to employment sector, being highest in the public sector and lowest in manufacturing and production and private-sector services. The CIPD is not the only organisation conducting such surveys, yet the results reported are broadly similar. The increased attention paid in recent years by companies to health, well-being and absence monitoring appears so far to have had little effect. Even world-wide recession and economic crisis have not brought numbers down much. Research by the Work Foundation (Silcox 2006) concluded that absence has remained broadly at the same level for the past thirty years with small fluctuations due to unemployment and the wider economic cycle.

WINDOW ON PRACTICE

Comparative absence figures

Lokke and her colleagues (2007) used data from the European Employee Index. The data was collected from employees, randomly selected, in 2004. Days absence per employee in 2004 were as follows: Denmark 2.8; Norway 3.5; Sweden 3.9; Finland 4.6. In each country absence in the public sector was higher than in the private sector, except for Sweden where there were no differences.

It is interesting to compare these figures with UK data for the same year where the CBI reports 6.8 working days lost per employee (CBI/AXA 2005) and the CIPD reports 8.4 (CIPD 2005). The differences might be explained by the choice of respondents, as the UK surveys collect data from managers about their employees, rather than directly from employees themselves. The TUC (2005) reported European comparisons based on figures produced by the University of Surrey. These indicate that short-term absence in the UK is lower than in any other country, apart from Denmark, and that long-term absence is lower than others except for Ireland, Austria and Germany.

There is a clear message that comparative figures are difficult to produce as so much depends on sources and methods.

Sources: Lokke, A., Eskildsen, J. and Jensen, T. (2007) 'Absenteeism in the Nordic countries', *Employee Relations*, Vol. 29, No. 1, pp. 16–29; TUC (2005) *Countering an Urban Legend: Sicknote Britain?* TUC: London; CBI/AXA (2005) *Who Cares Wins: Absence and labour turnover 2005*. CBI/AXA: London; CIPD (2005) *Absence Management: A survey of policy and practice*. CIPD: London.

In terms of the patterns of absence most surveys report that generally:

- absence is higher in larger organisations than in small ones;
- public-sector absence is higher than in the private sector;
- absence rates are higher for women, full-time workers and those under 30;
- managers, professionals and administrative professionals have lower levels of absence than other occupational groups (although this may be because they tend to have more flexibility in their working arrangements);
- unsurprisingly, absence was higher among manual workers.

The CBI reports that absence costs the UK economy around £13 billion per year and it constantly asserts that around 13% of all absence is not genuine, while unions point to the efforts that workers often make to attend work even when ill (see e.g. TUC 2005). Big sporting events, such as the World Cup, often attract attention in terms of their impact on absence levels, but organisations can use these events to their advantage given some thought. Smethurst (2006) reports on how Prudential and Egg responded to the World Cup by offering more flexible working over the period, with incentive schemes and themed competitions to incorporate interest in the event.

At a national cost of sickness absence is considerable to employers and to the taxpayer. In 2013 the UK, for instance, had over 2.6 million people claiming long-term sickness and disability benefit, considerably more than those claiming unemployment benefit.

WINDOW ON PRACTICE

International approaches to long-term absence

James and his colleagues (2002) explain how different countries have enacted legislation in respect of sickness absence. For example, in Sweden employers must ensure that they have assessed rehabilitation needs at an early stage, and are then obliged to put any relevant rehabilitation measures in place. In the Netherlands employers must submit a report on any employee who is unable to work within thirteen weeks of the start of the absence. They are required to submit this to a social security agency and must produce a 'work resumption plan'. In New South Wales, Australia, when workers have been absent for twelve weeks employers must establish a work rehabilitation programme, and if there are more than twenty people employed, they must appoint a rehabilitation coordinator and prepare plans for return to work.

Source: Summarised from James, P., Cunningham, I. and Dibben, P. (2002) 'Absence management and the issues of job retention and return to work', *Human Resource Management Journal*, Vol. 12, No. 2, pp. 82–94.

The organisational context

The CIPD (2006) found that over 90% of organisations in its survey considered absence to be a significant cost to the organisation, but less than half monitored this cost. The average cost was reported to be £598 per year per employee, which had risen to £673 in 2011 (CIPD 2012). Several studies (e.g. Barham and Leonard 2002; Bevan 2002) show that estimating the costs of absence is complicated, and that the estimate needs to include not only direct costs (i.e. paying salary and benefits for a worker who is not there), but also indirect costs such as replacement staff, overall reductions in productivity and administrative costs. Most employers underestimate the true costs of sickness absence, particularly long-term sickness; even the most sophisticated companies are not well equipped to calculate such costs.

Traditionally employers have concentrated on managing short-term absence, and while long-term absence accounts for only around 20% of absence incidents, it can represent more than 40% of total working time lost.

Process and causes of absence

The most frequently stated causes of absence are minor illness for short-term absence and back pain and minor illness (for manual workers) and stress and minor illness (for non-manual workers). For long-term illness the most frequent causes for manual workers are back pain and musculoskeletal injuries; and for non-manual workers stress remains the greatest, and an increasing, cause. The increase in stress as a cause may well be partly due to the fact that this is now a more legitimate reason for non-attendance than previously.

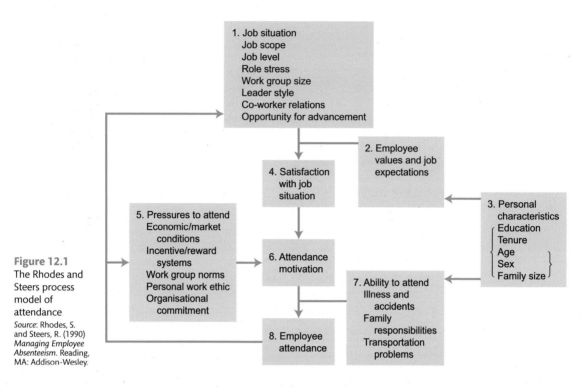

Figure 12.1
The Rhodes and Steers process model of attendance

Source: Rhodes, S. and Steers, R. (1990) *Managing Employee Absenteeism*. Reading, MA: Addison-Wesley.

It is important to bear in mind that recorded causes of absence in organisations will be those causes which employees perceive the organisation to view as legitimate.

The causes of absence are complex and interrelated and a process approach is generally agreed to be the most useful way of understanding absence behaviour, although there are criticisms that such models are not supported by the evidence. One of the most widely quoted models is from Rhodes and Steers (1990) and in our view this is the most useful of the process models. For an alternative model **see** Nicholson (1977).

The Rhodes and Steers model (see Figure 12.1) not only includes content information on the causes of absence, but also incorporates a range of interdependent processes. In essence the model focuses on attendance motivation and the ability to attend in terms of resulting attendance behaviour.

Rhodes and Steers suggest that *attendance motivation* is directly affected by two factors: *satisfaction with the job* and *pressure to attend*. Pressure to attend may result from such factors as market conditions. Examples include the likelihood that there will be redundancies at the individual's workplace and how easy it would be to get another job; incentives to attend, such as attendance bonuses; work group norms on what is acceptable in the work group and the effects of absence on other group members; personal work ethic producing internal pressure to attend based on beliefs about what is right; and commitment to the organisation through an identification with the beliefs and values of the organisation and an intention to remain with the organisation. On this basis threat of redundancies, attendance bonuses, team structures where team members have to cover the workload of an absent member, a personal ethic about the need to attend work wherever possible, and feelings of loyalty to the organisation should all promote the motivation to attend. All of these factors contribute to the current phenomenon of 'presenteeism', the opposite of absenteeism, which is explored in the Glossary at the end of the book.

Rhodes and Steers suggest that satisfaction with the job is determined by the *job situation* and moderated by *employee values and job expectations*. Factors in the job situation are identified as job scope and level of responsibility and decision making; role stress such as work overload, underload, difficult working conditions or hours; work group size; leadership style of an individual's immediate manager, particularly the openness of the relationship and how easy it is to discuss and solve problems jointly; strength of relationships with co-workers; and the opportunity for promotion. On this basis higher levels of responsibility and the opportunity to make decisions in relation to job demands, balanced workload and good working conditions, small work group size, an open relationship with the immediate manager, good relationships with colleagues and the opportunity for promotion should all improve attendance motivation.

However, job satisfaction is moderated by the values and expectations of the employee. Such values and expectations are shaped by both personality and personal characteristics and life experiences, but can also change during the course of one's life. The extent to which the job matches up to expectations and values will have a bearing on job satisfaction; a close match is more likely to lead to satisfaction than a mismatch.

Personality and personal characteristics influence expectations and values and job satisfaction. We have previously referred to the influence of age and sex on absence rates. Length of service has also been identified as having an influence. However, none of these relationships is clear cut, and different pieces of research often produce different findings. There is most evidence for suggesting that younger workers and female workers have the highest rates of absence, and it is argued that younger workers value free time to a greater extent than older workers.

This brings us to the last influence on attendance, which is the *ability to attend*. This influence is interposed between attendance motivation and actual attendance. For example, an employee could be highly motivated to attend, but may have insurmountable transportation difficulties, family or domestic responsibilities, or may be genuinely ill. In these cases motivation to attend does not result in attendance.

Managing for attendance

The complex interrelationship of the causes of absence needs to be taken into account in its management. Many policies for managing absence focus only on minimising short-term rather than long-term absence. The role of sickness in long-term absence has been given insufficient attention in the past, as has the fact that short-term absence, if badly handled, can lead to long-term absence. Long-term and short-term absence require different approaches. The causes of absence may be identified by patterns of absence and by enabling individuals to be open about why they are not at work. Measures range from proactive methods intended to reduce the risk of ill health, to measures intended to reduce spells of absence and those intended to reduce the length of absence. Typically there is a mix of processes both to discourage absence and positively encourage attendance, but these work differently with those on long- and short-term sickness absence.

Whatever approach is chosen, there is a great need for consistency in the construction and implementation of absence management policies and procedures, not only in terms of ensuring fairness and as a support for any disciplinary action taken, but also in terms of providing employees with clear expectations about how absence will be tackled, and promoting an attendance culture. While different approaches work in different sectors and with different types of staff, the policies themselves need to be consistent to encourage employee acceptance and line manager support. Dunn and Wilkinson (2002) report the difficulties of a line manager in a production company because manufacturing staff were subject to more stringent absence procedures than other staff in the company.

Inconsistent implementation also weakens any policy and procedures. The role of the line manager is key and there is much emphasis on giving the line manager ownership of absence and attendance issues, with support from the HR department. Whatever policies and procedures are set up, the line manager must have ownership of these and apply them in practice. James and his colleagues (2002) found that two-thirds of their interviewees in a long-term absence management study had problems in the way that line managers carried out their responsibilities. Managers frequently did not follow the guidelines in matters such as ongoing contact with absent employees, and consequently the HR department did not know what was going on and often had to step in and manage cases. James and his colleagues found that managers' behaviour resulted from time pressures, lack of awareness of what the procedure was and lack of training.

WINDOW ON PRACTICE

Managing absence at HBOS

McFadzean (2003) reports on a pilot project at HBOS which encouraged the HR department to look at absence from a different perspective. The project was intended to test two theories: first, that much absence had non-medical causes and therefore could be tackled by the HR department; and, second, that absence could be reduced without buying in any extra resources.

To introduce the project workshops were held with HR members and best practice guidelines were made available, HR advisers were then encouraged to go out and talk to managers about absence. The best practice model included an emphasis on finding the underlying cause of absence in terms of social or work-related issues, based on the belief that such issues are the root cause of much absence, and if not dealt with they will gradually produce medical symptoms. The skill was therefore in getting beyond the symptoms on the medical note to understand the underlying cause of absence. Once the underlying cause was understood then temporary or permanent changes could be made to help, such as reducing targets, hours and responsibilities or changing work patterns.

HBOS promoted an absence champion network in its first-tier approach which would adopt the best practice principles provided by the HR department, and would receive up-to-date information on absence and target cases for intervention (over twenty days' absence for long-term absence and four periods in a year for short-term absence). The HR department received consistent management information, and progress was monitored in all cases. A health provider network was also set up, as a second-tier approach (for long-term absence), to target high-risk areas and the top two causes of absence. Individuals were referred after ten days' absence in these cases, and the health provider network included a psychologist and a physiotherapist. Treatment was considered justified if there was deemed to be an 80% chance of return to work. HBOS feels that

rehabilitation back into work needs to become part of the business culture.

The project was only carried out in some areas and performance was measured against control groups. HBOS saved 21,000 days over the six-month period (6,000 headcount) and £880,000. Short-term absence was reduced by 35%, but there was no impact on long-term absence, which continues to creep up.

Source: After McFazdean, M. (2003) 'Managing absence', Paper presented at the CIPD National Conference, Harrogate, 22–24 October.

Some measures intended to manage absence actually increase it, so monitoring any new policies and procedures is critical. In terms of implementing a new absence strategy, the advice given by Huczynski and Fitzpatrick (1989) still holds good. The ALIEDIM process they suggest comprises the following stages:

- **A**ssess the absence problem
- **L**ocate the absence problem
- **I**dentify and prioritise absence causes
- **E**valuate the current absence control methods
- **D**esign the absence control programme
- **I**mplement the absence control programme
- **M**onitor the effectiveness of the absence control programme.

The mix of policies and methods chosen will be specific to the needs of the individual organisation.

Below are some of the most frequently used approaches to managing absence. Some are most appropriate for short-term absence, some are better suited to long-term absence, and others meet the needs of both.

Accurate records

Managing absence is almost impossible without an accurate picture of current absence levels and patterns, which requires identification of areas of high absence and the most common reasons for absence in the organisation. The CIPD (2006) found that 60% of those organisations reporting a reduction in absence attributed it to improved monitoring. However, such data collection is more often reported in the public sector and manufacturing industry than in the rest of the private sector. The HSE (Silcox 2005a) in a bid to aid employers has produced a computerised absence recording and management tool, SART, which encourages employers to record such data in a more consistent manner. Prior to its review of absence Carlsberg-Tetley (IDS 2001) did not have an accurate picture of sickness absence. Although some records were kept, absence was inconsistently measured and recorded, so there was no reliable information about level of absence and

Figure 12.2
The Bradford
factor formula for
scoring absence
Note: The score is
usually calculated
over a year.

Absence score = (spells of absence × spells of absence) × duration of absence

patterns. This was its first task in tackling absence. Carlsberg-Tetley decided to adopt the 'Bradford factor' method for scoring absence, where both frequency of absence spells and absence duration are used but with the weight being given to the former. The Bradford factor formula, devised by Bradford University, is shown in Figure 12.2. For further information on statistics see IDS (2005a).

WINDOW ON PRACTICE

Absence data at Brakes

AHP (Active Health Partners), who manage absence and attendance for Brakes, receive weekly updates from the payroll in order to update their absence data and produce reports. These reports are available to managers and include:

- details of who is absent and their expected return;
- individual data for each employee, including days lost, absence rate, longest absence spell, number of absence spells, any Monday and Friday absences;

- department breakdowns;
- details relating to those employees most frequently absent;
- reasons for absence overall;
- trend reports;
- number of accidents.

This information is regularly discussed, typically weekly at the conference call between all managers in a region.

Source: IDS (2005b) 'Brakes',
Absence Management, No. 801, November.
London: IDS.

Absence reports are frequently produced by the HR department and sent to line managers – and such reports will often include details of employees where trigger points have been hit and where intervention is required by the line manager. However, Dunn and Wilkinson (2002) found that the attention line managers gave to these reports varied, and some managers never even looked at the reports, because they did not agree that this was the best way to manage staff. As one manager commented, 'I know my staff well enough not to need these reports . . . at the end of the day it all comes down to good management and knowing your staff'. Some managers argued that the reports were of little use because the employees they managed often worked long hours (beyond contract) and came in at weekends. It was felt that to punish such employees, who were clearly committed to the company, because they had reached certain absence levels was unreasonable, and would be counter-productive.

Absence review and trigger points

In order to focus attention on those with less satisfactory absence records many organisations identify trigger points in terms of absence spells or length, or Bradford factor scores which indicate that action is needed when an individual's absence record hits the trigger. Such policies for reviewing absence appear to be critical in absence reduction, and the CIPD (2006) reports that 67% of organisations reporting a decrease in absence levels put this down to tightened policies for reviewing absence. The HBOS Window on practice above describes the trigger points that HBOS uses. However, such trigger points may be well known to employees, and Connex (IDS 2001) found that some employees were able to manipulate the system and regularly have absence levels just below the trigger point. To overcome this some organisations have a rolling year, rather than, say, a calendar year or a financial year, against which absence levels are assessed – on the grounds that it will be much more difficult for employees to keep track of their absence levels and manipulate the system. In fact Dunn and Wilkinson (2002) found organisations where the trigger system was avoided because it was felt that it would encourage employees to take off time until they were just under the trigger limit.

Some organisations have absence review groups, such as the absence champion network at HBOS, and the safety, health and absence unit at HM Customs and Excise (IDS 2001). While the role of these groups varies, they are frequently used to review all absences and identify those who have hit trigger points, which will then require intervention, such as an absence review meeting with the employee.

Absence targets and benchmarking

Many organisations have absence targets phrased in terms of a reduction on current absence levels or a lower absence level to attain. However, the CIPD (2006) found that although 80% of the organisations it surveyed believed that absence levels could be reduced, less than half of these had set targets for this, and only around 37% benchmarked their absence levels against other organisations. An alternative approach, used by some organisations, is to give managers absence targets for their group, and tie this into their performance review and performance payments. This is the approach used in Connex (IDS 2001). Such overall and local targets need to be carefully used, however, so as not to give the impression to employees that absence is not allowed.

ACTIVITY 12.1

We have noted that some organisations link improvements in absence levels in their departments to managers' performance assessments and performance-related pay.

1 What are the potential advantages of this approach?

2 What are the potential problems?

3 How else might managers be encouraged to treat absence levels as a key priority?

Training and support for line managers

Most organisations recognise that line managers play a key role in making absence procedures work and in reducing absence levels, and training is usually available when a new absence system is introduced. Connex (IDS 2001) has introduced a creative form of training. The company takes managers to an employment tribunal to view an absence-related case so that managers will understand the consequences of not dealing fairly and consistently with employees when they have to deal with similar situations at work. HM Customs and Excise (IDS 2001) uses training videos showing role plays of return to work interviews (see below). These demonstrate that such a meeting is not about accusation or recrimination. The idea is that managers watch the video with their team of supervisory staff and then discuss the issues that arise.

However, there is evidence that further training is needed. Both James *et al.* (2002) and Dunn and Wilkinson (2002) found managers who could not understand how 'sickness' could be managed, were scared of dealing with the situation and were embarrassed about asking personal questions about an employee's state of health.

Absence notification procedures

Many organisations specify that when employees phone in as absent they must phone themselves, rather than asking another person to phone on their behalf. Many also specify that the employees must speak to their direct line manager or nominated representative. This means that such a telephone conversation can be the first stage of the absence management process. The conversation is welfare based and the intention is that the manager is able to ask about the nature of the problem and the anticipated date of return to work. Brakes (IDS 2005b), interestingly, outsources potential absence reporting calls to a nurse helpline. The nurse gives confidential advice on how to manage symptoms but makes no recommendation about whether the individual should attend work or not. The nurse does, however, make a record of the call and notifies the appropriate line manager and also informs the line manager when the individual is ready to return to work. Apparently managers appreciate the removal of this burden and concentrate their attention on those employees whose absence level has reached a trigger point.

Some organisations, such as First Direct (IDS 2001), make every effort to offer alternative work. For example, a telephone operator who cannot do telephone work with a sore throat may be able to do other work, and managers are asked to bear this in mind when employees phone in sick and to try to encourage the employees to come in, where appropriate, to carry out other tasks. This telephone conversation is also seen as an important tool in reducing the length of the absence.

Better understanding of the causes of absence

Understanding absence requires sound data. Three measures are commonly used. The *absence rate* is the number of days of absence, when attendance would be expected, of all employees. The *absence percentage rate* is the absence rate divided by the total number of actual working days for all employees over the year, multiplied by 100. This simple percentage is widely used to compare absence level with national data and with data of other organisations in the same sector.

The *absence frequency rate* is the number of spells of absence over the period, usually a year. Comparing this and the absence percentage rate gives a key snapshot of the absence situation in the organisation. As well as making external comparisons, the same types of analysis can be used to compare departments, work groups, occupations, grades and so on.

Analysis of absence data may help employers develop absence management methods relevant to the most frequent causes. However, as we have said, the reasons employees give for absence will be those that the organisation considers legitimate, and further investigation may be necessary.

Organisations can encourage individuals to be open about the real cause for their absence; for example, a minor illness may be used as an excuse to cover for caring responsibilities, a stressful working environment or alcohol or drug problems. However, this is easier said than done. The London Borough of Brent (IRS 2002a) has decided that the next stage in its efforts to tackle long-term absence is to try to unpick the causes of such absence. This employer has a feeling that the explanation may be partly related to issues of stress and the nature and organisation of the work. Helping employees to feel that they can trust the employer sufficiently to admit the real cause of absence means that absence can then effectively be tackled by providing the appropriate form of support. Another key tool is risk assessment, so, for example, some organisations will assess the risk of back pain or stress and then training can be provided to meet identified needs. The CIPD (2006) found that organisations used risk assessments, training, staff surveys, policy development, flexible working, employee assistance programmes, focus groups and changes in work organisation as methods to identify and reduce stress. The HSE encourages the use of focus groups for stress identification and management; more details and examples can be found in Silcox (2005b).

WINDOW ON PRACTICE

Risk assessments for stress

Stress accounts for a large proportion of sickness absence in the NHS, so researchers from the Institute of Work, Health and Organisations at Nottingham University studied five groups of hospital staff working under pressure: nurses, healthcare assistants, technical and professional staff, catering staff and clerical/reception staff. The aim was to measure and tackle stress at work. The intervention began with risk assessment, and a well-being questionnaire was used to gather employee feelings about tiredness and exhaustion. Employees were asked to identify not only causes of stress, but also changes to management practice which would provide a solution. One of the examples provided is the catering team, who identified causes as peak-time high workloads, poorly maintained equipment and inadequate training. Resultant interventions included regular equipment maintenance, additional peak-time staff and regular team briefings.

Source: Summarised from HSE (2002a) *Interventions to Control Stress at Work in Hospital Staff*, HSE Contract Research Paper No. 435. London: HSE.

Ongoing contact during absence

Maintaining contact during absence is considered by many as a way of reducing the length of absence, demonstrating that there is continuing interest in the employee's welfare, so maintaining employee motivation. In some cases it is the line manager who will keep in touch, and, in others, such as Walter Holland and Son (IDS 2001), there are liaison officers who fulfil this role. Contact may be by telephone, and with longer periods of absence may involve home visits. A useful summary of a wide range of methods of keeping in touch with employees who are off sick is given in Silcox (2005c). The Employers Organisation for Local Government (EO) (HSE 2002b) suggests that more effort should be made to keep in touch with employees after operations, partly to keep them up to date, but also to see if it is possible for them to come back to work on light duties or on a part-time basis. In working out its policy of visits, Bracknell Forest

Council (IRS 2002b) pays due attention to the requirements of the Human Rights Act 1998. The council recommends one visit per month in working hours and considers this is reasonable in terms of the need to demonstrate 'respect for private and family life', and the wish to avoid putting pressure on employees to return to work too early.

Return to work interviews and formal absence reviews

Return to work interviews are used increasingly as a key part of attendance procedures. The CIPD (2006) reports that these were used by 81% of organisations in 2006 compared with 57% in 2000. The CIPD also reports that these interviews are regarded as the most effective way of managing short-term absence. For some organisations these interviews are mandatory, even following a single day's absence, but there is frequently some flexibility about the nature of the interview depending on the circumstances. The general purpose of such interviews is to: welcome the employee back and update him or her on recent events; check that the employee is well enough to resume normal duties and whether any further organisational support is needed; reinforce the fact that the employee has been missed and that attendance is a high priority in the organisation; and review the employee's absence record. Dunn and Wilkinson (2002) found managers in their research who said that there was not time to concentrate on return to work interviews, as the practicalities of getting the job done were more critical. They also found a view among line managers that they were just so glad to get the employee back that they did not want to 'rock the boat'. Where formal absence reviews are held these need to be handled with sensitivity and tact, and care needs to be taken so that the interview does not become recriminatory or accusatory.

Use of disciplinary procedures

If someone is genuinely ill and unable to work, disciplinary action whether threatened or real is unlikely to bring about a return to work. There are, however, situations in which people who are too ill to work have to be dismissed. Never a pleasant task, it often falls to the HR manager to carry it out. The key is to make sure that the dismissal is carried out in a legally sound manner. This issue is covered in greater detail elsewhere in this book (see Chapters 10 and 25), so it is only necessary here to summarise the main points:

1 Dismissing someone who is unable to work because of ill health is potentially fair under unfair dismissal law.

2 It is necessary to warn the individual concerned that he or she may be dismissed if he or she does not return to work and to consult with the individual ahead of time to establish whether a return in the foreseeable future is feasible.

3 It is necessary to act on whatever medical advice is available.

4 In larger organisations, except where a person's job is very specialised or senior, it is normally considered reasonable to refrain from dismissing a sick employee for at least six months.

5 In any case no dismissal should occur if the employee falls under the definition of 'disabled' as set out in the Disability Discrimination Act 1995. In these cases an

employee should only be dismissed once the employer is wholly satisfied that no reasonable adjustments could be made to accommodate the needs of the sick employee so as to allow him or her to return to work.

Where someone is persistently absent for short periods of time, the course of action taken will depend on whether there is a genuine underlying medical condition which explains most of the absences. If there is such a condition, the matter should be handled in the same way as cases of long-term absence due to ill health outlined above. If not, then it is feasible for the employer to take a tougher line and to threaten disciplinary action at an earlier stage. It is quite acceptable in law to dismiss someone whose absence record is unacceptably high, provided the individual has been warned ahead of time and given a fair opportunity to improve his or her attendance. It is also necessary to treat different employees in a consistent fashion. Taking disciplinary action in the form of issuing a formal warning is therefore credible and likely to be successful.

Absence levels and performance assessments

Some organisations include the review of attendance levels as a measure of performance in annual assessments. Dunn and Wilkinson (2002) found that in the three retail companies in their case sample, employees were assessed via a separate rating category on their absence levels. Employees with unacceptable absence levels would not be put forward for transfers or promotion. At HBOS (IDS 2005a) line managers have a key performance objective relating to employee absence, reflecting their enhanced roles in managing absence.

Attendance bonus and rewards

Some organisations pay bonuses direct to employees on the basis of their attendance records. For example, in Richmondshire District Council (Silcox 2005d) staff receive an additional day's leave for 100% attendance in the previous year. When this bonus and other absence management measures were employed, absence was reduced from ten days to eight days in the first year. The council argues not only that this is a cost saving, but that an anticipated day's holiday is much easier to manage than an unanticipated day's sickness absence. Connex (IDS 2001) will pay a quarterly attendance bonus of £155 at the end of each thirteen-week period for full attendance and an additional lump sum of £515 if an employee has had no sickness absence during a full calendar year. In addition Connex sends out letters commending employees for improving their absence record. The company considers that its absence scheme is a success as 80% of eligible employees now qualify for payments. However, some managers do not support attendance bonuses as they feel that employees are already paid to turn up, and they are effectively being paid twice. Connex also found managers who felt that attendance bonuses were a signal to employees that managers cannot control the work environment themselves and that they have relinquished all responsibility for managing absence. On the other hand, Dunn and Wilkinson (2002) found that managers felt attendance bonuses were unfair as they penalised those employees who were genuinely ill. A further problem is that such rewards may encourage employees to come into work when they are genuinely ill, which is not good for either the individual or the organisation. Such rewards therefore remain controversial.

ACTIVITY 12.2

In terms of your own organisation consider the approaches by which sickness absence is minimised in terms of proactive ill-health prevention methods, discouragement of sickness absence and encouragement of attendance:

1 Where is the emphasis in terms of approach?
2 Why do you think this is so?
3 Is this the most appropriate approach? Why?
4 To what extent are different employee groups treated differently?
5 Why do you think this is so?
6 Is this the most appropriate approach? Why?

Occupational health support, health promotion and well-being

A number of organisations carry out pre-employment screening to identify any potential health problems at this stage. Others screen employees for general fitness and for potential job hazards, such as working with radiation, or VDUs. General screening may involve heart checks, blood tests, eye tests, well-woman/man clinics, ergonomics and physiotherapy, and discussions about weight and lifestyle, such as smoking, drinking and fitness levels. The value of such screening is that problems can be identified at an early stage so that the impact on sickness absence will be minimised. In some organisations positive encouragement will be given to employees to follow healthy lifestyles, such as healthy eating, giving up smoking, taking up exercise routines. Increasing numbers of employers offer exercise classes and/or an on-site gym, or alternatively pay for gym membership. Healthier canteen menus are appearing, as well as healthier snacks in some vending machines. However, the CIPD (2006) found that barriers to such well-being initiatives were lack of resources, lack of senior management buy-in, and lack of employee buy-in, especially in manufacturing and production. The government has provided some funding (together with other organisations) for nine health promotion projects in England, and a good example of one of these is the 'Be Active 4 Life' Programme at Exeter City Council which will be evaluated soon after the time of writing by a team from Loughborough University. Details of this project and the eight others are provided by Silcox (2005e).

For long-term absence the CIPD (2006) reported that the involvement of occupational health professionals was the most effective management tool, although HSE (2002c) shows that only one in seven workers has the benefit of comprehensive occupational health support. However, such support does not have to be in-house and can be purchased; this is the course followed by the London Borough of Brent (IRS 2002a).

Physiotherapists, counsellors and psychologists are often employed, and the occupational health role may include remedial fitness training and exercise therapy for those recovering from an illness. Stress counselling as part of an employee assistance programme can reduce the liability in stress-related personal injury cases. Also training in stress management may be offered.

James and his colleagues (2002) found that the role of occupational health workers was ambiguous and problematic. Their respondents suggested that while occupational health professionals worked on behalf of the employer, they tended to see themselves as representing employee interests. They also found that employees were very sceptical about visiting occupational health workers as they saw it as the first step in termination of their employment.

Changes to work and work organisation

Many employers appear to offer flexible working hours, part-time work and working from home. Employers also sometimes consider offering light duties or redeployment. However, James and his colleagues (2002) found that operational factors often limited what was possible. In the three manufacturing organisations they visited it was not always feasible to offer light duties or make adjustments to the workplace. They also found that other departments were reluctant to accept someone who was being redeployed after sickness, partly because they felt the employee might have lost the work habit, and also because there might be problems with pay if the levels of the old and new job differed. They also noted that there might be no budget to pay for adaptations to equipment or to purchase further equipment.

WINDOW ON PRACTICE

Flexible working cuts sickness absence

People Management reports that the London Borough of Merton has halved its sickness absence rate and improved productivity by introducing flexible working as part of a work–life balance pilot project. The flexible patterns of work involved a compressed working week, working from home, career breaks, job sharing and special leave including compassionate leave. Keith Davis, the Assistant Chief Executive, explained that the management style had to change from managing attendance to managing output, and significant training was required. The council plans to roll out the scheme over the entire council.

Source: Summarised from *People Management* (2002) 'Flexible working cuts sickness absence', Vol. 8, No. 1, 10 January, p. 13.

Practical support

There are many ways in which the employer can provide practical support to minimise sickness absence. Many organisations have experienced frustrations while employees are on waiting lists for diagnostic procedures and operations. In order to speed up the medical treatment that employees need, some organisations are prepared to pay the medical costs for employees where there is a financial case to do this, for example the Corporation of London (Silcox 2005f). Training in areas such as stress management and time management may help employees minimise feelings of stress, childcare support may simplify childcare arrangements, and phased return to work after a long-term absence is also a useful strategy. For more details on phased return to work and some examples **see** Silcox (2005g).

SUMMARY PROPOSITIONS

12.1 Employee absence continues to be a major problem for both the country and business in terms of direct costs and lost performance.

12.2 The most often reported cause of short-term absence is minor illness; however, back pain for manual workers and stress for non-manual workers are the leading causes of long-term absence.

12.3 It is important to understand the true nature of the causation of absence, as remedies can only be developed with this knowledge. Absence can result from a complex interrelationship of factors.

12.4 Typical attendance management policies include absence monitoring and reporting, absence review and trigger points, training and support for line managers, absence notification procedures, better understanding of the causes of absence, risk assessments, ongoing contact during absence, return to work interviews and absence review interviews, use of disciplinary procedure, absence-influenced performance assessments, absence bonus and rewards, occupational health support, changes to work and work organisation, and practical support. The mix of policies and processes used needs to be tailored to the needs of the organisation.

GENERAL DISCUSSION TOPICS

1 In the Window on practice about Marissa Mayer we included a comment from an anonymous tweeter about needs for corporate survival overriding employment preferences. Do you agree or disagree?

2 To what extent do you consider that absence statistics underestimate the extent of absence in the UK, and why?

3 It could be argued that encouraging employees to engage in exercise and keeping fit will improve their work motivation and sense of well-being, and that this would reduce absence. To what extent do you agree with this notion?

THEORY INTO PRACTICE

Until recently Arthur and John worked as service engineers in a business that supplied deep cleaning equipment to the catering industry to service the company's equipment on customers' premises. Because of growing public concern about hygiene in industrial kitchens, the company is expanding rapidly and demand for equipment servicing is increasing even more rapidly because the equipment, once installed, is rarely properly maintained. By agreement with their employer, Arthur and John have set up a separate company offering a regular maintenance service for the range of equipment from their erstwhile employer, as well as that of rival suppliers, with the additional option of an annual deep clean of the entire kitchen. Some of their previous colleagues have joined them as engineers and other people have been employed to do some of the deep clean work. The new company is very successful, but the product offered has two attendance/absence problems: the work often exposes its employees to infection risk because of what they have to clean; and the hours are erratic because the customer needs to keep its business running. A work shift could be 12–14 hours, with a lot of weekends.

Question

Arthur and John are finding that absence is increasing. They would like some advice on what to do. What do you suggest?

FURTHER READING

Evans, A. and Walters, M. (2003) *From Absence to Attendance*, 2nd edn. London: CIPD.
A thorough text which covers absence measuring and monitoring; understanding the causes of absence; absence management policies; the disciplinary and legal framework of absence management; and developing and implementing absence management strategies.

James, P., Cunningham, I. and Dibben, P. (2006) 'Job retention and return to work of ill and injured workers: Towards an understanding of the organisational dynamics', *Employee Relations*, Vol. 28, No. 3, pp. 290–303.
This paper proposes a conceptual framework of policies and practices appropriate to the effective management of long-term ill and injured workers and makes some assessment of UK current practice in relation to this framework.

Robson, F. (2006) 'How to manage absence effectively', *People Management*, Vol. 12, No. 17, pp. 44–5.
This is a brief and well-focused summary of how to improve absence management.

Silcox, S. (2005) 'Absence essentials: The why and wherefores of sick notes', *IRS Employment Review*, No. 850, pp. 18–21.
This interesting article explains the current sickness certification system and explores the role of the GP in this. The GP perspective is outlined and the tensions between this and the government's proposed welfare reforms aimed at reducing long-term absence from work and the numbers receiving invalidity benefit.

REFERENCES

Barham, C. and Leonard, J. (2002) 'Trends and sources of data on sickness absence', *Labour Market Trends*, April. London: ONS, pp. 177–85.

Bevan, S. (2002) 'Counting the cost of absence', *IRS Employment Review*, No. 739, pp. 46–7.

CBI/AXA (2005) *Who Cares Wins: Absence and labour turnover 2005*. London: CBI/AXA.

CBI/AXA (2006) *Absence Minded: Absence and labour turnover in 2006. The lost billions: Addressing the cost of absence*. London: CBI.

CIPD (2005) *Absence Management: A survey of policy and practice*. London: CIPD.

CIPD (2006) *Employee Absence 2006*. London: CIPD.

CIPD (2009) *Absence Management Survey Report*. London: CIPD.

CIPD (2012) *Absence Management Survey Report*. London: CIPD.

Dunn, C. and Wilkinson, A. (2002) 'Wish you were here: Managing absence', *Personnel Review*, Vol. 31, No. 2, pp. 228–46.

HSE (2002a) *Interventions to Control Stress at Work in Hospital Staff*, HSE Contract Research Paper No. 435. London: HSE.

HSE (2002b) *Initiative Evaluation Report: Back in work*, HSE Research Report No. 441. London: HSE.

HSE (2002c) *Survey of the Use of Occupational Health Support*, HSE Research Report No. 445. London: HSE.

Huczynski, A.A. and Fitzpatrick, M.J. (1989) *Managing Employee Absence for a Competitive Edge*. London: Pitman.

IDS (2001) *Absence Management*, No. 702, January. London: IDS.

IDS (2005a) *Absence Management*, No. 810, November. London: IDS.

IDS (2005b) 'Brakes', *Absence Management*, No. 801, November. London: IDS.

IRS (2002a) 'Tackling long-term absence (2): London Borough of Brent', *IRS Employment Review*, No. 763, 11 November, pp. 44–6.

IRS (2002b) 'Tackling long-term absence in local government (1): Bracknell Forest Borough Council', *IRS Employment Review*, No. 762, 21 October, pp. 42–6.

James, P., Cunningham, I. and Dibben, P. (2002) 'Absence management and the issues of job retention and return to work', *Human Resource Management Journal*, Vol. 12, No. 2, pp. 82–94.

Lokke, A., Eskildsen, J. and Jensen, T. (2007) 'Absenteeism in the Nordic countries', *Employee Relations*, Vol. 29, No. 1, pp. 16–29.

McFadzean, M. (2003) 'Managing absence', Paper presented at the CIPD National Conference, Harrogate, 22–24 October.

Neal, L.F. and Robertson, A. (1968) *The Manager's Guide to Industrial Relations*. London: George Allen & Unwin.

Nicholson, N. (1977) 'Absence behaviour and attendance motivation: A conceptual synthesis', *Journal of Management Studies*, Vol. 14, pp. 231–52.

People Management (2002) 'Flexible working cuts sickness absence', Vol. 8, No. 1, p. 13.

Rhodes, S. and Steers, R. (1990) *Managing Employee Absenteeism*. Reading, MA: Addison-Wesley.

Silcox, S. (2005a) 'Making progress towards an absence-recording standard', *IRS Employment Review*, No. 820, pp. 18–19.

Silcox, S. (2005b) 'Absence essentials: Using focus groups in stress management', *IRS Employment Review*, No. 832, pp. 21–4.

Silcox, S. (2005c) 'Absence essentials: Maintaining contact', *IRS Employment Review*, No. 818, pp. 23–4.

Silcox, S. (2005d) 'Attendance incentives are on the HR agenda once again', *IRS Employment Review*, No. 832, pp. 18–20.

Silcox, S. (2005e) 'Exeter City Council wants its employees to "Be Active 4 Life"', *IRS Employment Review*, No. 836, pp. 19–21.

Silcox, S. (2005f) 'Corporation of London tackles long-term absence', *IRS Employment Review*, No. 834, pp. 19–21.

Silcox, S. (2005g) 'Absence essentials: Phased return to work', *IRS Employment Review*, No. 828, pp. 18–21.

Silcox, S. (2006) 'The CBI and EEF agree that absence is falling', *IRS Employment Review*, No. 850, pp. 22–3.

Smethurst, S. (2006) 'Sporting chance', *People Management*, Vol. 12, no. 13, pp. 32–4.

TUC (2005) *Countering an Urban Legend: Sicknote Britain?* London: TUC.

Part 4

DEVELOPMENT

CHANGING TIMES
RESOURCING
PERFORMANCE
DEVELOPMENT

Strategy
Competence(ies)
Learning and
development
Careers

Having set up appropriate methods of organisation and systems to ensure performance, we now have to consider in more detail the ways in which the organisation itself can be developed and how people acquire skill, knowledge and effectiveness in their capacity to perform.

In our fast-changing world, organisations need to be both proactive and responsive to change, and our first chapter in this part focuses on how such change can be most effectively implemented taking account of the natural difficulties which people experience when change is thrust upon them.

A key feature of development is the national framework within which vocational skills can be acquired. Here the individual employer relies on, and attempts to influence, the provision of the education and training system and the arrangements of professional and other bodies, which specify the appropriate standards for vocational competence.

Individuals are developed further within the business, especially in management development, where the skills and knowledge needed tend to be much more specific to the organisation within which they are employed, where the methods of development are geared to the ongoing processes of the business.

Talented people are key to organisational success and they require focused development in planning and supporting their career development as well as their current performance.

Chapter 13

ORGANISATIONAL CHANGE AND DEVELOPMENT

THE OBJECTIVES OF THIS CHAPTER ARE TO:

1   Review the nature of change, the traditional model of planned change and the limitations of this model

2   Explain how organisations may be designed to be more responsive to change

3   Explore the employee experience of change and the impact this may have on the success of change

4   Examine the nature of change when the organisation is conceptualised as a human living system

5   Explore organisational development (OD) as a specific approach to change in organisations, describe its evolution and consider its future

6   Summarise the role of HR professionals in change

We are all now familiar with change as a constant in our world and that its pace is ever increasing. In the 2011 WERS survey almost half the organisations experienced technological change over the previous two years and over a third experienced changes in each of the following areas: work techniques, work organisation and product/service innovation (van Wanrooy *et al*. 2013). Inevitably, therefore, leaders find themselves leading, promoting, encouraging and stimulating change, with a belief that they can 'manage' change.

All change, no matter how small, presents a challenge for everyone in the organisation. For leaders there is the challenge of making the required changes happen, and for everyone else there is the challenge of coping with changes over which they often have no control and for which they have potentially no desire. Such changes invariably involve them in engaging in new activities, behaviours and thinking, and the even more difficult task of letting go and unlearning old activities, behaviours and thinking.

It is therefore unsurprising that 70% of change programmes fail (Burnes and Jackson 2011). Soltani and colleagues (2007: 153) find that:

> very few change programmes produce an improvement in bottom-line, exceed the company's cost of capital, or even improve service delivery

while Beer and Nohria (2000: 133) recognise that the consequences of such programmes

> exert a heavy toll both human and economic.

However, change is considered to be a necessity in our complex world, for example changing the culture of financial institutions after the global financial crisis, and change in response to public spending cuts in many parts of Europe. Stephen Moir, Deputy Chief Executive of the Yorkshire Ambulance Service, notes that the HR function has the opportunity and responsibility to 'help to encourage and facilitate radical long-term thinking and embed the cultural changes we all need' (Maclachlan 2012: 14).

In this chapter we explore the ways in which organisations approach change; explore some of the reasons why change may be unsuccessful; and review current approaches to improving that success rate. We consider OD as a specific approach to change which may bring added benefits and conclude with a summary of the HR role in change.

The nature of change and the role of planned change

There are many reasons why a business has to change, such as competitor behaviour, customer expectations, development of technology and communications, response to a crisis, or a need to maximise shareholder value and for a thorough analysis of the causes of change – see, for example, Myers and colleagues (2012).

Table 13.1
Aspects of
change

Structure, size and shape	Formal and informal systems
	Processes and procedures
Culture, values and beliefs	People and behaviours at all levels

Sometimes change is an initiative to seize an advantage and make something happen (proactive); on other occasions it is an attempt to catch up with what is already happening (reactive). Other distinctions are made, for example whether the push for change comes externally or internally. The change may be revolutionary, sudden and dramatic, or incremental; it may be planned or evolutionary. However, underlying all of this is the fundamental reason for change, which is to enable organisations to survive and thrive in our complex global world.

The nature of change has also been hotly debated and the emphasis has increasingly been on transformational change. Transformational change is sometimes equated with revolutionary change, but evolutionary change can equally be transformational. Change may involve movements in organisational shape, size, structure which are technically termed 'hard' aspects, and which are very visible and perhaps more straightforward to implement, requiring less persuasion. Change may also involve 'softer' aspects such as rewards, values, beliefs, systems, procedures, roles, responsibilities, culture, tasks and behaviour, which are potentially more difficult to manage. In Table 13.1 we have summarised the different aspects of the organisation which change might affect.

While transformational change may involve all of the aspects shown in Table 13.1, transformational change is more than this and involves fundamentally new ways of understanding what the organisation is for and is doing. Beckhard (1992), for example, suggests that transformational change requires a re-examination of the organisation's mission and a vision of a different future state of the organisation. As Binney and Williams (2005) suggest, transformational change is about the change in mental models of what the organisation is about, sometimes referred to as change in the organisational paradigm, a completely different way of looking at things.

ACTIVITY 13.1

Think of a major change which you have experienced at work, university, school or in any other organisation. (You may even consider your family to be an organisation.)

Consider all of the different aspects of that change and then draw a table similar to Table 13.1 and allocate the different aspects of the change to each box.

It has been assumed that leaders can plan and manage change given the right processes and tools to use. There is a variety of models in the literature, and used by consultants, with most focusing on such stages as:

- identify the need for change;
- define the current state;
- envisage the future desired state;

- identify the gap;
- diagnose capacity for change including barriers and how they can be overcome;
- plan actions and behaviours needed to close the gap;
- implement required actions;
- manage the transition;
- constantly reinforce changes, sustain momentum and measure progress.

For more details on such processes see, for example, Hayes (2007) and Myers *et al.* (2012). Such models make this top-down change process sound very straightforward with a logical approach to what needs to happen, and may well involve a good degree of training to prepare people for what will happen and what they will need to do. However, as we highlighted in our introduction to this chapter, change is often both painful and unsuccessful.

In beginning to understand the great difficulties of achieving change it is helpful to address the limitations of the planned change model. On a practical level we have little time for such lengthy processes in our world of constant change and there is little opportunity to reinforce and embed a change as another change may be following closely on its heels and indeed may be happening at the same time. Organisations need to become more responsive to the need for change as well as proactive where possible.

A second difficulty with the planned approach to change is its underlying assumptions. It can be seen as allied to the metaphor of the organisation as a machine which emphasises rationality and ignores emotion (see e.g. Lewis *et al.* 2008; Morgan 2006). The machine develops a problem: the owners of the machine work out how to fix it: they put the plan into action and repair the machine. It is based on a scientific logical approach to problem solving in organisations, which may be appropriate for some problems, but is often inappropriate as it neglects the important fact that the organisational machine is made up of human beings who have a will of their own. Binney and Williams (2005) suggest that this approach deals inadequately with the unintended consequences of change, its messiness, the gap in perceptions between leaders and followers, the fact that visions often do not inspire. They also point out that it is based on the assumption that change is something which is done to organisations (and hence the people that make them up), rather like the assumption that leadership is done to followers rather than with them. The machine metaphor also focuses change on the observable, in other words behaviour, and does not allow for employee thinking processes, and fails to consider the employee experience of change and employees' potential contribution to change.

In the next three sections we address the above limitations of the planned change model.

How can organisations be responsive to change?

On a very practical level one way of trying to enable organisations to be more responsive to change is to *design* them so that they can change more easily. Lawler and Worley (2009) suggest that, given the increasing pace of change, organisations need to anticipate change and constantly reconfigure, and hence require a built-in capacity to change continuously. To do this Lawler and Worley suggest that organisations need to design themselves so that they can 'adjust their strategic intents, structures and human deployments as a matter of routine' (p. 28), and need to develop the ability to think creatively about the future to achieve sustained success.

WINDOW ON PRACTICE

Built-to-change

Lawler and Warley (2009) use the example of Capital One Financial Services to demonstrate a built-to-change approach.

1 **Strategising**: At Capital One change is a continuous forward-looking activity rather than an annual or biannual one and there is a 'test and learn' approach to drive growth. To do this Capital One identifies services, products and other elements that will, under a range of conditions, create high performance. These become strategic imperatives where capabilities must be developed.

2 **Structure**: The organisation is designed flexibly, ensuring that no one is more than one or two steps away from the external environment to ensure connection with the marketplace, regulators and so on.

3 **Information production and sharing**: Capital One employs processes to share internal and external information such as financial performance, market conditions, competitor performance, on the basis that people are more likely to accept change if they understand what needs to happen for the business to succeed.

4 **Job design**: New entrants to Capital One are rotated round the business so that they can

contribute in any area. This ensures flexibility and responsiveness to changing demands.

5 **Selecting the right people**: Capital One selects employees who enjoy change, are quick to learn and actively seek professional growth.

6 **Employment contract based on employee willingness to accept change**: Employees are expected to learn new skills and deliver high performance. Capital One cannot promise always to offer the training and support that employees need and if an individual's skills are outdated that person may no longer have a place in the organisation if the skills are readily available in the external labour market.

7 **Performance management and development**: This is a flexible, dynamic and interactive process with goals regarding performance and the development experiences that individuals will need to contribute to the business in the future. Appraisals focus on both performance achievement and the acquisition and application of skills and knowledge required for the future.

8 **Leadership**: Lawler and Worley propose that, given the complexity of change today, leadership needs to shift from a small group of people at the top of the organisation to all levels, where managers are urged to grasp leadership opportunities as soon as they arise.

Source: Adapted from Lawler, E. and Worley, C. (2009) 'The rebirth of change', *People Management*, Vol. 15, No. 3, 29 January, pp. 28–30.

ACTIVITY 13.2

How would you assess the advantages and disadvantages of working for the type of organisation described in the previous Window on practice?

This approach goes some way to address the needs of organisations in a constantly changing environment, but it does not address other fundamental problems with the planned change model.

Addressing the employee experience of change

There has been increasing recognition of the value of understanding the employee experience of HRM, with Boselie *et al*. (2005) suggesting that this is central to HRM research and practice, yet there remains a 'dearth of evidence on employee reactions to change' (Conway and Monks 2008: 73). Reactions are likely to be affected by the context of the change, for example whether the company is shrinking and fighting for survival or is expanding. The planned change model pays insufficient attention to employee perceptions of and reactions to change.

When our jobs and their context change significantly the psychological contract can be damaged and unable to support the employee. Particularly where change involves mergers and acquisitions it is possible that employees end up doing a job for which they did not apply, in a company for which they do not want to work, so it is not surprising that employees are likely to experience a breach of the psychological contract (CIPD 2009) as the deal for which they signed up appears to have been broken. When the psychological contract is breached employees may display behavioural symptoms such as holding back information, may make more errors or leave the organisation, and may express feelings such as frustration, anger and distrust.

Although the planned change model inevitably focuses on employee behaviour, as this is an essential part of the change being successful, it neglects other types of employee responses such as the emotions referred to above. If behaviour does not change in the required manner, there is a tendency for change agents and leaders to ascribe this to the fact that the planned change model was not applied rigorously enough (Lewis *et al*. 2008). Within this view there is an assumption that employee resistance to change is a characteristic of the individual psyche that, ultimately, has to be overcome, rather than that resistance stems from legitimate reasons and is partly a result of the way that change is conceived and led in the organisation.

Oreg (2006), for example, suggests that individuals react to change in three ways: affective (emotions), cognitive and behavioural. We would also add physical reactions, drawing on evidence from Worrall and Cooper (2006). Employee response to change is typically couched in terms of 'resistance' to change, a most unhelpful word, suggesting an illegitimate reaction, hence we use the term 'response', a neutral word, implying that this can be understood and developed. Table 13.2 shows the combination of individual responses to change.

Table 13.2
Individual response to change

Behavioural responses	Cognitive responses
Emotional responses	Physical responses

WINDOW ON PRACTICE

It depends on your perspective

How many times have you heard it said that the old system was more efficient than the new one? As a change is implemented it is almost inevitable that efficiency suffers as new procedures are being learnt, flaws in new procedures are identified and fixed, and sometimes old and new systems are run in parallel. So lack of efficiency is often a temporary matter. But not always. For example, the centralisation of administrative officers and systems in an organisation (usually associated with a reduction in staff numbers) may well permanently, or for a period of years, result in records being more difficult to access and amend, lengthier and more time-consuming processes, loss of accuracy of data and a loss of local knowledge. No matter how great the goodwill of all parties, the new system is less efficient than the old, and the frustrated and demoralised administrative staff and their contacts may feel they could have contributed to designing a more efficient system. Organisational leaders may, however, be very satisfied with the change as savings have been made, budgets are looking healthier and the share price has gone up.

As human beings our reactions to change are a mix of all four areas, which are bound up together and difficult to separate. A cognitive response to change may be to re-evaluate the advantages and disadvantages of working for a current employer or gaining alternative employment. When an organisation moves out of town, employees with marketable skills may not want the longer journey, higher costs and lack of lunchtime shopping. So a cognitive assessment results in the behaviour of leaving the organisation.

In an example focusing on cognitive and emotional responses, Jones *et al.* (2004) comment that in a restructuring/downsizing environment involving the removal or amalgamation of work units, employees may lose their role identity. In other words, they are unclear about where they fit in the new structure, cease to feel confident and may construe this loss of role identity as a threat to their self-esteem and work validation. The following Window on practice presents an alternative example of role identity being under threat.

WINDOW ON PRACTICE

Resisting change in an Australian credit union

Cutcher (2009) explains how the credit union Coast implemented changes affecting front-line staff in its branches in rural communities in New South Wales, and how staff resisted such changes.

In the context of the deregulation of financial services, management introduced a new sales strategy emulating that employed by the large retail banks. This shift from service to sales appeared to be accepted in the northern and central regions of the union which were more urban areas but resisted in the southern, poorer, rural region branches, labelled as problem branches by the general manager.

Coast's new strategy places a requirement on members to be profitable customers, with front-line staff focusing on increasing sales of new financial products in competition with each other. Employee performance was measured by level of sales against sales performance targets which had an influence on pay increases. Overall, 25% of Coast's employees left when the new strategy was introduced, and the remaining employees reported higher levels of stress.

Management blamed the problems in the southern region on the intransigence of staff but failed to recognise the contradictions within the new sales strategy and the complexity of the employee response to the changes.

Front-line staff continued to refer to members, rather than customers, two years after management changed the language. They also continued to refer to themselves as Member Service Officers rather than Sales Consultants (their new job title). Staff disliked the idea of targeting individuals in the queue and the competition to get to them first, knowing there was a possible sale of an insurance policy to be had. They cared more about knowing the people who used the union, whom they had known over many years, and who were satisfied with the service they got. They enjoyed being welcoming and friendly and valued going out of their way to help people. This was the basis of their work identity and they refused to accept the new discourse of 'enterprise'.

Staff explained that they did not want to compete against each other as they were all local women who had grown up together. Some described the branch as like a family – including staff and members. They did not want targets coming between them and entered the daily sales figures to show that the sales were shared equally between themselves irrespective of who had actually made the sales. They saw their work as a team effort, and were concerned to ensure that branch performance was good.

Their resistance to change was based on protecting their friendships both within the union and with members of their community. Managers had failed to take account of this.

Source: Adapted from Cutcher, L. (2009) 'Resisting change from within and without the organisation', *Journal of Organisational Change Management*, Vol. 22, No. 3, pp. 275–89.

In trying to understand employees' emotional reactions to change, managers have used models from other parts of the social sciences. An example is the Kubler-Ross (1997) change curve which tracks the stages an individual generally experiences when coping with loss, a model that was developed in the context of bereavement. This model suggests that individuals move through the stages of shock, denial, fear, anger, bargaining, depression, understanding and acceptance before moving on. Although the theoretical base for this is weak, it does have an intuitive appeal. Eriksson (2004) highlights the legitimate role of emotion, finding that change programmes resulted in employees exhibiting signs of depression and experiencing feelings of failure. He also draws attention to the work of Kanter (1983) who identifies change as exhilarating when done by us and disturbing when done to us. Truss and colleague (2012: 283) provide a useful set of people management strategies that can be used to help employees move through a similar transition curve.

Emotions have a powerful impact on our behaviour and are very personal to the individual, and we should not assume that emotions can be managed in line with organisational strategy. Individuals themselves have enough trouble managing their emotions, but it is known that suppressing them is not a healthy approach. In times of change it is important therefore for individuals to accept and address their emotions, and for change leaders to recognise that such emotions may be negative, and to be prepared to try and understand them and accept them, responding where possible, rather than trying to manipulate them. The role of emotions helps to explain why change leaders have such different perceptions about the success of change compared with employees. Loss of choice and uncertainty for employees can trigger a wide variety of emotional responses.

Middle managers in particular may experience difficulties in coping with the contradictions and tensions of top-down change and bottom-up pressures from change agents (see e.g. Conway and Monks 2011). And the managers in Worrall and Cooper's study (2006) felt that changes were a result of cost reductions and created work intensification and increased pressure to perform. This had negatively affected their morale (61%), sense of job security (56%), motivation (51%), sense of employee well-being (48%) and loyalty (47%). Managers felt they were subject to greater top-down control and greater scrutiny, and felt overloaded, having insufficient time and resources to do their job to the standard they felt appropriate.

Change can cause a wide range of physical reactions. Worrall and Cooper (2006) found that absence levels were significantly higher in those organisations with cost-cutting programmes, and larger proportions of managers reported insomnia, persistent headaches, appetite problems, muscular tension, constant tiredness and other symptoms; the researchers suggest that such levels of change are literally making managers ill. Such problems interestingly did not apply to the same extent to directors, who felt much more positively about the changes taking place, reporting lower levels of stressors.

Recognising the different feelings, physical reactions and perceptions that employees may have is the first step in helping change become more successful. There is a range of measures that may help. Communication is the first in helping to address the uncertainty associated with change.

WINDOW ON PRACTICE

Merging First Choice and Tui Travel

Jacky Simmonds, Tui Travel's HR Director, explains the challenge of merging two very different companies. To their credit they carried out a survey to see how staff were feeling. Although they had put a big effort into communications, they found from the survey that even more communication was required, and Simmonds comments that she was surprised by how much emotion the merger stirred up, even with senior staff, and recognised how difficult some people find it to cope with uncertainty: 'People want to be updated even if there isn't anything specific to say', she says.

Source: Syedain, H. (2009) 'A smooth landing', *People Management*, 29 March, pp. 18–22.

ACTIVITY 13.3

Consider a change which you instigated either at work or in your personal life.
Then consider a change that was forced upon you in your work or personal life.
    For each of these situations identify the emotions that you experienced and how you dealt with them.

Other measures that may help change leaders include involving different levels of employee in shaping some of the details of the change and allowing them some feelings of control. Discussing and, where possible, addressing concerns of staff and monitoring levels of engagement may also keep change leaders in touch with employees, as was done when BBC Scotland moved from the West End of Glasgow to Pacific Quay on the Clyde (Phillips 2008).

In helping employees through change and recognising their needs, Conway and Monks (2008) distinguish between management-centred and employee-centred HR practices and argue that employee-centred HR practices might be more important in encouraging employee commitment to change. In their research they found that basic HR practices such as communication, sufficient staffing and appropriate reward were important influences and explain how each is particularly relevant in a period of change. They also suggest that a positive employment relationship is an important factor measured by the industrial relations climate or the psychological contract. Iverson (1996) demonstrates, for example, that more favourable industrial relations (IR) climates were associated with greater acceptance of change.

Understanding the employee perceptions of and reactions to change takes us further towards a different approach to change whereby employees are viewed as human beings rather than cogs in a machine, and this is a step towards dealing with change in an alternative manner.

Reconceptualising change

In response to concerns about the leadership of change, Binney and Williams (2005), among others, suggest alternative ways in which change can be led by reconceptualising change, based on the metaphor of the organisation as a living system rather than a machine. They suggest that this perspective helps us see organisations as adaptive (as behaviour and thinking shift of their own accord in response to the pressure of events), as self-organising (to achieve an equilibrium), as interdependent with their environment (interacting in complex ways), and as dynamic. This is different to planned change models where there is a danger of assuming a static environment and constant environmental scanning may be neglected.

They propose that this perspective suggests change is natural, if painful, and that the challenge is to release the potential for change rather than drive it. In addition they identify the need for some stability as well as change. They suggest that this perspective encourages the view that managers cannot control change, and that the problem with a vision for the future is that it denigrates the present and the past of the organisation. This thinking fits well with the increasing attention being paid to the importance of continuity alongside change (see e.g. Saboohi and Saboohi 2011), and the idea of recognising current strengths and not destroying everything.

WINDOW ON PRACTICE

EE

In the merger between Orange and T-Mobile the company had a massive reorganisation to manage while fighting off competitors. It realised that a new culture was an important part of this and decided to retain the best from each legacy brand rather than starting from scratch.

An unnamed company

In a longitudinal study of a merger which was cancelled, one of the organisations was unable to return to its pre-merger strategy, and Mantrere et *al.* trace this failure to a lack of attention to continuity in making changes and question the view that managers need to destroy current organisational meaning in order to facilitate change.

Sources: Chynoweth, C. (2011) 'Upwardly mobile', *People Management*, September, pp. 44–7; Mantrere, S., Schildt, H. and Sillince, J. (2012) 'Reversal of strategic change', *Academy of Management Journal*, Vol. 55, No. 1, pp. 172–96.

The living organism approach also suggests that trying to copy excellence elsewhere is a fruitless task, as is a change consultant or chief executive telling people to change; changes, Binney and Williams suggest, emerge and the key is seeing the new pattern, drawing attention to it and reinforcing it. An acceptance that the future is unknowable and unpredictable is important, as is the need for leaders to recognise that they are also part of the problem, and to acknowledge that people are not rational and that feelings and emotion are legitimate. Binney and Williams characterise this approach to change as a learning approach rather than a leading approach, but recognise that both perspectives add value in a change situation; in order to reflect this they propose the concept of 'leaning into the future'. Figure 13.1 summarises their thinking.

If you look back to the characteristics of empowering leadership (see Chapter 11) you will be able to see the commonality between this and the learning approach to change suggested by Binney and Williams (2005). This analysis reminds us that there is a broad spectrum of leadership styles that may be employed in promoting change, and it is important that the balance of styles used matches the nature of the change and the context.

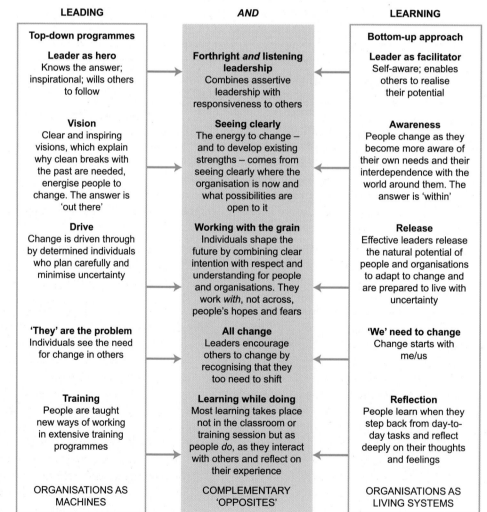

Figure 13.1
Leaning into the future

Source: Binney, G. and Williams, C. (2005) 'The myth of managing change', in G. Salaman, J. Storey and J. Billsberry (eds), *Strategic Human Resource Management: Theory and practice. A reader.* London: Sage/Open University, p. 317.

WINDOW ON PRACTICE

Leadership and change

Hope (2006) explains how Lady Marie Stubbs turned round an inner London school after its previous Head, Philip Lawrence, was murdered. Stubbs set out to make the children feel valued, first by physically transforming the building and, second, by welcoming them back to the school individually. Another way she approached this was to break down the division between teachers and pupils. For example, instead of locking the pupils out and the staff in at break times, she opened the school and created an atrium that students could use, with staff presence, and played music that the pupils would relate to. In the same vein she secured the part-time use of games pitches at Harrow Public School. She consulted the pupils on changes and gave them responsibility, such as handling reception for school visitors, focused on their aspirations and believed in them.

Sources: Hope, K. (2006) 'Lessons learnt',
People Management,
Vol. 12, No. 6, 23 March, pp. 30–1.

Organisational development as a specific approach to change

Organisational development (OD) is a specific approach to change, also based on the concept of the organisation as a living system, which we have discussed above. However, it is not only this systemic approach which distinguishes OD, but more importantly its legacy of humanistic values (see e.g. Garrow *et al*. 2009). These humanistic values, derived primarily from the work of Rogers (1961), underpin the work of an OD specialist. Humanistic values comprise:

- a respect for and the valuing of individuality;
- a belief that people are basically 'good' and do the best they can in the circumstances in which they find themselves;
- a belief that every individual is a set of potentials that can be realised;
- a belief that individuals have the capacity to strive for growth, dignity and self-determination in being all that they can (akin to achieving Maslow's self-actualisation).

There is also some resonance here with McGregor's theory 'y' of motivation, which has a similar positive view of workers wanting to do their best, being trustworthy, reliable and responsible, and that as long as managers treat them in this way, then this is what they are able to be. From an OD point of view individuals need to be given the environment and opportunity in the workplace which facilitates their striving to be themselves and realise their potential. Allied with humanistic values, OD work aims to make the organisation a better workplace for the benefit of both employees and the wider public that the organisation serves.

Alongside this respect for humanity, and with equal weight, OD specialists also focus on the efficient and effective running of the organisation. Such effectiveness is often expressed in terms of the alignment of the organisation with its environment so that it is responsive to it and interacts effectively with it. It is not surprising therefore that much current OD work is expressed strategically, as the organisation needs to review its mission and values and implement strategic interventions so that it is successful in a constantly changing world. Such interventions may include, for example, organisational learning, knowledge management and organisational design (for a fuller list see Yaeger and Sorensen 2006).

Internal alignment is also considered key so that all parts of the organisation interact effectively together. This may involve teambuilding and working on interpersonal and intergroup conflict. OD employs a systemic approach where work on any part of the organisation (such as a particular department) is never isolated but encompasses the impact of this on the rest of the organisation and its relationship with the environment.

WINDOW ON PRACTICE

School parking system

A high school asked parents not to park in the road near the front of the school when picking up their children. The school explained that this was causing hold-ups in the road for residents and other passing traffic and was a danger. The willing group of parents realised the next best place to wait was near the side entrance to the school which led into the next-door leisure centre car park. They therefore waited in the leisure centre car park, resulting in serious car park chaos for users of the leisure centre who found it difficult to get either in or out of the car park, causing them to be late for the leisure centre sessions they had booked. The school's best efforts at reducing chaos in one area resulted in the unanticipated consequence of chaos developing in another area! The school had neglected to consider the whole car parking system and just looked at one aspect of it in isolation.

ACTIVITY 13.4

1 If you work, or have worked, in an organisation, think of two or three organisation changes and identify both the intended and unintended impacts of these on different parts of the organisational system.

2 Alternatively think of two or three changes in school, university, sports teams, family or other membership groups to which you belong. Identify both the intended and unintended consequences of this on different parts of the whole system.

A key part of the OD approach is that in order to solve organisational problems and improve the organisation data need to be collected which enable members of the organisation to understand the nature of the problem or current state and upon which solutions may be built. Given OD's humanistic approach it is unsurprising that members of the organisation collect this information for and from themselves with the guidance of the OD specialist. This is the first step of the whole OD process which moves from data collection to diagnosis to action to evaluation, very much as in action research.

Finally OD specialists emphasise a processual approach where the focus of investigation and diagnosis is on the process of what is happening rather than on the content. For example, in a meeting we could summarise the content of what is discussed and agreed but from a processual approach we would be more interested in how the meeting was controlled, how different members contributed, how decisions were made and so on.

OD work is based on a broad base of behavioural science knowledge including social science, psychology and therapeutic psychology, and uses an eclectic mix of tools and techniques, for example CIPD (2012). OD practice is contextual (Garrow *et al.* 2009), meaning that how it is carried out depends very much on the context, so it is difficult to paint a clear picture of what it is as it is played out in many different ways in different organisations. It also depends very much on the practitioners themselves, and in a study of Dutch OD experts the authors concluded OD to be 'a loosely coupled community of practice, linking very diverse members' (Korten *et al.* 2010: 393). This reflects the many varied definitions of OD, but for the purpose of this chapter we suggest the following one identifying what OD work aims to achieve:

a pragmatic improvement of organisational capabilities – enhancing intra-organisational efficiency and performance, including those capabilities relating to individual health and psychological well-being at work.
(King and Anderson 2002)

So OD has twin foci: a humanistic approach to enabling people to become all that they can within the organisation; and a business imperative to help the organisation become effective and successful in its environment. The aim is sometimes expressed as achieving the best fit between organisational and individual goals. This is no mean task!

The evolution and future of OD

OD has been used in organisations for over fifty years, and just like HRM it has evolved. It reached some level of popularity in and around the 1960s and early 1970s but this tailed off and it is only recently that OD has regained a high profile, perhaps because of a stronger business focus. Interestingly Marshak and Grant (2008) make some helpful comparisons between classical earlier OD and newer approaches since the 1980s onwards. They characterise classical OD as having a positivist perspective, assuming that there is one objective reality, that the one truth can be uncovered using rational processes, that collecting data and using objective problem solving leads to change which can be planned and managed with the emphasis on changing behaviour. In contrast to this, newer approaches are based on a post-modernist perspective, where truth emerges and there are many socially constructed realities (in that we all perceive our world differently – see Chapter 14). In these approaches, creating new mindsets, possibly through negotiation, can lead to change which is continuous.

The contrast between these two approaches is very much in line with the traditional planned view of change and the alternative approach, characterised by Binney and Williams' (2005) learning approach to change. Some of the newer approaches to OD include appreciative inquiry (AI), which put simply includes the use of conversation to highlight, reinforce and encourage the spread of the positive aspects of what people currently do, rather than focusing on the negative ones. An excellent text on this growing approach is Lewis *et al.* (2008).

A key challenge for OD going into the future is whether the more traditional humanistic values of OD are still relevant or whether more weight should be given to pragmatic business considerations (Marshak and Grant 2008). For example, David Stephenson, Group Head of OD at Royal Mail, explained that the recession enabled OD specialists to engage with changes that would not have been possible otherwise, but he warned that both HR and OD professionals may be pressured by short-term demands to 'collude and command' (*People Management* 2009: 11) and that both sets of specialists are facing a challenge in 'keeping true to their values' (*People Management* 2009: 11). In this context of HR having to prove its value in terms of the maximisation of human capital, Nirenberg (2012) notes the worrying trend that many of the tools of OD have become integrated into mainstream management practice, but not for their original purpose.

OD is not a discipline but a field of practice and hence does not have an organisational home (see e.g. Garrow *et al.* 2009) when OD specialists are employed in-house. Indeed it does not have a professional and regulatory body, unless the OD specialist is a member of the British Psychological Society (BPS: OD Division). There have been moves of late to combine OD more closely with HRM and the latest set of ten professional standards from the CIPD, operational from 2010, have a whole standard devoted to OD. Job advertisements increasingly combine HR and OD. Indeed OD has been termed a 'strategic **HR tool**' (*HR Magazine* 2007), and OD has been similarly combined with learning and development functions. One of the challenges of combining is that HR is derived from different roots, which may form pressure to dilute the humanistic values characteristic of OD, and does not provide the OD specialist with sufficient distance from the organisation.

WINDOW ON PRACTICE

Recent literature questions whether 'western'-derived OD is appropriate or effective in global companies and whether OD values will be compromised. Working in different social, economic, political and cultural contexts presents a challenge to OD as there is likely to be a clash of values.

McKnight proposes a potential solution. She suggests that the individual OD specialist demonstrates OD values by being respectful of other cultures, being knowledgeable about them and prepared to learn continuously, and remaining authentic and demonstrating integrity. Through this demonstration and through encouragement and empowerment she suggests that OD values and work may be more easily assimilated.

Source: McKnight, L. (2012) 'Global consulting: The use of self to transfer OD values into national cultures', *Organisation Development Journal*, Vol. 30, No. 2, Summer. pp. 67–77.

Summary of the HR role in change

The discourse of strategic involvement suggests that in some organisations HR specialists may have a role in determining the need for change and the content of that change. In other organisations the HR role may be more limited to facilitating change and proposing, providing or supporting change processes, for example communication and training. HR specialists have a unique role in raising awareness of how employees and other stakeholders might respond to the intended changes; propose/provide/support processes for participation where this is appropriate; and propose other ways of engaging employees with the intended changes.

SUMMARY PROPOSITIONS

13.1   Change is constantly increasing and leaders use the planned change model in an attempt to manage change, but it has limitations.

13.2   It may be possible to design organisations to be more responsive to change.

13.3   It is important to take the employee experience into account and consider all four forms of response: behavioural; emotional; cognitive; physical.

13.4   Communication and involvement are important aspects of successful change management as are basic aspects of HRM such as sufficient staffing and appropriate reward.

13.5   An alternative approach to change is based on reconceptualising the organisation as a human living system rather than a machine.

13.6   OD is a specific approach to change and the key characteristics of OD are that it is based on humanistic values, aiming to get the best fit between both individual and organisational goals, and has a systemic and processual approach.

13.7   OD has received more attention of late and recent trends in OD encompass social constructivist principles and appreciative inquiry (AI). OD is increasingly paired with HRM.

13.8   In some organisations HR specialists may have a hands-on role in determining the need for and content of change, while in others they may be restricted to facilitating change.

GENERAL DISCUSSION TOPICS

1   'Change has to be planned and dictated from the top otherwise the organisation would be out of control.' Discuss reasons for agreeing or disagreeing with this statement.

2   'Organisation Development loses its unique contribution to the organisation if its humanistic values base is diluted; and this unique contribution is too important to lose.' Discuss reasons for agreeing or disagreeing with this statement.

THEORY INTO PRACTICE

Implementing change in the Norwegian civil aviation industry

'Avinor' was created as a government-owned private company from the government-administered civil aviation authority (Luftfartsverket) in response to economic challenges in the whole of the aviation industry. A major change initiative 'Take-off 05' was implemented to promote the survival of the business. The plan was to make some structural–technical changes such as reorganisation of administration and management structures and systems, reorganisation of some service areas and downsizing, and in addition to make changes to air traffic control which also involved downsizing and the closure of some operations. The context was one of predicted decrease in air passengers.

This initiative had broad support from employees including the air traffic controllers and the air traffic control union, who understood the dire situation that the organisation was in. They appreciated that this service was overweight, poorly structured and increasingly bureaucratic. The change process began as participative in terms of identifying the changes needed, and there was much cooperation and communication with staff and unions, producing a good level of engagement. Many cost savings were identified.

However, this consensus did not last because, when senior management unveiled the implementation plan, employees were shocked at the magnitude, speed and depth of change with 25% of employees being lost in the first two years, and more air traffic control centres to be closed than in the original plan. None of this matched expectations. Trust was breached and employee representatives who had participated felt undermined. The change had now become top-down driven and was no longer participative.

One part of the organisation – the air traffic controllers – had more power and had a history of resisting change; the union first asked for a delay to investigate and discuss matters, but senior management ignored this and pressed on. This led to resistance, yet the senior management became increasingly committed to the change in the face of this. Feeling overwhelmed the air traffic controllers said they no longer felt capable of operating safely and air traffic control over most of Norway ceased, stopping air traffic. At this point passenger numbers were actually increasing rather than decreasing as predicted, and this put increasing strain on the system which was being slimmed down. However, senior management had the support of the government and continued to push ahead with the changes. The only communication between the parties was through the media.

The situation changed dramatically when a new government was elected and ordered an independent investigation. The project collapsed in respect of the changes to air traffic control, although many of the other changes had been implemented successfully in a top-down manner (around 80% it is claimed with revenue savings). The director of air navigation services resigned and the CEO of Avinor was forced out.

Questions

1 Analyse the way that implementation was carried out and identify what caused the problems.

2 What recommendations would you make for the way that further changes should be implemented in Avinor?

Source: Lofquist, E. (2011) 'Doomed to fail: A case study of change implementation collapse in the Norwegian aviation industry', *Journal of Change Management*, Vol. 11, No. 2, pp. 223–43.

FURTHER READING

Cheung-Judge, M. and Holbeche, L. (2011) *Organisation Development: A practitioner's guide to OD and HR*. London: Kogan Page.
This a comprehensive handbook for senior leaders, OD and HR professionals involved in change. It combines theory and practice very well.

Hughes, M. (2006, reprinted 2010) *Change Management: A critical perspective*. London: CIPD.
A thoughtful text that brings together a wide range of views on how change may be understood. Concepts are clearly presented, and there are case studies and recommendations for further reading. This book is a good antidote to the 'how to do it' guides to change.

Self, D. and Schrader, M. (2009) 'Enhancing the success of organisational change: Matching readiness strategies with sources of resistance', *Leadership and Organisation Development Journal*, Vol. 30, No. 2, pp. 167–82.
Coming from the planned change perspective, this article summarises the resistance to change and the readiness to change literatures leading to recommendations for reducing resistance by specific readiness to change strategies.

REFERENCES

Beckhard, R. (1992) 'A model for the executive management of organisational change', in G. Salaman (ed.), *Human Resource Strategies*. London: Sage.

Beer, M. and Nohria, N. (2000) 'Cracking the code of change', *Harvard Business Review*, Vol. 78, May–June, pp. 133–41.

Binney, G. and Williams, C. (2005) 'The myth of managing change', in G. Salaman *et al.* (eds), *Strategic Human Resource Management: Theory and practice. A reader*. London: Sage.

Boselie, P., Dietz, G. and Boon, C. (2005) 'Commonalities and contradictions in HRM and performance research', *Human Resource Management Journal*, Vol. 15, No. 3, pp. 67–73.

Burnes, B. and Jackson, P. (2011) 'Success and failure in organisational change: An exploration', Vol. 11, No. 2, pp. 133–62.

Chynoweth, C. (2011) 'Upwardly mobile', *People Management*, September, pp. 44–7.

CIPD (2009) *The Impact of Mergers and Acquisitions*. London: CIPD.

CIPD (2012) *Organisation Development Factsheet*. London: CIPD.

Conway, E. and Monks, K. (2008) 'HR practices and commitment to change: An employee-level analysis', *Human Resource Management Journal*, Vol. 18, No. 1, pp. 72–89.

Conway, E. and Monks, K. (2011) 'Change from below: The role of middle managers in mediating paradoxical change', *Human Resource Management Journal*, Vol. 21, No. 2, pp. 190–203.

Cutcher, L. (2009) 'Resisting change from within and without the organisation', *Journal of Organisational Change Management*, Vol. 22, No. 3, pp. 275–89.

Eriksson, C. (2004) 'The effects of change programmes on employee emotions', *Personnel Review*, Vol. 33, No. 1, pp. 110–26.

Garrow, V., Varney, S. and Lloyd, C. (2009) *Fish or Bird? Perspectives on organisational development*. Brighton: Institute of Employment Studies.

Hayes, J. (2007) *The Theory and Practice of Change Management*, 2nd edn. Basingstoke: Palgrave Macmillan.

Hope, K. (2006) 'Lessons learnt', *People Management*, Vol. 12, No. 6, pp. 30–1.

HR Magazine (2007) 'Organisation development: A strategic HR tool', Vol. 52, No. 9, pp. 1–9.

Iverson, R. (1996) 'Employee acceptance of organisational change: The role of organisational commitment', *International Journal of Human Resource Management*, Vol. 14, No. 1, pp. 122–49.

Jones, L., Watson, B., Gardener, J. and Gallois, C. (2004) 'Organisational communication: Where do we think we are going?', *Journal of Communication*, Vol. 54, No. 4, pp. 722–50.

Kanter, R.M. (1983) *The Change Masters*. New York: Simon & Schuster.

King, N. and Anderson, N. (2002) *Managing Innovation and Change: A critical guide for organizations*. London: Thompson.

Korten, F., De Caluwe, L. and Geurts, J. (2010) 'The future of organisation development: A Delphi study among Dutch experts', *Journal of Change Management*, Vol. 10, No. 4, pp. 393–405.

Kubler-Ross, E. (1997) *On Death and Dying*. Washington, DC: Touchstone.

Lawler, E. and Worley, C. (2009) 'The rebirth of change', *People Management*, Vol. 15, No. 3, pp. 28–30.

Lewis, S., Passmore, J. and Cantore, S. (2008) *Appreciative Inquiry for Change Management: Using AI to facilitate organisational development*. London: Kogan Page.

Lofquist, E. (2011) 'Doomed to fail: A case study of change implementation collapse in the Norwegian aviation industry', *Journal of Change Management*, Vol. 11, No. 2, pp. 223–43.

Maclachlan, R. (2012) 'Public sector: A clear distinction is needed between HR and people management for transformation programmes to succeed', *People Management*, April, p. 14.

Mantrere, S., Schildt, H. and Sillince, J. (2012) 'Reversal of strategic change', *Academy of Management Journal*, Vol. 55, No. 1, pp. 172–96.

Marshak, R. and Grant, D. (2008) 'Organisational discourse and new organisational development practices', *British Journal of Management*, Vol. 19, pp. S7–17.

McKnight, L. (2012) 'Global consulting: The use of self to transfer OD values into national cultures', *Organisation Development Journal*, Vol. 30, No. 2, pp. 67–77.

Morgan, G. (2006) *Images of Organisation*. Thousand Oaks, CA: Sage.

Myers, P., Hulks, S. and Wiggins, L. (2012) *Organisational Change*. Oxford: Oxford University Press.

Nirenberg, J. (2012) 'Two roads to the bottom line: HR and OD', *Organisation Development Journal*, Vol. 30, No. 1, Spring, pp. 9–18.

Oreg, S. (2006) 'Personality, context and resistance to organisational change', *European Journal of Work and Organisational Psychology*, Vol. 15, No. 1, pp. 73–101.

People Management (2009) 'Recession benefits ODs who stay true to their values', 8 October, p. 11.

Phillips, L. (2008) 'Programme for change', *People Management*, Vol. 14, No. 9, pp. 18–23.

Rogers, C. (1961) *On Becoming a Person: A therapist's view of psychotherapy*. London: Constable.

Saboohi, N. and Saboohi, S. (2011) 'Revisiting organisational change: Exploring the paradox of managing continuity and change', *Journal of Change Management*, Vol. 11, No. 2, pp. 185–206.

Soltani, E., Lai, P. and Mahmoudi, V. (2007) 'Managing change initiatives: Fantasy or reality? The case of public sector organisations', *Total Quality Management*, Vol. 18, No. 1–2, pp. 153–79.

Syedain, H. (2009) 'A smooth landing', *People Management*, 29 March, pp. 18–22.

Truss, C., Mankin, D. and Kelliher, C. (2012) *Strategic Human Resource Management*. Oxford: Oxford University Press.

Van Wanrooy, B., Bewley, H., Bryson, A., Forth, J., Freeth, S., Stokes, L. and Wood, S. (2013) *The 2011 Workplace Employee Relations Survey: First findings*. London: Department for Business Innovation and Skills.

Worrall, L. and Cooper, C. (2006) 'Short changed', *People Management*, Vol. 12, No. 13, pp. 36–8.

Yaeger, T. and Sorensen, P. (2006) 'Strategic organisation development: Past to present', *Organisation Development Journal*, Vol. 24, No. 4, pp. 10–17.

Chapter 14

THE CONTEXT OF EMPLOYEE LEARNING AND DEVELOPMENT

THE OBJECTIVES OF THIS CHAPTER ARE TO:

1   Review the national UK picture of skills, training and development, and make some international comparisons

2   Explain the UK's skills aspirations and training framework, including skills pledges, apprenticeships, Investors in People and National Voluntary Qualifications

3   Explore the learning context in terms of behavioural competencies

4   Explore the learning context in terms of theories of learning and the process of learning from experience

Development, training and skills are at the heart of government policy as they impact on business and economic performance, unemployment levels, employability and social inclusion. Yet, the UK ranked twelfth for its high-level, eighteenth for its intermediate-level and seventeenth for its low-level skills base out of thirty-one OECD countries (UKCES 2010). In addition there has been constant concern with the management skills base. Successive governments have constantly changed and developed the national framework to encourage skills development and training by employers and reduce the skills gap between what employers need and what employees can offer. The skills gap, however, remains large. CIPD (2012a) reported that 82% of respondents to its 2012 Resourcing and Talent Planning Survey said they were still experiencing recruitment difficulties, mainly due to the lack of specialist and technical skills, and overall the hardest posts to fill were managers, professional and technical staff.

WINDOW ON PRACTICE

UK skills gaps

- The UK is investing in the offshore wind industry as a key part of meeting the 2020 EU targets for increasing the proportion of energy produced from renewable sources. However, the skills shortage in this area is a major barrier. Carol Frost, HR Director at Centrica Energy, claims we are capable of growing them but questions whether this can be done quickly enough (Smedley 2011).

- There was a significant shortage of trained and licensed security staff for the 2012 Olympics and the army had to be recruited in their stead (Brockett 2012).

- A shortage of IT skills has been identified for many years, yet a number of computer science graduates too frequently remain unemployed. 'Not all employers of IT professionals are looking for pure technical skills. Around 45 per cent of new IT professionals are recruited from other disciplines. These trends reflect the underlying skills shifts taking place in IT. For example there is a growing demand among employers for business-focussed, multi-disciplined technology professionals who understand how to use the technology to meet business goals' (representative of e-skills, the Technology Sector Skills Council, reported by Smedley 2009).

While everyone agrees that training and development is a good thing it is difficult to demonstrate a causal link between training and development and organisational and economic performance, partly because such terms are difficult to define precisely, and partly because the pay-off from development may not be seen in the short term. However, there is a clear employee demand for training and qualifications and unions are beginning to engage in bargaining for development.

The first part of this chapter focuses on the governmental framework of training in the UK and makes some international comparisons. The second part of the chapter looks at the nature and specification of learning as the other part of the context of learning and development in organisations.

The UK national picture and strategy

Employee development has traditionally been seen as a cost rather than an investment in the UK, although this is certainly changing in some organisations. For over thirty years UK organisations have given less support to training and development than our European

Table 14.1
The distribution of training days across different employee types (selected countries)

Country	Manual	Clerical	Professional/technical	Management	Average
EU average	4.14	4.71	7.88	7.20	5.98
UK	2.8	3.07	5.23	4.44	3.88
Estonia	5.11	6.78	13.10	12.66	9.41
Europe Non-EU average	4.35	5.49	8.43	9.16	6.86
Non-European average	6.36	7.17	9.23	9.04	7.95

Note: The non-European countries surveyed were Israel, Japan, Philippines, USA, Australia, Taiwan and South Africa.
Source: Cranet (2011).

partners. So, for example, in the Cranet international survey (2011) the UK spent 3.02% of payroll costs on training compared with an EU average of 3.72%, with only Austria, the Czech Republic, Denmark and France spending less than the UK. This lack of investment in training and development has been identified as a major factor in the UK's economic performance, and it has been argued that without such investment the UK will be trapped in a low-wage, low-skills economy (Wright *et al.* 2010), with the emphasis on competing on price rather than quality. Our national training framework is voluntarist, with the government's role limited to *encouraging* training rather than intervening, as in many other countries. In Table 14.1 the Cranet (2011) survey shows that the UK has the least average training days (3.88 days) of all seventeen EU countries, and there was only one country in the full survey of twenty-nine countries that had a lower average than the UK. This was Switzerland with an average of 3.77 days.

Alternatively it has been argued that it is not a lack of investment in training that is the problem but the way such investment is distributed: who it is spent on and the content of the training. Training spend is unevenly distributed with people at the lower end of the hierarchy and part-timers missing out on training. This imbalance of training days is true for many countries, as shown in Table 14.1, based on the Cranet survey (2011).

Hoque (2008) labels this very aptly as the 'training apartheid' and the WERS survey found that professionals, associated professionals, managers and those with most qualifications receive most training rather than low-skilled workers (Kersley *et al.* 2006).

WINDOW ON PRACTICE

Access to training: an international comparison with the USA

Finegold and his co-researchers (2005) investigated the access to training of temporary workers. They found that less than 25% of these workers took part in training and that educated and experienced individuals were more likely to be offered training. Lower-skilled individuals were, however, more likely to accept training when offered it. For temporary office staff, formal training was associated with significant wage growth in the following year. However, there was no such association for blue-collar workers. On-job skill development was associated with greater wage growth for both office and blue-collar temporary staff.

Source: Finegold, D., Levenson, A. and Van Buren, M. (2005) 'Access to training and its impact on temporary workers', *Human Resource Management Journal*, Vol. 15, No. 2, pp. 66–85.

In the aerospace and pharmaceuticals businesses, defined as high-skills sectors, Lloyd (2002) found a conflict of interests between employees' desire for training and development and managerial short-term aims, lack of accreditation of skills, structured development focused on key employees, access to training being dependent on individual initiative, senior managers viewing training as a minor issue to be dealt with by lower-level managers and insufficient resources. She suggests that there was underinvestment and lack of support for flexibility and employability. Much training is related to induction and particularly health and safety, as demonstrated in the WERS survey (van Wanrooy *et al.* 2013), which does nothing to drive the development of a knowledge-based economy. Employees in small organisations are at a disadvantage in terms of access to training, and evidence from the WERS survey suggests that the highest levels of training are in the public sector and larger organisations, particularly those with high levels of professional employees.

ACTIVITY 14.1

1 In your own organisation how is training/development shared out between employees?

2 Is there an explicit rationale for this? And if so what is it?

3 How would you explain the spread of training?

4 If you are not currently in employment choose five consecutive editions of *People Management* and analyse all articles and news items identifying the type of training/development being discussed and those for whom the training is provided.

The solution to this problem may be to increase state intervention, as voluntarism has had a limited effect. This would not necessarily mean a return to the levy system, where employers were forced to make an annual payment relative to profits which they could recoup by providing evidence that the equivalent money had been spent of training. But, for example, statutory rights for paid study leave and employer tax credits, and funding mechanisms to create a demand-led system, could be introduced.

The *Leitch Review* (Leitch 2006) provides a useful starting point in differentiating between a supply-led and a demand-led training system. The review characterises the supply-driven approach as being based on ineffectively articulated collective employer views of training needed and a central system of provision planned by the government to meet these needs, and predict future needs. The review suggests that employers and individuals find it difficult to articulate their needs partly because they are asked to provide input to a profusion of bodies, and because this approach results in too little investment by employers, too little responsibility being taken by individuals for their own training and a qualifications system divorced from the needs of the workplace. In contrast the review suggests a demand-led system is about directly responding to demand rather than planning supply. To achieve this, suppliers (such as colleges of further education) only receive funding as they attract customers (rather than being given block funding in advance, based on estimated demand), driving them to respond flexibly and immediately to employer demand, thus providing training provision which is more relevant, reflects the needs of customers and is likely to produce higher completion rates and better value for money. The Wolf Report (2011) endorsed this concept of funding following the learner, rather than the provider of training, and that it should be concentrated on economically valuable occupations.

If demand-led mechanisms are effective, training supply should be much more reactive to the real needs of employers; however, the limitations of this approach are that such a reactive approach focuses on current and short-term needs at the expense of anticipating and preparing for future needs, and does not address the structure of jobs in this country.

There is, however, a subtly different school of thought in relation to the supply/demand debate, which suggests the problem lies with the demand side of the equation rather than the supply side. In other words, the problem is not with government initiatives and measures to encourage training, development and learning, but with the way that skills are used and jobs are constructed, hence the employers' demand for training, development and learning. For example, Stevens (2002: 44) is concerned with 'whether the UK can generate enough jobs for people who have learnt and can learn' and Lloyd (2002) suggests that the country cannot solve its problems just by developing skills, as it is critical to change the structure of jobs:

All this suggests that we still have a situation in which the majority of organisations are using a reactive strategy: training only in response to the immediate short-term demands of the business, rather than being considered a strategic issue. (Ashton 2003: 23)

This implies that training and development needs to be considered at a strategic level in the business, but also, and perhaps more challenging, that employers need to change their business strategies to focus on quality rather than cost.

UK skills policy and framework

The UK training framework is complex, based on a number of reports and papers, and comprises implementing bodies and a range of specific initiatives. The framework constantly evolves, sometimes dramatically but most often in smaller changes as, for example, individual initiatives or bodies are introduced, changed or abandoned. We have chosen to discuss just some key government initiatives, rather than attempting to be comprehensive, as our system is complex:

A labyrinth, a maze and even a dog's breakfast. All three terms have been used by employers to describe the UK's skills landscape as it stands now, more than two years after Lord Leitch's review identified the reforms and simplifications necessary to secure the nation's economic competitiveness. A recent count identified a bewildering array of more than 3,000 government-funded training support schemes and 2,000 delivery agencies, costing more than £2.5 billion a year. (Phillips 2009: 21)

Skills policy in the UK includes the aims of upskilling the adult workforce and encouraging private investment in this; simplifying and improving the vocational training framework; stimulating the demand for skills and their better use; and improving management and leadership capability (CIPD 2012a). The purpose of the fundamental review of the national training framework undertaken by Lord Leitch in 2006 was to identify the UK's optimal skills mix for 2020 to maximise economic growth, productivity and social justice, to set out how responsibilities should be balanced for achieving that skills profile and to consider the policy framework required to support it. Lord Leitch proposed improved mechanisms and structures to encourage the extent and nature of employer training and development in order to narrow the skills gap, achieve a set of 2020 skills targets, and improve UK industrial performance. In summary, the vision he proposed is for the UK to become a world leader in skills by 2020 with reference to the top quartile of the thirty-one leading industrial countries (top eight) that make up the OECD. This required the almost doubling of skills attainment. He also proposed a set of principles, such as shared responsibility for skill development between employers, the individual and the government, a focus on economically valuable skills, demand-led, and a simplified framework.

Progress on the Leitch recommendations was reviewed in depth by the Innovation, Universities, Science and Skills (IUSS) Committee (now the Science and Technology Committee) in 2009, and it expressed a range of concerns (IUSS 2009). First, it questioned whether a demand-led system was appropriate, especially in a downturn, as it assumed that employers could predict which skills they required. The committee suggested that the targets were too ambitious and that targets based on qualifications only are problematic, suggesting that the focus should be on the skills themselves which may be more relevant to employers, and also be based on sectors rather than nationally.

The economic downturn has dictated that effort has been redirected from upskilling to reskilling so that those made unemployed can move into other sectors. In addition there is evidence that training is being used as an alternative to redundancy, as in Honda (Phillips 2009). However, the skills pledge is still being promoted, its original framework having been revamped and made more flexible. See **www.ukces.org.uk/ourwork/pledge**.

WINDOW ON PRACTICE

The Nissan Skills Pledge

We will develop and expand the contributions of all staff by strongly emphasising training and by the expansion of everyone's capabilities.

This means that it is part of our drive to improve our business that every eligible employee shall be:

- actively encouraged and supported to gain the basic skills they need to help our business succeed;
- actively encouraged and supported to achieve at least their first full level 2 qualification . . . including skills for life;
- actively encouraged and supported to achieve appropriate higher-level skills.

Source: IDS (2009) *Training Strategies: Nissan*, IDS HR Study No. 896, June, pp. 10–15.

The UK Commission for Education and Skills (UKCES), an independent strategic skills body, was set up in 2008 and its purpose is as follows:

We are a social partnership, led by Commissioners from large and small employers, trade unions and the voluntary sector. Our mission is to raise skill levels to help drive enterprise, create more and better jobs and economic growth. (**www.ukces.org.uk**, 2013)

In practice this means that UKCES advises the government on skills policy and monitors progress. The body is charged with simplifying government-funded training as it is generally agreed that there are too many brokers and providers. The UKCES remit is to reform structures and make it simpler for employers to get funding. Its report in 2010, however, concludes that given progress to date it is unlikely that the UK will be in the top eight

OECD countries in terms of skills by 2020. In 2013 it concluded that the evidence suggests the UK is making good progress in building its skills base, but other countries have made more rapid progress and the UK runs the risk of falling further behind (UKCES 2013).

A variety of other bodies currently operate in the skills arena including the Skills Funding Agency, the Young People's Learning Agency and the Sector Skills Councils. The latter SSCs aim to reduce skills gaps and shortages; improve productivity and performance; increase opportunities to develop skills and productivity; and improve the learning supply through National Occupational Standards, apprenticeships, and further education (FE) and higher education (HE).

National apprenticeship service

This service is responsible for increasing the number of apprenticeship opportunities, and works with employers and potential apprentices. It is simplifying the recruitment process for apprentices and has an online system for advertising new apprenticeships and enabling applications. Apprentices generally work for an employer alongside a skilled member of staff while undertaking an appropriate college course for one or two days a week, working towards NVQ level 2 and advanced apprentices towards level 3. Schemes vary by sector and employer but can take up to four years and are partly funded by the government. They are therefore a long-term training commitment and most often used by larger employers, the most well known being BT and British Gas. Traditionally these schemes have been used in manufacturing but have now been developed in a wider range of occupations such as retail, clerical and professional.

Apprenticeships are proving very popular and there were 665,000 apprentices in training in 2012 (NAS 2013). The range of apprenticeships has also been increased with graduate-level apprenticeships being introduced. The CIPD has also gained funding to develop a higher-level apprenticeship. As the number of apprenticeships increases, the proportion of older people (i.e. over 25 years) gaining them is increasing disproportionately and there has been some concern that this is disadvantaging young unemployed people (see e.g. Stevens 2011).

WINDOW ON PRACTICE

Apprenticeships

In January 2012 it was reported that 250 employers are to offer degree-level apprenticeships and include Burberry, Unilever, TNT and Leyland Trucks. The companies had to bid for funding and each was successful in getting a share of the £25 million pot available.

Sources: People Management (2012)
'bit.ly/apprenticeboost', January, p. 10.

Apprenticeships are not without criticism in terms of their quality. In a *Panorama* TV programme on 3 April 2013 examples were given of apprenticeships where there was no real job at the end or where the training was almost all college based or very limited, or where the apprenticeship was very short. The programme identified that the funding available for offering apprenticeships was attracting subcontractors whose work is not inspected and who cream off profits from the scheme.

WINDOW ON PRACTICE

German apprenticeships: current developments

The German apprenticeship system is highly valued and combines school-based learning with a greater amount, usually, of firm-based practical training. Employers train apprentices for the whole economy, beyond their specific needs, and to standards set by national committees. A wide range of firms contribute in this way to national skills development, not just the largest ones. Any in-house training may be monitored and supervised to ensure the national standards and being met. There is some state support but also a heavy reliance on private-sector sponsorship. There has of late been a decline in firm-based training due to the requirement for a different skills mix involving broader skills and more theoretical underpinning. Some of this is associated with the decline of the manufacturing sector. Fewer apprenticeships have been available, and there has been greater emphasis on school-based vocational training. The state and individuals themselves are taking on more financial responsibility for training thus easing the burden on employers.

Sources: Adapted from Thelen, K. (2007) 'Contemporary challenges to the German vocational training system', *Regulation and Governance*, No. 1, pp. 247–60; Brewster, C., Sparrow, P., Vernon, G. and Houldsworth, E. (2011) *International Human Resource Management.* London: CIPD.

Investors in People (IiP)

From 2010 UKCES became the champion and guardian of IiP. Compared with many government initiatives it has had a long-lasting impact since being introduced in 1991, although since then there have been several major revisions. More recent versions are increasingly less prescriptive and have more emphasis on outcomes rather than the process by which the business achieves IiP recognition. In addition attempts have been made to simplify the framework and make it more user friendly. There are now three principles, namely plan, do and review, and there are ten criteria in total set against the three principles in the latest 2009 framework. There are thirty-nine outcome-based evidence requirements in the plan–do–review cycle which are intended to give a full picture of how the business is managing its people and where improvements can be made. The current approach is more flexible, providing more opportunities to build on existing organisational processes; assessment no longer requires huge amounts of paperwork, as assessors now take on the responsibility of collecting mainly verbal evidence by interviewing a range of employees in relation to the standard.

Following the 2009 consultation with customers IiP launched three levels of recognition (bronze, silver and gold) beyond the standard, depending on the number of evidence-based requirements the organisation has met, and a new way of working with the framework, focusing more fully on the needs and priorities of the client in what IiP terms a 'choice-based' approach.

A commitment to IiP requires significant time and effort, and the benefits from gaining recognition of IiP status have been debated. Some studies have found that an increase in commitment to HR development, a belief in the value of the process and perceived performance gains (see e.g. Alberga *et al.* 1997) and that such firms are more likely to achieve organisational goals (Bourne 2008). Hoque (2008), reporting on the 2004 WERS survey data, found that training incidence and duration are higher in workplaces with the IiP standard and employees were more likely to agree with the statement 'Managers here encourage people to develop their skills.' However, the author found no evidence to suggest greater equality in the distribution of development opportunities and in fact IiP workplaces demonstrated less equality than non-IiP workplaces. In addition Hoque found that those workplaces with the standard were no better than others in respect of 'training apartheid' where the unskilled and those with no academic qualifications are provided with fewer training opportunities.

There is considerable evidence that the standard is sought for its 'stamp of approval' rather than because of a genuine commitment to improving training and it is often those organisations that have most to gain from pursuing the standard that are least likely to attempt to do this. There is a tendency in the IiP process to focus on formal qualifications, such as NVQs, and for the significance of informal development to be neglected.

ACTIVITY 14.2

Using an IiP-accredited organisation with which you, or someone you know, is familiar, consider the following:

1 How did the process of gaining accreditation impact on employees and managers?
2 What type of changes were experienced as a result of IiP accreditation?
3 Analyse the overall benefits and disadvantages of IiP accreditation.

National occupational standards and NVQs

NVQs are described in terms of national occupational standards, and are directed at developing the ability of trainees to perform specific tasks directly related to the job they hold or for which they are preparing, expressed in terms of performance outcomes.

The NVQ framework attempts to simplify UK qualifications by putting in place nine levels of NVQ (0–8) reflecting increased difficulty from 0, being basic numeracy and literacy, to 8, being high-level specialist skills. An NVQ framework has been put in place for all occupational areas, and an individual may gain the award by completing an NVQ directly and gaining a national qualification. Alternatively all other qualifications can now be expressed as NVQ equivalents so that it is clear for employers and individuals what the value of every qualification is. Even higher education is expressed in terms of the framework, with the first year of a degree course being level 4 and a PhD being 8.

The design of the standards is somewhat complex, although they have been simplified from earlier versions. The management standards were last updated in 2008.

WINDOW ON PRACTICE

Example: Management and Leadership Standards 2008

The standards divide into six key areas:

A Managing self and personal skills (3 units)
B Providing direction (12 units)
C Facilitating change (6 units)

D Working with people (17 units)
E Using resources (17 units)
F Achieving results (19 units)

Different combinations of units are relevant for different awards.

Inside one unit, for example **D7 'Provide Learning Opportunities for Colleagues'**, you will find:

List of relevant skills: for example, coaching, mentoring, providing feedback.

Outcomes of effective performance: for example, 'give colleagues fair and regular feedback on their work performance, discussing and agreeing how they can improve'.

Behaviour which underpins effective performance: for example, 'You recognise the achievements and success of others.'

Knowledge and understanding:

General: for example, 'how/where to identify and obtain information on different learning activities'.

Industry sector specific: for example, 'working culture and practices in the industry/sector'.

Context specific: for example, 'the current knowledge, skills and understanding of colleagues'.

The standards to be achieved are determined by designated standards-setting bodies some of which are SSCs, which involve or consult employers, practitioners and professional bodies, so that vocational standards are decided by those in charge of the workplace instead of by those in charge of the classroom. The standards-setting body for the management and leadership standards is the Management Standards Centre at **www.management-standards.org/**.

ACTIVITY 14.3

Try an experiment:

- On the Internet search and locate the full set of health and social care standards and identify the name of the standards-setting body.
- On the Internet search and locate the full set of management and leadership standards from the standards-setting body *without* typing in www.management-standards.org/ or 'management standards centre' in Google.

   1 How easy was it to complete these tasks?

   2 What difficulties did you experience with these tasks?

   3 What recommendations would you make for improving access to the standards?

There is an emphasis on being able to do rather than to know and the standards are designed so that the vast majority of work can be done 'on the job' with maybe small inputs from educational providers. This introduces greater flexibility into the learning process, so that career aspirants are not restrained by the elitist exclusiveness of either educational institutions or professional associations, and there are no artificial barriers to training, such that it is available only to people who have certain previous qualifications. Flexibility is further supported as candidates can stop and start their work towards the standard as it suits their personal or work needs, and they can complete the elements in any order. This means that standards can be worked on in line with business demands, and completed when the candidates can provide a portfolio of evidence demonstrating their competence, which can then be assessed.

There is evidence that some organisations adopting the management standards have been able to identify gaps in competence, identify competence development targets, develop a coherent structure for training and development, and identify clearer criteria for HR planning and career progression. In our own studies, again in relation to the management standards, it was found that participants developed self-confidence in their managerial role, became better organised and were motivated to focus on improvement and that following the standards was a rite of passage for those who were new to the managerial world.

In spite of early problems and reservations, and a slow initial take-up, NVQs have become embedded in the national training framework of the UK. One of the most common reservations about NVQs is the laborious nature of assessment, with candidates heavily engaged in a 'paper chase' to gather evidence of their competence, and this seemed to take over from the importance of the learning process and what was being learnt. It is also very difficult to ensure a satisfactory quality of assessment, where so much depends on a large number of individual assessors. The standards have been simplified from their original conception, though the framework remains complex.

Many standards now have both mandatory and optional units at each level so that the qualification itself gives only a partial indication of areas of competence. In relation to the management standards in particular, there is a criticism that the standards are reductionist. In other words, because the standards try to spell out the detail of what management entails, the complexity of management gets lost as it is difficult to specify this in the structure and language of the standards. It has also been argued that following the standards rubber-stamps the level of competence already achieved, rather than stimulating further development.

ACTIVITY 14.4

Interview at least three people who have followed the NVQ standards. They may be employees of your organisation, but this is not essential, so friends and family can be included. Ask your interviewees:

1 What were the most positive aspects of following the standards, and why?
2 What were the problematic aspects of following the standards, and why?
3 How might these negative aspects be overcome?

Behavioural competencies

While national occupational standards are output-based competencies (i.e. expressed in terms of job performance), behavioural competencies describe the behaviours which underpin performance (sometimes described as 'input' competencies).

Boyatzis (2008) in a development of his previous work defines a competency as an ability or capability expressed in a range of related behaviours attached to 'intent'. He uses the example of a range of listening and questioning behaviours which may be attached to the underlying intent of genuinely being interested in the other person's views. This competency might be described as 'understanding the other person'. Boyatzis maintains his position that a competency is 'an underlying characteristic of a person which results in effective and/or superior performance in a job' (Boyatzis 1982: 21), and in 2008 identifies three major groups of competencies relating to emotional intelligence, social intelligence and cognitive intelligence.

Boyatzis originally developed a common competency framework for managers but subsequently tailor-made competency frameworks have come thick and fast from the training and development specialists, and most large companies have produced such a framework. Most frameworks have clusters of competencies, like the Boyatzis model, and to each of the competencies within the cluster a list of behavioural indicators is usually attached. Some frameworks include level definitions encapsulating the simplicity or sophistication of the way that the competency is displayed, while others include positive and negative behaviours in relation to a competency, as shown in the following two Windows on practice.

WINDOW ON PRACTICE

An example of behavioural skills with level definitions from connexions

Working with others
The ability to work constructively within a group/team environment.

Level definitions	Examples of actions demonstrated at each level
Stage Three	
– Contributes to organisational success by defining, planning and implementing strategies for the future and building strategic relationships and alliances – Manages and allocates available resources, including financial, capital and people to best meet current and future requirements (2 of 4)	– Is able to recognise opportunities for organisation-wide networking – Develops and maintains strategic partnerships and alliances – Understands the strategic implications of working within different cultures (3 of 4)
Stage Two	
– Able to transfer knowledge – Challenges procedures – Develops best practice – Provides leadership to others (4 of 6)	– Builds confidence in others to take further responsibility – Provides constructive feedback to others on performance and impact on others – Maximises networking opportunities (3 of 7)
Stage One	
– Uses information to improve systems – Regularly acts on own initiative – Takes responsibility for own actions and decisions	– Understands team goals and objectives and works proactively for team success – Shares knowledge, skills and experience openly and honestly – Volunteers to work in projects or sub-committees – Helps others to achieve goals (4 of 10)
Foundation stage	
– Takes responsibility for own actions and decisions – Understands fundamental principles and applications – Refers to others for guidance – Follows procedures and processes	– Responsive, open and friendly in manner – Considers and relates well to all kinds of people – Personally enthusiastic, positive and approachable – Owns up to responsibility, even if mistakes happen; resilient (4 of 9)

Source: Connexions Cheshire and Warrington (but a national framework).

WINDOW ON PRACTICE

A sample competency from the police force

Respect for race and diversity – A

Behaviour category

Considers and shows respect for the opinions, circumstances and feelings of colleagues and members of the public, no matter what their race, religion, position, background, circumstances, status or appearance.

Understands other people's views and takes them into account. Is tactful and diplomatic when dealing with people, treating them with dignity and respect at all times. Understands and is sensitive to social, cultural and racial differences.

Positive indicators

- Sees issues from other people's viewpoints
- Is polite and patient when dealing with people, treating them with respect and dignity
- Shows understanding and sensitivity to people's problems, vulnerabilities and needs

- Makes people feel valued by listening to and supporting their needs and interests
- Understands what offends and adapts own actions accordingly
- Respects confidentiality wherever appropriate

[This is a selection from a full list of thirteen.]

Negative indicators

- Does not consider other people's feelings
- Does not encourage people to talk about personal issues
- Makes situations worse with inappropriate remarks, language or behaviour
- Is thoughtless and tactless when dealing with people
- Is dismissive and impatient with people
- Does not respect confidentiality
- Uses humour inappropriately

[This is a selection from a full list of eleven.]

Source: Police (Cheshire Constabulary).
(However, these are national competencies.)

Behavioural competencies are often seen as a means of expressing what is valued by the organisation as well as what characteristics have been seen to result in superior performance. In addition they are seen to provide a critical mechanism for the integration of HR practices which is considered essential to a strategic HR approach. Thus, once a competency framework has been researched and designed it can be used in recruitment, selection, training, performance management and reward (see e.g. IDS 2008). In this way employees are given consistent messages about what is valued and what is expected of them, and because not all competencies are equally developable it gives good direction as to which competencies need to be selected for in new employees. Westminster City Council, for example, has introduced a competency framework (CIPD 2006) which Tony Reynolds, Organisation Development Manager, describes as 'a golden thread running through the people management process' (p. 12); he also says that 'they are the behaviours we want to recruit, develop, manage and reward' (p. 12). However, in practice this link is often weak; for example, Abraham and his colleagues (2001) found organisations willing to identify a set of managerial competencies that described a successful manager, but did not place a corresponding emphasis on including these competencies in their performance appraisal. A further advantage of competency frameworks is that, because they can be expressed as behaviours, they are more easily measurable, and thus can be used explicitly in all HR processes. This means, for example, that in a development centre, assessors can be trained in how to observe a long list of behaviours.

Criticisms of the approach have been focused around the complex process required to research the appropriate competencies for the organisation, and, perhaps more importantly, the fact that such competencies, due to the research process itself, will be inevitably backward looking rather than future orientated. Hayes *et al.* (2000) also note that a competency framework may not include every aspect that is critical to superior performance, and also that while one set of competencies may result in high performance this does not necessarily mean that such performance may not be achieved via a different set of competencies. Whiddett and Kandola (2000) similarly argue that processes *solely* based on competencies are flawed and that a wider perspective needs to be taken. Without the wider perspective the scope for encouraging and using diversity may be diminished. We also need to remember that a person's behaviour is not necessarily consistent, and may be affected by the environment and the situation. Boyatzis (2009) does suggest that it is important to identify the 'tipping point' which identifies how often the relevant behaviours need to be displayed. Salaman and Taylor (2002) suggest that there are five inherent weaknesses where organisations limit themselves to a behavioural competency approach for managers including: marginalisation of the cultural, social and organisational context; the fact that such frameworks emphasise a narrow set of behaviours and attitudes with a lack of emphasis on the long-term processes of management development; and that competencies are founded on the questionable assumption that managers behave rationally and are achievement driven.

ACTIVITY 14.5

Research the use of behavioural competencies in your own organisation (if they are used), or one with which you are familiar.

1 What are the advantages of their use?

2 What are the disadvantages?

3 Compare views, if you can, from members of the HR function, line managers elsewhere and other professionals.

The nature of learning: theories

For the purpose of this text we consider the result of learning to be changed or new behaviour resulting from new or reinterpreted knowledge that has been derived from an external or internal experience. There are broadly four theoretical approaches or perspectives to understanding the nature of learning, and the training and development that organisations carry out reflects the explicit or implicit acceptance of one or more perspectives. We will look at each perspective in the evolutionary order in which they became important. There is no right or wrong theory – each has strengths and weaknesses.

The **behaviourist** perspective is the earliest, which, reflecting the label, concentrates on changes in observable behaviour. Experiments with animals formed the foundation of this theory, for example the work of Skinner, Watson and Pavlov. Researchers sought to associate rewards with certain behaviours in order to increase the display of that behaviour. The relevance of this for organisations today may be seen for example in telesales training where employees are taught to follow a script and calls are listened to, to ensure that the script is followed. Reward or punishment follows depending on behaviour.

Trainers are not interested in what is going on in the heads of employees, they merely want them to follow the routine to be learnt. This approach has also been used for a range of interpersonal skills training. One American company, for example, plays video sequences to trainees portraying the 'correct' way to carry out, say, a return to work interview. Trainees then practise copying what they have seen and are given cue cards to use when carrying out that particular interpersonal event. The problems with the perspective are that it is overtly manipulative, simplistic and limited. It may produce only temporary changes in behaviour and increase cynicism.

Cognitive approaches are based on an information-processing perspective and are more concerned with what goes on in the learner's head. This is a more technical perspective and maps out the stages of learning, such as: expectancy to learn (motivation); attention and perception required; experience is coded (meaning is derived); meaning is stored in long-term memory; meaning is retrieved when needed; learning is applied; feedback is received (which may supply reinforcement). The strengths of this perspective are that it stresses the importance of learner motivation and individual needs, it recognises that the individual has some control over what is learnt and it identifies feedback as an important aspect of learning. The weaknesses are that it assumes learning is neutral and unproblematic and it is a purely rational approach that ignores emotion. From this perspective useful development activities would be seen as formal courses offering models and ideas with lots of back-up paperwork. Activities to improve learning motivation are also important, for example helping employees to recognise their own development needs and providing rewards for skills development. Mechanisms for providing feedback to employees are also key.

The third perspective is based on **social learning theory**: in other words, learning is a social activity and this is based on our needs as humans to fit in with others. In organisations this happens to some extent naturally as we learn to fit in with things such as dress codes, behaviour in meetings and so on. Fitting in means that we can be accepted as successful in the organisation, but it is not necessary that we internalise and believe in these codes. Organisations often use role models, mentors and peer support, and 'buddies', to intensify our natural will to fit in. The disadvantages of this perspective are that it ignores the role of choice for the individual and it is based, to some extent, on a masquerade.

The **constructivist** perspective is a development of the information-processing perspective, but does not regard learning as a neutral process: it is our perception of our experiences that counts; there is no 'objective' view. This perspective accepts that in our dealings with the world we create 'meaning structures' in our heads and these are based on our past experiences and personality. New information and potential learning need to fit with these meaning structures in some way, which means that a similar new experience will be understood differently by different people. We tend to pay attention to things which fit with our meaning structures and ignore or avoid things that do not fit. As humans we are also capable of constructing and reconstructing our meaning structures without any new experiences. These meaning structures are mainly unconscious and therefore we are not aware of the structures which constrain our learning. We are generally unaware of how valid our meaning sets are, and they are deeply held and difficult to change. Making these structures explicit enables us to challenge them and to start to change them. This perspective recognises that learning is a very personal and potentially threatening process. We develop mechanisms to protect ourselves from this threat, and thus protect ourselves from learning. The implication of this is that learning support needs to encourage introspection and reflection, and providing the perspectives of others (e.g. as in 360-degree feedback, outdoor courses or relocations) may assist in this process.

The nature of learning: learning from experience

A significant amount of work has been done which helps us understand how managers, and others, learn from their experiences. Kolb *et al.* (1984) argue that it is useful to combine the characteristics of learning, which is usually regarded as passive, with those of problem solving, which is usually regarded as active. From this combination Kolb *et al.* developed a four-stage learning cycle, which was further developed by Honey and Mumford (1989).

The four stages, based on the work of both groups of researchers, are shown in Figure 14.1.

Each of these four stages of the learning cycle is critical to effective learning, but few people are strong at each stage and it is helpful to understand where our strengths and weaknesses lie. Honey and Mumford designed a questionnaire to achieve this which identified individuals' learning styles as 'activist', 'reflector', 'theorist' and 'pragmatist', and explain that:

- **Activists** learn best from 'having a go', and trying something out without necessarily preparing. They would be enthusiastic about role-play exercises and keen to take risks in the real environment.

- **Reflectors** are much better at listening and observing. They are effective at reflecting on their own and others' experiences and good at analysing what happened and why.

- **Theorists'** strengths are in building a concept or a theory on the basis of their analysis. They are good at integrating different pieces of information, and building models of the way things operate. They may choose to start their learning by reading around a topic.

- **Pragmatists** are keen to use whatever they learn and will always work out how they can apply it in a real situation. They will plan how to put it into practice. They will value information/ideas they are given only if they can see how to relate them to practical tasks they need to do.

Understanding how individuals learn from experience underpins all learning, but is particularly relevant in encouraging self-development activities. Understanding our strengths and weaknesses enables us to choose learning activities which suit our style, and gives us the opportunity to decide to strengthen a particularly weak learning stage of our learning cycle. Although Honey and Mumford adopt this dual approach, Kolb

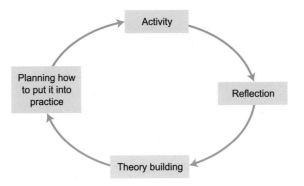

Figure 14.1
The learning cycle

firmly maintains that learners *must* become deeply competent at all stages of the cycle. There has been considerable attention on the issue of matching and mismatching styles with development activities and the matching and mismatching of trainer learning style with learner learning style.

SUMMARY PROPOSITIONS

14.1 There is currently a voluntarist approach to training and development in the UK, which means that employers make their own choices about the extent to which they train. The government attempts to influence what organisations do by a range of supply-side initiatives.

14.2 The UK aims to improve its skills base by 2020 so that it is in the top eight of OECD countries. UKCES has a responsibility in encouraging progress aided by a complex skills framework which includes employer skills pledges, apprenticeships, national occupational standards (output competencies) and NVQs.

14.3 Behavioural competencies (input competencies) outline the behaviours which underpin job performance.

14.4 There are four learning theories, namely behaviourist, cognitive, social learning and constructivist, which provide different explanations of how people learn, and in addition there are models of how we learn from experience.

14.5 The national context, behavioural competencies and learning theories all underpin practical employee development in organisations, which we look at in the following chapter.

GENERAL DISCUSSION TOPICS

1 'Both the UK as a whole and organisations themselves would benefit if the government adopted an interventionist approach to training.'

- Do you agree or disagree? Why?
- How might this intervention be shaped?

2 Should apprenticeships be restricted to the under 25s? List your arguments for and against and justify your conclusion.

THEORY INTO PRACTICE

The CIPD have produced a guide for employers illustrating how to create successful apprenticeships. As part of this they give two short case studies of individuals who have completed apprenticeships at Rolls-Royce. Below there is a short summary of each individual's perspective of what they gained from their experiences.

Gurjit Johal felt that her manufacturing/mechanical apprenticeship helped her develop both personally and professionally. She felt her life skills were enhanced, giving an example of teamworking: Gurjit and another apprentice were tasked with updating and collating new manufacturing instructions, which involved significant co-ordination with different departments to gain approval. She is proud that 15 years later these instructions are still being used and that she and her colleague moved these instructions from a manual to an electronic version for the first time.

Gurjit also appreciated the training available to her to strengthen her weaker skills, such as maths, and recognised that this improved her confidence. The can-do culture also struck Gurjit and made her feel that anything's possible, and her increased belief in herself and her abilities enabled her to complete two very different placements following the completion of her apprenticeship.

In retrospect, Gurjit, now a nuclear plant design engineer, is delighted that she has gained qualifications to degree level whilst working and being paid. Rolls-Royce are continuing to support her development in this new project management role. She feels her apprenticeship was special due to the support she received to gain the ability, skills and experience which provided a great start to her career.

Neeraj Sunger is currently a manufacturing engineering apprentice who feels that initially becoming a Young Apprentice at Rolls-Royce was the best decision he has ever made. He achieved a 'highly commended' in the Young Apprentice of the Year awards in 2009, of which he is very proud, and is not surprised that the scheme has been assessed as outstanding by Ofsted. In his current apprenticeship role he is studying for an NVQ3 in engineering maintenance and has one day a week off work to study for a foundation degree.

Neeraj wants to stay with Rolls-Royce (as 98% of apprentices do) and hopes that they will sponsor him to do a full engineering degree. He very much appreciates the guidance, support and knowledge he has gained so far, and feels that the apprenticeship is 'the opportunity of a lifetime'.

Questions

1 For what reasons are Gurgit and Neeraj satisfied by their apprenticeship experiences?

2 What issues do Rolls-Royce and other employers need to consider so that their apprenticeships are well resourced and successful?

3 Design an apprenticeship scheme for a specified job in your own organisation, or one with which you are familiar.

FURTHER READING

IDS (2012) *HR Studies: Competency Frameworks*. London: IDS.
Interesting up-to-date examples of competency frameworks in use with different employers.

Smith, A. and Collins, L. (2007) 'How does IIP deliver the lifelong learning agenda to SMEs?', *Education and Training*, Vol. 49, No. 8–9, pp. 720–31.
This paper based on a case study demonstrates the difficulties in matching IiP requirements with the individual requirements of SMEs. Business Link Advisers, acting as consultants to SMEs, find themselves in a difficult position trying to hit government-set targets for IiP and delivering a useful consultancy service at the same time which might not lead to IiP recognition.

REFERENCES

Abraham, S., Karns, L., Shaw, K. and Mena, M. (2001) 'Managerial competencies and the managerial appraisal process', *Journal of Management Development*, Vol. 20, No. 10, pp. 842–52.

Alberga, T., Tyson, S. and Parsons, D. (1997) 'An evaluation of the Investors in People standard', *Human Resource Management Journal*, Vol. 7, No. 2, pp. 47–60.

Ashton, D. (2003) 'Training trends: Past, present and future', in A. Booth and D. Snower (eds), *Reflections: New Developments in Training*. London: CIPD.

Bourne, A. (2008) *The Impact of Investors in People Standard on People Management Practices and Firm Performance*. Cranfield: Cranfield University.

Boyatzis, R. (1982) *The Competent Manager*. New York: Wiley.

Boyatzis, R. (2008) 'Guest editorial: Competencies in the 21st century', *Journal of Management Development*, Vol. 27, No. 1, pp. 5–12.

Boyatzis, R. (2009) 'Guest editorial: Competencies as a behavioural approach to emotional intelligence', *Journal of Management Development*, Vol. 28, No. 9, pp. 749–70.

Brewster, C., Sparrow, P., Vernon, G. and Houldsworth, E. (2011) *International Human Resource Management*. London: CIPD.

Brockett, J. (2012) 'Olympian task', *People Management*, August, p. 9.

CIPD (2006) 'Competency work pays off for Council', *People Management*, Vol. 12, No. 13, p. 12.

CIPD (2012a) *Factsheet: Skills policy in the UK*. London: CIPD.

CIPD (2012b) *Apprenticeships that Work: A guide for employers*. London: CIPD.

Cranet (2011) *Cranet Survey on Comparative Human Resource Management*. Cranfield: Cranfield University.

Finegold, D., Levenson, A. and Van Buren, M. (2005) 'Access to training and its impact on temporary workers', *Human Resource Management Journal*, Vol. 15, No. 2, pp. 66–85.

Hayes, J., Rose-Quirie, A. and Allinson, C. (2000) 'Senior managers' perceptions of the competencies they require for effective performance: Implications for training and development', *Personnel Review*, Vol. 29, No. 1, pp. 92–105.

Honey, P. and Mumford, A. (1989) *A Manual of Learning Opportunities*. Maidenhead: Peter Honey.

Hoque, K. (2008) 'The impact of Investors in People on employer-provided training, the equality of training provision and the "training apartheid" phenomenon', *Industrial Relations Journal*, Vol. 39, No. 1, pp. 43–62.

IDS (2008) *Competency Frameworks*, HR Study No. 865, March.

IDS (2009) *Training Strategies: Nissan*, IDS HR Study No. 896, June, pp. 10–15.

IUSS (2009) *Re-skilling for recovery: After Leitch, implementing skills and training policies – government response to the First Report from the Committee*, Session 2008–09.

Kersley, B., Alpin, C., Forth, J., Bryson, A., Bewley, H., Dix, G. and Oxenbridge, S. (2006) *Inside the Workplace: Findings from the 2004 Workplace Employment Relations Survey.* Abingdon: Routledge.

Kolb, D.A., Rubin, I.M. and McIntyre, J.M. (1984) *Organisation Psychology,* 4th edn. Englewood Cliffs, NJ: Prentice Hall.

Leitch, S. (2006) *Leitch Review of Skills: Prosperity for all in the global economy – final report,* December. London: The Stationery Office.

Lloyd, C. (2002) 'Training and development deficiencies in "high-skill" sectors', *Human Resource Management Journal,* Vol. 12, No. 2, pp. 64–81.

NAS (2013) *NAS Business plan 2012–13* at **www.apprenticeships.org.uk** (accessed 24 June 2013).

People Management (2012) 'bit.ly/apprenticeboost', January, p. 10.

Phillips, L. (2009) 'The skills maze', *People Management,* 7 May, pp. 21–4.

Salaman, G. and Taylor, S. (2002) 'Competency's consequences: Changing the character of managerial work', Paper presented at the ESRC Critical Management Studies Seminar: Managerial Work, The Judge Institute of Management, Cambridge.

Smedley, T. (2009) 'To a lesser degree', *People Management,* 10 September, pp. 24–9.

Smedley, T. (2011) 'Generating jobs', *People Management,* December, pp. 24–8.

Stevens, J. (2002) 'Balancing act', *People Management,* Vol. 8, No. 25, p. 44.

Stevens, M. (2011) 'Apprentices', *People Management,* December, p. 14.

Thelen, K. (2007) 'Contemporary challenges to the German vocational training system', *Regulation and Governance,* No. 1, pp. 247–60.

UKCES (2010) *Ambition 2020: World class skills and jobs for the UK: The 2010 Report.* London: UKCES.

UKCES (2013) *UK Skills Levels and International Competitiveness.* London: UKCES.

van Wanrooy, B., Bewley, H., Bryson, A., Forth, J., Freeth, S., Stokes, L. and Wood, S. (2013) *The 2011 Workplace Employee Relations Survey: First findings.* London: Department of Business Innovation and Skills.

Whiddett, S. and Kandola, B. (2000) 'Fit for the job?', *People Management,* 25 May, pp. 30–4.

Wolf, A. (2011) *Review of Vocational Education – The Wolf Report.* London: Department for Education.

Wright, J., Brinkley, I. and Clayton, N. (2010) *Employability and Skills in the UK: Redefining the debate,* A report prepared by the London Chamber of Commerce and Industry Commercial Education Trust. London: The Work Foundation.

Chapter 15

LEARNING AND DEVELOPMENT

THE OBJECTIVES OF THIS CHAPTER ARE TO:

1 Describe different ways in which learning needs can be identified

2 Explain the various methods of addressing learning and development needs

3 Investigate the nature of evaluation in this context

There has been a considerable shift in the way that individual development is understood and characterised. We have moved from identifying training needs to identifying learning needs, the implication being that development is owned by the learner with the need rather than by the trainer seeking to satisfy that need. This also has implications for who identifies the needs and the way that those needs are met. Current thinking suggests that needs are best developed by a partnership between the individual and the organisation, and that the methods of meeting these needs are not limited to formal courses, but to a wide range of on-the-job development methods and e-learning approaches. While a partnership approach is considered ideal, the phrase 'self-development' is key in our development lexicon, indicating that individuals increasingly own and take responsibility for their own development. There has also been a shift in the type of skills that are the focus of development activity: from technical skills to the development of personal skills, self-management and attitudes. Lastly, while the focus on development for the current job remains high, there is greater pressure for development to be future orientated. These shifts reflect the changes which we have already discussed in terms of global competition: fast and continuous change, and the need for individuals to develop their employability in an increasingly uncertain world.

In the UK the three most effective development methods are in-house development courses (52%), coaching by line managers (46%) and on-the-job training (39%), as identified in the CIPD 2012 *Learning and Talent Development Survey* (CIPD 2012a). Table 15.1 shows the most used learning methods in the Asia Pacific region according to the Cegos 2012 survey (Blain 2013).

Cegos compared these figures with its pan-European survey and note that classroom methods are used in 90% of organisations in Europe and online methods used in 43%.

Table 15.1 Methods of learning in the Asia Pacific region

Learning method	Percentage using this
Classroom	79
Online	58
Individual mentoring	42
Group mentoring	34
On the job	54
Blended	39

Identifying learning and development needs

The 'systematic training cycle' was developed to help organisations move away from ad hoc non-evaluated training and replace it with an orderly sequence of training activities, but this approach has been less prominent of late, as it does not necessarily reflect the messy world of practice and does not focus adequately on learning. In spite of this the cycle does retain some value, and we describe an adaptation of such a model to make it more applicable to today's environment. The model, shown in Figure 15.1, is set within an external environment and within an organisation strategy and an HR development strategy. Even if some of these elements are not made explicit, they will exist implicitly. Note that the boundary

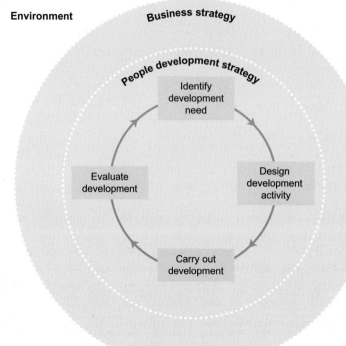

Figure 15.1
A systematic model of learning and training

lines are dotted, not continuous. This indicates that the boundaries are permeable and overlapping. The internal part of the model reflects a systematic approach to learning and to training. Learning needs may be identified by the individual, by the organisation or in partnership, and this applies to each of the following steps in the circle.

There are various approaches to analysing needs, the two most traditional being a problem-centred approach and matching the individual's competency profile with that for the job that person is filling. The problem-centred approach focuses on any perform- ance problems or difficulties, and explores whether these are due to a lack of skills and, if so, which ones. The profile comparison approach takes a much broader view and is perhaps most useful when an individual, or group of individuals, are new to a job. This latter approach is also useful because strategic priorities change and new skills are required of employees, as the nature of their job changes, even though they are still offi- cially in the same role with the same job title. The CIPD (2012a) also found that psycho- metric tests were used as a means of identifying learning needs. When a gap has been identified, by whatever method, the development required needs to be phrased in terms of a learning objective, before the next stage of the cycle, planning and designing the development, can be undertaken. For example, when a gap or need has been identified around team leadership, appropriate learning objectives may be that learners, by the end of the development, will be able 'to ask appropriate questions at the outset of a team activity to ascertain relevant skills and experience', and 'to check understanding of the task' or 'to review a team activity by involving all members in that review'. So you can see that learning objectives are phrased in terms of an activity that the learner will be able to perform once learning has been completed – hence they always begin with a verb.

ACTIVITY 15.1

Write learning objectives for the following individuals who are experiencing problems in their performance:

1 Tina, who always dominates meetings, and neglects the contribution of others.

2 Brian, who has never carried out a selection interview before, and is very unsure of how to go about this.

3 Mark, who feels he has lots of contributions to make at meetings, but never actually says anything.

4 Sara, who can never get to meetings on time.

The planning and design of learning will be influenced by the learning objectives and also by the HR development strategy, which for example may contain a vision of who should be involved in training and development activities, and the emphasis on approaches such as self-development, e-learning and social media. Once planning and design have been specified, the course, or coaching or e-learning activity, can commence, and should be subject to ongoing monitoring and evaluated at an appropriate time in the future to assess how behaviour and performance have changed.

Methods of learning and development

Off-job methods: education and training courses

Educational courses undertaken during a career are frequently done on a part-time basis leading to a diploma, degree or professional qualification. Masters degrees in management and MBAs are considered to provide value for both the employer and the participant; for debates around these and their advantages see for example *People Management* (2012) and Smedley (2012). This is an alternative approach to the NVQ route which we discussed in the previous chapter, which is more closely tied to on-the-job experiences and not concerned with 'education'.

In addition there are external consultancy courses, varying from a half-day to several weeks in length, and run by consultants or professional bodies for all comers. They have the advantage that they bring together people from varying company and occupational backgrounds providing new perspectives. They are relatively expensive and may be superficial but are good for swapping experiences among course members, and future networking. The most valuable courses of this type are those that concentrate on specific skills or knowledge, such as developing time management or interviewing skills, or being introduced to topical issues such as a new national initiative, or legislation where interpretation and sharing views is important.

In-house courses are often similar in nature to consultancy courses, and are sometimes run with the benefit of some external expertise. In-house courses can be particularly useful if the training needs relate to specific organisational procedures and structures, forthcoming organisational changes and ways of encouraging employees to work more effectively together. The drawbacks of in-house courses are that they suffer from 'organisational groupthink'.

Alternatively, there are outdoor-type courses, sometimes known as Outward Bound, after the organisation that pioneered them. Outdoor courses attempt to develop skills involved in working with and through others, and aim to increase self-awareness and self-confidence through a variety of experiences, including outdoor physical challenges. Their differential value is assumed to hinge on their separation from the political, organisational environment. A different environment is assumed to encourage individuals to forsake political strategising, act as their raw selves and be more open to new ideas, but this is perhaps more hope than reality. Learning experiences based on drama are increasingly popular; in these participants are engaged in improvisation through role play and exercises. For example, London Underground has a mock tube station 'West Ashfield' where underground staff can practise before going live, and fire, ambulance and police services can prepare for emergency situations such as mass evacuations and people falling under trains (Stevens 2010). We explore other forms of off-job simulation and experiential learning in a later section on the use of technology in learning.

WINDOW ON PRACTICE

Hazardous training

To make the most of an overnight closure of the M56 motorway, five fire crews from across Cheshire Warrington and Halton played out a scenario involving a multi-vehicle collision where a tanker containing hazardous chemicals had crashed into the central reservation. Actors and volunteers played the parts of casualties and the fire crews did not know what to expect when they attended the scene. It was felt that such realistic training experiences would be the best preparation for a real incident.

Source: Cheshire Fire and Rescue Service (2012) *Cheshire East Annual Report 2011/12*. Cheshire East.

One of the major concerns with these different types of off-job courses and activities is the difficulty of ensuring transfer of learning back to the workplace. Longenecker and Ariss (2002) asked managers what helped them retain what they had learnt and transfer it to the workplace. Developing goals/plans for implementing new skills was most frequently identified. In addition managers said that it helped to review materials immediately after the programme; be actively involved in the learning itself; make a report to peers/superiors on what they had learnt; review material and development plans with their mentor/manager; and include development goals in performance reviews. It is generally agreed that a supportive climate helps transfer (e.g. line manager interest and involvement) and Nielsen (2009) found that collaborative activities on return to the workplace aided trainees in transferring their course-based learning to the workplace. Santos and Stewart (2003), for example, found that transfer was more likely if reward such as promotion or pay was attached to developmental behaviour change, and also where there was a helpful management climate in terms of pre- and post-course briefings and activities.

WINDOW ON PRACTICE

Experiential activities: role reversal

Phillips (2006) provides an example of BUPA care staff in a retirement home. As part of a 'Personal Best' programme aimed at improving customer service, staff took the role of residents so as to see life through their customers' eyes. So, for example, they were fed puréed food and were hoisted in a mechanical sling from a chair into a bed. As a result staff behaviour towards residents has changed, for example explaining the hoisting procedure to residents and doing it more slowly.

Phillips, L. (2006) 'BUPA stars', *People Management*, Vol. 12, No. 22, 9 November, pp. 30–2.

Learning on the job

Natural learning and self-development

To some extent self-development may be seen as a conscious effort to gain the most from natural learning in a job, and to use the learning cycle, which was explained in the previous chapter, as a framework. Learners may start by understanding their own strengths and weaknesses in the learning cycle as this will inform their choice of development method and perhaps development goals.

ACTIVITY 15.2

1 If you have not already done so, obtain the Honey and Mumford questionnaire and work out your learning style(s).

2 Select your weakest style and try to identify two different learning activities which fit with this style, but that you would normally avoid.

3 Seek opportunities for trying out these learning activities. If you practise these activities on a regular basis this should help you strengthen the style you are working on.

4 Log your experiences and in particular what you have learnt about these 'new' learning activities.

The emphasis in self-development is that each individual is responsible for, and can plan, his or her own development, although he or she may need to seek help when working on some issues. Self-development can be focused in specific skills development, but often extends to attitude development and personal growth. It involves individuals in analysing their strengths, weaknesses and the way in which they learn, primarily by means of questionnaires and feedback from others. This analysis may initially begin on a self-development course, or with the help of a facilitator, but would then be continued by the individual back on the job. From this analysis individuals, perhaps with some help at first, plan their development goals and the way in which they will achieve them, primarily through development opportunities within the job. When individuals consciously work on and sometimes plan self-development they use the learning cycle in a more explicit way than in natural learning. They are also in a better position to seek appropriate opportunities and help, in their learning, from their manager. The following Window on practice gives an example.

WINDOW ON PRACTICE

Gwen is a management trainer in a large organisation running a number of in-house management courses. She has just moved into this position from her role as section leader in the research department; the move was seen as a career development activity in order to strengthen her managerial skills.

Gwen is working with her manager to learn from her experiences. Here is an extract from her learning diary based on the learning cycle:

Activity – I've had a go at running three sessions on my own now, doing the input and handling the questions.

Reflection – I find the input much easier than handling questions. When I'm asked a question

and answer it I have the feeling that they're not convinced by my reply and I feel awkward that we seem to finish the session hanging in mid-air. I would like to be able to encourage more open discussion.

Theory building – If I give an answer to a question it closes off debate by the fact that I have 'pronounced' what is 'right'. If I want them to discuss I have to avoid giving my views at first.

Planning practice – When I am asked a question rather than answering it I will say to the group: 'What does anyone think about that?' or 'What do you think?' (to the individual who asked) or 'What are the possibilities here?' I will keep encouraging them to respond to each other and reinforce where necessary, or help them change tack by asking another question.

David Megginson characterises learners by the extent to which they plan the direction of their learning and implement this, namely planned learning, and the extent to which they are able to learn from opportunistic learning experiences, namely emergent learning. Megginson (1994) suggests that strengths and weaknesses in these two areas will influence the way individuals react to self-development. These two characteristics are not mutually exclusive, and Megginson combines them to identify four learning types, as shown in Table 15.2.

Warriors are those who are strong at planning what they want to learn and how, but are less strong at learning from experiences they had not anticipated. They have a clear focus on what they want to learn and pursue this persistently. On the other hand, Adventurers respond to and learn from opportunities that come along unexpectedly; they are curious and flexible. However, they tend not to plan and create opportunities for themselves. Sages are strong on both characteristics, and Sleepers display little of either characteristic at present. To be most effective in self-development activities learners need to make maximum use of both planned and emergent learning. For a further explanation of this model also see Megginson and Whitaker (2007).

Many of the activities included in self-development are based on observation, collecting further feedback about the way the individual operates, experimenting with different approaches and in particular reviewing what has happened, why and what the individual has learnt. Self-development, however, is not a quick fix as it requires a long-term approach and careful planning, and attention needs to be paid to how the self-development process

Table 15.2
Planned and emergent learning

Learner type	Planned learning score	Emergent learning score
Sage	High	High
Warrior	High	Low
Adventurer	Low	High
Sleeper	Low	Low

Source: Adapted from Megginson, D. (1994) 'Planned and emergent learning: A framework and a method', *Executive Development*, Vol. 7, No. 6, pp. 29–32.

is to be supported. Extensive induction into the process is important as is an explanation of the theoretical underpinning, appropriate skill development, preparation for peer feedback, and further support in tracking progress.

Learning logs can be used as a mechanism for learning retrospectively as they encourage a disciplined approach to learning from opportunistic events. The log may be focused around one particular activity and is usually designed to encourage the writer to explain what happened, how he or she has reflected on this, what conclusions he or she has made and what future learning actions he or she wishes to make. Alternatively logs can be used in the form of a daily or weekly diary.

ACTIVITY 15.3

Identify a management skills area that you need to develop. (You may find it particularly helpful to choose an interpersonal area, for example assertiveness, influencing others, presentation, being more sociable, contributing to meetings, helping others.)

Keep a learning diary over the next few weeks, logging anything that is relevant to your development area. Use the framework which Gwen used in the previous Window on practice box.

At the end of the period review what you have learnt in your development area and also what you have learnt about the learning cycle.

Manager coaching and other internal and external coaching

The line manager's role in learning and development has increased with the devolution of HR tasks. Coaching is an informal approach to individual development based on a close relationship between the individual and one other person, either internal or external to the organisation. The coach is often the immediate manager, who is experienced in the task, but there is increasing use of external coaches, especially for more senior managers, or specially trained internal coaches. The CIPD (2012b) found that 43% of organisations used coaching to improve poor performance and 47% used it to build on good performance.

The line manager as coach helps trainees to develop by giving them the opportunity to perform an increasing range of tasks, and by helping them to learn from their experiences. Managers work to improve the trainee's performance by asking searching questions, actively listening, discussion, exhortation, encouragement, understanding, counselling and providing information and honest feedback. The manager coach is usually in a position to create development opportunities for the trainee when this is appropriate. For example, a line manager can delegate attendance at a meeting, or allow a trainee to deputise, where this is appropriate to the individual's development needs. Alternatively a line manager can create the opportunity for a trainee to join a working party or can arrange a brief secondment to another department. Coaches can share 'inside' information with the individual being coached to help him or her understand the political context in which the individual is working. For example, they are able to explain who will have most influence on a decision that will be made, or future plans for restructuring within a department.

Skilled coaches can adapt their style to suit the individual they are coaching, from highly directive at one end of the scale to non-directive at the other. The needed style may change over time, as the trainee gains more confidence and experience. IDS (2009) found that a good coach is one who had a genuine interest in the trainees; believes that everyone is capable of more and focuses on potential rather than past performance; knows that the coach does not have all the answers; believes a person's past is no indication of his or her future; understands that an open, supportive and mutual relationship is required for effective coaching; understands that results may be short or long term; and believes they should build awareness, responsibility and self-belief. A variety of barriers to coaching have been identified including performance pressures and a feeling that the role was not valued, but Anderson (2009) found that time pressures, lack of confidence to deal with difficult people and organisational culture were key. The emphasis in coaching on honest self-reflection suggests that there will be barriers in organisations where the culture is not one of openness and honesty.

There has been an increasing trend to broaden the concept of coaching in terms of both content and who carries out the coaching. Some organisations are now providing or arranging intensive training for designated internal coaches who operate broadly in the organisation, just in a coaching role. This is quite different from the basic training line managers are likely to receive. External executive coaching is often provided by consultancies and specialist coaching organisations. Various forms of coaching may include career coaching, performance coaching, skills coaching, business coaching and life coaching. Given the increasing professionalisation of coaching it is not surprising that the quality of the coaching experience is receiving attention. Supervision of practice is increasingly being used in a way that is similar to supervision for counsellors, which involves regular meetings with a more experienced practitioner to explore their client relationships and reflect on practice. Such individual supervision is carried out with a mind to client confidentiality; however, the use of group supervision of coaches and the desire of organisations to collect common coaching themes to inform organisational thinking put client confidentiality at greater risk.

WINDOW ON PRACTICE

Upwards coaching

The 'Pairing for Performance' scheme was introduced by the Department for Health as a form of upwards coaching. A more junior manager is paired with a senior manager and having observed the latter gives face-to-face feedback on his or her behaviour and the impact that this has on others. This increases the self-awareness of the senior managers, and allows them to adjust their behaviours where needed and experiment with new ones. The scheme was piloted as part of a leadership development programme for directors but is gradually being adopted by layers below. The junior of the pair is given training for the role, matched carefully with a more senior manager and takes on the responsibility for setting up meetings. Junior managers gain from the process through improved confidence and a better understanding of the pressures on senior managers.

Reverse mentoring

Clutterbuck (2004) provides an example in General Electric where at one time all top managers had young computer-literate mentors to help them keep up to date in new technologies.

Sources: Clutterbook, D. (2004) *Everyone Needs a Mentor*. London: CIPD; Arkin, A. (2011) 'The odd couple', *People Management*, October, pp. 44–6.

The emphasis on coaching is underlined by the journal *Coaching at Work*, and the development of the CIPD's coaching standards; organisations responding to the CIPD 2012 *Learning and Talent Development Survey* identified coaching as the second most effective development tool. Concerns for quality are being addressed, for example by a kitemarking scheme for coaching and mentoring qualifications, launched by the

European Coaching and Mentoring Council (see **www.emccouncil.org**), and the British Psychological Society now has a specialist interest group focused on coaching. The lack of evaluation of coaching has been identified and greater attention is being paid to the evidence base for coaching (CIPD 2012b).

Mentoring

Mentoring offers a wide range of advantages for the development of the mentee or protégé, coaching as described above being just one of the possible benefits of the relationship. The mentor may occasionally be the individual's immediate manager, but usually it is a more senior manager in the same or a different function. The CIPD (2012c) identifies the purposes of mentors as sharing their greater understanding of the workplace to enhance career advancement (such as increasing exposure and visibility and sponsorship), and building confidence. Fowler and O'Gorman (2005), on the basis of research with both mentors and mentees, describe eight individual mentoring functions which are: personal and emotional guidance; coaching; advocacy; career development facilitation; role modelling; strategies and systems advice; learning facilitation; and friendship. There is evidence that mentoring does benefit both parties, and Broadbridge (1999) suggests that mentors can gain through recognition from peers, increased job satisfaction, rejuvenation, admiration and self-satisfaction. Indeed reciprocity is expected in a mentoring relationship and there is evidence both mentor and mentee can make claims on each other (Oglensky 2008). The drawbacks to mentoring that were revealed in Broadbridge's research include the risk of over-reliance, the danger of picking up bad habits, the fact that the protégé may be alienated from other sources of expertise and the sense of loss experienced when a mentor leaves. In addition, the difficulty of dealing with conflicting views in such an unequal relationship was identified. Perceived benefits, however, considerably outweighed any drawbacks. There is a danger of assuming that mentoring is unquestionably good and Oglensky (2008) notes that mentoring can be a source of stress, conflict and dysfunction.

Managers are also seen as responsible for developing talent, and although a mentor/protégé relationship might not naturally occur, mentorship may be encouraged or formalised. For example, there are systems where all new graduates are attached to a mentor as soon as they join the organisation. The difficulties of establishing a formal programme include the potential mismatch of individuals, unreal expectations on both sides and the time and effort involved. Mentoring for women managers currently has a high profile (see e.g. Ehrich 2008; Maxwell 2009).

 WINDOW ON PRACTICE

Mentoring at fifteen

Liam Black, Director of Fifteen (Jamie Oliver's project to turn disadvantaged youngsters into cooks), initiated a structured programme to turn six members of staff into qualified mentors able to support the more vulnerable youngsters to aid retention. The staff are from different companies run by Oliver and are not directly working with the youngsters. The six are working towards a Certificate in Workplace Mentoring from the Oxford School of Coaching and Mentoring (accredited by Oxford Brookes University), which is suitably tailored to their work-based needs. The programme is a six-month blended learning package and the mentors will work with the youngsters setting goals, developing coping strategies and building their often non-existent self-esteem.

Cottee, P. (2006) 'Oliver's army', *People Management*, Vol. 12, No. 19, 28 September, pp. 44–5.

Peer relationships

Although mentor/protégé relationships have been shown to be related to high levels of career success, not all developing individuals have access to such a relationship, and even formal schemes are often reserved for specific groups such as new graduate entrants. Supportive peer relationships at work are potentially more widely available to the individual and offer a number of benefits for the development of both parties. Peer relationships can vary in depth, which can be expressed on a continuum. Some peer relationships share information and skills; some may provide job-related feedback and friendship, and share career planning; others may focus on emotional support, personal feedback, friendship and confirmation. Most of us benefit from one or a number of peer relationships at work but often we do not readily appreciate their contribution towards our development. Peer relationships most often develop on an informal basis and provide mutual support. Some organisations, however, formally appoint an existing employee to provide such support to a new member of staff through the first 12–18 months in the organisation. These relationships may, of course, continue beyond the initial period. The name for the appointed employee will vary from organisation to organisation, and sometimes the word 'buddy', 'coach' or 'mentor' is used – which can be confusing! The skills and qualities sought in peer providers are likely to include accessibility, empathy, organisational experience and proven task skills.

ACTIVITY 15.4

Consider each significant peer relationship that you have at work. Where does each fit on the continuum of relationships described above, and what contributions does it make towards your development?

If you are in full-time education consider the contribution that each of your relationships (whether at university, home or work) makes to your development.

Self-development groups

Peers can also be involved in self-development groups which usually involve a series of meetings where they jointly discuss their personal development, organisational issues and/or individual work problems. Groups may begin operating with a leader who is a process expert, not a content expert, and who therefore acts as a facilitator rather than, but not to the complete exclusion of, a source of information. The group itself is the primary source of information and may operate without outside help as its members' process skills develop. The content and timings of the meetings can be very flexible, although meetings will require a significant level of energy and commitment if they are to operate well. It is important that the members understand what everyone hopes to get out of the group, the role of the facilitator (if there is one), the processes and rules that the group will operate by and how the members agree to interact.

Learning contracts

Learning contracts are sometimes used within more formalised self-development groups but can also be used on other management courses; as part of a mentoring or coaching relationship; or in working towards a competency-based qualification. These contracts are a formal commitment by the learner to work towards a specified learning goal, with an identification of how the goal might be achieved. They thus promote a proactive approach to learning. Boak (1991) has produced a very helpful guide to the use of such contracts and suggests that they should include:

- an overall development goal;
- specific objectives in terms of skills and knowledge;
- activities to be undertaken;
- resources required;
- a method of assessment of learning.

The value that individuals gain from learning contracts is dependent on their choosing to participate, their identification of the relevant goal and the importance and value they ascribe to achieving it. Only with commitment will a learning contract be effective, because ultimately it is down to the individual learner manager to make it happen.

WINDOW ON PRACTICE

David wanted to improve his influencing skills and has sent the following draft learning contract to his manager for discussion:

Goal

To improve my influencing skills with both peers and more senior managers.

Specific objectives

- To prepare for influencing situations.
- To try to understand better the perspective of the other.
- To identify the interpersonal skills required – probably active listening, reflecting, summarising, stating my needs, collaboration (but maybe more).
- To be able to identify that I have had more influence in decisions made.

Activities

- Watch a recommended DVD on influencing skills.

- Reread my notes from the interpersonal skills course I attended.
- Watch how others in my department go about influencing.
- Ask other people (supportive ones) how they go about it.
- Identify possible influencing situations in advance, and plan for what I want and what might happen.
- Reflect back on what happened, and work out how to do better next time.
- Ask for feedback.

Resources

- DVD.
- Notes.
- The support of others.

Assessment

- I could ask for feedback from colleagues and my manager.
- My own assessment may be helpful.
- Make a log over time of decisions made and my originally preferred outcome.

E-learning and blended learning

E-learning can be defined as 'learning that is delivered, enabled or mediated by electronic technology' (Sloman and Rolph 2003: 1), and although this definition still holds good the nature of e-learning has changed dramatically over the years since then. The CIPD survey (2012a) found that 24% of respondents expected to use e-learning more widely in their organisations over the next two years, and 15% were expecting more use of Web 2.0 technology; however, only 11% identified e-learning as one of the three most effective learning and development practices. The history of e-learning has been one of exciting promise which has often not lived up to expectations.

E-learning, which began as an electronic form of distance learning, is now much more than that, with reliance on company intranets, the Internet and especially interactive Web 2.0 technology. E-learning provides the opportunity for learners to study flexibly in terms of time and topics which match up with immediate job demands. Learning can be done opportunistically and need not be in work time, and learners can progress at their own pace. E-learning also comes into its own when training has to be delivered to a large number of people in a short space of time, such as a new product launch – giving speed and cost-effectiveness. Also where training must be consistent yet regularly updated, such as health and safety training, e-learning has much to offer.

Increasingly, synchronous learning is used where all participants log on at the same time, with a tutor or facilitator being available online. Individuals can progress through material alone or network with others to complete a task and use chatrooms and have a dialogue with the tutor. Videoconferencing can also be used to bring participants together at the same time, with some MBA courses being delivered via videoconferencing rather than classroom-based teaching, and webinars (seminars delivered via the Web) are popular. Virtual reality can be used (as in gaming) and this is especially helpful in situations where it would be dangerous to learn solely on the job.

WINDOW ON PRACTICE

Second Life™

Virtual reality has been around for many years in the gaming world but it is only recently that learning and development professionals have begun to grasp the potential that this technology has to offer.

For example, Second Life, produced by Linden, is a site that can be used just for fun, but also for learning and development. In this 'second life' world an individual creates a virtual persona, called an avatar, and engages with other avatars, involving themselves in making and selling things, education, discussion groups and so on as in the real world.

Organisations that use it as a vehicle for people development may have a custom version of the world built for them, sometimes creating their office, store or campus so that learners experience a virtual world which mirrors their real one.

Virtual worlds can be used to give individuals experience of trying out new skills, learning new ideas and making mistakes. There is the potential for individuals to 'meet' and engage with others in ways that would be difficult in the real world. One way that the virtual worlds can be used for people development is for there to be a 'scripted' approach. This means that some of the avatars are controlled to create situations which can then be discussed afterwards. 'Open access' (i.e. not scripted) learning may also be used, for example for team exercises where teams address a challenge and are given feedback, just as on an 'outdoor' team training event.

Sources: **www.secondlife.com**; CIPD (2008) 'Virtual worlds and learning: Using Second Life at Duke Corporate Education', CIPD case study from **www.cipd.co.uk**; Syedain, H. (2008) 'Out of this world', *People Management*, Vol. 14, No. 8, 17 April, pp. 20–3.

Most recently the use of social media, such as Facebook and Twitter, is being explored as a learning and development tool. Such tools allow learners to be contributors as well as receivers of knowledge, and allow multi-way discussion and interpretation of content. This also allows communities to form around a topic, and enables learners to collaborate whatever their geographical location. Blogs and wikis can be used as well as social networking sites and some companies do develop their own sites. The CIPD (2011a) lists a range of ways in which tutors in educational centres can incorporate these media with other activities, and the ways in which these media support learning from a constructivist perspective.

WINDOW ON PRACTICE

Using Web 2.0 for knowledge development

The law firm Allen & Overy

Allen & Overy was attracted to using technology for knowledge development and sharing and decided to develop social business networking across its practice and have a number of networking communities. One is the 'HR exchange' for its eighty HR staff based in London and worldwide. Instead of passing on information via group or individual emails, HR staff are now encouraged to share information and experience using social networking technology. The site contains information on HR procedures and standard letter templates, but in addition there are discussion spaces where all HR staff can contribute on current projects and which encourage advice and knowledge sharing on HR practices.

Another site is for all staff, worldwide, who are parents and so far there are 250 members. Some content is generated by the firm, such as information on the availability of relevant training programmes (e.g. a seminar on parenting), and regular news feeds of items that busy parents might otherwise miss. However, much is contributed by members of the site, such as suggestions for school holiday activities and recommended websites for buying school clothes. In addition there are discussion forums and a monthly 'Ask the expert' series.

The biomedical and pharmaceutical company Pfizer

Pfizer has developed 'Pfizerpedia', which is similar to Wikipedia and open to all employees. The company says it is fast becoming a key resource for research and development staff seeking knowledge relevant to their jobs, and enables employees to share and access knowledge more quickly than before. Pfizer suggests that this is helping to break down 'silo protectionism' and avoids bureaucratic approval processes.

Source: Sloman, M. and Martin, G. (2008) 'Social climbers', *People Management*, Vol. 14, No. 23, 13 November, pp. 32–4.

Another major change is in the hardware that learners are using. Historically the move from desktops to laptops and notebooks has been well documented, but more recently tablets and smartphones are increasingly being used for learning. While this is progressing slowly in the west, in many Asia Pacific countries employees are leapfrogging traditional IT hardware to embrace tablets and mobile learning (Table 15.3). India in particular is ahead on this with 22% of employees already using smartphones for learning and development (Blain 2013) compared with 3% in the UK (CIPD 2012d). A US survey found that 22% of organisations were intending to invest in the use of mobile technologies in the coming months (Pace 2013).

Table 15.3
IT hardware for learning and development as reported in a survey across nine Asia Pacific countries by Blain (2013) on the use of different methods of accessing online learning

Desktop/laptop/large notebook	41%
Smartphone	15%
Tablet	28%
Emails	10%
Online messaging	6%

Source: Blain, J. (2013) *Major Learning Trends and Indicators for 2013 and Beyond Within the Asia Pacific Region*. Singapore: Cegos.

Progress, however, has been modest despite high expectations, and CIPD's e-learning survey (2011b) found low completion rates, poor user experience and firms focusing on the cost benefits of e-learning rather than learning quality. Elsewhere there is evidence of employees being unwilling to use e-learning. E-learning can still be a solitary activity and is often very dependent on individual self-discipline, and there are some learners who will simply find that an interactive Web-based learning unit does not compare with the conviviality and action associated with attending a course. Thus motivation dwindles unless there is other support to encourage learners to complete the units they need. Also using more sophisticated packages involving synchronous learning and joint learner tasks, bulletin boards and group/tutor dialogues can be very difficult at first for many employees, even though they may have good everyday computer skills, and they will need time to learn how particular packages work and how to use the facilities. If the right preparation and support are not made available employees can easily be put off by one difficult experience in which they found they could not keep up with the rest of the synchronous learning group.

In some organisations access to the appropriate equipment is still a problem, yet transferring to smartphones can bring other problems such as animations and interactions not working as well as on larger computers (Jass 2013). However, there is evidence that some initial concerns were perhaps unfounded. For example, in the Indian banking sector Mittal (2008) found that older age did not compromise the effectiveness of e-learning and neither did a lower job level.

There was much initial euphoria about what e-learning could contribute but increasingly it has been recognised that motivating learners is critical and most organisations now have much more realistic expectations of what e-learning can achieve, and the fit with other learning methods appears critical. At a very basic level e-learning can be very effectively used before a face-to-face course to do pre-work so that, for example, all attendees are starting from a roughly similar knowledge base. In this case those employees who have the knowledge base already can be exempt, while e-learning enables the others to get up to speed before the course begins. Similarly e-learning can be used effectively for course briefings and general preparation, such as the completion and analysis of pre-course questionnaires and other pre-work which saves time at the beginning of the event itself.

At the end of a course e-learning can be used for refreshers, for self-checking of understanding and planning how to apply the learning gained on the course. Similarly e-learning can be used in combination with manager coaching. This has led to the term 'blended learning', which is often used to indicate the blending of e-learning with face-to-face learning experiences, although it is increasingly used to indicate a blend of any approaches to learning. There is evidence that learning and training now involve a much wider range of activities; for example, Pickard (2006) reports on the blended learning approach at the Department for Work and Pensions which integrates self-managed learning, coaching and e-learning.

In conclusion, e-learning has a critical role to play but it would be dangerous to see it as the answer to all learning needs and the future of learning and development at work. Its value is best exploited where it is the most appropriate approach to meeting key development needs, such as preparing for dangerous tasks by using virtual reality, and where it can be combined with other learning activities to ensure a more complete learning experience and where it particularly suits the learning style of the individual learner.

WINDOW ON PRACTICE

Julie Scumming at AXA

Clarke (2006) recounts a very inventive learning experience at AXA, highly job based and involving a variety of activities. The exercise started with a Christmas card from a fictitious employee Julie Scumming. Posters followed announcing her arrival and then her fictitious husband entered the offices, shouting. After this there were diary entries on the intranet from both Julie and her boss which staff began to follow and picked up the story that Julie was a devout Christian who felt she was being discriminated against and bullied by her boss and peers. Dummy tabloid articles were circulated, a stand-up row in the canteen was performed by actors. Sticky notes were put on computers saying not to get 'stuck like Julie', and an advent calendar counted down the days to the main event, which was a tribunal hearing for managers. When the tribunal panel retired to consider their verdict actors acted out scenes which had led up to the tribunal. Meanwhile employees could log on to discussion forums to express their views about the case, and there was a poll about the anticipated results. Involvement in all of this was voluntary but many staff participated. The objective was to raise awareness about discrimination issues. Responses to questionnaires after the event demonstrated that managers were more aware of religious discrimination issues.

Source: Clarke, E. (2006) 'Julie diligent',
People Management,
Vol. 12, No. 14, 13 July, pp. 32–4.

Evaluation of training and development

One of the most nebulous and unsatisfactory aspects of the training job is evaluating its effectiveness, yet it is becoming more necessary to demonstrate value for money. While Campbell (2006) estimates that employer, public and individual spend on workforce training and development in the UK nears £30 billion each year, Phelps (2002) suggests there is no satisfactory return on investment calculation to prove its value, and that we remain unsure whether training breeds success or success breeds training. Evaluation is straightforward when the output of the training is clear to see, such as reducing the number of dispatch errors in a warehouse or increasing someone's typing speed. It is more difficult to evaluate the success of a management training course or a programme of social skills development, but the fact that it is difficult is not enough to prevent its being done. Cunningham (2007), however, suggests there is a danger that trainers and developers become too focused on trying to prove return on investment, and he works with an organisation where the focus of evaluation is for the trainees to present to their sponsors/managers their assessment of value that they and the organisation have gained from their learning.

A familiar method of evaluation is the post-course questionnaire, which course members complete on the final day by answering vague questions that require them to assess aspects of the course using only such general terms as 'good', 'very good' or 'outstanding'. The drawbacks with such questionnaires are, first, that there is a powerful halo effect, as the course will have been, at the very least, a welcome break from routine and there will probably have been some attractive fringe benefits such as staying in a comfortable hotel and enjoying rich food. Second, the questionnaire tends to evaluate the course and not the learning, so that the person attending the course is assessing the quality of the tutors and the visual aids, instead of being directed to examine what has been learnt.

Hamblin (1974), in a much-quoted work, identified five levels of evaluation: (1) evaluating the training, as in the post-course questionnaire above; (2) evaluating the learning, in terms of how the trainee now behaves; (3) evaluating changes in job performance; (4) evaluating changes in organisational performance; and (5) evaluating changes in the wider contribution that the organisation now makes. Perhaps the most well-referenced approach to evaluation is Kirkpatrick (1959) who suggested four levels of evaluation, somewhat similar to Hamblin: (1) reaction level; (2) learning level (have the learning objectives been met?); (3) behaviour (how has the individual's behaviour changed after returning to the job?); and (4) results and impact on the bottom line (what is the impact of training on performance?).

Measuring performance effectiveness after a learning intervention involves identifying changes in behaviour, knowledge, skills and attitudes, and it is important that the criteria for evaluation are built into development activities from the very beginning, not tagged on at the end. Lingham and his co-researchers (2006) provide a good example of how this can be done in practice. They describe an action research project where evaluation was built in from the outset and involved collaboration between organisational leaders, trainers, participants and evaluators. A four-phase approach was used:

- Phase 1: design of training programme (organisational leaders, trainers and evaluators agree design and methods to obtain feedback from participants after the initial runs of the training programme).

- Phase 2: launch and evaluation of initial programme (training conducted and agreed methods used to collect participants' views).

- Phase 3: feedback and design of evaluation instrument (organisational leaders, trainers and evaluators meet to review feedback and field notes and adapt the training programme where necessary, and a survey instrument needs to be designed for the evaluation of future iterations of the programme).

- Phase 4: ongoing training and evaluation (training programme conducted with new design/content, evaluation survey used and results fed back into Phase 3).

(Adapted from Lingham *et al.* 2006)

SUMMARY PROPOSITIONS

15.1 The emphasis has moved from training to learning, with individuals taking ownership of identifying and addressing their own learning needs, or at least contributing to this. To be effective learners we need to understand the nature of learning and our own strengths and weaknesses.

15.2 The emphasis on formal development programmes is declining in favour of greater interest in approaches to on-the-job development, such as coaching, mentoring, peer relationships and self-development.

15.3 The interest in e-learning continues; however, the extent to which employees take advantage of such opportunities will be affected by the context and the support available. E-learning is increasingly being blended with other forms of learning.

15.4 Evaluation of development is critical but difficult. It is most effective when built into the design of the development activity rather than tagged on at the end.

GENERAL DISCUSSION TOPICS

1   If learning is an individual process, why is so much training done in groups? What are the implications of moving towards more individualised learning?

2   Discuss the view that the role of the trainer/facilitator is critically important in the effectiveness of a training programme.

THEORY INTO PRACTICE

Micropower

Micropower is a rapidly growing computer software firm, specialising in tailor-made solutions for business. Increasingly, training for other businesses in its own and other software packages has occupied the time of the consultants. Micropower sees this as a profitable route for the future and such training is now actively sold to clients. Consultants both sell and carry out the training. As an interim measure, to cope with increasing demand, the firm is now recruiting some specialist trainers, but the selling of the training is considered to be an integral part of the consultant's role.

Micropower has just issued a mission statement which accentuates 'the supply of and support for sophisticated computer solutions', based on a real understanding of business needs. The firm considers that it needs to be flexible in achieving this and has decided that multiskilling is the way forward.

All consultants need to sell solutions and training at all levels, and be excellent analysts, designers and trainers. Some 200 consultants are now employed. Most have a degree in IT and most joined the firm initially because of their wish to specialise in the technical aspects of software development, and spent some years almost entirely in an office-based position before moving into a customer contact role. A smaller proportion were keen to concentrate on systems analysis, and were involved in customer contact from the start.

In addition there are 300 software designers and programmers who are primarily office based and rarely have any customer contact. It is from this group that new consultants are appointed. Programmers are promoted to two levels of designer and those in the top level of designer may then, if their performance level is high enough, be promoted to consultant. There is some discontent among designers that promotion means having to move into a customer contact role, and there are a growing number who seek more challenges, higher pay and status, but who wish to avoid customer contact. Another repercussion of the promotion framework is that around a quarter of the current consultants are not happy in their role. They are consultants because they valued promotion more than doing work that they enjoyed. Some have found the intense customer contact very stressful, feel they lack the appropriate skills, are not particularly comfortable with their training role and are unhappy about the increasing need to 'sell'.

Questions

1 What immediate steps could Micropower take to help the consultants, particularly those who feel very unhappy, perform well and feel more comfortable in their new roles?

2 In the longer term how can Micropower reconcile its declared aim of multiskilling with a career structure which meets both organisational and employee needs?

3 What other aspects of HR strategy would support and integrate with the development strategy of multiskilling?

4 Micropower wishes to develop a competency profile for the consultant role. How would you recommend that the firm progress this, and how might the profile be used in the widest possible manner in the organisation?

FURTHER READING

Harvey, M. (2012) *Interactional Coaching*. Abingdon: Routledge
A practical, accessible and business-focused book which includes the debate between directive and non-directive coaching, and also acknowledges the client's choice of whether to implement its learning in the workplace. Harvey focuses on three types of interactions in order to understand a situation: our relationship with time and how the past and future impact on the present; our interaction with our self, for example in terms of our values, beliefs and strengths; and our interactions with others.

London, M. and Hall, M. (2011) 'Perspectives: Web 2.0 support for individual, group and organisational learning', *Human Resource Development International*, Vol. 14, No. 1, pp. 103–13; 'Unlocking the value of Web 2.0 technologies for training and development: The shift from instructor-controlled adaptive learning to learner-driven, generative learning', *Human Resource Management*, Vol. 50, No. 6, pp. 757–75.

Using each stage of Kolb's learning cycle these articles demonstrate the ways in which Web 2.0 interactive learning can support generative learning, comparing this with more traditional training methods. The articles provide lots of practical learning methods that can be used for each approach.

Neilsen, A. and Norrekit, H. (2009) 'A discourse analysis of the disciplinary power of management coaching', *Society and Business Review*, Vol. 4, No. 3, pp. 202–14.

This is a fascinating and thought-provoking review of the literature on coaching from the point of view of control. The article finds that there are two approaches to coaching: employee coaching which seems to involve action control and direct monitoring; and executive coaching which appears to involve control of the spirit as well as results and achievements, the authors arguing that this acts as a constraint on the individual's self-realisation project. They conclude that coaching can be a stronger disciplining technique than control by targets/numbers.

Slotte, V. and Herbert, A. (2008) 'Engaging workers in simulation-based e-learning', *Journal of Workplace Learning*, Vol. 20, No. 3, pp. 165–80.

This is a lovely example of how simulation-based e-learning and face-to-face methods can be combined. The authors explain how this approach was used in a bookstore to develop customer service skills. The simulation package presented scenarios of different types of difficult customer and staff initially worked with a live coach to facilitate their discussions of how to approach each situation, and offer concepts where appropriate. They found this thought provoking and their discussions continued after the end of the one-day initial programme. Later they continued to use the simulation programme with virtual coaching from 'Esko' who gave continuous feedback. Some said they preferred this mechanical feedback to their responses to different scenarios in that it felt safer to try out alternatives and make mistakes.

REFERENCES

Anderson, V. (2009) 'Research: Line manager as coach', *People Management*, 21 May, p. 42.

Arkin, A. (2011) 'The odd couple', *People Management*, October, pp. 44–6.

Blain, J. (2013) *Major Learning Trends and Indicators for 2013 and Beyond Within the Asia Pacific Region*. Singapore: Cegos.

Boak, G. (1991) *Developing Managerial Competencies: The management learning contract approach*. London: Pitman.

Broadbridge, A. (1999) 'Mentoring in retailing: A tool for success?', *Personnel Review*, Vol. 28, No. 4, pp. 336–55.

Campbell, M. (2006) 'Demonstrating the value of learning, training and development', in *Latest Trends in Learning, Training and Development: Reflections on the 2006 Learning and Development Survey*. London: CIPD.

Cheshire Fire and Rescue Service (2012) *Cheshire East Annual Report 2011/12*. Cheshire East.

CIPD (2008) 'Virtual worlds and learning: Using Second Life™ at Duke Corporate Education', CIPD case study from **www.cipd.co.uk**.

CIPD (2011a) *Factsheet: Using social media in education: For tutors in centres*. London: CIPD.

CIPD (2011b) *E-learning Survey*. London: CIPD.

CIPD (2012a) *Learning and Talent Development: Annual survey 2012*. London: CIPD.

CIPD (2012b) *Sustainable Organisation Performance: Research report: Coaching – the evidence base*. London: CIPD.

CIPD (2012c) *Coaching and Mentoring Factsheet*. London: CIPD.

CIPD (2012d) *Research Insight: From e-learning to 'gameful' employment*. London: CIPD.

Clarke, E. (2006) 'Julie diligent', *People Management*, Vol. 12, No. 14, pp. 32–43.

Clutterbuck, D. (2004) *Everyone Needs a Mentor*. London: CIPD.

Cottee, P. (2006) 'Oliver's army', *People Management*, Vol. 12, No. 19, pp. 44–5.

Cunningham, I. (2007) 'Viewpoint: Sorting out evaluation of learning and development: Making it easier for ourselves', *Development and Learning in Organisations*, Vol. 21, No. 5, pp. 4–6.

Ehrich, L. (2008) 'Mentoring and women managers: Another look at the field', *Gender in Management: An International Journal*, Vol. 23, No. 7, pp. 469–83.

Fowler, J. and O'Gorman, J. (2005) 'Mentoring functions: A contemporary view of the perceptions of mentees and mentors', *British Journal of Management*, Vol. 16, pp. 51–7.

Hamblin, A.C. (1974) *Evaluation and Control of Training*. Maidenhead: McGraw-Hill.

IDS (2009) *Coaching and Mentoring*, HR Study No. 897, July. London: IDS.

Jass, B. (2013) 'Taking the mobile learning plunge', *Training and Development*, February, pp. 29–30.

Kirkpatrick, D. (1959) 'Techniques for evaluating training programs', *Journal of the American Society of Training Directors*, Vol. 13, pp. 3–26.

Lingham, T., Richley, B. and Rezania, D. (2006) 'An evaluation system for training programs: A case study using a four-phase approach', *Career Development International*, Vol. 11, No. 4, pp. 334–51.

Longenecker, C. and Ariss, S. (2002) 'Creating competitive advantage through effective management education', *Personnel Review*, Vol. 21, No. 9, pp. 640–54.

Maxwell, G. (2009) 'Mentoring for enhancing females' career development: The bank job', *Equal Opportunities International*, Vol. 28, No. 7, pp. 561–76.

Megginson, D. (1994) 'Planned and emergent learning: A framework and a method', *Executive Development*, Vol. 7, No. 6, pp. 29–32.

Megginson, D. and Whitaker, V. (2007) *Cultivating Self-development*. London: IPD.

Mittal, M. (2008) 'Evaluating perceptions on effectiveness of e-learning programs in Indian banks: Identifying areas for improvement', *Development and Learning in Organisations*, Vol. 22, No. 2, pp. 12–14.

Nielsen, K. (2009) 'A collaborative perspective on learning transfer', *Journal of Workplace Learning*, Vol. 21, No. 1, pp. 58–70.

Oglensky, B. (2008) 'The ambivalent dynamics of loyalty in mentorship', *Development and Learning in Organisations*, Vol. 61, No. 3, pp. 419–49.

Pace, A. (2013) 'Learning technology trends in 2013', *Training and Development*, February, p. 18.

People Management (2012) 'First person: Career clinic: Should I pursue an MBA?', August, p. 66.

Phelps, M. (2002) 'Blind faith', *People Management*, Vol. 8, No. 9, p. 51.

Phillips, L. (2006) 'BUPA stars', *People Management*, Vol. 12, No. 22, pp. 30–2.

Pickard, J. (2006) 'Suits ewe', *People Management*, Vol. 12, No. 12, pp. 36–7.

Santos, A. and Stewart, M. (2003) 'Employee perceptions and their influence on training effectiveness', *Human Resource Management Journal*, Vol. 13, No. 1, pp. 27–45.

Sloman, M. and Martin, G. (2008) 'Social climbers', *People Management*, Vol. 14, No. 23, pp. 32–4.

Sloman, M. and Rolph, J. (2003) *E-learning: The learning curve – the change agenda*. London: CIPD.

Smedley, T. (2012) 'Fast masters', *People Management*, February, pp. 49–52.

Stevens, M. (2010) 'Fake station offers real training', *People Management*, 28 January, p. 12.

Syedain, H. (2008) 'Out of this world', *People Management*, Vol. 14, No. 8, pp. 20–3.

Chapter 16

TALENT AND CAREER DEVELOPMENT

THE OBJECTIVES OF THIS CHAPTER ARE TO:

1 Clarify various definitions of talent

2 Explore ways in which talent can be identified

3 Review a strategic approach to talent and career development, and succession planning

4 Examine different talent and career development activities including managing talent in a developmental way, international development and the perspective of those labelled as 'talented'

5 Explain how organisations evaluate the practice of talent management

Since the 2008–9 economic downturn organisations in the UK have fought to protect and keep their talented employees, and the practice of talent 'hoarding' has become familiar in preparation for the upturn (see e.g. *People Management* 2013). This reflects the difficulty and cost of finding talent. Indeed some organisations see the downturn as an opportunity to pick up talent from competitors, but many anticipate focusing on retaining and developing talent rather than recruiting it (CIPD 2011a). This is very different from the previous downturn when many organisations let go of their talented employees and consequently did not have the talent resources to take advantage of the upturn when it came.

As the west is experiencing the retirement of the post-war baby-boomer generation and developing countries continue to grow in spite of the world downturn, there is a shortage of talent, with this being particularly severe in Asia (Ng Ek Heng 2012). As talent is so important in driving organisational competitiveness, transformation and long term success it is key that organisations develop a pool of talent and also secure a long-term leadership pipeline. Krinks and Strack (2008), in an international HR survey, found that managing talent was identified as the most important HR challenge in nine of the seventeen countries surveyed including the UK, USA, Singapore, Australia and Japan.

What is talent?

Definitions of talent are varied, and different organisations will use a definition appropriate to their needs. Michaels *et al*. (2001) were employees of McKinsey, and coined the term 'war for talent'. They initially limited talent to a small number of individuals with high potential to reach the top jobs in the organisation. This is an elitist definition which focuses on a few employees. For example, Bacardi-Martini focuses attention on the top 20% of the workforce who are the rising stars (Maynardleigh Associates 2009).

However, this approach may miss those who are most critical to business success and John Boudreau (Chubb and Phillips 2008) stresses the importance of linking talent to the organisation's strategy, maintaining that it is necessary to identify the talent in the organisation that when improved would be pivotal to the organisation's achievements. This gives room for a slightly different way of identifying which talent to focus on and Scott Snell (Pickard 2007) uses Ryanair as an example, arguing that its value is created by turnaround speed and therefore the most valuable, but not the highest paid or trained, jobs are ground staff. These jobs are critical to the competitive advantage of the organisation.

Both the above perspectives are selective and hence cut across equal opportunities. Focusing on talent development for the few can lead to greater individual competition rather than teamwork, and can be alienating for the remainder of employees. It can also mean that latent talent is never identified as these individuals are not offered the development they need, which would enable them to demonstrate and exploit their talent for the benefit of themselves and their organisation.

An alternative view is that *all* employees possess latent talent. This inclusive approach is about enabling everyone in the organisation to be their best by unlocking the talent that they have. This is exemplified by Stuart-Kotze and Dunn (2008: 2) who say:

WINDOW ON PRACTICE

Aviva

Aviva has a clear statement which reads 'If you work for Aviva you're talented', which John Ainsley, Group HR Director of Aviva, contrasts with star development programmes. He says that 'Everyone in Aviva has the same conversation about their development, so all our colleagues, wherever they are in the world, are covered by the same process.' He claims that this has increased employee engagement scores and that employees say they feel recognised. He says that Aviva provides strong encouragement for people to have honest and authentic conversations about their development.

Source: Smedley, T. (2012a) 'On my agenda', *People Management*, March, pp. 51–3.

There is no shortage of talented people. There is a shortage of people who know how to identify, develop, recruit and retain talent.

In a survey by Maynardleigh Associates (2009) half the respondent companies including Bourne Leisure and BSkyB adopted the view that talent is about everyone realising their full potential. They also found that during the recession Britannia also moved from an elitist approach concentrating on the top 100 employees to focusing on the whole 5,000 employees in the workforce. It is interesting that McKinsey has now adopted a more inclusive definition of talent (Guthridge and Lawson 2008), reflecting the human capital debate and the need for all to perform well, not just a few. However, there is evidence that a more restricted view of talent is predominant in the UK as demonstrated in the Window on practice below. Interestingly the CIPD (2012: 1) defines talent as:

Talent consists of those individuals who can make a difference to organisational performance either through their immediate contribution or, in the longer-term, by demonstrating the highest levels of potential.

WINDOW ON PRACTICE

The CIPD (2011a) carried out a survey of international learning and talent development covering the USA, India and the UK. In the UK, definitions of 'talent' most often referred to 'high-potential' employees, senior employees and graduates, with only 20% of respondents defining 'talent' as all employees. In India and the USA, 'talent' tends to be interpreted more broadly.

Source: International Learning and Talent Development comparison survey, 2011. London: CIPD.

A more recent approach to talent development, sometimes called blended, has been for organisations to identify different talent groups and provide different types of development and career planning for each. Hills (2012) provides an interesting model of four talent groups representing different ways in which organisations define talent, but which also demonstrates how organisations could potentially group different parts of the workforce. The four groups are listed below and indicate the focus of talent development:

- leadership and senior roles;
- high potentials;
- talent pools;
- all employees.

You will have identified how each group becomes broader.

In this chapter we generally focus on senior managers and leaders, high-potential employees and graduates, because we looked at the development of broader talent in the previous chapter.

ACTIVITY 16.1

1 How does your organisation define talent? (If you are a full-time student read one or two relevant cases in *People Management* and interpret these as 'your organisation'.)

2 Is this definition explicit or implicit?

3 What are the advantages and disadvantages of the approach taken?

4 Provide evidence to support your conclusions.

Identification of talent

The recruitment and selection process is one way to identify and then buy in talent, but too much emphasis on this can make other employees feel undervalued and can be unhelpful in the development of organisational culture. Lack of career development opportunities may encourage employees with potential to move elsewhere and may be a disincentive to be proactive and give of their best (see e.g. Crawshaw *et al.* 2012). A balance between external and internal talent is usually most appropriate and can be matched to the needs of the organisation.

WINDOW ON PRACTICE

Nando's approach to talent management

UK Learning and Development Manager, Marcelo Borges, says: 'Let's assume that everyone who works for us is talented, and let them grow and develop in their own environment.' The firm argues that its ability to fill jobs internally is proof that this approach to talent management is working. Almost half the managerial jobs are filled internally, as are around two-thirds of area managers and regional directors, and management retention is 22%, which is approximately double the sector average.

Source: Evans, J. (2007) 'Talent strategy feeds growth at Nando's', *People Management*, Vol. 13, No. 9, 3 May, p. 16.

For current employees, appraisal and potential ratings from the manager, 360-degree feedback and the evaluation of previous development experiences will be of value in the identification of talent. Assessment and development centres are commonly used to identify talent by means of psychometric tests, interviews, role play, business games and direct experiences of work tasks at higher or different grades. We have discussed these centres in some detail earlier (see Chapter 7), and when used internally they usually assess candidates against a set of competencies required or desired at higher job grades.

However, putting too much emphasis on assessing sets of competencies can be problematic. For example, Rob Goffe and Gareth Jones (Chubb and Phillips 2008) warn against assessing people against a rigid set of competencies as this provides a limited view of employees and minimises diversity within the organisation; and Cunningham (2007a) suggests that organisations go astray when they expect a total talent package from one individual, insisting that a person displays talent across a wide range of competencies in order to justify being labelled as talented. He goes on to suggest that people may have an enormous talent in one area but be weak in others, so jobs need to be designed around their talents to maximise them.

Also some may not display talent in their current junior role but they might in a higher-level role, or a different role. Alternatively someone displaying talent in a current role, such as a professional or technical role, may not have the talent for a managerial role. In addition talent needs to be identified for future needs and possibilities rather than just current needs. So a clear distinction needs to be made between current performance and potential future performance in a different role.

Cunningham (2007b) identifies two strategic approaches to talent management, first aligning roles with people (in other words, fitting talented people to current job roles) and, second, aligning people with roles (in other words, designing jobs to fit the talented people in the organisation). He suggests that both these strategies are critical and there needs to be a dynamic interaction between these two approaches.

ACTIVITY 16.2

1 In your own organisation what is the balance between growing and buying in talent? (If you are a student choose a case organisation from *People Management* magazine or elsewhere.)

2 How well does this balance work? Provide evidence for your conclusion.

3 What might be the disadvantages of an over-reliance on growing talent?

Before responding to this activity you might find it helpful to read the article by Hills (2009) in *Industrial and Commercial Training* as detailed in the References.

Strategic talent and career development

Since the acquisition, development and retention of talent is key to success, organisations are constantly advised to manage all aspects of talent in a strategic and integrated manner; however, they often fall short. Such a strategic approach, similar to the strategic criteria we discussed earlier (see Chapter 3), requires that:

- The approach needs to be embedded in the organisation and therefore requires senior management sponsorship rather than being led by the HR department.
- Talent development activities need to be integrated with each other and with other talent activities, and to be consistent.
- The approach needs to support the strategic objectives for the organisation. Garrow and Hirsh (2008) propose three questions that need to be answered in terms of focus on strategic objectives. The first is which job roles need to be managed in this way (e.g. senior leadership, IT specialists, airport ground staff, or all roles)? The second is where does the talent come from for these roles (e.g. from outside the organisation or is there potential to be developed within)? The third is what are the development outcomes required for individuals who have the potential to fill the specified job roles?
- The approach to talent needs to fit more generally with the organisation, its values and other activities. Garrow and Hirsh (2008) say there needs to be a fit with culture, the psychological contract in the organisation, other HR policies and practices, and the skills of the managers who will be implementing talent management. Powell and Lubitsh (2007) suggest talent activities need to be congruent with the aspirations of the organisation, its underlying systems and processes and core beliefs, and warn that a mismatch will cause confusion and cynicism.

Strategic talent development is most often expressed as a system incorporating a structured approach to job development and planned moves and there may be centralised monitoring of talent. Powell and Lubitsh (2007) further suggest that this works for some, but that such a traditional approach may not be suitable for all talented people and a more flexible approach may be required. A traditional approach focusing on integrating talent management and development activities is exemplified by the Civil Service example in the Window on practice below.

WINDOW ON PRACTICE

'Early talent' in the civil service

Allen (2008) spoke to Claire Wilson of the Department for Work and Pensions (DWP) who explains how there were three separate talent management programmes running but these were all aimed at niches and not linked together. 'Early talent' was devised to be open to all rather than being selective and for senior people; it was seen as an opportunity to link up with the senior programmes. The intention was to apply this approach across other government departments and produce a deeper talent pool, which involved creating consistent tools and frameworks. 'Early talent' is targeted at people who are identified as having the capability to rise rapidly by two Civil Service grades and falls into three stages:

- Stage 1: Any employee can use the STEP (Seeing Talent Emerge and Progress) website and use an online simulation tool introducing them to the challenges of a senior manager role. This is to help candidates decide if they are capable of carrying out such a role.

- Stage 2: If candidates decide they have the potential to carry out a senior role they progress to the first assessed test – the Situational Judgement test – designed to look at thinking and personal styles.

- Stage 3: Candidates who pass stage 2 then carry out capability-based assessments linked to the skills required in a given role.

After taking part in the last assessment candidates are provided with personal feedback, and all are encouraged to view this process as career development rather than a guarantee of promotion for those who pass, given the limited number of promotions available.

There is then an ongoing development programme with candidates working in small groups and action learning sets supported by a facilitator. There are also skills workshops and master classes and a business-critical project to carry out.

Source: After 'Bright and Early', *People Management*, Vol. 14, No. 7, pp. 30–2 (Allen, A.), Reproduced with the permission of the publisher, the Chartered Institute of Personnel and Development, London (**www.cipd.co.uk**).

A more flexible approach generally focuses on talent pools and their development rather than specific jobs and job moves. For example, Google adopts a more flexible approach as outlined in the Window on practice below.

WINDOW ON PRACTICE

Talent at Google

Brockett (2008) reports that Google uses rigorous recruitment and selection methods and has a very low attrition rate, but there are no specific 'talent programmes'. Google's argument for this approach is that it does not want to label people. It feels that people are attracted to work at Google because of the brand. Although the company is not hierarchical and there is little room for promotion it broadens jobs to allow people to develop and expand their skills, encouraging self-managing teams and autonomy.

So Google seems to focus on the appropriate management style for engaging clever people rather than a formal talent system. However, there is a career development system which emphasises internal moves rather than external recruitment, with a desire to tip the balance towards internal moves. Google promotes training and development, job shadowing with Europe/Asia Pacific and allows people time to innovate in their jobs. Meeting other employee needs, the company provides flexible working, free food, an on-site gym, sofas, and many offices have crèches.

Source: Adapted from Brockett, J. (2008) 'Finders keepers', *People Management*, Vol. 14, No. 9, 18 September, pp. 28–34.

However, while Tim Miller (Phillips 2008), Director of People, Property and Assurance at Standard Chartered Bank, says that the responsibility for talent management and development lies firmly with the line, the Hewlett UK Talent Survey found that 84% of managers do not have the time to do it (*People Management* 2008). In this survey 60% of the 240 respondents also thought that managers did not have adequate skills, although 88% thought talent management a top strategic priority. The main problem identified was that talent strategies were not filtering down to managers and their decisions did not reflect talent management strategies (55%).

Similarly in China (Wilson 2008), 76% of respondents to a Mercer survey did have a strategy in place that defined how to assess, develop and retain current and future leaders, but the problem seemed to be translating this into practice, having the skills and knowledge of where to start being the biggest barrier.

Promotion and succession planning

Focused succession planning can only accommodate a limited number of roles and individuals as it can be a time-consuming process – so it is usually reserved for top jobs and for individuals of high potential. A major strength of growing talent is the building of talent pipelines, which is a key aspect of the CIPD's Shaping the Future research, so that a depth of talent is available if a key employee leaves unexpectedly. This is important as it avoids long gaps between an employee leaving and a new recruit beginning, thus protecting service and production levels. Such a pipeline may involve both company-suggested lateral and upwards moves and applications for promotions from those on the talent track. Building flexible pools of talent ready to fill a wide range of roles within the business is different from older approaches to succession planning where specific individuals were groomed and developed to fill a specific job, or at best a very narrow range of jobs, when they became available in the future. Secondments and international experience often figure in development for succession planning based on the range of company experience that top jobs require.

Those identified on the talent track may move quickly through a number of job roles. This may be very stimulating for the individual, but there is a danger of becoming derailed later in career, despite earlier successes. As individuals only stay a short time in any position they may not have the experience of setbacks and recovering from them, and they may not be there long enough to experience the impact of any changes they make. In addition high flyers may alienate others on their way up and may not stay in any one place long enough to form a development and support network. To compensate for this it is critical that high flyers receive high levels of developmental feedback as they progress.

ACTIVITY 16.3

We noted above the difficulty that high flyers may experience later in their career.
What other developmental activities would you recommend for such employees? Explain why they would aid long-term career success.

Succession planning can assist retention if plans are shared with individuals, and especially if there is some form of consultation. This raises the issue of transparency, which would need to be carefully handled to avoid expectations which might not be fulfilled, as the pool of individuals covered by succession planning will inevitably be larger than the number of key roles to be filled. It is also difficult to plan with any certainty as frequent mergers and acquisitions change the nature of the organisation, different competencies become important, and the available talent pool changes.

WINDOW ON PRACTICE

China's talent management challenge

China has so far made minimal progress in building locally sourced talent according to Wilson (2008). She points out the shortage of entrepreneurial management talent in the current leadership generation and the following one, as such managers have grown up during the Cultural Revolution, when skills such as hard work, tenacity and perseverance enabled success rather than strategic, innovation and entrepreneurial skills.

China has used expatriates for key leadership positions and although this practice appears to be reducing, Wilson suggests that China has not achieved the best balance between growing and buying in

talent. Building a leadership pipeline is a long-term investment, and using expatriates to fill gaps is a useful short-term ploy but creates a long-term problem. She suggests that such use of expatriates creates a perceived 'glass ceiling' for locally born Chinese. While expatriates command very high salaries and benefits, the process of transitioning (i.e. moving from having a role filled by an expatriate to appointing a local person) is difficult, especially when the local person in that position will be paid much less that the outgoing expatriate. This creates feelings of inequity and frustration. The timescale for these moves is slow as many expatriates say that they do not have the time to develop their successors, and the growing complexity of the business environment means that developing the necessary skills is a long-term process. Wilson suggests that a strategy based only on buying in talent is unsustainable in the long term, but knowing where to start on development schemes seems to be a key barrier. Companies often have an appropriate strategy to develop local talent but implementation is weak. Wilson provides an example of a more proactive employer, Estee Lauder (in conjunction with Mercer), whose strategy for local managers starts with an assessment against region-specific leadership

behaviours, plus a twelve-month development programme with personal feedback, experiential learning modules, and a year-long business case supported by the all-important long-term commitment of the senior leadership.

Source: Adapted from 'Hidden dragons' *People Management*, Vol. 14, No. 16, pp. 18–23 (Wilson, B.), Reproduced with the permission of the publisher, the Chartered Institute of Personnel and Development, London (**www.cipd.co.uk**).

Developing talent and careers

We have already discussed a broad range of developmental activities in the previous chapter, some of which are considered to be particularly valuable for career and talent development, although different surveys produce slightly different views. The Cranet survey (2011) of twenty-nine countries found that the most common career development activities are project teamwork, special tasks/projects, cross-organisation and interdisciplinary tasks. The theme here appears to be gaining the broadest possible organisational understanding and networking. In the 2011 CIPD International Talent development survey covering the UK, India and the USA, the most effective development activities for leaders were identified as internal knowledge sharing, external conferences and events, and coaching by an external practitioner.

In addition to the usual development activities we would add another three methods which are particularly relevant to developing talent and careers: managing people in a developmental way; international experience; and working with employee perspectives of their careers.

Managing talent in a developmental way

Employers not only need to understand what people's capabilities are, but also need to give them scope to use and develop them. Charles Handy suggested that organisations should take more risks and allow talented people more power to make decisions. The way that talented people are managed will not only affect their performance and development, but also determine whether they wish to stay with the organisation.

Talented people generally want to display their talents and give of their best but can be alienated by a lack of empowerment within their job and by formal organisational procedures and processes. Managers need to engage talented employees by providing appropriate scope and decision-making capacity and manage them lightly on a day-to-day basis – you may wish to refer back to our discussion on organisation design and flexibility at this point (see Chapter 5). Managers also need to be prepared to manage talented employees' careers in a joint and flexible manner. As high flyers move through an organisation quickly there is evidence that they experience difficulties and therefore support needs to be available to them.

Goffee and Jones (2009), for example, recognise that while talented people may add most value to the organisation, they are often the hardest to manage. Some of the authors' recommendations for those who manage bright people are that they should: recognise their knowledge, accepting their independence and difference; try and align the goals of the individual with those of the organisation; win resources for them but allow them space to get on with things alone; encourage them to achieve external recognition; protect them from administrative matters which they may see as a distraction; and provide as few rules as possible.

In a similar vein Powell and Lubitsh (2007) propose that talented people know their worth to the organisation and have their own views on the direction of their career. They will often fail to respond to traditional management approaches and may respond unpredictably, not valuing hierarchy and avoiding being controlled.

International development

International experience has become a critical part of leadership preparation. This can be provided in a number of developmental ways such as frequent international travel, virtual international teams, short-term assignments/visits (say a few weeks) and international commuting. However, in spite of the costs, longer-term international assignments of two or more years remain well used.

From the organisation's point of view, international assignments provide not only vital management development, but also the opportunity for skills and knowledge transfer and a means of control of subsidiaries.

Careful preparation is critical and will often involve some language and cultural training as well as role-relevant preparation. A clear remit, support (such as a local manager, but also a mentor from the home country), development goals and performance expectations need to be agreed and set down before the assignment begins. Repatriation also needs to be carefully handled as repatriates will be partial outsiders on their return and need to be reintegrated as quickly as possible. It is also critical to match them on their return with a job which uses their newly acquired experience and skills (see especially Chapter 27). Some useful practical information on international assignments can be found in the CIPD factsheet (2011b).

WINDOW ON PRACTICE

Compelled to go abroad?

Pinto and her colleagues carried out an interview survey of Portuguese expatriates and repatriates and overall these employees found international experience to be valuable. However, around half of those interviewed felt themselves compelled to accept an international assignment, this being the third most popular motive for agreeing the assignment, after the opportunity for challenge and improvement of career prospects. They felt subtle pressure from the company indicating that their career prospects would be damaged if they did not accept, and that other opportunities would not be made available to them. Turning down an assignment indicated some sort of failure. The effects of feeling compelled had an impact on the assignment. These individuals experienced a longer and more difficult adjustment to their new location and were generally less satisfied with the assignment. The authors conclude by questioning the appropriateness of organisational pressure as they suggest it may also affect the long-term commitment of these employees to the company.

Pinto, L., Cabral-Cardoso, C. and Werther, W. (2012) 'Compelled to go abroad? Motives and outcomes of international assignments', *International Journal of Human Resource Management*, Vol. 23, No. 11, pp. 2295–314.

Valuing employees' perspective and meeting their needs

The Window on practice above indicates the potential different perspectives on career progression between employers and employees. In addition it is not just the high-potential few who seek development opportunities and career progression. Although an organisation may focus on them, it would be a mistake to ignore career support for all employees. For example, Vodafone launched 'career deal' for its workforce to improve engagement and perceptions of career development (Scott 2007). This involves a toolkit for employees where they can work through the questions: where am I now; where do I want to be; and how do I get there?

WINDOW ON PRACTICE

R&SA intranet aids career planning

R&SA is using a new intranet site to encourage staff to plan their careers. The site enables people to assess their strengths and weaknesses, their motivations and to set development goals. This site was produced in response to employee desire to understand the career opportunities available to them. It also provides

thumbnails of how various people from across the business reached their current role and has encouraged more career discussions with managers and inspired leaders to become more involved in career development. Users of the site are alerted to international vacancies so that staff see them even if they are not proactively looking for a new role.

Source: Chubb, L. (2008) 'R&SA intranet aids career planning', *People Management*, Vol. 14, No. 4, 21 February, p. 10.

Job role design and flexibility can also be important in retaining talent. We noted before that for the high-potential few, designing jobs which make the most of their strengths and contribution is worth consideration. In addition flexible working may retain older people who are talented but who may not wish to continue to work full time as the only alternative to retiring. Offering part-time and flexible hours is a way to hold on to the knowledge of talented people. At the other end of the spectrum many younger employees, 'generation Y', often expect a better balance between work and home life. As Jenny Watson, Chairwoman of the EOC (now the Equality and Human Rights Commission), says:

Failing to rethink about the way we've traditionally organised work is a chronic waste of talent. (Phillips 2007)

Flexible working may also help attract talent back after career breaks. It is important to engage people in discussions about their careers as their views may be surprisingly different from what senior managers may suppose. For example, work–life balance, the meaningfulness of a job, the interest in a job, travel opportunities, speed of promotion will all be valued differently by different individuals.

How organisations evaluate talent management

Measuring the outcomes of HR practices has a long history and has always been beset by difficulties, and talent management is no different. Internal HR measures are often used as these are easier to collect (such as internal promotions and retention rates) and these can be of great value if there is an identified problem around these issues. Linkerman (2007) warns against measuring processes and activities rather than outcomes. For example, an organisation may measure the numbers of people who have a development plan, but this does not tell us whether the development plan is actually used, whether intended development has been achieved or whether this has impacted on the individual's performance. At the other end of the scale there are external measures such as profit, share price and sales. As with any case of measurement, there is the hurdle of proving that the results obtained, such as increased retention or a higher share price, are indeed caused by the talent management activity that has been undertaken.

In the Cranfield School of Management study (Parry and Tyson 2007) of over 600 UK organisations only 15% systematically measured the return on investment (ROI) for talent management. They found that the most common measures were cost per individual (58%), overall cost of talent management (53%) and the individual cost of talent management techniques (33%). In addition costs of talent management were measured against retention (43%), other career progression (40%) and productivity. Yapp (2009) in her research with an unspecified number of global organisations found that the measures used were internal HR measures such as retention, engagement, promotion, succession and diversity.

In the CIPD's international study (2011a) the most popular methods of evaluation were feedback from employees covered by talent management initiatives and their managers and retention. Less than one-quarter in each country had clear success criteria at the outset, and only around 20% in each country considered the implementation of formal succession plans in evaluation. Around 10% admitted to no evaluation. All of these studies revealed little in terms of external measures such as business performance, revenue, margins and shareholder value.

WINDOW ON PRACTICE

Maynardleigh Associates (2009) found that only one company of the twenty they researched calculated the return on investment (ROI) of talent management activities in a formal way. This company used a comparative approach and calculated the value of graduate trainees by identifying the profit on revenue-generating projects they were involved in multiplied by the number of graduates. The company did a similar calculation with a non-graduate control group. The graduate group contributed more revenue and the company found that for every £1 of money spent on talent management (with the graduates) it received multiple returns in respect of extra sales.

Yapp (2009) describes a similar approach which she calls a micro ROI approach in npower. This company invested heavily in identifying and developing leaders and future leaders who could successfully drive culture change in the organisation by inspiring, promoting pride in the company, providing opportunities for personal growth and helping employees understand their role in the company. The leadership project was evaluated in terms of sales revenue and employee perceptions. In the first division to experience this initiative sales were up by 54% and productivity almost 5% and customer service complaints down by 14%. Employees' pride in working for npower increased by 14 points, and their willingness to recommend npower as an employer increased by 11 points. Staff retention also increased by 33%. Comparison figures with other divisions are, however, not provided.

Sources: Maynardleigh Associates (2009) *Talent Management at the Crossroads: How 20 of the UK's best employers are rising to meet the challenge of turbulent times*. London: Maynardleigh Associates; Yapp, M. (2009) 'Measuring the ROI of talent management', *Strategic HR Review*, Vol. 8, No. 4, pp. 5–10.

Yapp (2009) makes the point that if talent management and development is already accepted and is clearly satisfying the organisation's strategic priorities then measurement may not be necessary, and that for others internal HR measures may be of more relevance in the short term. For example, at Standard Chartered Bank (Syedain 2007) there was a concern with attrition, so that a lot of talent management is about staff engagement, personal development and career planning. The measures regularly taken are rates of attrition, internal v. external recruitment, promotion rates and whether people are achieving their personal development plans. Other measures we have not yet mentioned include external customer and competitor opinion.

SUMMARY PROPOSITIONS

16.1 Talent is sometimes defined exclusively as possessed by the high-potential few and sometimes inclusively as something that everyone has. Some organisations now identify different types of talent groups with different defined offerings for each one.

16.2 Talent may be bought in or home-grown and the organisation needs to decide the most appropriate balance between the two. Methods of identifying potential include assessment/development centres, 360-degree feedback and appraisal results.

16.3 Organisations are more likely to gain from a strategic and integrated approach to talent management and development which fits with organisational needs. A traditional approach will be structured and planful, and may include succession planning for key roles, whereas some organisations use a more flexible approach.

16.4 Key activities for talent and career development include: managing talent in a developmental way; providing international experience; and understanding employee perspectives on careers

16.5 Few organisations formally evaluate talent management and development, and those who do use internal HR measures to a greater extent than external outcomes.

THEORY INTO PRACTICE

Careers at Ernst & Young

Ernst & Young provide a thorough range of global career development activities for graduates, and there are three key aspects to provision: learning; job experiences; and coaching.

Learning focuses on building general business skills and acumen, constantly refreshing and enhancing technical skills across service lines to promote improved service and better client relationships. Building relationships and leading people are seen as key aspects of learning and career development.

In terms of job experiences, secondments are offered, as well as cross-border and cross-service line placements, on both a short- and long-term basis. Some are domestic and some international, but all will involve connecting with people from around the world and provide challenging and stimulating assignments. These are intended to help graduates develop an inclusive mindset and thrive in an increasingly global market while matching clients' needs. Graduates are also encouraged to use their professional skills to give back to the community, benefiting others but also enhancing their career and life – through development of leadership, communication or project management skills.

Graduates work closely with a coach who will put time and effort into becoming an expert in the individual and his or her career development. Coaches encourage learning and development, and help graduates to consider new ideas and challenges to ensure a stimulating and evolving career. High-quality feedback and support is offered to help graduates progress quickly. Mentoring provides support, insights and practical advice on a variety of professional development and career topics, and as graduates become more experienced they are encouraged to mentor less experienced colleagues.

Perhaps the most unusual aspect of a career at Ernst & Young is the view below, explained on the company website when addressing potential recruits:

The experience you gain with EY will last you a lifetime. In fact, whatever you go on to do in the future, you'll be able to take the knowledge and insights you've gained with you.

EY and you (EYU) is our career development framework, which is designed to provide you with the skills, knowledge and confidence you need to take ownership of your career.

Your development is at the heart of our culture, but it centres on giving you the tools to progress in the direction you desire. We believe you'll do the best work you can when you have the freedom to map your own career path. And ultimately that means our clients will benefit too. (**www.ernstandyoung.com**)

This provides an unusually strong focus on graduates developing their own career path, and even more unusually the focus on career development for graduates which they can then take with them to a new employer. Mike Cullen, Ernst & Young's Global Managing Partner, People, explains this position thus:

For every thousand graduates you recruit, you've only got 250 manager slots. . . . Most people who come through our doors (as recruits) *now live somewhere out there in the economy. How they feel about E&Y is crucial to our proposition. We want them to feel a lifetime member of one of the best business networks in the world.* (Smedley 2012: 30)

Alumni are positively encouraged to remain in touch through magazines sharing news from past colleagues and personal and business directories to enable searching for past colleagues. Ernst & Young wants people to feel proud of working for it and offer development for people who carry on their careers within or outside the company. Thus it develops future leaders for business and commerce generally and not just Ernst & Young. Cullen explains how external analysts were taken aback by this idea as conventional thinking at the moment is focused on retaining talent. The aim is to create career value for people that will last a lifetime.

Sources: Smedley, T. (2012b) 'On my agenda', *People Management*, August, pp 28–31; **www.ernstandyoung.com**.

Questions

1 What are the dangers and downsides of the Ernst & Young approach to career development?

2 Exactly how can Ernst & Young reap the advantages of its approach to careers?

3 In which type of organisations might this approach to careers be advantageous? What criteria are you using, and why?

4 Assess the potential value of the career development activities that Ernst & Young provides. What other activities would you include, and why?

FURTHER READING

Brewster, C., Sparrow, P., Vernon, G. and Houldsworth, E. (2011) *International Human Resource Management*. London: CIPD, Chapter 14.
This is a very useful all-round text for international HRM, but in particular Chapter 14 on managing expatriation is very useful here. This twenty-five-page chapter gives an excellent overview of selecting and preparing an individual for an international assignment as well as managing performance and repatriation. It also includes the career perspectives of the expatriates themselves.

Dickman, M. and Baruch, Y. (2011) *Global Careers*. New York: Routledge.
There are three parts to this text: the context of global careers; career strategies and processes; and practical application. Its strengths are in explaining a wide range of concepts relevant to global careers, and in particular taking a very wide view of global careers – far beyond expatriation and other methods that the organisation might use to provide international experience from a home base.

Tansley, C., Turner, P., Foster, C., Harris, L., Sempok, A., Stewart, J. and Williams, H. (2007) *Talent Strategy, Management and Measurement*. London: CIPD.
A very useful report from these Nottingham Trent Business School authors which looks in more detail at the nature of talent and provides good models on strategic linkages. Some useful case studies are also included.

REFERENCES

Allen, A. (2008) 'Bright and early', *People Management*, Vol. 14, No. 7, pp. 30–2.

Brockett, J. (2008) 'Finders keepers', *People Management*, Vol. 14, No. 9, pp. 28–34.

Chubb, L. (2008) 'R&SA intranet aids career planning', *People Management*, Vol. 14, No. 4, p. 10.

Chubb, L. and Phillips, L. (2008) 'A global approach to talent: The best of the world congress', *People Management*, Vol. 14, No. 9, pp. 12–13.

CIPD (2011a) *International Learning and Talent Development Comparison Survey, 2011*. London: CIPD.

CIPD (2011b) *Factsheet: International Mobility*. London: CIPD.

CIPD (2012) *Factsheet: Talent Management: An overview*. London: CIPD.

Cranet (2011) *Cranet Survey on Comparative Human Resource Management*. Cranfield: Cranfield University.

Crawshaw, J., Dick, R. and Brodbeck, F. (2012) 'Opportunity, fair process and relationship value: Career development as a driver of proactive work behaviour', *Human Resource Management Journal*, Vol. 22, No. 1, pp. 4–11.

Cunningham, I. (2007a) 'Disentangling false assumptions about talent management: The need to recognise difference', *Development and Learning in Organisations*, Vol. 21, No. 4, pp. 4–5.

Cunningham, I. (2007b) 'Viewpoint: Talent management – making it real', *Development and Learning in Organisations*, Vol. 21, No. 2, pp. 4–6.

Evans, J. (2007) 'Talent strategy feeds growth at Nando's', *People Management*, Vol. 13, No. 9, 3 May, p. 16.

Garrow, V. and Hirsh, W. (2008) 'Talent management: Issues of focus and fit', *Public Personnel Management*, Vol. 37, No. 4, pp. 389–402.

Goffee, R. and Jones, G. (2009) *Clever: Leading your smartest and most creative people*. Boston, MA: Harvard Business School Press.

Guthridge, M. and Lawson, E. (2008) 'Divide and survive', *People Management*, Vol. 14, No. 19, 18 September, pp. 40–4.

Hills, A. (2009) 'Succession planning: Or smart talent management?', *Industrial and Commercial Training*, Vol. 41, No. 1, pp. 3–38.

Hills, J. (2012) 'How firms define and execute talent strategy', *People Management*, September, pp. 42–4.

Krinks, P. and Strack, R. (2008) 'The talent crunch', *People Management*, Vol. 14, No. 3, pp. 30–1.

Linkerman, A. (2007) 'How to measure the success of talent management', *People Management*, Vol. 13, No. 4, pp. 46–7.

Maynardleigh Associates (2009) *Talent Management at the Crossroads: How 20 of the UK's best employers are rising to meet the challenge of turbulent times*. London: Maynardleigh Associates.

Michaels, E., Handfield-Jones, H. and Axelrod, B. (2001) *The War for Talent*. Boston, MA: Harvard Business School Press.

Ng Ek Heng (2012) 'Singapore Summit', *People Management*, October, p. 9.

Parry, E. and Tyson, S. (2007) *UK Talent Report*. London: Capital Consulting and Cranfield School of Management.

People Management (2008) 'Managers don't have time to develop talent', Vol. 14, No. 17, 21 August, p. 10.

People Management (2013) '"Labour hoarding" offers comfort', March, p. 11.

Phillips, L. (2007) 'Work flexibly or waste talent', *People Management*, Vol. 13, No. 3, p. 14.

Phillips, L. (2008) 'Talent management up to managers not HR', *People Management*, Vol. 14, No. 5, p. 10.

Pickard, J. (2007) 'Go with the flow', *People Management*, Vol. 13, No. 8, pp. 46–7.

Pinto, L., Cabral-Cardoso, C. and Werther, W. (2012) 'Compelled to go abroad? Motives and outcomes of international assignments', *International Journal of Human Resource Management*, Vol. 23, No. 11, pp. 2295–314.

Powell, M. and Lubitsh, G. (2007) 'Courage in the face of extraordinary talent: Why talent management has become a leadership issue', *Strategic HR Review*, Vol. 6, No. 5, pp. 24–7.

Scott, A. (2007) 'Engagement rings at Vodaphone', *People Management*, Vol. 13, No. 7, p. 14.

Smedley, T. (2012a) 'On my agenda', *People Management*, March, pp. 51–3.

Smedley, T. (2012b) 'On my agenda', *People Management*, August, pp. 28–31.

Stuart-Kotze, R. and Dunn, C. (2008) *Who Are Your Best People?* London: FT/Prentice Hall.

Syedain, H. (2007) 'A talent for numbers', *People Management*, Vol. 13, No. 12, pp. 36–8.

Wilson, B. (2008) 'Hidden dragons', *People Management*, Vol. 14, No. 6, pp. 18–23.

Yapp, M. (2009) 'Measuring the ROI of talent management', *Strategic HR Review*, Vol. 8, No. 4, pp. 5–10.

Part 5

EMPLOYEE RELATIONS

CHANGING TIMES
RESOURCING
PERFORMANCE
DEVELOPMENT
EMPLOYEE RELATIONS

Strategy
Involvement
Health
Equality
Diversity
Grievance/Discipline
Skills

The past thirty years have witnessed a sea change in the UK employee relations scene. Most of the once well-established norms in UK industry have been abandoned or have withered away as the nature of the work that we do and the types of workplace in which we are employed have evolved. To an extent, cultural change has accompanied this structural change too, creating a world of work in which employee attitudes towards their employers and employer attitudes towards their employees have developed in new directions. Ongoing change of one kind or another has affected and continues to affect most areas of HRM activity, but it is in the field of employee relations that the most profound transformations have occurred.

That said, it is important to appreciate that change in this field proceeds at a different pace in different places. There remain many workplaces, particularly in the public sector and in the former public-sector corporations, in which more traditional models of employee relations continue to operate despite attempts by successive governments to change them. What we now have, therefore, is a far greater variety of approaches in place across the different industrial sectors than was the case in past decades.

Overt conflict between labour and management representing different *sides* with fundamentally different interests persists, but usually alongside a newer rhetoric that reflects aspirations towards greater partnership and employee involvement in decision making. In these organisations trade union membership remains high, while terms and conditions of employment continue to be established through formal collective bargaining mechanisms. Negotiations are, however, increasingly carried out at local rather than industry level with individual employers and not with employers' associations as was once common.

This model of employee relations no longer exists in most private-sector organisations where there is little effective collective employee consciousness on the part of employees and where trade unions are irrelevant if they have any serious presence at all. Here too the rhetoric of partnership and voice is common, but the extent to which there is any meaningful employee involvement in important decision making can be very limited indeed.

Profound though these changes in employee relations may be, it remains the case that all jobs have the potential to be alienating, making the job holder indifferent or hostile both to the job and to management. Employee relations activity continues to be largely concerned with preventing or alleviating that type of alienation. In doing so, however, managers are increasingly required to take account of regulation. Indeed, so great has been the growth of employment law that we now have a situation in which employment rights are protected through the law and the employment tribunal system to a much greater extent than they are by trade unions.

Regulation is one, but by no means the only, reason behind the growth of interest in equality and diversity issues. The same is true of health, safety and welfare. The law has plenty to say about these areas of HR practice, but there is also a compelling business case linking the presence of a healthy and diverse workforce to positive business outcomes. The law also determines the framework and broad approaches employers take when dealing with disciplinary matters and handling formal grievances lodged by their staff. There remains, however, plenty of scope to manage these difficult matters in different ways.

Chapter 17

EMPLOYEE VOICE

THE OBJECTIVES OF THIS CHAPTER ARE TO:

1 Introduce the main methods used by employers to involve employees in decision making

2 Assess the extent of information sharing and its purpose

3 Set out the case for formal and informal consultation with employees and their representatives

4 Explore situations in which co-determination occurs in UK and overseas organisations

It is quite possible to run a successful organisation without involving employees in management activities to any meaningful extent, but the chances of sustained success are higher when employees have a 'voice', that is they are involved in and can influence what happens in the organisation. Objectives are more effectively and efficiently achieved if employees have some say in decision making, especially as it affects their own areas of work. This is for two principal reasons:

1 Ultimately it is for managers to make decisions and to be held accountable. Such decisions can be difficult, but the chances that they will make the right decision are enhanced if they listen to the views of others and allow their own ideas to be subjected to a degree of scrutiny and constructive criticism. Moreover, involvement allows managers to tap into the ideas and suggestions of staff. The best new ideas often originate from people lower down organisational hierarchies because they are closest to the operational coalface and often to customers.

2 Employees like having a voice. They appreciate having their opinions listened to and acted upon, particularly in matters that directly concern their day-to-day activities. The chances of their being positively satisfied with their work are thus greatly improved if they are genuinely able to be involved. The knock-on effects include lower staff turnover, lower levels of absence, the ability to attract more recruits and higher levels of performance. The effective management of change is especially enhanced by employee involvement because people are always happier to support what they helped to create.

There is an emerging stream of research to demonstrate these positive outcomes (Holland *et al.* 2012). Jønsson and Jeppesen (2013), for example, demonstrate that voice arrangements improve employee commitment while Park *et al.* (2010) and Kaine (2012) show the effect of voice in reducing labour turnover and absenteeism.

Employee voice comes in many different forms. It can be formal or informal, direct or indirect, one-off or sustained over time, central to an organisation's core business or relatively peripheral. In recent years the number and extent of voice mechanisms have increased. This is partly due to the requirements of the law and partly because they have a part to play in many of the more common, contemporary HRM initiatives we have discussed elsewhere in this book – becoming an 'employer of choice', 360-degree appraisal and employee engagement. The exercise of employee influence is also a central element of an effective psychological contract (Guest and Conway 1998).

Our aim in this chapter is to discuss the major forms employee voice takes, to explore the difficulties that can be experienced in the implementation of initiatives and to evaluate their contribution to the achievement of an organisation's objectives.

Terminology

A variety of labels are used to describe employee voice. Although some writers have sought to make distinctions between them, there is no generally accepted usage. Hence you will read about 'involvement', 'employee participation', 'industrial democracy' and 'empowerment'. Each of these terms differs subtly and suggests a different perspective; Urwin *et al.* (2007), for example, suggest that voice mechanisms are associated with

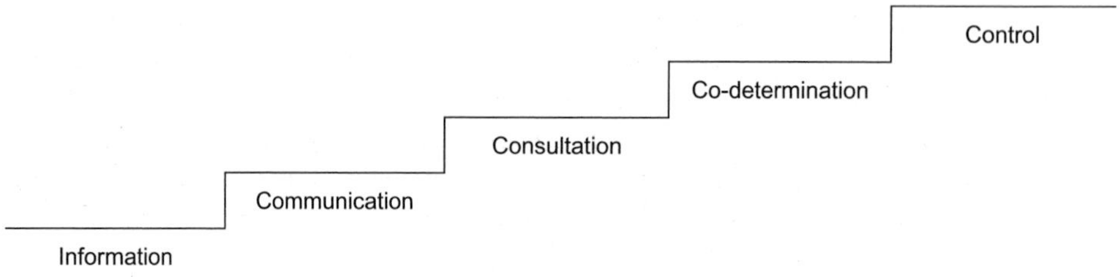

Figure 17.1
The escalator of participation
Source: Marchington, M. and Cox, A. (2007) 'Employee involvement and participation', in J. Storey (ed.) *Human Resource Management: A critical text*, 3rd edn. London: Thomson Learning, p. 179, fig 10.1.

trade union representation whereas HR practices tend to give rise to employee involvement. All terms are used to a greater or lesser extent to describe a situation in which employees are given, gain or develop a degree of *influence* over what happens in an organisation. The extent and nature of that influence, however, vary considerably.

Marchington and Cox (2007) helpfully distinguish between the major categories of voice with their 'escalator' model (Figure 17.1).

At the bottom of the escalator are organisations where there is no voice at all, managers taking all decisions without taking any meaningful account of what employees might think. By contrast, at the top of the escalator are organisations or parts of organisations which are controlled by employees rather than by a distinct group of managers. Employee control is very rare in the UK at the level of the organisation, although there are one or two examples of companies which are communally owned and run by staff in a partnership arrangement. A substantial degree of control is much more often exercised, however, by employees at the level of an individual department or team within a larger organisation.

Between 'no involvement' and 'employee control', there are three further stages, each in turn representing a deepening of the extent of involvement. The first is 'communication', signalling a very limited degree of involvement. At this stage employer and employees simply exchange information. Managers disclose defined classes of information, ensuring that employees are aware of the decisions they are taking, the economic situation and their objectives. Employees are also given an opportunity to respond, to voice concerns or put their own ideas forward. But decision making remains exclusively in the management realm. The next step up the escalator is 'consultation'. Here information is exchanged, often through formalised channels. Decision making is still the responsibility of managers, but full and proper consideration is given to the views expressed by staff (or their elected representatives) before key decisions are taken. Finally, a further step up the escalator takes us to co-determination or joint decision making. This is relatively rare in a formal sense in the UK, although it happens informally all the time. It is very common in Northern European countries where the law requires the agreement of a works council before significant decisions affecting employment can be taken.

At each of these stages voice initiatives can be either direct or indirect in nature. The term 'direct' relates to situations in which managers enter into a dialogue with, consult with or co-determine decisions with employees as individuals. People thus have a direct input in some shape or form. By contrast, the term 'indirect' refers to a situation in which employers take account of employee views through the filter of a representative institution. This may be a trade union, or it may be another kind of body such as a works council, a working party or a consultative committee. Either way, indirect involvement occurs through representatives of the workforce as a collective group. Academic research into employee voice often encompasses payment arrangements such as profit sharing and employee share ownership schemes which are referred to as types of 'financial participation'. These help to develop a community of interest between employers and their staff and can lead to situations in which individual employees cast votes at annual general meetings. We will discuss them later (see Chapter 22). The remainder of this chapter will focus on the major information-sharing, consultation and co-determination initiatives.

Research by Gollan and Lewin (2013) demonstrates that, while voice mechanisms have increased substantially over recent decades (around 82% of UK employees now have access), types of mechanisms have changed. From 1945 to 1975, trade union voice was dominant in the UK and many other western countries. Since this time, trade union representation has declined and less than 20% of UK private-sector employees were covered by collective pay bargaining arrangements in 2011. Even in the public sector, this proportion rose only to just over 50% (van Wanrooy *et al*. 2013). Non-union voice has thus increased markedly with practices like team briefing being adopted by around 70% of UK workplaces (Gollan and Lewin 2013). These changes are not confined to the UK, as we see in the following Window on practice.

WINDOW ON PRACTICE

Changing patterns of employee voice in Australia

Falling levels of union density and the relaxing of employment regulation have led to the continuing growth of non-union representation and direct voice mechanisms in Australia. These have been typically individualistic in nature, allowed a high degree of management prerogative and are now the preferred means of determining terms and conditions of employment and supporting employee involvement in decision making. There has been a particular interest in joint consultative committees which arise from management initiatives (as opposed to legislative provisions) and can vary in terms of the powers they afford to employees, the level of organisational operation, how they are composed and the issues that they deliberate upon.

Source: Holland *et al*. (2012).

Information sharing

According to the 2011 Workplace Employment Relations Survey (WERS) formal systems of communication between managers and employees are present in the vast majority of UK organisations (van Wanrooy *et al*. 2013). In many cases, however, the communication is carried out at the local level (e.g. line managers meeting with employees individually), there being no formal mechanisms provided for more senior managers to communicate directly with their staff or vice versa. Moreover, where a degree of formality is reported it can be limited simply to the posting of important data on noticeboards or ad hoc circulation of information by email.

The extent to which the disclosure of information by managers can be regarded as a form of employee involvement is debatable. After all, merely being told about an organisation's plans or its financial results does not in any way give employees influence. Nonetheless it can help to make employees feel a sense of involvement or at least of inclusion in the circle of those 'in the know'. It also enables employees, either individually or collectively, to exercise informal influence locally, simply because they are in a position to develop and articulate credible alternative approaches to those their immediate line managers would otherwise impose. Alternatively they are in a position to help improve or refine their strategies. It is often rightly stated that 'knowledge is power' and it therefore follows that spreading relevant knowledge beyond the ranks of management to employees is an empowering activity. This is why managers may hold back information from their staff. Except in a crisis situation in which there is a need to promote calm and keep everyone focused on their jobs, often no damage would be done to the organisation by disclosing the information and labelling it 'confidential'. Refusing to disclose it serves to enhance managers' own sense of personal authority and power.

However reluctant line managers may be to share information to which they are privy, there is substantial evidence to back up the view that regular, extensive information sharing has positive outcomes for organisations. This occurs because it improves levels of commitment among staff (Peccei *et al.* 2005) and because in a practical sense it helps everyone to clarify what their roles are in the wider organisation. It thus enhances communication and coordination across divisions. It also helps to prevent false understanding developing among staff due to the inevitable 'rumour mills' that operate in all organisations and can make employees view change initiatives with less cynicism than otherwise might be the case (Brown and Creagan 2008).

Two-way communication, by contrast, especially when it takes the form of a formal exercise, clearly falls into the category of employee involvement. Staff are being asked to respond to a suggested new approach, asked their opinion, being invited to make suggestions for improvements or given an opportunity to point out flaws in current systems or management thinking. Provided the exercise is not merely cosmetic, and that the views of staff are given serious consideration, influence is gained. Trust in management is, however, vital if staff are to become involved in two-way communication, as Kim *et al.* (2009) demonstrate in a South Korean context.

WERS 2011 identifed the most common methods of information sharing as: workplace meetings (80% of organisations); team briefings (66%); disclosure of financial information (55%); employee attitude surveys (37%); and quality circles (problem-solving groups, 14%). We discuss a number of these methods below.

Team briefing

Team briefing is an initiative that attempts to do a number of different things simultaneously. It provides authoritative information at regular intervals, so that people know what is going on, the information is geared to achievement of production targets and other features of organisational objectives, it is delivered face to face to provide scope for questions and clarification, and it emphasises the role of supervisors and line managers as the source of information. It is used to cascade information down the organisation, usually to teams in a common production or service area, for example a shop in a retail organisation. A trained team leader will undertake the briefings on a regular basis and should allow for questions from employees.

With goodwill and managerial discipline, team briefing can be a valuable contributor to employee involvement, as it deals in that precious commodity, information. Traditionally, there has perhaps been a managerial view that people doing the work are not interested in anything other than the immediate and short term and that the manager's status partly rests on knowing what others do not know. For this reason all the managers and supervisors in the communications chain have to be committed to making it a success, as well as having the necessary training.

Team briefing gets easier once it is established as a regular event. The first briefing will probably go very well and the second will be even better. It is important that management enthusiasm and commitment do not flag just as the employees are getting used to the process.

During economic recessions there is a boost to the team briefing process because so many managements have so much bad news to convey. When you are losing money and profitability, there is a great incentive to explain to employees exactly how grim the situation is, so that they do not look for big pay rises (Kersley *et al.* 2006: 135).

Sometimes, instead of cascading information down a management hierarchy, senior managers in larger organisations like to brief larger groups of employees about significant developments directly. Roadshows or 'interactive executive sessions' of this kind are common and are seen by managers as being almost as effective a means of passing information to employees as more conventional forms of team briefing (IRS 2005a: 11).

Quality circles

Originating in Japanese firms, quality circles comprise small groups of employees (10–15 maximum) who meet regularly to generate ideas aimed at improving the quality of products and services and of organisational productivity. They can also be used as problem-solving groups and as a means by which employee opinion is transmitted to senior management. Some quality circles consist of staff who work together within a team or organisational function, others are cross-functional and focus on interdepartmental issues. They have numerous objectives, such as to generate ideas, encourage cooperative working relationships and drive change (Marchington and Cox 2007). Not only, therefore, are quality circles a potential source of useful ideas for improving systems and saving costs, but also they give people a welcome opportunity to contribute their thoughts and experience. A generally positive impact on employee attitudes should thus result. WERS 2011 indicates that they are used by 14% of UK organisations, a small decline of 3% since 2004.

News sheets

Another common form of employee involvement occurs through the regular publication of in-house journals or news sheets in either paper or electronic form. On one level they simply provide a means by which information concerning finances, policy and proposed change can be transmitted by managers to employees. This is a limited form of employee involvement which does little more than improve the extent to which employees are informed about what is going on elsewhere in their organisations. This will engender a perception of greater involvement and belonging, but does not directly involve employees in any type of decision making. For that to occur the news sheet must be interactive in some way. It may, for example, be used as a means by which employees are consulted about new initiatives, or may provide a forum through which complaints and ideas are voiced.

Attitude surveys

Regular surveys of employee opinion are very useful from a management point of view, particularly where there are no unions present to convey to management an honest picture of morale and commitment in the organisation. Indeed, in their study of workplace bullying, Pate and Beaumont (2010) suggest that attitude surveys are one of the leading employee voice mechanisms. In order to be effective (i.e. honest), responses must be anonymous, individuals stating only which department they work in so that interdepartmental comparisons can be made. It also makes sense to ask the same questions in the same format each time a survey is carried out, so that changes in attitude and/or responses to initiatives can be tracked over time.

The major problems with attitude surveys are associated with situations in which they reveal serious problems which are then not properly addressed. This can easily lead to cynicism and even anger on the part of the workforce. The result is a poorer employee relations climate than would have been the case had no survey taken place. It is counterproductive to involve employees if their contribution is subsequently ignored, yet this appears to happen in many of the organisations where regular surveys are conducted. IRS (2005b) found that the main reasons employers in their sample gave for carrying out employee surveys were to 'take the pulse of the organisation' and to 'demonstrate commitment to employee views'. Only a minority subsequently used the information gathered to shape decision making, even in the HR arena.

Suggestion schemes

A common system of formal bottom-up communication employed by organisations involves encouraging staff to make suggestions about how practices and processes could be improved to make them more effective, efficient or safe. Employees are often best placed to observe in detail what happens operationally on the front line because they have the greatest level of interaction on a day-to-day basis with customers, equipment and organisational procedures. Many organisations go to great lengths to encourage suggestions from employees, as we illustrate in the Window on practice that follows.

WINDOW ON PRACTICE

Tube Lines staff are pitching business ideas to a panel of bosses in the style of the BBC2 television programme *Dragons' Den*. The firm, responsible for the infrastructure of three London Underground lines, rewards workers whose schemes save the company money with £1,000 worth of retail vouchers. Runners-up get £500 and £200 in vouchers.

The Change Challenge Cup, which takes place every three months, is designed to encourage employees to improve the way the business operates. The fifteen-strong panel of judges, chaired by Chief Executive Terry Morgan, is made up of the firm's Change Council, which monitors the organisation's improvements.

The first competition was won jointly by two employees. One developed a new way to clean iron filings from the trackside train position detectors, which has the potential to save the company £1.3 million a year in avoided train delays.

The other winning suggestion was to fit a metal platform across the track to the tunnel wall, allowing workers to cross safely. Morgan said: 'Tube Lines can only continue to move forward if employees are encouraged to come up with better ways of working.'

Source: Adapted from *People Management* (2008) 'Tube lines launches "Dragons' Den" scheme', 21 August, p. 14.

Managers often only become aware of problems when their employees report them, and without such reports can have no opportunities for improving things. So it makes sense to encourage staff to put forward suggestions; having a formal scheme enhances the chances that they will do so. IDS (2005) describes several types of scheme and draws together from these examples of some good practice points. IDS argues that employees should be recognised financially or otherwise when they make a suggestion which is taken up, that systems for submitting ideas should be as uncomplicated as possible, that feedback should be given to all who submit ideas, that past suggestions should be revisited periodically and that schemes must be regularly publicised to remind staff of their existence. IDS also found that organisations are increasingly benefiting from schemes which operate electronically. Suggestions are submitted via email or a form placed on an intranet and filed systematically by an evaluator. Feedback is then given electronically and the successes of the whole scheme publicised regularly through email bulletins sent to all staff.

ACTIVITY 17.1

Despite plenty of evidence that demonstrates how beneficial two-way information sharing can be for organisations, only a minority of non-union employers operate formal systems. Why do you think this is? What are the likely consequences? What arguments would you use to persuade a team of managers of the need to listen to the views of staff and to take them seriously?

Consultation

After information sharing, the next step up the 'escalator' is consultation. Here employees are asked either directly or through representatives to express views which management takes into account when making decisions. Such processes fall short of negotiation or co-determination because there is no ultimate expectation of agreement if the views of staff and management diverge. In some organisations regular meetings are held to enable consultation to take place about a wide range of issues. In others consultation exercises take place irregularly and focus on specific areas such as organisational restructuring or policy changes. Consultation is generally regarded as a hallmark of good management and UK employers have legal obligations to consult with employees (see Chapter 18). An employer who fails to consult properly, particularly at times of significant change, is likely to be perceived as being unduly autocratic. The result will be dissatisfaction, low levels of motivation, higher staff turnover and poorer levels of customer service. Moreover, consultation has important advantages as a means by which good ideas are brought forward and weak ones challenged.

In workplaces where unions are recognised it is usual for consultation to take place over a range of issues through permanent consultative institutions. The joint consultative committee (JCC) is the most common form, being a forum in which managers and staff representatives meet on a regular basis. In more traditional unionised organisations JCCs are kept distinct from negotiating forums – despite the fact that the membership is often the same. A clear divide is thus established between areas which are to be the subject of negotiation (typically terms and conditions of employment) and matters which are the subject of consultation such as health and safety or training. In recent years as partnership agreements have become more common (see Chapter 18), there has been a shift from negotiation towards consultation, the aim being to downplay the adversarial nature of the union–employer relationship and to widen the range of topics about which both sides can engage constructively. Butler *et al.* (2011) argue that partnership arrangements have been resilient forms of voice even in difficult economic circumstances.

The recent WERS 2011 indicates that 7% of workplaces have a JCC. This percentage is the same as in 2004 and halts a previously declining trend (van Wanrooy *et al.* 2013). It is unusual for the very largest workplaces not to have some form of consultative forum which meets periodically, although in some multi-site corporations formal consultation with employee representatives is restricted to the corporate level and does not take place in individual workplaces. JCCs are four times as common in union workplaces than in those where unions are not recognised (van Wanrooy *et al.* 2013), suggesting that they are mostly still used in parallel with collective bargaining machinery. However, some have argued that they are used in some workplaces as a substitute for collective bargaining or as a means of discouraging the development of a union presence. Managers in such workplaces believe that unions are less likely to gain support and request recognition if the employer keeps the staff informed of issues that affect them and consults with them before taking decisions. Consultative forums in non-union firms also provide a means whereby managers can put their case effectively without the presence of organised opposition. Here employee representatives may be appointed who do not have a connection with a trade union and who may indeed not operate within a JCC. This type of employee representative has been increasing and is now to be found in 13% of UK workplaces (van Wanrooy *et al.* 2013).

From a management perspective, the danger with consultation is that people come to believe that management is not genuinely interested in hearing their views or in taking them on board. This is referred to as 'pseudo-consultation' in which managers are really doing little more than informing employees about decisions that have already been taken. This is borne out by WERS 2011 (van Wanrooy *et al.* 2013: 23):

> Half (52%) of employees considered that management were 'Very good' or 'Good' at seeking their views. However, this is just the first step in the decision-making process. Employees were less likely to rate managers as 'Very good' or 'Good' at responding to suggestions and, in particular, allowing employees influence over final decisions (34%).

Cynicism results because there is perceived to be an attempt on the part of managers to use consultative forums merely as a means of legitimising their decisions. They can say that consultation has taken place, when in truth it has not. Pseudo-consultation typically involves assembling employees in large groups with senior managers present. The management message is then put across strongly and a short time is given for others to respond. In such situations employees have no time to give proper consideration to the proposals and are likely to feel too intimidated to articulate criticisms. The result is often worse in terms of employee morale and engagement with the changes than would have been the case had no consultation been attempted.

Even where managers genuinely intend to undertake meaningful consultation, they can very easily create an impression that it is no more than a 'pseudo'-exercise. It is therefore important to avoid the approaches outlined above. Employees should be informed of a range of possible ways forward (not just the one favoured by management) and invited to consider them in small groups. The results of their deliberations can then be fed back to senior managers and given proper consideration. In this way the appearance of pseudo-consultation, as well as the reality, can be avoided.

WINDOW ON PRACTICE

IRS (2006) describes how a marketing company called BI increased its profitability and halved its staff turnover, in part by introducing a range of employee involvement initiatives. The early years had seen company revenues decline markedly, leading to a pay freeze and staff turnover of 60%.

In 2004, following the appointment of a new chief executive and HR director, a wide range of measures was introduced to tackle these problems. Improving employee involvement was a priority, to signal very clearly the adoption of a new management style, to promote a positive culture and to encourage staff to identify problems and possible solutions. The initiatives included the following:

- weekly email bulletins to staff from senior managers explaining major developments;

- annual letters to staff from the managing director thanking them and setting out key achievements;
- quarterly company meetings at which all staff are briefed about financial matters and strategy;
- an intranet site updated daily with fresh information about the company's activities;
- monthly meetings at which the HR director talks in confidence to ten randomly selected employees about their concerns;
- regular meetings of a 'people forum' at which representatives from each team are consulted about developments.

As a result of these involvement activities many changes were made to operational processes and also to HR practices. Hours of work were made more flexible, and staff discouraged from working more hours than was necessary. A scheme was also introduced to allow people to trade some of their salary for additional holiday.

Co-determination

In the UK, important decision making in organisations is nearly always the preserve of managers. Decisions in the employment area are often taken after extensive and genuine consultation, or after negotiation with union representatives, but anything approaching serious co-determination with employees is very rare indeed. Nevertheless, it must be pointed out that at the level of the individual team, a degree of informal co-determination is common. Indeed, in recent years it has become more common as organisations have tended to de-layer, reducing the number of managers and levels of hierarchy. Increasingly employees and team leaders have found themselves 'empowered' to take decisions for themselves that once they would have had to refer to a manager. It is important not to overestimate the significance of this trend, as any discretion that is given operates within tightly defined boundaries. What gets done is still determined by managers, but there is greater flexibility about when and how exactly it gets done.

Elsewhere in Europe the extent of co-determination at the level of the team and of individual empowerment varies from country to country. In Southern European nations such as France, Italy and Spain managers at the local level tend to guard their autonomy more tightly than typical UK line managers. Co-determination at the local level over day-to-day workplace activities is thus rarer than in the UK. In Northern Europe, by contrast, a far greater degree of team-based autonomy is common. The best-known examples of teams assuming responsibility and decision-making authority are in the Scandinavian countries. The approach involves organising a workforce into small groups of about a dozen members, who are mutually supportive and who operate with minimal supervision. Managers set performance targets (often after consultation) and allocate tasks, but it is for the team to decide exactly how these are to be achieved. The team members organise their own activities, appoint their own leaders and work out themselves how to overcome problems. Teamworking can thus be characterised as a form of worker control, even though it operates within heavily prescribed limits. Managers refrain from giving day-to-day supervision, but are on hand to give advice or more direct assistance where necessary. Disciplining staff, for example, is a task carried out by managers and not by team members. Teamworking is often associated with situations in which several regionally based teams compete with each other to meet or exceed performance targets. Team-based remuneration then accounts for a proportion of the total pay received.

While practice varies at the local team level across Europe, at the level of the organisation co-determination is a great deal more established and widespread in most countries than is the case in the UK. It occurs through two distinct mechanisms:

1 through the legal empowerment of works councils or enterprise committees;

2 by reserving places on executive boards for worker directors.

Both approaches are famously used in Germany, where co-determination over employment matters is standard practice in organisations of any size. In the UK most of the activities described in this book are the preserve of managers, while in Germany they are decided jointly between managers and workforce representatives. German managers cannot impose any decision relating to changing workplace rules, disciplinary procedures, working hours, holidays, bonus payments, overtime arrangements, health and safety matters, training or selection methods without first securing the agreement of their organisation's works council. Moreover, their autonomy to make decisions about any changes relating to the nature of the work their employees do or the physical environment in which it is performed is subject to their first consulting with the works council and taking its objections and suggestions into account. In addition the law requires that managers share a great deal of financial and planning information with works councils that goes well beyond the employment sphere (Budd 2004: 129). Seats are also reserved on the supervisory boards of German companies for workforce representatives. In companies employing more than 500 people, a third of the seats are reserved. Where over 2,000 are employed, half the seats are taken by worker representatives. Such national variations are likely to be the cause of some difficulty for multinational corporations operating in a number of companies. A recent study by Marginson *et al.* (2010) showed that such employers are engaging in significant innovations in representation and voice arrangements in order to address these variations.

ACTIVITY 17.2

In many European companies works councils or enterprise committees tend to be dominated by trade unions, even where a majority of the staff are not members. Why do you think this is? What do you think are the major advantages and disadvantages of trade union representatives also acting as works council members or worker directors?

SUMMARY PROPOSITIONS

17.1 Genuine employee voice serves to increase commitment and to improve decision making in organisations.

17.2 Information sharing is common in the UK. Team briefing, news sheets and suggestion schemes are the most common mechanisms adopted.

17.3 The use of formal consultation processes is common in larger UK organisations. Joint consultative committees are found in most unionised workplaces.

17.4 Co-determination at the level of the organisation or workplace is rare in the UK, but common in many other EU countries.

17.5 Co-determination at the level of teams is increasing in the UK, but is limited in the extent to which it empowers employees.

GENERAL DISCUSSION TOPICS

1 Why do you think employers in the UK are more reluctant to involve employee representatives in strategic decision making than is the case in a country such as Germany?

2 How far do you agree with the view that information sharing barely constitutes employee involvement at all?

3 In what ways would you like to see increased or decreased employee involvement in your organisation, and why?

THEORY INTO PRACTICE

Kaufman (2013) reports a study of the Delta Air Lines employee involvement programme, which forms part of the organisation's attempt to maintain a high-commitment model of employment relations. In essence, Delta sees employee involvement as a way to improve efficiency and communication and to ensure that employees feel valued and well treated. Providing voice mechanisms is also seen as a way to reduce the demand for external representation and underpins Delta's partnership and non-union approach. Kaufman argues that the breadth, depth and formal structure of Delta's employee involvement mechanisms make it one of the leading non-union employee involvement companies in the USA, particlarly in respect of representative councils and forums.

Delta adopts a three-stage formal employee involvement strucure:

1 An organisation-wide consultative committee with five employee representatives, one from each of the major divisions.

2 Four employee involvement groups at divisional level, including: flight attendants, customer service and cargo, technical operations and reservation sales/city ticket offices. The first three of these have a two-layered structure with elected representatives at both city/base forums and system-wide forums.

3 In excess of 100 project teams which operate either across divisions or at particular sites, depending on the nature of the project.

These structures are supplemented by six organisation-wide groups to support employee diversity and, in some divisions, by a peer-review dispute resolution system. There are also a substantial number of other employee involvement activities including monthly CEO breakfasts and phone-ins where employees can ask questions of and provide feedback to senior executives.

Employee involvement mechanisms were central to Delta's merger with Northwest Airlines (NA). Twenty-seven project teams were established to address a whole range of matters, from strategic to low-level operational issues. These project teams comprised equal numbers of Delta and NA employees to foster a spirit of shared identity. Employee involvement was also central to integrating NA employees, from a unionised adversarial culture, into Delta's high-commitment culture. Promises made at the time of the merger, for example that pay rises would be made, were kept, NA employees were included in the councils and forums described above, and 'get acquainted' meetings were held. Former NA employees expressed surprise that the forums were able to achieve positive outcomes and offer protection to employees. Indeed, employee involvement is widely seen as a means to build a successful company and ensure that benefits accrue to all stakeholders, rather than a form of 'anti-union' mechanism. Kaufman attributes this to three things:

1 Some forum representatives are also union supporters and will not tolerate anti-union activity.

2 There is recognition that both organisation and employee representatives lose credibility if they tolerate or support anti-unionism.

3 Delta does not want to create an environment where union representation might seem desirable or take action that might prompt calls for union representation.

It is noteworthy that when, post-merger, there were calls for union recognition, the unions lost all the elections by a relatively wide margin.

Kaufman summarises Delta's approach to employee involvement as being quite successful, although he notes that it was introduced in a piecemeal fashion across the 1990s without any overarching HR vision. Nevertheless, employee involvement has supported a transition from employee commitment based upon a paternalistic employment relationship to commitment premised upon a mutual gains scenario in which management and workers cooperate to drive high performance that benefits both parties.

Questions

1 Using Marchington and Cox's 'escalator' model, how would you categorise Delta's approach to employee voice?

2 What other mechanisms could Delta use to offer employee voice?

3 To what extent do you agree that Delta's approach to employee voice makes union representation unnecessary?

Source: Adapted from Kaufman, B. (2013) 'Keeping the commitment model in the air during turbulent times: Employee involvement at Delta Air Lines', *Industrial Relations*, Vol. 52, pp. 343–77.

FURTHER READING

Benson, J. and Brown, M. (2010) 'Employee voice: Does union membership matter?', *Human Resource Management Journal*, Vol. 20, No. 1, pp. 80–99.
In this article, the authors explore the relationship between trade union membership and employee perceptions of voice. Their findings are counter-intuitive, that trade union membership has a significantly negative impact upon employee perceptions of voice, and they set about explaining why this might be the case.

Dundon, T. *et al*. (2005) 'The management of voice in non-union organisations: Managers' perspectives', *Employee Relations*, Vol. 27, No. 3, pp. 307–19.
In this article Tony Dundon and his colleagues explore the views of managers about the role played by consultative forums in seven non-union organisations. They conclude that commentators have often been too hasty to dismiss these practices as inconsequential or ineffective.

Harley, B., Hyman, J. and Thompson, P. (2005) *Participation and Democracy at Work: Essays in honour of Harvie Ramsay*. Basingstoke: Palgrave Macmillan.
A book of articles by leading academic researchers which covers every aspect of informing, consulting and involving employees.

Gollan, P. and Lewin, D. (2013) 'Employee representation in non-union firms: An overview', *Industrial Relations*, Vol. 52, pp. 173–93.
This special issue of *Industrial Relations* contains eight articles, authored by scholars from the USA, UK, Canada and Australia, that develop understanding of forms of non-union employee representation internationally.

REFERENCES

Brown, M. and Creagan, C. (2008) 'Organisational change cynicism: The role of employee involvement', *Human Resource Management*, Vol. 47, pp. 667–86.

Budd, J. (2004) *Employment with a Human Face*. Ithaca, NY: Cornell University Press.

Butler, P., Glover, L. and Tregaskis, O. (2011) '"When the Going Gets Tough" . . . : Recession and the resilience of workplace partnership', *British Journal of Industrial Relations*, Vol. 49, pp. 666–87.

Gollan, P. and Lewin, D. (2013) 'Employee representation in non-union firms: An overview', *Industrial Relations*, Vol. 52, pp. 173–93.

Guest, D. and Conway, N. (1998) *Fairness at Work and the Psychological Contract*. London: Institute of Personnel and Development.

Holland, P., Cooper, B. and Pyman, A. (2012) 'Trust in management: The role of employee voice arrangements and perceived managerial opposition to unions', *Human Resource Management Journal*, Vol. 22, pp. 377–91.

IDS (2005) 'Suggestion schemes', *IDS Study No. 812*. London: IDS.

IRS (2005a) 'Dialogue or monologue: Is the message getting through?', *IRS Employment Review*, No. 834. London: IRS.

IRS (2005b) 'More questions than answers? Employee surveys revealed', *IRS Employment Review*, No. 820. London: IRS.

IRS (2006) 'BI bounces back with culture of employee engagement', *IRS Employment Review*, No. 839. London: IDS.

Jønsson, T. and Jeppesen, H. (2013) 'A closer look into the employee influence: Organisational commitment relationship by distinguishing between commitment forms and influence sources', *Employee Relations*, Vol. 35, pp. 4–19.

Kaine, S. (2012) 'Regulation and employee voice in the residential aged care sector', *Human Resource Management Journal*, Vol. 22, pp. 316–31.

Kaufman, B. (2013) 'Keeping the commitment model in the air during turbulent times: Employee involvement at Delta Air Lines', *Industrial Relations*, Vol. 52, pp. 343–77.

Kersley, B., Alpin, C., Forth, J., Bryson, A., Bewley, H., Dix, G. and Oxenbridge, S. (2006) *Inside the Workplace: Findings from the 2004 Workplace Employment Relations Survey*. London: Routledge.

Kim, T., Rosen, B. and Lee, D. (2009) 'South Korean managerial reactions to voicing discontent: The effects of employee attitude and employee communication styles', *Journal of Organisational Behaviour*, Vol. 30, pp. 1001–18.

Marchington, M. and Cox, A. (2007) 'Employee involvement and participation', in J. Storey (ed.) *Human Resource Management: A critical text*, 3rd edn. London: Thomson Learning.

Marginson, S., Edwards, P., Edwards, T., Ferner, A. and Tregaskis, O. (2010) 'Employee representation and consultative voice in multinational companies operating in Britain', *British Journal of Industrial Relations*, Vol. 48, pp. 151–80.

Park, R., Appelbaum, E. and Kruse, D. (2010) 'Employee involvement and group incentives in manufacturing companies: A multi-level analysis', *Human Resource Management Journal*, Vol. 20, pp. 227–43.

Pate, J. and Beaumont, P. (2010) 'Bullying and harassment: A case of success?', *Employee Relations*, Vol. 32, pp. 171–83.

Peccei, R., Bewley, H., Gospel, G. and Willman, P. (2005) 'Is it good to talk? Information disclosure and organisational performance in the UK', *British Journal of Industrial Relations*, Vol. 43, pp. 11–39.

People Management (2008) 'Tube lines launches "Dragons' Den" scheme', 21 August, p. 14.

Urwin, P., Murphy, R. and Michielsens, E. (2007) 'Employee voice regimes and the characteristics of conflict: An analysis of the 2003 survey of employment tribunal applications', *Human Resource Management Journal*, Vol. 17, pp. 178–97.

Van Wanrooy, B., Bewley, H., Bryson, A., Forth, J., Freeth, S., Stokes, L. and Wood, S. (2013) *The 2011 Workplace Employment Relations Study: First findings*. London: BIS.

Chapter 18

THE LEGAL FRAMEWORK OF WORK

A regulatory revolution

One of the most important contemporary developments which has shaped HR practice in organisations has been the seemingly relentless increase, year on year, of new employment regulation. Forty years ago it was commonly and correctly stated that UK workplaces and labour markets were among the most lightly regulated in the industrial world. It was a long-standing tradition for the state to make a virtue of not intervening in the relationship between employers and employees except when it was absolutely necessary to do so. As a result, with the exception of basic health and safety entitlements, laws preventing the exploitation of child workers and the basic principle that the terms of all contracts of employment were legally enforceable, there was hardly any such thing as 'employment law' in the UK. Since then the position has wholly reversed. Though still less tightly regulated by comparison with some European countries, the UK now has one of the most highly regulated labour markets in the world. As far as the regulation of work is concerned, the past fifty years can truly be characterised as a revolutionary period.

Today a wide range of legally imposed restrictions severely limit employers' freedom to manage people and run their organisations as they please. Regulation plays a role in almost every area of HRM from recruitment and selection, through arrangements for paying people, managing working time, determining rights to leave from work, ensuring a decent level of health and safety, dealing with trade unions, managing retirements and dismissals. One aim is to provide some rebalancing of the power relationship between employers and employees, helping to restrict the extent to which managers can abuse their power by exploiting their employees unfairly or acting in an unjustly arbitrary manner towards them. Another is to promote good practice in people management via flexible working and partnership with unions and other employee representatives. We have already covered dismissal law thoroughly (see Chapter 9). Our purpose here is to introduce the other major areas of UK employment law, principally contracts of employment, discrimination law, family-friendly and health and safety regulation, and the law relating to pay and working time.

WINDOW ON PRACTICE

In 2006 Helen Green, an Assistant Company Secretary employed in London, won her case in the High Court. She had suffered two nervous breakdowns which were due, it was found, to Ms Green having been bullied at work by five colleagues. Over a period of four years she claimed to have been verbally abused, ignored and denigrated by them to such an extent that she became seriously ill, at one point being placed on 'suicide watch' in hospital. On her return to work following the first breakdown, she found that little had changed and she suffered a relapse a few months later. Her employment was subsequently terminated when it became clear that she was unlikely to be able to return to work in the foreseeable future. Having found in favour of Ms Green, her former employers, Deutsche Bank, were ordered to pay her compensation of £35,000 for pain and suffering, £25,000 for disadvantage in the labour market, £128,000 for lost earnings and a massive £640,000 for loss of future earnings and pension. In addition to this total of £828,000 damages, the bank was ordered to pay Ms Green's legal costs, taking its total pay-out to around £1.5 million – and that is before taking its own costs into account.

The day after the ruling and on subsequent days the newspapers covered the story in some depth. This was partly because of the size of the award (sizeable indeed for a woman who was earning £45,000 a year prior to her breakdown), partly because Ms Green is a good-looking young woman whose photograph editors were keen to publish, and partly because the nature of the 'bullying and harassment' that she had suffered appeared to many to have amounted to no more than the kind of banter and political game playing that goes on regularly in the majority of larger UK organisations.

Many opinion articles and letters appeared in the papers. Some supported Ms Green, arguing that it was about time employers were required to take bullying of the kind she had suffered more seriously. Many, however, were critical, in one case accusing her of acting like a 'gold-digging cry-baby' who had seriously put back the cause of women seeking careers in the financial services industry. The net result was a great deal of negative publicity for Deutsche Bank, particularly when it later emerged in newspaper interviews that the bank had sought both to undermine Ms Green's case by suggesting that her breakdowns were due to unfortunate circumstances in her earlier life (she had been sexually abused by her

adoptive father) and had tried unsuccessfully to find evidence to demonstrate that her mother had suffered from a serious mental illness.

Yet in many respects it can be plausibly argued that Deutsche Bank was unlucky in this case. The bank had after all kept Helen Green's job open for her and had paid her a full salary for over two years before dismissing her. It had promoted her twice before her breakdown, had provided a counselling service and had sent her on a stress management training programme. Moreover, some of the specific incidents that had led to Ms Green's breakdowns do appear on the face of it to be childish in nature and unlikely to offend most people to anything like the same extent. They included removing her name from a circulation list, hiding her post, blowing raspberries at her and, on one occasion, a colleague 'crossing her arms in a very dramatic way and staring at Ms Green'.

Whatever the rights and wrongs of the ruling in this case, it demonstrates clearly how employers can easily find themselves on the wrong side of the law in their dealings with employees and how the results can be costly in terms of compensation, staff time and lost reputation.

Sources: BBC (2006); Tait (2006); Guest (2006); and *The Times* (2006).

The contract of employment

Although a great deal is written about 'psychological contracts' and 'contracts for performance', the association between employer and employee remains at base a legal relationship governed by 'a contract of employment'. Whatever expectations employers and employees have of one another when the employment begins, the basic terms and conditions will be agreed and understood at the start and may, if necessary, be enforced in a court. In law the existence of such a contract confers on both parties important obligations as well as giving the employee access to significant legal rights which are not available to people who work under different contractual arrangements.

Employment contracts are very varied, and in recent years all industrialised countries have seen a trend away from what are usually described as being 'traditional' arrangements in which employees are employed on an open-ended basis for thirty-eight hours or so over a five-day standard 'working week' towards a variety of different alternative types of contract. In some industrial sectors we have seen a move away from employment altogether as people have chosen, or been required, to switch to self-employment or agency working. However, as far as the law is concerned, over 80% of people who work in the UK are employees. This means that they have a contract of employment with their employer, with the duties and privileges that that implies. As far as the law is concerned,

Table 18.1
Access to
statutory
employment
rights

Employment rights which apply to all workers	Employment rights which apply only to employees
Equal pay for equal work	Right to a statement of terms and conditions of employment
Right not to be discriminated against on grounds of sex, race, religious belief, sexual orientation, age or disability	Right to an itemised pay statement
Right not to have unauthorised deductions from pay	Statutory Sick Pay
Basic health and safety rights	Time off for public duties
Minimum wage	Nine months' maternity pay
Working time regulations	Trade union rights
Data protection rights	Minimum notice periods
Time off to care for dependants	Fixed-term employment regulations
Part-time workers regulations	Parental leave (after one year's service)
Twelve months' maternity leave	Unfair dismissal rights (after one or two years' service)

they are working under 'a contract of service'. This derives from the old notion of a master and servant relationship and indicates that the employee (or servant) has obligations to the employer or master, and vice versa. In contrast, those who are self-employed or subcontractors have greater autonomy, but no one standing between them and legal accountability for their actions. The law makes an important distinction between the two groups, employees having access to a wider range of legal rights than non-employees. While some areas of employment law apply to all workers, others only apply to employees. Non-employees are deemed to be working under 'a contract for services' rather than 'a contract of service'. In 2013 the main statutory rights that applied to each were those shown in Table 18.1.

In addition to the statutory rights conferred by Acts of Parliament, a range of common law duties are owed by employers to employees and vice versa which do not apply in the case of other forms of relationship. The major obligations are as follows:

Owed by employers to employees:

- a general duty of care
- a duty to pay agreed wages
- a duty to provide work
- a duty not to treat employees in an arbitrary or vindictive manner
- a duty to provide support to employees
- a duty to provide safe systems of work.

Owed by employees to employers:

- a duty to cooperate
- a duty to obey reasonable/lawful instructions
- a duty to exercise reasonable care and skill
- a duty to act in good faith.

Owed by employers to employees and vice versa:

- to maintain a relationship of mutual trust and confidence.

Owed by employees and ex-employees:

- duty of fidelity.

A contract of employment, contrary to common perception, need not exist in written form. It is much more satisfactory for both parties if there is documentary evidence of what terms and conditions have been offered and accepted, but a contract of employment exists whether agreed verbally on the telephone or sealed with no more than a handshake. Where there is any doubt about whether someone is an employee or not, the courts look at the evidence presented to them concerning the reality of the existing relationship between the two parties. If they consider, on balance, that it is governed by a 'contract of service' rather than a 'contract for services', they will consider the worker to be an employee and entitled to the full range of rights outlined above.

WINDOW ON PRACTICE

A case heard in the House of Lords (now reinvented as The Supreme Court) illustrates the importance of employee status. Mrs Carmichael and a colleague were employed as tour guides at a power station run by National Power PLC. They started working for the company on a casual basis in 1989, undertaking about four hours' work each week as and when they were needed. By 1995 they each were working around twenty-five hours a week, so they decided to ask for written particulars of their terms and conditions of employment. The company refused on the grounds that they were casual workers and not employees. The women won their case in the lower courts, but the company decided to appeal right up to the House of Lords. At this stage the women lost their case on the grounds that there was no mutuality of obligation. They could have, and indeed had, turned down requests to work without suffering any disciplinary action. They were therefore not employees and not entitled to the rights associated with full employment status.

ACTIVITY 18.1

Substantial and growing groups of people in the UK work under atypical sets of terms and conditions, for example on casual or agency contracts. As a rule such staff are classed as 'workers' rather than 'employees' because they are not deemed to be working under 'contracts of service'. As a result many important employment rights are denied to them (see Table 18.1).

What do you think are the main arguments for and against extending full employment rights to these groups? Where do you stand in this debate, and why?

Discrimination law

Most anti-discrimination law is now covered by European treaties or directives and thus applies in all member states of the EU. In the UK the passing of the Equality Act 2010 brought together in one statute most of these regulations. There remain important differences in the rights that relate to each 'protected characteristic' set out in the Act, but there is now a greater degree of harmonisation as far as core principles and terminology are concerned. The protected characteristics are as follows:

- sex
- race, ethnicity and national origin
- sexual orientation
- religion or belief
- age
- disability
- pregnancy and maternity
- marital status
- transsexuality.

In each case the details differ somewhat, but the same broad principles apply. Below we illustrate these by describing sex discrimination law at some length, going on briefly to explain how and why some of the other fields of discrimination law employ slightly different approaches.

Sex discrimination law

In the UK, extensive law in the area of sex discrimination has been on the statute books since 1975. This has been amended on several occasions since then and has been interpreted in different ways as a result of new case law, but the core tenets have always remained the same. There are four separate headings under which a case can be brought: direct sex discrimination, indirect sex discrimination, sexual harassment and victimisation.

Direct discrimination

Direct discrimination is straightforward. It occurs simply when an employer treats someone less favourably for a reason related to their gender. In judging claims the courts use the 'but for' test, asking whether the woman would have received the same treatment as a man (or vice versa) but for her sex. Examples of direct sex discrimination include advertising for a man to do a job which could equally well be done by a woman, failing to promote a woman because she is pregnant or dismissing a married woman rather than her single colleague because she is known to have a working husband.

If an employer is found to have discriminated *directly* on grounds of sex, except in one type of situation, there is no defence. The courts cannot, therefore, take into account any mitigating circumstances or make a judgment based on the view that the employer acted reasonably. Once it has been established that direct discrimination has occurred, proceedings end with a victory for the claimant.

The one exception operates in the area of recruitment, where it is possible to argue that certain jobs have to be reserved for either women or men. For this to be acceptable the employer must convince a court that it is a job for which there is an 'occupational requirement' on grounds such as:

- authenticity (e.g. acting or modelling jobs);
- decency (e.g. lavatory or changing room attendants);
- personal services (e.g. a counsellor engaged to work in a rape crisis centre).

Direct discrimination on grounds of pregnancy or maternity has long been assumed automatically to constitute unlawful sex discrimination. This means that there is no defence of reasonableness whatever the individual circumstances. It is thus unlawful to turn down a job application from a well-qualified woman who is eight months pregnant, irrespective of her intentions as regards the taking of maternity leave.

Indirect discrimination

Indirect discrimination is harder to grasp, not least because it can quite easily occur unintentionally. It occurs when a 'provision, criterion or practice' is set or operated which has the effect, in practice, of disadvantaging a significantly larger proportion of one sex than the other. In other words, if substantially fewer women than men can comply with the condition, even if it is applied in exactly the same way to both men and women, it is potentially unlawful. A straightforward example is a job advertisement which specifies that applicants should be taller than 5 feet 10 inches. This is indirectly discriminatory because a substantially smaller proportion of women are able to comply than men.

Indirect discrimination differs from direct discrimination in that there is a defence that an employer can deploy. An employer can objectively justify the condition or requirement it has set 'on grounds other than sex', in which case it may be lawful. An example might be a job for which a key requirement is the ability to lift heavy loads. It is reasonable in such circumstances for the employer to restrict recruitment to people who are physically able to comply, for example by including a test of strength in selection procedures. The fact that more men than women will be able to do so does not make the practice unlawful, provided the lifting requirement is wholly genuine. In judging cases of this kind the tribunal has to decide whether or not the provision, criterion or practice constitutes 'a proportionate means of achieving a legitimate aim'. If the tribunal decides it does, the employer wins, if not the employee wins.

It is not sufficient for the employer to show that the practice was convenient or administratively desirable – that does not amount to objective justification; to form the basis of an acceptable defence it must be shown to be genuinely necessary for the achievement of a legitimate business objective.

WINDOW ON PRACTICE

The Equality and Human Rights Commission

Employer actions in the area of discrimination are policed to some extent by the Equality and Human Rights Commission (EHRC) which is required to keep the legislation under review, to conduct formal investigations into employer actions where it has reason to suspect there has been a contravention of the law, to issue codes of practice and to provide legal assistance to employees who consider themselves to be victims of unfair discrimination. On occasions the EHRC itself represents employees before employment tribunals. It also brings its own test cases in a bid to push back the frontiers of the law.

The EHRC began operating in 2007, replacing three well-established commissions: the Equal Opportunities Commission, the Commission for Racial Equality and the Disability Rights Commission. However, its remit extends much further than those of the commissions it replaced to encompass fields covered by the Human Rights Act 1998 as well as discrimination law.

Sexual harassment

Sexual harassment is defined as unwanted conduct of a sexual nature or based on sex, which affects the dignity of men and women at work. It can be physical or verbal in nature, leading *either* to material detriment (i.e. it affects promotion, pay, access to training, etc.) *or* to the creation of an intimidating or humiliating work environment.

Although the law applies equally to men and women, the vast majority of cases are brought by women. The employer's liability in harassment cases arises from the application of the doctrine of **vicarious liability**, under which employers are held responsible for the commitment of civil wrongs by employees when they are at work.

In judging cases the courts focus on the reaction of the victim and do not apply any general definitions of what types of conduct do and do not amount to unlawful harassment. Hence conduct which may not offend one person in the slightest can be found to constitute sexual harassment when directed at someone else who is deeply offended.

For an employer the only valid defences relate to the notion of vicarious liability. An employer can, for example, claim ignorance of the incident of which the victim is complaining or can claim that vicarious liability does not apply because it occurred away from the workplace and outside office hours. Finally the employer can defend itself by showing that all reasonable steps were taken to prevent the harassment from occurring or continuing. In order to succeed here, the employer needs to produce evidence to show that initial complaints were promptly acted upon and that appropriate action, such as disciplining the perpetrators or moving them to other work, was taken.

Victimisation

In the field of sex discrimination the term 'victimisation' means the same as it does in other areas of employment law. An employer victimises workers if it disadvantages them in any way simply because they have sought to exercise their legal rights or have assisted others in doing so. An employee would thus bring a claim of victimisation to a tribunal if the employee had been overlooked for promotion having recently successfully settled an equal pay claim. Importantly victimisation covers situations in which someone threatens to bring an action or plans to do so even if no case is ultimately brought.

Other fields of discrimination law

These same core principles apply across the other fields of discrimination law covered by the EU's Equal Treatment Framework Directive and the Equality Act 2010. There are, however, some significant differences in the case of age discrimination and disability discrimination law:

- In age discrimination law it is permissible to discriminate directly if the act is objectively justified. In such cases the same defence that applies in cases of indirect discrimination must be complied with if the employer is to be able to show that it has acted lawfully, namely that the act of discrimination amounted to 'a proportionate means of achieving a legitimate aim'. This means that, in practice, mandatory retirement at the age of 65 or above remains lawful across most of the EU.

- Disability discrimination law permits employers to discriminate against a disabled person, a job applicant or an existing employee who becomes seriously ill, provided they have first genuinely considered whether any 'reasonable adjustments' could be made to enable that person to work or continue working. This typically involves adjusting working practices to accommodate someone's particular needs or making alterations to premises.

WINDOW ON PRACTICE

Religion or belief

Under EU law it is a requirement that all member states have in place regulations to deter employers from discriminating against their staff on grounds of 'religion or belief'. Back in 2003 when this law was first introduced, the UK government was keen to ensure that members of extreme political organisations could not use it to defend themselves when an employer objected to their views by, for example, refusing to promote them or even dismissing them. The UK law was thus phrased in terms of discrimination on grounds of 'any religion or similar philosophical belief'. This formulation soon proved to be unsatisfactory and hard to justify because it excluded people who did not have any religious belief and who were found, quite lawfully, to have been excluded from work in religious organisations and faith schools on these grounds. The wording was thus altered in 2006 to 'any religious or philosophical belief', the aim being to include people with deeply held beliefs about 'life, the universe and everything', whether or not they were religious in character. The new wording still sought to exclude instances in which people are discriminated against because of their political opinions or stance on an issue, but exactly who and what beliefs met the definition remained unclear.

In 2009 the issue became further confused when the Employment Appeals Tribunal (EAT) gave judgment in the case of *Grainger PLC & others* v. *Nicholson*. Here the claimant, Mr Nicholson, alleged that he had been made redundant from his post as Head of Sustainability at Grainger, in part, because of his belief in climate change – a point of view he expressed and acted on while at work with some passion. The EAT ruled that such a belief did fall within the new definition and found in his favour.

In the process the EAT set out a list of criteria which tribunals will now have to use when determining whether or not 'a philosophical belief' is or is not covered by the regulations. These are as follows:

- it must be a belief and not merely an opinion or viewpoint based on current information;
- the belief must be genuinely held;
- the belief must concern a weighty and substantial aspect of human behaviour;
- the belief must have a 'certain level of cogency, seriousness, cohesion and importance';
- the belief must be 'worthy of respect in a democratic society, not incompatible with human dignity and not in conflict with the fundamental rights of others'.

The aim here is presumably to steer a careful path so that beliefs that are racist, unpleasant or perverse cannot be protected, while 'allowing through' other deeply held and sincere beliefs. The trouble is that it leaves many questions unanswered, hence creating less clarity than was there before. In short, how can an employer now know whether or not it is or is not acting lawfully when faced with decision in this field? A great deal is now left to the subjective opinion of tribunal members.

In 2012 the European Court of Human Rights ruled against the UK government on this issue, finding in favour of a bus driver called Mr Redfearn who had been dismissed when he was elected to his local council as a representative of the British National Party (BNP). The court was concerned that Mr Redfearn had no legal avenue open to him to challenge his dismissal. This case demonstrates that the law probably still has some way to develop before a settled position on the scope of 'religion or belief' is reached.

Remedies

Victorious claimants in discrimination cases are awarded damages of two kinds. First they can claim from the employer compensation for any financial losses they have sustained as a result of the unlawful discrimination they have suffered. This may be very limited, but where someone has resigned or been dismissed there can be extensive sums awarded to compensate for lost earnings and potential future losses. The second category is 'injury to feelings'. The sums awarded here range from £500 for one-off incidents that cause very limited distress (e.g. being turned down for a job at the shortlisting stage when the individual had little expectation of being successful at interview) up to £30,000 where someone has, for example, been subjected to a lengthy campaign of racial harassment.

Equal pay law

The Equal Pay Act 1970 was the first legislation promoting equality at work between men and women. It came into force in December 1975 and was subsequently amended by the Equal Pay (Amendment) Regulations 1983. Its provisions are also now contained in the Equality Act 2010. These regulations are used to bring a case to tribunal when there is inequality between a man's contract of employment and that of a woman. In practice the majority of cases are brought by women and concern discriminatory rates of payment, although there have been some important cases brought by men focusing on aspects of pension provision. Three distinct types of claim can be brought:

1 **Like work**: where a woman and a man are doing work which is the same or broadly similar – for example, where a woman assembly worker sits next to a male assembly worker, carrying out the same range of duties.

2 **Work rated as equivalent**: where a man and a woman are carrying out work which, while of a different nature, has been rated as equivalent under a job evaluation scheme.

3 **Work of equal value**: where a man and a woman are performing different tasks but where it can be shown that the two jobs are equal in terms of their demands, for example in terms of skill, effort and type of decision making.

Unlike sex discrimination law where the 'but for test' permits the use of hypothetical comparators, in order to bring a case under the Equal Pay Act the claimant must be able to point to a comparator of the opposite gender with whom he or she wishes to be compared. The comparator must be employed by the same employer or at an establishment covered by the same collectively negotiated terms and conditions. When an equal value claim is brought which an employment tribunal considers to be well founded, an 'independent expert' may be appointed to carry out a job evaluation exercise in order to establish whether or not the two jobs being compared are equal in terms of the demands they make.

Employers can employ two defences when faced with a claim under the Equal Pay Act. First, they can seek to show that a job evaluation exercise has been carried out which indicates that the two jobs are not like, rated as equivalent or of equal value (see Chapter 21). To succeed the job evaluation scheme in use must be both analytical and free of sex bias. Second, the employer can claim that the difference in pay is justified by 'a material factor'. For this to succeed, the employer has to convince the court that there is a good business reason for the unequal treatment and that there has thus been no sex discrimination. Examples of genuine material factors that have proved acceptable to the courts are as follows:

- different qualifications (e.g. where a man has a degree and a woman does not);

- performance (e.g. where a man is paid a higher rate than a woman because he works faster or has received a higher appraisal rating);

- seniority (where the man is paid more because he has been employed for several years longer than the woman);

- regional allowances (where a man is paid a London weighting, taking his pay to a higher rate than that of a woman performing the same job in the Manchester branch).

When a claimant wins an equal pay claim the claimant is entitled to have his or her pay equalised with that of the chosen comparator and is also paid compensatory back-pay for a period of up to six years.

Health and safety law

Health and safety law, like discrimination law, is now largely derived from European directives, the same broad principles applying across all EU member states. In the UK the law can be neatly divided into two halves, representing criminal and civil spheres. The first is based in statute and is policed both by the Health and Safety Executive and by local authority inspectorates. The second relies on the common law and allows individuals who have suffered injury as a result of their work to seek damages against their employers. The former is intended to be preventative, while the latter aims to compensate individuals who become ill as a result of their work.

Criminal law

Health and safety inspectors potentially wield a great deal of power, but their approach is to give advice and to issue warnings except where they judge that there is a high risk of personal injury. They visit premises without giving notice beforehand in order to inspect equipment and make sure that the appropriate monitoring procedures are in place. They have a general right to enter premises, to collect whatever information they require and to remove samples or pieces of equipment for analysis. Where they are unhappy with what they find, inspectors issue improvement notices setting out recommended improvements and requiring these to be put in place by a set date. In the case of more serious lapses, where substantial risk to health is identified, the inspectors issue prohibition notices which prevent employers from using particular pieces of equipment until better safety arrangements are established. Breach of one of these statutory notices is a criminal offence, as is giving false information to an inspector. Over a thousand prosecutions are brought each year for non-compliance with a Health and Safety Executive Order, leading to fines of up to £20,000.

The Health and Safety at Work etc. Act 1974 is the source of most health and safety law in the UK, under which more detailed sets of regulations are periodically issued. Its main purposes are as follows:

- to secure the health, safety and welfare of people at work;

- to protect the public from risks arising from workplace activities;

- to control the use and storage of dangerous substances;
- to control potentially dangerous environmental emissions.

The Act places all employers under a general duty 'to ensure, as far as is reasonably practicable, the health, safety and welfare at work' of all workers. In addition there are specific requirements to maintain plant and equipment, to provide safe systems of working, to provide a safe and healthy working environment, to consult with trade union safety representatives, to maintain an accident reporting book and to post on a noticeboard a copy of the main provisions contained in the 1974 Act.

Since 1974 numerous sets of regulations have been issued, many of a very specialised nature, to add to the more general principles established in the Health and Safety at Work Act. The most significant have been the following, most of which originate at the European level:

- The First Aid Regulations 1981 place employers under a general duty to provide adequate first aid equipment and facilities.
- The Control of Substances Hazardous to Health (COSHH) Regulations 1988 concern the safe storage and usage of potentially dangerous substances.
- The Management of Health and Safety at Work Regulations 1992 place a variety of duties on employers. Examples include regulations on the safe lifting of heavy loads, the prolonged use of video display units (VDUs) and the particular health and safety needs of pregnant workers.
- The Health and Safety (Consultation with Employees) Regulations 1996 require employers to consult collectively with their employees about health and safety matters irrespective of whether a trade union is recognised.
- The Health Act 2006 bans smoking in public spaces, including most workplaces and company vehicles in England. Equivalent legislation has been passed by the Scottish Parliament and the Welsh and Northern Irish Assemblies.

ACTIVITY 18.2

Devise a health and safety policy for your organisation. Include information about:

- General policy on health and safety.
- Specific hazards and how they are to be dealt with.
- Management responsibility for safety.
- How the policy is to be implemented.

Or:

Obtain the Health and Safety Policy from any organisation and assess the policy in the light of these four points.

Civil law

While distinct in origin and nature from the criminal sanctions, civil cases relating to health and safety are often brought alongside criminal proceedings in connection with the same incident. When someone is seriously injured or suffers ill health as a direct result of their work the health and safety authorities will bring a criminal prosecution, while the injured party will sue for damages in the civil courts. Most claims are brought under the law of negligence, the injured party alleging that the employer acted negligently in allowing him or her to become injured.

In such cases the courts have to be satisfied that the employer failed to act reasonably and that the injury or illness was sustained 'during the course of employment'. Central here, as in the criminal law, are the notions of foreseeability and risk assessment. Cases often hinge on what the employer knew at the time the injury was sustained and whether or not reasonable precautions in the form of training or the provision of equipment had been taken. Employers can thus defend themselves effectively by satisfying the court that little else could have been done by any reasonable employer to prevent the accident from occurring. Importantly the principle of vicarious liability applies in this field, so employers are legally liable for the negligence if one employee causes another to become injured.

In recent years, as is demonstrated by the *Green* v. *Deutsche Bank* case described at the start of this chapter, people suffering from psychiatric injuries brought about from undue workplace stress have successfully brought claims. In practice, however, as was the case with Helen Green, large sums by way of damages are only won where employees suffer two serious breakdowns, both of which are work related. Otherwise it is very difficult to satisfy a court that the risk of injury was genuinely 'reasonably foreseeable' and hence that the employer is liable.

Working time

Some of the most significant recent developments in the field of health and safety law have derived from the Working Time Regulations (1998), an example of law that was introduced into the UK rather reluctantly in order to meet European treaty obligations. The basic 'headline' entitlements are as follows:

- a limit of forty-eight hours per week;
- twenty-eight days paid leave each year;
- twenty minutes rest in any period of work lasting six hours or more
- eleven hours' rest in any one twenty-four-hour period;
- twenty-four hours' rest in any seven-day period;
- night workers limited to eight hours' work in any one twenty-four-hour period;
- free health checks for night workers
- special regulations restricting working time of young workers (i.e. 16–18 year olds)

On the surface this looks clear cut and straightforward, but this is not the case. The regulations are complex, running to more than 100 pages in length. What is more, parts of them do not apply in some situations, meaning that many workers in the UK are, in practice, either unprotected or only partially protected:

- The regulations allow for considerable flexibility because they allow employers to average time worked over a seventeen-week reference period.
- Anyone can if they wish formally 'opt out' of the forty-eight-hour week restriction by signing or writing a written declaration. Employers in the UK are lawfully able to

make the signing of such an opt-out a requirement of employment. Staff are at any time to 'opt' back in by informing their employer in writing and giving notice and cannot be victimised for exercising this right. This 'opt-out' arrangement only applies in the UK, and from time to time other European governments and institutions campaign for its removal.

● Workforce agreements can be established which allow an employer to vary the working time regulations in various ways. Where the majority of the workforce assent to a proposal in a vote, by signing up directly or via a trade union agreement a workplace can adapt its interpretation of the working time regulations to suit its needs.

ACTIVITY 18.3

What is your view of the opt-out arrangement maintained by the UK? Should employers be able to make it a condition of employment that new starters sign such an agreement? Aside from the cost implications, what other disadvantages might follow from an employer perspective were opt-outs to be outlawed?

Family-friendly employment law

In recent years a significant contribution to the development of workplaces which offer a better work–life balance has been made via the introduction of new and enhanced employment rights which require employers to take account of the needs of people with family responsibilities. These are straightforward but have been highly significant both for employers who have to find ways of accommodating them and for the many employees who have benefited considerably. The key rights are as follows:

● The right for pregnant employees to take reasonable time off work to attend ante-natal medical appointments without losing any pay.

● The right for a mother to take time off before, during and after her baby is born. Most employed women are entitled to take six months' 'ordinary maternity leave' followed by a further six months' 'additional maternity leave'.

● The right to Statutory Maternity Pay (SMP) for a period of nine months while maternity leave is being taken. SMP is paid at the 'higher rate' for the first six weeks (90% of salary) and thereafter at the 'lower rate' (£136.78 per week in 2013).

● A right for both parents of a child the right to take up to eighteen weeks' unpaid leave during the first five years of the child's life or during the five years following the adoption of a child. This right currently only extends to employees who have completed a year's continuous service with their employer.

● A right for fathers of new babies to take two weeks' paid paternity leave within the first fifty-six days of the birth, and subsequently to 'take over' any remaining maternity leave left after the child's mother has returned to work twenty weeks after starting her leave.

- A right for parents and carers to take reasonable amounts of time off during working hours for urgent family reasons, employers being informed of the intention to take the leave 'as soon as is reasonably practicable'.

- A right for parents of children aged up to 18 and carers of sick adults to request flexible working. The procedure requires the parent or carer to write formally to his or her employer asking for a one-off change in terms and conditions, together with an explanation as to how the request could be accommodated in practice. The employer can turn the request down, but only when one of eight specific business reasons applies.

- Equivalent rights for parents of adopted children, one being able to claim maternity rights, the other paternity rights.

Further substantial extension of rights in this area is planned for 2015 when it is intended that a couple will be able to divide their maternity/paternity leave rights between one another far more flexibly. This is likely to result in many couples taking paid leave at the same time for an extended period following the birth of a new baby. A general extension of the right to request flexible working is also planned.

The National Minimum Wage

Since 1999 most workers in the UK have been entitled in law to be paid a minimum hourly rate for the work that they do. The rate of the National Minimum Wage (NMW) is not linked to any formula, but is set by the Secretary of State for Business after consultation with the Low Pay Commission. The aim is always to set the highest rate possible that will not appreciably have an adverse impact on employment levels. In practice the level of the NMW is increased in October each year, and in recent years the increases have sometimes been well in excess of the prevailing rate of inflation. In 2013 it stood at £6.19 an hour.

Not everyone, however, is entitled to the full amount. There are some groups who are excluded altogether, such as people engaged in family work (au pairs, nannies, etc.), people working in sheltered work schemes run for homeless persons, apprentices, barristers' pupils and students undertaking periods of work experience as part of a course of higher education. Other groups are only entitled to a lower 'development rate' (£4.98 an hour in 2013). This applies to people who are aged 18–22 and those over that age who are in the first six months of a new job during which at least twenty-six days are being spent training to achieve a National Vocational Qualification (NVQ) or Scottish Vocational Qualification (SVQ). Finally, there is a third lower 'youth rate' for 16–17 year olds (£3.68 an hour in 2013).

The government has appointed a team of inspectors to investigate incidents of wilful refusal to pay the NMW. They have the right to inspect records of hours worked and wages paid so as to establish whether or not the NMW has been and is being been paid. Where an employer knowingly refuses to comply with the NMW regulations, it can be charged with a criminal offence and fined. Fines are calculated according to the following formula:

Twice the rate of the minimum wage at the time of the charge multiplied by the number of employees who have been paid below the level of the NMW multiplied by the number of working days they have not been paid the NMW.

In addition, of course, workers who are found not to have been paid the NMW are entitled to receive their full entitlement in the future and to receive back-pay too by way of compensation.

ACTIVITY 18.4

At the time when the National Minimum Wage was introduced some groups representing employers argued that it would have a negative impact on both the level of unemployment and the level of inflation. Why do you think there is a danger of these effects when minimum wages are introduced? Why do you think they have not occurred in practice in the UK as a result of the National Minimum Wage?

Deductions from wages

All employees in the UK are entitled in law to receive an itemised pay statement which sets out the gross rate of pay for the month or week and any deductions that have been made. The Employment Rights Act 1996 sets out what deductions can lawfully be made, the implication being that other types of deduction are unlawful and can lead to action in the employment tribunal. The list of permissible deductions includes those authorised by legislation such as tax and National Insurance contributions and those authorised in the contract of employment such as trade union subscriptions or pension fund contributions. Sometimes courts issue 'attachment orders' requiring an employer to pay a fine or a debt on behalf of an employee and to make an equivalent deduction from the pay package, and from time to time mistakes are made in salary administration resulting in overpayments to employees that need to be recovered. In both these situations deductions are lawful. Importantly, however, it is unlawful for an employer to levy any kind of fine on an employee as a punishment when a disciplinary offence has been committed or where an individual's performance in the job is unsatisfactory. In such circumstances, along with any others in which underpayments of agreed wages are made, aggrieved employees have the right to take their case to an employment tribunal and to argue that they should be reimbursed.

Is employment law a benefit or a burden for businesses?

It is common for managers and owners of small businesses, as well as the journalists, politicians and employers' associations who support their interests, to argue that the extent of employment regulation is now so great as to be having a substantial, negative impact. At base this argument concerns economic competitiveness, it being said that regulation both adds unnecessary costs and stifles the capacity of organisations to act flexibly and opportunistically. The result is reduced international competitiveness because so many rival organisations are based in countries which have far less regulation to contend with. It follows, according to its critics, that employment law acts as a disincentive to job creation and also provides an incentive for UK-based organisations to 'export jobs' by relocating aspects of their operations overseas or by subcontracting them to overseas-based suppliers (CBI 2000).

There is no question that employment regulation adds to employers' costs, not least by taking up a good deal of management time. A survey carried out by the Chartered Institute of Personnel and Development found that two-thirds of HR managers in the UK spend over 20% of their time 'dealing with employment law issues', a further 25% spending over 40% of their time in this way (CIPD 2002). In addition to time spent making sure that an organisation is complying, there are further direct costs associated with the introduction of new measures. In recent years, as the scope of employment law has widened, unsurprisingly the number of claims being brought has increased too, as has the complexity of many of these claims. The number of claims lodged with employment tribunals in the UK is now over 120,000 a year, compared with 30,000 or so twenty years ago (Taylor and Emir 2012: 6). To this additional cost burden we can plausibly add lost opportunity costs. Although impossible to quantify at all accurately, it is reasonable to ask what benefits could accrue if managers were free to devote the time they spend dealing with employment law matters on value-adding activities instead?

A further argument contends that the effect of employment law, even if it is not the intention of legislators, is to harm the career interests of those groups who are afforded the most legal protection (e.g. ethnic minorities, disabled people and mothers with dependent children). This occurs because it makes organisations less likely to employ them.

The main arguments in favour of employment law relate to social justice and the need to reduce the extent to which people suffer unreasonably at the hands of prejudiced, negligent or bullying managers abusing the power their position gives them. It is necessary to protect employees via the law, just as it necessary to protect other vulnerable groups from injustice. Such arguments are strong, straightforward and accepted by most, although disagreements will always persist about where the balance should lie between protecting the interests of employees and that of employers. However, there are also influential economic arguments in favour of extensive employment protection legislation. The implication here is that regulation of the employment relationship does not just benefit employees, but that organisations and the economy generally have also stood to gain from its extension in recent decades.

There are a number of distinct strands that make up the economic argument in favour of employment law. The first has tended to be used by ministers introducing new legislation in the face of business opposition, it being argued that the most productive workplaces are those in which people are managed effectively and fairly. In requiring managers to treat their staff with dignity, fairness and in an equitable manner, employment regulation helps to raise employment standards. In turn this has positive benefits for businesses in terms of higher levels of motivation and productivity, lower levels of staff turnover and a healthy, high-trust employee relations climate. Employment law, it is argued, should hold no fears whatever for good employers. All it aims to do is to bring all employment practice up to that same broad standard.

The second strand of the argument relates directly to the issue of growing skills shortages among some key professional groups. The starting point here is the view that the inability of many employers to recruit and retain people with the skills and experience that they need constitutes a significant national economic problem which holds back economic growth (see Frogner 2002). It follows that the amelioration of skills shortages should properly be a significant public policy objective. Improving employment standards by forcing employers to treat their employees well helps to achieve this because it makes work more attractive than it otherwise would be. It follows that more people with a choice about whether to work or not choose to do so in a world of regulated employment than would if the employment relationships were unregulated. The result is a higher economic participation rate as women with young children, people with long-term ill-health issues and those who could afford to retire if they wanted to put their skills, at least for part of the time, at the disposal of the economy. High standards also help to attract into the country highly skilled migrant workers from overseas who might otherwise choose to work elsewhere.

The final, third strand of the argument concerns the UK economy's competitive position internationally. It is argued that highly developed economies such as the UK's cannot sustain themselves in the face of competition from developing and newly industrialised countries by competing on the basis of cost. There is no future for such a business strategy because wage levels in China, India and elsewhere are invariably much lower than is the case in Europe and, as a result, the goods and services that they produce will always be far cheaper (see Chapter 2). It follows that the UK, like many other countries, needs clearly to position itself as a high-wage, knowledge-based economy which produces innovative hi-tech goods and provides upmarket services. In order to achieve this organisations need to be encouraged to work in partnership with their employees and, particularly, to invest in their training. There is little economic incentive for employers to devote resources to extensive employee development programmes in environments characterised by high staff turnover and low-trust employment relationships. The government thus needs to intervene to push employers in this direction and employment law is one of several public policy tools that are used to achieve this. The long-term aim is thus to help sustain economic growth in a rapidly changing and highly competitive business environment.

The most persuasive conclusion to reach is that employment regulation is both a burden and a benefit to UK employers, although it is of less benefit to and a much greater burden for smaller businesses without the expertise and resources to ensure that they are managing within its requirements. It is a burden because it adds substantial costs and because it limits the freedom managers have to run their businesses in ways that they might otherwise wish to. However, it is also a benefit because it helps to raise employment standards throughout the country, making work more attractive to people who have skills and experience that they might otherwise choose not to make use of in the employment context. In the process it contributes to reduced staff turnover, helps to encourage later retirement, helps to create the conditions in which superior individual performance is more likely and, crucially, in which low-trust, adversarial industrial relations are less likely to emerge.

ACTIVITY 18.5

Where do you stand in this debate about employment legislation? Does it serve to underpin economic prosperity or reduce international competitiveness? What further measures would you welcome and which would you oppose?

SUMMARY PROPOSITIONS

18.1   In the space of a single generation UK workplaces have gone from being among the least regulated in the world to being among the most highly regulated.

18.2   At base the employment relationship is contractual. A legally binding agreement is formed when an employee starts working for an employer. Neither side can lawfully breach that contract and cause the other some kind of detriment without risking legal action and the requirement to pay some compensation.

18.3   Discrimination law has grown rapidly in recent years, extending to new grounds such as age, sexual orientation and religion or belief. Equal pay law requires men and women to be paid the same wage for doing work which is the same or which can be shown to be of equal value unless the employer can justify a difference on grounds other than sex.

18.4   The legal framework for health and safety includes both the criminal and civil law. The former is policed by health and safety inspectors; the latter provides a vehicle for those who suffer illness or injury as a result of their work to claim damages.

18.5   Family-friendly employment law has been very much extended in recent years and will be further extended in the future. It aims to help people better combine their work and domestic responsibilities.

18.6   Two major recent additions to employment regulation have been the National Minimum Wage and the Working Time Regulations. Both have had, and continue to have, a major impact on HR practice in organisations.

18.7   Employment regulation increases the cost burden for employers and reduces their freedom of action, but in helping to ensure that reasonably high minimum standards are maintained in employee relations it also brings economic advantages to organisations.

GENERAL DISCUSSION TOPICS

1   How far do you think that UK discrimination law is effective in achieving its aims? What could be done to make it more effective?

2   To what extent do you agree with the view that employment regulation now imposes so many restrictions and costs on employers as to make businesses based in European countries uncompetitive internationally?

THEORY INTO PRACTICE

Trouble at the Big Top

All around towns across the country brightly coloured posters proclaim the imminent arrival of Geraldo Pecorino's traditional, family, travelling circus. Geraldo's round red face smiles out inviting all to gaze and wonder at Alice and Maximillian's amazing feats on the flying trapeze, to gasp in amazement as Little Fat Stan the human cannon ball is propelled at speed across the circus ring, to laugh at the crazy antics of Micky the clown and his chums, and to applaud as Daisy the elephant dances daintily on her hind legs. But in reality, Geraldo is not smiling at all. He is very worried about the future of his circus. His star performers may help bring in the crowds, but they are also causing him a variety of managerial headaches.

Alice is his longest-serving artiste. For thirty-five years, partnered by a succession of male trapeze stars, she has nightly swung and somersaulted high in the air above a safety net, before descending to take her bow. Unfortunately, over time the once lissom Alice has become less agile and has put on a great deal of weight. As a result, when she enters the ring in her leotard and climbs up to her trapeze the audience increasingly see her as a figure of fun. When she carries out her final triple somersault and falls into the safety net, the structure wobbles alarmingly, causing the audience to scream with laughter. The contrast with the much younger and very athletic Maximillian is becoming more and more obvious, and he is not happy. 'Find me a new partner', he says, or 'I will find a better circus to work for'. But what can Geraldo do? Alice is well paid and popular among the troupe. For several months he has been able to placate Maximillian by saying that he cannot find a replacement for Alice, but now a perfect new partner for Maximillian has become available. A beautiful 18-year-old trapeze artist called Melanie who has the rare capacity to carry out a Russian-style, back-flip, quadruple somersault has left a rival circus and is begging Geraldo for a job. Can he sack Alice? Can he redeploy her? Redeployment would be preferable but the only suitable job he has for her would involve performing with Micky and his crazy clowns. Alice would get the laughs, but it would be much less well-paid work and undignified for a senior artiste with years of loyal service behind her.

Geraldo's second managerial headache concerns another long-serving employee. Jethro has for many years acted as keeper and trainer of Daisy the elephant. They are devoted to one another. Every day Jethro feeds her, cleans her wagon, takes her for walks, washes her and then, in the evening, the two of them perform together to the delight of the audience. For many this act is the highlight of the circus. But six months ago an unfortunate accident occurred. In the middle of their act a large light bulb exploded above the circus ring, which gave Daisy a terrible fright. She panicked and instead of continuing to dance, she charged at Jethro and tossed him into the air. He sustained serious back and neck injuries in this accident and has been in and out of hospital ever since. Geraldo now realises that Jethro will not be able to return to work again for many more months. Daisy is back to her old self and has apparently bonded well with her new keeper, Geraldo's daughter Romola. Jethro visits her when he can, but he comes with his carer and is unable to get up out of his wheelchair. What should Geraldo do? He is still paying Jethro but cannot afford to continue doing so for ever. Can he dismiss him? Should he try to reach a financial settlement, and if so would his insurance company reimburse him?

And finally, what is Geraldo to do about Little Fat Stan, his much-loved, but increasingly awkward human cannon ball? Stan has worked in the circus for years, delighting generations of audiences with his acts. He started out as a tumbler, then as he got older he turned to fire-eating and knife swallowing, before winding up being fired nightly from a cannon across the ring through several paper hoops, and landing spectacularly in a meticulously placed bouncy castle. Stan is not happy. He feels his life is unfulfilled and he wants to change direction. Stan has dealt with his depression in the past by drinking heavily, but has now managed to stop. Instead he has found great solace by becoming an active Christian. He attends churches in each town that the circus visits and continually regales the other performers with stories about how his faith has changed his life. But this has caused difficulties for Geraldo because Stan has said that he will not in future be available to perform on Sundays or at any time over the Christmas and Easter periods. He has asked Geraldo if he could give up performing and assist him in a management role, taking responsibility for publicising the circus. Failing that he would like to run the box office. But these jobs are already taken and are not, in truth, suitable for Stan. Geraldo insists that he can only employ him as a specialist performer. What should Geraldo do? Mondays and Tuesdays are the days the circus does not put on a performance and on which everyone takes time off. Two performances are mounted every Sunday, and Easter and Christmas are periods when audiences increase substantially. Should he threaten to sack Little Fat Stan? Could he employ someone else to be a human cannon ball on Sundays, and reduce Stan's wages to compensate?

The worry of what to do about Stan, Jethro, Maximillian and Alice causes Geraldo to suffer many sleepless nights.

Questions

1 Geraldo decides that he has no choice but to employ Melanie as a replacement for Alice. He tells Alice that from next week onwards she will have to perform alongside Micky and his clowns. Her role will be to act as his foil and a victim of his many practical jokes. For the next six months she will be paid the same salary that she currently earns. After this date it will be reviewed.

   Assuming that she is unhappy with Geraldo's decision, what possible legal claims might Alice be able to bring? What defences might Geraldo be able to deploy were Alice to take her case to an employment tribunal?

2 Geraldo decides to dismiss Jethro, offering him a one-off payment of £25,000 by way of a full and final settlement.

   What possible legal claims could Jethro bring were he to reject Geraldo's offer? What action could Geraldo take to minimise his chances of losing these cases in court?

3 Geraldo decides to allow Little Fat Stan to take Sundays off and to take his annual leave over the Christmas and Easter periods. Another performer will be trained up to take his place at these times. In return Geraldo will reduce Stan's pay by 20%.

   What possible legal claims might Stan be able to bring? How might Geraldo be able to defend himself were the dispute to reach a tribunal hearing?

FURTHER READING

An excellent book which analyses UK employment regulation in the round, explaining its purpose and debating its strengths and weaknesses from a variety of perspectives, is *Perspectives on Labour Law* by A.C.L. Davies (2009).

Sandra Fredman has written extensively on discrimination law. The key debates are discussed concisely and effectively in her book entitled *Discrimination Law* (2011).

There are several good textbooks on employment law. Those aimed primarily at management students rather than lawyers include those authored by Janice Nairns (2011), David Lewis, Malcolm Sargeant and Ben Schwab (2011), Brian Willey (2012) and Stephen Taylor and Astra Emir (2012).

REFERENCES

BBC (2006) 'Bullied City worker wins £800,000', BBC News website, 1 August.
CBI (2000) *Cutting through red tape: The impact of employment legislation.* London: Confederation of British Industry.
CIPD (2002) *Employment Law: Survey Report.* London: CIPD.
Davies, A.C.L. (2009) *Perspectives on Labour Law*, 2nd edn. Cambridge: Cambridge University Press.
Fredman, S. (2011) *Discrimination Law*, 2nd edn. Oxford: Oxford University Press.
Frogner, M.L. (2002) 'Skills shortages', *Labour Market Trends*, January.
Guest, K. (2006) 'Why I deserve every penny of the £800,000, by the bullied City exec', *Independent*, 6 August.
Lewis, D., Sargeant, M. and Schwab, B. (2011) *Essentials of Employment Law*, 11th edn. London: CIPD.
Nairns, J. (2011) *Employment Law for Business Students*, 4th edn. London: Longman.
Tait, N. (2006) 'Courts take bullying by the horns', *Financial Times*, 6 August.
Taylor, S. and Emir, A. (2012) *Employment Law: An Introduction*, 3rd edn. Oxford: Oxford University Press.
The Times (2006) Letters page, 8 August 2006.
Willey, B. (2013) *Employment Law in Context*, 4th edn. London: FT/Prentice Hall.

LEGAL CASES

Grainger PLC & others v. *Nicholson* (2010) IRLR 4.
Green v. *Deutsche Bank* (2006) EWHC 1898.

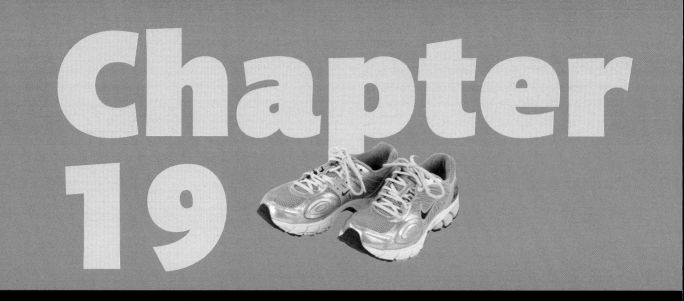

Chapter 19

EQUAL OPPORTUNITIES AND DIVERSITY

THE OBJECTIVES OF THIS CHAPTER ARE TO:

1 Review the current employment experiences of the members of some socially defined minority groups

2 Analyse the differing approaches to achieving equality for those groups, in particular contrasting the more traditional equal opportunities approach with the management of diversity approach

3 Explore the implications which managing diversity has for organisations

In today's times of globalisation and demographic change, the workforce is becoming increasingly diverse and it is more important than ever for organisations to develop equal opportunity and diversity strategies to attract and retain talent to improve workforce performance. Legislation, voluntary codes of practice and equality initiatives have resulted in some progress towards equality of treatment for minority groups, but there remains inescapable evidence of continuing discrimination. More recent approaches under the banner of management of diversity include the economic and business case for equality, the valuing and managing of diversity in organisations, culture change and the mainstreaming of equality initiatives. Such approaches are partly a response to the insufficient progress made from the equal opportunities route, yet there is only limited evidence that they have made a difference. While diversity approaches offer some useful perspectives and practices, the underlying concepts also raise some issues and concerns. We consider issues relating to both equality of opportunity and diversity management in this chapter.

How 'equal' is the workforce?

The workforce in the UK has changed radically in the past fifty years, becoming more diverse in terms of gender, age, race and ethnicity, sexual orientation and political and religious beliefs, to name just some of the criteria on which employees may differ. Diversity can also extend beyond social category to include informational diversity (differences in terms of education, tenure and functional background) and value diversity (which includes differences in personality and attitudes) (CIPD 2011). We have therefore been necessarily selective in the groups we have chosen to discuss here and include the top five equality and diversity issues identified in a recent survey (CIPD 2012a), namely gender, racial/ethnic minorities, people who are disabled, older people and individuals who are lesbian, gay, bisexual or transsexual. We present evidence of the equality of opportunity available to these diverse employee groups.

Gender

If **participation** in the labour force is an indication of decreasing discrimination then recent figures are encouraging. From 1971 to 2012, the UK female participation rate in employment increased from 56% to over 70% and 51% of the UK workforce is now female (van Wanrooy *et al.* 2013). Further, women have been less adversely affected by the economic downturn than men, possibly as a result of working more often in the public sector or in part-time jobs. As we noted earlier (see Chapter 5), however, part-time employment is often low paid, low skilled and insecure, so the over-representation of women in this type of employment hardly creates equality of opportunity.

Some of the more obvious signs of discrimination, such as in recruitment advertising, may have disappeared, and there is some evidence to suggest that women are beginning to enter some previously male-dominated occupations. For example, women have now been ordained as priests in the Church of England. Similarly men are beginning to enter some previously female-only occupations, such as midwifery. However, there remains a high degree of subtle discrimination, for example in access to training and support for development and promotion, and not-so-subtle discrimination, as in the continued

gender segregation in terms of both type and level of work. Care work is, for example, largely a female occupation (Atkinson and Lucas 2012) and senior management, particularly at board level, continues to be dominated by men (Broughton and Miller 2009). This is not simply a UK phenomenon, as both Ross (2010) and Metz and Harzing (2012) demonstrate in their respective accounts of female board-level exclusion in Australia and women's under-representation on international academic journal editorial boards.

WINDOW ON PRACTICE

Getting women on boards: the new girls' network

Clegg (2012) reports that while more women in the UK are joining boards, the rate of increase is slow and there is still a rejection of quotas. There is a growing acceptance of the need for women to network and be mentored in order to build knowledge, confidence and to make themselves more visible to corporate decision makers. While this may sound like a female version of the 'old boy network' Clegg argues that it is essential to address the market's failure to promote women on their own merits.

Source: Adapted from Clegg (2012).

Pay differentials between men and women are still evident. While these began to narrow in the UK when the Equal Pay Act 1970 came into force in 1975, progress has been slow, and a gender pay gap still exists. According to a recent Annual Survey of Hours and Earnings (ONS 2012), the average weekly rate for full-time women is £499 as against £546 for full-time men, some 10% lower. Similar international patterns are again apparent, for example in Canada (Drolet and Mumford 2012) and Denmark (Gupta and Eriksson 2012). IDS (2004) identifies a range of unintentional consequences of pay systems which prove to be a barrier to achieving equal pay, and these are shown in Table 19.1.

Table 19.1
Barriers to the achievement of gender-based equal pay

Starting pay is frequently individually negotiated	As men usually have higher previous earnings this means they can negotiate a higher starting rate
Length of service	Men generally have longer service and fewer career breaks, and while this may result in greater experience early in a career it is less of a performance-influencing factor as general length of service increases
Broadbanding	There is a lack of transparency in such systems and there is a lack of structured progression; managers are likely to have high levels of discretion and may be unaware of biases
Lack of equal access to bonus payments	There is evidence that appraisal ratings and assessments discriminate unfairly against minority groups
Market allowances not evenly distributed	Such allowances are more likely to be given to men
Different pay structures and negotiating bodies	As some jobs are done primarily by women and some primarily by men, direct comparisons are harder to make
Job evaluation	Such schemes often perpetuate old values and may be subject to managerial manipulation

Source: Based primarily on material in IDS (2004) 'Employers move on equal pay', *IDS Report*, No. 897, January, pp. 10–18.

Racial and ethnic groups

Racial and ethnic minority groups constitute around 9% of the UK labour market (van Wanrooy *et al*. 2013). Their labour market participation rates are, however, typically lower than for other groups in both the UK and elsewhere. This is thought to result from discrimination and is not restricted to the UK. In the Netherlands, for example, there is evidence of ethnic minority groups being marginalised, stigmatised and discriminated against in the labour market (der Laan Bouma-Doff 2008). There is also segregation in the UK across occupations, with ethnic minority male employees being disproportionately employed in sectors such as hotel and catering and manufacturing industry. Ethnic minorities further tend to be under-represented at senior levels of organisations, a recent study by Cook and Glass (2009) even suggesting that the appointment of ethnic minorities to senior positions in organisations can adversely affect share price. Racial discrimination may also happen less blatantly. Rana (2003) reports on a project designed to understand why ethnic minority managers are under-represented in senior levels of local government. The researchers found that in 360-degree feedback results the line managers' assessments of ethnic minority employees were less favourable for each individual than all other assessments, which were generally similar. This discrepancy did not occur when considering the ratings of white employees.

People with a disability

About 2% of the UK workforce is classified as disabled (van Wanrooy *et al*. 2013). Woodhams and Danieli (2000) demonstrate that people who have a disability face common barriers to full integration into society and yet are a very varied group in that impairments can vary in severity, stability and type. People with a disability are more likely to be unemployed than their able-bodied counterparts, and once unemployed they are likely to remain so for a longer period. Choice of job is often restricted for people with a disability, and where they do find work it is likely to be in low-paid, less attractive jobs, although disability discrimination legislation may have improved the lot of the disabled worker in the past decade (Woodhams and Corby 2007).

Age

Demographic changes, legislation and labour shortages have led to an increased recognition of the need for age equality. In the UK labour market 24% of workers are over 50 and this proportion continues to grow (van Wanrooy et al. 2013). However, research continues to report that age discrimination remains a significant problem, with older workers being commonly disadvantaged in terms of promotion and training, and these age biases being deeply ingrained (Riach 2009). For example, line managers have negative perceptions of older workers, seeing them as less able to cope with change, training or technology and less interested in their careers, more likely to be sick and to cost more money to employ. There are also, however, some positive stereotypes depicting older workers as more loyal and conscientious, having better interpersonal skills and lower turnover rates, more efficient and that their experience counteracts any age-related factors lowering productivity. The young also face labour market discrimination (Snape and Redman 2003) with over 1 million young people in the UK being not in employment, education or training (NEETs) (Burnham 2012).

Sexuality

Lesbian, gay, bisexual and transgender (LGBT) discrimination is the most difficult to identify due to the fact that group membership may not be revealed, usually due to the anticipation of discrimination. It is therefore difficult to quantify the extent to which these groups experience active discrimination. The Business & Human Rights Resource Centre (**www.business-humanrights.org**) suggests that, despite policy rhetoric, homophobia and discrimination are still common in certain sectors, for example financial services. Rumens and Broomfield's research (2012), however, reports that gay policemen feel able to disclose their sexuality and are valued organisational members. There is also some evidence of pay discrimination on the grounds of sexuality, although these relationships are not well understood (Ahmed *et al.* 2011).

Stonewall (2010) adopts a Workplace Equality Index analysing the policies of organisations which support LGBT employees. Each year, it makes awards to the best 100 employers in the UK. While this represents great progress in eradicating discrimination for these groups of employees, there is still a distance to go in achieving equality. Many of the top 100 employers in the Workplace Equality Index are large firms, smaller firms perhaps being slower to respond with formal policies on sexual orientation. Research by Day and Greene (2008), however, suggests that small firms may have advantages in promoting inclusiveness in terms of a positive work climate.

In summary

Discrimination and inequality are difficult to measure. Fevre *et al.* (2011), for example, analyse the UK government's Citizenship Survey to demonstrate that in 2011 nearly half the population felt they had been discriminated against in the previous year, but that most people did not think that they themselves were prejudiced. Nevertheless, discrimination and inequality remain in the workplace and are particularly evident for certain groups. We now turn to the theoretical debate which underpins different organisational approaches to tackling discrimination and inequality.

ACTIVITY 19.1

Talk to people you know across a range of socially defined groups – gender, race, disability and older workers, for example. What are their experiences of discrimination in the workplace? To what extent do you think equality for these groups is apparent?

Different approaches to equality

There has been a continuing debate concerning the action that should be taken to alleviate the disadvantages that minority groups encounter. One approach, generally referred to as equal opportunities or a liberal approach, supports legislative action. Most recently in the UK this takes the form of the Equalities Act (2010), which prevents discrimination on the grounds of a number of 'protected characteristics' including race, disability, gender reassignment, sex, marriage and civil partnership, pregnancy and maternity, religion and belief, sexual orientation and age (also see Chapter 18). A second approach, managing diversity, argues that legislation will not be effective and that a fundamental change to the attitudes and preconceptions held about these groups is required. The initial emphasis on legislative action was adopted in the hope that this would eventually affect attitudes. A third, more extreme, radical approach, which enjoys less support, comes from those who advocate legislation to promote positive or reverse discrimination to compensate for a history of discrimination against specified groups and to redress the balance more immediately. In the UK, legislation provides for positive action, such as special support and encouragement, for disadvantaged groups, but not positive or reverse discrimination (discriminating in their favour), except for disability legislation. The labels 'equal opportunities' and 'management of diversity' are used inconsistently, and to complicate this there are different perspectives on the meaning of managing diversity, so we shall draw out the key differences which typify each of these approaches, and offer some critique of their conceptual foundations and effectiveness.

The equal opportunities approach

The equal opportunities approach seeks to influence behaviour through legislation so that discrimination is prevented. It has been characterised by a moral and ethical stance promoting the rights of *all* members of society. This liberal approach concentrates on the equality of opportunity rather than the equality of outcome found in more radical approaches. The approach is based on the understanding that some individuals are discriminated against, for example in the selection process, due to irrelevant criteria. These irrelevant criteria arise from assumptions based on the stereotypical characteristics attributed to them as members of a socially defined group, for example that women will not be prepared to work away from home due to family commitments or that a person with a disability will have more time off sick. The equal opportunities approach therefore seeks to formalise procedures so that relevant, job-based criteria are used (using job descriptions and person specifications) and discrimination is based on fair criteria, that is the ability to do the job.

The rationale, therefore, is to provide a 'level playing field' on which all can compete on equal terms. Differences between socially defined groups are glossed over, and the approach is generally regarded as one of 'sameness'. Positive action, not positive discrimination, is allowable in order that some may reach the level at which they can compete equally. For example, an organisation may advertise its vacancies in publications which target particular under-represented ethnic groups. Once it has generated a pool of applicants, however, it must not then use ethnic origin as a selection criterion.

Equal opportunities approaches stress disadvantaged groups, and the need, for example, to set targets for those groups to ensure that their representation in the workplace reflects their representation in wider society. Targets are needed in occupations where they are under-represented, such as firefighters, police officers and in the armed forces, where small numbers of ethnic minorities are employed or senior management roles where there are small numbers of women. These targets are not enforceable by UK legislation, in contrast to some other countries, but organisations have been encouraged to commit themselves voluntarily to improvement goals, and to support this commitment by putting in place measures to support disadvantaged groups such as special training courses and flexible employment policies.

Questioning quotas: diversity management practices in the United Arab Emirates

While not formalised in UK legislation, the use of quota systems to improve diversity is common in many countries. Quotas are, for example, cited in many Northern European countries as having made a substantial contribution to women's board-level representation. In the United Arab Emirates (UAE), quotas have been adopted to force the employment of home nationals who are often unemployed as a result of the appointment of foreign expatriate workers. There are, however, problems with the use of quotas.

In the UAE, for example, they lead to the negative stereotyping of home nationals and to insecurity for expatriates, some of whom considered the quotas themselves to be discriminatory. While quotas have been in place for over a decade, less than 1% of private-sector employees are home nationals. This failure can be ascribed to numerous causes, central to which were discourses of efficiency, merit and performance amid concerns that the employment of home nationals would negatively impact on business performance. Scepticism about government penalties for non-compliance largely rendered the quota system ineffective.

Source: Adapted from Forstenlecher *et al.* (2012).

Problems with the equal opportunities approach

There is an assumption in the equal opportunities approach that equality of outcome will be achieved if fair procedures are used and monitored. In other words, if this is done it will enable any minority groups to achieve a fair share of what employment has to offer. Once such minority groups become full participating members in employment, the old stereotypical attitudes on which discrimination against particular social groups are based will gradually change, as the stereotypes will be shown to be unhelpful.

The assumption that fair procedures or procedural justice will lead to fair outcomes has not been borne out in practice. The focus of equal opportunities is on formal processes and yet it is it not possible to formalise everything in the organisation. In addition there has been criticism of the assumption that once members of minority groups have demonstrated their ability to perform in the organisation, this will change attitudes and beliefs in the organisation. Further, there can be a general lack of support within organisations, partly because equality objectives are not linked to business objectives and partly because equal opportunities have often been viewed as the concern of the HR function. A focus on disadvantaged groups may also alienate the large sections of the workforce not identified as such; for example, Atkinson and Hall (2009) demonstrate that workers adopting standard patterns resent the extra burden that colleagues (mainly female) working flexibly impose upon them.

In summary the equal opportunities approach is considered simplistic and to be attempting to treat the symptoms rather than the causes of unfair discrimination.

The management of diversity approach

The management of diversity approach concentrates on individuals rather than groups, and includes the improvement of opportunities for *all* individuals and not just those in minority groups. Hence managing diversity involves everyone and benefits everyone, which is an attractive message to employers and employees alike. Separate groups are not singled out for specific treatment.

The CIPD (2011) argues that managing diversity involves recognising the differences in people and valuing, respecting and using these differences to support business performance. So the focus is on valuing difference rather than finding a way of coping fairly with it. Whereas the equal opportunities approach minimised difference, the managing diversity approach treats difference as a positive asset.

This brings us to a further difference between the equal opportunities approach and the managing diversity approach, which is that the managing diversity approach is based on the economic and business case for recognising and valuing difference, rather than the moral case for treating people equally. Rather than being purely a cost, equal treatment offers benefits and advantages for the employer if it invests in ensuring that everyone in the organisation is valued and given the opportunities to develop his or her potential and make a maximum contribution. The practical arguments supporting the equalisation of employment opportunities are thus highlighted. The CIPD (2012b) suggests that business benefits can be summed up in three broad statements: that diversity enhances customer relations and market share; that it enhances employee relations and reduces labour costs; and that it improves workforce quality and performance in terms of diverse skills, creativity, problem solving and flexibility.

For example, a company that discriminates, directly or indirectly, against older or disabled people, women, ethnic minorities or people with different sexual orientations will be curtailing the potential of available talent. The financial benefits of retaining staff who might otherwise leave due to lack of career development or due to the desire to combine a career with family are stressed, as is the image of the organisation as a 'good' employer and hence its attractiveness to all members of society as its customers. Although the impact on performance is more difficult to assess, it is reasonable to assume that more satisfied and committed employees will lead to reduced absence and turnover levels. In addition, the value of different employee perspectives and different types of contribution is seen as providing added value to the organisation, particularly when organisational members increasingly reflect the diverse customer base of the organisation. This provides a way in which organisations can better understand, and therefore meet, their customer needs. The business case argument is likely to have more support from managers as it is less likely to threaten the bottom line. While these arguments may hold good in a buoyant economic climate, the recession does pose a threat to the business case argument as labour markets become less competitive. The CIPD (2012c) presents case studies of organisations which have sustained their diversity efforts even where their business case is less compelling, while Fenwick *et al.* (2011) demonstrate acceptance of the business case for diversity in Australia.

WINDOW ON PRACTICE

London 2012 puts diversity at its heart

The London 2012 games were the first Olympics to be organised with diversity and inclusion as one of the central goals. Stephen Frost, Head of Diversity and Inclusion at LOCOG, the organising committee for the games, said that unlike previous Olympiads, the capital's diversity was central to the 2012 brand and helped inspire young people from all communities to take up sport.

'It might surprise some people that we are a private-sector company, funded by private-sector sponsors. Therefore, we aren't bound by public-sector duties and motivated by compliance – we are doing this because we really believe it will benefit our games', Frost said. The LOCOG workforce started with just 150 people and swelled to around 200,000 during the games once temporary workers were added. This demand for talent made it essential to engage local communities. The organisation had a prominent diversity board to provide leadership on the issue and every manager making hiring decisions was directly responsible for ensuring the diversity of their team. External efforts to recruit a more diverse range of people included recruitment evenings aimed at specific communities, blogs by BME (Black and Minority Ethnic) staff detailing their

experiences and job adverts being read out along with the call to prayer in London mosques. With the Paralympic Games an important part of the package, there was also an emphasis on hiring disabled workers. LOCOG launched Access Now – a scheme that guaranteed disabled people an interview if they meet basic criteria. The organisation also operated a talent pool, so that unsuccessful disabled candidates were kept in mind for other posts as they arose.

Source: Adapted from Brockett, J. (2009) 'London 2012 puts diversity at its heart', BBC Radio 4, PM Online, 19 November.

Organisational culture is also central to managing diversity. Equal opportunity approaches tend to concentrate on behaviour and, to a small extent, attitudes, whereas management of diversity approaches recognise a need to go beneath this. So adopting a culture where one treats people as individuals and supports them in developing their potential is critical, although the difficulties of culture change make this a very demanding task. Also, depending on the approach to the management of diversity, the culture of different groups within the organisation comes into play. For example, men and women may need managing and developing in different ways. Attending to the organisation's culture suggests a move away from seeing the individual as the problem, and requiring that the individual needs to change because he or she does not fit the culture. Rather, it is the organisation that needs to change so that traditional assumptions of how jobs are constructed and how they should be carried out are questioned, and looked at afresh.

In summary, managing diversity is considered to be a more integrated approach to implementing equality. Whereas equal opportunities approaches were driven by the HR function, managing diversity is seen to be the responsibility of all managers. And, as there are business reasons for managing diversity, it is argued that equality should not be dealt with as a separate issue, as with equal opportunities approaches, but integrated strategically into every aspect of what the organisation does; this is often called mainstreaming.

Table 19.2 summarises the key differences between equal opportunities and managing diversity.

Problems with the managing diversity approach

While many saw the management of diversity approach as revitalising the equal opportunities agenda, and as a strategy for making more progress on the equality front, this progress has been slow to materialise. In reality, there remains the question of the extent to which approaches have really changed in organisations. Redefining equal opportunities in terms of its 'business case' may just be a way of making it more palatable in today's climate. Indeed, only a small number of organisations are ever quoted as management of diversity and the workforces of those that are so described are not necessarily more

Table 19.2
Major differences between 'equal opportunities' approaches and 'management of diversity' approaches

Aspect	Equal opportunities	Managing diversity
Purpose	Reduce discrimination	Utilise employee potential to maximum advantage
Approach	Operational	Strategic
Case argued	Moral and ethical	Business case – improved profitability
Whose responsibility?	HR/personnel department	All managers
Focuses on	Groups	Individuals
Perspective	Dealing with different needs of different groups	Integrated
Benefits for employees	Opportunities improved for disadvantaged groups, primarily through setting targets	Opportunities improved for all employees
Focus on management activity	Recruitment	Managing
Remedies	Changing systems and practices	Changing the culture
Monitoring success	Changed processes	Business outcomes

diverse than those of other organisations. Apart from this there are some fundamental problems with the diversity management approach and different approaches are also apparent internationally, as we outline in the following Window on practice.

WINDOW ON PRACTICE

'Hard' diversity policies and ethnic minority representation

This study (Verbeek and Groeneveld 2012) investigates the effectiveness of three types of diversity policy in improving ethnic minority representation. These are:

- assigning responsibility for the policy within the organisation;
- tiebreak preferential treatment (i.e. selecting the ethnic minority candidate if the applicants are equally qualified);
- use of quotas.

These policy types are not legislated for in all countries but are legal in the Netherlands where the study was conducted.

The study demonstrated difficulties with all three policy types and their failure to increase ethnic minority representation. Assigning organisational responsibility for diversity matters did not lead to substantial action as it was 'content empty': that is, a policy instrument without a goal. Similarly, the use of quotas was 'form empty': that is, a goal without a policy instrument. Tiebreak preferential treatment was no more effective as it was either not implemented or implemented with effects opposite to those intended.

Source: Adapted from Verbeek and Groeneveld (2012).

Even within a single legislative framework, diversity management is complex and subject to differing interpretations, which we have so far ignored, and which focus on the prominence of groups or individuals. One approach is to identify and celebrate individual differences, and to expose and challenge prejudices via training. The second, more orthodox, approach is where the organisation seeks to develop the capacity of all.

The most common approach to the management of diversity is based on individual contribution rather than on group identity. The *individualism* approach is based on dissolving random differences, not those that accrue due to membership of a particular social group. The advantage of this approach is that it is inclusive and involves all members of the organisation. An alternative emphasis in the management of diversity is that of *valuing differences* based on the membership of different social groups. Following this approach would mean recognising and highlighting differences, and being prepared to give special training to groups which may be disadvantaged and lack self-confidence, so that all in the organisation feel comfortable. This could, however, lead to reinforcement of group-based stereotypes and, indeed, problems which can result from a more diverse workforce, for example increased conflict.

A significant criticism of managing diversity is its basis in the 'business case'. The business case is unreliable because it will only work in certain contexts (Atkinson and Hall 2009). For example, where skills are easily available there is less pressure on the organisation to promote and encourage the employment of minority groups. Not every employee interacts with customers, so if image and customer contact are part of the business case this will apply only to some jobs and not to others. Also some groups may be excluded. For example, there is no systematic evidence to suggest that disabled customers are attracted by an organisation which employs disabled people. UK managers are also driven by short-term budgets and the economic benefits of equality may only be reaped in the longer term. The CIPD (2006a) argues that the evidence of performance improvements resulting from diversities is weak, which may mean that the business case is in fact potentially detrimental to equality.

In terms of implementation of a diversity approach there are also difficulties. Foster and Harris (2005) in their research in the retail sector found that it was a concept that lacked clarity for line managers in terms both of what it is and of how to implement it within anti-discrimination laws, and some were concerned that it may lead to feelings of unfairness and claims of unequal treatment. There are also concerns about whether diversity management, which originated in the USA, will travel effectively to other countries where the context is different, especially in terms of the demographics and the history of equality initiatives. Indeed, there are concerns about whether diversity can be managed at all given that individual differences derive from complex societal constructions far beyond the organisation's influence.

Equal opportunities or managing diversity?

Are equal opportunities and managing diversity completely different things? If so, is one approach preferable to the other? For the sake of clarity, earlier in this chapter we characterised a distinct approach to managing diversity which suggests that it is different from equal opportunities. However, as we have seen, managing diversity covers a range of approaches and emphases, some closer to equal opportunities, some very different.

Much of the management of diversity approach suggests that it is superior to and not compatible with the equal opportunities approach. There is, however, increasing support for equal opportunities and managing diversity to be viewed as mutually supportive and for this combination to be seen as important. Dickens (2006) suggests that social justice and economic efficiency are increasingly being presented as complementary, although there is so far a lack of guidance about how this can be done in practice. To see equal opportunities and management of diversity as *alternatives* threatens to sever the link between them and may therefore be detrimental to organisational objectives. Legislation on equality may support diversity approaches in preventing discrimination which arises from market forces (Dickens 2006) and be of value in setting minimum standards (Woodhams and Lupton 2006).

Implications for organisations

Equal opportunities and managing diversity: strategies, policies and plans

The Workplace Employee Relations Survey 2011 (WERS) found that 76% of organisations had equal opportunities or diversity policies or statements, up from 73% in 2004 and 64% in 1998 (van Wanrooy *et al.* 2013). The public sector and larger organisations were more likely to have policies than smaller ones, which means that the majority of the labour force are in organisations where such a policy exists. In addition a policy was more likely to exist in organisations where there was union recognition and where there was an employment relations specialist (even allowing for size). It would be a mistake, however, to assume that all policies cover all potentially disadvantaged groups: the CIPD (2006b) found that while 93% of organisations which responded to its survey did have a diversity policy, the disadvantaged groups covered by these were very variable, and many did not cover all the groups for which there is legislative protection. Similarly, policies may not cover all organisational activity. Woodhams and Corby (2007) suggest, for example, that many organisations have policies in place which cover the recruitment but not the promotion or career progression of those with disabilities. Further, WERS indicates that, despite having a policy, few organisations seek actively to prevent discrimination; for example, the overwhelming majority do not monitor recruitment and selection or promotion policies or review relative pay rates.

Despite the prevalence of policies there is always the concern that having a policy is more about projecting the right image than about reflecting how the organisation operates. For example, reports abound that job applications from those of minority ethnic origin are less favourably received than those from white UK applicants. Creegan *et al.* (2003) investigated the implementation of a race equality action plan and found a stark difference between paper and practice. Line managers who were responsible for implementing the plan were operating in a devolved HR environment and so had to pay for advice, training and support from HR specialists. The consequence of this was that in order to protect their budgets they were reluctant to seek help. Employees felt that there was no ownership of the strategy or the plan within the organisation by senior or middle managers. Further, Kirton and Healey's (2009) study of the use of competencies to promote equality and diversity in the selection of judges suggests that, while competencies can give an impression of fairness, they are nevertheless interpreted by human actors. This gives rise to the continuing exercise of bias and prejudice.

ACTIVITY 19.2

Consider the equal opportunities and diversity policies in your own organisation, or another with which you are familiar.

1 To what extent does practice match policy?

2 Explore the reasons for the achievement of a match or mismatch.

A process for managing diversity

There are many prescriptions for developing diversity policies and strategies. We draw here on the key elements suggested by a recent CIPD report (2012a):

- Strategy: policies must have board- and senior-level support and this must be sustained over a lengthy period, not as a one-off initiative. The strategy should support business goals, support fairness and inclusion and be legally compliant. Line managers should be supported in policy implementation and empowered to take decisions at local level. The strategy should also be integrated with other HR policies and be effective internationally (where applicable).

- Workplace behaviour: respect and dignity must be consistently valued and all organisational members should understand their role in promoting equality. Bullying and harassment must not be tolerated.

- Communication: open communications and consultation are essential and should draw on a variety of methods such as intranets and organisational magazines.

- Training: equality and diversity concepts should be central to all training and awareness-raising programmes may be helpful. The concepts should also be part of induction and line manager training.

- Measurement: regular audits are essential to review and evaluate progress and demonstrate business benefits. Both organisational and employee data, possibly using employee attitude surveys, should be used. Equality and diversity objectives should be built into job descriptions and performance review. Benchmarking, networking and celebrating success will also promote and reinforce equality and diversity.

While the ideal may be for organisations to work on all aspects of diversity in an integrated manner, the reality is often that organisations will target specific issues or groups at different times.

ACTIVITY 19.3

Prepare a strategy for managing diversity which would be appropriate for your organisation, or one with which you are familiar.

SUMMARY PROPOSITIONS

19.1 The essence of much HR work is to discriminate between individuals. The essence of equality is to avoid unfair discrimination. Unfair discrimination often results from people being treated on the basis of limited and prejudiced understanding of the groups to which they belong rather than on the basis of an assessment of them as individuals. People are not always aware when they are discriminating unfairly.

19.2 Legislation can have only a limited effect in achieving equality, and does not change attitudes, beliefs and cultures and structures. Organisations and their cultures, processes and structures are founded on the needs of the majority group and individuals from other groups are expected to adapt to this norm. This explains why progress towards equality of opportunity has been very slow.

19.3 Equal opportunities approaches highlight the moral argument for equal treatment, whereas managing diversity highlights the business case.

19.4 Actual changes in practice relating to equalising opportunity are taking place very slowly, and only long-term organisational transformation is likely to support equality.

19.5 Equal opportunities approaches and the management of diversity are best viewed not as alternatives, but as complementary approaches which need to be interrelated.

GENERAL DISCUSSION TOPICS

1   To what extent are equality of opportunity and managing diversity mutually supportive?

2   Thinking about Cook and Glass's (2009) findings that the appointment of racial/ethnic minorities to top management positions can have a negative impact on share price:

   • Why do you think that this is the case?

   • How could organisations try to address this?

THEORY INTO PRACTICE

A key skill of the international manager is harnessing diversity across a huge variety of cultures. This requires consideration of varying legal, cultural and demographic influences and, outside of Europe, anti-discrimination legislation may be lacking. Indeed, there may well be an absence of policy or organisational interventions to promote equality and diversity. Understanding of diversity management is essentially a western concept that may not translate well into other cultural or national contexts. Business strategies that develop understanding of local contexts and circumstances are, therefore, essential to the international manager, as are coping strategies to deal with ethical dilemmas that may arise. There are a series of questions that managers can ask themselves to determine appropriate actions in difficult situations, which include:

- Is the practice of concern acceptable? Different approaches may apply and derive from the host country's level of development. If this is the case, would the manager's home country have tolerated the practice at a similar stage? If so, the practice should be accepted. If it would not have been tolerated at a similar stage of development in the home country, further questioning is required.

- Is it possible to continue to trade in the host country while accepting the practice? Does the practice violate fundamental human rights? Dependent on the answers, the manager may have to refuse to accept the practice and may need to challenge the practice.

The international manager should, however, proceed with caution and take advice as to the implications of this refusal and how best to frame it.

The international manager must draw heavily on diversity as an effective mechanism of team management. A secure environment for the expression of ideas and communication should be created and recognition of cultural differences should again be recognised. In certain cultures, for example, it may be seen as disrespectful to express views that challenge those of the manager. It is also essential to be aware of and account for local cultural influences that may impact on working practices. Religion is a good example in that it may both affect working patterns, given for example the need to pray, and create work group tensions, where for example the group comprises members drawn from different religions. Similarly, if there is a dominant group, they may have undue influence and other important diversity issues may be neglected. It is important to be alert to cultural issues that may influence working relationships in order to build respect and value dignity.

Gender is also a critical issue. Most international managers are men, which may result from organisations' reluctance to send women abroad. This is particularly so where it is unusual for women to work, especially at senior levels, in the host country. This male dominance itself leads to limited diversity understanding among international managers.

Questions

1 What examples of cultural diversity likely to be faced by the international manager can you think of?

2 What impact might these examples have on work groups and how could this be addressed?

3 How could the dominance of men as international managers be addressed?

Adapted from CIPD (2011) *Diversity and International Management: Factsheet*. London: CIPD.

FURTHER READING

Cook, A. and Glass, C. (2009) 'Between a rock and a hard place: Managing diversity in a shareholder society', *Human Resource Management Journal*, Vol. 19, No. 4, pp. 393–412.

This is a fascinating study examining whether the appointment of racial/ethnic minorities to top management positions has a different impact on share price than the appointment of Caucasians to equivalent positions. The findings suggest that market reaction to the appointment of racial/ethnic minorities in corporate leadership positions is significant and negative, while the market's reaction to the appointment of Caucasians is significant and positive. The authors suggest, however, that the negative market reaction to the appointment of racial/ethnic minorities can be mitigated by the explicit incorporation of diversity into organisation strategy.

Fagan, C., Rubery, J., Grimshaw, D., Smith, M., Hebson, G. and Figueiredo, H. (2005) 'Gender mainstreaming in the enlarged European Union: Recent developments in the European employment strategy and social inclusion process', *Industrial Relations Journal*, Vol. 36, No. 6, pp. 568–91.

This article provides some excellent data comparing progress in the UK with that in other members of the EU in relation to employment rates and gender gaps.

Rumens, N. and Broomfield, J. (2012) 'Gay men in the police: Identity disclosure and management issues', *Human Resource Management Journal*, Vol. 22, pp. 283–98.

This is an interesting article which provides a useful counterpoint to much of the more negative literature which reports discrimination and stereotyping of LGBT workers, especially in traditionally masculine cultures such as the police force. The authors argue that gay police officers do not expect to be stigmatised and seek opportunities to disclose their sexuality. They appear to be openly managed and valued as organisational members.

WEB LINKS

www.business-humanrights.org
www.equalityhumanrights.com
www.gov.uk/rights-disabled-person

REFERENCES

Ahmed, A., Andersson, L. and Hammarstedt, L. (2011) 'Inter- and intra-household earnings differentials among homosexual and heterosexual couples', *British Journal of Industrial Relations*, Vol. 49, s258–78.

Atkinson, C. and Hall, L. (2009) 'The role of gender in various forms of flexible working', *Gender, Work and Organisation*, Vol. 16, pp. 650–66.

Atkinson, C. and Lucas, R. (2012) 'Policy and gender in adult social care work in England', *Public Administration*, doi: 10.1111/j.1467-9299.2012.02040.x.

Brockett, J. (2009) 'London 2012 puts diversity at its heart', BBC Radio 4, PM Online, 19 November.

Broughton, A. and Miller, L. (2009) 'Encouraging women into senior management positions', *Research Report 462*. London: Institute for Employment Studies.

Burnham, J. (2012) 'Young jobless Neets still top one million' [Online]. London: BBC. Available at: **www.bbc.co.uk/news/education-20444524** (accessed 24 February 2013).

CIPD (2006a) *Managing Diversity: Measuring success*. London: CIPD.

CIPD (2006b) *Diversity in Business: How much progress have employers made? First findings*. London: CIPD.

CIPD (2011) *Diversity and International Management: Factsheet*. London: CIPD.

CIPD (2012a) *Diversity and Inclusion: Fringe or fundamental?* London: CIPD.

CIPD (2012b) *Diversity in the workplace: An overview: Factsheet*. London: CIPD.

CIPD (2012c) *Game on! How to keep diversity progress on track*. London: CIPD.

Clegg, A. (2012) 'Getting women on boards: The new girls' network', *People Management*, www.cipd.co.uk/pm/peoplemanagement/p/paymentgateway.aspx?returnURL=/pm/peoplemanagement/b/weblog/archive/2012/03/26/getting-women-on-boards-the-new-girls-network-2012-03.aspx&blogid=2&postid=95953 (accessed 24 June 2013).

Cook, A. and Glass, C. (2009) 'Between a rock and a hard place: Managing diversity in a shareholder society', *Human Resource Management Journal*, Vol. 19, No. 4, pp. 393–412.

Creegan, C., Colgan, F., Charlesworth, R. and Robinson, G. (2003) 'Race equality policies at work: Employee perceptions of the "implementation gap" in a UK local authority', *Work, Employment and Society*, Vol. 17, pp. 617–40.

Day, N. and Greene, P. (2008) 'A case for sexual orientation diversity management in small and large organisations', *Human Resource Management*, Vol. 47, pp. 637–54.

Der Laan Bouma-Doff, W. (2008) 'Concentrating on participation: Ethnic concentration and labour market participation of four ethnic groups', *Journal of Applied Social Science Studies* Vol. 128, pp.153–73.

Dickens, L. (2006) 'Re-regulation for gender equality: From "either/or" to "both"', *Industrial Relations Journal*, Vol. 37, pp. 299–309.

Drolet, M. and Mumford, K. (2012) 'The gender pay gap for private-sector employees in Canada and Britain', *British Journal of Industrial Relations*, Vol. 50, pp. 529–53.

Fenwick, M., Costa, C., Sohal, A. and D'Netto, B. (2011) 'Cultural diversity management in Australian manufacturing organisations', *Asia Pacific Journal of Human Resources*, Vol. 49, pp. 494–507.

Fevre, R., Grainger, H. and Brewer, R. (2011) 'Discrimination and unfair treatment in the workplace', *British Journal of Industrial Relations*, Vol. 49, s207–35.

Forstenlecher, I., Lettice, F. and Ozbilgin, M. (2012) 'Questioning quotas: Applying a relational framework for diversity management practices in the United Arab Emirates', *Human Resource Management Journal*, Vol. 22, 299–315.

Foster, C. and Harris, L. (2005) 'Easy to say, difficult to do: Diversity in retail management', *Human Resource Management Journal*, Vol. 15, pp. 4–17.

Gupta, N. and Eriksson, T. (2012) 'HRM practices and the within-firm gender wage gap', *British Journal of Industrial Relations*, Vol. 50, pp. 554–80.

IDS (2004) 'Employers move on equal pay', *IDS Report*, No. 897. London: IDS.

Kirton, G. and Healey, G. (2009) 'Using competency-based assessment centres to select judges: Implications for diversity and equality', *Human Resource Management Journal*, Vol. 19, pp. 302–18.

Metz, I. and Harzing, A. (2012) 'An update of gender diversity in editorial boards: A longitudinal study of management journals', *Personnel Review*, Vol. 41, pp. 283–300.

ONS (2012) 'Annual Survey of Hours and Earnings, 2012 Provisional Results', *Statistical Bulletin*. London: ONS.

Rana, E. (2003) 'Council appraisals discriminate', *People Management*, Vol. 9, p. 11.

Riach, K. (2009) 'Managing difference: Understanding age diversity in practice', *Human Resource Management Journal*, Vol. 19, pp. 319–35.

Ross, E. (2010) 'AHRI: Mind the gap', *People Management,* April, www.peoplemanagement.co.uk/pm/articles/2010/04/ahri-mind-the-gap.htm (accessed 5 June 2013).

Rumens, N. and Broomfield, J. (2012) 'Gay men in the police: Identity disclosure and management issues', *Human Resource Management Journal*, Vol. 22, pp. 283–98.

Snape, E. and Redman, T. (2003) 'Too old or too young? The impact of perceived age discrimination', *Human Resource Management Journal*, Vol. 13, pp. 78–89.

Stonewall (2010) *Workplace Equality Index*. London: Stonewall.

Van Wanrooy, B., Bewley, H., Bryson, A., Forth, J., Freeth, S., Stokes, L. and Wood, S. (2013) *The 2011 Workplace Employment Relations Study: First Findings*. London: BIS.

Verbeek, S. and Groeneveld, S. (2012) 'Do "hard" diversity policies increase ethnic minority representation? An assessment of their (in)effectiveness using administrative data', *Personnel Review*, Vol. 41, pp. 647–64.

Woodhams, C. and Corby, S. (2007) 'Then and now: Disability legislation and employers' practices in the UK', *British Journal of Industrial Relations*, Vol. 45, pp. 556–80.

Woodhams, C. and Danieli, A. (2000) 'Disability and diversity: A difference too far?', *Personnel Review*, Vol. 29, pp. 402–17.

Woodhams, C. and Lupton, B. (2006) 'Gender-based equal opportunities policy and practice in small firms: The impact of HR professionals', *Human Resource Management Journal*, Vol. 16, pp. 74–97.

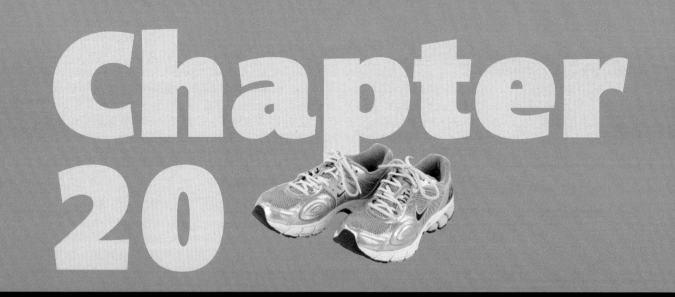

Chapter 20

GRIEVANCE AND DISCIPLINE

THE OBJECTIVES OF THIS CHAPTER ARE TO:

1   Examine the nature and explain the place of grievance and discipline in the employment contract

2   Review the Milgram experiments with obedience and use them to explain our response to authority

3   Explain the framework of organisational justice in the business

4   Explain grievance and discipline procedures

In 2009 there was a change in UK legal requirements about formal grievances to give employees the right to take a grievance directly to a tribunal without necessarily going through internal procedures. The employee must still advise the employer of the complaint, but does not need to set out the full basis of it until invited to a meeting with the employer. This is a further reason for employers to take complaints seriously and to ensure that their internal procedures are effective and fully respected.

The words grievance and discipline describe the breakdown of mutual confidence between employer and employee, or between managers and managed. When someone starts working in an organisation there are mutual expectations from the forthcoming working relationship. Maintaining the validity of those mutual expectations is the central purpose of HRM. Both parties will have expectations of what is to come. Employees are likely to expect, for instance, a congenial working situation with like-minded colleagues, opportunities to use existing skills and to acquire others, work that does not offend their personal value system, acceptable leadership and management from those more senior, and opportunities to grow and mature. Employers will have expectations such as willing participation in the team, conscientious and imaginative use of existing skills and an ability to acquire others, compliance with reasonable instructions without quibbles, acceptance of instructions from those placed in authority and a willingness to be flexible and accept change.

That working relationship will sometimes go wrong. If the employee is dissatisfied, then there is potentially a grievance. If the employer is dissatisfied, there is the potential for a disciplinary situation. The two complementary processes are intended to find ways of avoiding the ultimate sanction of the employee quitting or being dismissed, but at the same time preparing the ground for those sanctions if all else fails.

Usually, authority exercised in a business is impersonalised by the use of roles in order to make it more effective. If a colleague mentions to you that you have overspent your budget, your reaction might be proud bravado unless you knew that the colleague had a role such as company accountant, internal auditor or financial director. Everyone in a business has a role. Most people have several roles, each conferring some authority. The canteen assistant who tells you that the steak and kidney pudding is off is more believable than the managing director conveying the same message. Normally in hospitals people wearing white coats and a stethoscope are seen as being more authoritative than people in white coats without a stethoscope.

Dependence on role is not always welcome to those in managerial positions, who are fond of using phrases like, 'I know how to get the best out of people' or 'I have a loyal staff'. This may partly be due to their perception of their role being to persuade the reluctant and command the respect of the unwilling by the use of personal leadership qualities, and it is indisputable that some managers are more effective with some groups of staff than with others, but there is more to it than personal skill: we are predisposed to obey those who outrank us in any hierarchy.

The Milgram experiments with obedience

Stanley Milgram conducted a classic and controversial series of experiments to investigate obedience to authority and highlighted the significance of obedience and the power of authority in our everyday lives (Milgram 1974). His work remains a standard explanation of how we all behave.

Subjects were led to believe that a study of memory and learning was being carried out which involved giving progressively more severe electric shocks to a learner who gave incorrect answers to factual questions. A correct answer was rewarded with a further question; an incorrect answer was punished with a mild electric shock. Each shock was more severe than the previous one. The 'learner' was not actually receiving shocks, but was a member of the experimental team simulating progressively greater distress, as the shocks were supposedly made stronger. Eighteen different experiments were conducted with over 1,000 subjects, with the circumstances between experiments varying. No matter how the variables were altered, the subjects showed an astonishing compliance with authority even when delivering 'shocks' of 450 volts. Up to 65% of subjects continued to obey throughout the experiment in the presence of a clear authority figure and as many as 20% continued to obey when the authority figure was absent. If you believe that people no longer behave so submissively in the twenty-first century, an interesting copy of the experiment was carried out in 2009 (Nick and Eltchaninoff 2010), in which volunteers were also asked to inflict electric shocks to a screaming victim. The key difference was that the volunteers were told they were piloting a new reality TV show. Almost all of the eighty participants continued to the end.

Milgram was dismayed by his results:

> With numbing regularity good people were seen to knuckle under to the demands of authority and perform actions that were callous and severe. Men who are in everyday life responsible and decent were seduced by the trappings of authority, by the control of their perceptions, and by the uncritical acceptance of the experimenter's definition of the situation into performing harsh acts. (1974: 123)

This demonstrates that we all have a predilection to obey instructions from authority figures, even if we do not want to. The act of entering a hierarchical system (such as any employing organisation) makes people see themselves acting as agents for carrying out the wishes of someone else, and this results in these people being in a different mental state, 'the agentic state', which is the opposite of the state of autonomy when individuals see themselves as acting on their own initiative. The factors that lay the groundwork for obedience to authority are:

1 **Family.** Parental regulation inculcates a respect for adult authority. Parental instructions form the basis for moral imperatives, as commands to children have a dual function. 'Don't tell lies' is a moral injunction carrying a further implicit instruction: 'And obey me!' It is the implicit demand for obedience that remains the only consistent element across a range of explicit instructions. Parents reading this will laugh in disbelief, but angry defiance, insolence and all the other familiar behaviours are not the same as absolute refusal to obey.

2 **Institutional setting.** Children emerge from the family into an institutional system of authority: the school. Here they learn how to function in an organisation. They are regulated by teachers, but can see that the head teacher, the school governors and central government regulate the teachers themselves. Throughout this period they are in a subordinate position. When, as adults, they go to work it may be found that a certain level of dissent is allowable, but the overall situation is one in which they are to do a job prescribed by someone else.

3 **Rewards.** Compliance with authority is generally rewarded, while disobedience is frequently punished. Promotion within the hierarchy not only rewards the individual, but also ensures the continuity of the hierarchy.

4 **Perception of authority.** Authority is normatively supported: there is a shared expectation among people that certain institutions typically have a socially controlling figure. Also, the authority of the controlling figure is limited to the situation. In an aircraft you may ignore the safety demonstration by the cabin crew, but you do buckle your safety belt; you would not readily allow the same person, no longer in uniform, to calmly jump the queue ahead of you in a supermarket. Where authority is expected it does not have to be asserted, merely presented.

5 **Entry into the authority system.** Having perceived an authority figure, an individual must then define that figure as relevant to the subject. The individual not only takes the voluntary step of deciding which authority system to join (at least in most of employment), but also defines which authority is relevant to which event. The fire-fighter may expect instant obedience when calling for everybody to evacuate the building, but not if asking employees to use a different accounting system.

6 **The overarching ideology.** The legitimacy of the social situation relates to a justifying ideology. Science and education formed the background to Milgram's experiments and provided a justification for actions carried out in their name. Most employment is in realms of activity regarded as legitimate, justified by the values and needs of society. This is vital if individuals are to provide willing obedience, as it enables them to see their behaviour as serving a desirable end.

Managers are positioned in an organisational hierarchy in such a way that others will be predisposed, as Milgram demonstrates, to follow their instructions. Managers put in place a series of frameworks to explain how they will exact obedience: they use *discipline*. Because individual employees feel their relative weakness in the hierarchy, they seek complementary frameworks to challenge the otherwise unfettered use of managerial disciplinary power: they may join trade unions, but they always need channels to present their *grievances*.

In later work Milgram (1992) made an important distinction between obedience and conformity, which had been studied by several experimental psychologists, most notably Asch (1951) and Abrams *et al.* (1990). Conformity and obedience both involve abandoning personal judgement as a result of external pressure. The external pressure to conform is the need to be accepted by one's peers and the resultant behaviour is to wear similar clothes, adopt similar attitudes and adopt similar behaviour. The external pressure to obey comes from a hierarchy of which one is a member, but in which certain others have more status and power than oneself:

There are at least three important differences. . . . First, in conformity there is no explicit requirement to act in a certain way, whereas in obedience we are ordered or instructed to do something. Second, those who influence us when we conform are our peers (or equals) and people's behaviours become more alike because they are affected by example. In obedience, there is somebody . . . in higher authority influencing behaviour. Third, conformity has to do with the psychological need for acceptance by others. Obedience, by contrast, has to do with the social power and status of an authority figure in a hierarchical situation. (Gross and McIlveen 1998: 508)

We are here concerned only with discipline and grievance within business organisations, but it is worth pointing out that managers are the focal points for the grievances of people outside the business as well, but those grievances are called complaints. Whatever you may complain *about*, you complain *to* a manager.

HR managers make one of their most significant contributions to business effectiveness by facilitating and administering grievance and disciplinary issues. First, they devise and negotiate the procedural framework of organisational justice on which both discipline and grievance depend. Second, they are much involved in the interviews and problem-solving discussions that eventually produce solutions to the difficulties that have been encountered. Third, they maintain the viability of the whole process: they monitor to make sure that grievances are not overlooked and so that any general trend can be perceived, and they oversee the disciplinary machinery to ensure that it is not being bypassed or unfairly manipulated.

Grievance and discipline handling is one of the roles in HRM that few other people want to take over. Ambitious line managers may want to select their own staff without HR intervention or by using the services of consultants. They may try to brush their HR colleagues aside and deal directly with trade union officials or organise their own management development, but grievance and discipline are too hot a potato.

HR people must be both knowledgeable and effective in explaining the requirements regarding grievance handling and the legal framework to avoid unfair dismissal come together to produce a combination that provides a valuable platform for influencing other aspects of management. The HR manager who is not skilled in grievance and discipline is seldom in a strong organisational position.

Everything so far presupposes both hierarchy and the use of procedures. You may say that we have already demonstrated that hierarchy is in decline and that there is a preference for more flexible, personal ways of working than procedure offers. Why rely on Milgram's research, which is now forty years old? Surely we have moved on? Our response is simply that hierarchical relationships continue, although deference is in decline. We still seek out the person 'in authority' when we have a grievance and managers readily refer problems they cannot resolve to someone else with a more appropriate role. Procedures may be rigid and mechanical, but they are reliable and we use them even if we do not like them.

What do we mean by discipline?

Discipline is regulation of human activity to produce a controlled performance. It ranges from the guards' control of a rabble to the accomplishment of lone individuals producing spectacular performance through self-discipline in the control of their own talents and resources.

In *managerial* discipline everything depends on the leader from start to finish. There is a group of people who are answerable to someone who directs what they should all do. Only through individual direction can that group of people produce a worthwhile performance, like the person leading the community singing in the pantomime or the conductor of an orchestra. Everything depends on the leader.

Team discipline is where the quality of the performance depends on the mutual dependence of all, and that mutual dependence derives from a commitment by each member to the total enterprise: the failure of one would be the downfall of all.

This is usually found in relatively small working groups, like a dance troupe or a design team.

Self-discipline is like that of the juggler or the skilled artisan, where a solo performer is absolutely dependent on training, expertise and self-control. One of the few noted UK researchers working in the field of discipline concluded that self-discipline has become much more significant, as demonstrated in the title of his work, 'Discipline: Towards trust and self-discipline' (Edwards 2000).

Discipline is, therefore, not only negative, producing punishment or prevention. It can also be a valuable quality for the individual who is subject to it, although the form of discipline depends not only on the individual employee, but also on the task and the way it is organised. The development of self-discipline is easier in some jobs than others and many of the job redesign initiatives of recent years have been directed at providing scope for job holders to exercise self-discipline and find a degree of autonomy from managerial discipline. However, even the most accomplished solo performer has at some time been dependent on others for training and advice, and every team has a coach.

ACTIVITY 20.1

Note three examples of managerial discipline, team discipline and self-discipline from your own experience.

Managers are not dealing with discipline only when rebuking people or threatening them with dismissal, they are also developing the coordinated discipline of the working team, engendering that *esprit de corps* which makes the whole greater than the sum of the parts. They are training the new recruit who must not let down the rest of the team, puzzling over the reasons why A is fitting in well while B is still struggling. Managers also provide people with the equipment to develop the self-discipline that will give them autonomy, responsibility and the capacity to maximise their powers. The independence and autonomy that self-discipline produces also bring the greatest degree of personal satisfaction, and often the largest pay packet. Furthermore the movement between the three forms represents a declining degree of managerial involvement. If you are a leader of community singing, nothing can happen without your being present and the quality of the singing depends on your performance each time. If you train jugglers, the time and effort you invest pays off a thousand times, while you sit back and watch the show.

There has long been an instinctive tendency to put discipline together with punishment, however limited this notion may be. The legislation on unfair dismissal is to most managers the logical final point of disciplinary procedures, yet it covers dismissal on the grounds of capability and ill health as well as more obvious forms of indiscipline. Because of this general feeling that disciplinary procedures imply disobedience, there is an emerging trend to have separate procedures to cover capability, so as to avoid the stigma, but being unsatisfactory in any way is difficult for many people to cope with. No matter how hard one tries, the prefix 'in-' causes problems. To be indisciplined is unwelcome (and does not actually appear in the dictionary): to be incapable is even worse.

What do we mean by grievance?

We distinguish between the terms 'dissatisfaction', 'complaint' and 'grievance' as follows:

- **Dissatisfaction.** Anything that disturbs an employee, whether or not the unrest is expressed in words.
- **Complaint.** A spoken or written dissatisfaction brought to the attention of a manager or other responsible person. This is the first stage of formal procedure.
- **Grievance.** A complaint that has been formally presented to an appropriate management representative or to a union official.

This categorisation separates out grievance as a formal, relatively drastic step, compared with simply complaining. It is much more important for management to know about dissatisfaction, much of which never turns into complaint, as something happens to make it unnecessary. It evaporates with a night's sleep, after a cup of coffee with a colleague, or when the cause of the dissatisfaction is in some other way removed. The few dissatisfactions that do produce complaint are also most likely to resolve themselves at that stage. The person hearing the complaint explains things in a way that the dissatisfied employee had not previously appreciated, or takes action to get at the root of the problem.

Grievances are rare since few employees will openly question their superior's judgement, whatever their private opinion may be, and fewer still will risk being stigmatised as a troublemaker. Some people do not initiate grievances because they believe nothing will be done. HR managers have to encourage the proper use of procedures to discover sources of dissatisfaction. Managers in the middle may not reveal the complaints they are hearing, for fear of showing themselves in a poor light. Employees who feel insecure, for any reason, are not likely to risk going into procedure, yet the dissatisfaction lying beneath a repressed grievance can produce all manner of unsatisfactory work behaviours from apathy to arson. Individual dissatisfaction can lead to the loss of a potentially valuable employee; collective dissatisfaction can lead to industrial action.

In dealing with complaints it is important to determine what lies behind the complaint; not only verifying the facts, which are the *manifest* content of the complaint, but also determining the feelings behind the facts: the *latent* content. An employee who complains of the supervisor being a bully may actually be expressing something rather different, such as the employee's attitude to any authority figure, not simply the supervisor.

ACTIVITY 20.2

Think of an example from your own experience of dissatisfaction causing inefficiency that was not remedied because there was no complaint. Why was there no complaint?

The framework of organisational justice

The business requires a framework of justice so that managers and supervisors, as well as other employees, know where they stand when dissatisfaction develops. An illustration of this is in Figure 20.1.

Organisation culture and management style

The culture of an organisation develops behavioural norms that are hard to alter and which provide a pattern of conformity. If, for instance, everyone is in the habit of arriving ten minutes late, a manager will struggle to change the habit. Equally, if everyone is in the habit of arriving punctually, then a new recruit who often arrives late will come under strong social pressure to conform, without need for recourse to management action. Culture also affects the freedom and candour with which people discuss dissatisfactions with their managers without allowing them to fester.

The style of managers in handling grievances and discipline reflects their beliefs. The manager who sees discipline narrowly as being punishment, and who regards grievances as examples of subordinates getting above themselves, will behave in a relatively autocratic way, being curt in disciplinary situations and dismissive of complaints. The manager who sees disciplinary problems as obstacles to achievement that do not necessarily imply incompetence or ill will by the employee will seek out the cause of the problem. That problem may then be revealed as one requiring firm, punitive action by the manager, or it may be revealed as a matter requiring management remedy of a different kind. The manager who listens out for complaints and grievances, gets to the bottom of the problems and finds solutions will run little risk of rumbling discontent from people obsessed by trivial problems.

Figure 20.1
The framework of organisational justice

Rules

Every workplace has rules; the difficulty is to have rules that people will honour. Some come from legislation, such as the requirement for drivers to have a licence, but most are tailored to meet the particular requirements of the organisation in which they apply: rules about personal cleanliness are essential in a restaurant but less stringent in a garage.

Rules should be clear and readily understood; the number should be sufficient to cover all obvious and usual disciplinary matters. For general compliance it helps if rules are jointly determined, but it is more common for management to formulate the rules and for employee representatives eventually to concur with them. Employees should have ready access to the rules through the employee handbook and noticeboard, and the HR manager will always try to ensure that the rules are known as well as published.

Rules can be roughly grouped into various types:

1 **Negligence** is failing to do the job properly and is different from incompetence because the employee is capable of doing the job properly, but has not.

2 **Unreliability** is failing to attend work as required, such as being late or absent.

3 **Insubordination** is refusing to obey an instruction, or deliberate disrespect to someone in a position of authority. It is not to be confused with the use of bad language. Some of the most entertaining cases in employment tribunals have involved weighty consideration of whether or not colourful language was intended to be insubordinate or was merely 'customary banter'.

4 **Interfering with others' rights** covers a range of behaviours that are socially unacceptable. Fighting is clearly identifiable, but harassment or intimidation may be more difficult to establish.

5 **Theft** is another clear-cut aspect of behaviour that is unacceptable when it is from another employee. Theft from the organisation should be supported by very explicit rules, as stealing company property is regarded by many offenders as one of the perks of the job. How often have you taken home a box of paper clips or a felt tip pen without any thought that you were stealing from the employer?

6 **Safety offences** are those aspects of behaviour that can cause a hazard.

Rules provide guidelines on what people should do, as the majority will comply. It is extremely difficult to apply rules that do not command general acceptance.

WINDOW ON PRACTICE

In a recent discussion with a group of senior managers, employees identified the following as legitimately taken at will:

- paper clips, pencils, disposable pens, spiral pads, local telephone calls, plain paper, computer CDs, adhesive tape, overalls and simple uniform.

Among the more problematic were:

- **Redundant or shop-soiled stock**. One DIY store insisted that the store manager should personally supervise the scrapping of items that were slightly damaged, to ensure that other items were not slightly damaged on purpose.
- **Surplus materials**. One electricity supplier had some difficulty in eradicating the practice of surplus cable and pipe being regarded as a legitimate perquisite of fitters at the end of installation jobs, as they suspected their engineers were using the surplus for private work. Twelve months later the level of material requisition had declined by 14%.

Ensuring the rules are kept

Rules are only effective if they are observed. How do we ensure that employees obey the rules?

1 **Information.** Everyone must know what the rules are. Most people conform to the behaviour of their colleagues, so informal methods of communication are just as important as formal statements.
2 **Induction.** Rules can be explained, so that people not only know the rules, but also understand why they should be obeyed.
3 **Placement or relocation.** Placing a new recruit with a working team that has high standards of compliance can avoid the risk of rules being broken. If there are signs of disciplinary problems in the offing, then a quick relocation can put the problem employee in a new situation where offences are less likely.
4 **Training.** There will be new working procedures or new equipment from time to time and training, by improving self-confidence and self-discipline, will reduce the risk of safety offences, negligence or unreliability.
5 **Reviewing the rules periodically.** This ensures that the rules are up to date and that their observance is a live issue. The simple fact of the rules being discussed maintains the general level of awareness of what they are.
6 **Penalties.** These make the framework of organisational justice firmer if there is an understanding of what penalties can be imposed, by whom and for what. It is not feasible to have a fixed scale, but neither is it wise for penalties to depend on individual managerial whim. The following are some typical forms of penalty:
   (a) **Rebuke.** The simple 'Don't do that' or 'Smoking is not allowed in here' or 'If you're late again, you will be in trouble' is all that is needed in most situations, as someone has forgotten one of the rules, had not realised it was to be taken seriously, or was perhaps testing the resolution of the management. Too frequently, managers are reluctant to risk defiance and tend to wait until they have a good case for more serious action rather than deploy their own, there-and-then authority.
   (b) **Caution.** Slightly more serious and formal is the caution, which is then recorded. This is not triggering the procedure for dismissal, it is just making a note of a rule being broken and an offence being pointed out.
   (c) **Warnings.** When managers begin to issue warnings, great care is required because unfair dismissal legislation has made the system of warnings an integral part of disciplinary practice, which must be followed if the employer is to succeed in defending a possible claim of unfair dismissal at tribunal. For the employer to show procedural fairness there should normally be a formal oral warning, or a written warning, specifying the nature of the offence and the likely outcome if the offence is repeated. It should also be made clear that this is the first, formal stage in the procedure. Further misconduct could then warrant a final written warning containing a statement that further repetition would lead to a penalty such as suspension or dismissal. All written warnings should be dated, signed and kept on record for an agreed period. The means of appeal against the disciplinary action should also be pointed out.
   (d) **Disciplinary transfer or demotion.** This is moving the employee to less attractive work, possibly carrying a lower salary. The seriousness of this is that it is public, as the employee's colleagues know the reason. A form of disciplinary transfer is found on assembly lines, where there are some jobs that are more attractive and carry higher status than others. Rule breakers may be 'pushed down the line' until their contempt is purged and they are able to move back up.

(e) **Suspension.** This tactic has the benefit of being serious and is not as long lasting as demotion. The employer has a contractual obligation to provide pay, but not to provide work, so it is easy to suspend someone from duty with pay either as a punishment or while an alleged offence is being investigated. It may also be possible to suspend the employee for a short period without pay.

The important general comment about penalties is that they should be appropriate in the circumstances. Where someone is, for instance, persistently late or absent, suspension would be a strange penalty. Also penalties must be within the law. An employee cannot be demoted or transferred at managerial whim, and unpaid suspension can only be imposed if the contract of employment allows it.

Procedural sequence

This is the clear, unvarying logic of procedure, which should be well known and trusted. Procedure makes clear, for example, who does and who does not have the power to dismiss. The dissatisfied employee, who is wondering whether or not to turn a complaint into a formal grievance, knows who will hear the grievance and where an appeal could be lodged. This security of procedure, where step B always follows step A, is also needed by managers, as it defines their authority as well as limiting the scope of their actions.

Although it is essential to get the procedure right, there is also great value simply in its existence as line or operational managers are typically reluctant to get into procedure because of its very rigidity; they much prefer informal methods. Jones and Saundry (2012: 259) illustrate the reluctance of operational managers to move into procedure with this comment by a project manager: 'You're then going into a performance improvement programme which takes six months' worth of little meetings, giving tasks, and if the manager's not willing to spend the time to correct it, they'll just ignore it and let it go.'

In most cases the manager would not 'let it go' but try to resolve the issue informally.

Managerial discipline

This preserves general respect for the justice framework by managers exercising self-discipline in how they work within it. With very good intentions some senior managers maintain an 'open door' policy with the message: 'My door is always open . . . call in any time you feel I can help you.' This has many advantages and is often necessary, but it has dangers for matters of discipline and grievance if it encourages people to bypass middle managers. Also employees come to see the settlement of their grievances as being dependent on the personal goodwill of an individual rather than on the business logic or their human and employment rights.

Managers need consistency in handling discipline and grievance issues. Whatever the rules are, they will be generally supported only as long as they deserve support. If they are enforced inconsistently they lose any moral authority, and will be obeyed only because of employees' fear of penalties. Equally, the manager who handles grievances quickly and consistently will enjoy the support of a committed group of employees.

The other need for managerial discipline is to test the validity of the discipline assumption. Is it a case for disciplinary action or for some other remedy? There is little purpose in suspending someone for negligence when the real problem is lack of training. Many disciplinary problems disappear under analysis, and it is sensible to carry out the analysis before making a possibly unjustified allegation of indiscipline.

Grievance procedure

Some managers resent the formality of grievance procedure, arguing that it introduces unnecessary rigidity into the working relationship: 'I see my people all the time. We work side by side and they can raise with me any issue they want, at any time they want'. The problem is that many people will not raise issues with the immediate superior that could be regarded as contentious, in just the same way that managers frequently shirk the rebuke as a form of disciplinary penalty. Formality in procedure provides a structure within which individuals can reasonably air their grievances and avoids the likelihood of managers dodging the issue when it is difficult. It avoids the risk of inconsistent ad hoc decisions, and the employee knows at the outset that the matter will be heard and where it will be heard. The key features of grievance procedure are fairness, facilities for representation, procedural steps and promptness.

1 **Fairness** is needed, to be just and to keep the procedure viable. If employees believe that the procedure is only a sham, then its value will be lost and they will seek other ways to deal with grievances. Fairness is best supported by the obvious even-handedness of how grievances are handled

2 **Representation** can help the individual employee who lacks the confidence or experience to take on the management single-handedly. A representative, such as a union official, has the advantage of having dealt with a range of employee problems and may be able to advise the aggrieved person whether the claim is worth pursuing. There is always the risk that the presence of the representative may produce a defensive management attitude that is affected by a number of other issues on which the manager and union official may be at loggerheads. Therefore the managers involved in hearing the grievance have to cast the representative in the correct role for the occasion.

3 **Procedural steps** are best limited to three. There is no value in having more just because there are more levels in the management hierarchy. This will lengthen the time taken to deal with matters and may bring the procedure into disrepute. The reason for advocating three steps is that three types of management activity are involved in settling grievances. Nevertheless, it is quite common for there to be more than three steps where there is a steep hierarchy, within which there may be further, more senior, people to whom the matter could be referred. The reason for there being more steps has nothing to do with how to process grievances but is purely a function of the organisation structure.

   • The first step is the *preliminary*, when the grievance is lodged with the immediate superior of the person with the complaint. In the normal working week most managers will have a variety of queries from members of their departments, some of which could become grievances, depending on the manager's reaction. Mostly the manager will satisfy the employee or the employee will decide not to pursue the matter. Sometimes, however, a person will want to take the issue further. This is the preliminary step in procedure, but it is a tangible step as the manager has the opportunity to review any decisions made that have caused the dissatisfaction, possibly enabling the dissatisfied employee to withdraw the grievance. In our experience it is rare for matters to be taken any further unless the subject of the grievance is something on which company policy is being tested.

- The *hearing* gives the complainant the opportunity to state the grievance to a more senior manager, who is able to take a broader view of the matter than the immediate superior and who may be able to see the issue more dispassionately and to perceive solutions that the more limited perspective of the immediate superior obscured. It is important for the management that the hearing should finalise the matter whenever possible, so that recourse to appeal is not automatic. The hearing should not be seen by the employees as no more than an irritating milestone on the way to the real decision makers. This is why ideally procedural steps should be limited to three.

- If there is an *appeal*, this will usually be to a designated more senior manager, and the outcome will be either a confirmation or a modification of the decision at the hearing. This three-step approach has now been incorporated in legislation on dismissal, which requires dismissal to be preceded by these steps, although they are called letter, meeting and appeal.

4 **Promptness** avoids the bitterness and frustration that comes from delay. When an employee 'goes into procedure', the action is not taken lightly and is in anticipation of a swift resolution. Furthermore, the manager whose decision is being questioned will have a difficult time until the matter is resolved. The most familiar device to speed things up is to incorporate time limits between the steps, specifying that the hearing should take place no later than, say, four working days after the preliminary notice and that the appeal should be no more than five working days after the hearing. This gives time for reflection and initiative by the manager or the complainant between the stages, but does not leave time for the matter to be forgotten.

Where the organisation has a collective disputes procedure as well as one for individual grievances, there needs to be an explicit link between the two so that individual matters can be pursued with collective support if there is not a satisfactory outcome. An outline grievance procedure is given in Figure 20.2.

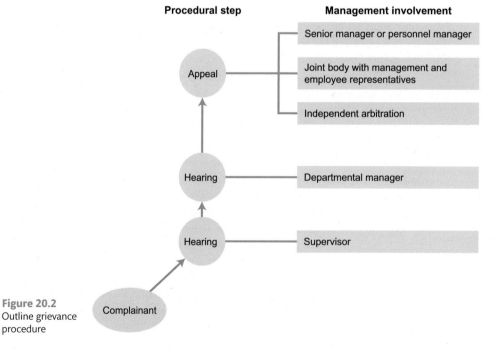

Figure 20.2
Outline grievance
procedure

Disciplinary procedure

Procedures for discipline very similarly depend on fairness, promptness and representation. There are some additional features (Figure 20.3).

Authorisation of penalties

The law requires that managers should not normally be able to dismiss their immediate subordinates without reference to more senior managers. Whatever penalties are to be imposed should only be imposed by people who have that specific authority delegated to them. Usually this means that the more serious penalties are left to more senior people, but there are some businesses where such decisions are delegated to the HR department.

Investigation

The procedure should also ensure that disciplinary action is not taken until before confirming that there is a problem that justifies the action. The possibility of suspension on

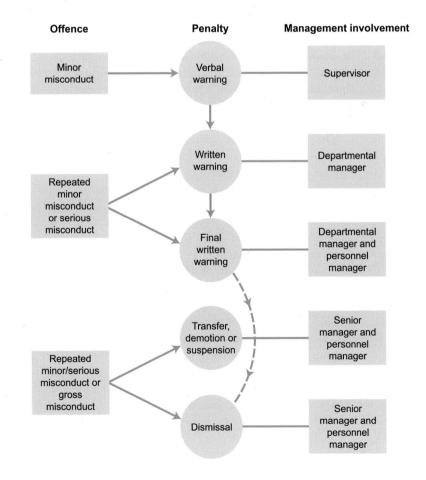

Figure 20.3
Outline
disciplinary
procedure

full pay is one way of allowing time for the investigation of dubious allegations, but the stigma attached to such suspensions should not be forgotten.

Information and explanation

If disciplinary action is possible, the person to be disciplined should be told of the complaint, so that an explanation can be made, or the matter denied, before any penalties are decided. If an employee is to be penalised, then the reasons for the decision should be explained to make sure that cause and effect are appreciated. The purpose of penalties is to prevent a recurrence.

Are grievance and discipline processes equitable?

For grievance and discipline processes to work they must command support, and they will only command support if they are seen as equitable, truly just and fair. At first it may seem that concern for the individual employee is paramount, but the individual cannot be isolated from the rest of the workforce. Fairness should therefore be linked to the interests that all workers have in common in the business, and to the managers who must also perceive the system as equitable if they are to abide by its outcomes.

Procedures have a potential to be fair in that they are certain. The conduct of employee relations becomes less haphazard and irrational: people 'know where they stand'. The existence of a rule cannot be denied and opportunities for one party to manipulate and change a rule are reduced. Procedures also have the advantage that they can be communicated. Formalising a procedure that previously existed only in custom and practice clarifies the ambiguities and inconsistencies within it and compels each party to recognise the role and responsibility of the other. By providing pre-established avenues for responses to various contingencies, procedures make it possible for the response to be less random and so more fair. The impersonal nature of procedures offers the possibility of removing hostility from the workplace.

The achievement of equity may not match the potential. Procedures cannot, for instance, impart equity to situations that are basically unfair. Thus attempting to cope with an anomalous pay system through a grievance procedure may be alleviating symptoms rather than treating causes. It is also impossible through a grievance procedure to overcome accepted norms of inequity in a company, such as greater punctuality being required of manual employees than of white-collar employees.

All procedures adopt certain legalistic mechanisms, such as the right of individuals to be represented and to hear the case against them, but some aspects of legalism, such as burdens of proof and strict adherence to precedent, may cause the application of standard remedies rather than the consideration of individual circumstances.

There is a nice irony in the fact that equity is best achieved when procedures are not used. Procedure is there in the background and expresses principles for fair and effective management of situations. All the time that the **principles** are followed and the framework for organisational justice is observed, procedure is not invoked. The advantage of this is that individuals, whether employees or managers, are not named and shamed so that matters are much easier to deal with. Only when the matter is dealt with badly does the procedural step come closer.

WINDOW ON PRACTICE

The 'red-hot stove' rule of discipline offers the touching of a red-hot stove as an analogy for effective disciplinary action:

1 The burn is immediate. There is no question of cause and effect.

2 You had warning. If the stove was red hot, you knew what would happen if you touched it.

3 The discipline is consistent. Everyone who touches the stove is burnt.

4 The discipline is impersonal. People are burnt not because of who they are, but because they touch the stove.

ACTIVITY 20.3

Think of an attempt at disciplinary action that went wrong. Which of the features of the red-hot stove rule were missing?

Notions of fairness are not 'givens' of the situation; they are socially constructed and there will never be more than a degree of consensus on what constitutes fairness. Despite this, the procedural approach can exploit standards of certainty and consistency, which are widely accepted as elements of justice

SUMMARY PROPOSITIONS

20.1 The authority of managers to exercise discipline in relation to others in the organisation is underpinned by a general predilection of people to obey commands from those holding higher rank in the hierarchy of which they are members.

20.2 The exercise of that discipline is limited by the procedural structures for grievance and discipline.

20.3 Grievance and discipline handling are two areas of HRM that few other people want to take over, and provide HR managers with some of their most significant contributions to business effectiveness.

20.4 Discipline can be understood as being managerial, team or self-discipline, and the three types are connected hierarchically.

20.5 Dissatisfaction, complaint and grievance form another hierarchy. Unresolved employee dissatisfaction can lead to the loss of potentially valuable employees. In extreme cases it can lead to industrial action.

20.6 Grievance and disciplinary processes both require a framework of organisational justice.

20.7 The procedural framework of disciplinary and grievance processes is one of the keys to their being equitable.

20.8 Effective management of both discipline and grievance is achieved by following the principles of the procedures without necessarily invoking them in practice.

GENERAL DISCUSSION TOPICS

1 What examples can individual members of the group cite of self-discipline, team discipline and managerial discipline?

2 'The trouble with grievance procedures is that they encourage people to waste a lot of time with petty grumbles. Life at work is rarely straightforward and people should just accept the rough with the smooth.'

What do you think of that opinion?

THEORY INTO PRACTICE

EITHER

The Milgram experiments – what is their contemporary relevance to HR?

This chapter has relied heavily on the work of Stanley Milgram, first published in *The Journal of Abnormal Psychology* in 1963. In view of all the social changes that have taken place since then, is there still any relevance to the twenty-first-century world?

What has this to do with HR anyway? Here are some more points about the study.

Milgram was strongly criticised for deceiving the subjects in his experiments, many of whom were distressed by the experience. He was also criticised for 'explaining away' Nazi atrocities in the Holocaust, especially as he was a Jew (e.g. Baumrind 1964). The validity of his analysis is now a standard feature of the study of psychology, although its cogency is slightly muted by the studies of conformity by Asch, which Milgram accepted. Due to the notoriety of the experiment, it was never seriously repeated. His 1974 book is still in print and is fascinating reading.

The 2010 series of experiments (Nick and Eltchaninoff 2010) made no claim to academic rigour or validity. They were simply a device for a popular TV programme. Nevertheless they produced an incredible level of compliance to instructions to virtually electrocute a human being. The authority figure issuing the instructions in the TV studio was very different from the bearded, bespectacled figure in a white coat in the 'elegant interaction laboratory at Yale University'. However, the incentive was a moment of fame rather than $4.50, including 50 cents car fare. Milgram's subjects were American men aged between 20 and 50. The French volunteers were of both sexes.

Questions

1 How do you understand the agentic state and to what extent do you think that you and your work colleagues will do things you dislike or the reasons for which you think are invalid, providing that someone else accepts the responsibility for your actions?

2 If you, as an HR person, had to deliver a message that you knew would be unwelcome to your audience, such as a pay freeze, would you 'sell' it or would you disclaim any responsibility, 'I don't agree with this, but I've been instructed to tell you that . . .'?

3 Some years ago an American, Scott Myers, expressed a common managerial uncertainty in a paper 'If I'm in charge why is everybody laughing?'. To what extent do you recognise that anxiety?

OR

Who is in charge anyway?

Reread the first six pages of this chapter and then read the article by Jones and Saundry (2012), which describes a small piece of research examining the relationship between HR and operational managers on matters of discipline in light of the current emphasis on operational managers taking responsibility for disciplinary issues, with HR to monitor and advise. It also refers to the long-standing dream by HR people to have a strategic role in the business.

Questions

1 Does the article describe a place for HR in discipline that will contribute to their having a distinct and useful role in discussing and formulating strategy with other senior managers?

2 The article describes the view of one of the interviewees that in a disciplinary situation an operational manager would not want to devote the time and energy involved in a programme of performance improvement and would just 'let it go'. What are the implications of that attitude?

3 This chapter has had a theme of seeing discipline and grievance as both being a means of solving problems before the extremes of dismissing the employee or the employee resigning.
    After reading the article do you agree with this attitude to discipline, or do you feel it is really always punishment?

FURTHER READING

Advisory, Conciliation and Arbitration Service (2011) *Code of Practice on Disciplinary Practice and Grievance Procedures at Work*. London: The Stationery Office.

BIS (2009) *Avoiding and Resolving Discipline and Grievance Issues at Work*. London: Department for Business Innovation and Skills.

CIPD (2012) *Discipline and Grievances at Work*. London: Chartered Institute of Personnel and Development.

Each of these sets out the current legal situation in the UK about the two central issues, taking slightly different perspectives.

Taylor. S., and Emir, A (2012) *Employment Law*, 3rd edn. Oxford: Oxford University Press, chapters 13 and 14.

This standard text is a comprehensive account of UK employment law and the chapters suggested deal with the background to the material in this chapter.

REFERENCES

Abrams, D., Wetherell, M., Cochrane, S., Hogg, M.A. and Turner, J.C. (1990) 'Knowing what to think by knowing who you are: Self categorisation and norm formation', *British Journal of Social Psychology*, Vol. 29, pp. 97–119.

Asch, S.E. (1951) 'Effect of group pressure upon the modification and distortion of judgements', in H. Guetzkow (ed.), *Groups, Leadership and Men*. Pittsburgh, PA: Carnegie Press.

Baumrind, D. (1964) 'Some thoughts on ethics of research after reading Milgram's "Behavioural study of obedience"', *American Psychologist*, Vol. 19, pp. 421–3.

Edwards, P. (2000) 'Discipline: Towards trust and self-discipline', in S. Bach and K. Sisson (eds), *Personnel Management*, 3rd edn. Oxford: Blackwell.

Gross, R. and McIlveen, R. (1998) *Psychology: A new introduction*. London: Hodder & Stoughton.

Jones, C. and Saundry, R. (2012) 'The practice of discipline: Evaluating the roles and relationship between managers and H.R. professionals', *Human Resource Management Journal*, Vol. 22, No. 3, pp. 252–66.

Milgram, S. (1963) 'Behavioural study of obedience' *Journal of Abnormal Psychology*, Vol. 67, pp. 372–8.

Milgram, S. (1974) *Obedience to Authority*. London: Tavistock.

Milgram, S. (1992) *The Individual in a Social World*, 2nd edn. New York: Harper & Row.

Nick, C. and Eltchaninoff, M. (2010) *L'Experience Extreme*. Paris: Don Quichotte.

Part 6

REWARD: THE CONTRACT FOR PAYMENT

CHANGING TIMES
RESOURCING
PERFORMANCE
DEVELOPMENT
EMPLOYEE RELATIONS
REWARD

Strategy
Salaries
Incentives
Pensions and benefits
Skills

Reward is clearly central to the employment relationship. Although there are plenty of people who enjoy working and who claim that they would not stop working even if they were to win a big cash prize in a lottery, most of us work in large part because it is our only means of earning the money we need to sustain us and our families in the style to which we are accustomed. How much we are paid and in what form is therefore an issue which matters hugely to us. These questions are also central ones for the HRM function because money spent on salaries, benefits and other forms of reward typically accounts for well over half an organisation's total costs. For commercial organisations it is thus a major determinant of both profitability and competitive advantage. In the public sector the cost of rewarding staff is determined by, and in turn helps determine, the level of taxes that we pay.

For these reasons, to a greater extent than is the case in other areas of HR practice, the management of reward is heavily constrained by the financial position of the organisation. The aim is to design competitive reward packages which serve to attract, retain and motivate staff, while at the same time keeping a lid on the costs so as to ensure the organisation's commercial and financial viability. This is not an easy task, and it is made harder because of the great significance that employees themselves attach to their pay, and particularly to the level of pay they receive vis-à-vis other people. Getting it wrong has major, negative consequences, because it can demotivate in quite serious ways, leading to the departure of good performers, higher absence levels, less effort and the deterioration of the organisation's employee relations climate. Over time, of course, these too serve to reduce an organisation's effectiveness and damage its financial performance.

As markets for goods and services become more competitive and global, the extent to which employers are able to use payment systems as a means of achieving their HR objectives is increasingly constrained. Profit margins are tighter than they used to be in most industries, making it less possible than it once was to tackle skills shortages or to raise the quality of job applications simply by increasing the salaries on offer. The need to restrain labour costs is particularly significant in the public sector as, in recent years, governments have cut their expenditure in order to reduce high levels of public debt. As a result employers are having to think more creatively and more broadly about the rewards that they offer, looking for ways of motivating and retaining valued staff, without increasing their pay bills. For these reasons the concept of 'total reward' has become attractive and significant in recent years. This involves thinking about the reward package in a very broad sense, not only the aspects that involve payment, but a range of other elements too. Organisations may be increasingly constrained in terms of how much more they can pay someone, but there is a good deal less constraint when it comes to providing them with career development opportunities, flexible working patterns or even a stimulating and pleasant working environment.

The other major contemporary development in this field of HR practice is the increasing prominence in many organisations of well-articulated reward strategies. Over time managers are taking a less reactive approach to the management of their payment systems. Increasingly they are thinking about how the approaches they use to rewarding staff can be designed so as to achieve specific longer-term objectives. If increasing the level of skills in the organisation is a priority, the response is thus to make salary progression or bonus payments conditional on the attainment of new or increased skills. By contrast, where the overriding aim is to increase productivity, payment systems are developed which reward people or teams for the quantity of their output. Reward strategies are thus about encouraging a confluence of interest between employees and the organisation.

This approach has often been described as 'the new pay' by researchers working in the field of reward management (see Druker and White 2009), and this is an appropriate label because it is only over the past two or three decades that reward management has attained a strategic dimension in the generality of organisations. In the UK change started in the private sector during the 1980s, later becoming prevalent in many public-sector organisations too. It was associated with the decline in trade union influence we introduced earlier (see Part 5), and in particular with the breaking down of the national collective bargaining system. In the recent past managers in many organisations were thus restricted to deciding who should be employed on which grade, how they should progress up the grade hierarchy, what should be paid by way of an annual increment and how much overtime they worked. In the UK, as in many other countries, this system of multi-employer bargaining declined steeply during the 1980s and 1990s, so that by 2004 only 36% of public-sector employees and just 1% of those employed in the private sector had their pay determined by such arrangements (Kersley *et al*. 2006: 184), figures which have declined further in more recent years (van Wanrooy *et al*, 2013: 22).

In this part of the book we explore the major elements that make up the reward package, including an introduction to 'total reward' thinking. We will look first at how salaries are determined and at how organisations go about deciding how much each employee should be paid in comparison with others (Chapter 21). Our focus will then turn to incentives and bonus payments of one kind or another (Chapter 23) and to pensions and benefits (Chapter 24).

REFERENCES

Druker, J. and White, G. (2009) 'Introduction', in G. White and J. Druker (eds), *Reward Management: A critical text*, 2nd edn. London: Routledge.

Kersley, B., Alpin, C., Forth, J., Bryson, A., Bewley, H., Dix, G. and Oxenbridge, S. (2006) *Inside the Workplace: Findings from the 2004 Workplace Employment Relations Survey*. Abingdon: Routledge.

Van Wanrooy, B., Bewley, H., Bryson, A., Forth, J., Freeth, S., Stokes, L. and Wood, S. (2013) *The 2011 Workplace Employment Relations Study: First findings*. London: Department for Business, Innovation and Science.

Chapter 21

SETTING PAY

THE OBJECTIVES OF THIS CHAPTER ARE TO:

1 Set out the different elements that can make up a reward package

2 Evaluate the alternative methods of setting base pay rates

3 Explore major current developments in the management of salary progression systems

4 Explain the concept of 'total reward' and the reasons for its increasing prominence

Introducing reward management

It is helpful to think about reward management in terms of two key decisions:

1 How much should we pay each person in our organisation?
2 How should the payment package be made up?

These are among the most important decisions HR managers have to take because they have such significant outcomes. On the one hand they are a major determinant of organisational profitability vis-à-vis competitors and may help determine whether an organisation thrives or even survives. On the other they also help determine the standard of living that individual employees are able to enjoy, the choices they are able to make about how they and their families live their lives, when they can retire and how many hours a week they are obliged to work. Importantly they also play a large part in determining whether employees are motivated at work and prepared to demonstrate discretionary effort. When poor decisions about pay are made the result is demotivation, higher levels of absence, reduced productivity and an increased chance that an adversarial, low-trust employee relations climate will develop. Finally, of course, these decisions are crucial to an organisation's ability to recruit and retain effective staff in competitive labour markets. Organisations are obliged to compete with one another for good staff as well as for customers, and as Charles Cotton points out in a CIPD survey of reward practices, 'respondents report that employees can be just as discerning as their customers in what they want from their employer' (CIPD 2007: 33). In tight labour markets, where it is harder to recruit and retain the best-qualified people, more pressure there is placed on employers to develop reward packages that suit employees as much as they suit their own needs. By contrast, where labour markets are loose and the skills that employers need to source are in plentiful supply, competitive pressure tends to force wage levels down.

For these reasons great care must be taken when answering the two core questions set out above, and it makes sense to think about how they should be answered in strategic terms. This leads us to asking and looking for answers to a range of further questions:

- What are we seeking to achieve in designing or in redesigning our payment systems?
- What are our competitors doing?
- How do we wish to position ourselves as an employer so as to compete effectively in the labour market?
- What constraints do we face when designing our reward systems?
- How can we avoid demotivating employees when making decisions about how much and in what way we pay them?
- To what extent should employees or their representatives be involved in helping to determine who is paid how much and in what form?

According to Armstrong and Brown (2009: 34) there are four key components in a written reward strategy. First of all there needs to be a statement of intentions setting out, in general terms, what the reward strategy of the organisation is seeking to achieve and which reward initiatives have been chosen in order to achieve these core objectives.

Second, these ideas are expanded through a more detailed 'rationale', which explains the objectives in greater depth and shows how the various elements that form the organisation's reward policy support the achievement of those objectives. In effect this amounts to a statement of the business case that underpins the strategy. To that end the rationale should include costings, a statement of the benefits that will accrue, and an indication of the means that will be used to evaluate its success. The third element is an explanation of the guiding principles or values that have been used in developing the initiatives and will be used to adapt them in the future. Typically this will include statements which deal with ethical issues or which reiterate a commitment to core principles such as equality between men and women, fair dealing or rewarding exceptional individual performance. The final component is an implementation plan, setting out exactly what initiatives are being brought forward and when, who has responsibility for their introduction and what their cost will be.

ACTIVITY 21.1

Consider the following list of jobs and job holders. In each case think about how much you think each currently receives annually in basic pay (i.e. excluding benefits, overtime, bonuses, etc.) and about how much you think each *should* be paid. Make a list of the key criteria you are using in making your decisions.

Primary school head teacher

The Prime Minister

Private soldier

Chief Executive of British Telecom

Newly qualified junior doctor

Experienced firefighter

Lollipop lady/man

Wayne Rooney

The elements of payment

The payment of any individual employee will be made up of one or more elements from those shown in Table 21.1. Fixed elements are those that make up the regular weekly or monthly payment to the individual, and which do not vary other than in exceptional circumstances. Variable elements can be varied by either the employee or the employer.

Table 21.1
The potential
elements of
payment

Bonus	Profit allocation Discretionary sum	**Variable elements** • Irregular
Incentive	Group calculation basis Individual calculation basis	• Variable amount • Usually discretionary
Overtime payment		
Premia	Occasional Contractual	

Benefits	Fringe benefits
	Payments in kind Other
	                        Accommodation
	                        Car
		Fixed elements
		• Regular
		• Rarely variable
		• Usually contractual

	Benefit schemes Other
	                      Pension
	                      Sick pay	

Plussage	'Fudge' payments Special additions	
Basic rate of payment		Basic

Basic rate

The irreducible minimum rate of pay is the basic. In some cases this is the standard rate also, not having any additions made to it. In other cases it is a basis on which earnings are built by the addition of one or more of the other elements in payment.

Plussage

Sometimes the basic has an addition to recognise an aspect of working conditions or employee capability. Payments for educational qualifications and for supervisory responsibilities are quite common.

Benefits

Extras to the working conditions that have a cash value are categorised as benefits and can be of great variety. The most common are company cars, subsidised meals, childcare vouchers, private health insurance, staff discounts and occupational pensions.

Premia

Where employees work at inconvenient times – or on shifts or permanently at night – they receive a premium payment as compensation for the inconvenience. Sometimes this is built into the basic rate or is a regular feature of the contract of employment so that the payment is unvarying. In other situations shift working is occasional and short-lived, making the premium a variable element of payment.

Overtime

It is customary for employees working more hours than are normal for the working week to be paid for those hours at an enhanced rate, usually between 10% and 50% more that the normal rate according to how many hours are involved. Overtime is earned by 19% of full-time workers in the UK (National Statistics 2012: 25). Where overtime is paid it can account for a major portion of an individual's gross pay.

Incentive

Incentives are elements of payment linked to the working performance of an individual or working group, usually as a result of prior arrangement. This includes payment by results schemes that reward people for the quantity of their output (e.g. sales commission) as well as other forms of performance-based payment. Incentives are paid to 58% of employees in the UK private sector, compared with only 22% in the public sector (van Wanrooy *et al*. 2013: 25).

Bonus

A different type of variable payment is the gratuitous payment by the employer that is not directly earned by the employee: a bonus. The essential difference between this and an incentive is that the employee has no entitlement to the payment as a result of a contract of employment and cannot be assured of receiving it in return for a specific performance. The most common example of this is the Christmas bonus.

ACTIVITY 21.2

If you could design your own 'remuneration package' which could be made up from any of the items in Table 21.1, what proportion of each item would you choose and why? Does your answer suggest ideas for further development of salary policies?

Setting base pay

One of the most important decisions in the development of reward strategies concerns the mechanism or mechanisms that will be used to determine the basic rate of pay for different jobs in the organisation. In practice employers enjoy rather less freedom when making this decision than is the case when deciding how the total package should be made up. There are two main reasons for this:

1 In many countries the law imposes restrictions directly through the operation of a national minimum wage (£6.19 an hour in the UK in 2013) and indirectly through the operation of equal pay law (see Chapter 18). Moreover, in many countries incomes

policies are operated as tools of inflation control. These restrict the amount of additional pay that people can receive in any one year while remaining in the same job.

2   There is a limit on how much any employer can afford to pay if it is to remain competitive in its industry. On the other hand there is a limit below which it becomes impossible to attract or retain people with the required skills and experience. Hence, as Gerhart (2009: 225) points out, product and labour market pressures effectively set a ceiling and a floor to overall pay levels for any one job or individual.

It is possible, notwithstanding the above restrictions, to identify four principal mechanisms for the determination of base pay. They are not entirely incompatible, although one tends to be used as the main approach in most organisations.

External market comparisons

In making external market comparisons the focus is on the need to recruit and retain staff, a rate being set which is broadly equivalent to 'the going rate' for the job in question. The focus is thus on **external relativities**. Research suggests that this is always a major contributing factor when organisations set pay rates, but that it increases in significance higher up the income scale. Some employers consciously pay over the market rate in order to secure the services of the most talented employees. Others 'follow the market', by paying below the going rate while using other mechanisms such as flexibility, job security or longer-term incentives to ensure effective recruitment and retention. In either case the decision is based on an assessment of what rate needs to be paid to compete for staff in different types of labour market. Going rates are more significant for some than for others. Accountants and craftworkers, for instance, tend to identify with an external employee grouping. Their assessment of pay levels is thus greatly influenced by the going rate in the trade or the district. A similar situation exists with jobs that are clearly understood and where skills are readily transferable, particularly if the employee is to work with a standard piece of equipment. Driving heavy goods vehicles is an obvious example, as the vehicles are common from one employer to another, the roads are the same, and only the loads vary. Other examples are secretaries, switchboard operators and computer operators. Jobs that are less sensitive to the labour market are those that are organisationally specific, such as much semi-skilled work in manufacturing, general clerical work and nearly all middle management positions.

There are several possible sources of intelligence about market rates for different job types at any one time. A great deal of information can be found in published journals such as the pay bulletins issued by Incomes Data Services (IDS) and Industrial Relations Services (IRS), focusing on the hard-to-recruit groups such as computer staff. More detailed information can be gained by joining one of the major salary survey projects operated by firms of consultants or by paying for access to their datasets. Information on specific types of job, including international packages for expatriate workers, is collected by specialised consultants and can be obtained on payment of the appropriate fee. In addition there are more informal approaches such as looking at pay rates included in recruitment advertisements in newspapers, at job centres and on Web-based job-board sites. New staff, notably HR people, often bring with them a knowledge of pay rates for types of job in competitor organisations and can be a useful source of information. Finally, it is possible to join or set up salary clubs. These consist of groups of employers, often based in the same locality, who agree to share salary information for mutual benefit.

Internal labour market mechanisms

Just as there is a labour market of which the company is a part, so there is a labour market within the organisation which also needs to be managed so as to ensure effective performance. According to Doeringer and Piore (1970), there are two kinds of internal labour market: the enterprise and the craft. The enterprise market is so called because the individual enterprise defines the boundaries of the market itself. Such will be the market encompassing manual workers engaged in production processes, for whom the predominant pattern of employment is one in which jobs are formally or informally ranked, with the jobs accorded the highest pay or prestige usually being filled by promotion from within and those at the bottom of the hierarchy usually being filled only from outside the enterprise. It is, therefore, those at the bottom that are most sensitive to the external labour market. Doeringer and Piore point out that there is a close parallel with managerial jobs, the main ports of entry being from management trainees or supervisors, and the number of appointments from outside gradually reducing as jobs become more senior. This modus operandi is one of the main causes of the problems that redundant executives face.

Recent US research has stressed the importance of this kind of internal labour market in determining pay rates. Here the focus is on **internal differentials** rather than external relativities. An interesting metaphor used is that of the sports tournament in which an organisation's pay structure is likened to the prize distribution in a knock-out competition such as is found, for example, at the Wimbledon Tennis Championships. Here the prize money is highest for the winner, somewhat lower for the runner-up, lower again for the semi-final losers and so on down the rounds. The aim, from the point of view of the tournament organisers, is to attract the best players to compete in the first round, then subsequently to give players in later rounds an incentive to play at their peak. According to Lazear (1995: 26–33), the level of base pay for each level in an organisation's hierarchy should be set according to similar principles. The level of pay for any particular job is thus set at a level which maximises performance lower down the hierarchy among employees competing for promotion. The actual performance of the individual receiving the pay is less important.

The second type of internal labour market identified by Doeringer and Piore is the craft market, where barriers to entry are relatively high, typically involving the attainment of a formal qualification. However, once workers are established in the market, seniority and hierarchy become unimportant as jobs and duties are shared among the individuals concerned. Such arrangements are usually determined by custom and practice, but are difficult to break down because of the vested interests of those who have successfully completed their period of apprenticeship. Certain pay rates are expected by those who have achieved the required qualification and it is accepted by everyone that this is a fair basis for rewarding people.

Job evaluation

Job evaluation involves the establishment of a system which is used to measure the size and significance of all jobs in an organisation. It results in each job being scored with a number of points, establishing in effect a hierarchy of all the jobs in the organisation ranging from those which require the most knowledge and experience and which carry a great deal of responsibility to those which require least knowledge and experience and require the job holder to carry relatively low levels of responsibility. Each job is then assimilated to an appropriate grade and payment distributed accordingly. The focus is thus on the relative worth of jobs within an organisation and on comparisons between these rather than on external relativities and comparisons with rates being paid by other employers. Fairness and objectivity are the core principles, an organisation's wage budget being divided among employees on the basis of an assessment of the nature and size of the job each is employed to carry out.

Usage of job evaluation has increased in recent years. It is currently used by almost 40% of organisations in the UK, and by a higher proportion still in larger ones (CIPD 2012: 20). It is a well-established technique, having been developed in all its most common forms by the 1920s. In recent years it has received a series of boosts. First, various types of incomes policy between 1965 and 1974 either encouraged the introduction of job evaluation or specifically permitted expenditure above the prevailing norm by companies wishing to introduce it. In the 1980s the use of job evaluation became the hinge of most equal pay cases. More recently organisations have found it useful as part of moves towards single-status contractual arrangements and resolving pay issues following organisational mergers. Much of the recent growth has been in the public sector, local authorities and the NHS being examples of major employers establishing new schemes, but the surveys suggest that job evaluation is very widely used in the private sector as well. Moreover, few organisations abandon it, once introduced. The maxim that 'job evaluation is the one management tool that refuses to go out of fashion' thus continues to hold true.

Despite its popularity it is often misunderstood, so the following points have to be made:

- Job evaluation is concerned with the job and not the performance of the individual job holder. Individual merit is not assessed.

- The technique is systematic rather than scientific. It depends on the judgement of people with experience, requiring them to decide in a planned and systematic way, but it does not produce results that are infallible.

- Job evaluation does not eliminate collective bargaining where trade unions are recognised. It determines the differential gaps between incomes; it does not determine pay levels or annual pay rises.

- Only a structure of pay rates is produced. Other elements of earnings, such as premia and incentives, are not determined by the method.

There are many methods of job evaluation in use and they are summarised by Armstrong and Murlis (2007: 129–64). Where a non-analytical or 'whole job' scheme is used a panel of assessors examines each job as a whole, in terms of its difficulty or value to the business, to determine which should be ranked more highly than others. No attempt is made to break down each job into its constituent parts. By contrast, an analytical scheme requires each element or factor of the job to be assessed. Since 1988 it has been the practice of courts only to accept the results of analytical schemes in equal pay cases. The most widely used analytical schemes are based on points-rating systems, under which each job is examined in terms of factors such as skill, effort and responsibility. Each factor is given a weighting indicating its value relative to the others and for each factor there are varying degrees. A score is then given depending on how demanding the job is in terms of each factor, with the overall points value determining the relative worth of each job – hence its grade in the organisation's pay structure.

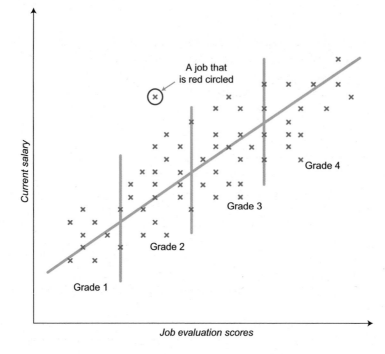

A job that
is red circled

Current salary

Grade 4

Grade 3

Grade 2

Grade 1

Job evaluation scores

Figure 21.1
Job evaluation
analysis

In recent years there has been great growth in the use of highly sophisticated computer-assisted job evaluation systems marketed by leading firms of consultants which award scores to each job on the basis of information gathered from job analysis questionnaires.

The points values eventually derived for each job can be plotted on a graph or simply listed from the highest to the lowest to indicate the ranking. Then – and only then – are points ratings matched with cash amounts, as decisions are made on which points ranges equate with various pay grades. This process is illustrated in Figure 21.1, each cross representing a job. The most common approach involves using a graph on which one axis represents the *current salary* for each job evaluated and the other the number of *job evaluation points* awarded. A line of best fit is then drawn and each job assigned to a grade. Salary-modelling software is widely available to help with this process.

It is virtually inevitable that some jobs will be found to be paid incorrectly after job evaluation has been completed. If the evaluation says that the pay rate should be higher then the rate duly rises, either immediately or step by step, to the new level. The only problem is finding the money, and introducing job evaluation always costs money. More difficult is the situation where evaluation shows the employee to be overpaid. It is not feasible to reduce the pay of the job holder without breaching the contract of employment. There have been two approaches. The first is buying out. The overpaid employee is offered a large lump sum in consideration of the fact of henceforth being paid at the new, lower rate. The second device used is that of the personal rate or red circling, so called because the job is circled in red on the job evaluation chart. The outcome is that current job holders continue to be paid at the present level, but their successors are paid at the lower job-evaluated rate.

Collective bargaining

The fourth approach involves determining pay rates through collective negotiations with trade unions or other employee representatives. Forty years ago this was the dominant method used for determining pay in the UK, negotiations commonly occurring at industry level. The going rates for each job group were thus set nationally and were adhered to by all companies operating in the sector concerned. Recent decades have seen a steady erosion of these arrangements, collective bargaining being decentralised to company or plant level in the manufacturing sector, where it survives at all. Meanwhile the rise of service sector organisations with lower union membership levels has ensured that collective bargaining arrangements now cover only a minority of UK workers. According to van Wanrooy *et al.* (2013: 22) only 23% now have any of their terms and conditions determined in this way, collective bargaining over any kind of issue continuing in only 13% of workplaces. The experience of many other countries is similar, but there remain regions such as Eastern Europe and Scandinavia where collective bargaining remains a major determinant of pay rates. Where separate clusters of employees within the same organisation are placed in different bargaining groups and represented by different unions, internal relativities become an issue for resolution during bargaining.

In carrying out negotiations the staff and management sides make reference to external labour market rates, established internal pay determination mechanisms and the size of jobs. However, a host of other factors come into the equation too as each side deploys its best arguments. Union representatives, for example, make reference to employee need when house prices are rising and affordable accommodation is hard to find. Both sides refer to the balance sheet, employers arguing that profit margins are too tight to afford substantial rises, while union counterparts seek to gain a share of any increased profits for employees. However good the case made, what ultimately makes collective bargaining different from the other approaches is the presence of industrial muscle. Strong unions which have the support of the majority of employees, as is the case in many public-sector organisations, are able to ensure that their case is heard and taken into account. They can thus sometimes 'secure' a better pay deal for their members than market rates would allow.

ACTIVITY 21.3

Which of the four mechanisms outlined above do you think is usually most efficient for setting the following?

- Base pay
- Annual cost of living increases
- Executive remuneration packages
- Bonus schemes

The importance of equity

Whatever methods are used to determine pay levels and to decide what elements make up the individual pay package, employers must ensure that they are perceived by employees to operate equitably. It has long been established that perceived inequity in payment matters can be highly damaging to an organisation. Classic studies undertaken by Adams (1963) found that a key determinant of satisfaction at work is the extent to which employees judge pay levels and pay increases to be distributed fairly. These led to the development by Adams and others of equity theory, which holds that we are very concerned that rewards or 'outputs' equate to our 'inputs' (defined as skill, effort, experience, qualifications, etc.) and that these are fair when compared with the rewards being given to others. Where we believe that we are not being fairly rewarded we show signs of 'dissonance' or dissatisfaction which leads to absence, voluntary turnover, on-job shirking and low-trust employee relations. It is therefore important that an employer not only treats employees equitably in payment matters, but is *seen* to do so too.

While it is difficult to gain general agreement about who should be paid what level of salary in an organisation, it is possible to employ certain clear principles when making decisions in the pay field. Those that are most important are the following:

- a standard approach for the determination of pay (basic rates and incentives) across the organisation;
- as little subjective or arbitrary decision making as is feasible;
- maximum communication and employee involvement in establishing pay determination mechanisms;
- clarity in pay determination matters so that everyone knows what the rules are and how they will be applied.

These are the foundations of procedural fairness or 'fair dealing'. In establishing pay rates it is not always possible to distribute rewards fairly to everyone's satisfaction, but it should always be possible to do so using procedures which operate equitably.

WINDOW ON PRACTICE

Countries vary considerably in terms of how much different groups are paid, some being a good deal more equal than others in terms of how organisations pay people at different levels and how far income is subsequently redistributed via taxation and state benefits.

International statistics on inequality are published each year by the United Nations in its *Human Development Reports*. The level of equality in a society is measured using the Gini coefficient, an internationally accepted measurement tool. It operates on a scale of 0–100. Were a country to be reported as having a Gini coefficient of 100 it would mean that all the wealth was in the hands of a single individual (i.e. as unequal as it is possible to be). By contrast, a Gini coefficient of 0 would indicate a society in which all wealth was distributed wholly equally between everyone. The reported figures for 2012 show that the most unequal country in the world (or at least the most unequal country that reports its figures to the UN) was Namibia with a Gini coefficient of 70.7. Other African countries also report very high levels of inequality as do most countries in South America. Among the western industrialised countries the most unequal is the USA (Gini coefficient of 45), the UK following behind with a figure of 36. By contrast some Northern European countries are a great deal more equal. The Gini coefficient in Sweden was just 23, Denmark also being very equal with a figure of 24. Japan and Germany also come close to the top of the equality table.

Although wealth varies across international borders for many reasons, the level of pay plays a major part. The same patterns are reflected in the figures on pay equity in industrialised countries published regularly by the OECD. One measure that it uses is the difference between the gross male full-time average earnings of the top and bottom deciles in a population.

According to the most recent OECD statistics, dating from 2010, the difference in the USA is 5.01, meaning that the top 10% earned just over five times more than the bottom 10%. In the UK the difference in 2010 was 3.6, in Germany it was 3.2 and in France 2.9. Here too the lowest figures are reported in Scandinavian countries: in Finland it was 2.5, and in Sweden only 2.2.

While the precise figures for each country fluctuate from year to year, the overall pattern across most of the world during the past thirty years has been towards greater inequality as measured by both these indices.

Sources: OECD Employment Database, **www.oecd.org/ employment/emp/onlineoecdemploymentdatabase**; United Nations, *Human Development Report* (2009; 2012).

International diversity in reward management

Despite globalisation and the rise of multinational corporations, there remain distinct national variations in the way that pay is determined. In a number of industrialised countries there remains resistance to the primacy of market comparisons. Instead, pay scales and/or pay arrangements are agreed/determined at industry level, to a considerable extent removing pay as a factor in labour market competition. To this fundamental divide between national approaches can be added different attitudes towards incentive payments, employee attributes that should be rewarded and huge differences in taxation and social security regulation. The extent of the diversity is best illustrated with some examples.

The US/UK approaches

These approaches are characterised by a high degree of decentralisation. Aside from setting a minimum wage and requiring that men and women are treated equally, the state by and large refrains from interfering in pay determination matters. Even in the public sector, while overall budgets are set by government ministers and while they deal with major public policy questions (like public-sector pension arrangements), ministers leave the detailed negotiation of pay packages to local managers or to pay review bodies which are independent of government. In the private sector, trade unions now play only a limited role, management effectively deciding who should be paid what and in what way. Pay is thus set according to what an organisation can afford and what the market requires. Individual pay negotiation is now the standard approach. Performance-related pay (PRP) is very common in the private sector and is becoming a great deal more common in the public sector too, while the overall value of occupational pensions has been significantly eroded in order to reduce company exposure to financial risk.

Meanwhile executive pay has rocketed upwards, way ahead of the increases seen in other countries.

The German approach

In Germany there is a good deal more centralisation, but pay is largely determined at the industry level, not at governmental level. The majority of workers in Germany have their basic pay set through legally sanctioned, industry-level collective bargaining arrangements. The agreements set out the grading structure for each industry and, in many cases, also determine the job evaluation factors to be used in assigning jobs to grades. Employers are not permitted to undercut agreed minima (they are seen as being basic contractual rights), although they can supplement them with locally agreed discretionary emoluments. Typical discretionary payments vary from 5% in the financial sector to 25% in engineering industries. In larger firms, only the most senior managers are employed on individual contracts – equivalent to 2% of the total workforce. Stock option schemes, however, are a good deal less common in Germany than the UK due to unfavourable tax treatment. Incentive payments are common in Germany. There are many piecework and individual performance-based schemes, as well as government-sponsored profit-sharing arrangements. An attractive feature of German remuneration is the wide existence of 'thirteenth-month' bonus payments in December.

The Japanese approach

The Japanese system resembles that of Germany in that it comprises industry-level pay scales agreed between firms. It differs, however, in that it is person based rather than job based. Collective bargaining also plays a lesser role as Japanese unions are all enterprise based. Three separate factors determine each individual's pay:

1 the career category

2 age/seniority

3 rank and class.

There are five accepted career categories into which employees are allocated. Each has its own pay scales. The five are as follows:

- general administration
- scientific/engineer
- secretarial/office
- technician/blue collar
- contingent.

Within each category, base pay is determined with reference to age (around 60% of pay) and skill/effort (typically 40%). In a country with traditions of 'lifetime' or long-term employment in one enterprise, seniority is central to reward. Earnings go up with each year of service until the age of 50, after which they decline steadily. The skill-based element operates in a similar way to traditional UK public-sector grade/incremental systems. In Japan, however, progression is discretionary. Seniority plays a part in the skill-based payments too, as there is usually a minimum time to serve in each class before promotion can be gained. Bonus payments are mostly group based and typically equal two months' pay. The result is a high degree of pay compression and an adherence to the maxim that 'a nail standing too high will be pounded down'.

The Scandinavian approach

In Norway, Sweden and Finland payment arrangements tend to be very much more centralised than elsewhere, the government playing a decisive role that extends across most industries. Collective agreements that cover salaries, benefits and all other conditions of work are negotiated at national level between trade unions and employers associations under the auspices of government agencies. These are typically long-term deals that, once agreed, last three years or more. Government agencies arbitrate when agreement cannot be reached. One result is a high degree of similarity in grading schemes across industries. Another is a relatively low level of social inequality. Top executives in Scandinavian countries are typically paid eleven or twelve times the average wage, whereas in the UK and, especially in the USA, the differential is now typically over fifty times. PRP is very common in Scandinavian countries, but it tends to be team based rather than individual.

Total reward

So far in this chapter we have focused on transactional or tangible rewards, by which we mean those which are financial in nature, and this will remain our focus in the other chapters in this part. However, it is important to remember that employees also value the intangible (or relational) rewards which they gain from coming to work, all of which we have made extensive reference to in earlier chapters. These include opportunities to develop both career-wise and more generally as a human being, the social life which is associated with working in communal settings, recognition from managers and colleagues for a job well done and for the effort expended, and more generally from a sense of personal achievement. Increasingly the opportunity to work flexibly so as to achieve a better 'work–life balance' is discussed in this context too. The trend towards viewing reward policies and practices as extending well beyond the realms of payment has led to widespread interest in the concept of 'total reward' which involves managers viewing the way that they reward employees in the round, taking equal account of both the tangible and intangible ingredients that together help to make work and jobs 'rewarding' in the widest sense of the word. The idea is effectively illustrated in graphical form by Armstrong and Brown (2009: 25) in their model adapted from work by the Towers Perrin reward consultancy (see Figure 21.2). Here four distinct categories of rewards are identified, the implication being that each has equal potential significance as a source of reward from the employee perspective.

The change in perspective away from a narrow focus on payment towards a broader focus on 'total reward' has come about largely because of developments in the commercial environment. Year on year, organisations operating in the private sector are facing greater competitive pressure in their product markets leading them to search for ways of reducing their costs while retaining or improving the levels of quality they achieve. In the

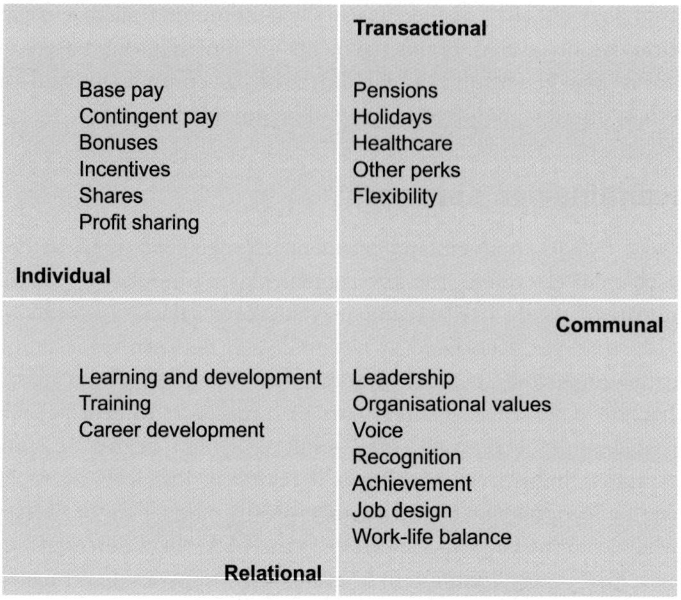

	Transactional
Base pay Contingent pay Bonuses Incentives Shares Profit sharing	Pensions Holidays Healthcare Other perks Flexibility
Individual	**Communal**
Learning and development Training Career development	Leadership Organisational values Voice Recognition Achievement Job design Work-life balance
	Relational

Figure 21.2
Categories of reward

public sector competitive forces increasingly play a role too, but here pressure to keep costs down comes primarily from taxpayers seeking good value for their money. The trouble is that these pressures are being faced simultaneously with tighter labour market conditions, making it difficult for employers to recruit, retain and motivate the staff they need without substantially increasing pay levels. There are a variety of responses to this conundrum that organisations are embracing. One involves employing fewer, but more highly paid people to carry out existing work more efficiently. Another involves keeping a lid on payment levels while simultaneously looking for other ways of rewarding staff effectively. It is this latter approach which has led managers to think about the 'total reward' package that they offer.

As a rule managing the tangible components (i.e. the financial ones) is relatively unproblematic provided basic principles are adhered to and the correct technical decisions are made. While they enable organisations to secure a degree of competitive advantage in their labour markets, these tangible parts of a total reward package are readily imitated by competitors. It is much harder, in practice, to replicate intangible rewards. Over the longer term it is thus in the interests of organisations to improve the perceived value of the intangible elements, but that is a great deal harder both to achieve and to evaluate. Moreover, several important intangible rewards are 'intrinsically' rather than 'extrinsically' motivating, and by definition cannot be directly provided by managers. These are terms used by psychologists to distinguish between sources of positive motivation which are external to individuals and *given* to them by their employer, such as money or praise, and those which are internally generated. An example of intrinsic motivation is someone putting a great deal of effort into a project at work simply because they find it interesting or enjoyable. The result may be very considerable satisfaction on the part of the employee concerned, but this has not resulted directly from any management action. All managers can do is try to create and sustain a culture in which individual employees can achieve intrinsic motivation and hence experience work which is rewarding.

ACTIVITY 21.4

How far do you agree with the proposition that managers should think in terms of 'total reward' as a means of recruiting, retaining and motivating their staff? Are praise and career development as important as pay? Would you trade some of your pay for greater recognition and development opportunities?

WINDOW ON PRACTICE

Total reward at the Crown Prosecution Service

In 2006 the Crown Prosecution Service (CPS) launched a new reward system which was heavily influenced by the 'total reward' concept. Until 1996 when responsibility for reward management was devolved, the CPS's 8,500 staff were paid on standard terms and conditions which were negotiated nationally for civil servants working across all government departments. After devolution incremental changes were introduced that aimed to meet the particular needs of the CPS, culminating in this major overhaul. Labelled 'Invest', the new approach aims to underpin the CPS's evolving agenda.

The first priority for the CPS is to manage successfully a major programme of expansion. New responsibilities taken over from the police require that the CPS employs 300 new lawyers and 500 new administrators. 'Invest' is designed to increase the attractiveness of a career within the CPS and to help retain staff more effectively. An explicit objective of the CPS is to make itself 'an employer of choice' for lawyers and people seeking a career in public administration. A second aim is substantially to improve performance. The CPS has as its central corporate objective a mission to become recognised as 'a world-class prosecution authority'. This requires cultural change and the acquisition by staff of a range of new skills and attributes.

The new strategy aims to meet these objectives in a number of ways. First, a job evaluation system has been introduced to ensure that each job is fairly graded according to the skills its holders require and the responsibilities they shoulder. Second, a new performance appraisal system has come into effect to strengthen links between pay and individual effort and contribution. The existing Civil Service benefits package has been enhanced with new elements such as childcare services and a counselling service, the whole package being promoted with greater coherence at the recruitment stage. A major element is enhanced training and development opportunities for staff, allowing easier career progression within the CPS. Employees are sponsored to attain professional qualifications, and e-learning packages have also been developed to support career development. Finally, flexible working initiatives have been developed, including a great deal more home-working, which aim to meet the needs of both the CPS and its employees. In the future it is intended to introduce long-service awards and to recognise individual achievements with formal letters of recognition from senior managers.

Source: Suff (2006).

SUMMARY PROPOSITIONS

21.1 Until relatively recently many employers in the UK were greatly restricted in their capacity to design reward strategies which met their priorities by the prevailing system of multi-employer or industry-level collective bargaining. The experimentation that followed the disintegration of this system has led to both successful and unsuccessful outcomes.

21.2 The main elements of payment are basic rate, plussage, benefits, premia, overtime, incentives and bonus.

21.3 There are four main alternative methods of setting base pay rates: external labour market comparisons, internal labour market mechanisms, job evaluation and collective bargaining.

21.4 Procedural equity is essential to the design of successful payment systems.

21.5 Simultaneous competition in product and labour markets has led employers increasingly to think in terms of 'total reward' when developing reward strategies. This involves incorporating all management initiatives which may have the effect of adding value to the experience of working in an organisation.

GENERAL DISCUSSION TOPICS

1 Can payment ever be truly fair?

2 Do you think it is possible to identify 'best practice' in payment policy? What elements would you consider should make up any such package?

3 'Job evaluation does not produce equitable payment: it merely produces a ramshackle method of justifying the status quo.' Do you agree with this statement?

4 Why have we seen increased interest in the concept of 'total reward' in recent years? Why might interest grow still further in the future?

THEORY INTO PRACTICE

The following article by Lucy Kellaway is light-hearted and witty, but it also raises several interesting questions about relative pay levels and how we should determine them.

Pandora's pay packet

Imagine if you got into work to find you had been sent an email listing the salaries and bonuses of everybody in your company.

You'd fall on it, read it greedily. And then read it again. You'd scan the list for all those paid more than you. All those paid less. You'd look up the salaries of your most comparable colleagues. you'd look for those of the cocky ones whom you've never rated.

Assuming that you had started the day feeling reasonably content with your salary, by the end it would be a different story. Either you'd be seething at the higher salaries paid to people you think less deserving than yourself, or you'd be feeling sheepish about those talented hardworking people earning considerably less than you.

This is what happens in a case study in the latest *Harvard Business Review*. A disaffected employee unearths a complete salary and bonus list and promptly emails it to the entire staff. Sure enough, all hell breaks loose.

The four labour market experts wheeled on by the magazine to discuss the case agree on one thing. The forced disclosure will do some good – it will bring about a more open culture and a fairer pay system.

I think this is optimistic. Openness is not a good thing *per se*. It is good only when the occasion calls for it.

Pay is the last taboo. Pay is full of iniquities and will always be so. Better, therefore, not to draw attention to it.

If you meet someone at a dinner party, you can ask them about their religion. You can ask them which way they are going to vote. You can ask what they paid for their house. (In fact, I consider this to be the height of bad manners but people ask, nevertheless.)

You may even, if circumstances are right, be able to ask about their sex lives. What you cannot do, under any circumstances, is ask how much they are paid.

You could say that this reticence is misplaced and that in time pay will go the way of all the other taboos.

The reason salaries are so sensitive is that they are the only 'objective' way we have of comparing your labour to mine. Your salary is a clear measure of what someone else is prepared to pay for you.

This makes pay more revealing than other kinds of financial information.

If I know you paid a lot for your house I can conclude any number of things. That your salary is huge. Or that your wife's is. That one or other of you inherited some money. Or that you made a couple of lucky property moves in the past. There are all kinds of possibilities.

But your salary measures only one thing: it sums up your worth. Only as we all know, it does nothing of the kind.

While it may be dangerous to discuss salaries at a dinner party, where bankers may be cheek by jowl with teachers, to discuss them in the office canteen is dynamite.

If salaries in your company were determined fairly, according to some commonly agreed principle, secrecy might not be necessary. but they aren't determined like that, are they? In the real world, your salary reflects a thousand different things, your 'worth' being only one of them.

When did you join the company? Was the job market tight at the time? Which department are you in? How well does your boss like you? How good are you at complaining? All these things affect your pay.

In the public sector people traditionally knew what others were paid, because for each grade and each task there was a rate. But now, thanks to performance-related pay, salary discussion is becoming taboo there too.

Some trendy new companies have experimented with full salary disclosure. This tends to work when the company is very young but as it grows and the outside labour market bears down, transparency seems like less of a good thing.

It could be argued that by publishing all salaries in a company you shock the system into greater 'fairness'. But even if this did happen, it is doubtful whether it would be desirable. Would you want to own shares in a company that could not hire good people from the outside at higher wages for fear of alienating existing employees?

We have, under our noses, a good example of what happens when individual salaries are forcibly outed. For the past few years, directors of public companies have had to disclose in full, gory detail how much they are paid. The aim of this was to rein in the worst of the fat cat pay increases.

Yet it is debatable whether it has in fact achieved that. Pay levels of top directors have continued to soar and the supposed performance criteria they have held up to justify their bonuses have proved to be laughably easy to meet. Maybe they would have risen still further if disclosure had not been required; maybe they would not.

What transparency at the top has certainly done is to make everyone else's sense of outrage and envy all the greater. Now that the fat cat is out of the bag, we can all see how fat it really is – and the sight does us no good at all.

So I am not going to tell you what I earn, either. More than anything else, I do not want to share this information with my colleagues.

Yet suppose when I get into work tomorrow I find that email waiting for me. Will I heed the above and simply press the 'delete' button? Like hell. I'll fall on it, read it greedily, then read it again.

Source: **FT.com**, 14 May 2001.

Questions

1 Is pay really 'the last taboo' as is argued in this article?

2 Why is it only 'dangerous' to discuss salaries at a dinner party, but 'dynamite' to discuss them in the office canteen?

3 Is the author right to argue that more openness in the area of pay is not something to be welcomed?

FURTHER READING

The Chartered Institute of Personnel and Development carries out a big annual survey of reward management policy and practice which is published in February each year. It can be downloaded from the institute's website. In addition the CIPD publishes the results of other research projects that focus on reward.

Reward management continues to be an area of HRM practice which is heavily researched. Good summaries of the most important recent contributions are the following:

Kessler, I. (2013) 'Remuneration systems', in S. Bach and M. Edwards (eds). *Managing Human Resources*, 5th edn. Chichester: Wiley.

Guthrie, J. (2007) 'Remuneration: Pay effects at work', in P. Boxall *et al.* (eds), *The Oxford Handbook of Human Resource Management*. Oxford: Oxford University Press.

Gerhart, B. (2009) 'Compensation', in A. Wilkinson *et al.* (eds), *The Sage Handbook of Human Resource Management*, London: Sage.

White, G. and Druker, J. (eds) (2009) *Reward Management: A critical text*, 2nd edn. London: Routledge.

REFERENCES

Adams, J.S. (1963) 'Towards an understanding of inequity', *Journal of Abnormal and Social Psychology*, Vol. 67, pp. 422–36.

Armstrong, M. and Brown, D. (2009) *Strategic Reward: Implementing more effective reward management*. London: Kogan Page.

Armstrong, M. and Murlis, H. (2007) *Reward Management: A handbook of remuneration strategy and practice*. London: Kogan Page.

CIPD (2007) *Reward Management: Annual survey report 2007*. London: CIPD.

CIPD (2012) *Reward Management: Annual survey report 2012*. London: CIPD.

Doeringer, P.B. and Piore, M.J. (1970) *Internal Labour Markets and Manpower Analysis*. Washington, DC: Office of Manpower Research, US Department of Labor.

Gerhart, B. (2009) 'Compensation', in A. Wilkinson *et al.* (eds), *The Sage Handbook of Human Resource Management*. London, Sage.

Lazear, E.P. (1995) *Personnel Economics*. Boston, MA: Massachusetts Institute of Technology.

National Statistics (2012) *2011 Annual Survey of Hours and Earnings*. London: National Statistics.

Suff, R. (2006) 'Investing in excellence at the Crown Prosecution Service', *IRS Employment Review*, No. 841, 17 February, pp. 24–7.

United Nations (2009) *Human Development Report*. New York: United Nations.

United Nations (2012) *Human Development Report*. New York: United Nations.

Van Wanrooy, B., Bewley, H., Bryson, A., Forth, J., Freeth, S., Stokes, L. and Wood, S. (2013) *The 2011 Workplace Employment Relations Study: First findings*. London: Department for Business, Innovation and Science.

Chapter 22

INCENTIVES

Incentive payments remain one of the ideas that fascinate managers as they search for the magic formula. Somewhere there is a method of linking payment to performance so effectively that their movements will coincide, enabling the manager to leave the workers on automatic pilot, as it were, while attending to more important matters such as strategic planning or going to lunch. This conviction has sustained a continuing search for this elusive formula, which has been hunted with all the fervour of those trying to find the Holy Grail or the crock of gold at the end of the rainbow.

In recent years incentives of all kinds have been the source of much debate among HR professionals, consultants, trade unionists and academic writers. While particular attention has been given to the pros and cons of individual performance-related reward systems, much has also been written in support of and against the use of team-based incentives and those which reward the acquisition of defined skills. Profit sharing and employee share ownership have been the subject of significant government initiatives and have thus also become topics about which a great deal is written.

Basic choices

While incentive payment systems are common in the UK and in many other countries, there are millions of employees who do not receive this kind of reward and many employers who use them only in a limited way (often in the remuneration of senior managers). It is thus perfectly possible, and some would argue desirable, to recruit, retain and motivate a workforce by paying a simple, fixed rate of pay for each job in the organisation. There is other equipment in the HR manager's toolkit which can be used to reward effort and maintain good levels of job satisfaction. The most fundamental question is therefore whether or not to use an incentive payment system at all. In the opinion of Sisson and Storey (2000: 123–4) many organisations in the UK have introduced schemes for 'ideological reasons' as a means of impressing stock market analysts, reinforcing management control or undermining established collective bargaining machinery. These, they suggest, are poor reasons which have generally met with little long-term success. Incentive schemes should only be used where they are appropriate to the needs of the business and where they can clearly contribute to the achievement of organisational objectives.

There is a long tradition in the academic literature of hostility to incentive schemes in general and those which focus on the individual in particular. In 1966, Frederick Herzberg argued that pay was a 'hygiene factor' rather than a 'motivator'. He claimed that its capacity to motivate positively was limited, and it can very easily demotivate when managed poorly. It follows that there is little to be gained and a great deal to lose from the introduction of incentive schemes. Others (e.g. Thompson 2000) have focused on the way that incentives are perceived by employees as tools of management control which reduce their autonomy and discretion. This, it is argued, causes resentment and leads to dissatisfaction and industrial conflict. A third source of criticism is the considerable additional costs which invariably mount up when organisations introduce incentive schemes. Cox (2006: 1493) labels these 'costly side-effects' and shows that they are both considerable and largely unanticipated at the time a new scheme is introduced.

A different school of thought argues in favour of incentives on the grounds that they reward effort and behaviours which the organisation wishes to encourage (Gerhart 2009: 226). As a result they not only are a fair basis for rewarding people, but also can enhance organisational effectiveness and productivity. Advocates of expectancy theory hold this position with their belief that individual employees will alter their behaviour (e.g. by working harder or prioritising their actions differently) if they believe that in so doing they will be rewarded with something they value. Hence, where additional pay is a valued reward, employees will seek it and will work to secure it. A positive outcome for both employer and employee is achievable provided the incentive is paid in return for a form of employee behaviour which genuinely contributes to the achievement of organisational objectives.

In addition, many reward specialists point to a significant sorting effect which leads employees who are willing and able to perform to a higher standard to be attracted to jobs in which their superior relative contribution will be properly rewarded. At the same time, it is argued, existing employees who perform relatively poorly are more likely to seek alternative employment than colleagues who perform well and are rewarded for doing so. Hence, over time, the quality of employees rises as a result of the presence of incentive schemes. Conversely, of course, it can be plausibly argued that employers who fail to recognise superior individual contribution in their payment systems are more likely to lose higher-performing people because they perceive themselves to be being inadequately rewarded for their skills and efforts.

The research evidence is patchy on the question of how far incentives actually lead to performance improvements at the organisational level. Some studies suggest a correlation between superior performance and some types of incentive scheme (e.g. Huselid 1995; Lazear 2000; Piekkola 2005; Gielen *et al.* 2006; Cadsby *et al.* 2007; Gerhart and Trevor 2008), while others (e.g. Pearce *et al.* 1985; Thompson 1992; Makinson 2000; Marsden 2004) have found no significant evidence of any link. In any case, as Corby *et al.* (2005: 5–6) point out, there are very few published studies which focus on performance or productivity levels before and after the introduction of a new scheme. What we have are correlation studies which link superior organisational performance to the presence of incentive schemes, but no proof of any causal relationship. Much seems to depend on the circumstances. Incentives are not universally applicable, but can play a role in enhancing individual effort or performance where the conditions and scheme design are right. Problems occur when the wrong system is imposed, on the wrong people, in the wrong circumstances or for the wrong reasons.

Where an incentive scheme is used, the next choice relates to the way the scheme is to operate. There are two basic approaches that can be used: bonus payments and incremental progression. In the case of the former, the employee is rewarded with a single payment (possibly made in stages) at the end of a payment period. In the case of profit sharing it will often be an annual payment, while sales commission is usually paid monthly. Whatever the timing, the key principle is that the pay is variable. Good performance in one period is rewarded, but the same individual could earn rather less in the next if his or her performance deteriorates. Some writers refer to such systems as putting 'pay at risk', because earnings vary from period to period depending on how much incentive is earned. The alternative approach involves making incremental progression up to the next grade dependent on the individual's contribution. The reward takes the form of a general pay rise over and above any cost of living increment being paid in a particular year. The incentive payment thus becomes consolidated into overall earnings and is not variable or 'at risk' after it has been earned.

ACTIVITY 22.1

What in your view are the main advantages and disadvantages of these alternative approaches from a management perspective? Would you be more motivated by the prospect of a pay rise or a one-off bonus payment?

Another basic choice concerns the extent of the incentive. In practice this is a decision of rather greater importance than the type of incentive scheme to be used, although it is given rather less coverage in the literature. There is the world of difference, in terms of cost and employee perception, between a scheme which rewards people with 3% or 4% of salary and one which pays a sum equivalent to 25%. Studies undertaken in the USA, reported by Bartol and Durham (2000: 14), suggest that the minimum level of bonus or pay rise 'necessary to elicit positive perceptual and attitudinal responses' is between 5% and 7% of salary. Piekkola (2005), in her studies of links between incentives and firm performance in Finland, found that a positive impact on productivity only began to kick in once the incentive exceeded 3.6% of salary. Lesser payments are thus unlikely to provide meaningful incentives and will have only a peripheral impact. According to Hendry *et al.* (2000: 54), this has been a major problem for schemes introduced in the public sector where incentives have tended to be worth a maximum of only 2% or 3% of salary.

The final choice concerns the level at which the incentive will be paid. Some schemes reward individuals for individual performance, others reward a group of employees or team for their collective performance. Finally there are schemes which share incentive payments out among all employees in the organisation or within individual business units. Team-based incentives have tended to get a better press in recent years than individual incentives, a major problem with the latter being their tendency to undermine teamworking in situations where it is an important contributor to competitive advantage (see Pfeffer 1998: 218–20; Gerhart 2009: 232), but the different forms of incentive are by no means mutually exclusive. It is possible, for example, to reward a salesperson with three types of incentive, one from each level. The basic pay would thus be enhanced with commission calculated individually, with a performance-based payment made to all in the person's sales team to reflect excellent customer feedback, and finally with a profit-related bonus paid to all employees in the organisation. Indeed, the more recent research suggests that employers are increasingly mixing different types of incentive scheme so as to enable them to help meet a range of distinct organisational objectives. It is not at all uncommon, as a result, for more senior employees to have an opportunity to earn additional income from three or four different types of bonus, some individual, some group-based, some leading to a pay rise, others resulting in a one-off bonus payment. The schemes themselves also appear to be becoming increasingly sophisticated and administratively complex (IDS 2005: 7).

WINDOW ON PRACTICE

Peter and Patrick are sales consultants for a financial services company and both had business targets for a six-month period. Peter met his target comfortably and received the predetermined bonus of £6,000 for reaching on-target earnings. Patrick failed to reach his target because his sales manager boss left the company and poached two of Patrick's prime customers just before they signed agreements with him, whose bonus was therefore £2,000 instead of £6,250.

Joanne was a sales consultant for the same company as Peter and Patrick. Before the sales manager left, he made over to her several promising clients with whom he had done considerable preparatory work and who were not willing to be 'poached' by his new employer. All of these signed agreements and one of them decided to increase the value of the deal ten-fold without any reference to Joanne until after that decision was made, and without

knowing that she was now the appropriate contact. Her bonus for the period was £23,400.

Henry is a production manager in a light engineering company with performance pay related to a formula combining output with value added. Bonus payments were made monthly in anticipation of what they should be. One of Henry's initiatives was to increase the gearing of the payment by results scheme in the factory. Through peculiarities of company accounting his bonus payments were 'justified' according to the formula, but later it was calculated that the production costs had risen by an amount that cancelled out the value-added benefits. Also 30% of the year's output had to be recalled due to a design fault.

Patrick had his bonus made up to £6,250. Joanne had her bonus reduced to £8,000, but took legal advice and had the amount cut restored, whereupon Peter and Patrick both threatened to resign until mollified by *ex gratia* payments of £2,000 each. Peter resigned three months later. Henry was dismissed.

The extent to which incentives are paid

There is conflicting evidence about how widespread incentive payments are in the UK and about whether or not they are becoming more or less common. Until 2005, each year the government's New Earnings Survey selected a sample of over 100,000 employees from across the country and asked their employers to fill in a form outlining their earnings in the previous tax year. One of the questions asked about incentive payments 'such as piecework, commission, profit sharing, productivity and other incentives/bonuses'. The survey results persistently showed that only around 15–20% of employees were receiving such payments, most of which were accounted for by traditional piecework or PBR systems operated in manufacturing organisations. The incidence of individual incentives paid to non-manual workers was low. However, other surveys have long painted a rather different picture. The authors analysing the 2011 Workplace Employment Relations Survey (van Wanrooy *et al.* 2013: 24–5) concluded that 54% of the workplaces in their sample operated some form of incentive payment system, 40% using schemes that tie pay to individual performance and 38% to group performance. Even allowing for a strong degree of overlap between schemes as a result of employers operating different payment systems simultaneously, these figures show that incentive payments form at least some part of some people's reward packages in a good majority of UK workplaces.

The CIPD's annual survey of reward practice covers a much smaller sample of employers, but it too suggests both high usage of incentives in the UK and considerably increased usage of incentives over recent years. In 2012 the CIPD reported that 66.8% of its respondents rewarded staff with individual performance-related bonuses, while 56.5% gave merit pay rises and 38.1% operated a profit-sharing scheme. While such approaches are used by a sizeable minority of employers in the public and voluntary sectors, it is in the private sector that activity is focused.

It is not easy to reconcile the diverse results produced by these surveys. One possibility is that the different results may reflect the different samples used. The New Earnings Survey covered workplaces of all sizes, including the very smallest, while the others tend to focus on somewhat larger employers. It could therefore be the case that incentive schemes are largely used in bigger firms with more sophisticated management practices. Another possibility is that many of the schemes in operation only apply to senior managers and not to the generality of staff. Either way, there is clear evidence of growth in the extent to which employers make use of incentive payment systems. Moreover, this is very much an international trend and one which is associated with all industrial sectors (Marginson 2009: 103; IRS 2009).

ACTIVITY 22.2

Why do you think the proportion of workplaces using individual incentive payment systems seems to have grown so much in recent decades?

PBR schemes

Historically, the most widely used incentive schemes have been those which reward employees according to the number of items or units of work they produce or the time they take to produce them. This approach is associated with F.W. Taylor and the phase in the development of personnel management described under the heading 'Humane bureaucracy' (see Chapter 1). Little attention has been paid to the operation of piece-work schemes in recent years and there is some evidence to show that traditionally designed schemes are in decline, both in terms of the proportion of total pay which is determined according to PBR principles and in terms of the number of employees paid in this way (Bryson and Forth 2008: 499). However, PBR is still widely used in some shape or form by employers of manual workers (Cox 2006) and, in the form of sales commission, continues to account for a good portion of the earnings of people with selling roles. PBR schemes tend to take one of five major alternative forms:

1 **Individual time-saving schemes** involve incentives being paid for time saved in performing a specified operation. A standard time is derived for a work sequence, the employee receiving an additional payment for the time saved in completing a number of such operations. If it is not possible to work due to shortage of materials or some other reason, the time involved is not counted when the sums are done at the end of the day.

2 **Measured daywork schemes** work by paying employees a fixed sum as long as they maintain a predetermined and agreed level of working. Employees thus have far less discretion over the amount of effort they expend. The advantage of measured daywork over time-saving schemes, from the management point of view, is the greater level of management control that is exercised.

3 **Group incentives** involve applying the principles of individual time saving to group rather than individual output to improve group performance and to promote the development of teamworking. Where jobs are interdependent, group incentives can be appropriate, but it may also put great pressure on the group members, aggravating any interpersonal animosity that exists and increasing the likelihood of stoppages.

4 **Plant-wide bonus schemes** ensure that all employees in a plant or other organisation share in a pool bonus that is linked to the level of output, the value added by the employees collectively or some similar formula. Theoretically, employees are more likely to identify with the organisation as a whole when paid in this way and will cooperate more readily with the management and each other. The difficulties lie in the fact that there is no tangible link between individual effort and individual reward, so that those who are working effectively can have their efforts nullified by others working less effectively.

5 **Commission** paid on sales secured is a widespread practice about which surprisingly little is known as these schemes have not come under the same close scrutiny as incentive schemes for manual employees. They suffer from some of the same drawbacks as manual incentives, except that they are linked to business won rather than to output achieved.

ACTIVITY 22.3

A problem with sales commission is its tendency to reward the quantity of goods sold without having regard to the quality of service provided by sales staff. In which circumstances might this have negative consequences? How could a commission-based incentive scheme be adapted to incorporate measures of quality as well as quantity?

PRP

Arguments about the advantages and disadvantages of individual PRP have been some of the most hotly contested in recent decades. The topic has formed the basis of numerous research studies and remains one which attracts much controversy, as was shown in recent debates about the introduction of PRP for teachers working in state schools. The main reason is the apparent contrast between the theoretical attractiveness of such systems – at least from a management perspective – and their supposed tendency to disappoint when operated in practice. While there are many different types of scheme available, all involve the award of a pay rise or bonus payment to individual employees following a formal assessment of their performance over a defined period (normally the previous year). Two distinct varieties of scheme can be identified:

1 **Merit-based systems** simply involve the immediate supervisor undertaking an appraisal of each subordinate's work performance during the previous year. This will typically be done following a formal appraisal interview and often requires the completion of standard documentation drawn up by an HR department. A proportion of future remuneration is then linked to a score derived from the supervisor's assessment. Some systems require supervisors to award a percentage mark against different criteria, while others oblige them to assess individual performance as 'excellent', 'good', 'satisfactory' or 'inadequate'. Merit-based systems are generally regarded as unsatisfactory because they allow considerable scope for assessors to make subjective judgements or to allow personal prejudice to colour their assessments. There is also a tendency to give undue weight to recent events at the expense of achievements taking place early in the appraisal period.

2 **Goal-based systems** are more objective, but are not appropriate for all kinds of job. They are, however, particularly well suited for the assessment of managerial work. Here the supervisor and subordinate meet at the start of the appraisal period and agree between them a list of objectives which the appraisee will seek to meet during the coming months. Examples would be the completion of particular projects, the establishment of new initiatives, undertaking a course of training or making substantial progress towards the solving of a problem. Many employers nowadays seek to link individual objectives directly to defined organisational goals for the year as a means of reinforcing their significance and ensuring that all are pulling in the same direction. At the end of the year the employee is assessed on the basis of which objectives have or have not been met. A score is then derived and a bonus payment or pay rise awarded. Where performance in a job can meaningfully be assessed in this way, such systems are recommended because they are reasonably objective and straightforward to score. Where the nature of the job involves the consistent achievement of a defined level of performance, and cannot usefully be assessed in terms of the achievement of specific objectives, the goal-based approach has less to offer. It may still be possible to assess part of the job in this way, but there will also have to be a merit-based element if the appraisal is to reflect all of a person's activity during the appraisal period.

ACTIVITY 22.4

Make a list of five jobs that you consider would be best rewarded by a merit-based system and five more that are best rewarded via the goal-based approach.

The attractions of PRP

It is not difficult to see why PRP has attracted the interest of managers, consultants and government ministers. Its theoretical attractions are considerable and include the following:

- attracting and retaining good performers;

- improving individual and corporate performance;

- clarifying job roles and duties;

- improving communication;

- improving motivation;

- reinforcing management control;

- identifying developmental objectives;

- reinforcing the individual employment relationship at the expense of the collective;

- rewarding individuals without needing to promote them.

In short PRP aims to provide a flexible and cost-effective means of distributing rewards fairly between the good and poorer performers while also contributing towards improved organisational performance. Moreover, it is based on principles to which most people, employees as well as managers, seem to adhere (Brown and Armstrong 2000: 11–13). Most of us are very happy to see individuals rewarded for superior performance and/ or effort and would like payment decisions to be based on such criteria. The problems arise when attempts are made to put the principles into practice. A system which is fair and objective in theory can easily fail to achieve these objectives when implemented.

Critiques of PRP

PRP attracted a great amount of criticism from academic researchers in the 1980s and 1990s during a period when its virtues were frequently asserted by HR managers and consultants. The attacks came from several quarters. Occupational psychologists tended to question the ability of PRP to motivate positively (e.g. Kohn 1993), while sociologists saw it as a means of reinforcing management control at the expense of worker autonomy (e.g. Hendry *et al.* 2000). A further source of criticism has come from those who suspect that PRP is used as a means of perpetuating gender inequality in payment matters (e.g. Rubery 1995). However, the most colourful and damning criticisms have come from management thinkers such as W. Edwards Deming who advocate total quality management approaches and for whom PRP represents exactly the wrong kind of initiative to introduce. The whole basis of their philosophy is the substitution of 'leadership' for 'supervision', removing organisational hierarchies and managing people with as little direction and control as possible. They see PRP as having the opposite effect. It reinforces the hierarchy, enhances the power of supervisors and strengthens management control.

For many critics, including those cited above, PRP has fundamental flaws which cannot be overcome. Kohn, for example, argues that incentives can only succeed in securing temporary compliance. Their use cannot change underlying attitudes, while the attempt to do so ultimately damages the long-term health of an organisation by undermining relationships and encouraging employees to focus on short-term aims. Managers who insist that the job won't get done right without rewards have failed to offer a convincing argument for behavioural manipulation. Promising a reward to someone who appears unmotivated is a bit like offering salt water to someone who is thirsty. Bribes in the workplace simply can't work (Kohn 1993: 60).

A second stream of criticism is more moderate, arguing that PRP can have a role to play in organisations, but that its positive effects are limited. Moreover, while not fundamentally flawed, PRP is very difficult to implement effectively in practice. As a result, systems fail as often as they succeed. The arguments are summarised well by Gomez-Mejia and Balkin (1992: 249–55), Cannell and Wood (1992: 66–101), Pfeffer (1998: 203–4), Purcell (2000) and more recently by Armstrong and Brown (2009: 47–9) and Gerhart (2009). The major points made by these authors are as follows:

- Employees paid by PRP, especially where the incentive is substantial, tend to develop a narrow focus to their work. They concentrate on those aspects which they believe will initiate payments, while neglecting other parts of their jobs.

- PRP, because of its individual nature, tends to undermine teamworking. People focus on their own objectives at the expense of cooperation with colleagues.

- PRP, because it involves managers rating employees according to their perceptions of performance, can lead to a situation in which a good proportion of staff are demotivated when they receive their rating.

- Employees are rarely in a position wholly to determine the outcomes of their own performance. Factors outside their control play an important role, leading to a situation in which the achievement or non-achievement of objectives is partially a matter of chance.

- Even the most experienced managers find it difficult to undertake fair and objective appraisals of their employees' performance. Subjective judgements are often taken into account leading to perceptions of bias. Some managers deliberately manipulate ratings for political reasons, allowing their judgement to be coloured by the effect they perceive the outcome will have on particular employees. Low ratings are thus avoided, as are very high ratings, where it is perceived this will lead to disharmony or deterioration of personal relationships.

- In organisations subject to swift and profound change, objectives set for the coming year may become obsolete after a few months. Employees then find themselves with an incentive to meet goals which are no longer priorities for the organisation.

- PRP systems tend to discourage creative thinking, the challenging of established ways of doing things and a questioning attitude among employees.

- Budgetary constraints often lead managers to reduce ratings, creating a situation in which excellent individual performance is not properly rewarded.

- It is difficult to ensure that each line manager takes a uniform approach to the rating of their subordinates. Some tend to be more generously disposed in general than others, leading to inconsistency and perceptions of unfairness.

- When the results of performance appraisal meetings have an impact on pay levels, employees tend to downplay their weaknesses. As a result development needs are not discussed or addressed.

- PRP systems invariably increase the pay bill. This occurs because managers fear demotivating their staff by awarding low or zero rises in the first years of a system's operation. Poorer performers are thus rewarded as well as better performers.

- PRP systems can be too successful, leading people to take unnecessary risks or to act recklessly in order to secure higher rewards.

WINDOW ON PRACTICE

One of the fundamental problems associated with PRP derives from the so-called 'Lake Wobegon Effect' (Guthrie 2007: 350). The label derives from the words the great American humorist Garrison Keillor uses each week on his radio show when completing his monologue about the goings on in his fictional, but archetypal, small rural town:

And that's the news from Lake Wobegon where all the women are strong, all the men are good looking, and all the children are above average.

Just as it is not mathematically possible for all children to be 'above average', neither is it possible for all employees to be so. Yet whenever people are asked to rate their own performance they have a very strong tendency to rate themselves as being 'above average'. The inevitable consequence is a situation in which most employee ratings of their own performance are considerably higher than those of their managers. The result is disappointment when manager ratings are revealed, and a tendency for most people to be demotivated.

Using PRP effectively

Despite the problems described above it is possible to implement PRP successfully, as is shown by the experience of case study companies quoted by Brown and Armstrong (2000), IRS (2005a; 2005b) and IDS (2005). It will only work, however, if it is used in appropriate circumstances and if it is implemented properly. Part of the problem with PRP has been a tendency in the HR press to portray it as universally applicable and as a panacea capable of improving performance dramatically. In fact it is neither, but is one of a range of tools that have a useful if limited role to play in some situations. Gomez-Mejia and Balkin (1992) specify the following favourable conditions:

- Where individual performance can be objectively and meaningfully measured.
- Where individuals are in a position to control the outcomes of their work.
- Where close teamworking or cooperation with others is not central to successful job performance.
- Where there is an individualistic organisational culture.

A consensus now appears to be emerging in support of the view that PRP does not generally work as well in the public sector as it does in the private sector (OECD 2005; Prentice *et al.* 2007). Only a minority of public-sector workers appear to be motivated positively by PRP, while some groups find that it actively undermines their motivation simply because they are not primarily motivated by pay. Introducing PRP thus cuts across the established professional culture and is not compatible with their perceptions of 'the public-sector ethos'. By contrast PRP does seem to fit better with cultures in some of the growing private-sector industries. Armstrong and Brown (2009) focus particularly on knowledge-intensive work and on customer service, finding in both cases that the circumstances are often, if not always, suited to individualised rewards such as PRP.

Brown and Armstrong (2000) also point to the importance of careful implementation and lengthy preparation prior to the installation of a scheme. Moreover, they argue that PRP should not be looked at or judged in isolation from other forms of reward, both extrinsic and intrinsic. Success or failure can hinge on what else is being done to maximise motivation, to develop people and to improve their job security.

Ultimately PRP has one great advantage which no amount of criticism can remove: it helps ensure that organisational priorities become individual priorities. Managers can signal the importance of a particular objective by including it in a subordinate's goals for the coming year. If the possibility of additional payment is then tied to its achievement, the chances that the objective concerned will be met increases significantly. Organisational performance is improved as a result. Where the achievement of such specific objectives forms a relatively minor part of someone's job, PRP can form a relatively minor part of their pay packet. Other rewards can then be used to recognise other kinds of achievement.

WINDOW ON PRACTICE

Many job descriptions for supervisory positions include reference to responsibility for ensuring that the appropriate health and safety at work regulations are adhered to. Few supervisors, however, left to themselves would see this aspect of their work as a priority. In one organisation known to the authors it was decided to try to raise the profile of health and safety issues by including objectives in this field into managers' annual performance targets. It therefore became clear that the level of PRP in the following year would, in part, be determined by the extent to which the health and safety objectives had been met. The result was the swift establishment of departmental health and safety committees and schemes whereby staff could bring safety hazards to the attention of supervisors.

Skills-based pay

A further kind of incentive payment scheme is one which seeks to reward employees for the skills or competencies which they acquire. It is well established in the USA and became fashionable in the UK during the 1990s and early 2000s. Since then interest has waned, most recent texts on reward management paying it relatively little attention. It is most useful as a means of rewarding technical staff, but there is no reason why the principle should not be extended to any group of employees for whom the acquisition of additional skills might benefit the organisation.

There are several potential benefits for an employer introducing a skills-based pay scheme. Its most obvious effect is to encourage multiskilling and flexibility enabling the organisation to respond more effectively and speedily to the needs of customers. A multi-skilled workforce may also be slimmer and less expensive. In addition it is argued that, in rewarding skills acquisition, a company will attract and retain staff more effectively than its competitors in the labour market. The operation of a skills-based reward system is proof that the sponsoring employer is genuinely committed to employee development.

Most skills-based payment systems reward employees with additional increments to their base pay once they have completed defined skill modules. A number of such schemes are described in detail in a study published by Incomes Data Services (IDS 1992). Typical is the scheme operated by Venture Pressings Ltd where staff are employed on four basic grades, each divided into ten increments. Employees progress up the scale by acquiring specific skills and demonstrating proficiency in them to the satisfaction of internal assessors. New starters are also assessed and begin their employment on the incremental point most appropriate to the level of skills they can demonstrate. In many industries it is now possible to link payment for skills acquisition directly to the attainment of National Vocational Qualifications (NVQs) for which both the setting of standards and the assessment of individual competency are carried out externally.

A skills-based pay system will only be cost effective if it results in productivity increases which are sufficient to cover the considerable costs associated with its introduction and maintenance. A business can invest a great deal of resources both in training its workforce to attain new skills and in rewarding it once those skills have been acquired, only to find that the cost of the scheme outweighs the benefit gained in terms of increased flexibility and efficiency. Furthermore, in assisting employees to become more highly qualified and in many cases to gain NVQs, an employer may actually find it harder to retain its staff in relatively competitive labour markets.

The other major potential disadvantage is associated with skills obsolescence. Where a business operates in a fast-moving environment and needs to adapt its technology regularly, a skills-based payment system can leave the organisation paying enhanced salaries for skills which are no longer significant or are not required at all. Employers seeking to introduce skills-based systems of payment therefore need to consider the implications very carefully and must ensure that they only reward the acquisition of those skills which will clearly contribute to increased productivity over the long term.

ACTIVITY 22.5

A number of commentators praise skills-based pay as a system which avoids some of the pitfalls associated with PRP schemes. Look back at the list of practical problems with PRP schemes above and consider which do and which do not apply to skills-based incentive systems.

Profit sharing

There are a number of different ways in which companies are able to link remuneration to profit levels. In recent decades governments all over the world have sought to encourage such schemes and have actively promoted their establishment with advantageous tax arrangements. The EU has been particularly interested in promoting these types of scheme. Underlying government support is the belief that linking pay to profits increases the employee's commitment to his or her company by deepening the level of mutual interest. As a result, it is argued that such schemes act as an incentive encouraging employees to work harder and with greater flexibility in pursuit of higher levels of take-home pay. Other potential advantages for employers and governments described by Pendleton (2009) are better cost flexibility, changed attitudes on the part of employees and the discouragement of union membership.

Cash-based schemes

The traditional and most common profit-sharing arrangement is simply to pay employees a cash bonus, calculated as a proportion of annual profits, on which the employee incurs both an income tax and a National Insurance liability. Some organisations pay discretionary profit bonuses on this basis, while others allocate a fixed proportion of profits to employees as a matter of policy. Gain sharing is a variation on cash-based profit sharing which is widely used in the USA and which can be used in non-profit-making organisations as well as those operating in the commercial sector. Here the bonus relates to costs saved rather than profit generated in a defined period. So if a workforce successfully achieves the same level of output at lower overall cost, the gain is shared between employer and employees.

Share-based schemes

There are several methods of profit sharing which involve employees being awarded shares rather than cash. Here too there are government-sponsored schemes in operation which involve favourable tax treatment. There are several distinct schemes available for employers to use, some of which are more tax efficient than others. Traditionally senior managers have been paid, in part, through share-based reward systems, but companies are increasingly seeing an advantage in extending these arrangements to a greater proportion of their staff. The purpose is to increase commitment by giving employees a significant financial stake in the future of the business they work for, at the same time helping to align employees' interests with those of shareholders. The result should be improved staff retention and higher levels of individual performance, but it is difficult to prove that such outcomes result in practice from the introduction of these schemes. For most ordinary employees the level of reward is too low, and the extent to which their actions impact on a firm's performance too indirect, for there to be a clear-cut incentive effect. Cohen (2006) and IDS (2007) provide concise and clear guides to the whole range of systems. The two most common are the following:

1 **Savings-Related Share Option** schemes permit companies to grant share options to directors and employees in a tax-effective manner. This means that they are given the opportunity to buy shares in their own companies at a future date, but at the current price. The hope is that the value will have increased in the meantime, allowing the purchaser to cash in a tidy profit. This particular government-sponsored scheme requires participants to put between £5 and £250 of their monthly pay aside and then to use the proceeds of the accumulated fund, after three, five or seven years, to buy shares at a discount of 20% of the price they were when the plan started. The scheme is popularly known as 'save as you earn' or 'sharesave'.

2 **Inland Revenue Approved Share Incentive Plans** (previously called All-Employee Share Schemes) allow employees to obtain shares in their own companies while avoiding tax and National Insurance contributions. Employers can give such shares to employees to a maximum value of £3,000 per year. Some can be given in recognition of individual or team performance, making it possible to award some employees more shares than others. Where employees subsequently hold these shares for three years or more, there is no tax liability when they are sold. In addition, under the scheme, employees can buy up to a further £1,500 worth of shares out of pre-tax income and

subsequently avoid a proportion of the tax owed when they are sold. Companies are also allowed to give 'free' matching shares for each share purchased by an employee under the scheme. Employers as well as employees gain tax advantages from operating these schemes. Deductions in corporation tax can be made equivalent to the amount of salary used by employees to purchase shares, as well as monies used in establishing and operating the scheme.

Disadvantages of profit-related schemes

The obvious disadvantage of the schemes described above from the employee's point of view is the risk that pay levels may decline if the company fails to meet its expected profit levels. If no profit is made it cannot be shared. Share values can go down as well as up. Companies are not permitted to make guarantees about meeting payments and will have their schemes revoked by the Inland Revenue if they do so. In any event it is likely that profit-based incentives will vary in magnitude from year to year.

For these reasons it is questionable to assert that profit-sharing schemes do in fact act as incentives. Unlike PRP awards they do not relate specifically to the actions of the individual employee. Annual profit levels are clearly influenced by a whole range of factors which are both internal and external to the company. An employee may well develop a community of interest with the company management, shareholders and other employees but it is unlikely seriously to affect the nature of his or her work. Furthermore, both poor and good performers are rewarded equally in profit-related schemes. The incentive effect will therefore be very slight in most cases and will be restricted to a general increase in employee commitment.

WINDOW ON PRACTICE

For many years government ministers from across the political spectrum in the UK have developed schemes which provide incentives to firms to share profits with their employees. These have often taken the form of plans which make it tax efficient to reward staff with shares. The model operated by the John Lewis Partnership (owners of the John Lewis department stores and the Waitrose supermarket chain) is often cited as one which government would like other companies to imitate.

John Lewis is controlled by a trust which has the task of running the company in the interest of its employees, all of whom are partners in the enterprise for as long as they remain employed by the company. The trust appoints the chairman and deputy chairman, who in turn appoint five members of the executive board. The remaining five places are occupied by people who are nominated by the Partnership Council, an eighty-two-strong body of whom 80% are elected by the partners through a branch network. The result is a company which is highly successful commercially, but which also provides its people with terms and conditions of employment that are very generous by comparison with those provided by other retailers. Each year in January all partners receive a bonus payment which is linked directly to the profits generated in the previous year. This is calculated as a percentage of their annual salary, the same percentage being received by everyone regardless of seniority. Because the company is successful and growing, bonus payments have tended to be quite high in recent years, averaging between 10% and 20% of salary. In 2012–13 the company made a net profit of £406.6 million, of which £210.8 million was distributed to partners in the form of profit sharing. This gave each of them a bonus payment equivalent to 17% of their annual salaries. Pension and holiday entitlements are also very generous, all partners who complete twenty-five years service being rewarded with a six-month period of paid leave.

SUMMARY PROPOSITIONS

22.1 Incentive schemes should be used where they are appropriate to the needs of the business and where they can clearly contribute to the achievement of organisational objectives.

22.2 The extent to which different types of incentive arrangement are used in the UK is unclear. There is evidence of growth in recent years, but the majority of employees are not covered by such schemes.

22.3 Methods of payment by results include individual time saving, group incentives, measured daywork, plant-wide schemes, productivity schemes and commission.

22.4 Performance-related pay systems are either merit based or goal based. They have been the subject of notable debate in recent years, many researchers finding a mismatch between their theoretical attractions and practical outcomes.

22.5 Skills-based pay involves linking incentives to the achievement of defined competencies or qualifications. It rewards what people bring to the job rather than the results of their efforts.

22.6 Profit sharing has been promoted by governments for many years. The share incentive plan is one of several government-sponsored schemes aimed at encouraging employees to hold shares in their own companies.

GENERAL DISCUSSION TOPICS

1 What are the relative advantages of: (a) a system of straight salary that is the same each month; and (b) a system of salary with an individual performance-related addition so that the total payment each month varies?

2 In what circumstances might it be appropriate to base individual payment on team performance?

3 What do you think about Peter, Patrick, Joanne and Henry in the Window on practice box early in this chapter?

THEORY INTO PRACTICE

Performance-related pay at the Cavendish Hall Hotel

Daphne Jones has recently been appointed as Personnel Manger of the Cavendish Hall Hotel, a 200-bedroom, four-star country house hotel located in rolling hills a few miles south of a major northern industrial conurbation. The hotel provides a wide range of conference and banqueting facilities and is a popular wedding location. Despite poor reviews from guests concerning the cost of drinks and the quality of the food on offer, the hotel is financially successful, having recently recorded increased annual profits.

Soon after her appointment Daphne decides that it is necessary and desirable to introduce a new payment system which links reward to individual effort and competency. She is concerned that the present system of paying everyone in a job role the same rate irrespective of their individual performance is unfair and tends to demotivate the best performers. She therefore decides to take a different approach when determining this year's annual pay rises:

1 Each member of staff will receive a 1% salary increase regardless of performance to take account of the increased cost of living.

2 Each line manager will be required to score their staff based on their individual performance over the past year. There are four options:

- excellent
- good
- satisfactory
- unsatisfactory.

3 Staff scored as 'excellent' will receive a 4% pay rise (3% plus the 1% cost of living increase), those marked as 'good' will receive 3% and those as 'satisfactory' 2%. People who are marked as 'unsatisfactory' will simply receive the 1% cost of living increase.

The hotel has not hitherto operated any kind of formal performance management system. There are no annual appraisals or development reviews. Managers vary greatly in the extent to which they communicate with their staff at all, let alone to discuss their individual performance. For many the only indicator they have that they are doing a good job is the amount they receive from guests in the form of tips. As a result, when the new scheme is announced in a series of staff meetings, there is enormous excitement. There is massive anticipation among staff in the days and weeks running up to the announcement of the pay awards.

At the last minute, however, there are hitches and as a result the announcement is delayed for a week. This occurs because Daphne finds herself disagreeing profoundly with the scores awarded by two of her managers.

George Clapham, the Head Porter, has awarded all his staff excellent ratings. When Daphne questions him about this, he replies that he thinks all his lads are wonderful, that they have all worked very hard over the last year and that they all deserve the full 4%. Surely, Daphne argues, he cannot give Graham Dudd an excellent rating? Not only has he been absent most of the past year, but he is regularly found away from his post chatting up chambermaids in the staff room?

George argues that Graham means well and is greatly liked by his colleagues. Daphne insists he is downgraded to 'satisfactory'.

Henry Oldham-Down, the Head Chef, has awarded two of his senior staff excellent ratings, but has rated all the commis chefs and kitchen porters as 'unsatisfactory'. When questioned about this, Henry says that they are all 'crap' and a waste of space as far as he is concerned and that giving them the 1% cost of living rise is much more than they deserve. Daphne lists some names of kitchen staff who she thinks do a good job. After each name is mentioned Henry just says 'crap'.

Daphne insists that one or two of the staff are upgraded to 'satisfactory'.

The following week letters are sent to all staff telling them how they have been rated by their managers and what the implications are for their pay. At the end of the letter is a sentence that asks staff who are unhappy with their pay rises to see Daphne Jones.

The following day a long line of disappointed staff forms outside Daphne's office. There is a perceivable drop in morale and this leads to reduced effort. In the coming weeks absence rates increase and guest complaints rise. There are particular problems in the kitchen, leading several guests to write very strongly worded letters of complaint.

Daphne is not surprised that poor performers are disappointed, but she finds it hard to understand why so many strong performers who have been rated 'good' are so negative about the whole exercise. What is more, she finds herself under fire from the finance director of the company which owns the hotel. He says that the pay bill is now too high and that it will have to be cut back next year.

The general manager of Cavendish Hall thinks that the problems with the scheme have mainly been caused by different managers rating people according to different criteria. Next year, he says, a forced ranking system will be used. This will mean that each line manager will be asked to rank their staff in order of performance. The top 25% will then receive the excellent rating and highest pay rise. Those in the second quartile will be scored as 'good' and those in the third and fourth quartiles as 'satisfactory' and 'unsatisfactory' respectively. This system also means that a budget can be set and that it will be adhered to in practice.

Questions

1 What was wrong with the design of the payment system?

2 What was wrong with the way it was introduced?

3 What do you think of the new 'forced ranking system' that is planned for next year?

4 What alternative type of system would you argue should be introduced and why?

FURTHER READING

Brown, D. and Armstrong, M. (2000) *Paying or Contribution: Real performance-related pay strategies*. London: Kogan Page.

Kohn, A. (1993) 'Why incentive plans cannot work', *Harvard Business Review*, September–October, pp. 54–63.
The debate about the merits of individual performance-related pay is so polarised that it is rare to find a balanced account that sets out the views of those who are for and those who are against. It is best to read the partisan accounts. Kohn's (1993) article contains an eloquent and damning critique of such schemes, while Brown and Armstrong (2000) paint a more positive picture.

Incomes Data Services: various publications.

Industrial Relations Services: various publications.

Information about trends in the design of incentive payment schemes is regularly provided in the IDS and IRS publications. They also commonly feature case studies which show exactly how the various schemes operate in practice as well as regular surveys of current practice that can be used for benchmarking processes.

Gerhart (2009) is a very good, comprehensive summary of academic research on incentives of all kinds, reviewing the major studies and reaching sound, balanced conclusions.

REFERENCES

Armstrong, M. and Brown, D. (2009) *Strategic Reward: Implementing more effective reward management*. London: Kogan Page.

Bartol, K.M. and Durham, C.C. (2000) 'Incentives: Theory and practice', in C. Cooper and E. Locke (eds), *Industrial and Organisational Psychology*. Oxford: Blackwell.

Brown, D. and Armstrong, M. (2000) *Paying for Contribution: Real performance-related pay strategies*. London: Kogan Page.

Bryson, A. and Forth, J. (2008) 'The theory and practice of pay setting', in P. Blyton *et al.* (eds), *The Sage Handbook of Industrial Relations*. London: Sage.

Cadsby, C., Song, F. and Tapon, F. (2007) 'Sorting and incentive effects of pay-for-performance: An experimental investigation', *Academy of Management Journal*, Vol. 37, pp. 554–79.

Cannell, M. and Wood, S. (1992) *Incentive Pay: Impact and evolution*. London: IPM.

CIPD (2012) *Reward Management: Annual survey report 2012*. London: CIPD.

Cohen, S. (2006) *Employee Share Plans: Supporting business performance*. London: CIPD.

Corby, S., White, G. and Stanworth, C. (2005) 'No news is good news? Evaluating new pay systems', *Human Resource Management Journal*, Vol. 15, No. 1, pp. 4–24.

Cox, A. (2006) 'The outcomes of variable pay systems: Tales of multiple costs and unforeseen consequences', *International Journal of Human Resource Management*, Vol. 16, No. 8, pp. 1475–97.

Gerhart, B. (2009) 'Compensation', in J. Storey *et al.* (eds), *The Routledge Companion to Strategic Human Resource Management*. London: Routledge.

Gerhart, B. and Trevor, C. (2008) 'Merit pay', in A. Varma *et al.* (eds), *Performance Management Systems: A global perspective*. London: Routledge.

Gielen, A.C., Kerkhofs, M.J.M. and Van Ours, J.C. (2006) *Performance-related Pay and Labour Productivity*, IZA Discussion Paper 2211. Berlin: Institute for the Study of Labour (IZA).

Gomez-Mejia, L. and Balkin, D. (1992) *Compensation, Organisational Strategy and Firm Performance*. Cincinnati, OH: South Western Publishing.

Guthrie, J. (2007) 'Remuneration: Pay effects at work', in P. Boxall *et al.* (eds), *The Oxford Handbook of Human Resource Management*. Oxford: Oxford University Press.

Hendry, C., Woodward, S., Bradley, P. and Perkins, S. (2000) 'Performance and rewards: Cleaning out the stables', *Human Resource Management Journal*, Vol. 10, No. 3, pp. 46–62.

Herzberg, F. (1966) *Work and the Nature of Man*. Cleveland, OH: World Publishing.

Huselid, M. (1995) 'The impact of HRM practices on turnover, productivity and corporate performance', *Academy of Management Journal*, Vol. 38, pp. 635–72.

IDS (1992) *Skills-based Pay*, IDS Study No. 500. London: Incomes Data Services.

IDS (2005) *Bonus Schemes*, IDS Study No. 794. London: Incomes Data Services.

IDS (2007) *Share Incentive Plans*, IDS Study No. 840. London: Incomes Data Services.

IRS (2005a) 'Pay 4 Performance at Yorkshire Water', *IRS Employment Review*, No. 833, pp. 31–5.

IRS (2005b) 'Performing flexible reward at Severn Trent Water', *IRS Employment Review*, No. 834, pp. 30–3.

IRS (2009) 'Charity employers are turning to performance-related pay', *IRS Employment Review*, No. 914, January.

Kohn, A. (1993) 'Why incentive plans cannot work', *Harvard Business Review*, September–October, pp. 54–63.

Lazear, E.P. (2000) 'Performance pay and productivity', *American Economic Review*, Vol. 90, No. 5, pp. 1346–61.

Makinson, J. (2000) *Incentives for Change*. London: HMSO.

Marginson, P. (2009) 'Performance pay and collective bargaining: A complex relationship', in S. Corby *et al.* (eds), *Rethinking Reward*. Basingstoke: Palgrave.

Marsden, D. (2004) 'The role of performance-related pay in renegotiating the "effort bargain": The case of the British public service', *Industrial and Labour Relations Review*, Vol. 57, No. 3, pp. 350–70.

OECD (2005) *Performance-related Pay Policies for Government Employees*. Paris: OECD.

Pearce, J.L., Stevenson, W.B. and Perry, J.L. (1985) 'Managerial compensation based on organisational performance: A time series analysis of the effects of merit pay', *Academy of Management Journal*, Vol. 28, pp. 261–78.

Pendleton, A. (2009) 'Employee share ownership in Europe', in S. Corby *et al.* (eds), *Rethinking Reward*. Basingstoke: Palgrave.

Pfeffer, J. (1998) *The Human Equation: Building profits by putting people first*. Boston, MA: Harvard Business School Press.

Piekkola, H. (2005) 'Performance-related pay and firm performance in Finland', *International Journal of Manpower*, Vol. 7, No. 8, pp. 619–35.

Prentice, G., Burgess, S. and Propper, C. (2007) *Performance Pay in the Public Sector: A review of the issues and evidence*. London: Office of Manpower Economics.

Purcell, J. (2000) 'Pay per view', *People Management*, 3 February, pp. 41–3.

Rubery, J. (1995) 'Performance-related pay and the prospects for gender pay equity', *Journal of Management Studies*, Vol. 32, No. 5, pp. 637–54.

Sisson, K. and Storey, J. (2000) *The Realities of Human Resource Management*. Buckingham: Open University Press.

Thompson, M. (1992) *Pay and Performance: The employer experience*, Institute of Manpower Studies Report 218. London: IMS.

Thompson, M. (2000) 'Salary progression systems', in G. White and J. Druker (eds), *Reward Management: A critical text*. London: Routledge.

Van Wanrooy, B., Bewley, H., Bryson, A., Forth, J., Freeth, S., Stokes, L. and Wood, S. (2013) *The 2011 Workplace Employment Relations Study: First findings*. London: Department for Business, Innovation and Science.

Chapter 23

PENSIONS AND BENEFITS

THE OBJECTIVES OF THIS CHAPTER ARE TO:

1   Introduce the different types of pension scheme provided by the state, by employers and by financial services organisations

2   Explain the causes and significance of current trends in the provision of occupational pensions

3   Outline the roles played by HR professionals in the field of occupational pensions

4   Distinguish between Statutory Sick Pay (SSP) and Occupational Sick Pay (OSP)

5   Assess developments in the provision of company cars by UK employers

6   Explore the potential of flexible benefits systems in the UK context

Employee benefits commonly used to be known as 'fringe benefits', suggesting a peripheral role in the typical pay packet. The substantial growth in the value of most benefits packages over the past twenty or thirty years means that the title 'fringe' is no longer appropriate. An increasing proportion of individual remuneration is made up of additional perks, allowances and entitlements which are mostly paid in kind rather than cash. The total value of benefits 'paid' by employers to employees commonly represents between 20% and 50% of an organisation's salary budget, depending on what is included. Pensions alone can easily account for 20%, to which must be added the costs of providing some or all of the following: company cars, sick pay, meals, live-in accommodation, parking facilities, private health insurance, crèche facilities, mobile phones, Christmas parties, staff discounts, relocation expenses and any holiday or maternity allowances paid in excess of the required statutory minima. Wright (2009a: 184) shows that these extra elements of pay are distributed unevenly between members of staff. Those earning at the top of the scale (especially directors and senior managers) tend to gain rather more than average employees, 30% or 50% of their take-home pay being accounted for by benefits of various kinds.

This is an area of HRM policy in which practice varies considerably from country to country. In the USA, for example, there is no legal entitlement to paid holiday and it is usual for people to take just two weeks leave in a year. Yet the extent and generosity of employer-provided private health insurance and pensions is as good as anywhere in the world. By contrast, in France holiday entitlements and redundancy payments are very generous, but pensions are rarely provided for most employees at all. In the UK statutory paid maternity leave and associated rights are among the most generous in the world, have become increasingly generous in recent years, yet are still exceeded by many employers. Occupational pensions are in decline in the UK, but still cover many more employees than is the case in most European countries. Generally speaking, however, everywhere in the world the long-term trend is towards the provision of a wider range of benefits, and for this element of the total pay package to increase as a proportion of the whole.

Despite these developments, there remains a big question mark over how far employees value the benefits provided to them by their employers or appreciate the extent of the costs involved in their provision. Surveys of both employers and employees regularly demonstrate that staff have little understanding of the value of the benefits they receive and that there is thus little by way of any positive motivational effect generated by their presence (see Accor 2008; Thomson Online 2007). This does not mean, of course, that employers can easily stop offering benefits. While the full cost may not be appreciated by employees, they are generally in favour of the benefits and would resent their removal. Poor publicity would also inevitably follow the withdrawal of rewards such as pensions which are generally seen as being the hallmark of a good employer. The alternative courses of action involve communicating the true value of benefits to employees more effectively and providing them with a degree of choice as to which benefits they wish to receive. The latter approach, involving the provision of 'flexible' or 'cafeteria' benefits, has become very common in the USA and has received a great deal of attention in the UK too.

Pensions

The role of employers in providing pensions has moved up the public policy agenda for several reasons in recent years, but underlying all of them are the long-term demographic trends which have called into question the ability of the established UK pension system to provide an adequate income to older people after they retire. First and foremost, people are living increasingly longer and thus require a bigger pension to provide them with an income across their years of retirement. In 1950 men aged 65 in the UK could expect to live for a further twelve years on average, and women for a further fifteen. The figures are now over nineteen years for men and twenty-two for women, and with rapid developments in medical science there is every reason to expect life expectancy rates to accelerate further in the coming fifty years. It is likely, according to many projections, that over half of the people born in the 1980s will live into their 90s and beyond. Second, fewer children are being born, birth rates in the UK having been at below replacement rates since the late 1960s (Pemberton *et al.* 2006: 4). These trends are soon going to lead to a steady increase in the dependency ratio, by which is meant the proportion of retired people vis-à-vis working people in the economy. At present in the UK 27% of the adult population is aged over 65. By 2050, according to the Government Actuary, the proportion will be 48% (Turner 2004: 4). Demographic trends are thus leading us steadily towards a situation in which the funding of adequate pensions using established approaches is going to become harder and harder to achieve. The trend for more young people to stay at school until the age of 18 and for many more to go on to university makes the problem more acute because it further reduces the proportion of the population which is economically active.

The UK is by no means unique in facing this long-term problem. Indeed, in many other industrialised countries the situation is worse because fertility rates are lower still and there is a tradition of greater reliance on the state to provide pension income than has hitherto been the case in the UK. Everywhere it is increasingly being realised that action needs to be taken now in order to avoid a future scenario in which either the elderly live in unacceptable poverty or taxation has to be increased to economically unsustainable levels in order to fund a decent level of state pension.

In the UK the situation has been made worse over the past fifteen years by some most unwelcome trends in the occupational pensions sector. Until the 1990s the UK could boast that it had one of the most extensive and well-funded systems of occupational pension provision in the world. Well over half of the workforce were members of reasonably generous, well-funded occupational pension schemes provided for them by their employers, while millions of retired employees drew a substantial income from the schemes which supplemented their state pensions. This system was likened by commentators who drew international comparisons to the goose that laid the golden egg. It meant that the UK had a great deal less to worry about from population ageing than other countries because so much more of our pension income was sourced privately through both individual savings and these huge, long-established occupational pension funds. Unfortunately, the goose has now stopped laying the golden eggs and the long-established system is in terminal decline. Employers are less likely to offer membership of occupational schemes than they were, and where they still do, it is on a less satisfactory financial basis when seen from the perspective of most employees.

A combination of factors is responsible, but the core problem is the hugely increased costs that are now associated with the provision of good pensions for staff. This is due to taxation changes, to increased life expectancy and to the need to keep topping up pension funds whenever the stock market suffers falls of the kinds it has in recent years.

The government has responded to this situation in a way that most commentators have welcomed, although some argue that the plans it has put in place do not go far enough. In 2002 Adair Turner (now Lord Turner), a former Director General of the Confederation of British Industry (CBI), was appointed by the Department of Work and Pensions to lead an extensive review of future pension provision in the UK. The Turner Commission has since produced three substantial reports setting out its findings and recommendations. The government accepted the vast majority of these and brought forward legislation in the form of the Pensions Act 2007 to encourage later retirement and significantly greater levels of saving into pension funds. It also makes important changes to the established state pension system which are aimed particularly at improving the position of women. At the same time other steps have been taken by the government to ease the pressures on the pension system caused by demographic trends. The equalisation of state pension ages between men and women is such a step, as in many respects is the recent substantial growth in immigration. Other measures include new incentives for people who are not working (e.g. single parents and early retirees) to re-enter the workforce.

ACTIVITY 23.1

The UK has always been unusual in having such a substantial occupational pensions sector. There is a similar system in the Netherlands and in the Republic of Ireland, but in most EU countries most employers see no reason why they should be involved in the provision of pensions. Why do you think these differences persist? What arguments would you advance to persuade a company based in an EU country of the need to offer occupational pensions to employees in a new UK subsidiary?

State schemes

In the UK the state currently runs two schemes: a basic scheme and the State Second Pension (S2P) scheme, although the latter will soon be phased out and replaced with a single, more generous, basic old age pension benefit. By 2020 the pensionable age for both men and women will be 65 and in the years running up to this date the pensionable age for women is gradually increasing from 60 where it was for many decades. The government has announced plans to push back the state pension age for men and women once equalisation has been achieved. It will increase to 66 from 2024, to 67 from 2034 and to 68 from 2044, but changes may in fact come in considerably earlier than this.

The state pension scheme is organised on a pay-as-you-go basis. This means that there is no state pension fund as such, and the money that is paid to today's pensioners comes from today's taxes and National Insurance contributions. The money that will be paid to today's contributors, when they become pensioners, will come not from the investment of their and their employers' contributions, but from the contributions of the workforce and its employers in the future. This is why there is concern about the ability of future governments to be able to fund state pensions for many more retired people beyond a basic subsistence level, and why a raft of new regulation is currently being introduced which aims to increase pension saving (see below).

Occupational schemes

The UK has had, for many years, one of the most extensive and effective systems of occupational pension provision in the world. According to the most recent government statistics, there are around 44,000 separate schemes in operation with combined assets worth approximately £1.9 trillion. Just over 8 million people are members of occupational pension schemes, while around 9 million pensioners draw an income from their funds (ONS 2012a). Although there has been some reduction recently in the proportion of the workforce covered by occupational pensions, they remain by far the most significant employee benefit in terms of their cost to employers.

Occupational schemes provide an additional retirement pension on top of the state pension, providing better and wider-ranging benefits than the state schemes and a great deal more flexibility. They are most often found in large organisations and the public sector, but some smaller organisations also run such schemes. Men and women have equal access to occupational schemes and, since 1990, have had to be treated equally in respect of all scheme rules. Yet, in spite of this, men and women continue to fare differently in terms of pension benefits due to the typical pattern of women's employment being different from male patterns and women's longer average life expectancy. A higher proportion of managerial and professional workers have occupational pensions than other groups, unskilled workers being the least likely to be in schemes. It is no longer lawful for an employer to exclude part-time or temporary workers.

With the exception of one or two in the public sector, occupational schemes do not pay their pensioners in the pay-as-you-go manner operated by the state, but create a pension fund, which is managed separately from the business. The advantage of this is that, should the organisation become bankrupt, the pension fund cannot be seized to pay debtors because it is not part of the company. The money in the pension fund is invested and held in trust for the employees of the company at the time of their retirement. However, where a company becomes insolvent at a time when its pension fund is in deficit, employees can lose all or part of their pensions. This has happened in one or two high-profile cases recently, leading the government to establish a central fund to provide a measure of compensation to those whose pensions are reduced as a result of their employer's insolvency.

Larger organisations traditionally administer their own pension funds through an investment or fund manager. The manager will plan how to invest the money in the fund to get the best return and to ensure that the money that is needed to pay pensions and other benefits will be available when required. An actuary can provide mortality tables and other statistical information in order to assist planning and must be hired regularly to carry out a formal actuarial assessment of the scheme's assets and liabilities. Smaller organisations tend to appoint an insurance company or a bank to administer their pension funds, and so use their expertise. Pension funds can be invested in a variety of different ways, and are often worth more than the market value of their sponsoring companies. As a result they have come to dominate investment on the stock market.

Defined benefit schemes

Defined benefit schemes dominated in the final decades of the twentieth century, but the number of people with access to them has declined hugely in the last ten years. Virtually all the public-sector schemes still take this form, but 87% of the private-sector schemes have now been closed to new members (NAPF 2013). They remain operational only for the purposes of paying pensions to retired members and for the benefit of employees who joined before their closure. Here contributions are made into a single organisation-wide fund which is invested on behalf of members by a fund manager. Retired employees then draw a pension from the fund calculated according to a defined formula. Most defined benefit schemes take the final salary form, in which the value of the pension is determined by the level of salary being received by each individual at the time of retirement. In the private sector it is common for this to be calculated on a 'sixtieths' basis, whereby the retiree is paid an annual pension equivalent to $1 \div 60$ (1.67%) of their final salary multiplied by the number of years' pensionable service they have completed. In the public sector it is usual for the figure to be based on 'eightieths', with a tax-free lump sum being paid in addition at the time of retirement. In either case the size of pension is heavily related to the length of scheme membership, the maximum pension payable equalling two-thirds of final salary. Examples of final salary calculations are given in Table 23.1.

Another form of defined benefit scheme bases the pension calculation on the average salary earned over a period of 5, 10 or 20 years prior to retirement rather than on pay in the final year. Unless most of someone's pensionable service has been spent earning close to the final salary level, such schemes are less generous than the final salary variety in terms of the amount of pension paid. High levels of inflation also reduce the value of pensions calculated on an average salary basis. The government has signalled that it wishes over time to convert the public-sector schemes from the final salary to an average salary formula, while also removing the right previously enjoyed by many public-sector workers to retire on a full pension at the age of 60.

Most defined benefit schemes are contributory. This means that monies are paid into the fund on a regular basis by both the employer and the employee. In the case of

Table 23.1
Final salary schemes – examples of various contribution periods with a 1/60th and a 1/80th scheme

Sixtieths scheme:	
Final salary	= £24,000
Contributions for 5 years	= 1/60 × 24,000 × 5
Pension	= £2,000 per year
Final salary	= £24,000
Contributions for 25 years	= 1/60 × 24,000 × 25
Pension	= £10,000 per year
Final salary	= £24,000
Contributions for 40 years	= 1/60 × 24,000 × 40
Pension	= £16,000 per year
Eightieths scheme:	
Final salary	= £24,000
Contributions for 25 years	= 1/80 × 24,000 × 25
Pension	= £7,500 per year
Lump sum	= 3/80 × 24,000 × 25 = £22,500

employees the contribution is fixed as a percentage of salary (typically 5%), a sum which is subject to tax relief. Employers, by contrast, are obliged only to pay in sufficient funds to ensure that the scheme remains solvent. When the pension fund is in surplus, as many were in the 1980s and 1990s, employers can take 'contribution holidays'. By contrast, when the fund is in deficit, the employer has to contribute whatever is necessary to ensure that assets are sufficient to meet possible liabilities.

This means that the amount of employer contribution can vary considerably, year on year, in an unpredictable fashion. In 2012 contribution rates for employers were averaging over 15% of salary (ONS 2012b). However, employers, like employees, gain from tax relief on contributions paid.

In some industries, as well as parts of the public sector, it has been traditional for occupational pensions to be non-contributory. In such schemes the employee makes no contribution at all, but nonetheless draws a pension calculated according to the final salary. Civil servants benefit from this kind of arrangement, as do many employees in the banking and finance sectors. Defined benefit schemes also typically offer extra benefits such as ill-health pensions for those forced to retire early and death-in-service benefits for widows and widowers.

Defined contribution schemes

Defined contribution schemes (also known as money purchase schemes) are organised in a totally different way from defined benefit arrangements. There are no promises about what the final level of pension will be. Instead employees and employers both contribute a fixed percentage of current salary to these schemes, usually 5% to 8% on a monthly basis. The pension benefits received are then entirely dependent on the money that has been contributed and the way that it has been invested. Where investments perform well, a good level of pension can be gained. Where investments are disappointing, the result is a low level of pension. Further uncertainty derives from the way that money purchase schemes result in the payment of a single lump sum to the employee when he or she retires. This is then used to buy an annuity from an insurance company from which a weekly or monthly income is paid for life. Annuity rates vary considerably from year to year, and there is also considerable variation between the deals offered by different providers. In essence this means that the risk associated with pension investments is carried by the employee in a defined contribution arrangement, rather than by the employer as in a final salary scheme. For this reason defined contribution schemes are generally less satisfactory than defined benefit schemes when seen from an employee's perspective. Investments have to perform unusually well while inflation remains low for a money purchase scheme to give an equivalent level of benefit. However, despite these drawbacks, money purchase schemes are more flexible and more easily transferable than defined benefit arrangements. For people changing jobs frequently or working on a self-employed basis for periods of time, particularly during the early years of a career, they can thus be a more attractive option.

In recent years there has been a strong trend away from defined benefit schemes and towards defined contribution provision. The majority of newly established schemes take the defined contribution form, while many organisations now offer only a money purchase scheme to new employees (Dobson and Horsfield 2009). The trend has coincided with a period in which long contribution holidays have come to an end and in which the amount of regulation to which defined benefit schemes are subject has increased substantially. Employers have thus taken the opportunity to reduce their own liabilities and to move to a form of provision which is more predictable financially from their point of view, but which is likely to pay a far lower level of pension to their employees when they retire.

Hybrid schemes

Hybrid schemes too are becoming more common, although as yet they represent a small minority of UK pension funds. These, in various different ways, combine elements of the defined benefit and defined contribution forms of provision. The most common form is the 'money purchase underpin' which is basically a final salary arrangement, but one which calculates pensions and transfer values on a money purchase basis where these are higher. Such schemes seek to combine the best aspects of both main types of scheme. They offer a generous, secure and predictable pension, but also incorporate the flexibility associated with defined contribution schemes.

In the USA some organisations have moved towards the provision of cash-balance pension plans which work on a final salary basis, but pay out a single lump sum at retirement rather than a monthly pension (Field *et al*. 2009: 185). The employee uses the money to purchase an annuity, so the level of pension received varies considerably depending on market rates at the time of retirement. Such schemes make the financial commitment more predictable from the employer's perspective, but tend to result in lower pensions than a conventional final salary arrangement.

ACTIVITY 23.2

Which of these three types of occupational pension scheme would you find most attractive at the current stage in your career? Under what circumstances might you change your preference?

Group personal pensions

Since the 1980s there has been substantial growth in the market for personal pensions. Self-employed people have always used these, but increasingly as employers have withdrawn from occupational pensions, employees have had to start up personal pensions too. More general attention has been focused on this area due to increasing job mobility and the perceived greater portability of personal pensions. A personal pension is arranged, usually through an insurance company, and the individual pays regular amounts into his or her own 'pension fund' in the same way that the individual would with a company fund. The employer may also make a contribution to the fund, but at present there are very few employers who have chosen to do so.

An alternative arrangement is a Group Personal Pension plan (GPP) set up by an employer instead of an occupational pension scheme. From a legal and taxation perspective a GPP is no different from any individual personal pension arrangement, but charges are lower because the employer is able to arrange a bulk discount. The scheme is administered by an insurance company, the employer making contributions as well as the employee. Pensions are calculated on the same basis as an occupational money purchase scheme, but tend to be less extensive because employees are responsible for paying some of the administrative charges. From an employee's perspective a GPP is inferior to an occupational pension scheme, but is better than a situation in which no employer provision is made at all. Such arrangements are mainly entered into by small firms, but one or two big companies have also set them up in place of conventional occupational pensions. A key difference is that a GPP is contract based rather than trust based. This means that unlike an occupational pension there is no board of trustees appointed to oversee the running of the scheme; instead a contract is signed with an external provider.

Auto-enrolment

The Pensions Act 2008 contained a range of measures designed to increase the amount of money being saved in private pension funds and also to encourage employer contributions. At the time of writing (2013) these are in the process of being phased in. The requirements are complex and apply at different times to different organisations depending on their size in terms of staff. The first 'staging date' was 1 October 2012. There are forty-two in all, only businesses employing fewer than five people being exempt for the time being.

Ultimately, once all staging dates have passed in October 2017, all employees in the UK who earn over £9,440 (in 2013) and are over the age of 22 will have to be enrolled either in an occupational pension scheme or in the new government-sponsored 'personal pension account scheme'. People will be able to opt out if they wish, but otherwise they will be automatically enrolled into one scheme or the other, including any new starters after the relevant staging date. Employees will contribute 4% of their earnings (up to £41,450 in 2013) into their fund and employers will contribute 3%, tax relief effectively meaning that a further 1% is contributed by the government.

The aim is to achieve a situation by the middle of the century whereby 60% of retirement income is provided from private sources and only 40% by the state. At present 60% is state provided and only 40% from private sources.

Occupational pensions and HRM

Although occupational pension schemes are governed by a board of trustees which includes member representatives, in most organisations the pensions manager and pensions department are part of the HR function. It is thus important that HR professionals are familiar with the types of scheme offered and the main operating rules so that they can give accurate and timely advice to staff and to potential recruits. They also need to be familiar with the regulatory environment for occupational pensions, which has changed considerably in recent years. Aside from new legislation outlawing discrimination on grounds of sex or against part-time and temporary staff, several other important regulatory changes have been made and new regulatory bodies established. The Pensions Act 1995 sets out in detail what information must be disclosed to scheme members on request and what must be sent to them automatically each year. The Act also requires all occupational funds to meet a defined minimum funding level so that they are always able to meet their liabilities in the event of the employing company being wound up. Moreover, strict restrictions are now placed on 'self-investment', making sure that fund assets cannot be invested in property or other business ventures controlled by the sponsoring organisation.

The Social Security Act 1985 put in place a series of measures to protect 'early leavers', ensuring that people who switch employers during their careers do not suffer substantial loss in the value of their pensions. Early leavers now have one of three options in making their pension arrangements when they begin work for a new employer. One option is to claim back the contributions that the individual has made into the former employer's pension scheme. Deductions are made in accordance with tax laws and, of course, the employer's contribution is lost, but a substantial sum can be reinvested in the new employer's scheme or in a personal pension. Another alternative involves opting for a preserved pension. With a final salary scheme, if there were no inflation, and if the individual progressed very little up the career ladder, a preserved pension from an old employer plus a pension from the recent employer would equate well with the pension the individual would have received had he or she been with the new employer for the whole period. However, if these conditions are not met, which in recent times they have not been, individuals who have had more than one employer lose out in the pension stakes. Past employers are required to revalue preserved pensions in line with inflation (to a maximum of 5%), but the value of such a pension remains linked to the level of salary at the date of leaving.

The third option is usually preferable, but is only open to people who have completed two years' membership of a scheme. This involves the transfer of the pension from the old employer's fund into that of the new employer. The process is straightforward in the case of a money purchase scheme, because the worth of each person's pension is readily calculated. It is simply the value of the employee's contributions, plus those of the employer, together with funds accrued as a result of their investment. The process is more complicated in the case of a final salary scheme, the transfer value being calculated according to standard actuarial conventions which take account of the employee's age, the length of pensionable service, the level of salary at the time of leaving and the current interest rate. All things being equal, 'early leavers' still fare worse than 'stayers' in terms of final pensions, but the difference is a great deal less than used to be the case.

Aside from giving advice and taking overall responsibility for pensions issues, HR managers are concerned with determining their organisations' pension policy. Is an occupational pension to be offered? If so, what form should it take? What level of contribution is the employer going to make? It is quite possible to make a judgement in favour of generous occupational provision simply on paternalistic grounds. Many organisations have thus decided that they will offer pensions because it is in the interests of their staff that they should. Occupational schemes represent a convenient and tax-advantageous method of providing an income in old age; it therefore makes sense to include a pension in the total pay and benefits package. The problems with such a commitment, particularly in the case of defined benefit schemes, are the cost and the fact that the long-term financial consequences are unpredictable. This, combined with the fact that many employees do not seem to appreciate the value of an occupational pension, is one of the reasons that many employers have been questioning their commitment to final salary schemes and to pension provision in general.

Research suggests that interest in and understanding of occupational pensions varies considerably from person to person (Taylor 2009). Older people, professional workers and those working in the financial services sector usually have a clearer perception of their value than other groups of staff. For these groups pensions are important, and their labour market behaviour will be affected as a result. A firm which does not offer a good pension will thus find it harder to recruit and retain them than one which does. By contrast, a firm which largely employs younger people, and/or workers in lower-skilled occupations, may find that it makes more sense to offer additional pay in place of an occupational scheme.

ACTIVITY 23.3

It has been argued that by making occupational pensions readily transferable, by increasing the complexity of the regulatory regime and by increasing taxation levied on pension funds, successive governments have provided a major disincentive to employers considering the establishment of a scheme. To what extent do you agree with this point of view?

Sick pay

As with pension schemes, the provision of sick pay is seen as the mark of a good employer. Sick pay is an important issue due to the need for control and administration of absence. Research suggests that sickness absence represents around 4% of working time (CBI 2008), although there are large differences between sector and job type. The HR manager and the HR department have a variety of roles to play in relation to sick pay, particularly in relation to the administration of Statutory Sick Pay.

Statutory Sick Pay

Statutory Sick Pay (SSP) is a state benefit that has been in existence for several decades. It provides a basic income (£76.70 per week in 2013) to employees who are incapable of going to their normal place of work as a result of illness. SSP, however, is not claimed from a benefit office; it is administered by employers and paid through the payroll according to regulations set out in statute.

Employers are required to take full financial responsibility for SSP for the first four weeks of absence, after which they can claim back a portion of the costs from the state through reduced employer National Insurance contributions. However, the method of calculation used ensures that smaller employers are able to claim back a considerably higher proportion of the costs than larger employers who usually have to fund it all themselves. Most employees are entitled to State Sickness Benefit; however, there are some exceptions: employees who fall sick outside the EU; employees who are sick during an industrial dispute; employees over pensionable age; and part-timers whose earnings are below the lower earnings limit (£109 per week in 2013). These groups, as well as self-employed people, are obliged to claim State Incapacity Benefit instead. SSP is built around the concepts of qualifying days, waiting days, certification, linked periods, transfer to the Department for Work and Pensions (DWP) and record periods.

- **Qualifying days** are those days on which the employee would normally have worked, except for the fact that he or she was sick. For many Monday-to-Friday employees this is very straightforward. However, it is more complex to administer for those on some form of rotating week or shift system. Sick pay is only payable for qualifying days.

- **Waiting days** have to pass before the employee is entitled to receive sick pay – at present the number of days is three. These three days must be qualifying days, and on the fourth qualifying day the employee is entitled to sickness benefit, should he or she still be away from work due to sickness.

- **Certification** from a doctor is required after seven days of sickness absence. Prior to this the employee provides self-certification. This involves notifying the employer of absence due to sickness by the first day on which benefit is due – that is, immediately following the three waiting days.

- **Linked periods** of illness mean that the three waiting days do not apply. If the employee has had a period of incapacity from work (PIW) within the previous eight weeks, then the two periods are linked and treated as just one period for SSP purposes, and so the three waiting days do not have to pass again.

The employer does not have to administer SSP for every employee indefinitely. Where the employee has been absent due to sickness for a continuous or linked period of twenty-eight weeks the responsibility for payment passes from the employer to the state. A continuous period of twenty-eight weeks' sickness is clearly identifiable. It is not so clear when linked periods are involved. An employee who was sick for five days, back at work for four weeks, sick for one day, at work for seven weeks and then sick for two days would have a linked period of incapacity of eight days. Alternatively, an employee who was sick for four days, back at work for ten weeks and then sick for five days would have a period of incapacity this time of five days. The DWP requires employers to keep SSP records for three years so that these can be inspected.

Occupational Sick Pay

There is no obligation on employers to pay employees for days of absence due to sickness beyond what is required under the state's SSP scheme. However, most employers choose to do so via a benefit known as Occupational Sick Pay (OSP). The most common approach is to continue paying the full salary for a set period of time, but other schemes involve reducing the pay rate for days taken off as a result of illness. In either case a sum in excess of the statutory minimum is paid, the portion accounted for by SSP being reclaimed from the state where possible. Paying the full salary is straightforward for those staff who receive a basic salary with no additions. It is more difficult to define for those whose pay is supplemented by shift allowances or productivity bonuses.

OSP arrangements tend to be most generous in unionised environments and in the public sector, although professional and managerial employees are usually well covered in most organisations. The common public-sector approach involves paying full pay for the first six months of an illness, once three years' service have been completed, before moving the employee on to half-pay for a further six months. Thereafter OSP ceases. At the other end of the scale are employers who pay no OSP at all. They take the view that OSP will be abused and so pay only what is due under the state scheme. Another approach involves paying a predetermined flat rate in addition to money provided via SSP.

OSP schemes also vary according to the period of service required. Some employers provide sick pay for sickness absence from the first day of employment. Others require a qualifying period to be served. For some this is a nominal period of four weeks, but the period may be three or six months, or a year or more. There is a major difference here between OSP and SSP. With SSP, pay is available immediately after employment has begun.

Company cars

A form of employee benefit which is a great deal more common in the UK than in other countries is the company car, but it is a good deal less common than it used to be. In 2000, 84% of companies offered a car to at least some of their staff. By 2012 the proportion had fallen to 54% (CIPD 2012). Managers from overseas often take some persuading that cars are necessary to attract and retain high-calibre managers, but the received wisdom is that they are. Their importance to employees is demonstrated by the comparative lack of take-up of cash alternatives where these are offered (Smith 2000a: 161). After pensions, they are the second most significant employee benefit in cost terms.

There are a number of sound reasons underlying the provision of company cars. First, for some there is a need as part of their jobs to travel very widely and regularly. Not everyone can be assumed to own a reliable car, so it is sometimes necessary to provide one simply to enable an employee to carry out his or her day-to-day job duties. In the case of sales representatives and senior managers the impression created when travelling on company business can be important. It is therefore often considered necessary to provide them with upmarket and up-to-date models to ensure that clients and potential clients are suitably impressed. A case can also be made on cost efficiency grounds for people who clock up a great number of business miles each year. The cost of paying them a reasonable mileage allowance to drive their own cars is often greater than the cost of providing them with a company vehicle; it costs £9,000 a year to reimburse someone who has travelled 30,000 miles at 30p per mile.

However, most possessors of company cars do not fit either of the above categories. Their car entitlements simply come as an expected part of the pay package for middle and senior managers. As such, they signify the achievement of a certain level of status. Indeed, in many companies the cars offered become steadily more imposing as people climb up the corporate hierarchy. Being upgraded to a more impressive car thus signifies in a very manifest way the company's approval. Downgrading, of course, has the opposite effect.

One of the reasons that company cars are so significant in the UK is historical. Until 1994 they were a highly tax-efficient benefit. It was a good deal cheaper to drive a company car than to purchase one's own out of taxed income, so it made sense for people to be 'paid' in part with a car. This is now far from being the case.

The current tax regime introduced in 2002 encourages employers to lease or purchase cars which are environmentally friendly. Formerly company cars were simply taxed according to the number of miles driven on company business, the annual tax paid by the driver being equivalent to a percentage of the car's list price. The more business miles clocked up, the less tax was paid. In addition there were substantial discounts for people who drove older cars. Since 2002 the tax paid depends on carbon emissions or engine size and there are no reductions for people who drive a great number of miles or use an older vehicle. So there is a substantial incentive for people who drive a great deal as part of their jobs to use smaller cars or larger ones with low carbon emissions. Most employers offer cash alternatives equal to the tax payable on the car, but many of those eligible choose not to take these up despite the fact that there are no longer any obvious tax advantages associated with driving a company car. This is partly because company cars tend to be more expensive than individuals could justify spending from their own income, but mainly because of the substantial savings that still accrue in terms of insurance, maintenance and repair costs. The tax changes have, however, led to a preference for 'trading down'. This means that, where a choice is given, employees are increasingly opting for a smaller car and more cash in their pay packets.

ACTIVITY 23.4

Assume that you have been offered a new job which comes with either the use of a new company car or a cash allowance. The salary is £35,000 per year. The car is worth £15,000, giving you an annual tax bill of £5,250. This is also the amount being offered by way of an annual cash allowance. Which option would you choose and why?

Flexible benefits

Flexible benefits or 'cafeteria plans' have proliferated in the USA over recent years where they are specifically recognised in the tax regime. By contrast, take-up of the idea in the UK has tended to be slow (Wright 2009b: 207). However, several high-profile organisations have now moved towards greater flexibility and there is unquestionably a great deal more interest in the approach developing among UK employers more generally. This has been driven by skills shortages and to initiatives in the work–life balance arena. The CIPD (2012: 41) reports that 24% of the respondents to its reward management survey operated some form of flexible benefits scheme.

The case for flexible benefits from an HRM perspective is strong, but the systems themselves can prove to be very costly to operate. The approach involves giving individual employees a choice as to how exactly their pay packet is made up. The overall value of the package is set by the employer, but it is for employees to choose for themselves what balance they wish to strike between cash and the different kinds of benefit. Those who have children, for example, can opt for benefits that are of value to them, such as childcare vouchers, access to a company crèche or additional holidays. A young person in their first job might well prefer to forgo most benefits in return for higher take-home pay, while an older person may wish to purchase additional years of pensionable service in exchange for cash or perhaps a car.

There are a number of good reasons for considering such an approach. First, it helps ensure that employees are only provided with benefits which they are aware of and appreciate. Resources that would otherwise be wasted by providing unwanted benefits are thus saved. The employer gets maximum value per pound spent, while at the same time allowing employees to tailor their own 'perfect' benefits mix. The result should be improved staff retention and a better motivated workforce.

WINDOW ON PRACTICE

In 1998 a large-scale merger took place between two of the world's largest professional services firms – Price Waterhouse and Coopers & Lybrand. The merged firm, called PricewaterhouseCoopers, employs 150,000 people in 150 different countries. While the two organisations were culturally similar, they had rather different traditions in the provision of benefits. Rather than continue with different people employed on different sets of terms and conditions, the partners decided to harmonise everyone as soon as was possible. This process was made a great deal easier and less contentious by the decision to develop a new flexible benefits scheme called 'Choices'. It allows employees to trade cash for additional holiday, a choice of car, childcare vouchers, retail vouchers, insurance of various kinds and a pension. No one was required to alter their existing benefits package as a result of the merger unless they wished to.

Source: Franks, O. and Thompson, D. (2000) 'Rights and rites of passage', *People Management*, 17 February.

Flexible benefits plans take many different forms, the main distinction being between those that are 'fully flexible' and those that allow a degree of flexibility within prescribed limits. The former allow employees a free hand to make up their own package and to change it at regular intervals. Under such a regime an employee could theoretically swap all benefits for cash, or could double his or her holiday entitlement in exchange for a pay cut. A degree of restriction is more common, a compulsory core of benefits being compulsory, with flexibility beyond that. Under such a scheme everyone might be required to take four weeks' holiday and invest in a minimal pension, but be allowed freedom to determine whether or not they wished to benefit from private health insurance, gym membership, discounts on company products, etc. Typical plans also permit some choice of the make and model of car.

A third approach is administratively simpler but is more restrictive in terms of employee choice. This involves 'prepackaging' a number of separate benefits menus designed to suit different groups of employees (rather like a pre-set banquet menu in a Chinese restaurant). Employees must then opt for one package from a choice of five or six, each having the same overall cash value. One is typically tailored to meet the needs of older staff, another is for those with young families, a third for new graduates and so on.

A number of disadvantages with flexible benefits systems can be identified which may well explain their relatively slow development in the UK. These are summarised by Smith (2000b) as follows:

Objections include difficult administration; problems connected with handling individual employee choices; the requirement for complex costing and records; difficulty in getting employees to make effective choices; employees making mistakes (for example leaving themselves with inadequate pension cover); employees' circumstances changing over time leaving his or her package inappropriate and giving the employer the costly headache of re-designing the package; and finally the possible hiring of expensive specialist or consultant skills and financial counselling to support the move to flexibility.

Uncertainty about the future tax position may also be a deterrent, especially where changes have the potential to throw a whole system out of kilter (as happened in 1997 when the Chancellor of the Exchequer substantially extended taxation on pension fund investments).

SUMMARY PROPOSITIONS

23.1   Between 20% and 50% of the typical employer's pay bill is spent on the provision of supplementary benefits. Evidence suggests that most employees do not appreciate the true financial value of such benefits.

23.2   Occupational pensions are a tax-efficient means of providing funds for retirement in excess of what is provided by state and personal pension schemes.

23.3   Employers are required to facilitate the payment of Statutory Sick Pay to employees who are away from work as a result of an illness. Most pay Occupational Sick Pay in addition either as a result of moral obligation or in order to attract, retain and motivate their workforces.

23.4   Company cars are commonly provided by UK employers for senior staff. The tax regime aims to discourage demand for larger cars which are not environmentally friendly.

23.5   In theory flexible benefits plans have a great deal to offer employees. It is likely that their use will grow more widespread in the next few years.

GENERAL DISCUSSION TOPICS

1   Why do you think so few people seem to have an appreciation of the value of their occupational pensions and other benefits? What could be done to raise awareness of the costs involved in their provision?

2   Draw up three flexible benefits packages: one aimed at new graduates; one at employees in their 30s; and one for those aged over 50.

THEORY INTO PRACTICE

According to the 2012 Annual Reward Management Survey carried out by the Chartered Institute of Personnel and Development, the following benefits are provided for employees by over 20% of UK employers:

- Twenty-five paid holiday days a year in addition to bank holidays
- Training and career development
- Childcare vouchers
- Free tea and coffee
- Christmas party
- On-site car parking
- Eye-care vouchers
- Employee assistance programme (i.e. counselling advice helpline)
- Life assurance
- Enhanced maternity and paternity leave
- Dress-down days
- Cycle-to-work loans
- Subsidised dining
- Travel season ticket loans
- Unpaid sabbaticals
- Discounts on own products and services
- Flu-jabs
- Paid leave for military activities
- Private medical insurance
- Company picnic or barbeque.

Source: After *Reward Management: Annual Survey Report 2009*, London: Chartered Institute of Personnel and Development (CIPD 2009), Reproduced with the permission of the publisher, the Chartered Institute of Personnel and Development, London (**www.cipd.co.uk**).

Questions

1 Over time the proportion of employers who offer these benefits is increasing. Why do you think this is?

2 What other benefits might you have expected to see listed here?

3 Which of these benefits would you consider to have value for you personally? How far might their presence or absence from a reward package influence your interest in working for a company?

FURTHER READING

Taylor, S. (2009) 'Occupational pensions', in G. White and J. Druker (eds), *Reward Management: A critical text*. London: Routledge.

Wright, A. (2009a) 'Benefits', in G. White and J. Druker (eds), *Reward Management: A critical text*. London: Routledge.

Field, S., Olsen, C. and Williams, R. (2009) 'The pensions revolution', in S. Corby *et al.* (eds), *Rethinking Reward*. Basingstoke: Palgrave.

Wright, A. (2009b) 'Flexible benefits', in S. Corby *et al.* (eds), *Rethinking Reward*. Basingstoke: Palgrave. Between them, these four chapters in two edited books published fairly recently cover the issues raised in this chapter very effectively. All review the contemporary research and explain trends in a clear and concise manner.

The Turner Report (2004) contains several chapters looking at the background to pension provision over the next few decades, including demographic and funding issues.

Incomes Data Services

IDS regularly publishes issues of its HR Studies that are focused on employee benefits. The approach is practical, case studies being provided to illustrate the approaches that employers are currently choosing to take. Two excellent editions are Study 856 on employee benefits and Study 811 on flexible benefits.

REFERENCES

Accor (2008) *Reward to Engage: Rewards, benefits and employee engagement in today's organisations*. London: Accor Services.

CBI (2008) *CBI/AXA Absence Survey 2008*. London: Confederation of British Industry.

CIPD (2012) *Reward Management: Annual Survey Report 2012*. London: CIPD.

Dobson, C. and Horsfield, S. (2009) *Defined Contribution Pension Provision*, Research Report 608. London: Department for Work and Pensions.

Field, S., Olsen, C. and Williams, R. (2009) 'The pensions revolution', in S. Corby *et al.* (eds), *Rethinking Reward*. Basingstoke: Palgrave.

Franks, O. and Thompson, D. (2000) 'Rights and rites of passage', *People Management*, 17 February.

NAPF (2013) 'Final salary pensions shut at record rate in private sector', Press release, 20 January.

ONS (2012a) *Occupational Pension Scheme Survey 2011*. London: Office for National Statistics.

ONS (2012b) *Pension Trends*. London: Office for National Statistics.

Pemberton, H., Thane, P. and Whiteside, N. (2006) *Britain's Pension Crisis: History and policy*. Oxford: The British Academy.

Smith, I. (2000a) 'Benefits', in G. White and J. Druker (eds) *Reward Management: A critical text*. London: Routledge.

Smith, I. (2000b) 'Flexible plans for pay and benefits', in R. Thorpe and G. Homan (eds), *Strategic Reward Systems*. London: Financial Times/Prentice Hall.

Taylor, S. (2009) 'Occupational pensions', in G. White and J. Druker (eds), *Reward Management: A critical text*. London: Routledge.

Thomson Online (2007) Employee Rewards Watch 2007, available at **www.thomsons.com**.

Turner, A. (2004) *Pensions: Challenges and choices. The first report of the Pensions Commission*. London: The Stationery Office.

Wright, A. (2009a) 'Benefits', in G. White and J. Druker (eds), *Reward Management: A critical text*. London: Routledge.

Wright, A. (2009b) 'Flexible benefits: Shaping the way ahead?', in S. Corby *et al.* (eds), *Rethinking Reward*. Basingstoke: Palgrave.

Part 7

CONTEMPORARY ISSUES

CHANGING TIMES
RESOURCING
PERFORMANCE
DEVELOPMENT
EMPLOYEE RELATIONS
REWARD
CONTEMPORARY ISSUES

Ethics
Work–life balance
HR function
Future of work
Measuring HR
Future of work
Skills

As we come to the close of the book, we have a different sort of part. In this part we are not considering activities in a specific functional grouping, but issues that tend to influence all functional areas. We start with the ethical dimension of management in general and HRM in particular which has aroused great interest recently.

The management of the HR function is undergoing some changes and those engaged in the area need to be aware of these and how changes may move forward. Structures continue to be adapted and the HR function strives to operate strategically. The effectiveness of the HR function is frequently questioned so all HR people need to consider how valuable their contribution is and how it can be effectively measured.

Health and well-being at work continue to be important in terms of an ethical approach to employment and also as a means of encouraging higher performance.

Finally we look at managing an international workforce, as this becomes more prevalent. We need to understand why HR practices may differ across borders and the role of different cultures, and the challenges these provide for organisational integration.

ETHICS AND CORPORATE SOCIAL RESPONSIBILITY

THE OBJECTIVES OF THIS CHAPTER ARE TO:

1   Introduce the topic of ethics and corporate social responsibility

2   Consider the particular aspects of ethics that affect HRM

3   Review the variations of ethical practice across national boundaries

4   Suggest particular ethical questions facing HRM people in the future

WINDOW ON PRACTICE

In January 2004 the Treasury Select Committee of the British Parliament criticised chief executives of large insurance companies for taking big pay rises at a time when the profitability of their companies and the value of endowment policies were falling, both after a period during which endowment policies had been mis-sold. The chairman of the committee said, 'The industry is going downhill like a slalom skier. . . . Why do you think you're worth so much?'

The committee chairman was demonstrating that committee members believed the chief executives were behaving unethically. Five years later British Members of Parliament were strongly criticised because many of them claimed expenses by means that were within the rules but seemed quite unreasonable by the country's electorate: their behaviour was regarded as unethical. More recent examples include a Member of Parliament resigning his seat after being imprisoned for deception and a member of the French government with specific responsibility for stopping tax evasion was forced to resign after it was discovered that he had held accounts in Singapore and Switzerland for twenty years.

This could be a starting point for the fourth general discussion topic at the end of this chapter.

The ethical dimension

In 2009 a female music teacher in an English girls' school was jailed for engaging one of her pupils in a sexual relationship that had begun when the girl was under 15. Two days later an anonymous letter to a national newspaper commented that the writer had had a similar relationship as a teacher with a pupil, but had no feelings of guilt, 'It may have been unethical, but it was not wrong.' That makes a distinction that implies that rule breaking is wrong, but unethical behaviour is a matter of personal choice and nothing to do with anyone else. So what do we mean by ethics and what are the ethical dimensions of HRM?

In western thought the major set of ideas are those set out by Aristotle 2,300 years ago, that virtues, such as generosity, charity and justice, impel people possessing them to act in a way that benefits them and their surrounding society. This benign concept remains persuasive, perhaps because of its common-sense attractiveness and its reflection in the Judaeo-Christian tradition that dominates the western world, being further clarified by philosophers such as the German, Immanuel Kant, and Jeremy Bentham and John Stuart Mill, who defined ethical behaviour as that which produces the greatest good for the greatest number. It is relatively simple to see that every member of the business will seek to behave, and to carry out their duties, in a way which they individually regard as ethical although they may find that their personal ethics conflict with aspects of law or company policy.

This suggests that law out scores ethics in employment matters. In several western countries this has been demonstrated in attitudes to aspects of dress with, for instance, schoolgirls in France not being allowed to wear the burka and some UK employers not permitting employees to incorporate religious insignia such as the cross into their clothing. Whatever one may think of a law, it remains the law until it is changed, no matter how offensive to one's personal views. Equally, company official policy overrides anyone's personal ethical stance.

Can a business have ethical standards? Kenneth Blanchard is an American academic and consultant of considerable reputation, including being the author of the best-selling *The One-Minute Manager*. He teamed up with Norman Vincent Peale, who had written *The Power of Positive Thinking*, which had sold no fewer than 20 million copies. Together they produced a slim, popular book about ethics in management which they described as follows:

ethical behaviour is related to self-esteem. We both believe that people who feel good about themselves have what it takes to withstand outside pressure and to do what is right rather than do what is merely expedient, popular or lucrative. We believe that a strong code of morality in any business is the first step towards its success. We believe that ethical managers are winning managers. (Blanchard and Peale 1988: 7)

Aristotle would have been proud of them! It is interesting that the idea is 'sold' as a means to an end rather than as an end in itself, and it sounds almost as 'expedient, popular or lucrative' as the alternative that they are disparaging. We will return to the general management interest in business ethics later in the chapter, but we can get Blanchard and Peale in clearer perspective if we consider some definitions.

Any dictionary will indicate that ethics describe:

a social, religious or civil code of behaviour considered to be correct, especially that of a particular group or profession.

In the business context ethics are part of the culture of the individual business corporation that sets norms of behaviour by which people in the business will abide because the norms have some moral authority as well being convenient. They are also guidance to a set of guidelines followed by people in a particular group or profession because it makes practical sense in enabling them to do their jobs. Barristers will not represent two different clients if there is likely to be a conflict of interest between the clients. Doctors will generally refrain from sexual relationships with their patients. In both cases there are sound practical reasons, quite apart from any moral dimension. The medical profession is, however, an interesting point of comparison because the importance of ethics is so obvious, public discussion of medical ethics is regular, academic examination of medical ethics is widespread and there is a history that goes back at least 2,400 years to the Greek 'father of medicine', Hippocrates.

Among the contemporary attempts to formulate a universal code of medical ethics, the most widely reported is described by Gillon (2003) as having four principles, their longevity being demonstrated by three of them being given a definition in Latin as well as in English:

Beneficence – a practitioner should act in the best interest of the patient. (*Salus aegroti suprema lex.*)
Non-maleficence – 'first, do no harm' (*primum non nocere*).
Autonomy – the patient has the right to refuse or choose treatment. (*Voluntas aegroti suprema lex.*)
Justice – concerns the distribution of scarce health resources, and the decision of who gets what treatment.

Gillon explains how this affects the individual practitioner:

> The best moral strategy for justice that I have found for myself as a health care worker is first to distinguish whether it is I or an organisation, profession, or society itself that has to make a decision. For example, 'how should I respond to a particular patient who wants an abortion?' is distinct from, 'what is this hospital's organisational view on abortion?' and 'what is the medical profession's collective view on abortion?' and 'what is society's view as expressed in law and practice?'
>
> Firstly, for decisions that I must take myself I must try to exclude decisions that have no moral basis or justification. Neither pursuit of my own self interest – for example, accepting bribes from patients, hospitals, or drug manufacturers – nor action that discriminates against patients on the basis of personal preference or prejudice can provide a just or morally acceptable basis for allocating scarce health care resources or for any other category of justice. Moreover, it is not my role as a doctor to punish patients; withholding antibiotics from smokers who do not give up smoking or refusing to refer heavy drinkers with liver damage induced by alcohol for specialist assessment on the grounds that they are at fault is not a just or morally acceptable basis for rationing my medical resources. (Gillon 2003: 267)

Although these comments are directed at medical practitioners or healthcare workers, it is an interesting intellectual exercise to substitute the word 'employee' for 'patient' to see how helpful and practical they might be. A book by four American academics (Wicks *et al.* 2010: 10) writing for a *business* readership enlarges the Hippocratic principles, *without any reference to their origin*, into a Standards of Conduct Decision Guide:

> *Beneficence* – People should provide help to others.
> *Non-maleficence* – People should avoid doing harm to others, especially intentional and direct harm.
> *Autonomy* – People should be free to make their own choices, particularly when they relate to their own welfare and life projects.
> *Justice* – People ought to give others what they are due and operate with a sense of fair play.
> *Responsibility* – People have certain expectations of themselves, and feel certain obligations to themselves, which they expect in return from others.

This discussion demonstrates four aspects of ethics for managers:

1 Ethics are about behaviour which stems from personal conviction.

2 If personal conviction conflicts with law or specific company policy, then law prevails.

3 Managerial interest in ethics is the extent to which they can emphasise, extend or transcend desirable behaviours within the general framework of company policy.

4 Some ethical standards may be determined by a professional body of which an employee is a member, and with which the employee will feel obliged to comply, even if such compliance leads to behaviours in conflict with company policy and practice.

Early management concern with ethics

The early management concern with ethics was led by philanthropic industrialists in the nineteenth century, such as Cadbury, Lever, Salt and Rowntree, later criticised for their intrinsic paternalism. An American contemporary was Andrew Carnegie, who was born in Scotland but made a considerable fortune after emigrating to the USA and devoted the last years of his life to giving most of it away. In 1900 he wrote a book called *The Gospel of Wealth*, which set out a statement of corporate social responsibility that was quite as paternalist as that of his UK counterparts. He believed that corporate social responsibility had two principles, charity and stewardship. The more fortunate in society had an obligation to aid the less fortunate (charity) and those with wealth should see themselves as owning that wealth in trust for the rest of society by using it for purposes which were socially legitimate (stewardship).

Carnegie was very influential, largely because he dispensed charity on such a massive scale, but paternalism gradually drew more and more criticism and the involvement in social responsibility waned. It was more or less destroyed altogether by Milton Friedman, who argued that those in business were not qualified to decide on the relative urgency of social needs. He contended that managers who devoted corporate resources to pursuing personal interpretations of social need might be misguided in their selection and would unfairly 'tax' their shareholders, employees and customers:

> There is one and only one social responsibility of business: to use its resources and energy in activities designed to increase its profits as long as it stays within the rules of the game, engaging in open and free competition, without deception and fraud. (Friedman 1963: 163)

Renewed interest in business ethics

The 1980s saw the return of interest in business ethics, although to many people it remains an incongruous concept:

> Many persons educated in the humanities (with their aristocratic traditions) and the social sciences (with their quantifying, collectivist traditions) are uncritically anti-capitalist. They think of business as vulgar, philistine, and morally suspect. . . . Three accusations come up.
>
> (a) In pursuit of profits, won't businesses act immorally whenever necessary?
>
> (b) Aren't executive salaries out of line? Isn't dramatic inequality wrong?
>
> (c) Isn't it wrong to subject workers and middle managers in their mature years to so much insecurity? Isn't it wrong to let people go abruptly and without a parachute?
>
> (Novak 1996: 7–8)

That was an American perspective, but it would be echoed by many people in Europe. There is also the more general feeling that any commercially driven activity has dominant motivations that are inevitably opposed to social considerations. Another version of the same view is that those in management positions should not make moral judgements as they have no authority to do so. Instead they should respond to public opinion as expressed by customers' purchasing decisions, demonstrations by pressure groups or trade unions or by government legislation.

WINDOW ON PRACTICE

One relatively recent form of control on management decision making is whistle-blowing, which describes the practice of an employee metaphorically blowing a whistle to attract attention from the outside to some ethical malpractice within the business. Originally this was done by lone individuals taking great risks with their employment, but the method has now altered through the establishment of a charity, Public Concern at Work, which gives free legal advice to potential whistle-blowers. Its director claims that most issues are now settled within the business:

90 per cent of clients who follow our advice report a successful outcome. This has much to do with our policy that, if raised responsibly within the organisation, concerns about malpractice will be addressed properly by those in charge. (Dehn 1997)

A further development of Dehn's work is in Borrie and Dehn (2002).

The need for ethical guidelines

The logic supporting the need for ethical guidelines is that actions in business are the result of decisions by human beings, and human beings tend to seek justification for their actions beyond the rule of value for money. This can be grotesque rationalisation. The various Mafia families apparently have a very robust code of conduct, based on strong family cohesion and a convenient interpretation of the Roman Catholic faith. This 'justification' enables them to peddle drugs, launder money, run large-scale prostitution and extortion, to say nothing of killing people, without a sense of guilt. Many jihadists are apparently motivated by a personal interpretation of Islam that legitimises terrorism.

Fortunately, most people do not resort to such extreme behaviour, but will still seek to justify to themselves actions they take that can have unpleasant consequences for others. The person who is totally rational in decision making is a rare creature in business life. Earlier we referred to Milgram's work (see Chapter 20), which showed people acting in a most extreme way when they were put in an 'agentic state', whereby the responsibility lay somewhere else, absolving individuals of any guilt or responsibility associated with their actions. Recent concern about responsibility for fatal accidents has created great interest in the concept of corporate manslaughter. Who is responsible for a train crash, the train driver or those in overall charge of the business who did not arrange for suitable training, supervision or other facilities?

Moral justification

Sometimes the moral justification comes from a value system that is independent of the business itself and where individual opinions can be sharply divided. Some doctors and nurses are happy to work in abortion clinics, while others refuse. Some people are enraged about the destruction of green land to build motorways, while others are enthusiastic. Other actions and decisions are more generally supported by the external value system. Few would disagree that people at work should be honest and that claims about a product or service should be accurate. Most would also agree with the general proposition of equal opportunity for all, although there may be sharp disagreement about what exactly that means in practice.

Ethical principles

Some standards of ethics derive from voluntary agreement by members of a particular industry, such as editors of national newspapers, or statutory 'watchdogs' such as those monitoring the activities of privatised public utilities. The problem of pensions and similar financial services being mis-sold produced the Personal Investment Authority, which was dissolved in 2009 with its powers being transferred to the Financial Services Authority with swingeing powers intended to prevent a repetition of that sort of problem. Then there are the ethical standards that are generated within a particular business. The Royal Dutch/Shell Group of Companies relies largely for its international effectiveness on the values shared by all its companies and employees. No new joint venture will be developed unless the partner company accepts them:

The business principles are a set of beliefs which say what the Shell group stands for and covers in general terms its responsibilities to its principal stakeholders, its shareholders, employees, customers and society. They are concerned with economic principles, business integrity, political activities, the environment, the community and availability of information. (Haddock and South 1994: 226)

These principles were first set out in 1976 and were not imposed from the top, but were a codification of already accepted behaviour. The principles are revised from time to time and one of the challenging tasks for the central HR function was to introduce a code of practice relating to drugs and alcohol, which took considerable discussion and consultation before agreement could be reached:

At the heart of our Business Principles are three core values: honesty; integrity and respect for people. Consistently behaving with integrity requires clear and simple requirements (like our zero tolerance for bribes and fraud); effective procedures to check and reward compliance, and a company culture that does not tolerate dishonest or illegal practices. (Royal Dutch Shell 2009)

Individuals encounter moral dilemmas frequently in their working lives and are likely to find them very difficult. In carrying out research a few years ago about performance appraisal practice in a large building society, it was possible to see the rise in sickness absence at the time of the annual appraisal discussion, and this was most marked among appraisers: those who had to pass on bad news. We saw previously that few managers wish to take over responsibility for grievance and discipline from HR people (see Chapter 20), and making the decision to dismiss someone for almost any reason other than gross misconduct is a most unpopular management task because it seems that the interests of the business are being considered at the expense of the interests of individual employees. At times like this managers are very anxious to find some justifying framework for their actions.

Codes of ethics

The key issue with ethical codes is the extent to which they are supported by the people to whom they apply. They are not rules that can be enforced by penalties for non-compliance. It is necessary that they are understood, appreciated and willingly honoured by the great majority of those who are affected. There will then be considerable social pressure on the few who do not wish to comply. Imposing ethics is very tricky. When examining equal opportunities some years ago, researchers found an interesting situation in an American computer company with a rapidly growing UK subsidiary. The company had a high-profile commitment to 'positive action to seek out and employ members of disadvant-aged groups'. This was reinforced in the annual appraisal system for managers, who had to indicate what they had done in the previous twelve months to implement a 'pro-gramme of employment and development for minorities'. The company annual report made a claim that this initiative was advancing at all international locations. In the UK, however, it was found in practice that:

> Without exception, all managers to whom we spoke ignored that part of their appraisal. . . . They put a line through the offending clause and wrote 'not applicable in the UK' . . . despite the corporate objective of 'citizenship', applicable in the UK, requiring recruitment officers to seek out the disadvantaged in the community. . . . Suggestions by the researchers that such an active recruitment policy was an obligation on the part of management . . . invoked the reaction, 'we're not a welfare organisation'. (Torrington *et al.* 1982: 23)

Ethics and HRM

HR interest in ethics

HR people have long held a strong interest in ethics, although it was usually caricatured as welfare. Some of the academic critics argue that personnel managers should remain aloof from the management hurly-burly so that 'professional values will be paramount and prevail over other interests' (Hart 1993: 30). The problem with that simplistic argument is that HR people do not have a separate professional existence from the management of which they are a part. HRM is a management activity or it is nothing. The company doctor and the company legal adviser are bound by codes of professional ethics different from those of managers, but they are employed for their specialist, technical expertise and they are members of long-established, powerful professional groupings with their own normal places of work. When they leave their surgeries or their courtrooms to align themselves with managers in companies, they are in a specialised role. They can maintain a non-managerial, professional detachment, giving advice that is highly regarded, even when it is highly unpopular. Furthermore, they advise; they do not decide. For instance, any dismissal on the grounds of ill health is a management decision and not a medical decision, no matter how explicit and uncompromising the medical advice may be.

HR specialists do not have separate places and conventions of work which they leave in order to advise managements. They are employed in no other capacity than to participate closely in the management process of the business. They do not even have the limited degree of independence that company accountants have, as their activities are not sub-ject to external audit, and it is ludicrous to expect of them a fully fledged independent, professional stance, although there is a move in that direction since the professional body became chartered. The *chartered* personnel practitioner can only retain that particular cachet after regular reassessment of professional competency.

The change in general management orientation during the 1980s and 1990s towards the idea of leaner and fitter, flexible organisations, downsizing, delayering, outplacement and all the other ideas that eventually lead to fewer people in jobs and fewer still with any sort of employment security has usually been implemented by HR people. HR and personnel managers cannot behave like Banquo's ghost and be silently disapproving of their colleagues' actions. What they can do is to argue vigorously in favour of what they see as the best combination of efficiency and justice, but they can only argue vigorously if they are present when decisions are made. If they are not generally 'on side', they do not participate in the decision making and they probably do not keep their jobs. Either they are a part of management, understanding business needs and priorities, valued by their colleagues, despite their funny ideas, or they are powerless. There are no ivory towers for them to occupy, and no more employment security for them than for any other member of the business.

HR people can still be critical of proposed management actions, if they are valued by their managerial colleagues for the wholeness of their contribution, and if they accept the fact that they will often lose the argument: they cannot do it by masquerading as an unrepresentative shop steward. They have no monopoly of either wisdom or righteousness, and other members of the management team are just as likely as they are to be concerned about social values.

HR managers have not abandoned their interest in welfare; they have moved away from an approach to welfare that was trivial, anachronistic and paternalist. In the HR vocabulary the term 'welfare' is code for middle-class do-gooders placing flowers in the works canteen. HR managers increasingly shun the traditional approach to welfare not for its softness, but because it is ineffectual. It does not satisfy the HR obsession with getting progress in the employment of people, and it certainly does not do enough to satisfy the people who are employed. In many undertakings HR specialists are taking their management colleagues along with them in an enthusiastic and convinced attempt to give jobs more meaning and to humanise the workplace. Their reasoning is that the business can only maintain its competitive edge if the people who work there are committed to its success, and that commitment is volitional: you need hearts and minds as well as hands and muscle. Investment in training and the dismantling of elaborate, alienating organisation structures do more for employee well-being than paternalistic welfare programmes ever did.

Ethics across national boundaries

The international dimension of the social responsibility question has still to be developed. Logging operations in South America are ravaging the rainforests, which are essential to life continuing on the planet. Error, or neglect, in the management of manufacturing processes can produce a tragedy like that of Chernobyl in Ukraine or the various discharges of crude oil that have occurred all over the world. Since the first formal warning by the US Surgeon General about the risks of smoking, tobacco consumption has been falling in western countries, so the tobacco companies have increased their marketing in less developed countries, which is widely regarded as a most dubious practice.

Ethical standards vary. Becker and Fritzsche (1987) carried out a study of different ethical perceptions between American, French and German executives: 39% of the

Americans said that paying money for business favours was unethical; only 12% of the French and none of the Germans agreed. In the USA, Japanese companies have been accused of avoiding the employment of ethnic minority groups by the careful location of their factories (Cole and Deskins 1988: 17–19). On the other hand, Japanese standards on employee health and safety are as high as those anywhere in the world (Wokutch 1990). In South East Asia the contrast in prosperity between countries such as Malaysia and Singapore on the one hand and Indonesia and the Philippines on the other means that there are ethical questions about the employment of illegal immigrants that are superficially similar to those applying to Cubans and Mexicans in the USA, but which do not occur in other parts of the world. There are very low wages and long working hours in China and in much of India.

The various high-profile cases over the last decade of offering inducements to individuals in order to obtain business has led the UK government to introduce the Bribery Act of 2010. This makes it an offence (a) to offer or pay a bribe, (b) to request or receive a bribe, or (c) to bribe a foreign public service official, and there is also (d) a corporate offence of failing to prevent a bribe being offered or paid on behalf of the business.

The disparate nature of ethical standards between countries will be one of the key HR issues to be addressed in the future. There will gradually be a growing together of national practice on working hours, but it will take much longer for rates of pay to harmonise. One can visualise common standards on health and safety developing much more quickly than equality of opportunity between the sexes and across ethnic divisions.

Games are played between governments and multinational companies. Among the most recent examples is the long-running saga of General Motors/Opel/Vauxhall. General Motors is an American business that also owns Opel, with plants in Belgium and Germany, and Vauxhall, with plants in the UK. By 2008 General Motors was in serious financial difficulties and the sale of Opel and Vauxhall seemed its best hope for survival. The UK and German governments were immediately concerned about the likely implications for their two economies and attempted to influence the sale process in their favour by offering financial inducements. For some months the sale was to be made to a Canadian company, which duly received similar blandishments. In the autumn of 2009 General Motors suddenly announced that its financial situation had improved so the sale was off. So UK and German officials had to dust off some of their earlier files and start all over again. In both countries the issue of jobs was of crucial importance, but General Motors still needed to save money. It had overcapacity in manufacturing in Europe and the possibility of plant closures continues.

Some current and developing ethical dilemmas

We conclude this chapter by suggesting some of the less obvious ethical dilemmas for those in management positions. Issues such as the environment and equalising opportunity are extensively discussed, but there are others that receive less attention.

Life in the business

What sort of quality does working life have and what sort of quality will it have in the future? Thirty years ago a team of experts were employed by the UK government in a

Quality of Working Life Unit. Their task was to suggest ways in which that quality could be improved, mainly through job redesign initiatives. Since then the general belief is that quality of working life has declined, partly through overwork and partly through fear of losing employment. At the beginning of the twenty-first century, workplace stress is one of the most common causes of absence and the place of work is an arena where newspapers would have us believe that harassment, poor supervision and bullying are rife. We include a piece on dealing with bullying in the skills miscellany (see Part 8).

> Few people go off to work these days with a song in their hearts . . . many people dread each day because they have to work in places where they feel abused and powerless. What is happening to us? Why are talented, productive people being thwarted and sabotaged? Why do we treat each other so badly? Why are tyrannical bosses tolerated? Does the bottom line really justify the hurt and frustration we experience? (Wright and Smye 1996: 3)

We now lack the comfortable feelings of security that the employing organisation used to provide. Whether people really are more or less secure in their jobs is debatable, but there is no doubt that they feel less secure. Furthermore, delayering and downsizing to become leaner and fitter have mainly affected people in middle-range posts, who used to be the most secure and who valued their security most highly.

We shall have to find ways that make work less stressful and more satisfying, despite the absence of certain of its traditionally most attractive features: security and community.

Information technology and the workplace

We have plenty of predictions of what the computer, the Internet and the microprocessor can do and what will in due course logically happen: manufacturing will progressively be taken over by robots, there will be rapid transfer and manipulation of data, the paperless office, people working from home instead of coming into a centre, and so forth – the golden age of the post-industrial society and the World Wide Web. The ethical dilemma is to wonder what will be done to make up for what the computer will take from us: the conviviality and communal feeling of organisational life.

Managers have long had the opportunity to spend more of their time, and make more of their decisions, by rational planning and operational research methods than in fact they do. The strange thing is that there continues to be a preference among managers in general and HR managers in particular to spend their time talking with people and to make their decisions as a result of discussion and shrewd judgement. Will managers now begin to eschew face-to-face discussion in favour of face-to-terminal decision making, or will they continue to confer and keep busy while others feed to them an ever-increasing flow of processed information requiring interpretation, evaluation and further discussion? Research findings suggest that managers work in the way that they do at least partly because they like it that way. Nobody saw it more clearly than one of the management greats, Henry Mintzberg:

> The manager actually seems to prefer brevity and interruption in his work. Superficiality is an occupational hazard of the manager's job. Very current information (gossip, hearsay, speculation) is favoured; routine reports are not. The manager clearly favours the . . . verbal media, spending most of his time in verbal contact. (Mintzberg 1973: 51–2)

The date and male gender of that quotation may be significant. Most of the studies of managerial work have been of men and of men and women working in a male-dominated culture. It may be that the increasing proportion of managerial jobs done by women will alter the stereotype. The women authors of *Corporate Abuse* are quite clear about the need to care for souls:

Studies of work flow suggest there is five times more opportunity to experience joy in the workplace on a daily basis than in the home environment if it is a workplace that is in tune with the needs of the soul. . . . Once we have a community of fully nurtured souls, the possibility of creativity is limitless. Everyone in the workforce will be tapped into his or her own power source as well as being part of a larger community of effort and partnership. (Wright and Smye 1996: 248–9)

This rings strangely in management ears, but maybe this is the way to rediscover the sense of community that employing organisations used to provide.

How great will the influence of the computer on HRM work actually become? How will we make up for what the computer takes away? If there is a general tendency for people to work at home, taking their laptop with them, how popular will that turn out to be? It is over a century since the household ceased to be the central productive unit and the men, and later the women, began to spend a large part of their waking hours at a different social centre: the factory, shop or office – the organisational entity. To be housebound has become a blight.

WINDOW ON PRACTICE

Jeremy is a newspaper journalist who works from home. Having a young family he needed more space for an office, so he had a 'posh shed' erected in his garden, with heating and light, to accommodate him at work. After a few months this ideal environment became not so ideal and Jeremy now spends most mornings with his laptop and his mobile phone in a local café.

The World Wide Web may not turn everyone into a home-worker, but it is still having a significant impact. There is the slightly isolating nature of the work that computerisation produces. The individual employee is not one of many in a crowded workshop, but one of a few scattered around a mass of busy machines. The clerical employee spends more time gazing at a computer terminal and less talking to colleagues. What employee behaviour will this engender and what attitudes will be associated with that behaviour?

WINDOW ON PRACTICE

Susan is not a high-flyer, but an extremely competent and conscientious PA/secretary who is happy to work part time so as to maintain an active family role. She explains what she has progressively 'lost':

When I started I worked for one boss. He was a bit of a pain at times, but I got very involved, partly because he was so disorganised. He relied on me and I could follow all the ups and downs of his office politics. There was good camaraderie with other secretaries, who really ran the place. Not at all PC, but interesting and worthwhile. Nowadays there is more concentration on just doing the basic job of setting out letters and endless hours staring at that bloody screen. I feel more and more isolated.

The central ethical dilemma seems to be that we are allowing information technology gradually to take away the social institution of the organisation on which we have become so dependent. How will this scenario unfold?

ACTIVITY 24.2

What difference has the computer made to your working life so far? What further effect do you expect it to have in the next five years? How readily would you be (or are you) a home-worker?

Employment

If employing organisations are not to provide the security of a job for life, how will people find employment, both as a way of earning their livelihood and as a means of finding their place in society? There has been much brave talk of people managing their own careers and concentrating on ensuring their continuing employability. Charles Handy enunciated his concept of portfolio living, whereby people put together a portfolio of different activities so that they could control their own lives without becoming dependent on a single employer. This is fine for the able, well educated and independently minded, but human society has not evolved to the point where that description fits everyone; it probably fits only a minority.

There have always been large proportions of any society who were dependent. The golden age of Ancient Greece was based on slavery, as was the earlier Pharaonic period in Egypt. The lord of the manor had his tenants, mass production required masses of people and the world has always required large numbers for its armies. Not only were there dependent people, but society depended on them. We are now moving into this strange new world where there seems to be no place for that large proportion of the population.

It is unrealistic to expect every middle-aged redundant unskilled operative or every school-leaver without GCSEs to develop their own flexible employability. They need someone or something to provide them with the opportunity to work. Current economic wisdom is that jobs can only come through the activity of the market. This is one of the common political debating points: where are the jobs going to come from? Surely, however, it is one of the salient questions for HRM. If HR managers have social responsibility, how will they improve job prospects in the economy?

Self-improvement

For a long time we have lived with inflation that was, in many ways, the engine of growth. Not only did we spend in order to avoid higher prices next month, but we always felt we were making progress when our take-home pay kept going up. Rationally we knew that we were not necessarily doing better at all, but it vaguely felt as if we were. Recently the level of inflation in most western countries has been so firmly controlled that we no longer have that spurious feeling of making progress, as cost of living adjustments either do not exist or seem so small.

Without the mirage of progress provided by inflation, people need to have a more genuine sense of being able to do better. We have already considered the advantages and drawbacks of relating pay to performance, which is the main way in which it has been possible recently to see an improvement in one's material circumstances, but this really pays off only for a minority.

Delayering has taken out another yardstick of progress, as the scope for promotion is much reduced. This may reduce costs and may replace the phoney improvement of promotion by the possibility of real improvement through finding new opportunities, but we should remember that the business that is 'lean and mean' feels very mean indeed to the people who are inside it.

A nice HR challenge is to develop novel aspects of corporate culture that will recognise achievement and give a sense of progress for all those who seek it, without generating envy:

Conspicuous privilege, ostentation, and other forms of behaviour, even when not necessarily wrong, typically provoke envy. Unusually large salaries or bonuses, even if justified by competition in a free and open market, may offer demagogues fertile ground on which to scatter the seeds of envy. It is wise to take precautions against these eventualities. (Novak 1996: 144)

Personal (note: not personnel) management

One ethical challenge in HRM is to ensure that the processes of management are seen to be carried out by people who can be seen, talked to, argued with and persuaded.

While it is clearly important for managers to avoid an over-preoccupation with procedural trivia, which reinforces the status quo and inhibits change, management is not all about strategy, and HRM has only a modest strategic element. It is the operational or technical aspects that require the skill and confer the status. Is there anything harder for a manager to do well than carry out a successful appraisal interview? Are there many more important jobs to be done than explaining strategy, or making the absolutely right appointment of someone to a key role? This is operational management for HR specialists, yet so often we find that they have retreated to the strategy bunker to think great thoughts and discuss the shape of the world with like-minded people, consuming endless cups of coffee, while the appraisal and the selection and the communication are left to 'the line'.

There used to be a management approach known as MBWA, or Management By Walking About. This exhorted managers to get out of their offices and walk about to see what was going on and to be available. We have already referred in this chapter to the apparent preference among managers to spend their time in face-to-face discussion rather than in solitary activities. The trouble is that more and more of their contacts are with other managers rather than with people in the front line.

We suggest that it is important to maintain the work of HR as largely 'a contact sport', dealing face to face with people in all sorts of jobs in all parts of the business, so that, although the business employs the HR managers, they are agents of that employing business with whom employees can reason and debate.

Future HR managers will need a shrewd strategic sense and a set of operational managerial skills. They will also need an ethical sense, able to set management action in its context, understanding the implications for the enterprise, for each person and for the community at large. Many aspects of management work can be developed into a science: successful HRM is an art.

Corporate social responsibility

There has recently developed an interest in corporate social responsibility or CSR. This is an interest in a wide range of matters where some companies wish to review their activities and includes topics like climate change, pollution, charitable contributions, customer care and others that are not narrowly the province of HR and therefore lie outside the scope of this book, although Maureen Stapley describes an interesting broad-based approach at Mondial Assistance that has generated the useful by-product of short-term absence declining from 2007 to 2009 from 3.76 days to 3.2 while staff turnover fell from 22.68% to 6.4%. She offers the obvious reservation:

> While these decreases were driven by a number of factors within the business, our team of executive directors . . . firmly believe that the commitment and focus on CSR were a very strong contributing factor. (Stapley 2010: 55)

However, there are signs of HR pushing for HR to absorb CSR. This, of course, is at the same time that environmental issues are currently the most fashionable aspect of ethical concern. What special expertise in environmental matters is vested in HR is unclear.

Reviewing the development of CSR, Stefan Stern made the following comment:

> CSR is bound to fail in companies where it is adopted simply for reasons of public relations. . . . It may be successful in changing attitudes to your company in the short term, but if your activities are morally dubious they will eventually be exposed. CSR, if it is to mean anything, cannot be a bolted-on attitude or a departmental annexe. . . . It is not about 'putting something back' – it is about how you make your money in the first place. (. . . In any case, if you really feel the need to 'put something back', doesn't that suggest you have taken too much already?) (Stern 2004: 35)

How can HR people behave ethically in a way that all of its members accept and follow and which is more than complying with employment law?

HRM has always had an ethical dimension. The early days of personnel management were characterised, and later scorned, for a preoccupation with employee welfare regardless of the development of the business. The odd thing is that practitioners have for so long been trying to bury this aspect, while academic commentators have grumbled that HR practitioners fail to deliver on it. In 1977 Peter Anthony reminded his readers of an earlier statement by Michael Fogarty at an IPM conference, 'the business of business is business', before adding his own comment, 'it is the business of the industrial relations specialist to make sure that the business can get done'.

SUMMARY PROPOSITIONS

24.1 In the business context, ethics are part of the corporate culture that sets norms of behaviour by which people in the business will abide because they have some moral authority as well as being convenient.

24.2 Ethical standards vary between different national cultures, making international standards difficult.

24.3 Ethical codes are only valid if they are appreciated and willingly implemented by the great majority of those to whom they apply.

24.4 Personnel management has always had a strong ethical dimension, although personnel managers and the practice of HRM are regularly criticised for failure in social responsibility.

24.5 The CIPD has a code for its members, setting standards of conduct in accuracy, confidentiality, counselling, developing others, equal opportunities, fair dealing and self-development.

24.6 Among current and developing ethical dilemmas are the quality of life in the business, information technology in the workplace, employment, self-improvement and personal management.

GENERAL DISCUSSION TOPICS

1 The chapter opens by explaining that personnel managers for years played down their ethical/welfare role. Why do you think this was?

2 To what extent do you regard Tim Hart's criticisms as valid?

3 What examples can you think of that would make you feel that the demands of your job conflicted with what you regarded as being right? How would you deal with this and how do the Milgram experiments on obedience (see Chapter 20) explain, or fail to explain, your actions?

4 Most people agree that differences in rates of pay according to value or effort are justified, but that some differences are 'obscene'. What criteria would you suggest for setting pay differentials within a business that both are seen as fair and are effective in being able to attract and retain appropriate people from the labour market?

Here is an ethical dilemma on HR decisions.

Eric

Thirty years ago, before the days of wheelie bins, Eric was deaf, mute and suffered from cerebral palsy. He had been unemployable all his adult life, but in his late twenties he started to follow round the local authority refuse collectors emptying dustbins. As the lorry reached the end of a street, Eric would go ahead of it and drag dustbins out from behind the houses to the front. His handicap made it a very slow and painful process, but it was something he could do and he was exhausted. This completely unofficial arrangement was accepted by the refuse collectors as they were able to complete their rounds more quickly and they were on an incentive payment arrangement. Eric's participation enabled them to complete their rounds in slightly less time. At the end of the week they had a collection and gave Eric a few pounds. This transformed his life, as he had a purpose and had some mates. Setting aside, for a moment, issues about legal entitlement to benefit . . .

Questions

1 Do you feel that Eric was being exploited by the refuse collectors? Local authority officials heard about what Eric was doing and said it had to stop.

2 Why do you think they made this decision? Do you agree with it? A personnel manager in the neighbourhood heard about Eric and arranged for him to be taught to operate a sewing machine. He was then employed in the personnel manager's factory to maintain and repair all the overalls, a straightforward job carried out skilfully and conscientiously.

3 Do you feel that Eric was being exploited by the personnel manager?

4 As Eric was able to draw invalidity benefit, do you feel that the job should have been offered first to someone who was able-bodied? In the following three years investigations twice demonstrated that the overalls could be repaired more cheaply by subcontracting the work to another company, but that decision was not taken. Eric carried on as an employee.

5 Why do you think that decision was not made? Do you agree with it?

FURTHER READING

Fisher, C. and Lovell, A. (2009) *Business Ethics and Values*, 3rd edn. Harlow: Prentice Hall. This is a fairly weighty textbook providing an integrated discussion of ethical issues for managers in general. There are sections of particular interest to HRM people, including some careful treatments of international comparisons and ethical differences. Pages 139–45 provide an interesting evaluation framework for an individual manager or business to assess the ethical validity of a particular course of action.

People Management (2003) and (2012).
The first issue, from July 2003, is dedicated to examining corporate social responsibility. The second, from December 2012, pp. 24–7, has an article devoted to whistle-blowing.

Wicks, A.C., Freeman, R.E., Werhane, P.H. and Martin, K.E. (2010) *Business Ethics: A managerial approach*. Upper Saddle River, NJ: Prentice Hall.
An American text that takes an unashamedly managerial approach and sometimes blurs difficult issues, but still a useful text to provide a distinctly different approach to Fisher and Lovell.

REFERENCES

Becker, H. and Fritzsche, D.J. (1987) 'A comparison of the ethical behavior of American, French and German managers', *Columbia Journal of World Business*, Winter, pp. 87–95.
Blanchard, K. and Peale, N.V. (1988) *The Power of Ethical Management*. London: Heinemann.
Borrie, G. and Dehn, G. (2002) *Whistleblowing: The new perspective*. London: Public Concern at Work.
Cole, R.E. and Deskins, D.R. (1988) 'Racial factors in site location and employment patterns of Japanese auto Firms in America', *California Management Review*, Fall, p. 11.
Dehn, G. (1997) 'Blow the whistle, save a life', *The Times*, 8 April.
Fisher, C. and Lovell, A. (2009) *Business Ethics and Values*, 3rd edn. Harlow: Prentice Hall.
Friedman, M. (1963) *Capitalism and Freedom*. Chicago, IL: University of Chicago Press.
Gillon, R. (2003) 'Four scenarios', *Journal of Medical Ethics*, Vol. 29, pp. 267–8.
Haddock, C. and South, B. (1994) 'How Shell's organisation and HR practices help it to be both global and local', in D.P. Torrington (ed.), *International Human Resource Management*. Hemel Hempstead: Prentice Hall International.
Hart, T.J. (1993) 'Human resource management: Time to exorcise the militant tendency', *Employee Relations*, Vol. 15, No. 3, pp. 29–36.
Mintzberg, H. (1973) *The Nature of Managerial Work*. London: Harper & Row.
Novak, M. (1996) *Business as a Calling: Work and the examined life*. New York: Free Press.
Stapley, M. (2010) 'How HR made a difference at work', *People Management*, February, p. 55.
Stern, S. (2004) 'The perils of CSR', *Royal Society of Arts Journal*, January.
Torrington, D.P., Hitner, T.J. and Knights, D. (1982) *Management and the Multi-Racial Workforce*. Aldershot: Gower.
Wicks, A.C., Freeman, R.E., Werhane, P.H. and Martin, K.E. (2010) *Business Ethics: A managerial approach*. Upper Saddle River, NJ: Prentice Hall.
Wokutch, R.E. (1990) 'Corporate social responsibility, Japanese style', *Academy of Management Executive*, May, pp. 56–72.
Wright, L. and Smye, M. (1996) *Corporate Abuse*. New York: Macmillan.

Chapter 25

MANAGING THE HUMAN RESOURCE FUNCTION

THE OBJECTIVES OF THIS CHAPTER ARE TO:

1   Identify and explain the purpose and role of the HR function and potential structures that may be used to manage the function

2   Explore the extent to which the HR function operates strategically

3   Examine the use of self-service HR, shared services, outsourcing and the benefits and drawbacks of these approaches

4   Explore the role of line managers in HRM

5   Debate and critique the current developments in the management of the HR function

The purpose and structure of the personnel/HR function has developed considerably since its earliest welfare function, through a range of different incarnations, and in order to manage the function effectively we need to pay attention to its current purpose. Historically the HR function has been encouraged to gain greater power and credibility, and more recently play a greater strategic role. If HR is strategic to business success then HR needs to be a strategic player and:

> the case for HR being a strategic partner is becoming stronger, as it rests on the reality that human capital and how it is organised are increasingly pivotal to organisational effectiveness. (Lawler and Boudreau 2009: 15)

In the first two decades of the twenty-first century there has been a great deal of attention on how HR purpose, roles and structures are changing and much opinion of how they should change in the future.

Purpose and roles of the HR function

The purpose of the HR function has historically been expressed as a variety of different roles that the function plays in the organisation, the most well-known typologies, based on the analysis of empirical data, being Tyson and Fell (1985) and Storey (1992). See Truss *et al.* (2012) for more details of these and other typologies.

More recently, on the basis of work with leading-edge organisations in the USA, Ulrich proposed four HR roles in 1997 and, on the basis of further research, Ulrich and Brockbank (2005a; 2005b) provided a view of the way these roles had evolved since, focusing on what an HR professional has to do to create value. In Table 25.1 we list both the 1997 and the 2005 role sets and link them together.

Table 25.1
Comparison of HR roles in the Ulrich and Brockbank (2005b) model and the Ulrich (1997) model

Roles in Ulrich and Brockbank (2005b)	Explanation of 2005 role	Equivalent role in Ulrich (1997)
Employee advocate	Caring for, listening to, understanding and responding to employee needs, covering issues such as grievances, the impact of strategy on employees, equality, diversity, health and safety, discipline. All of these are played out in a context of the realities of the firm and the performance standards required of individuals	Employee champion
Human capital developer	Based on the premise that people are a critical asset of the organisation and thus need to be developed proactively with a focus on maximising their potential and contribution in the future. Such human capital developers would be located in Centres of HR Expertise, and often act as coaches working on behaviour and attitudes	Employee champion
Strategic partner	Multiple dimensions including business expert, change agent, knowledge manager and consultant. Aligning HR with business strategy is key, alongside transformation and cultural change	Combination of strategic partner and change agent
Functional expert	Application of the HR body of knowledge through HR practices. There are two categories of HR practices, those for which HR has direct responsibility (such as recruitment) and those for which responsibility is indirect (such as communications) Some practices are delivered through administrative efficiency and others through policies and interventions.	An expansion of administrative expert
Leader	Leading the HR function, establishing the function's agenda within the firm and acting as a role model demonstrating the importance of HR in the way they lead their own function. Also contributing to the leadership of the organisation. This role requires that the functions of the four roles above are met	Similar to the business partner role in that it requires the functioning of all other roles, but goes beyond this

One of the fundamental features of Ulrich's approach is his view that HR effectiveness can only be achieved if all business needs relating to HR are met, and therefore all roles are fulfilled. Thus, Ulrich argues that HR must deliver on both a strategic and an administrative level, although there is less focus on administration in the 2005 roles. This view has been echoed elsewhere, with comments that operational HR excellence is an essential precursor for the involvement of HR professionals at a strategic level (e.g. Caldwell 2003). However the 'business or strategic partner' roles have unsurprisingly attracted most attention in terms of job advertisements and new job titles. However, while making the case for strength from fulfilling all roles, Ulrich does acknowledge the paradox created by this, such as representing employee needs at the same time as implementing a management agenda, and it is interesting that the 'employee advocate role' and 'human capital development' roles are now more prominent. This reflects the imperative to explore and understand the employee voice and employee well-being and a recognition that these are important for the individual and the organisation and were under-represented in earlier thinking and practice in HRM.

ACTIVITY 25.1

Using a sample (say, two or three) of the most recent issues of *People Management* analyse the job titles referred to in the articles and any advertisements:

1 How do the job titles quoted compare with the roles identified by Ulrich (1997) and Ulrich and Brockbank (2005b)?

2 Look for evidence of where job titles/remits have changed and note the reason for changes where they are given.

Most recently research has focused on the fundamental purpose of the HR function, and how it needs to change in new environments, as this is seen to be more important than limited roles and structures. The 'Next Generation' research conducted by the CIPD (2011) uncovered a range of HR purposes, generally along the lines of 'people and performance', 'creating a great place to work' and 'landing strategy through people and culture'. However, the CIPD also found some HR leaders who identified the purpose of the HR function as building organisations that would last, focusing on the fitness for purpose of the business now and in the future; in other words, 'supporting sustainable performance'. A key interpretation of the research is that four levels of purpose can be identified which the CIPD arranges in a pyramid:

'actively seeking out growth opportunities' (4) at the top;
'ensuring the business is able to deliver its business strategy' (3);
'seeking competitive advantage through shaping the organisation's culture and people capabilities' (2); and
continuously improving core people processes (1) at the bottom.

The CIPD suggests that the purpose of the HR function has gradually moved up through the pyramid, and that it is most important that the purpose of HR covers all levels. The research suggests that it is more important for HR to take a situational and imaginative approach to the needs and demands of its own organisation rather than merely following generic prescriptions of best practice such as the fulfilment of specific roles.

Structure of the HR function

The purpose and roles of HR in any organisation will have an influence on the structure of the function in any business/business unit, and this becomes more complex in a corporation which comprises several business units, which may or may not be related. Decisions need to be taken about the location of HR professionals between corporate HQ, business HQ and functions and departments, and a range of geographical locations complicates this further. HR professionals and policy/decision making can be either fully centralised or fully decentralised, or any point on this continuum to suit business needs. This is often reflected in reporting lines: for example, does the business HR manager report to the business CEO or to HR at corporate HQ? The level of involvement of line managers in HR is part of this mix and we deal with this specifically later in the chapter. Further complexity is added in global corporations.

A second and equally critical aspect of structure is the extent to which the HR function is an integrated department of generalists across the business, or whether there is some segregation on the basis of expertise, such as recruitment or reward or development across the business; or in terms of client departments, such as research or marketing each having their own dedicated HR generalist. The two approaches may, of course, be taken together, so structures may be very complex.

A more recent and extreme structure is that derived from Ulrich's work on roles. Initially he proposed a three-legged structure comprising:

- **strategic/business roles**;
- **shared service centres/outsourcing/intranet support**; and
- **centres of HR expertise**.

There is evidence that in some large organisations (see e.g. Chesters 2011) a version of this structure has replaced the integrated model where one HR team carried out this full range of roles. However, although popular, it is not as prevalent in its pure form as much of the publicity surrounding the model suggests. It has been criticised for fragmenting the HR function and there are now examples of organisations seeking greater collaboration between the different structural parts of HR, as in the Window on practice, next.

WINDOW ON PRACTICE

Amey redesigns its HR structure and philosophy

Amey had grown considerably through Transfer of Undertakings (Protection of Employment), or TUPE, transfers, and the HR function had found the growth in job titles, large numbers of temporary agency workers and unspecified numbers of people managers a complex challenge. There was an HR service centre but this had been badly received. To transform the HR function to become a strategic driver in the business, greater collaboration within the function was needed. Centres of excellence and shared service teams were brought together and there was increased interaction and movement across the business. Communication with line managers was improved and an HR intranet, telephone support and a self-service system introduced. HR career pathways and succession plans were introduced and links made to CIPD competencies. Amey won the CIPD 'Building HR Capability' award in 2011, the judges concluding that it had redesigned the HR structure and philosophy in a go-ahead way which was commercially successful.

Source: Riddoch, V. (2011) 'Built-in success', *People Management*, November, pp. 40–1.

After further work with organisations, Ulrich and his colleagues (2009) have developed and expanded the model to better reflect the complexity of modern organisations, and this has five elements which are explained as distinct but overlapping:

- **Corporate HR**: being concerned with corporation-wide integration and initiatives, working with top management.
- **Centres of expertise**: providing specialist support to the service centres, providing expert advice and being involved in the design of HR policy and activities.
- **Embedded HR**: those who focus on the strategic needs of the business unit rather than the corporation, working with the leadership team and sometimes line managers, and having a wide range of role titles such as including 'business partner' and 'HR generalist'.
- **Operational executors**: who are based within the business unit dealing with operational HR issues and occasionally administrative work that cannot be dealt with by service centres, enabling 'embedded HR' to focus on strategic issues.
- **Service centres/e-HR**: focusing on administrative and routine issues.

Thus there are now more opportunities for strategic and business partner involvement. The emphasis in this work is on the importance of the HR structure matching the structure of the larger business, for example in the extent to which it is decentralised, giving much greater priority to context than the previous model. Ulrich *et al.* also suggest that the five-element model fits most closely with an organisation comprising allied/diversified businesses rather than a single business or a holding company comprising vastly different businesses.

WINDOW ON PRACTICE

Influences on HR structure in a global setting

A major challenge for global companies is to decide the degree of centralisation in the business and the HR function. High levels of centralisation engender a 'one-company approach' where employees receive the same experience wherever they are in the world. Such standardisation is often cost effective provides high levels of consistency, as long as centralised policies and practices are not subverted. Alternatively some organisations pay more attention to the local context: for example, as Reilly (2012) points out, there are likely to be differences in attitudes and legal provisions relating to data protection; in attitudes to age and seniority; in the acceptability of nepotism; in social obligations. There are of course more differences than these and local cultures can be very resilient to corporate dictates. Working with the local culture may be productive in terms of goodwill, flexibility, commitment and performance. Responsiveness to local cultures generally works best with a corporation which is a holding company for a group of very different specific businesses which keep their separate identities. However, it may be more difficult to clarify shareholder expectations and there are greater risks of unacceptable behaviour.

Whatever balance is chosen in terms of centralisation will impact not only on HR strategies, but also on the positioning and structure of the function and its reporting lines as it works to support corporate and business strategies.

HR strategic contribution

There is much evidence that the strategic or business partner role is the one which has been most attractive, with these job titles used very heavily initially, although a greater variety of titles is now emerging. To offer a strategic contribution HR has to be credible and it has been suggested that such credibility needs to come from being involved in a wider range of business agendas, such as branding, ethics, risk management and corporate social responsibility, and there is some evidence of this happening.

It is worth bearing in mind, however, that the term 'business partner' is often used as a synonym for strategic partner, and used interchangeably (Francis and Keegan 2006), although this is not what Ulrich was originally suggesting. Business partners may be located alongside line managers, building a relationship with them and helping to solve issues, yet in other organisations partners have a more strategic role, providing consultancy to senior managers and becoming involved in the wide range of business issues. So, different organisations are interpreting the role in a variety of ways.

Focusing on senior HR managers in a local government context, Griffiths (2005) reports an Employers' Organisation survey which found that 68% of senior HR managers had a strategic partner role as their primary role; however, the survey report suggests reasons for this high figure, one of which is that there are varied interpretations of that role. Lawler and Boudreau (2009: 18) put it well when they say:

> It is one thing to say that HR should be a strategic partner; it is quite another to define what it looks like and what it takes to make it happen.

While some commentators have found a greater HR involvement in strategy, others suggest that there remains a wide gap between rhetoric and reality. Indeed, Lawler and Boudreau (2009), looking at trends in their surveys from 1998 to 2007, found no increase in the HR role in strategy. So changes in job titles may not reflect changes in roles.

In addition to the lack of clarity about the nature of the strategic role, another problem with assessing the extent of strategic involvement is that many surveys on the HR role are completed by HR specialists alone, and it has often been demonstrated that others in the organisation will not necessarily share the view of the HR specialist on this and other topics. In a survey which included an assessment of the HR strategic role in India, Bhatnagar and Sharma (2005) found that line managers and HR managers differed significantly in their assessment of the HR strategic partner role, with HR managers having a much more positive view of their involvement in this capacity.

WINDOW ON PRACTICE

Reality of HR: strategy or administration?

Brewster and Less (2006) conducted research in sixty international non-governmental organisations (NGOs), many small, but including some large ones such as the Roman Catholic Church. They found HRM issues were neglected and not regarded as strategic, and that the emphasis was on campaigning programmes rather than on enhancing the employee experience and performance. Where HR specialists did exist they were rarely represented at senior levels. Yet internally there was dissatisfaction with HR, particularly among fieldworkers. HR managers felt their role was purely administrative and reactive, and that they lacked involvement in strategic planning and had no presence on trustee boards. Line managers lacked the skills to promote employee commitment via concern for employee capability and work–life balance.

Source: Summarised from Brewster, C. and Less, S. (2006) 'The success of NGOs hinges on their people – but HR is neglected in the sector', *People Management*, Vol. 12, No. 6, 23 March, p. 44.

The extent to which the HR function is involved in both organisational and HR strategy development is dependent on a range of factors, including the overall philosophy in the organisation towards the management of its employees, and there are clear examples of organisations where the HR role remains administrative. The presence of an HR director is considered important and this has previously been used as a proxy for strategic involvement. In a survey of HR directors, Caldwell (2011) found that the benefits of board membership were: having greater involvement and influence in business planning; experiencing more positive perceptions of HR performance; anticipating their CEOs to have higher ratings of the HR function; and a belief that there was greater integration between HR and business strategy. Although Caldwell found other mechanisms for involvement in business strategy, such as executive committees and personal networks, board membership appeared to confer 'symbolic capital', which was significant and attractive.

Long-term historical evidence suggests that HR board membership has increased, although HR director roles can come and go depending on the context, and HR does not yet have an automatic right to be on the board – the function has to earn its place. The focus on assessing trends in HR directorships has weakened more recently with the emphasis moving to strategic contributions in a variety of different HR roles, as we have previously seen, the competencies for strategic capability being a key theme.

It is suggested that HR managers need to use business and financial language; describe the rationale for HR activities in terms of added value; use strategic thinking; act as a business manager first and an HR manager second; appoint line managers into the HR function; concentrate on priorities as defined by the business; understand the business they work in, display business acumen; use relationship building (especially with the CEO) and networking skills; and offer well-developed change-management skills that can be used immediately. Sheehan (2005) argues that the business expertise and credibility of the senior HR specialist can either support or prevent strategic HR integration. More recently the 'Next Generation' research (CIPD 2011) focuses on the importance of insight-led HR in making a strategic contribution. Such insight is based on three savvys: business savvy (in-depth understanding of how the business makes money, its current and future commercial health); organisational savvy (in-depth understanding of people and culture and how things get done in this internal context); and contextual savvy (in-depth understanding of context, for example in terms of demographics, competitor behaviour and geo-politics). However well equipped HR professionals are, there is a further challenge of being able to let go of previous operational duties (e.g. Pritchard 2010).

Self-service HR

Sometimes referred to as employee self-service (ESS) or manager self-service (MSS), these systems allow employees and managers to update records, or get information to solve their queries online, rather than contacting a service centre. These interactive intranets, are also termed e-HR, which Gainey and Klaas (2008: 51) define as 'using computer-based technologies to put HR activities in the hands of "customers"'.

As with other initiatives, much of the drive for such systems has come from the need to reduce the time that the HR function spends on administrative tasks to allow it to focus on more strategic matters. Improvements in efficiency, service delivery, standardisation and organisational image are commonly cited as reasons for introducing self-service systems. Some organisations cite empowering employees as a reason for introduction. In terms of impact of the system Gainey and Klaas (2008) found improvements in delivery of HR (e.g. time and accuracy); improved communications; cost reductions; HR strategic involvement; and employee involvement. In their study Parry and Tyson (2011) did find improvements in service delivery, standardisation and efficiency, and some evidence that the HR function was more able to support the organisation in achieving its business strategy, but there was no evidence of increased HR involvement in business decision making.

Facilities can be wide ranging and are summarised in Table 25.2. Clearly some of the items in the table are password protected because confidential information is involved,

Table 25.2
Self-service HR
facilities

Type of facility	Examples
Information and communication	HR policies and procedures Online employee handbooks Induction information Benefits information Available training courses News/newsletters
Downloading of forms	Expenses claim forms Overtime forms Application forms Training request
Interrogation of recorded data	Provision of personal information to employee or line manager such as absence or leave taken to date Pension forecasts
Queries via email to be answered by an HR specialist	Training requests Requests for advice
Uploading information	Change of address and personal details Attendance data Submitting forms such as expenses Choosing flexible benefits from a menu Responding to a staff survey
Managing HR processes	Performance management uses with ongoing recording of performance and development goals, progress and outcomes by employee and manager, maybe including salary review

and employees and their line managers may have different levels of access. Such systems are often introduced along with HR service centres, the intention being that the system should be the first port of call. In this way the pressure on service centres, using a version of these systems themselves, should be reduced in the long run. Some of these applications will clearly require changes in the organisational culture. There are also issues about access to computers and the computer literacy of some staff. Some companies have introduced kiosks where computers can be used by a range of staff, but there are issues about the extent to which staff will prefer to use their coffee breaks booking holidays on the computer.

In addition, such systems may offer cost-saving advantages, but can pose special problems of their own inducing feelings of remoteness, dehumanisation and lack of customer friendliness. In addition there are concerns about the loss of the personal touch and security of information. *People Management* (2006) reports on a study by Roffey Park Institute which investigated line manager perceptions of HR self-service. The two negative aspects reported most frequently were that line managers felt they had insufficient training on the system, and that employees were penalised when they did not keep their records up to date. Managers also felt that they spent too much time on HR administration and that online help available was of poor quality. There is evidence from Voermans and van Veldhoven (2007) that the availability of greater support is likely to lead to a more favourable response from line managers, and Alleyne and colleagues (2007) found that line manager satisfaction with such systems was influenced by level of communication and training.

ACTIVITY 25.2

We referred to the 'loss of the personal touch' in this discussion of these alternative means of providing HR services.

How important is 'the personal touch' to the employees of today and why do you think this is so?

HR shared services

Shared services refers to one element out of the five in Ulrich's model of the HR function, and service centre staff deal with transactional HR issues for both line managers and employees. They are usually remote call centres and replace local HR officer/administrative staff, with service centre staff having electronic access to personal employee details and HR policies and other information, and are sometimes referred to as partnership service centres or insourcing. Reasons for introducing them revolve around costs savings, the creation of more effective HR services for line managers and employees, and enabling embedded HR/business partners to focus on strategic rather than transactional issues. A Towers Watson survey (2012) of 628 global firms found that in nearly half of those businesses surveyed the HR function was to be reorganised over the forthcoming year with 40% of these moving to a shared services environment and just over 30% extending their use of shared services. No firms anticipated moving away from shared services.

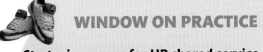

WINDOW ON PRACTICE

Strategic reasons for HR shared service centres in the Netherlands

Farndale and his colleagues (2009) contacted all the companies in the Netherlands using HR shared services and found that the four most common reasons for their introduction were:

52%   Improve professionalisation – customer orientation

48%   Reorganisation of the HR function to be more customer focused

32%   Improve quality, flow and management of work processes

32%   Cost savings.

Source: Summarised from Farndale, E., Paauwe, J. and Hoeksema, L. (2009) 'In-sourcing HR: Shared service centres in the Netherlands', *International Journal of Human Resource Management*, Vol. 20, No. 3, pp. 544–61.

Service centres may be shared across all geographical locations of a business and some provide services shared with other functions such as IT and finance. HR service centres may provide for transactional needs on an even wider basis, such as across a number of different businesses in a corporation where the businesses have enough in common. Alternatively, in the public sector the most frequent form of shared services is a centre which serves two or more public bodies, such as local councils. Lastly a shared service centre may be an independent unit jointly owned by the organisation and an external supplier. In almost every case this form of HR delivery is supported by a self-service intranet as the first port of call, and is usually accompanied by a push to devolve operational HR tasks to line managers.

The centre typically has front office staff who deal with phone calls and back office staff who are involved with a variety of other transactional work such as sending out interview invitations, preparing contracts and so on. Work is sometimes structured by specialist function, for example training or recruitment, or by client group. A more recent innovation is allocating staff on an employee life-cycle basis where a new starter will always be dealt with by the same member of service centre staff wherever they move in the organisation (Pickard 2009a). There is usually a system of escalation whereby queries can be fed up to the next level or tier if the original call centre operator cannot resolve them, so for example there would be access to a functional specialist for non-routine or complex queries.

Shared services are a form of centralisation which avoids duplication but which can also be responsive to local needs. Benefits are expected from efficiency savings and lower transaction costs, a more consistent HR approach across the whole of a company and an HR service which is more customer focused and more responsive to business needs. In addition there are potentially increased opportunities for shared learning. One of the advantages of such centres is the metrics that can be derived to assess their performance. Examples are call waiting time, call count, call length, time taken to resolve queries, accuracy and satisfaction measures from users.

Four councils combine shared services

Cotswold District Council, West Oxfordshire District Council, Forest of Dean District Council and Cheltenham Borough Council are building shared services covering HR, finance, payroll and procurement. They are also moving towards a self-service offering and centres of excellence. The aim is to enable HR to focus on strategic issues and streamline transactional processes, sharing best practice and avoiding duplication. There are 1,400 full-time equivalent staff and currently 26 HR posts which will be reduced. Savings expected are £3.4 million over ten years.

Source: Stevens, M. (2011) 'Local authority shared services "secure HR's future"', *People Management*, 24 February, p. 9.

The problems with the service centre structure are that local knowledge and business solutions may be lost in the changeover, many low-level administrative roles are created with little potential for career development and there may be an obsession with measurement at the expense of service delivery. However, anecdotal evidence suggests that in some organisations line managers have difficulty getting through to the centre and eventually give up. In a survey Reilly (2008) found gaps in service provision and difficulties in defining and communicating the boundary with other parts of HR. He also found that customers did not like standardised services and having various different contact points. Higher staff turnover was also found as employees saw these HR jobs as dull, and cost savings were not always sustained.

Outsourcing HR

Outsourcing is an alternative approach to shared services but typically involves the same delivery channels: self-service HR and an outsourced service centre.

Police forces share and outsource HR services

The first HR services shared between three police forces will be between Leicestershire, Derbyshire and Nottinghamshire, in the East Midlands, and will be delivered by Capita. It is expected that each force will save £900,000 annually and the contract costs £2.3 million over five years.

Source: *People Management* (2012) 'Strategy and OD', July, p. 8.

HR administration, for example pensions and payroll and recruitment, has typically been outsourced. But more specialist aspects have been subject to outsourcing too, such as training and legal work, and in its 2010 survey IDS found that the most popular activity to be outsourced was health and well-being/occupational health. ACAS (2012) note an increasing trend for higher-value HR processes to be outsourced, such as recruitment and training, in addition to routine transactional activities. The definition of outsourcing is somewhat elastic and there is a lack of consensus as Woodall (2009) points out, but she separates out traditional subcontracting of low-skilled tasks from outsourcing business processes where an external provider owns, manages and administers them. Outsourcing the whole of HR (sometimes called end-to-end outsourcing) is also a very different proposition from outsourcing differentiated activities, which has been happening in an ad hoc manner for a much longer time.

The key drivers for outsourcing HR are usually reducing costs and improving service delivery. Outsourcing appears to encourage the measurement of the value of HR, through the need for service-level agreements and key performance indicators with a greater focus on customer satisfaction. Sometimes current HR inefficiencies drive the move to outsourcing. Most of the publicity surrounding HR outsourcing focuses on larger global companies but outsourcing is a slightly different proposition for smaller organisations.

WINDOW ON PRACTICE

Outsourcing in a smaller organisation: Dartford Borough Council

In a deal believed to be the first of its kind Dartford Borough Council has outsourced its entire HR and payroll function. The authority has 400 staff and was originally supported by five members of HR and one member of payroll. The new five-year contract with Northgate means that there are no internal HR employees, but one member of Northgate will be on site and others can be contacted remotely. A major driver was dissatisfaction with the current HR service and it is estimated that the Council will save £50,000 a year. When asked whether the Council would miss out on the strategic element of HR, Brooks, Head of Finance and Resources, who will handle the outsourced relationship, countered that the contract will enable the Council to gain strategic expertise from Northgate.

Source: Brockett, J. (2008) 'Dartford Council outsources HR in ground-breaking deal', *People Management*, Vol. 14, No. 5, 6 March, p. 10.

Some of the benefits of outsourcing are that the organisation can concentrate on its core business; potentially save money due to the supplier's economies of scale; and achieve greater numerical flexibility with less risk. Outsourcing has also been introduced as a vehicle for effecting changes that would be hard to implement internally. For example, in large organisations outsourcing has been used to bring different parts of the organisation together to reduce costs, apply common standards, share best practice, and access innovative IT solutions. A further advantage that is claimed is that the internal HR function can now concentrate on driving the direction of HR rather than carry out more mundane tasks. Truss *et al.* (2012) provide a very useful summary of the advantages and disadvantages of outsourcing.

WINDOW ON PRACTICE

BP and Hewitt renew HR outsourcing deal

There was speculation as to whether BP would renew its outsourcing contract with Hewitt, but when BP did it expanded the contract to cover worldwide operations rather than just the UK and USA as previously. However, most aspects of recruitment have been taken back in-house, and highly complex ex-pat administration was handed back as early as 2006. BP was the first company to secure a major outsourcing contract in 1998 but has experienced problems reflected in the reduction of the scope of the contract.

Source: Pickard, J. (2009b) 'BP and Hewitt renew outsourcing deal', *People Management*, Vol. 15, No. 4, 12 February, p. 10.

However, time is needed to select and develop a relationship and trust with a service provider, and fit with the service provider is important. There is evidence to suggest that the HR function is not the key mover in outsourcing (Woodall 2009) and the CIPD (2009) found that the involvement of HR professionals in the outsourcing process was limited, although considered important. Decisions were generally made by senior executives in the organisation. Outsourcing providers are more likely to find themselves negotiating with the purchasing department, which is more likely to be concentrating solely on cost, rather than the HR function.

Although there has been increasing attention to end-to-end outsourcing, few companies outsource the whole of the function, but outsourcing discrete processes in a tactical way remains most evident (Reilly 2008). There is also evidence that big outsourcing contracts are being replaced by smaller deals, although some are focused on less typical areas such as staff surveys and mediation (Syedain 2009), thus resembling traditional subcontracting.

It will be some time before the full impact of such major long-term outsourcing relationships can be assessed. However, a range of problems is beginning to come through and many large contracts continue to be renegotiated due to problems such as suppliers bidding at too low a price and not being able to fulfil the deal, not knowing which processes need to stay in-house and lack of clarification of roles.

ACTIVITY 25.3

We noted that outsourcing the whole of the HR function is a different proposition from outsourcing some specific aspects. In the context of your own organisation, or one with which you are familiar:

1 If you were to outsource some specific aspects of HR, what would they be and why would you choose them?

Or:

What aspects of HR are already outsourced, how effective has this proved to be and why?

2 If you were to outsource the whole HR function, what reactions would you anticipate from employees and line managers, why do you think they would react like this and what could be done to support them through this change?

Or:

If your organisation has already outsourced the entire HR function, how effective has this proved to be and why?

WINDOW ON PRACTICE

BT and Accenture: Managing a global multi-process outsourcing contract

Julie Clapham, HR Transformation Director for BT, characterises outsourcing as an evolutionary journey as BT continues to renegotiate its second contract with Accenture, three years into it. She suggests that too little attention is paid in advance to the details of what needs to be done and who will do what; and more effort should be made to decide which processes to outsource and which need to stay in-house as they are culture dependent. She also suggests that the time needed for negotiating and managing the contract is much greater than anticipated, and that there are huge hidden costs with ongoing commitment, such as developing retained HR staff to adapt to the changes.

Source: Pickard, J. (2009c) 'Taught in the act', *People Management Guide*, Vol. 14, No. 6, 20 March, pp. 8–10.

Main (2006) suggests the lack of success of some outsourcing experiences is due to the fact that outsourcing is seen as a way to get rid of a problem (such as cost and inadequate computer systems) and the view that once activities are outsourced management responsibility for them ends. Overall problems include the potential loss of skill, knowledge and capacity, limiting the development of a distinctive HR contribution; short-term disruption and discontinuity, and potentially a longer-term reduction in the quality of services, damaging the HR relationship with the line. The loss of HR employee morale and motivation, partly due to more limited career prospects, has also been identified, as has damage to long-term competitiveness. In addition Woodall (2009) found that rather than cost savings there were sometimes increases in costs. Some organisations have even brought HR back in-house, but as Reilly (2008) points out this is very often difficult due to the lack of infrastructure, resources and knowledge.

WINDOW ON PRACTICE

LV= brings HR back in-house

LV= was formerly Liverpool Victoria and is a mutual insurance company employing around 4,000 staff.

In this growing company Dave Smith, HR Director of LV=, was given the opportunity to redesign the HR function and one of the first things he did was to bring the outsourced HR function back in-house. The Chief Executive saw HR strategy as integral to the growth of and change in the company so there was support from the top. Smith stated that the savings made by bringing HR back in-house were estimated to be £3 million over the past year.

Source: People Management (2009)
'In-house HR saves £3m for insurance group',
24 September, p. 10.

The role of line managers in HR

For some time there has been an emphasis on the devolution of HR management by integrating HR activities with day-to-day line management. We use the word 'devolution' here to mean the reallocation of HR tasks to managers outside the HR function, focusing on the line taking ownership of HR activities, enabling HR specialists to act as consultant, coach, facilitator and strategic partner. Such devolution of operational day-to-day HR tasks has been described by Hope-Hailey *et al.* (2005) as devolving the employee champion role, and it is considered to be a means of strengthening the relationship between the employee and his or her manager, resulting in a more positive management approach to employee performance. The importance of the role of the line manager in delivering HR is well documented, especially by Hutchinson and Purcell (2004: ix), as in their research they found that first-line manager behaviour is:

the most important factor explaining the variation in both job satisfaction and job discretion, or the choice that people have over how they do their jobs. It is also one of the most important factors in developing organisational commitment.

Hutchinson and Purcell suggest that line managers bring HR policies to life, and have a direct impact on employee performance, with a poorly implemented HR practice, for example appraisal, being worse than having no practice at all.

However, the difficulties of devolving HR activities to first-line managers have also been consistently highlighted, and Purcell and Hutchinson (2007) identify a gap between what is formally required in the HR policy and what line managers actually deliver. In our research, we found that implementation was difficult, sometimes being described as a game of tennis. Although there was a deliberate policy to devolve HR activities, and managers were encouraged to take them on, these often bounced straight back to HR specialists. The idea that line managers need to take on more day-to-day HR activities has been countered by line managers' lack of skills and interest in this. For example, Hope-Hailey *et al.* (2005) found that line managers neither were motivated nor had the ability to take on people management responsibilities. Interestingly McConville (2006), in the context of the NHS, the armed forces and the fire services, found that middle managers wanted to be pro-active in HR, were committed to it, and exceeded their job requirements to carry out HR activities, but their already substantial workload created the greatest barrier. Caldwell (2004) found that managers resisted taking full ownership of HR and conversely HR professionals wanted to retain control over HR policy. His interviewees were generally reluctant to take devolution 'too far', as ultimately too much devolution may result in the HR role itself being devalued. Devolution has also been identified as problematic due to the lack of consistency of HR decisions, increased potential for inappropriate decisions, and lack of integration resulting in more difficulties in implementing HR strategy. Yet in spite of the risks more devolution to the line is considered key to realising the full potential of the workforce (Churchard 2012).

Maxwell and Watson (2007), on the basis of their investigation into line manager and HR manager perspectives of line management involvement in HR in Hilton Hotels, propose three types of line manager buy-in which are key to their active involvement in HR activities. These are:

- a conceptual understanding of the reasons for their involvement;
- the ability to implement these activities effectively through a clear HR role and having sufficient capability; and
- belief that their involvement in HR is valuable.

Interestingly the authors also found a general lack of shared understanding between line managers and HR specialists about the role of line managers in HR, and some indications that the more similar the perceptions of HR and line managers, the better the hotel performance, whereas the more divergent their perceptions, the weaker the hotel performance. The importance of communication and shared understanding is underlined by Keegan *et al.*'s research (2012) in the Netherlands, Austria, UK and USA. They found that line and project managers were more comfortable carrying out HR tasks if they had direct access to HR specialist as opposed to online support.

Critique of changes in the management of the HR function

There is evidence that the HR function has had greater strategic involvement in some large companies, that line managers are more involved in HR, and that the use of outsourcing and shared services is popular. However, we have also shown that these changes are not universal and are difficult to implement, and sometimes have adverse consequences. It is also important to separate the rhetoric from the reality.

The HR function may be able to become more strategic, but the employee experience may deteriorate (see e.g. Hope-Hailey *et al.* 2005). The concentration on strategic roles appears to have gone hand in hand with the abandonment of the role of employee champion or advocate. Evidence suggests that concern for employee well-being is seen as a signal that the HR function is being dragged back to its old welfare role, with consequent loss of status and credibility. In an interview one senior CIPD adviser stated that 'nobody wants to be an employee champion. They all think it's ideologically unsound' (Francis and Keegan 2006).

This role may also be undermined by increasing use of self-service and outsourcing (Harris 2006). Harris suggests that as the HR function becomes distanced from the workforce and line managers, the consequent loss of knowledge of operational issues means that the function is less able to act as an employee advocate. She found that employees were less likely to see HR as a form of support and advice and suggests they are more likely to approach the union or use legal redress, making the employment relationship more adversarial. She proposes that this loss of touch hinders rather than enables a strategic role, and that lack of opportunity to build relationships and trust with both the line and employees may have a negative impact on promoting employee commitment (Harris 2007).

Along the same lines Francis and Keegan (2005) found the employee champion role was disintegrating in almost all of the organisations they looked at. They found growth of the business partner role and the parallel restructuring of the HR function which appeared to downgrade the employee-facing role, a reduction in the number of HR specialists and devolution of face-to-face HR to line managers. They identified a loss of employee trust and confidence and a cost to employee well-being. Respondents believed employees were losing out because line managers did not have time to prioritise HR issues, or their training, and often HR advisers were geographically distant, so employees were more likely to turn to the union for advice. The unions appear very aware of the chasm they might fill (*People Management* 2005).

Not only do these developments have potential consequences for employees, but they also have consequences for HR practitioners who do not consider employee champion roles as career-enhancing moves, and yet may be disenchanted that the 'people' element of the job was diminishing, which is often why professionals enter HR. The split between strategic and non-strategic HR roles not only hinders strategic parts of the role and therefore the fulfilment of the HR role overall, but also can create barriers between different groups of HR professionals with those in non-strategic roles experiencing low morale and feeling undervalued (see e.g. Pritchard 2010). Career progression in the function becomes more problematic.

The fragmentation of the HR function and devolution and decentralisation create problems for consistency and integration. Caldwell (2003) also suggests that the decentralisation of HRM to the business unit level has resulted in HRM being under more pressures associated with costs, value and delivery and suggests that this has been the driver for the fragmentation or balkanisation of HR into specialist sub-tasks with some parts outsourced externally or to the line. Caldwell suggests that the main risk here is de-professionalisation of the function, and that decentralisation may cause the HR contribution to shift constantly, thereby diminishing the clarity of its role or function. He suggests that the function remains dogged by ambiguity and conflict.

There is a current focus on more effectively managing the HR function across boundaries (see e.g. ACAS 2012), greater collaboration between different parts of the HR function so that it is better connected, and even reintegrating the HR function (Riddoch 2011). The emerging consensus appears to be that there is too much emphasis on models and not enough on skills, people and delivery in context, and that there is a need for the HR function to be agile and flexible in response to the needs of the organisation and consequently for the less rigid application of models (see e.g. CIPD 2006).

SUMMARY PROPOSITIONS

25.1 For many years categorisations of the HR role have been proposed. Most recently Ulrich and Brockbank have identified five roles: employee advocate; human capital developer; strategic partner; functional expert; and leader, with a compound role.

25.2 The focus is moving on from specifying roles to examining the purpose of HR in building a sustainable organisation, with a focus on context and HR capability. The purpose of the HR function will influence its structure.

25.3 There is some evidence of larger organisations employing Ulrich's recommended three-legged HR department structure, but the model is often tailored to meet the needs of the organisation.

25.4 The extent to which HR specialists are involved in HR strategy is influenced by the environment of the business, its culture, the perspective of the chief executive, HR board membership and the qualities, characteristics and working relationships of the most senior HR specialist.

25.5 Although there have been some early problems with outsourcing and shared services, these continue to be pursued by many organisations, and often involve cost savings and staff reductions.

25.6 Devolution of HR activities to line managers enables HR professionals to focus on strategic issues. But line managers often do not have the required motivation, skills or time to carry out HR activities effectively.

25.7 There are concerns that the focus on the business partner role has been at the expense of the employee champion/advocate role, with the consequence that employee well-being is compromised.

25.8 The current trends in HR roles and structure are fragmenting the HR function, resulting in a lack of integration and consistency, and difficulties in effective strategic HR. Collaboration between different parts of the HR function is very important.

GENERAL DISCUSSION TOPICS

1   Does it really matter whether the most senior HR person is on the board of directors, or are personal work relationships, political alliances and personal track records more important?

2   'Outsourcing may be an effective solution in the medium term, but it brings short-term disruption and long-term damage to organisational capability and success.' To what extent do you agree or disagree with this statement?

3   Debate the following comment: 'There has always been a debate about the extent to which day-to-day HR activities should be shared between the professional function and the line. In essence nothing has really changed.'

THEORY INTO PRACTICE

ARM Holdings

This is a continuation of the case study we used earlier (see Chapter 3). You should reread this first to remind yourself about the company. Then read the extract below:

> ARM has one centralised way of doing things across 17 countries. 'Twenty years ago, people used to bang on about "Act global, think local",' says Parsons. "Whereas we fundamentally don't do that. If you join our company community, we have a certain way of doing things. If you operate in many countries and you have many ways of doing the same thing, you are setting yourself up for complexity by definition." For example, an annual equity stake is paid to ARM employees worldwide. Rather than tweak or change the amount according to local laws, tax regimes, or norms, it is simply one rule for all. Not only does it make it easier to administer but, says Parsons, it 'gives the message that we are one company, one community, one everything'. (Smedley 2011: 26)

Questions

1   What are the potential disadvantages of this approach for ARM?

2   What other potential advantages are there for ARM in addition to the ones noted?

3   How would you structure the HR function in ARM so that it supports ARM's one-company approach? Justify your structure.

Source: Extract from Smedley, T. (2011) 'A light touch', *People Management*, October, pp. 24–8.

FURTHER READING

Caldwell, R. (2008) 'HR business partner competency models: Re-contextualising effectiveness', *Human Resource Management Journal*, Vol. 18, No. 3, pp. 275–94.
Based on survey and interview evidence Caldwell provides a useful insight into the value of competency models, finding them to be weak at predicting performance in business partner roles. He also highlights the importance of contextual factors such as the degree of change within the HR function, patterns of centralisation/decentralisation, the consistency of the implementation of business partnering and overall levels in the reduction of transactional HR work.

CIPD Factsheets relevant to this chapter: *HR Shared Service Centres* (2012), *HR Outsourcing* (2011), *HR Business Partnering* (2011) and *The Role of Line Managers in HR* (2012).
Each of these factsheets provide useful definitions; a helpful summary of the key issues; an analysis of advantages and disadvantages; and practical guidance on implementation.

Delmotte, J. and Sels, L. (2008) 'HR outsourcing: Threat or opportunity?', *Personnel Review*, Vol. 37, No. 5, pp. 543–63.
This article reports research in the Belgian context which provides some interesting data on a key debate: whether outsourcing is a means of cost cutting and reducing the numbers in HR or whether it is an instrument for creating more time for HR to play a more strategic role.

Ulrich, D. and Allen, J. (2009) 'Grow your own', *People Management*, 3 December, pp. 32–4.
An insightful summary of the recent five-element model of HR structures. This is an informative yet quick read if you do not have time for the full book or the lengthier academic articles.

REFERENCES

ACAS (2012) *Outsourcing and the Fragmentation of Employment Relations: The challenges ahead*, ACAS Future of Workplace Relations discussion paper series. London: ACAS.

Alleyne, C., Kakabadse, A. and Kakabadse, N. (2007) 'Using the HR intranet: An exploratory analysis of its impact on managerial satisfaction with the HR function', *Personnel Review*, Vol. 36, No. 2, pp. 295–310.

Bhatnagar, J. and Sharma, A. (2005) 'The Indian perspective of strategic HR roles and organisational learning capability', *International Journal of Human Resource Management*, Vol. 16, No. 9, pp. 1711–39.

Brewster, C. and Less, S. (2006) 'The success of NGOs hinges on their people – but HR is neglected in the sector', *People Management*, Vol. 12, No. 6, p. 44.

Brockett, J. (2008) 'Dartford Council outsources HR in ground-breaking deal', *People Management*, Vol. 14, No. 5, p. 10.

Caldwell, R. (2003) 'The changing roles of personnel managers: Old ambiguities, new uncertainties', *Journal of Management Studies*, Vol. 40, No. 4, pp. 983–1004.

Caldwell, R. (2004) 'Rhetoric, facts and self-fulfilling prophecies: Exploring practitioners' perceptions of progress in implementing HRM', *Journal of Management Studies*, Vol. 35, No. 3, pp. 196–215.

Caldwell, R. (2011) 'HR directors in UK boardrooms: A search for strategic influence of symbolic capital?', *Employee Relations*, Vol. 33, No. 1, pp. 40–63.

Chesters, J. (2011) 'Creating strategic HR impact: It's the how, not what', *People Management*, August, pp. 32–5.

Churchard, C. (2012) 'HR "must devolve to line managers despite risks"', *People Management*, April.

CIPD (2006) *The HR Function: A report on an event to discuss the changing shape of the HR function*. London: CIPD.

CIPD (2009) *HR Outsourcing and the HR Function: Threat or opportunity?* London: CIPD.

CIPD (2011) *Next Generation HR: Insight driven*. London: CIPD.

Farndale, E., Paauwe, J. and Hoeksema, L. (2009) 'In-sourcing HR: Shared service centres in the Netherlands', *International Journal of Human Resource Management*, Vol. 20, No. 3, pp. 544–61.

Francis, H. and Keegan, A. (2005) 'Slippery slope', *People Management*, Vol. 11, No. 13, pp. 26–31.

Francis, H. and Keegan, A. (2006) 'The changing face of HRM: In search of balance', *Human Resource Management Journal*, Vol. 16, No. 3, pp. 231–49.

Gainey, T. and Klaas, B. (2008) 'The use and impact of e-HR: A survey of HR professionals', *People and Strategy*, Vol. 31, No. 3, pp. 50–5.

Griffiths, J. (2005) 'Local heroes?', *People Management*, Vol. 11, No. 5, pp. 12–13.

Harris, L. (2006) 'Have council changes eroded HR's role as employee champion?', *People Management*, Vol. 12, No. 21, p. 72.

Harris, L. (2007) 'The changing nature of the HR function in UK local government and its role as "employee champion"', *Employee Relations*, Vol. 30, No. 1, pp. 34–47.

Hope-Hailey, V., Farndale, E. and Truss, C. (2005) 'The HR department's role in organisational performance', *Human Resource Management Journal*, Vol. 15, No. 3, pp. 49–66.

Hutchinson, S. and Purcell, J. (2004) *Bringing Policies to Life: The vital role of front-line managers in people management*, Executive Briefing. London: CIPD.

IDS (2010) *The HR Function*, HR Study 928, October. London: IDS.

Keegan, A., Huemann, M. and Rodney Turner, J. (2012) 'Beyond the line: Exploring the HRM responsibilities of line managers, project managers and the HRM department in four project-orientated companies in the Netherlands, Austria, the UK, and the USA', *International Journal of Human Resource Management*, Vol. 23, No. 15, pp. 3085–104.

Lawler, E. and Boudreau, J. (2009) 'The strategic partner role', *People and Strategy*, Vol. 32, No. 1, pp. 15–22.

Main, C. (2006) 'How to manage an outsourcing contract', *People Management*, Vol. 12, No. 13, pp. 44–5.

Maxwell, G. and Watson, S. (2007) 'Perspectives on line managers in human resource management: Hilton International's UK Hotels', *International Journal of Human Resource Management*, Vol. 17, No. 6, pp. 1152–70.

McConville, T. (2006) 'Devolved RM responsibilities, middle-managers and role dissonance', *Personnel Review*, Vol. 35, No. 6, pp. 637–53.

Parry, E. and Tyson, S. (2011) 'Desired goals and actual outcomes of e-HRM', *Human Resource Management Journal*, Vol. 21, No. 3, pp. 335–54.

People Management (2005) 'Address people needs, not just business needs, advises GMB', Vol. 11, No. 6, p. 10.

People Management (2006) 'e-HR can alienate managers', *People Management*, Vol. 12, No. 4, p. 16.

People Management (2009) 'In-house HR saves £3m for insurance group', 24 September, p. 10.

People Management (2012) 'Strategy and OD', July, p. 8.

Pickard, J. (2009a) 'Calling in the shots', *People Management*, 2 July, pp. 20–3.

Pickard, J. (2009b) 'BP and Hewitt renew outsourcing deal', *People Management*, Vol. 15, No. 4, p. 10.

Pickard, J. (2009c) 'Taught in the act', *People Management Guide*, Vol. 14, No. 6, pp. 8–10.

Pritchard, K. (2010) 'Becoming an HR strategic partner: Tales of transition', *Human Resource Management Journal*, Vol. 20, No. 2, pp. 175–88.

Purcell, J. and Hutchinson, S. (2007) 'Front-line managers as agents in the HRM-performance causal chain: Theory, analysis and evidence', *Human Resource Management Journal*, Vol. 17, No. 1, pp. 3–20.

Reilly, P. (2008) 'Should you branch out?', *People Management*, Vol. 14, No. 6, pp. 16–17.

Reilly, P. (2012) 'HR's future in a global setting', *Human Resource Management International Digest*, Vol. 20, No. 3, pp. 3–5.

Riddoch, V. (2011) 'Built-in success', *People Management*, November, pp. 40–1.

Sheehan, C. (2005) 'A model for HRM strategic integration', *Personnel Review*, Vol. 32, No. 2, pp. 192–209.

Smedley, T. (2011) 'A light touch', *People Management*, October, pp. 24–8.

Stevens, M. (2011) 'Local authority shared services "secure HR's future"', *People Management*, 24 February, p. 9.

Storey, J. (1992) *Developments in the Management of Human Resources*. Oxford: Blackwell.

Syedain, H. (2009) 'Out of the ordinary', *People Management*, 5 November, pp. 20–2.

Towers Watson (2012) *Emerging Choices and Enduring Changes: Creating service delivery in an era of new opportunities*. New York: Towers Watson.

Truss, C., Mankin, D. and Kelliher, C. (2012) *Strategic Human Resource Management*. Oxford: Oxford University Press.

Tyson, S. and Fell, A. (1985) *Evaluating the Personnel Function*. London: Hutchinson.

Ulrich, D. (1997) *Human Resource Champions: The next agenda for adding value and delivering results*. Boston, MA: Harvard Business School Press.

Ulrich, D. and Brockbank, W. (2005a) 'Role call', *People Management*, Vol. 11, No. 13, pp. 24–8.

Ulrich, D. and Brockbank, W. (2005b) *The HR Value Proposition*. Boston, MA: Harvard Business School Press.

Ulrich, D., Allen, J., Brockbank, W., Younger, J. and Nyman, M. (2009) *HR Transformation*. Maidenhead: McGraw-Hill.

Voermans, M. and van Veldhoven, M. (2007) 'Attitude towards e-HRM: An empirical study at Phillips', *Personnel Review*, Vol. 36, No. 6, pp. 887–902.

Woodall, J. (2009) 'Making the decision to outsource human resources', *Personnel Review*, Vol. 38, No. 3, pp. 236–52.

chapter 200

HEALTH AND WELL-BEING

THE OBJECTIVES OF THIS CHAPTER ARE TO:

1 Discuss the nature of health and well-being in an organisational context
2 Outline the range of initiatives that sit within a health and well-being agenda
3 Explain the principles of job design and its role in well-being
4 Explore the impact of health and well-being initiatives on individuals and organisations
5 Examine criticisms of health and well-being initiatives

The nature of health and well-being

The links between employee health and performance were identified long ago. Indeed, the origins of personnel management lie with social reformers such as the Cadbury family who, in the late nineteenth century, began to provide housing, healthcare and education to their workforces. Welfare officers, the early incarnation of today's HR officers, were appointed to oversee the well-being of the workforce. Although altruism played a part in this paternalistic approach towards employees, there was also a strong business case underpinning these practices. Healthy and well-educated workforces are more productive than those struggling in poor accommodation and with insufficient access to education and healthcare. The impact of this focus on well-being on workers' lives was substantial, as can be seen in Cadbury's museum in Bourneville which documents these early attempts at improving employee health and well-being.

As we explained earlier (see Chapter 1), however, the development of personnel management into HRM has had many stages and, since those early days, there has been little enthusiasm to associate the function with what came to be viewed as a 'tea and sympathy role'. Certainly the supposed evolution of personnel into HR management in the 1980s, and its preoccupation with the strategic aspects of business, left little room for considerations of employee health. In recent years, however, health and well-being have again become central to the HR agenda. Indeed, the CIPD has demonstrated significant interest in health and well-being, suggesting that attempts to promote this focus upon:

creating an environment to promote a state of contentment which allows an employee to flourish and achieve their full potential for the benefit of themselves and their organisation. (CIPD 2007: 4)

While some might argue that contentment is not the desired state for employees, it is one of a range of states within well-being which organisations seek to promote. Thus health and well-being go beyond the typically narrower concerns of absence management to include a holistic approach to employees which seeks to promote physical, mental, emotional and social health (Wilson *et al.* 2004). Although a widely agreed definition is lacking, there is a general consensus that health and well-being create 'contented' employees who perform well and are productive: a sound business case clearly underlies attempts to ameliorate the lot of employees.

The re-emergence of health and well-being in the HR agenda can perhaps be explained by the changes to the employment relationship which have been widely reported since the mid-1980s. Changes to the psychological contract have given rise to far less job security for employees, organisational restructuring has led in many sectors to work intensification and the negative consequences for employee morale have been widely reported. Alongside this, there has been an explosion in stress-related illness and absence. A need to refocus on employee well-being to prevent detriment to organisations became apparent. A further impetus has derived from the increasing interest in corporate social responsibility within firms. Employers have a responsibility to create healthy workplaces for reasons beyond performance, bearing a responsibility to society to ensure employees are well treated and healthy. See, for example, IBM's website where information on its wellness programme is presented in its corporate social responsibility section:

www.ibm.com/ibm/responsibility/employee_well_being_management.shtml.
Promoting the work environment as a source of better health and improving health in
the workplace acts as means to reduce social inequality through employment.

In the UK, these developments have coincided with a prominent government interest
in health and well-being, aimed at reducing sickness absence and tackling developing
social phenomena such as obesity. There are many government agencies with remits to
improve public health and national productivity offering employers advice, for example:

> a healthier, more engaged workforce makes good business sense. A motivated, healthy workforce is more likely to
> perform well. Employers and employees benefit through improved morale, reduced absenteeism, increased
> retention and improved productivity. (DH 2004: 3)

There are thus seen to be strong links between health and individual/organisational
performance and ultimately national performance. The emphasis within UK government
programmes has been upon proactive employee support, good employment practice to
reduce prospects of ill health and injury, and effective return to work and rehabilitation
strategies. As with many other areas of the employment relationship, the government
has to a large extent eschewed regulation and exhorted employers to action based upon
the business case, developing a range of policies to support this. For example, a ten-year
strategy to improve occupational health, 'Securing Health Together', was implemented
in 2000 by a range of government agencies, as was a 'Health, Work and Wellbeing' strategy in 2005 and the Department for Work and Pensions' health and well-being initiatives
(**www.dwp.gov.uk/health-work-and-well-being/about-us/**).

As we noted above, health and well-being agendas seek to deal holistically with employees
and encompass a wide range of issues. This breadth is evident in the Management Standards
on workplace stress introduced by the Health and Safety Executive in 2004 (HSE 2004).
The HSE estimates the costs to society of work-related stress to be around £4 billion each
year, while 13 million working days were lost to stress in 2012. Indeed, stress-related conditions are now one of the two most common causes of sickness absence (**www.hse.gov.uk/
statistics/dayslost.htm**). The HSE's Management Standards outline six key areas in which
employers and employees should work together in order to reduce stress and improve well-
being (HSE 2009). We outline these in the Window on practice below.

WINDOW ON PRACTICE

HSE's Management Standards on managing stress in the workplace

Demands – includes workload, work patterns and
the work environment.

Control – how much say a person has in the way
they do their work.

Support – includes the encouragement, sponsorship
and resources provided by the organisation, line
management and colleagues.

Role – whether people understand their
role within the organisation and whether the
organisation ensures that they do not have
conflicting roles.

Change – how organisational change (large or
small) is managed and communicated in the
organisation.

Relationships – promoting positive working
to avoid conflict and dealing with unacceptable
behaviour.

Source: **www.hse.gov.uk/stress/standards/**.

The role of HR practitioners across these six areas is evident in, for example, designing involvement policies that devolve control to employees and ensuring that roles are clearly designed and meet employees' social and psychological needs (see below). The conception of health and well-being by HR practitioners, however, tends to be much more narrowly drawn as we discuss in the following section.

Health and well-being initiatives

As a fairly recent CIPD survey demonstrates (Table 26.1), the HR health and well-being agenda focuses on initiatives which deal mainly with physical and mental health. As we note later in the chapter, this narrow approach draws a great deal of criticism.

These initiatives are widely adopted, particularly in the public sector where the government encourages its agencies to lead by example and be 'model employers'. As can be seen, there is a significant, and narrow, focus on initiatives related to physical and mental health, the latter dealing particularly with workplace stress. To this end, 55% of organisations, 87% in the public sector, offer counselling services, 32% offer employee assistance programmes and a quarter offer stress risk assessments.

While there is not a great deal of academic literature on the types of initiatives presented in Table 26.1, entering 'employee health and well-being' into an Internet search

Table 26.1
Organisational well-being initiatives

	Organisations (%)					
	Total	Manufacturing and production	Private services	Non-profit organisations	Public services	Ireland
Advice on healthy eating	25	29	18	15	40	43
Healthy menu in employee canteen	25	28	20	17	37	40
Healthy snacks in vending machines	13	21	10	1	11	22
In-house gym	12	7	9	8	27	9
Subsidised gym membership	28	21	30	25	43	28
Exercise classes provided on work premises	9	4	6	7	25	13
Support to stop smoking	34	40	21	31	57	34
Regular health checks	28	40	18	17	30	42
Private health insurance	60	71	77	31	12	76
Personalised healthy living programmes for employees	2	2	2	1	5	5
Employee assistance programme	32	25	32	47	40	42
Access to counselling service	55	49	46	62	87	52
Stress risk assessment	25	23	20	29	44	13
Access to physiotherapy	21	26	12	17	29	15
Massage	9	4	10	10	12	12

Source: From *What's Happening with Wellbeing at Work?*, CIPD (2007), Table 2. With the permission of the publisher, the Chartered Institute of Personnel and Development, London (**www.cipd.co.uk**).

engine returns a plethora of consultancies offering advice on the subject (see e.g. www.workandwellbeing.com), alongside a large number of organisations outlining such policies and suggesting that employee health and well-being are important to their success. This is so across both the public and private sectors. Wiltshire County Council, for example, has introduced a range of awards for its business partners, which include promoting physical health, healthy eating and innovative walking routes. It is an international, not just a UK, phenomenon. IBM, for example, outlines a range of initiatives across its global subsidiaries: **www.ibm.com/ibm/responsibility/employees_global_wellness.shtml.**

ACTIVITY 26.1

Look at a health and well-being policy on a corporate website – this might be IBM's (see above) or another one you can find. To what extent do you think these policies set out to address the corporate social responsibilities of organisations?

Even more notable, however, is the number of practices which relate to physical health.

A key concern here is obesity, which, with its links to illnesses such as cancer and heart disease, has emerged as one of the most significant threats to health in modern times in the western world. While its causes are complex, diet and exercise are thought to be two major contributory factors and government policy has sought to encourage both individuals and employers to adopt healthier lifestyles. This is clearly reflected in organisational policy which is focused upon healthy eating, mechanisms to promote physical exercise such as gym membership, health checks and support with giving up smoking. Indeed, such is the emphasis on promoting physical health that it has even found its way into building design, as we outline in the Window on practice below.

WINDOW ON PRACTICE

Get fit while you work

The Broadgate Centre in the City of London was redesigned with fitness in mind. It is one example of a new generation of 'fit' office buildings being designed by architects to encourage employees to become healthier by making them walk while they are at work. The design policy is for fitter people and a fitter environment. Meeting rooms, canteens and car parks are being put at appreciable distances from desks so workers have to expend energy getting to them.

Source: DH (2004).

The range of practices adopted by organisations in attempts to promote employee health and well-being is vast, and many are not captured in Table 26.1. Our own experiences, and those of colleagues and other contacts, suggest that it is common for employers to offer free fruit, various forms of massage, free cholesterol tests, cycle to work schemes, dance and yoga classes, meditation – the list is seemingly endless! This is certainly the message in a recent article on health and well-being schemes in UK universities, demonstrated in the next Window on practice.

WINDOW ON PRACTICE

Well-being in UK universities

Examples of health and well-being initiatives in UK universities are presented on the website **www.wellbeing.ac.uk**. The emphasis on physical and mental health is again apparent in a range of initiatives focusing on stress, counselling and physical activity. City University, for example, offers health and stress checks and 'body MOTs', while Birmingham City University includes among its initiatives information on alcohol abuse, workshops on relaxation techniques, healthy eating and t'ai chi.

Source: Adapted from Newman, R. (2010) 'Get happy and get on with it', *Times Higher Education*, 21–27 January, pp. 32–6.

For information and inspiration, readers should visit the Investors in People website, which offers a database of suggestions for health and well-being initiatives. The CIPD (2013) has also produced a helpful factsheet on health and well-being.

ACTIVITY 26.2

What health and well-being initiatives are offered by your employer or an organisation on **www.wellbeing.ac.uk**?

What is your opinion on the usefulness of these initiatives? How likely are they to improve employee health and well-being?

A narrow emphasis on physical and mental health, however, overlooks other key aspects of employee well-being. An increasing body of research demonstrates the impact of work overload, role conflict, lack of control or autonomy at work, job insecurity and unsupportive working environments in reducing employee well-being (see e.g. Alfes *et al*. 2012; Greasley *et al*., 2012). We argue that effective job design can alleviate many of these problems and move on now to explain job design and outline its role in well-being.

Job design

Job design is the process of putting together a range of tasks, duties and responsibilities to create a composite for individuals to undertake in their work and to regard as their own. It is crucial: not only is it the basis of individual satisfaction and achievement at work, but also it is necessary to get the job done efficiently, economically, reliably and safely. As long as there have been organisations, there has been debate on the best way to design the jobs within them and for much of this time the interest in job design has centred round attempts to improve employee satisfaction with the working situation.

The focus has changed from designing jobs which ensure employee compliance to designing those which generate employee commitment. In this way, job design is seen to be integral to efforts to improve employee well-being and thus organisational performance. The recent WERS 11 (van Wanrooy *et al.* 2013) has reinforced the relationship between elements of job design such as job autonomy and improved employee well-being. This UK-based evidence is supported by international research as we show in the following Window on practice.

WINDOW ON PRACTICE

Stress and health and well-being in a Chinese University

Research into stress in a Chinese university studied the impact of certain 'job stressors' on employee health and well-being. The stressors included work relationships, work–life balance, job control, job overload, job insecurity, resources and communication, and pay and benefits. The overall context was one of increasing staff/student ratios and hard performance management in which academic workloads had increased. The study identified negative relationships between these stressors and both psychological well-being and physical well-being. It also predicted that those with better psychological well-being would have better physical well-being. These findings are clear evidence that job design has an important role to play in overall employee well-being.

Source: Sang *et al.* (2013) 'Modelling occupational stress and employee health and well-being in a Chinese higher education institution', *Higher Education Quarterly*, Vol. 67, pp. 15–39.

The first attempts at job design were influenced by F.W. Taylor and the scientific school of management. This approach was founded on the division of labour into simple jobs and rigid allocations of individuals to narrowly defined tasks. Concerns centred around efficiency, time and motion studies, for example ensuring tasks were structured in a way that allowed workers to conduct them in the most efficient manner. This led to highly specialised jobs, workers at Ford's factories on assembly lines each carrying out, for example, very narrow specified elements of the construction of a motor car. Scientific management was premised upon the idea of 'man as machine', that is rational, unemotional and focused upon economic concerns. Incentives, such as bonuses, were designed to meet the extrinsic motivations of employees. Jobs were, however, routine, repetitive and monotonous, leading to boredom and industrial unrest among workers.

The recognition that workers had needs beyond economic ones led, from the 1940s on, to worker motivation being a key concern within job design. Abraham Maslow, for example, suggested that there was a hierarchy of needs within workers and that job design should meet a range of needs, such as social, rather than simply focusing on economic concerns. In the period 1940–60, a range of motivational theories influenced job design. We do not have the space here to provide a comprehensive review of motivation theory and suggest the reader refers to an organisational behaviour text for further information. We do intend, however, to focus in some detail on one of the most influential pieces of research on job design, namely Hackman and Oldham's (1976) Job Characteristics Model (JCM, Figure 26.1, cited in CIPD 2008). Despite first appearing in the 1970s, it has resonance and influence to this day (see e.g. Wood and Wall 2007).

The JCM specifies certain aspects which must be designed into a job in order to ensure the positive outcomes of meaningful work, responsibility and knowledge. Achieving these will lead to high internal motivation and links to enhanced individual and organisational performance.

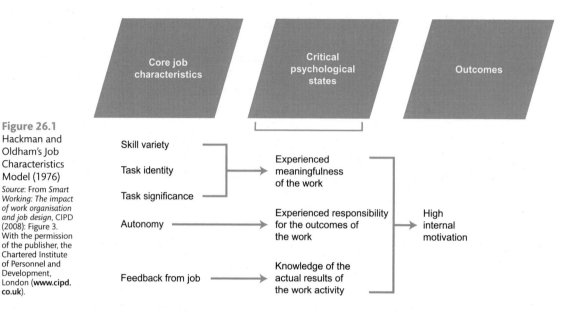

Figure 26.1
Hackman and
Oldham's Job
Characteristics
Model (1976)
Source: From *Smart
Working: The impact
of work organisation
and job design*, CIPD
(2008): Figure 3.
With the permission
of the publisher, the
Chartered Institute
of Personnel and
Development,
London (**www.cipd.
co.uk**).

Skill variety

Skill variety is the extent to which the tasks in a job require a range of skills and abilities. Jobs designed in accordance with scientific management principles were highly special-ised, requiring a narrow range of skills and abilities, and the negative outcomes arising from the boredom and monotony created by this became evident. The JCM suggested that jobs should require workers to use a wide range of skills and abilities and led to a focus on **job enrichment**, the process of incorporating more skills and abilities into jobs. Wood and Wall (2007) make a case for the continuing importance of job enrichment in job design, arguing that it has been overlooked in strategic HRM and that it should continue to be a key element within HRM endeavour.

Task identity

Task identity refers to the degree to which a job provides the opportunity to undertake a whole and identifiable piece of work. Completing such a piece of work is critical to positive psychological outcomes, the negative impact of not doing this again being apparent from, for example, the alienation caused by working on an assembly line. Car manufacturers such as Volvo have over the years experimented with principles such as autonomous work teams, where a team are tasked with the construction of an entire car, rather than individuals being tasked with specified elements of it, in order to provide this task identity. While such experiments have not been unproblematic, they are an attempt to design jobs so as to provide workers with meaningful work.

Task significance

Task significance is the extent to which a job has an impact, whether on the organisation, its employees or customers. The more impact a job is seen to have, the better the psychological outcomes for the worker. A key aspect of job design is thus that workers should understand the contribution made by their job to the organisational endeavour. An oft quoted example in this respect is the hospital cleaner who sees his or her job not as cleaning but helping to deliver high-quality patient care. When conceptualised in this way, the cleaner's job takes on a high level of task significance.

Together, skill variety, task identity and task significance comprise the 'meaningfulness' of the work undertaken. Job design should aim to achieve all three in order to promote motivation in workers and thus higher performance. Although some organisations have worked to design jobs to achieve this, there are still many contemporary organisations which adopt somewhat Taylorist principles. One only has to think of the level of routine and specialisation in jobs such as call centre operatives or fast food restaurant workers to see that the principles of the JCM are by no means universally adopted. This may go some way to explaining the typically high level of labour turnover in such organisations.

Autonomy

Autonomy describes the extent to which the individual undertaking the job has the discretion to make decisions about how it is done, including scheduling the work and deciding upon the procedures used to carry it out. Autonomy creates the positive outcome of responsibility, which again influences motivation. The flattening organisation structures discussed earlier in this chapter have led, since the mid-1990s, to an organisational preoccupation with worker autonomy in the guise of 'empowerment' (see e.g. Cooney 2004). Empowerment devolves responsibility to workers and removes the need for close supervision control – impossible given the removal or reduction of middle managers in many organisations. Working time flexibility, which we discuss below, can also create more worker autonomy (Hall and Atkinson 2006). More recently, the concern to create worker autonomy has been reflected in high-performance work organisation designs focusing on employee involvement mechanisms, as discussed earlier (see Chapter 17).

Feedback

Feedback is about receiving direct and clear information about levels of performance. This leads to worker knowledge which again, according to the JCM, leads to higher motivation. Krasman (2013) presents an interesting study of feedback in relation to the JCM and its positive outcomes. It is this need for feedback which underpins many contemporary performance management systems (see Chapter 10).

The JCM led to a paradigm shift in which jobs were designed which required a range of skills and abilities, provided greater freedom to workers, who often worked in autonomous teams, and adopted flexible working practices. Its principles impacted on models of the flexible firm in the 1980s, high-performance work systems in the 1990s and through to the organisational development approaches of this century. Job design is, however, still dependent on individual characteristics; some workers will, for example, be more receptive to being stretched and challenged than others. Morgeson and Humphrey (2006) also argue that its effectiveness will depend on organisational context, as we see in the Window on practice below which considers role redesign for midwives in the NHS.

WINDOW ON PRACTICE

The redesign of midwives' roles

A central premise of HRM strategies in the NHS is the need to redesign workforce roles and develop new ones, while at the same time expanding the scope of jobs so that staff can take on new responsibilities and skills. The effect of this for midwives was to design 'extended' roles, expanded to include work traditionally performed by doctors, with some aspects of their previous role being delegated to maternity support workers. Midwives felt, however, that the extended roles often prevented them from providing individualised woman-centred care, as they spent time going from one woman to another performing repetitive technical tasks. Work was often described as a 'production line' and a case of 'get them in, get them delivered, and ship them out'. They also felt that there was greater ambiguity in their role and that its extension reduced autonomy and recognition, de-skilling them as they became reliant on technology rather than expertise. In order to undertake the extended roles, the delivery of care, where midwives obtain the greatest job satisfaction and their highest intrinsic motivation, was delegated to maternity support workers. The professional boundaries of midwifery and its traditional social and emotional skills are thus being eroded or replaced as midwives take on more technical roles previously undertaken by doctors and reluctantly relinquish their traditional social and caring roles to maternity support workers.

Critics of the HRM policies of the NHS suggest that role redesign, rather than improving work satisfaction, is being used to reduce labour costs, de-skill staff and promote greater flexibility of labour. The demotivational effects of this upon midwives raises questions about government assumptions that NHS role redesign will improve midwives' productivity.

Source: Adapted from Prowse, J. and Prowse, P. (2008) 'Role redesign in the National Health Service: The effects on midwives' work and professional boundaries', *Work, Employment and Society*, Vol. 22, No. 4, pp. 695–712.

ACTIVITY 26.3

Thinking of a job you have held, or one you have observed (e.g. your interactions with workers in fast food restaurants), analyse it in terms of the Job Characteristics Model. To what extent does it offer:

- Skill variety
- Task identity
- Task significance
- Autonomy
- Feedback?

What are the implications of your analysis for worker motivation and well-being?

The impact of health and well-being initiatives on individuals and organisations

Despite our own view that job design is central to well-being, many organisations emphasise physical health and fitness in health and well-being initiatives. Such initiatives are not cheap: one university spent £50,000 on a programme to encourage staff to keep fit, and this level of expenditure is not unusual. Clearly employers expect that there will

Table 26.2
Benefits of health and well-being initiatives

Recruitment	Many organisations promote their health and well-being policies in order to attract applicants for vacancies that they advertise. They seek to be 'employers of choice' in demonstrating concern for employees
Improved performance	Achieved through more productive employees and better service via a reduced dependence on replacement employees
Competitive advantage	GlaxoSmithKline suggests that investing in health and well-being will help to build competitive advantage through employees: **www.gsk.com/uk/careers/why-gsk/protecting-your-well-being-and-the-planet.html**
Positive employee attitudes	Employees will be more engaged, committed and contented and these positive employee attitudes have been demonstrated to be performance enhancing
Retention	Fewer employees will be lost due to ill health and intention to quit employment is likely to be reduced as a result of positive employee attitudes.

be substantial returns on this investment, often in the form of improved employee attendance, as discussed earlier (see Chapter 12). But returns are expected to go significantly beyond reduced sickness absence, as we outline in Table 26.2. Indeed, one survey suggests that there is a return of £4.17 for every £1 spent on employee well-being (Newman 2010).

Crush (2009) reports on Royal Mail's health and well-being initiatives. While he recognises that their contribution can be hard to assess, he cites an international survey which suggests that well-being is one of the prime drivers of employee engagement. We summarise part of his work in the Window on practice which describes Royal Mail's health and well-being policy and practices and their outcomes and considers the wider implications of health and well-being for economic performance.

WINDOW ON PRACTICE

Royal Mail Group's health and well-being 'blueprint' could provide a £1.45 billion boost to the UK's struggling sectors: innovative measures help the organisation cut absence by 25% and save £227 million in three years.

Health and well-being initiatives introduced by Royal Mail Group could hold the key to reducing the impact of absence across the UK's worst performing sectors and deliver savings of £1.45 billion a year, a study by the London School of Economics revealed. In its 'Value of Rude Health' report – the result of a unique, year-long study – the London School of Economics also calculated that the value of Royal Mail Group's approach to tackling absence could bring more than 94,000 people absent through illness or injury back into work more quickly.

The study revealed that Royal Mail Group's health and well-being activities have:

- Slashed absence by 25% between 2004 and 2007.
- Brought 3,600 employees absent through illness or injury back into work.
- Saved more than £227 million in terms of direct costs (wages and benefits).

Royal Mail Group's success in cutting absence by a quarter has been achieved through:

- Health screening for employees and occupational support services including physiotherapy and occupational therapy.
- Health clinics in more than ninety Royal Mail Group sites to help people return to work and prevent them getting ill.
- Fitness centres run by trained instructors in larger sites.
- Health promotion campaigns targeting smoking and back pain.
- Increased support and training for managers to improve the effectiveness of absence to attendance policies.

And the business is continuing its activities to improve the health and well-being of its people through two new initiatives – an online health check-in and assessment service and the recruitment of health trainers to help fellow workers improve their health through advice and practical support.

David Marsden, a Professor in the Centre for Economic Performance at the London School of Economics and author of the report, commented:

Our study suggests that the 13 sectors of the economy least effective at addressing employees' health and well-being could benefit significantly from Royal Mail Group's 'blueprint'. Following the organisation's example in bringing high rates of absence in specific sites to average levels would deliver huge financial gains and provide a boost to the performance of a range of companies and organisations.

These include:

- Bringing more than 94,000 workers absent through illness or injury back into work.
- Adding an extra 21 million days worked by UK employees a year.
- Annual cost savings of £1.45 billion to the UK economy.

At a time when absence is an increasing priority for employers, the London School of Economics' 'Value of Rude Health' report has created one of the most compelling investment cases to date for health and well-being policies. One of the UK's largest employers, Royal Mail Group has invested £46 million over three years in approaches that address the biological, social and psychological causes of absence, delivering a return on investment of five to one.

Source: Adapted from Marsden and Moriconi (2009) 'The value of rude health: Employee's well being, absence and workplace performance', *CEP Discussion Paper No. 919*. London: Centre for Economic Performance.

Criticisms of health and well-being initiatives

There are a variety of criticisms of health and well-being initiatives, ranging from questions of definition to challenges to the HR conception of the issue. While health and well-being programmes have grown in popularity in recent years, there is a suggestion that they contain little new, rather that they are a rebranding of absence management programmes. Even where they are seen to contain practices of merit, it is argued that lack of resources or senior management buy-in can lead them to be largely ineffective. Such initiatives may also be beyond the financial means of many smaller firms, which form the majority of organisations.

A further concern is the extent to which organisations have the right to interfere in employees' lives. While employers may have a responsibility to tackle work-related stress, there is an argument that an employee's weight and fitness levels are nobody's business but the employee's own. Indeed, many employees have expressed concern about information obtained by employers as part of these programmes being put to inappropriate use, in, for example, redundancy or promotion selection decisions. When Walmart launched its wellness campaign in 2005, requiring employees to volunteer information on weight and take steps to reduce this if appropriate, there were accusations of heavy-handedness and even fascism from employees and their representatives.

The major criticism of health and well-being initiatives as conceived by the HR community, however, is their narrow focus on concerns such as fitness and healthy eating (see e.g. CIPD 2012). As we noted earlier, academic treatments of health and well-being take a much wider view on what they constitute. Recent work, for example, has defined employee

Table 26.3
Organisational
and individual
well-being in
context

Organisational well-being	Individual well-being
• Values-based working environment and management style • Open communication and dialogue • Teamworking and cooperation • Clarity and unity of purpose • Flexibility, discretion and support for reasonable risk taking • A balance between work and personal life • The ability to negotiate workload and work pace without fear of reprisals or punishment • Being fairly compensated in terms of salary and benefits	• Maintaining a healthy body by making healthy choices about diet, exercise and leisure • Developing an attitude of mind that enables the employee to have self-confidence, self-respect and to be emotionally resilient • Having a sense of purpose, feelings of fulfilment and meaning • Possessing an active mind that is alert, open to new experiences, curious and creative • Having a network of relationships that are supportive and nurturing

Source: Adapted from CIPD (2007).

well-being as a combination of employee happiness, health and relationships (see e.g. Atkinson and Hall 2011; de Voorde *et al.* 2012) and academic publications on the subject rarely concern the kinds of initiatives outlined earlier. Rather, they consider issues such as job design and the extent to which workers have autonomy and experience job satisfaction (Holman 2002). It has been suggested that these narrow approaches are a facade to conceal the fact that the employer is seeking to get more out of employees for less:

> Overall, 'wellness' is a sham. It is aimed at distracting attention from more stressful work, more bullying and the weakness of unions which means that workers have less 'voice' at work. (Newman 2010: 36)

Table 26.3 outlines both organisational and individual aspects of health and well-being from this broader perspective. It is evident from this that physical health is a relatively small part of overall individual well-being and that organisational responsibilities are significant and draw on much wider aspects of HR practice than providing healthy food in canteens or free gym membership.

Holman's (2002) work on employee well-being in call centres, the findings of which are outlined in the Window on practice below, reinforces the point that organisations have broad responsibilities in supporting health and well-being. He suggests, for example, that autonomy and limited but supportive supervision are the fundamentals of health and well-being.

WINDOW ON PRACTICE

Employee well-being in call centres

Call centres are often perceived to have a negative impact on employee well-being, mainly attributed to four factors: job design, performance monitoring, HR practices and team leader support. This article reports on a survey of 557 customer service representatives that examined the relationship of these factors to four measures of well-being: anxiety, depression and intrinsic and extrinsic job satisfaction. One distinctive feature of this article is its focus on anxiety and depression, two major dimensions of well-being not addressed in call centre research to date. Results demonstrated that the factors most highly associated with well-being were high control over work methods and procedures, a low level of monitoring and a supportive team leader. Evidence also indicates that the level of well-being in some call centres is similar to that in other comparable forms of work.

Source: Adapted from Holman, D. (2002) 'Employee wellbeing in call centres', *Human Resource Management Journal*, Vol. 12, No. 4, pp. 35–50.

Our argument thus far has been that current HR initiatives are too narrowly drawn and there is growing weight to this argument. A recent article in the UK higher-education press makes the point strongly that there is more to health and well-being than massage and free fruit (Newman 2010). It may also be that this is becoming apparent to HR practitioners. In the Window on practice below, we draw from two speeches by senior HR professionals, both of whom suggest that a narrow focus on physical and mental health is unhelpful and that the HR perspective on health and well-being needs to be widened. A greater focus is needed on the fundamentals of the workplace that may lead to poor health, rather than presenting solutions to problems that have already emerged.

WINDOW ON PRACTICE

What drives employee well-being?

'What HR professionals need to decide is whether health and wellbeing is about providing lettuce for lunch or about far less obvious but potentially more effective things,' says David Batman, Group Medical Officer, Nestlé UK. 'Simply giving staff more autonomy in their jobs will reduce the level of stress they suffer. This impacts blood pressure and heart conditions. To me, just giving people the opportunity to do their job will have a far more significant impact on the health of a company's employees than persuading them to give up smoking and eating more healthily in the staff canteen.'

'Old-style wellbeing is like walking downstream of a river, rescuing employees who are flailing around in the water, needing saving,' says Margaret Samuel, Chief Medical Officer at EDF Energy. 'What we need to do is turn around and walk upstream to find out why so many of these employees are ending up in the water in the first place; we need to find the source of the emergency.'

Source: Crush, P. (2009) 'Health and wellbeing: The science of employee wellbeing', *Human Resources*, 1 July. Available at: **www.hrmagazine.co.uk/hr/features/1014936/health-wellbeing-the-science-employee-wellbeing**.

ACTIVITY 26.4

What are the key causes of reduced productivity and/or commitment in an organisation with which you are familiar? To what extent do you think that these issues will be improved or resolved by the initiatives outlined in Table 26.1?

SUMMARY PROPOSITIONS

26.1 The links between health and well-being and employee performance were identified long ago, although there was little emphasis on them from an HR perspective for much of the twentieth century.

26.2 The past decade has seen a substantial increase in interest in employee health and well-being from both an organisational and a governmental perspective. This has been driven by social, economic and political changes.

26.3 Initiatives within a health and well-being policy have typically focused narrowly on employees' physical and mental health. This focus has attracted a great deal of criticism.

26.4 Effective job design is fundamental to employee well-being.

26.5 It is suggested that health and well-being initiatives have a range of positive outcomes including improvements in recruitment, performance, engagement and retention, more positive employee attitudes and enhanced competitive advantage.

26.6 There are many criticisms of the narrow HR approach to health and well-being. These include assertions that such approaches differ little from traditional absence management, are likely to lack management buy-in and are financially beyond the reach of the many smaller firms in the economy.

26.7 Other concerns surround the argument that an employee's health is no concern of the employer and, most fundamentally, that health and well-being initiatives often tackle the symptoms of poor employment practice. Better job design and more worker autonomy would be much more effective in improving the lot of the employee.

26.8 There is some evidence that HR practitioners are beginning to recognise the need for wider conceptions of health and well-being.

GENERAL DISCUSSION TOPICS

1 'The positive outcomes from health and well-being initiatives justify their significant cost.' Discuss this statement.

2 'An organisation does not have the right to concern itself with the weight and fitness levels of its employees.' To what extent do you agree with this statement?

3 Evaluate the suggestion that organisations would obtain more significant benefits from designing jobs well than from providing access to free fruit and low-cost gym membership.

THEORY INTO PRACTICE

Employee stress and burnout

Read: Churchard, C. (2012) 'One in three employees threatened by burnout', *People Management*, 19 November.

Questions

1 To what extent do you think job design is important in promoting employee well-being?

2 '53 per cent of employees agreed that their stress levels at work are manageable, although less than a third said that their leaders supported health and wellbeing policies to help them cope with it.'

　　To what extent can health and well-being policies addressed mainly at employee fitness help to alleviate stress levels at work?

3 Are the issues discussed in the case mainly restricted to the UK or are they to be found internationally? If the latter, find evidence of these issues in other countries.

4 Why is well-being important for organisational performance?

Source: **www.cipd.co.uk/pm/peoplemanagement/b/weblog/archive/2013/01/29/one-in-three-employees-threatened-by-burn-out-finds-study-2012-11.aspx.**

FURTHER READING

CIPD (2007) *What's Happening with Wellbeing at Work?* London: CIPD.
This report presents detailed information on a range of health and well-being initiatives. It provides case study evidence that workplaces which invest in the well-being of their employees have high workplace standards and also help those people to improve their own well-being.

De Voorde, K., Paauwe, J. and Van Velhoven, M. (2012) 'Employee well-being and the HRM–organisational performance relationship: A review of quantitative studies', *International Journal of Management Reviews*, Vol. 14, pp. 391–407.
This paper reviews thirty-six research studies to explore the relationship between employee well-being and organisational performance. A broad conceptualisation of well-being as comprising happiness, health and relationships is adopted. The authors argue that where well-being relates to happiness and relationships, both the individual and the organisation benefit. Where it relates to health, the organisation benefits at the expense of employees. The paper is valuable in reviewing a broad range of literature in the field and in demonstrating the benefit of considering well-being to be more than just health and fitness.

Marsden, D. and Moriconi, S. (2009) 'The value of rude health: Employees' well being, absence and workplace performance', *CEP Discussion Paper No. 919*. London: Centre for Economic Performance. This report reflects the interest of businesses and government in health and well-being. It explores one organisation's approach to managing health and well-being and demonstrates that it benefits both people and business. Its effects on business performance – from employee morale to productivity and other indicators of business performance – are clearly laid out in this report.

WEB LINKS

www.ibm.com/ibm/responsibility/employee_well_being_management.shtml (IBM website, section on corporate social responsibility, accessed 24 March 2013).

www.ibm.com/ibm/responsibility/employees_global_wellness.shtml (IBM website, section on international wellness initiatives, accessed 24 March 2013).

www.investorsinpeople.co.uk (website of Investors in People, accessed 24 March 2013).

www.well-being.ac.uk (website of well-being funded by the HEFCE and the Scottish Funding Council to investigate and promote well-being in higher education, accessed 24 March 2013).

www.workandwell-being.com (website of Work and Well-being Ltd, a consultancy, accessed 24 March 2013).

www.dwp.gov.uk/health-work-and-well-being/about-us/ (accessed 24 March 2013).

REFERENCES

Alfes, K., Shantz, A. and Truss, C. (2012) 'The link between perceived HRM practices, performance and well-being: The moderating effect of trust in the employer', *Human Resource Management Journal*, Vol. 22, pp. 409–27.

Atkinson, C. and Hall, L. (2011) 'Flexible working and happiness in the NHS', *Employee Relations*, Vol. 33, pp. 88–105.

CIPD (2007) *What's Happening with Wellbeing at Work?* London: CIPD.

CIPD (2008) *Smart Working: The impact of work organisation and job design.* London: CIPD.

CIPD (2012) *Building a Culture of Organisational Well-being.* London: CIPD.

CIPD (2013) *Health and Well-being at Work: Factsheet.* London: CIPD.

Cooney, R. (2004) 'Empowered self-management and the design of work teams', *Personnel Review*, Vol. 33, pp. 677–92.

Crush, P. (2009) 'Health and well-being: The science of employee well-being', *Human Resources*, 1 July.

De Voorde, K., Paauwe, J. and van Veldhoven, M. (2012) 'Employee well-being and the HRM–organisational performance relationship: A review of quantitative studies', *International Journal of Management Reviews*, Vol. 14, pp. 391–407.

DH (2004) *Choosing Health: Making healthy choices easier*, Cm 6374. London: The Stationery Office.

Greasley, K., Edwards, P., Baker-McClearn, D. and Dale, J. (2012) 'Why do organisations engage in HR initiatives? A test case of a health and well-being intervention', *Employee Relations*, Vol. 34, pp. 443–62.

Hall, L. and Atkinson, C. (2006) 'Improving working lives: Flexible working and the role of employee control', *Employee Relations*, Vol. 28, pp. 374–86.

Holman, D. (2002) 'Employee well-being in call centres', *Human Resource Management Journal*, Vol. 12, pp. 35–50.

HSE (2004) *Management Standards for Work-related Stress.* London: Health and Safety Executive.

HSE (2009) *How to Tackle Work-related Stress: A guide for employers on making the Management Standards work.* London: Health and Safety Executive.

Krasman, J. (2013) 'Putting feedback-seeking into "context": Job characteristics and feedback-seeking behaviour', *Personnel Review*, Vol. 42, pp. 50–66.

Marsden, D. and Moriconi, S. (2009) 'The value of rude health: Employees' well being, absence and workplace performance', *CEP Discussion Paper No. 919*. London: Centre for Economic Performance.

Morgeson, F. and Humphrey, S. (2006) 'The Work Design Questionnaire (WDQ): Developing and validating a measure for assessing job design and the nature of work', *Journal of Applied Psychology*, Vol. 91, pp. 1321–39.

Newman, R. (2010) 'Get happy and get on with it', *Times Higher Education*, 21–27 January, pp. 32–6.

Prowse, J. and Prowse, P. (2008) 'Role redesign in the National Health Service: The effects on midwives' work and professional boundaries', *Work, Employment and Society*, Vol. 22, No. 4, pp. 695–712.

Sang, X., Teo, S., Cooper, C. and Bohle, P. (2013) 'Modelling occupational stress and employee health and well-being in a Chinese higher education institution', *Higher Education Quarterly*, Vol. 67, pp. 15–39.

Van Wanrooy, B., Bewley, H., Bryson, A., Forth, J., Freeth, S., Stokes, L. and Wood, S. (2013) *The 2011 Workplace Employment Relations Study: First findings*. London: BIS.

Wilson, M., Dejoy, D., Vandenberg, R., Richardson, H. and McGrath, A. (2004) 'Work characteristics and employee health and well-being: Test of a model of a healthy work organisation', *Journal of Organisational and Occupational Psychology*, Vol. 77, pp. 565–88.

Wood, S. and Wall, T. (2007) 'Work enrichment and employee voice in human resource management: Performance studies', *International Journal of Human Resource Management*, Vol. 18, pp. 1335–72.

THE INTERNATIONAL DIMENSION

THE OBJECTIVES OF THIS CHAPTER ARE TO:

1 Provide an overview of research and practice in international HRM

2 Explore the major dimensions of cultural difference between workplaces based in different countries

3 Assess how institutional differences help account for differences in HRM practice across national borders

4 Explain how international HRM practice varies from nationally based HRM practice

5 Review aspects of communication and coordination in international organisations

6 Discuss the major steps necessary to ensure the successful deployment of expatriate staff.

Earlier we explained how the globalisation of economic activity over recent decades and, in particular, its acceleration in the last twenty years have had a huge impact on the context in which HRM activity now takes place (see Chapter 2). Most organisations in the private sector are now obliged to compete, either directly or indirectly, with others based overseas. This is vastly increasing the extent of competition, is making the business environment more volatile and is thus a key driver behind many of the contemporary developments in HRM practice which we have introduced in this book. Globalisation is also providing both the rationale and the opportunity for organisations which once restricted their activity to a national market to expand overseas and become multinational corporations (MNCs) with interests in several countries and an international workforce to manage. Estimates of the number of people employed directly in MNCs vary considerably, but it is probably in the region of 100 million people worldwide (see Marginson and Meardi 2009). Public-sector organisations are also affected by globalisation, being required to benchmark their performance with other equivalent bodies overseas and to take on approaches that have been found to work well in other countries. Labour markets are becoming increasingly international as organisations seek to source elsewhere key skills that are in short supply at home. In recent years, for example, the NHS has recruited heavily from overseas countries. While the numbers have reduced somewhat recently, at their peak between 2000 and 2006 well over 10,000 nurses a year were registering in the UK having trained in other countries. This represented more than half of all new nurses recruited (Buchan and Seccombe 2009: 11–13).

Unsurprisingly, as globalisation has picked up its pace, international HRM has become one of the most widely researched and written about fields of study. Numerous books and articles have been published over the past twenty years examining all aspects of practice in international organisations, a number of fascinating debates evolving about what is happening, what should happen and about the longer-term direction of travel. In one short chapter we can only begin to introduce this subject, so we will focus on two or three key issues that have generated the most interest to date. We start by introducing some studies in the field of comparative HRM, exploring why it is that the way people are managed, and expect to be managed, varies so much from country to country. We go on to discuss key issues in the management of people in international corporations, focusing in particular on communication and coordination difficulties. Finally we introduce some specific issues that arise in connection with the employment of expatriate staff.

WINDOW ON PRACTICE

Deresky (2008: 5) reproduces a whimsical description of globalisation 'from an unknown source', relating to the death of Princess Diana in Paris:

Princess Diana was an English princess
With an Egyptian boyfriend
Who crashed in a French tunnel,
Driving in a German car with a Dutch engine,
Driven by a Belgian who was drunk on Scotch whisky,
Followed closely by Italian paparazzi,

On Japanese motorcycles.
She was treated by an American doctor,
Using Brazilian medicines.
This is sent to you by an American Indian,
Using Bill Gates's technology.
You are probably reading this on your computer
That uses Taiwanese chips
And a Korean monitor,
Assembled by Bangladeshi workers in a Singapore plant,
Transported by Indian lorry drivers,
Unloaded by Sicilian longshoremen
And trucked to you by Mexican immigrants.

Cultural variations

In recent decades a number of extensive, questionnaire-based studies have been carried out among employees and managers working in different countries, the results subsequently being 'mapped'. The dominant features of business cultures across the globe have thus been categorised into readily understood types which demonstrate how they differ one from another. The best known studies are those by:

- Kluckohn (1954)
- Strodtbeck (1961)
- Hofstede (1980; 1991; 2001)
- Hall and Hall (1990)
- Trompenaars (1993)
- Lewis (1996)
- House *et al.* (2004).

Inevitably this process oversimplifies matters to a considerable extent, downplaying the extent of cultural variation between organisations, generations and regions within countries, as well as changes over time, while emphasising cultural differences between countries. However, because the researchers have all, without exception, found that work cultures vary much more between countries than they do within national boundaries, these studies can claim to be both valid and useful.

Although it may be simplistic, there is a great deal of truth in the finding across all these studies that the UK's dominant workplace culture is one in which organisations tend to have less formal hierarchical structures than elsewhere, much more decentralisation of authority, a relatively relaxed view of change and a preference for keeping emotions hidden. The observation is thus useful, particularly as the basis for making broad international comparisons, but it must also be recognised that there are also plenty of organisations, communities and individuals who do not share these cultural norms, so care has to be taken not to simply 'read off' a set of national characteristics from the published typologies and assume it applies everywhere, equally within any single country.

Despite being subjected to a great deal of criticism over the years, Gert Hofstede's work in this field remains by far the most widely quoted and cited, making it a truly seminal contribution to the study of HRM. Hofstede's studies remain unrivalled in terms of their scale and scope, comprising the analysis of detailed questionnaires issued to many thousands of IBM employees in seventy different countries over a long period. The studies have led to the publication of several detailed books, including a number of editions of *Culture's Consequences*, which was originally published in 1980 but has been updated on several occasions since. Hofstede's organisation also runs a most interesting website which explains his work and allows all manner of charts to be downloaded which show how different countries 'score' on all his dimensions (**www.geert-hofstede.com**).

Hofstede defines national culture as 'the collective mental programming which distinguishes one nation from another'. He originally identified four dimensions that allow different national characteristics to be classified or mapped. These are as follows:

1 **Individualism**: This is the extent to which people expect to look after themselves and their family only. The opposite is collectivism, which has a tight social framework and in which people expect to have a wider social responsibility to discharge because others in the group will support them. Those of a collectivist persuasion believe they owe absolute loyalty to their group.

2 **Power distance**: This measures the extent to which the less powerful members of the society accept the unequal distribution of power. In organisations this is the degree of centralisation of authority and the exercise of autocratic leadership.

3 **Uncertainty avoidance**: The future is always unknown, but some societies socialise their members to accept this and take risks, while members of other societies have been socialised to be made anxious about this and seek to compensate through the security of law, religion or technology.

4 **Masculinity**: The division of roles between the sexes varies from one society to another. Where men are assertive and have dominant roles these values permeate the whole of society and the organisations that make them up, so there is an emphasis on showing off, performing, making money and achieving something visible. Where there is a larger role for women, who are more service orientated with caring roles, the values move towards concern for the environment and the quality of life, putting the quality of relationships before the making of money.

Hofstede found some clear cultural differences between nationalities and from this he concluded that countries emphasising large power distance and strong uncertainty avoidance were likely to produce forms of organisation that relied heavily on hierarchy and clear orders from superiors: **a pyramid of people**. In countries where there is small power distance and strong uncertainty avoidance, there would be an implicit form of organisation that relied on rules, procedures and clear structure: **a well-oiled machine**. The implicit model of organisation in countries with small power distance and weak uncertainty avoidance was a reliance on ad hoc solutions to problems as they arose, as many of the problems could be boiled down to human relations difficulties: **a village market**. The picture is completed by the fourth group of countries where there is large power distance and weak uncertainty avoidance, where problems are resolved by constantly referring to the boss who is like a father to an extended family, so there is concentration of authority without structuring of activities. The implicit model of organisation here is: **the family**. Table 27.1 shows which countries are in the different segments.

The implicit form of organisation for the UK is a village market, for France it is a pyramid of people, for Germany it is a well-oiled machine and for Hong Kong it is a family. If we can understand the organisational realities and detail in those four countries, then this can provide clues about how to cope in Denmark, Ecuador, Austria or Indonesia because they each share the implicit organisational form and implicit organisational culture of one of the original four.

ACTIVITY 27.1

Identify your country and its type from those shown in Table 27.1. If it is not there, pick one with which you are familiar.

1 Do you agree with Hofstede's description of the type of organisation that is implicit?

2 Think of examples of how that implicit type of organisation affects HR activities.

Table 27.1

Pyramid of people	Well-oiled machine	Village market	Family
Arab speaking	Austria	Australia	East Africa
Argentina	Costa Rica	Canada	Hong Kong
Belgium	Finland	Denmark	Indonesia
Brazil	Germany	Ireland	India
Chile	Israel	Netherlands	Jamaica
Colombia	Switzerland	New Zealand	Malaysia
Ecuador		Norway	Philippines
France		South Africa	Singapore
Greece		Sweden	West Africa
Guatemala		UK	
Iran		USA	
Italy			
Japan			
Korea			
Mexico			
Pakistan			
Panama			
Peru			
Portugal			
Salvador			
Spain			
Taiwan			
Thailand			
Turkey			
Uruguay			
Venezuela			
Yugoslavia			

It is not quite as easy as that, because the clusters show only relative similarities and, inevitably, other studies do not entirely agree with Hofstede (e.g. Ronen and Shenkar 1985), but there is sufficient agreement for us to regard the four-way classification as useful, if not completely reliable.

Hofstede later produced a refinement of the uncertainty avoidance dimension: 'Confucian dynamism', or long-term versus short-term orientation. Working with the Canadian Michael Bond, Hofstede used a Chinese value survey technique in a fresh study and uncovered the cultural variable of long-term orientation that none of the original, western, questions had reached. The highest scoring countries on this dimension were China, Hong Kong, Taiwan, Japan and South Korea. Singapore was placed ninth. Hofstede argues that countries in the west have derived their culture largely from the three religions of Judaism, Christianity or Islam, all of which are centred on assertion of truth that is accessible to true believers, whereas none of the religions of the east are based on the assertion that there is a truth that a human community can embrace. The 'Confucian' values found attached to this long-term orientation included perseverance, clearly maintained status differentials, thrift, and having a sense of shame. In many ways these values are valuable for business growth, as they put social value on entrepreneurial initiative, support the entrepreneur by the willing compliance of others seeking a place in the system, encourage saving and investment, and put pressure on those who do not meet obligations.

Hofstede's work is interesting in that it demonstrates that cultures (or collective mental programming) among a national people remain strikingly and persistently divergent despite convergence in areas such as technology and economic systems.

Hence he found huge differences in culture between the OECD countries, that is the most industrially advanced countries, indicating that economic development does not have a major impact on culture. On uncertainty avoidance, for example, among OECD countries Greece is five times higher than Denmark. On the masculinity index, Japan is eighteen times higher than Sweden and Norway.

From a strategic perspective cultural diversity has many implications for HRM. Hodgetts and Luthans (2000: 36) selected some of these where the culture of a society can directly affect management approaches:

- **The centralisation of decision making**: In some societies (especially the pyramid of people type) all important decisions are taken by a small number of managers in senior positions. In other societies (like the village markets) decision making is more decentralised. In a joint venture between two dissimilar societies, not only will these differences of approach need to be recognised, but management systems will have to enable members of the two cultures to understand each other and work together.

- **Rewards and competition**: The level of financial rewards between countries can be a problem, when those in country A appear to receive much more money than those in country B for doing the same job, but a more subtle difference is the way in which rewards are disbursed. In some instances there is a culture favouring individual recognition, while elsewhere there is a convention of group rewards. Similarly some societies encourage competition rather than cooperation, and in others the reverse applies.

- **Risk**: As Hofstede demonstrated in his first study, attitudes towards taking risks are a clear discriminator between cultures, with marked variations of uncertainty avoidance.

- **Formality**: The well-oiled machine cultures place great emphasis on clear procedures and strict rules, while the pyramid of people cultures emphasise clear hierarchies and observance of rank. This contrasts strongly with the village market types of societies where relationships are more informal and ad hoc action more likely.

- **Organisational loyalty**: In Japan there tends to be a strong sense of loyalty to one's employer, while in the UK and USA there is a growing sense of identification with one's occupational group, rather than with a particular employer. The long-standing importance of professional bodies and the declining long-term reliability of corporations to look after career development have increased this loyalty to one's occupation rather than to one's employer.

- **Short- or long-term orientation**: Hofstede's identification of an eastern predilection to the long term is beginning to influence strategic decisions on where to locate those organisational activities for which long-term thinking is particularly appropriate.

Institutional variations

The work of Hofstede and others who have carried out similar studies all emphasise cultural differences between countries, the implication being that different approaches to the management of people are required in each place if an organisation is to maximise its ability to recruit, retain, engage and motivate its staff. In recent years, however, studies have been published which question this point of view. There is general agreement that HR systems and policies do vary from country to country, but the extent to which this is due to cultural differences is disputed. Instead it is strongly argued that institutional differences offer a better explanation (Whitley 1999; Edwards and Rees 2006; Wright and de Voorde 2009). This conclusion has been reached from a reading of many studies looking at how HR practices vary across different locations within the same MNC. A widely advanced view is that the following factors have a major influence on how HR is practised on a day-to-day basis:

- local laws
- enforcement mechanisms/agencies
- government and local government policies
- collective bargaining structures
- labour market institutions
- national training systems
- pension arrangements
- social security systems.

Moreover, it is further argued that over time these become so well embedded as to become management norms in the countries concerned:

In the local context, the labour laws and regulations restrict the range of possible HRM practices, local managers have taken-for-granted views about good management practices that influence the policies and practices that they suggest for the subsidiary, strong professional norms may exist, and processes of institutionalisation might also take place among MNCs in the focal country. (Bjorkman 2006: 465)

While there is now a degree of international convergence as far as employment law is concerned, due to the efforts of bodies such as the International Labour Organization and the European Union (EU), national systems remain very different from one another. Even within the EU where so many employment law principles apply in all member states, considerable differences persist. Dismissal law, for example, the most fundamental of all employment rights, is completely different depending on the country in which someone loses their job (see Chapter 9). In the UK many are excluded from bringing unfair dismissal cases at all, while those who can are unlikely to win much by way of damages unless they are older with many years' service and have difficulty finding alternative employment. In many other EU countries a suspected unfair dismissal can give rise to criminal proceedings, the case being brought not by the aggrieved employee, but by a local labour inspectorate. Damages are also far higher in many jurisdictions, fines also being levied by way of punishment. The presence in law of such different approaches to dismissal inevitably has a profound effect on the way that people are managed and their expectations about work.

Ultimately the debate about which factors, cultural or institutional, best explain differences between the dominant approaches to HR practised across borders is of little practical relevance. Both play a part to a greater or lesser extent in different types of situation. De Cieri (2007: 519–20) demonstrates this by looking at recruitment and selection practices. These, she argues, in part vary from country to country because of cultural differences. In Anglo-Saxon cultures selection processes tend to be competitive and objective, the aim being to secure the services of the person who is likely to perform best in the job. Elsewhere in the world where personal networks and relationships play a stronger role in the business culture and where power distance (as defined by Hofstede) is great, it is the norm for employees to be appointed due to family or clan connections, on personal recommendation, or, on occasion, because a bribe of some kind has been paid. These are cultural explanations for the differences. But there are also institutional explanations. In countries such as the UK and USA discrimination law serves to deter employers from selection on anything other than objective grounds. De Cieri goes on to give other examples of HRM practices in which both institutional and cultural factors play a role in shaping international divergence, exploring performance appraisal and diversity management in particular.

ACTIVITY 27.2

What other examples of HR practices or established employment norms can you think of which differ from country to country? How far are these explained by cultural or by institutional differences, or is there some other explanation?

HRM in international organisations

In terms of its aims and objectives, IHRM (i.e. HRM in an international organisation) is no different from HRM in an organisation based in one country. The purpose is to mobilise an appropriately qualified workforce, and subsequently to retain it, motivate it and develop it. IHRM, however, is more complex and necessarily has a rather different emphasis:

- IHRM involves working with an organisational structure that is more complex.
- There are a greater number of more diverse stakeholder groups to take account of.
- There is greater involvement in people's private/family lives because of the expatriation element.
- Diversity is necessary in terms of management style.
- There are greater numbers of external influences and risks to understand and manage.

IHRM is also harder because of the communication difficulties that arise due to distance and language differences as well as cultural and institutional traditions and assumptions such as those we discussed above. This makes effective knowledge management and change management harder to achieve in particular. International HR managers thus need to have a somewhat different skill set from domestically focused HR managers and tend to develop careers exclusively in international organisations.

A particular issue of significance for international organisations concerns the design of internal structures and reporting lines. While these are complex issues at the best of times for large organisations, they are made a great deal more involved when geographically diverse workforces are included. The major alternatives are as follows:

- by product group
- by organisational function
- by geographical region
- matrix structures.

In the latter case individuals may report to two or three different people for different purposes, a direct line manager based in the same geographical location, a regional manger working in the same specialist area of activity but based in another country, and others with responsibility for particular projects and initiatives being run internationally from a corporate headquarters based elsewhere.

Linked to the question of the overall structure is the issue of who should manage plants or other units located in countries other than that of the corporate headquarters. Most international companies are firmly rooted in a home country and wish to appoint home country nationals in sufficient numbers around global operations as a means of exercising financial control. However, in a truly global organisation, where the original location of the corporate headquarters is irrelevant to staffing policy, and perhaps where ownership is no longer concentrated in one country, the nationality of each unit manager is less of an issue. This is also true of many international organisations that are not commercial (e.g. the EU, the UN and its associated bodies). Here corporate culture tends to supersede separate national cultures, and it becomes possible simply to promote people to new positions across different countries on the basis of individual merit. Deresky (2008: 343–6) identifies the following three approaches.

The **ethnocentric approach** is to fill key overseas positions with people from headquarters. This is typical of businesses that are at the internalisation stage of expansion and retain a strong, centralised structure. The people appointed have a full understanding of the company ethos, products and technology, and may be essential where there is a shortage of appropriately skilled and experienced local personnel. This approach, however, denies promotion opportunities to local managers and prevents the business from making use of its full overseas staff potential.

The **polycentric approach** employs local managers to fill key positions in their own countries. This has the obvious advantage that they are familiar with the culture, language and ways of doing business in their own country and probably already have many useful contacts as a basis of their essential network. Once this step is taken, there is the potential problem of maintaining effective coordination across the business as a whole. The benefits of strong centralisation are lost. The US company, for instance, that has Americans in all its local CEO positions has people with a common national culture and background, as well as familiarity with the company's products and procedures. If that company opts instead to appoint CEOs who are from the local country, there is no longer the same degree of what can be taken for granted in shared values, attitudes and understanding. Will the CEO in Taiwan have the same understanding of the business use of bribes (or 'sweeteners', 'gifts in appreciation', 'special fees' and so on) as the CEO in Kuwait, in Detroit or in Stockholm? If polycentric staffing becomes widespread, will the social understanding and cultural awareness at headquarters become increasingly less effective in relation to the subsidiaries?

The **global** approach is where the most appropriate person for a particular job is recruited from anywhere in the group, or even outside, so that the entire management cadre gradually becomes internationalised with a shared global view as well as local understanding. This usually works only in a mature and very large business with great international experience.

Communication

Communicating across geographical, ethnic and national boundaries is a major challenge for HR people. There are various ways in which expectation determines communication content and all can impair the accuracy of message transmission. Such problems are compounded by geographical distance, cultural differences and subtleties of language.

Cognitive dissonance does more than lead to misunderstanding; it can also distort or inhibit action. Not only do recipients of information find it difficult to understand, remember and take action, but they will also grapple with the dissonance that the problematical new information presents. One of the ways in which they do this is to distort the message so that what they actually hear is what they expect to hear and can easily understand rather than the difficult, challenging information that is being put to them. There are particular problems with jargon, where a word or a phrase has a specialised meaning that is immediately understandable by those in the know, but meaningless or misleading to those who do not share the specialised knowledge.

There is a need for constant communication throughout the business to disseminate information and to sustain changing values. The organisation must operate holistically. It is not the sum of its parts: the whole exists in every part, like the human body. If you are ill a doctor can obtain information about your illness from any part of you. A sample of your blood or taking your temperature is just as good wherever it comes from. If you are to be protected against cholera, which attacks the intestines, you have an injection in your arm. If you are about to be shot in the chest, your entire body will shiver in fear.

When a company is operating internationally, one logical main channel for communication could be the work flow pattern. If a washing machine is produced by manufacturing electronic components in California, subassemblies and wiring harnesses in Korea and final assembly in Scotland, there is an easy sequence to follow. Job instructions, guidance notes, queries, telephone calls, specifications, requisitions, authorisations, order forms are some of the many ways in which groups of people communicate with those before and after them in the work flow, or critically adjacent to the process, like the HR people. Among the most effective international communicators are airlines, as their entire business is moving not only customers but also staff constantly across national boundaries to different organisational outposts of the business: the business activity creates the communications. All international businesses require centralised, coordinated communications to create common purpose and to share ideas and benefits, but those that do not have a natural work flow link across national boundaries will have this need more highly developed.

The communications management challenge for IHRM is at two extremes. At one is the personal behaviour and skill of individual people in making themselves understood, persuading others to do things, negotiating agreements with people from different cultural backgrounds, overcoming language barriers, appreciating different frames of reference and developing heightened sensitivity to varying behavioural norms and conventions. Communication is an individual activity, reflecting personal style, and the HRM requirement is for cultural awareness and perhaps language training. In this type of communication the manager is a skilled solo performer. The other extreme is impersonal and systemic, more concerned with channels of communication than with individual behaviour, and more concerned with the systematic distribution of carefully chosen information and the organisation of communications opportunities. In this type of communication the manager metaphorically writes the score and then conducts the orchestra.

WINDOW ON PRACTICE

An expression that is often repeated in the French workplace is *Pourquoi le faire simple si l'on peut le faire compliqué?* (Why make something simple if one can make it complicated?). This slightly ironic comment encapsulates the French practice of opting for elaborate and time-consuming work systems rather than less complicated alternatives.

A similar point of view was expressed by Ann Moran (1994), who was involved in a merger between a UK company and a French one. She describes some of the cultural differences and their impact:

the effort needed to communicate has doubled. The French expect a response from the person to whom a communication was sent and not from a delegated person. To reply otherwise is taken as a slight.

More upwards and more complicated communications are needed whilst keeping [within] the formal hierarchical framework that is normal in French companies. Open questioning of superiors by the French is not common.

In meetings French colleagues do not feel constrained to follow the agenda and sometimes walk out of the meeting for a private discussion.

Source: Moran (1994), pp. 112–13.

Coordination

Managers working internationally give themselves major problems of coordination by adopting measures that they see as necessary for business success. On the one hand they have to encourage diversity of local action, so that what is done fits local circumstances. On the other hand their global thinking requires careful coordination as the way to synergy, so that the global business does more and better together than it could possibly achieve as a number of independent units.

Bartlett and Ghoshal (1989) described three conventional approaches to coordination that were used, stemming from the nationality of the parent company, namely the Japanese, the American and the European.

Japanese centralisation

The typical Japanese approach is where a strong headquarters group maintains for itself all major decisions and frequently intervenes in the affairs of overseas subsidiaries. This appears to stem from its difficulty in dealing with foreigners:

a major strategic challenge for Japanese firms is to accept that non-Japanese must somehow be given more direct responsibility and opportunity for promotion within the company at local level . . . there has to be letting-go from the centre. But this is no easy thing. For companies must overcome severe impediments associated with wariness, distrust and lack of knowledge about the world beyond Japan. (Holden 1994: 127)

American formalisation

The American approach is described as formalisation. Power is vested not in headquarters or in the managers of local companies, but in formal systems, policies and standards, so that it is the systems that drive the business. Many American businesses went international at the time when the use of control systems was being rapidly developed to cope with the large size of the businesses. The idea of delegation and holding others accountable by means of extensive computerised information systems seemed eminently suitable for operating the increasing number of overseas units, especially when one remembers the apparent unpopularity of overseas postings among American managers (e.g. Tung and Miller 1990).

European socialisation

In European companies the approach to coordination is described as socialisation. There has been a reliance on key, highly skilled and trusted individuals. These people were carefully selected and developed a detailed understanding of the company's objectives and methods. Their personal development included the establishment of close working relationships and mutual understanding with colleagues. Once groomed these key decision makers were despatched to manage the subsidiaries, so that the headquarters and the subsidiaries were both strengthened:

because it relies on shared values and objectives, it represents a more robust and flexible means of co-ordination. Decisions reached by negotiations between knowledgeable groups with common objectives should be much better than those made by superior authority or by standard policy. (Bartlett and Ghoshal 1989: 163)

These three different approaches worked best for companies headquartered in those three regions of the globe. As the world becomes smaller and companies become more diverse with subsidiaries that are fully mature, more sophisticated methods are needed: companies are not international, but global. The influence of the parent company's national culture remains strong, but there is a cosmopolitan tendency gradually blurring some of the traditional boundaries.

Harmonisation

Across all decision making in IHRM, however organisations are structured, however good the communication systems and however well coordinated they are, there runs an ever-present and highly significant tension. This relates to the degree of harmonisation and centralisation that is possible or desirable.

Organisations want to develop strong corporate cultures and take active steps to manage culture and cultural change in order to achieve this. In nationally based corporations shaping corporate culture is straightforward provided it runs with the grain of the national culture. However, when a strong centralised corporate identity is imposed on an international company, inevitably it will run against the grain of some national cultures. The same is true of HR policies and practices. What works well in one national culture will jar in another, leading to demotivation, reduced performance, lower levels of trust and recruitment/retention problems.

In-depth knowledge of local labour market conditions, expectations and attitudes is the only means of judging where to strike a balance between centralisation and diversity. A long-held mantra which sums up the best approach to take is simple:

Think global, act local.

This means developing HR strategies for the whole global operation, but implementing them differently so as to take account of local cultural and institutional differences.

ACTIVITY 27.3

1 Think of where you work, or where you have worked, and identify three activities where global thinking needs to influence local action. What are the local people management implications of this?

2 In the same situation what aspects of local action influence, or should influence, global thinking?

Managing expatriates

A feature of HRM in international organisations which makes it different from HRM in a nationally based organisation is the need, on a regular basis, to post people overseas. International organisations need to have on their payroll substantial numbers of people who originate in one country, often where corporate headquarters is located, but work elsewhere in an international operation. Overseas employees can be divided into a number of distinct categories:

- Engineers are staff who regularly spend short periods of a week or two overseas, often working on specific projects such as setting up new production processes.
- Cosmopolitans are a small elite group who are familiar with different countries and are comfortable dealing with different cultural contexts all the time. They travel from location to location throughout their working year, spending little more than a week or two in each country before moving on.
- Occasional parachutists are firmly based in one country, but whose work takes them from time to time to sites based in other countries for a few days at a time.
- Expatriates are staff whose normal place of work is in one country, but who are sent on secondment for a period of two or three years to work overseas, usually in a relatively senior position, before returning home to their original workplace.

The management of all these groups requires some specialist knowledge and experience if it is to be carried out well, but it is expatriates who pose the biggest challenge. Unlike cosmopolitans they are not used to living overseas and will often find it hard to adjust, particularly when they take their families overseas with them. But unlike the engineers and occasional parachutists their role is long term and for the duration of their period working abroad they form an integral part of the overseas operation they are being sent to manage or work in. They also expect to be repatriated and anticipate that they will benefit from their overseas experience by gaining promotion to a more senior post.

Whether male or female the expatriate's spouse is nearly always placed in a position of total or partial dependency by corporate expatriation: one career is subordinated to another. This dependency is not just economic, it affects the social position and status that a couple have while overseas. For expatriate spouses with a professional career in suspension, this can require considerable ingenuity to adapt. Because of the demands that expatriation makes on both individuals and families, it thus has to be managed carefully and thoroughly.

Selection for expatriation

The possibility of an extended overseas assignment can come as a shock, which may or may not be welcome, presenting all the problems of considering the potential career handicap of turning down the opportunity and the potential domestic problems of accepting it. Employers seldom have the luxury of a large number of appropriately qualified people readily available to fill any vacancy, but the most satisfactory general approach to selection for expatriation is through the combination of performance management and career planning.

A feature of annual appraisal can be a discussion of whether people are interested in working overseas at all, the degree of technical expertise and managerial experience they possess and the domestic/social constraints that would affect the timing of such a move. That can then be developed by identifying timings that would be appropriate for such a move, preferred locations and even some language training. As with all career management initiatives, this sets up expectations of the future that the management may not be able to deliver because of changes in business activity, but it provides a cadre of people who would welcome an overseas move.

The particular location is the next most important determinant in matching the person to the job. Among the most important issues are the following:

- **Culture**: How different from home is the culture of the country – religion, the social position of women, the degree of political stability/instability, personal security and petty crime, local press and television, cable television, availability of foreign newspapers, health hazards?

- **Economic development**: How well developed is the economy of the country – standard/cost of living, availability of familiar foods and domestic equipment, transport, post and telephone, local poverty, health and education facilities, availability of international schools?

- **Geographical location**: How far away is it and where is it – climate, in a cosmopolitan city or more remote, the importance/unimportance of language proficiency, the size of the local expatriate community, employment prospects of spouse?

- **The job**. What has to be done and what is the situation – the nature of the organisation, proportion of expatriates, technical, commercial and managerial demands of the job, staffing and support, the extent of role in managing local nationals?

The most important aspect of selection is making sure that the potential appointee and family members have a full understanding of what will be involved. It is essential, however, that those proceeding on an overseas posting should be appropriate for it. If there is not an appropriate person in the organisation, then recruitment from outside is preferable to assigning someone about whose suitability there are doubts. There is no profile of the ideal expatriate, but here are some selection issues arranged under the four headings used already.

Culture

How well prepared is the expatriate family for an unfamiliar culture? In many ways the developed countries of Western Europe present fewer problems than those of further afield, but English is spoken more widely in Singapore than, for instance, in France. Malaysia is a multi-ethnic society, but with a Muslim majority in the population. The Muslim dominance of life in most Middle East countries has profound implications for expatriates, requiring a degree of puritanism that will be unfamiliar and a social role for women that is quite unlike that which western women experience. In the developing countries of the Far East there may be superb hotels, but little else to do in the evening. Manila and Bangkok have plenty of after-dark facilities for men on their own, but little for couples and even less for women on their own. Whatever the culture is, open-mindedness and tolerance are essential qualities for the expatriates to develop.

Economic development

Many Asian countries now enjoy a standard of living and material convenience that matches or surpasses that of people in the west, so that the expatriate will find excellent systems of transportation and postal and telecommunication systems that will be similar to those of the home country. Elsewhere the situation will be very different and everyday life will require a great deal more adjustment once the expatriate is outside the air-conditioned cocoon of the MNC's offices. Medical and dental facilities may be sparse and few expatriate families can avoid being affected by the conditions of those among whom they live. Not only may they be distressed by the living conditions they see in most parts of Africa, for instance, but also they will have to contend with very high rates of urban crime in some places.

Geographical location

This is a further twist to the economic development question. The heat and humidity of tropical climates are supportable when moving from an air-conditioned home, via an air-conditioned car to an air-conditioned office or shopping mall. Those moving to more remote areas have greater problems in coping with the climate and the relative isolation, so they need to be emotionally self-sufficient and not too dependent on outside stimulation. The distance from home is another determinant of personal suitability to the posting. The Parisian working in Brussels could easily contemplate weekly commuting: someone from Brussels working in Madagascar could not. There will be a smaller expatriate community in most Italian cities than in Hong Kong, so that the expatriate family may have to work harder at establishing social contacts, and will therefore require considerable social skill and self-confidence. The geographical location will also determine the importance of local language proficiency for all members of the expatriate family.

The job

In a global business questions about the job may initially seem unproblematic. Many expatriates are simply moving to exercise their well-developed company expertise in a different location. The situation will, however, always be different no matter how similar the conventions and procedures. The various demands of the job need to be thoroughly considered, especially what may be involved in managing local nationals, where the subtleties of response to leadership and expectations of authority will probably still baffle the expatriate when finally on the way home from the tour of duty.

Preparing for expatriation

If circumstances permit a relatively lengthy period of preparation, language training can make real progress. This comes to life most effectively when there is a strong flavour of cultural orientation and familiarisation as well, so that two of the basic requirements of preparation are dealt with simultaneously. The nature of the language training provided is usually slightly different for the expatriate employee and for the expatriate spouse. The employee will concentrate on technical and business terms, while the spouse concentrates on what will be useful in everyday matters like shopping and trying to get the washing machine repaired, or in local social contacts.

More general aspects of cultural familiarisation can be achieved by various means, often depending on the individual. Some will read avariciously, both travel books and the range of novels that have been written about most parts of the world. Others prefer film and video. Can there be any better preparation for Australian suburban life than watching several episodes of *Neighbours*?

Some companies use returned expatriates to write and present case histories about the country, with the obvious advantages that the potential expatriate can discuss with someone face to face personal experiences in a situation which they are about to undergo. It should also be automatic for the potential expatriate to meet socially with any nationals from the country of expatriation who may be visiting the host company during the pre-departure stage.

The success of an overseas assignment will be enhanced by some previous experience overseas and some experience of the location, but brief business trips scarcely qualify as previous experience. A holiday could be better, as people on holiday usually go at least partly to see the country and the people. Much better is a visit before the move, which is made to prepare for the move. By this method it is possible to deal with such crucial issues as housing. Nothing reassures one about impending relocation so much as knowing where one is going to live. If there are children, arrangements for their schooling can also be made.

Continuing back-home arrangements while abroad can be extensive. There may be children remaining in boarding schools, or elderly relatives to be catered for and pets to worry about, as well as renting the family home and many more arrangements. There may be a need for some company help, especially with financial and similar matters.

Travel arrangements themselves are relatively straightforward, but still have to be organised. There may be a need for family visas and one or more work permits, removal of household effects as well as personal baggage, health checks and whatever range of 'jabs' and medication are required.

Repatriation

Coming back from an overseas assignment seldom receives the attention it needs. It is not expected to be problematic and therefore receives little attention: all the problems are expected to be about getting out and getting settled. Why should there be problems about coming home?

> The long-term implications of ineffective repatriation practices are clear: few good managers will be willing to take international assignments because they see what happened to their colleagues . . . the only people willing to take on foreign assignments in the future will be those who have not been able to succeed on the home front.
> (Deresky 2008: 370)

The first potential problem is the nature of the overseas experience. If it has been thoroughly satisfactory for all members of the family, with an enhanced lifestyle, plenty of career development and scope for the employee, plenty of money and exciting experience for the family in an agreeable climate, then there may not be much initial enthusiasm for returning, so that it will be like coming back from an extended holiday, with all the reluctance about leaving good friends and stimulating experiences to return to dreary old Barnstaple, or Dusseldorf or Des Moines.

On the other hand, if the overseas experience has been difficult, with a loss of social life, disagreeable climate, frustrations and disappointment at work and all sorts of petty inconveniences, then the prospect of returning home can become an obsession, with the days ticked off on the calendar and a great buildup of anticipation. When the day of return to hearth and home at last comes, Barnstaple (or Dusseldorf or Des Moines) may soon seem just a little ordinary compared with the wonderful picture that had been built up in expectation.

The second major problem is the career situation of the returning expatriate. Virtually all repatriated personnel experience some personal difficulty in reintegrating on return. There may be loss of status, loss of autonomy, lack of career direction and lack of recognition of the value of overseas experience. It may not be considered a management responsibility to fuss over a manager's personal readjustment, but an American study (Adler 1991: 238) showed that the effectiveness of expatriates took between six and twelve months to return to an acceptable level on repatriation, so there are some hard-headed reasons for taking it seriously.

ACTIVITY 27.4

Expatriate assignments frequently end in failure, in that the posting is not completed or fails to meet its initial objectives. Briscoe *et al.* (2009: 179) identify three types of expatriate failure:

- dropout (the expatriate returns home early);
- brownout (the expatriate performs poorly while overseas);
- turnover upon repatriation (the expatriate resigns shortly after returning home);

What different factors do you think contribute to each of these three types of failure? What steps can IHRM specialists take to reduce the likelihood of their happening?

SUMMARY PROPOSITIONS

27.1 The rise and proliferation of multinational organisations is both a consequence and cause of globalisation.

27.2 Understanding cultural diversity is crucial to managing an international organisation effectively. Work by Hofstede has identified four distinguishing factors of national culture: individualism, power distance, uncertainty avoidance and masculinity. He later added a fifth: Confucian dynamism or time orientation.

27.3 Institutional variation is another major determinant of differences between the prevalent approaches to HRM found in different countries.

27.4 Problems of communication in any international business are made more difficult by different frames of reference, stereotyping, cognitive dissonance and language.

27.5 Traditional forms of coordination can be roughly stereotyped as Japanese centralisation, American formalisation or European socialisation. More particular forms of coordination include evangelisation, standards and norms, systems and locating capability.

27.6 In order to maximise the likelihood that an expatriate posting will be successful, particular care must be taken when selecting, preparing and the repatriating expatriate staff.

GENERAL DISCUSSION TOPICS

1 Multinational companies tend to be unpopular with social activists, who mount demonstrations against their apparent greed and serious impact on some of the societies in which they operate. What are the arguments for and against this point of view?

2 Can an HR manager from one culture carry out a line management role working in a different culture?

THEORY INTO PRACTICE

You work in the HR department of a large corporation which operates a well-known chain of fashion stores (Large Co). Your company has outlets on the high streets of all the major UK cities and is steadily increasing its presence in out-of-town shopping complexes and airports. In addition, recent years have seen the start of what is intended to be a major expansion overseas with the opening of new flagship stores in a number of European cities. International online sales are also growing rapidly.

As part of its overseas expansion plans, a few weeks ago, your company took over another organisation (Small Co) which operates high street fashion outlets in South East Asian cities and also supplies garments to a range of retailers in the UK from its factories. It employs around a hundred staff at its UK headquarters and several hundred in Asia.

You have been seconded for a year to work at Small Co which has not to date ever employed a professionally qualified HR manager. Soon after your arrival at Small Co, you become aware of various management practices which you are uneasy about and which are very different indeed from what you are used to at Large Co.

Pay rates, for example, do not appear to be established using any rational system. While some UK staff are paid at the level of the National Minimum Wage, others are appointed at a variety of rates according to what they were able to negotiate at interview. There are also a good number of junior managerial staff who are working in excess of sixty hours each week. Trade union membership is actively discouraged and training and development opportunities are minimal. There is no formal induction provided and no staff handbook. Health and safety procedures appear to be minimal. In the past year alone the company has had seventeen employment tribunal claims lodged against it, all of which were settled out of court. Staff turnover is running at 35%.

You are even more concerned when you visit some of the stores and garment factories that Small Co operates in Asia. Here pay is very low and hours of work are long. The more senior posts all seem to be held by male relatives of top managers (all themselves men), and people seem to be hired and fired on a whim.

Although the managers you meet deny bullying their staff, this is not what the staff themselves say to you when you speak to them confidentially. Moreover, while it is denied that anyone under the age of 15 is employed, some staff look to you to be considerably younger. You are also concerned to observe that water contaminated with dyes and fixing agents appears to be being channelled directly into a river behind one of the factories you visit.

You are taken aback by what you observe in your first few weeks at Small Co. You are used to working in Large Co with its big HR division, range of 'good practice' employment policies and prominent corporate code of ethics. None of these exist at Small Co and there is no sign at all that any kind of ethical culture has been developed. It is, however, a very profitable business.

Questions

1 What are the main strands of the business case you could make in support of the introduction across Small Co's operations, as a matter of priority, of an ethical culture alongside ethically sound HR policies and practices? What counter-arguments might you expect to have to answer?

2 What barriers would you expect to come up against when promoting new standardised HR practices across the whole company in the following areas:

- recruitment and selection;
- performance management and reward;
- employee relations;
- HR devlopment?

3 What role might expatriate managers play in helping to develop a more progressive management culture across the company's global operations?

FURTHER READING

Numerous books and articles are published each year about the different aspects of HRM introduced in this chapter. Three edited volumes containing articles by academic researchers and which cover the field effectively are:

Handbook of International Human Resource Management, edited by Paul Sparrow (2009).

Handbook of Research in International Human Resource Management, edited by Gunter Stahl and Ingmar Bjorkman (2006).

Research Handbook of Comparative Employment Relations, edited by Michael Barry and Adrian Wilkinson (2011).

Communications and cultural issues are introduced and discussed in *Management Across Cultures* by Richard Steers, Carlos Sanchez-Runde and Luciara Nardon (2010).

REFERENCES

Adler, N.J. (1991) *International Dimensions of Organisational Behaviour*. Boston, MA: PWS Kent.

Barry, M. and Wilkinson, A. (2011) *Research Handbook of Comparative Employment Relations*. Cheltenham: Edward Elgar.

Bartlett, C.A. and Ghoshal, S. (1989) *Managing Across Borders*. London: Random House.

Bjorkman, I. (2006) 'International human resource management research and institutional theory', in G. Stahl and I. Bjorkman (eds), *Handbook of Research in International Human Resource Management*. Cheltenham: Edward Elgar.

Briscoe, D., Schuler, R. and Claus, L. (2009) *International Human Resource Management: Policies and practices for multinational enterprises*, 3rd edn. New York: Routledge.

Buchan, J. and Seccombe, I. (2009) *Difficult Times, Difficult Choices: The UK nursing labour market review 2009*. London: Royal College of Nursing.

De Cieri, H. (2007) 'Transnational firms and cultural diversity', in P. Boxall *et al.* (eds), *The Oxford Handbook of Human Resource Management*. Oxford: Oxford University Press.

Deresky, H. (2008) *International Management*, 6th edn. Upper Saddle River, NJ: Pearson Education.

Edwards, T. and Rees, C. (2006) *International Human Resource Management: Globalisation, National systems and multinational companies*. London: FT/Prentice Hall.

Hall, E. and Hall, M. (1990) *Understanding Cultural Differences*. Yarmouth, ME: Intercultural Press.

Hodgetts, R.M. and Luthans, F. (2000) *International Management*. New York: McGraw-Hill.

Hofstede, G. (1980) *Culture's Consequences: Comparing values, behaviors, institutions, and organisations across nations*. Beverly Hills, CA: Sage.

Hofstede, G. (1991) *Cultures and Organisations: Software of the mind*. London: McGraw-Hill.

Hofstede, G. (2001) *Culture's Consequences: Comparing values, behaviors, institutions, and organizations across nations*. Thousand Oaks, CA: Sage.

Holden, N.J. (1994) 'Management language and Euro-communications: 1992 and beyond', in M. Berry (ed.), *Cross-Cultural Communication in Europe*, Proceedings of the Conference on Cross-Cultural Communication, Helsinki. Turku: Institute for European Studies.

House, R., Hanges, P., Javidan, M., Dorfman, P. and Gupta, V. (2004) *Culture, Leadership and Organisations: The GLOBE study of 62 societies*. Thousand Oaks, CA: Sage.

Kluckhohn, C. (1954) *Culture and Behaviour*. New York: Free Press.

Lewis, R.D. (1996) *When Cultures Collide: Managing successfully across cultures*. London: Nicholas Brealey.

Marginson, P. and Meardi, G. (2009) 'Multinational companies and collective bargaining: Employment profile of MNCs', European Industrial Relations Observatory Online, **www.eurofound.europa.eu/ areas/industrialrelations/dictionary/definitions/europeanindustrialrelationsobservatory.htm** (accessed 24 June 2013).

Moran, A. (1994) 'Ferranti-Thomson Sonar Systems: An Anglo-French venture in high tech collaboration', in D.P. Torrington, *International Human Resource Management*. London: Prentice Hall International.

Ronen, S. and Shenkar, O. (1985) 'Clustering countries on attitudinal dimensions: A review and synthesis', *Academy of Management Review*, Vol. 10, No. 3, pp. 435–54.

Sparrow, P. (2009) *Handbook of International Human Resource Management*. Chichester: Wiley.

Stahl, G. and Bjorkman, I. (eds) (2006) *Handbook of Research in International Human Resource Management*. Cheltenham: Edward Elgar.

Steers, R., Sanchez-Runde, C. and Nardon, L. (2010) *Management Across Cultures*. Cambridge: Cambridge University Press.

Strodtbeck, K. (1961) *Variations in Value Orientations*. Westport, CT: Greenwood.

Trompenaars, F. (1993) *Riding the Waves of Culture: Understanding cultural diversity in global business*. London: McGraw-Hill.

Tung, R.L. and Miller, E.L. (1990) 'Managing in the twenty-first century: The need for global orientation', *Management International Review*, Vol. 30, pp. 5–18.

Whitley, R. (1999) *Divergent Capitalisms: The social structuring and change of national business systems*. Oxford: Oxford University Press.

Wright, P. and Van de Voorde, K. (2009) 'Multilevel issues in IHRM: Mean differences, explained variance and moderated relationships', in P. Sparrow (ed.), *Handbook of International Human Resource Management*. Chichester: Wiley.

Part 8

SELECTED HUMAN RESOURCE SKILLS

CHANGING TIMES
RESOURCING
PERFORMANCE
DEVELOPMENT
EMPLOYEE RELATIONS
REWARD
CONTEMPORARY ISSUES
SELECTED HUMAN RESOURCE SKILLS

Skills

I n this part we change to a quite different structure and style. Chapters are split into short distinct sections, there are very few references and we are aiming narrowly on how to do specific things that are part of the HR job. They are *our suggestions*; there may well be better ways, and methods frequently need to be adapted to particular circumstances, but these usually work. First we have those relating to communication and relating to other people, then we move to the more analytical types of activity.

Most of the skills in management are generic in that they are equally important to all those in managerial roles, no matter what their specialism, but here we consider the skills which are the essence of HRM, even though some of them are important to other managers as well.

We consider first skills in face-to-face situations, such as selection, appraisal, training and coaching, grievance and discipline, negotiation and mediation. Professor Tom Lupton was the second Director of Manchester Business School and a distinguished industrial relations academic. When addressing a national conference of the Institute of Personnel Management he stressed the importance of personnel people being involved in strategy because, 'otherwise all you have left is selling it to the lads'. Yet 'selling it to the lads' is a prime example of a rare and vital skill: not working out what to do, but getting people to share that understanding and then make it happen.

We also have five areas of quite different types of skill. Job analysis is fundamental to selection and training. There are some simple statistical techniques applicable to measurement in a number of aspects of HR. Then we suggest the elements of designing procedures, designing questionnaires and how to use consultancy services, so that you receive and use the service you need rather than what the consultant will provide if not given the necessary steer and carefully managed.

FURTHER READING

Barker, A. (2010) *Improve Your Communication Skills*, 2nd edn, rev. London: Kogan Page.

Books on communication skills mainly come and go quite quickly, but this was first published in 2000 with a second edition in 2006, which was reprinted twice in 2007, with a further revision in 2010, so is recommended as a general introduction at this stage.

Chapter 28

SKILLS SET 1: FACE-TO-FACE AND OTHER COMMUNICATION SKILLS

I Being good with people

Effective face-to-face people are likely to have some basic qualities. *Poise* enables a person to be at ease in a wide variety of social situations, often enjoying them, and able to talk with different types of people in a relaxed and self-confident way. This self-confidence comes partly from the feedback of willing responses constantly provided by other people.

Another element of poise is knowing what you are talking about; we demonstrate our poise much more in situations with which we are familiar than we do in strange circumstances. There is less fear of what the other may say and less apprehension about appearing naive. Questions, and even criticism, are easier to deal with and are often wanted, so stimulating the interchange.

Poise is often associated with maturity, due to a person having succeeded in developing a rounded view of themselves without feeling too much anxiety about the possible adverse opinions of others. The process of acquiring poise can be accelerated by the experience of meeting a variety of people from differing backgrounds.

A necessary feature of poise is being *responsive* to the needs, feelings and level of understanding in other people. This prevents poise from becoming too egocentric. The teacher, for instance, will be looking for signs of misunderstanding in the student so that the message can be restated or clarified, and the market research interviewer will be looking for signals that the question has been accurately construed, or that it needs elaboration. Responsiveness can also include offering rewards, like friendliness, warmth, sympathy and helpfulness, as features of general style or as part of a relationship with other participants. These not only sustain the relationship, but also may be held back as a means of trying to get one's own way.

Certain general problems impair effectiveness. They mostly concern the way that people tend to hear what they expect to hear rather than what they are being told.

The *frame of reference* is the standpoint from which a person views an issue, and understanding of the issue will be shaped by that perspective rather than any abstract 'reality'. It is a set of basic assumptions or standards that frame our behaviour. These are developed through childhood conditioning, through social background, education and through our affiliations. Differences in the frames of reference held by participants in interactions present inescapable problems. How can those who manage and direct ever fully appreciate the point of view of those who are managed and directed?

The frame of reference on any particular matter is largely determined by opinions developed within a group with which we identify, as few of us alter our opinions alone. We both follow and help to shape opinion in our group, and most of us are in a number of such reference groups. Because of this, complexities arise: some people can be vociferously anti-union as citizens and voters in general elections, yet support a union of which they are members at their workplace.

The *stereotype* is the standardised expectation we have of those who have certain dominant characteristics: typical stereotypes are that all Americans are brash and self-confident, Scandinavians are tall and blond, women are more caring than men and men are more aggressive than women. The behaviour of some people in a category makes us expect all those in that category to behave in the same way. This is obviously invalid, but is a tendency to which we are prone. We have to listen to what people are actually saying to us rather than hearing what we think a person of that type *would say*.

Making use of stereotypes is necessary at the start of working relationships; it is not feasible to deal with every individual we meet as being a void until we have collected enough information to know how to treat them, so we always try to find a pigeon-hole in which to put someone. We begin conversations with a working stereotype, so that, for example, we stop someone in the street to ask directions only after we have selected a person who looks intelligent and sympathetic. If we are giving directions to a stranger we begin our explanation having made an assessment of that person's ability to understand quickly, or their need for a more detailed, painstaking explanation. The stereotype becomes a handicap only when we remain insensitive to new information enabling us to develop a fuller, more rational appraisal of the individual with whom we are interacting.

Being aware of the dangers of stereotyping others, and trying to exercise self-discipline, can reduce the degree to which you misunderstand other people, but you still have the problem that your respondents will put *you* into a stereotype and hear what you say in accordance with whatever their predetermined notion may be.

Cognitive dissonance is the difficulty we all have in coping with doing something that is not consistent with our beliefs. Such behaviour will make us uncomfortable and we will try to cope with the dissonance in various ways in order to reduce the discomfort. Either we persuade ourselves that we believe in what we are doing, or we avoid the necessary behaviour. We all interpret or decode words that we hear in order to make sense of them. If we decode the words we hear in a way that does not match what we believe, then we tend to reinterpret them in a way that we can believe.

Different types of face-to-face situation

We can categorise interactions into three broad types, namely enquiry, exposition and joint problem solving, with conflict resolution as a subset of joint problem solving.

Enquiry is that group of situations where you need to find things out from someone else, with the selection interview being the classic example. What needs to be found out may be factual information, attitudes, feelings, levels of understanding or misunderstanding. The main skill is in types of questioning.

Exposition is almost the direct opposite. Instead of finding things out, you are trying to convey information, to develop in the other person a level of knowledge and understanding, acceptance of an argument or agreement with a proposition. Although some questioning is often an integral part of exposition, the main skill is in clear articulation, fluency, good organisation of material and effective illustration. You may think, for instance, that the above explanation of cognitive dissonance could have been improved with an illustration. So, sorry for the oversight, try this: a medication was recently developed enabling small children to be protected against measles, mumps and rubella by a single injection rather than three. A spurious piece of research was published apparently demonstrating an increased risk of autism among children immunised in this way rather than with separate injections. Few people read the article publishing the findings, but rumours spread and large numbers of parents *believed* the rumours rather than rational explanation and authoritative rebuttals, they refused the single injection for their children and the incidence of infections rose.

Joint problem solving involves developing an exchange in which both parties work together to unravel a problem or understand a situation which neither fully understands beforehand. It is not one person transferring an 'answer' to another, but both trying to understand together something which they can only partly understand alone. The skills involve some questioning and explanation, but also careful listening and feedback.

Joint problem solving assumes that both parties trust each other and see a common interest in helping the other. *Conflict resolution* begins without that mutual confidence, as the parties have interests that inevitably conflict and they are not likely to trust each other fully. The skills here are, first, those of presentation and then of listening, questioning and feedback.

The fundamentals of setting the tone

Any interaction begins by someone setting the tone of what is to follow. The HR specialist will set the tone of a selection interview, for instance, by explaining what is to happen and providing other contextual information that will enable the candidate to engage in the process constructively. There will also be a process of conveying more subtle messages to say, 'I'm in charge; I know what I'm doing; you can trust me'. In other interactions the way of setting the tone is different, but some features are common:

- Speak first.
- Smile, looking confident and relaxed (much easier said than done).
- Have *brief*, harmless exchanges that enable the parties to speak to each other without the answers mattering (weather, travel problems, etc.), but always react appropriately to answers.
- Explain your understanding of what is to happen.
- Check that that is understood and accepted.

The fundamentals of listening

Giving attention

Inclining the body towards the other person is a signal of attentiveness, so our posture should be inclined forward and facing the other squarely with an open posture: folded arms can be inhibiting.

Eye contact is crucial to good listening, but is a subtle art. You need to show interest and a desire to listen; look away occasionally but only briefly; not repeatedly looking away, staring or looking blank.

We also show *physical responses* in our attentiveness. We have to avoid distracting the other person by physical behaviour unrelated to what is being said; fiddling with a pen, playing with car keys, scrutinising fingernails, wringing hands, brushing specks of dust off our sleeves are a few typical behaviours that indicate inattention. Skilled listeners not only suppress these, but also develop minor gestures and posture variants that are directly responsive to what the other is saying.

Being silent helps you to listen by providing space for incoming messages, but it also provides opportunities to observe the other person and to think about what is being said. Most people are uncomfortable with silence and try to fill it with inconsequential chat, but this interferes with listening. Silence still has to be attentive and the longer the silence, the harder it is to be attentive.

The fundamentals of questioning

Closed questions seek precise, terse information and are useful when you want clear, straightforward data. Most interactions feature closed questioning at some point.

Open-ended questions avoid terse replies by inviting respondents to develop their opinions without the interviewer prescribing what the answer should be. The question does little more than introduce a topic to talk about. The main purpose of such questions is to obtain the type of deeper information that the closed question misses, as the shape of the answer is not predetermined by the questioner. You are informed not simply by the content of the answers, but by what is selected and emphasised.

Indirect questions take an oblique approach on a difficult matter. A blunt 'Did you like that job?' almost suggests you did not, or at least raises the suspicion that the interviewer thinks you did not. Put indirectly as 'What gave you the most satisfaction in that job?', it has the merit of concentrating on the work rather than the person.

The *probe* is a form of questioning to obtain information that the respondent is trying to conceal. When you realise that the other person is doing this you have to make an important, and perhaps difficult, decision: whether to respect the candidate's unwillingness and let the matter rest, or to persist with the enquiry. Reluctance is quite common in selection interviews where a candidate may wish to gloss over an aspect of recent employment history. The most common sequence for the probe takes the following form: (a) direct questions, replacing the more comfortable open-ended approach ('What were you doing in the first six months of 2013?'). Careful phrasing may avoid a defensive reply, but those skilled at avoiding unwelcome enquiries may still deflect the question, leading to (b) supplementaries, which reiterate the first question with different phrasing ('Yes, I understand about that period. It's the first part of 2013 that I'm trying to get clear: after you came back from Belgium and before you started with Amalgamated Widgets'). Eventually this should produce the information the questioner needs. (c) Closing. If the information has been wrenched out like a bad tooth and the interviewer looks horrified or sits in stunned silence, then the candidate will feel badly put down. The interviewer needs to make the divulged secret less awful than the candidate had feared, so that the interview can proceed with reasonable confidence ('Yes, well you must be glad to have that behind you'). It may be that the interviewer will feel able to develop the probe by developing the answer with a further question such as 'And how did that make you feel?' or 'And how did you react to that? It must have been a terrible blow.' It is only reasonable to do this if the resultant exchange adds something useful to the questioner's understanding of the client: simple nosiness is not appropriate.

WINDOW ON (MAL)PRACTICE

One dubious version of the probe is to offer an exaggerated explanation for something being avoided. In the imaginary situation described above the selector might do this:

Selector: Yes, I understand about that period. It's the first part of 2013 that I'm trying to get clear: after you came back from Belgium and before you started with Amalgamated Widgets. You weren't in prison or anything, were you?

Candidate: Oh no. I had a nervous breakdown.

The explanation offered by the selector is so appalling that the candidate rushes to offer a less appalling explanation. This is not recommended, but it is interesting to know about. It might happen to you one day.

Some common lines of questioning should be avoided because they can produce an effect that is different from what is intended.

Leading questions ('Would you agree with me that . . . ?') will not necessarily produce an answer that is informative, but an answer in line with the lead that has been given.

Multiple questions give the candidate too many inputs at one time ('Could you tell me something of what you did at university, not just the degree, but the social and sporting side as well, and why you chose to backpack your way round the world? You didn't travel on your own, did you?'). This sort of questioning is sometimes adopted by interviewers who are trying very hard to efface themselves and let the respondent get on with the talking. However helpful the interviewer intends to be, the effect is that the candidate will usually forget the later parts of the question, feel disconcerted and ask, 'What was the last part of the question?' By this time the interviewer has also forgotten, so they are both embarrassed.

Taboo questions are those that do not respect the reasonable personal privacy of the other person. Some questions have to be avoided, especially in selection interviews, as they could be interpreted as biased. It is potentially discriminatory, for instance, to ask women how many children they have and what their husbands do for a living. Questions about religion or place of birth should also be avoided. Some questions may do no more than satisfy the idle curiosity of the questioner. If there is no point in asking them, they should not be put.

The fundamentals of feedback

As well as listening one has to provide feedback, indicating that you have received and understood what you are being told. There are six basic methods.

In *reflection*, the listener picks up and restates the content of what has just been said. In a difficult situation the listener picks out the emotional overtones of a statement and 'reflects' them back to the respondent without any attempt to evaluate them. The interviewer expresses neither approval nor disapproval, neither sympathy nor condemnation.

At a more prosaic level, there is *summary and rerun* to show you are listening and providing the opportunity for any misunderstanding to be pointed out. In appraisal, for instance, the appraisee will produce lots of information in an interview and you will be selecting that which is to be retained and understood. From time to time you interject a summary sentence or two with an interrogative inflection. This shows that you are listening, gives the respondent the chance to correct any false impressions and reinforces the key points that are being retained. It is also a useful way of making progress, as the interjection is easily followed by another open-ended question, 'Now perhaps we can turn to . . .'.

The standard method in both reflection and summary is *paraphrasing*, by which the listener states the essence of what has been said. This is done concisely, giving the other person a chance to review what has been said and, perhaps, to correct it.

We all respond positively when a listener shows *interest* in what is being said. If it is possible also to agree with what is being said, the reinforcement of the respondent will be greater.

The most common form of *affirmation* in feedback is the head-nod, and many public speakers look for head-nods (not to be confused with nodding off) as a way of judging the supportive mood of the audience. Other ways of affirming involve the use of the eyes. These are too subtle and individual to describe, but we each have a repertoire of signals to indicate such reactions as encouragement, surprise and understanding. When the eyes are part of a smile, there will be stronger reward to the talker. There are also words and phrases: 'Really?', 'Go on . . .', 'Yes . . .', 'Of course . . .', 'My word . . .', 'You were saying . . .'.

Interaction contains a variety of *noise*s that are ways of feeding back to the other party. They are impossible to reproduce in words but are usually variations of a theme of 'Mmm . . .' and they form a part of the exchanges that is inarticulate yet meaningful, keeping things going without interrupting.

SUMMARY PROPOSITIONS

I.1 Face-to-face skills are fundamental to all managerial work.

I.2 Effectiveness in interaction is aided by poise and being responsive to others, as well as by understanding the effects of the frame of reference, stereotyping and cognitive dissonance.

I.3 The basic types of interaction can be categorised as enquiry, exposition and joint problem solving.

I.4 Listening skills include giving attention, eye contact, physical responses and being silent.

I.5 The main types of question are closed, open ended, indirect and the probe. Inappropriate questions are leading, multiple and taboo.

I.6 Methods of feedback include reflection, summary and rerun, paraphrasing, showing interest, affirmation and using appropriate noises.

GENERAL DISCUSSION TOPICS

1 What are the advantages of face-to-face conversation compared with a combination of email, fax, text messages and telephone calls? To what extent is videoconferencing adequate as an alternative to meeting face to face?

2 If a central part of HRM is getting things done by other people, what is the difference between telling them what to do and asking them to do things? In what sort of situations would each approach be appropriate?

FURTHER READING

Argyle, M. (1994) *The Psychology of Interpersonal Behaviour*. Harmondsworth: Penguin.
This classic was first published in 1967 and remains the ideal introduction to understanding the dynamics of interpersonal skills.

Caro, M. (1994) *The Body Language of Poker*. Secaucus, NJ: Carol Publishing Group.
An analysis of the ways in which poker players try to conceal their reactions to different stages of play, especially as cards are dealt.

Collett, P. (2003) *The Book of Tells*. London: Doubleday.
A comprehensive explanation of non-verbal behaviours that reveal a person's true feelings. The author is a social psychologist who has combined research at the Oxford University Department of Experimental Psychology with acting as resident psychologist for the television programme *Big Brother*.

Anderson, W. (2012) *Communication Skills for the Workplace*. Eugene, OR: NorthStar.

II The selection interview

In the selection interview the interviewer is trying to obtain information from an applicant in order to form a judgement about that person for a particular job or position in an organisation, working with a particular group of working colleagues. At the same time those being interviewed are presenting information to influence that decision and collecting information that will help them decide whether they want the job or not. This fact of *exchange* has led personnel/HR texts to describe the interview as 'a two-way conversation with a purpose'. This comfortable axiom, like many axioms, is largely accurate but misses an important element, that the interviewer is in charge, setting the agenda, controlling the development, deciding when to close and making the key judgement: yes or no. Candidates may decide not to take your lousy job; even if it is offered, they would still like to have the ego boost of refusing. Candidates need the interviewer to set the agenda and to lead the interview, otherwise they tend towards making an ego-centric pitch that does more for their self-esteem than for their job prospects.

A second important point about the selection interview is that the approach and skills used are similar to those needed in other working situations in which your purpose is to obtain information face to face from someone else, such as assessing the merit of a computer system that is being sold to you, assessing the situation when trying to mediate between two colleagues, dealing with the facts of a disciplinary situation and so on.

Varieties of selection interview

There is a range of employee participation in the employment process which correlates with the type of work. There are working situations where the amount of discussion between the parties is limited to perfunctory exchanges about trade union membership, hours of work and rates of pay, labourers on building sites and extras on film sets being two examples. As interviews move up the organisational hierarchy there is growing equilibrium, with the interviewer becoming more courteous and responsive to questions from the applicant, who will probably be described as a 'candidate' or someone who 'might be interested in the position'. For the most senior positions it is less likely that people will be invited to respond to vacancies advertised in the press, although equality legislation is leading to more senior positions being openly advertised. It is more likely that individuals will be approached, either directly or through consultants, and there will be an elaborate ritual in which each party tries to persuade the other to declare an interest first.

The purpose of the selection interview

The interview is a *controlled* conversation with a purpose. These are:

- to collect information in order to predict how well the applicants would perform in the job for which they have applied, by measuring them against predetermined criteria;
- to provide candidates with full details of the job and organisation to facilitate their decision making;
- to conduct the interview in such a way that candidates feel that they have been given a fair hearing.

Handling this most crucial of encounters is a key skill for personnel and other managers as the interview has a number of important advantages which cannot be provided by any other means. It cannot be bettered as a means of exchanging information and meeting the human and ritual aspects of the employment process.

Human and ritual aspects

An interview can be used to assess matters that cannot be approached in any other way, such as the potential compatibility of two people who will have to work together. Both parties need to meet before the contract begins, to 'tune in' to each other and begin the process of induction. The interview is valuable in that way to both potential employee and potential employer. It gives applicants the feeling that they matter, as another person is devoting time to them and they are not being considered by a computer. Also, giving applicants a chance to ask questions underlines their decision-making role, making them feel less helpless in the hands of the all-powerful interviewer. Selection interviewing has important ritual elements, as the applicants are seeking either to enter, or to rise within, a social system. This means that they defer to the interviewer more than they would in other situations.

At the same time those who are already inside and above display their superiority and security, even unconsciously, in contrast with the behaviour of someone so obviously anxious to share the same privileged position. Reason tells us that this is inappropriate in the twenty-first century as the books are full of advice to interviewers not to brandish their social superiority, but to put applicants at their ease and to reduce the status differentials. This, however, still acknowledges their superiority as they are the ones who take the initiative; applicants are not expected to help the interviewer relax and feel less apprehensive. Also the reality of the situation is usually that of applicants anxious to get in and selector choosing among several. Status differentials cannot simply be set aside. The selection interview is at least partly an initiation rite, not as elaborate as entry to commissioned rank in the armed forces, nor as whimsical as finding one's way into the Brownie ring, but still a process of going through hoops and being found worthy in a process where other people make all the rules.

ACTIVITY II.1

For a selection interview in which you recently participated, either as selector or as applicant, consider the following:

1 What were the ritual features?

2 Were any useful ritual features missing?

3 Could ritual have been, in any way, *helpfully* reduced?

Interview strategy

The approach to selection interviewing varies considerably from the amiable chat in a bar to the highly organised, multi-person panel.

By far the most common is the approach which has been described as *frank and friendly*. Here the interviewer is concerned to establish and maintain a constructive tone for the exchanges; English has no better descriptor of this than the French *rapport*. This is in the belief that if applicants do not feel threatened, and are relaxed, they will be more forthcoming in the information that they offer. It is straightforward for both interviewer and interviewee and has the potential advantage that applicants will leave with a favourable impression of the business.

A variation is the *problem-solving approach*. The interviewer presents the candidate with a hypothetical problem and evaluates the answer. The questions asked are derived from the job description. Candidates are required to imagine themselves as the job holder and describe what they would do in a variety of hypothetical situations. This method is most applicable to testing elementary knowledge, such as the colour coding of wires in electric cables or maximum dosages of specified drugs. It is less effective for testing understanding and ability.

There is no guarantee that the candidate would actually behave in the way suggested. The quick thinker will score at the expense of those who can take action more effectively than they can answer riddles.

The *biographical* method focuses on the candidate's past behaviour and performance, which is a more reliable way of predicting future performance than asking interviewees what they would do in a certain situation. Candidates are asked to describe the background to a situation and explain what they did and why; what their options were; how they decided what to do; and the anticipated and real results of their action. The success of this method depends on in-depth job analysis, and preferably competency analysis, in order to frame the best questions. We have already seen that the focus on competencies is growing (see Chapter 7), as it deals first with the applicant's record and other evidence like test results and then moves to consider the work that is needing to be done. For both the biographical approach is an excellent method.

Number of interviews and interviewers

There are two broad traditions governing the number of interviewers. One says that effective, frank discussion can only take place on a one-to-one basis, so candidates meet one interviewer, or several interviewers, one at a time. The other tradition is that fair play must be demonstrated and nepotism prevented, so the interview must be carried out, and the decision made, by a panel of interviewers. Within this dichotomy there are various options.

The individual interview

The individual interview gives the greatest chance of establishing rapport, developing mutual trust and is the most efficient deployment of time in the face-to-face encounter, as each participant has to compete with only one other speaker. It is usually also the most satisfactory method for the candidate, who has to tune in to only one other person instead of needing constantly to adjust to different interviewers. The candidate can more readily ask questions and it is the least formal type of interview. The disadvantages lie in the reliance placed on the judgement of one person, although this can be mitigated by a series of individual interviews. A sole interview with the line manager is very popular in the selection of people for manual work, being used in a third of all interviews. It is less popular for administrative and management posts.

Sequential interviews

Sequential interviews are a series of one-to-one interviews. The most frequent combination is an interview with the line manager and one with a representative of the HR department. For managerial posts this will be extended to interviews with other departmental managers, top managers and significant prospective colleagues. Sequential interviews can give the employer a broader picture of the candidate and they also allow the applicant to have contact with a greater number of potential colleagues. However, for the advantages of sequential interviews to be realised there is a need for effective organisation and for all interviews to be held on the same day. It is important that all interviewers meet beforehand to agree on the requirements of the post and to decide how each will contribute to the overall theme. Immediately after the interviews candidates can be jointly evaluated at a further meeting. One disadvantage is the organisation and time that it takes from both the employer's and the candidate's point of view. It requires considerable commitment from the candidate, who may have to keep repeating similar information and whose performance may deteriorate throughout the course of the interviews due to fatigue.

Panel interviews

The panel interview method has the specious appeal of sharing judgement and may appear to be a way of saving time in interviewing as all panel members are operating at once. It is also possible to legitimise a quick decision, always popular with candidates, and there can be no doubt about the ritual requirements being satisfied. Panel interviews reduce the likelihood of personal bias in interviewing, particularly in guarding against possible infringements of legal requirements.

They can also ensure the candidate is acceptable to the whole organisation, and allow the candidate to get a good feel for the business and its culture. The drawbacks lie in the tribunal nature of the panel. They are not having a conversation with the candidates; they are sitting in judgement upon them and assessing the evidence they are able to present in response to the panel's requests. There is little prospect of building rapport and developing discussion, and there is likely to be as much interplay between members of the panel as there is between the panel and the candidate.

Panel interviews tend towards over-rigidity and give ironic point to the phrase 'it is only a formality'. They are ritualistically superb, but dubious as a useful preliminary to employment. However, the benefits of the panel interview can be increased, and the disadvantages reduced, if the interviewers are properly trained and the interview well organised, thoroughly planned and made part of a structured selection process.

ACTIVITY II.2

In your organisation how many interviews and interviewers are used? How effective is this approach and why? In what ways could the approach be improved?

The selection interview sequence

Preparation

The preliminaries of job analysis, recruitment and shortlisting are complete and the interview is now to take place. The first step is for the interviewers to brief themselves by checking the job description or similar details of the post to be filled, a candidate specification or statement of required competencies and the application forms or curricula vitae of the candidates.

If there are several people to be interviewed the interview timetable needs greater planning than it usually receives. The time required for each interview can be determined beforehand only approximately. A rigid timetable will weigh heavily on both parties, who will feel frustrated if the interview is closed arbitrarily at a predetermined time. If an interview that has 'finished' is drawn out to complete its allotted timespan it becomes increasingly artificial and exasperating. However, the disadvantages of keeping people waiting are considerable and underrated.

Most candidates will have competing calls on their time, as they will have taken time off to attend and have earmarked the anticipated interview time to fit in a busy schedule. Some may have other interviews to go to. An open-ended waiting period can be worrying, enervating and a poor preliminary to an interview. If the dentist keeps you waiting you may get distressed, but when the waiting is over you are simply a passive participant and the dentist does not have the success of the operation jeopardised. The interview candidate has, in a real sense, to perform when the period of waiting is over and the success of the interaction could well be jeopardised.

The most satisfactory timetable is the one that guarantees a break after all but the most voluble candidates. If candidates are asked to attend at hourly intervals, for example, this would be consistent with interviews lasting between forty and sixty minutes. This would mean that each interview began at the scheduled time and that the interviewers had the opportunity to review and update their notes in the intervals. The whole plan can still go wrong if one or more candidates fail to turn up.

Reception

Candidates arrive on the premises of their prospective employer on the lookout for every scrap of evidence they can obtain about the business and its people. A candidate is likely to meet at least one and possibly two people before meeting the interviewer. First will be the receptionist. There is frequently also an emissary from the HR department to shepherd them from the front door to the waiting room. Both are valuable sources of information, and interviewers may wish to prime such people so that they can see their role in the employment process and can be cheerful, informative and helpful.

The candidate will most want to meet the interviewer, the unknown but powerful figure on whom so much depends. Interviewers easily forget that they know much more about the candidates than the candidates know about them, because the candidates have provided a personal profile in the application form. Interviewers do not reciprocate. To bridge this gap it can be useful to introduce themselves to the candidate in the waiting room, so that contact is made quickly, unexpectedly and on neutral territory. This makes the opening of the interview itself rather easier.

Candidates wait to be interviewed. Although there are snags about extended, open-ended waiting periods, some time is inevitable and necessary to enable candidates to compose themselves. It is a useful time to deal with travelling expenses and provide some relevant background reading about the employing organisation.

Setting

The setting for an interview has to be right for the ritual and right from the point of view of enabling a full and frank exchange of information. It is difficult to combine the two. Many of the interview horror stories relate to the setting in which it took place. A candidate for a senior local authority post was interviewed on a stage while the panel of seventeen sat in the front row of the stalls, and a candidate for a head teacher post came in to meet the interview panel and actually moved the chair on which he was to sit. He only moved it 2 or 3 inches because the sun was in his eyes, but there was an audible frisson and sharp intake of breath from the members of the panel.

Remaining with our model of the individual interviewer, here are some simple suggestions about the setting:

- The room should be suitable for a private conversation.

- If the interview takes place across a desk, as is common, the interviewer may wish to reduce the extent to which the desk acts as a barrier, inhibiting free flow of communication.

- All visitors and telephone calls should be avoided, as they do not simply interrupt: they intrude and impede the likelihood of frankness.

- It should be clear to the candidates where they are to sit.

Interview structure

There are several important reasons why the employment interview should be structured, making use of the application or CV:

- The candidate expects the proceedings to be decided and controlled by the interviewer and will anticipate a structure within which to operate.

- It helps the interviewer to make sure that all relevant areas are covered and irrelevancies avoided.
- Structure can be used to guide the interview and ensure that it makes sense.
- It assists the interviewer in using the time available in the most effective way.
- The application form can be used as a memory aid by the interviewer when making notes directly after the interview or during it.
- It makes it easier to compare candidates.

The interview

There are several different ways to structure the interview. We recommend the form set out in Table II.1. This divides activities and objectives into three interview stages: opening, middle and closing. While there are few, if any, alternative satisfactory ways for conducting the beginning and the end of the interview, the middle can be approached from a number of different angles, depending on the circumstances.

The interviewer needs to work systematically through the structure that has been planned, but not too rigidly, abandoning his or her own route whenever the candidate chooses one that seems more promising.

The opening of the interview is the time for mutual preliminary assessment and tuning in to each other. A useful feature of this phase is for the interviewer to sketch out the plan or procedure for the interview and how it fits into the total employment decision process. The application form may provide an easy, non-controversial topic for these opening behaviours.

One objective is for the two parties to exchange words so that they can feel reasonably comfortable with each other. Interviewers who can do this can then further develop a relationship in which candidates trust the interviewer's ability and motives so that they speak openly and fully. The interviewer's effectiveness will greatly depend on being skilled at this process.

We are working on the assumption that candidates will behave in a reasonably genuine way, provided the interviewer can convince them that the process is fair. Some candidates do not and such people have been labelled as 'white-collar psychopaths',

Table II.1
Interview structure: a recommended pattern

Stage	Objectives	Activities
Opening	To put the candidate at ease, develop rapport and set the scene	Greet candidate by name Introduce yourself Explain interview purpose Outline how purpose will be achieved Obtain candidate's assent to outline
Middle	To collect and provide information	Ask questions within a structure that makes sense to the candidate, such as biographical areas of the application form, or competencies identified for the job Listen Answer questions Summarise interview
Closing	To close the interview and confirm future action	Check candidate has no more questions Indicate what happens next and when

although it has to be said that they are rare. They are very good at presenting themselves as being exactly what the interviewer is looking for. Not only are they manufacturing the truth about their experience, but also the trait (or psychopathic tendency) that drives them causes them to wreak havoc once they are appointed. A New York psychologist cites the example of 'Ron' who was appointed to a sales post in a pharmaceuticals company:

Ron fiddled his sales figures, charged call girls to the company and nearly succeeded in using his charm to get his new boss fired when he was questioned about his behaviour. Psychopaths are motivated by three things: thrill-seeking, game-playing and hurting people. Once inside the organisation they build networks of influence that make it very difficult to get rid of them and can help them join the management fast track. (Paul Babiak, quoted in Butcher 2004)

There are some suggestions for spotting false claims on a CV in *People Management* (2012).

For the middle of the interview the biographical approach is the simplest. It works on the basis that candidates at the time of the interview are the product of everything in their lives that has gone before. To understand the candidate the interviewer must understand the past and will talk to the candidate about the episodes of his or her earlier life, education and previous employment.

The advantage of this is that the objectives are clear to both interviewer and interviewee; there is no deviousness or 'magic'. Furthermore, the development can be logical and so aid the candidate's recall of events. Candidates who reply to enquiries about their choice of A-level subjects will be subconsciously triggering their recollection of contemporaneous events, such as the university course they took; questions about choice of university subject are likely to come next in the interview. The biographical approach is the simplest for the inexperienced interviewer to use as discussion can develop from the information provided by the candidate on the application form. Some version of sequential categories, such as employment, education and training, seems the most generally useful, but it will need the addition of at least two other categories: the work offered and the organisational context in which it is to be done. The middle of the interview can be structured by systematically working through items of the job description or the person specification. Increasingly, where competencies have been identified for the job, these are used as the basis of the structure.

In the preparatory stage of briefing, the interviewer will also prepare notes on two elements to incorporate in the plan: key issues and checkpoints. Key issues will be the two or three main issues that stand out from the application form for clarification or elaboration. This might be the nature of the responsibilities carried in a particular earlier post, the content of a training course, the reaction to a period of employment in a significant industry, or whatever else strikes the interviewer as being productive of useful additional evidence. Checkpoints are matters of detail that require further information: grades in an examination, dates of an appointment, rates of pay and so forth.

At the close of the interview the explanation of the next step needs especial attention. The result of the interview is of great importance to the candidates and they will await the outcome with anxiety. Even if they do not want the position they will probably hope to have it offered. The great merit of convention in the public sector is that the chosen candidate is usually told before the contenders disperse: the great demerit is that they are asked to say yes or no to the offer at once.

In the private sector it is unusual for an employment offer to be made at the time of the interview, so there is a delay during which the candidates will chafe. Their frustration will be greater if the delay is longer than expected and they may start to tell themselves that they are not going to receive an offer, in which case they will also start convincing themselves that they did not want the job either! It is important for the interviewer to say as precisely as possible when the decision will be made, but ensuring that the candidates hear earlier rather than later than they expect, if there is to be any deviation.

The interviewer will need to call into play certain key aspects of method:

1   Some data can be collected by simple observation of the candidate. Notes can be made about dress, appearance, voice, height and weight, if these are going to be relevant (and not unlawfully discriminatory), and the interviewer can also gauge the candidate's mood and the appropriate response to it by the non-verbal cues that are provided.

2   The remainder of the evidence will come from listening to what is said, so the interviewer has to be very attentive throughout, not only listening to the answers to questions, but also listening for changes in inflection and pace, nuances and overtones that provide clues on what to pursue further. The amount of time that the two spend talking is important, as an imbalance in one direction or the other will mean that either the candidate or the interviewer is not having enough opportunity to hear information. Being silent and deliberately leaving verbal lulls in face-to-face situations provide the opportunity for the other person to say more, perhaps more than was initially intended. Silence still has to be attentive and the longer the silence, the harder it is to be attentive.

3   In order to have something to hear, the interviewer will have to direct the candidate. This, of course, is done by questioning, encouraging and enabling the candidate to talk, so that the interviewer can learn. The art of doing this depends on the personality and style of the interviewer, who will develop a personal technique through a sensitive awareness of what is taking place in the interviews.

    The selection interviewer needs to distinguish between different types of question. In our introduction to face-to-face and communication skills we explained the difference in nature and usage of various questioning methods.

4   The best place for the interviewer to make notes is on the application form or CV. In this way they can be joined to information that the candidate has already provided and the peculiar shorthand that interviewers use when making notes during interviews can be deciphered by reference to the form and the data that the note is embellishing. It also means that the review of evidence after the interview has as much information as possible available on one piece of paper. An alternative is to record notes on the interview plan where the structure is based on job description, person specification or competencies. Interviewers are strangely inhibited about note taking, feeling that it in some way impairs the smoothness of the interaction. This apprehension seems ill founded as candidates are looking for a serious, businesslike discussion, no matter how informal, and note taking offers no barrier, provided that it is done carefully in the form of jottings during the discussion, rather than pointedly writing down particular comments by the candidate which make the interviewer seem like a police officer taking a statement.

5   Data exchange marks a change of gear in the interview. Establishing rapport is necessarily rather rambling and aimless, but data exchange is purposeful, with the interviewer

controlling both the direction and the pace of the exchanges. Candidates will be responsive throughout to the interviewer's control, and the better the rapport, the more responsive they will be. Skilled interviewers close off areas of discussion and open fresh ones. They head off irrelevant reminiscences and probe where matters have been glossed over. They never abandon control. Even when the time has come for the candidates to raise all their queries, they will do this at the behest of the interviewer and will constantly look for a renewal of the mandate to enquire by using conversational prefixes such as, 'Can I ask you another question?', 'If it's not taking up your time, perhaps I could ask . . .?', 'I seem to be asking a lot of questions, but there was just one thing . . .'.

6 Closing the interview can be as skilful as opening it. Most of the suggestions so far have been to encourage a response, but it is easy to nod and smile your way into a situation of such cosy relaxation that the respondent talks on and on . . . and on. A surprising number of interviewers have great difficulty closing. These methods can help:

- *Braking* slows the rate of talking by the candidate by working through a series of steps. You will seldom need to go beyond the first two or three, but five are described in case you have to deal with a really tough case. (a) One or two closed questions to clarify specific points may stem the tide. (b) The facial expression changes with the brow furrowed to indicate mild disagreement, lack of understanding or professional anxiety. The reassuring nods stop and the generally encouraging, supportive behaviours of reward are withdrawn. (c) Abstraction is when the eyes glaze over, showing that they belong to a person whose attention has now shifted away from the respondent and towards lunch. (d) To look at one's watch during a conversation is a very strong signal indeed, as it clearly indicates that time is running out. Other, milder ways of looking away are: looking for your glasses, looking at your notes or looking at the aircraft making a noise outside the window. A rather brutal variant is to allow your attention to be caught by something the respondent is wearing, a lapel badge, a tie, a ring or piece of jewellery, maybe. Putting on your glasses to see it more clearly is really going too far! (e) If all else fails, you simply have to interrupt.

- *Closing* requires the interview to end smoothly. Future action is either clarified or confirmed. Also, candidates take a collection of attitudes away with them, and these can be influenced by the way the interview is closed. There is a simple procedure. (a) First signal, verbal plus papers. The interviewer uses a phrase to indicate that the interview is nearing its end ('Well now, I think we have covered the ground, don't you? There isn't anything more I need to ask you. There's nothing further you want from me?'). In this way the interviewer signal the impending close at the same time as obtaining the candidate's confirmation. There is additional emphasis provided by some paper play. A small collection of notes can be gathered together and stacked neatly, or a notebook can be closed. (b) Second signal, the interviewer confirms what will happen next ('There are still one or two people to see, but we will write to you no later than the end of the week'). (c) The final signal is to stand up: the decisive act to make the close. By standing up the interviewer forces the candidate to stand as well and there remain only the odds and ends of handshakes and parting smiles.

SUMMARY PROPOSITIONS

II.1 Despite criticisms and shortcomings, the selection interview remains a central feature of the recruitment and selection process.

II.2 Typical interview strategies are frank and friendly, problem solving, biographical and stress.

II.3 Aspects of interview preparation are timetabling, reception and deciding the right setting.

II.4 Features of the interview itself are the opening for preliminary mutual assessment; data gathering, involving a logical sequence, key issues and checkpoints; and the closure, which prepares candidates for the next step in the process.

GENERAL DISCUSSION TOPICS

1 This analysis of the selection interview assumes that the candidate is seeking to become an employee. How would the interview be different if the candidate were being interviewed with a view to becoming a freelance consultant doing work for the organisation rather than being an employee in it?

2 'HR are constantly wanting to "involve me" in their recruitment and selection of staff. I'm too busy to spend time doing that. I want HR to do their job properly and send the people through to me when everything is sorted out and a new recruit is ready to start.' How do you react to that comment from an operations manager in an airline?

THEORY INTO PRACTICE

For this exercise you need a cooperative, interested relative, or a very close friend, who would welcome interview practice.

1 Follow the sequence suggested in Table II.1 to give your partner practice in being interviewed for a job, and giving yourself practice in interviewing and note taking.

2 After the interview, discuss your mutual feelings about the process around questions such as:

Selector   Did you ever feel you were being misled? When? Why?
Did you feel the interview got out of your control? When? Why?
How could you have avoided the problem?
How was your note taking?
What, if anything, made you bored or cross?
What did you find most difficult?
How comprehensive is the data you have collected?

Candidate   Were you put at your ease?
Were you at any time inhibited by the selector?
Did you ever mislead the selector? When? How?
Did the selector ever fail to follow up important points? When? Which?
Were you in any way disconcerted by the note taking?
Has the selector got a comprehensive set of data about you, so that you could feel any decision made about you would be soundly based?
What did you think of the interview experience?

3 Now swap roles.

FURTHER READING

Anderson, N. and Shackleton, V. (1993) *Successful Selection Interviewing*. Oxford: Blackwell.

Newell, S. and Shackleton, V. (2000) 'Recruitment and selection', in S. Bach and K. Sisson (eds), *Personnel Management: A comprehensive guide to theory and practice*. Oxford: Blackwell.
Both of these books provide full treatment of the selection interview in all its forms.

Brewster, C. and Tyson, S. (eds) (1991) *International Comparisons in Human Resource Management*. London: Pitman.

Lawler, J.J., Zaidi, M.A. and Atriyanandana, V. (1989) 'Human resources strategies in South East Asia: The case of Thailand', in A. Nedd *et al.* (eds), *Research in Personnel and Human Resources Management*, Supplement 1. Greenwich, CT: JAI Press, pp. 201–23.

Tan, K.H. (1995) *Planning, Recruiting and Selecting Human Resources*. Shah Alam: Federal Publications.
Each of these works provides research findings on interview validity.

McDaniel, M.A., Whetzel, D.A., Schmidt, F.L. and Maurer, S.D. (1994) 'The validity of the employment interviews', *Journal of Applied Psychology*, Vol. 79, No. 19, pp. 599–616.

Williamson, L.G. *et al.* (1996) 'Employment interview on trial: Linking interview structure with litigation outcomes', *Journal of Applied Psychology*, Vol. 82, No. 6, pp. 900–12.
Selection interviewing varies considerably across different cultures. This skill unit and most of the available literature is rooted in Anglo-American practice. Some insights into practice in other situations can be found in the three works given above.

WEB LINKS

www.thedevco.com (the Development Company).
www.bps.org.uk (British Psychological Society).
www.opp.co.uk (Oxford Psychologists Press).
www.shlgroup.com/uk (Saville and Holdsworth, test developer/supplier).
www.psl.net (test developer).
www.intest.com is the website of the International Test Commission which has provided guidelines on computer-based and Internet-delivered testing.

REFERENCES

Babiak, P. (2004) quoted in Butcher, S. (2004) 'When the ideal applicant is too good to be true', *Financial Times*, 12 January, p. 12.

People Management (2012) "Can you spot a fraudulent CV?", December, pp. 38–9.

III The appraisal interview

Throughout the first years of the twenty-first century the UK government ran various programmes within its Civil Service departments to manage performance by setting specific targets by which senior civil servants' performance would be judged and rewarded. This is a common enough feature of employment outside the Civil Service, however varied its effectiveness, but novel in government service. In the middle of 2006 a survey by the Prime Minister's Delivery Unit cast doubt on the impact of this policy. The survey assessed four of the largest departments of state. On a four-point scale, with 4 at the top, they all scored 2 for managing performance and even less well for providing value for money. The Prime Minister said the departments needed to transform the way they deliver services to meet growing public expectations and that government ministers could not 'micro-manage' services. Most people would probably say 'Thank God for that!', but it is a common cry in business circles as well, with senior managers confidently inhabiting the sunlit uplands of strategy formulation and therefore being far to busy to 'micro-manage' performance. Although the Prime Minister's claim that ministers could not micro-manage civil servants was welcomed, some people grumbled that ministers had used a different pattern of micro-managing by setting lots of targets, which were not always mutually compatible and usually linked to some form of individual bonus.

This part of the skills package is unequivocally about a crucial act of micro-management: appraising performance *face to face*. It is linked to our previous thorough discussion of performance management (see Chapter 10). We open with an examination of the performance appraisal process, with particular reference to the appraisal interview. We have seen the place of leadership and motivation in producing a situation where effective performance is likely. Face-to-face appraisal is crucial in the whole process of achieving effective focused performance by individuals. It may be undertaken in conversations with our colleagues, our bosses and perhaps our customers or clients, both by assessing how things are going and by providing a basis for future development. We move forward in our understanding of how we are doing and how we are going to be where we need to be. Usually it is an erratic sequence of a word here, an observation there, a complaint, an argument, an explanation of why something failed or was brilliantly successful. As we build up our understanding of who we are, where we want to be, what we want to do and how we can make progress towards whatever our goals may be, we piece together the products of dozens of such inputs. Occasional landmark conversations crystallise our thinking. These are most likely to be appraisal interviews, and they are landmarks because of their relative formality, their official nature and because they are dedicated solely to bringing our personal performance up to an even higher level than it is already.

Our objectives in this skill unit are:

1 To explain the purpose and nature of the appraisal interview.
2 To suggest a model sequence for conducting appraisal interviews.

The appraisal interview

The novelist, the textbook writer, the popular vocalist, the newspaper editor, the sculptor or painter, the athlete or the owner of a corner shop all have in common the fact that their performance is measurable in an absolute way by numbers. When Adele releases an album, she can see the effectiveness of her performance in the irrefutable logic of the numbers sold. When Usain Bolt races, that performance is measured by the time taken. These measurements can then be compared with those of competitors. There are no mitigating circumstances. The writer may feel that the publisher should have done a better job (not often!) or that the reviewers were incompetent (usually), but that has no weight compared with the inescapable fact of the numbers. The shop owner may grumble about local authority planners or about unfair competition from the local hypermarket, but that explanation will not stop customers from drifting away.

Few working people have that same absolute measure for their own personal performance, which is all part of an integrated corporate endeavour. Individual effectiveness is rarely measurable by a market indicator, as so many other people contribute to the effectiveness or ineffectiveness of any individual's activity. The inexorable logic of the marketplace or other external arena has to be replaced by internal measures, mediated by managerial judgement. This is tricky.

Appraising performance is not a precise measurement but a subjective assessment based on hard evidence about the performance, and that evidence has to be put together and assessed. The assessment has a long history of being damned for its ineffectiveness at the same time as being anxiously sought by people wanting to know how they are doing. It is difficult to do, it is frequently done badly with quite serious results, but on the rare occasions when it is done well it can be invaluable for the business, and literally life transforming for the appraisee. It is probably the most demanding and skilful activity for any manager to undertake and is dreaded by both appraisers and appraisees. Recent research about appraising the performance of UK school teachers found that the appraisal itself was often accompanied by long periods of sickness absence due to stress. To a great extent this centred on the difficulty of appropriate criteria for judgement, particularly where head teachers link capability to personal qualities such as 'open-minded and prepared to adapt and take on new skills' or 'attitude' or where generalised descriptions such as 'unable to do the job properly' or 'not meeting standards' are offered. Measurement is also inevitably imprecise when it is subjective, making the judgement difficult to substantiate and prone to challenge. This leads to the risk that the yardsticks of acceptable performance chosen are those that can best be justified rather than those that are most important (Torrington et al. 2003).

We all seek approval and confirmation that we are doing the right thing, and we could all do better.

Once installed, appraisal schemes are frequently modified or abandoned, and there is widespread management frustration about their operation. Despite the problems, the potential advantages of appraisal are so great that organisations continue to introduce them and appraisal can produce stunning results. Here is an extract from a CIPD examination answer:

I have had [an] annual appraisal for three years. Each time it has been a searching discussion of my objectives and my results. Each interview has set me new challenges and opened up fresh opportunities. Appraisal has given me a sense of achievement and purpose that I had never previously experienced in my working life. (from an insurance company)

We have to try and reduce the tendency for qualitative appraisal to be unstructured, avoiding awkwardness and being unsuitable for comparison. There are two difficulties: the first is the potential lack of the *systematic* reporting that is looked for in attempts at management control of, and information about, the process; second, qualitative appraisal interviewing is not easy and requires a high level of *mutual trust* between appraiser and appraisee. How many appraisees are appraised by a paragon in whom they can trust?

Frances Storr described an approach to performance appraisal that sought to take out almost all the formality. It included the appraisees choosing their own appraisers and usually the feedback is face to face, with virtually no form filling:

its purpose is stated clearly: to improve performance and enable people to learn and grow. We emphasise that appraisal is as much about celebrating people's achievements, as it is about helping them to identify areas in which they can improve. Within that framework it is up to individuals to decide how they will carry out their own 360 degree appraisal. In more than 90 per cent of cases, feedback is given face to face, with people talking to their appraisers as a group. Any written material . . . belongs to the appraisee, with the result that the appraisal has become a dialogue rather than a survey. (Storr 2000: 39)

ACTIVITY III.1

A managerial approach to appraisal is to *control* performance. Those being appraised are interested in *developing* their performance. Can the benefits of both approaches be achieved in a single scheme?

Who does the appraisal?

Individuals are appraised by a variety of people, including their immediate superior, their superior's superior, a member of the HR department, themselves, their peers or their subordinates.

Some of the problems for appraisers are:

- **Prejudice**: some appraisers may be prejudiced against the appraisee, or be over-anxious not to be prejudiced; either could distort their judgement.

- **Insufficient knowledge of the appraisee**: appraisers often carry out appraisals because of their position in the hierarchy rather than because they have a good understanding of what the appraisee is doing.

- **The 'halo effect'**: the general likeability, or the opposite, of an appraisee can influence the assessment of the work that the appraisee is doing.

- **The problem of context**: it is difficult to distinguish the work of appraisees from the context in which they work, especially when there is an element of comparison with other appraisees.
- **The paperwork**: documentation soon gets very cumbersome in the attempts made by scheme designers to ensure consistent reporting.
- **The formality**: although appraisers are likely to try to avoid stiff formality, both participants in the interview realise that the encounter is relatively formal, with much hanging on it.

ACTIVITY III.2

Think of jobs where it is difficult to disentangle the performance of the individual from the context of the work. How would you focus on the individual's performance in these situations?

Other common problems, which often cause appraisal schemes to fail, are:

- **Outcomes are ignored**: follow-up action for management to take, although agreed in the interview, does not happen.
- **Everyone is 'just above average'**: most appraisees are looking for reassurance that all is well, and the easiest way for appraisers to deal with this is by stating or inferring that the appraisee is doing at least as well as most others, and better than a good many. It is much harder to deal with the situation of presenting someone with the opinion that they are average; who wants to be average?
- **Appraising the wrong features**: sometimes issues other than real work are evaluated, such as time-keeping, looking busy and being pleasant, because they are easier to see.

The appraisal interview style

The different styles of appraisal interview were succinctly described fifty years ago by the American psychologist Norman Maier (1958). His three-fold classification remains the most widely adopted means of identifying the way to tackle the interview. The *problem-solving* style can be summarised as an opening in which the appraiser encourages appraisees to review their performance, evaluate it and identify any problems. The appraiser then takes a more active role by sharing in reviewing the problems that the appraisee has first identified and jointly discussing possible solutions. Any evaluation comes as a result of the discussion rather than being a unilateral judgement by the appraiser.

This is certainly the most effective style provided that both the appraiser and appraisee have the skill and ability to handle it, but it is not the only style. Maier's alternatives included, first, *tell and sell*, where the appraiser acts as judge, using the interview to tell the appraisee the result of the appraisal and how to improve. This 'ski instructor' approach can be right for appraisees who have little experience and who lack the self-confidence to analyse their own performance. *Tell and listen*, the second alternative, still casts the appraiser in the role of judge, passing on the outcome of an appraisal that has already been completed and listening to reactions. Both of these approaches could sometimes change the assessment, as well as enabling the two people to have a reasonably frank exchange.

It is tempting to identify the problem-solving approach as 'the best', because it appears to be the most civilised and searching, but not all appraisal situations call for this style, not all appraisees are ready for it.

The appraisal interview sequence

Certain aspects of the appraisal interview are the same as for selection. The appraiser determines the framework of the encounter, there is a need to open in a way that develops mutual confidence as far as possible and there is the use of closed and open-ended questions, reflection and summarising. It is also a difficult meeting for the two parties to handle.

The appraiser needs a degree of confidence and personal authority that few managers have in their relationship with all those whom they have to appraise. The most contentious aspect of many appraisal schemes is that appraisees have no part in deciding who the appraiser should be.

For the appraisee there are concerns about career progress, job security, the ongoing working relationship with the appraiser and the basic anxieties relating to self-esteem and dealing with criticism.

The fundamental difference between selection and appraisal is that the objective is to reach an understanding that will have some impact on the future performance of the appraisee: it is not simply to formulate a judgement by collecting information, as in selection. A medical metaphor may help. A surgeon carrying out hip replacements will select patients for surgery on the basis of enquiring about their symptoms and careful consideration of the evidence. The surgeon asks the questions, makes the decision and implements that decision. A physician examining a patient who is overweight and short of breath may rapidly make the decision that the patient needs to lose weight and take more exercise. It is, however, not the physician but the patient who has to implement that decision. The physician can help with diet sheets, regular check-ups and terrifying advice about the alternative; the real challenge is how to get the patient to respond.

The easy part of appraisal is sorting out the facts; bringing about a change in performance is the difficult bit. The interview, like the discussion in the physician's consulting rooms, is crucial in getting a change of attitude, fresh understanding and commitment to action.

Preparation

The appraiser should brief the appraisee on the form of the interview, possibly asking for a self-appraisal form to be completed in advance. To some extent this is setting the tone, making the opening of the eventual interview easier.

Asking for the self-appraisal form to be completed will only be appropriate if the scheme requires this. As we have seen, self-appraisal gives the appraisee some initiative, ensures that the discussion will be about matters which the appraisee can handle and on 'real stuff'. The appraiser has to collect and review all the available evidence on the appraisee's performance, including reports, records or other material regarding the period under review. Most important will be the previous appraisal and its outcomes.

Most of the points made about preparing for the selection interview also apply to appraisal, especially the setting. Several research studies (e.g. Anderson and Barnett 1987) have shown the extremely positive response of appraisees who felt that the appraiser had

Table III.1
Structure for a
performance
appraisal
interview

1 Purpose and rapport or setting the tone	Agree purpose with appraisee Agree structure for meeting Check that pre-work is done
2 Factual review	Review of known facts about performance in previous period Appraiser reinforcement
3 Appraisee views	Appraisee asked to comment on performance over the last year: what has gone well and what has gone less well; what could be improved; what they liked; what they disliked; possible new objectives
4 Appraiser views	Appraiser adds own perspective, asks questions and disagrees, as appropriate, with what appraisee has said
5 Problem solving	Discussion of any differences and how they can be resolved
6 Objective setting	Agreeing what action should be taken, and by whom

taken time and trouble to ensure that the setting and supportive nature of the discussion were considerate of the appraisee's needs.

Interview structure

A recommended structure for a performance appraisal interview is shown in Table III.1. Alternative frameworks can be found in Anderson (1993: 112–13) and Dainow (1988).

Rapport or setting the tone is unusual because it attempts to smooth the interaction between two people who probably have an easy social relationship, but now find themselves ill at ease. They are not used to having this sort of conversation together, so they have to find new ground-rules. The appraisal interview itself may be easier to introduce and handle if, as generally recommended, there are mini-reviews throughout the year. This should ensure that there are no surprises, and the two people concerned get used to having performance-focused meetings, however informal. There is still the problem of appraisee reaction to the tentative presentation of things the appraisees are not doing properly. A minority will misconstrue comments to focus on the good at the expense of the not so good, while a different minority will do the exact opposite: demoralised collapse at facing a suspended sentence. The majority will react sensibly and most appraisees will have the simple guts to face up to issues that are problematic.

The opening of the interview itself still needs care. The mood needs to be light, but not trivial, as the appraisee has to be encouraged towards candour rather than gamesmanship and the appraiser needs to concentrate on the basis of feedback, which we considered in introducing face-to-face skills.

ACTIVITY III.3

What do you think of the following openings to appraisal interviews heard recently?

(a) 'Well, here we are again. I'm sure you don't like this business any more than I do, so let's get on with it.'

(b) 'Now, there's nothing to worry about. It's quite painless and could be useful. So just relax and let me put a few questions to you.'

(c) 'I will be straight with you if you will be straight with me. All right?'

(d) 'Right. Let battle commence!'

Factual review is reviewing aspects of the previous year's work that are unproblematic. The appraiser begins by reviewing the main facts about the performance, without expressing opinions about them but merely summarising them as a mutual reminder, perhaps reviewing previous objectives set and including the outcome of the previous appraisal. This will help to key in any later discussion by confirming such matters as how long the appraisee has been in the job, any personnel changes in the period, turnover figures, training undertaken and so forth.

The appraiser will still be doing most, but not all, of the talking, and can isolate those aspects of performance that have been disclosed which are clearly satisfactory, mention them and comment favourably. This will develop rapport and provide the basic reassurance that the appraisee needs in order to avoid being defensive. The favourable aspects of performance will to some extent be *discovered* by the factual review process. It is important that 'the facts speak for themselves' rather than appraiser judgement being offered. Not, for instance:

> Well, I think you are getting on very well. I'm very pleased with how things are going generally.

That sort of comment made at this stage would have the appraisee waiting for 'but . . .' as the defences have not yet been dismantled. A different approach might be:

> Those figures look very good. How do they compare with . . . ? That's X per cent up on the quarter and Y per cent on the year. . . . That's one of the best results in the group. You must be pleased with that. . . . How on earth did you do it?

This has the advantage of the evidence, including that collected throughout the year as we suggested earlier, being there before the eyes of both parties, with the appraiser pointing out and emphasising. It is also specific rather than general, precise rather than vague. This type of approach invariably raises the question from appraisers about what to do in a situation of poor performance. Appraising stars is easy; what about the duds? The answer is that all appraisees have some aspects of their performance on which favourable comment can be made, and the appraisal process actually identifies strengths that might have been previously obscured by the general impression of someone who is not very good – the opposite of the halo effect. The appraiser may discover something on which to build, having previously thought the case was hopeless. If there is not some feature of the performance that can be isolated in this way, then the appraiser probably has a management or disciplinary problem that should have been tackled earlier. If the system is one in which appraisees complete a self-report beforehand, then much of the factual review could be centred on this.

The appraiser then asks for the *appraisee's views* on things that are not as good as they might be in the performance, areas of possible improvement and how these might be addressed. These will only be offered by the appraisee if there has been effective positive reinforcement in the previous stages of the interview. People can only acknowledge shortcomings about performance when they are reasonably sure of their ground. Now the appraisee is examining areas of dissatisfaction by the process of discussing them with the appraiser, with whom it is worth having the discussion, because of the appraiser's expertise, information and 'helicopter view'. There are three likely results of debating these matters:

- some will be talked out as baseless;
- some will be shown to be less worrying than they seemed when viewed only from the single perspective of the appraisee, and ways of dealing with them become apparent;
- some will be confirmed as matters needing attention.

This stage in the interview is fraught with difficulties for the manager, and is one of the reasons why an alternative style is sometimes preferred. Some people prefer to be told on the basis that the appraiser is the one whose judgement matters and they do not like having to make the running, perhaps exposing themselves to criticism before they have been able to work out what the appraiser's position is.

This is particularly likely in the high-power distance cultures that we discussed earlier (see Chapter 2). Many countries do not aspire to the particular type of social sophistication which western nations regard as the height of cool. These, however, are problems to be recognised and overcome; they are not reasons for not bothering to try.

Appraiser views can now be used in adding to the list of areas for improvement. In many instances there will be no additions to make, but usually there are improvement needs that the appraisee cannot, or will not, see. If they are put at this point in the interview, there is the best chance that they will be understood, accepted and acted upon. It is not possible to guarantee success. Demoralised collapse or bitter resentment is always a possibility, but this is the time to try, as the appraisee has developed a basis of reassurance and has come to terms with some shortcomings that he or she had not already recognised. The appraiser has to judge whether any further issues can be raised and, if so, how many. None of us can cope with confronting all our shortcomings, all at the same time, and the appraiser's underlying management responsibility is to ensure that the appraisee is not made less competent by the appraisal interview. There is also a fundamental moral responsibility not to use a position of organisational power to damage the self-esteem and adjustment of another human being.

Problem solving is the process of talking out the areas for improvement that have been identified, so that the appraisee can cope with them. Underlying causes are uncovered through further discussion. Gradually huge problems come into clearer and less forbidding perspective, perhaps through being analysed and broken up into different components. Possibilities for action, by both appraiser and appraisee, become clear.

These central stages of the interview, namely factual exchange, appraisee views, appraiser views and problem solving, need to move in that sequence. Some may be brief, but none should be omitted and the sequence should not alter.

The final stage of the encounter is to agree what is to be done: *objective setting*. Actions need to be agreed and nailed down, so that they actually take place. One of the biggest causes of appraisal failure is with action not being taken, so the objectives set must be not only mutually acceptable, but also deliverable. It is likely that some action will be needed from the appraiser as well as some from the appraisee.

Making appraisal interviewing work

Appraisers need training in how to appraise and how to conduct appraisal interviews. Appraisees will also need some training if they have any significant involvement in the process. An excellent performance appraisal system is of no use at all if managers do not know how to use the system to best effect.

In all appraisal situations where the style is problem solving or tell and listen, rather than tell and sell, the interview must be given appropriate salience in the whole process: it must fit and other features must fit with it. If the outcome of the overall appraisal is predetermined then tell and sell is better. This can often be the emphasis where appraisal is directly linked to pay rather than to development or improvement.

SUMMARY PROPOSITIONS

III.1 Performance appraisal has a poor track record, but it has considerable potential, when done well.

III.2 Among the problems of appraisal are prejudice, insufficient knowledge by the appraiser of the appraisee, the halo effect, the problem of context, the paperwork, the ignoring of outcomes, appraising the wrong features and the tendency for everyone to be appraised as just above average.

III.3 Three alternative approaches to the appraisal interview are problem solving, tell and sell, and tell and listen.

III.4 Features of the interview itself are the opening for preliminary mutual assessment; factual review; appraisee views on performance; appraiser views, to add perspective; problem solving; and objective setting.

III.5 Appraisers must follow up on interviews, making sure that all agreed action (especially that by the management) takes place.

III.6 Training in appraisal is essential for appraisers and for appraisees.

GENERAL DISCUSSION TOPICS

1 'What right does he have to ask me questions about my motivation and objectives? I come here to do a job of work and then go home. What I want to do with my life is my business.' How would you react to that comment by someone who had just emerged from an appraisal interview?

2 In what situations have you seen outstanding individuals depress the performance of a team where the other people were demoralised by the dominance of that individual? How do you cope with this?

THEORY INTO PRACTICE

For this you need a fellow learner who is to practise appraising and being appraised. You need to be in similar work so that you can understand what the other person is talking about, but without any hierarchical relationship with each other. You also have to trust each other to be ultra-discreet about what you hear.

A interviews B about what B did at work last week, what went well, what less well, problems and disappointments (15 minutes).

B interviews A about what A did at work last week, what went well, what less well, problems and disappointments (15 minutes).

This to obtain information, not to discuss except for clarification. You both now separately review what you have learnt and identify two or three issues that the other seems to have difficulty with.

A and B then take it in turns to lead the other in a discussion about possible ways forward with the difficult issues, following the suggested sequence for the appraisal interview.

FURTHER READING

Fletcher, C. (1999) *Appraisal: Routes to improved performance*. London: CIPD.

Lowry, D. (2002) 'Performance management', in J. Leopold (ed.), *Human Resources in Organisations*. London: Prentice Hall.

The appraisal interview has not been the subject of much research in recent years, but the above reviews provide practical suggestions.

Milliman, J., Nason, S., Zhu, C. and De Ciere, H. (2002) 'An exploratory assessment of the purposes of performance appraisals in North and Central America and the Pacific Rim', *Human Resource Management*, Vol. 41, pp. 87–102.

This is an interesting piece of work comparing the way in which performance appraisal is carried out in contrasting cultures.

Redman, T., Snape, E., Thompson, D. and Kaching Yan, F. (2000) 'Performance appraisal in the National Health Service', *Human Resource Management Journal*, Vol. 10, No. 1, pp. 1–16.

Torrington, D.P., Earnshaw, J.M., Marchington, L. and Ritchie, M.D. (2003) *Tackling Underperformance in Teachers*. London: Routledge Falmer.

The above are both reviews of practice in two parts of public-sector employment in the UK.

Ling Sing Chee (1994) 'Singapore Airlines: Strategic human resource initiatives', in D. Torrington, *International Human Resource Management*. London: Prentice Hall, pp. 143–60.

Dr Ling Sing Chee's chapter includes an account of how the Thai office had difficulty in writing negative comments because of Buddhist beliefs about reincarnation, and the office needed to adapt various aspects of its embryonic performance management system to accommodate cultural differences.

REFERENCES

Anderson, G.C. (1993) *Managing Performance Appraisal Systems*. Oxford: Blackwell.

Anderson, G.C. and Barnett, J.G. (1987) 'The characteristics of effective appraisal interviews', *Personnel Review*, Vol. 16, No. 4, pp. 18–25.

Dainow, S. (1988) 'Goal-orientated appraisal', *Training Officer*, January, pp. 6–8.

Maier, N.R.F. (1958) *The Appraisal Interview: Objectives, methods and skills*. New York: Wiley.

Storr, F. (2000) 'This is not a circular', *People Management*, May, pp. 38–40.

Torrington, D.P., Earnshaw, J.M., Marchington, L. and Ritchie, M.D. (2003) *Tackling Underperformance in Teachers*. London: Routledge Falmer.

IV Coaching

Although this section is about coaching, we need to remember the frequent close connection with mentoring, which has been explained previously (see Chapter 16). Coaching is not teaching people how to do things, but helping them to do even better things that they have already learnt. It is a form of learning that is highly personal and flexible, largely driven by the protégé rather than led by the coach.

Coaching is as important for the proficient or expert as it is for beginners. The more expert a person becomes, the more important a coach is to hone performance, to take a broad view of the context in which the learner's career is developing and how it may proceed. Coaching is a skill but more than just an encounter to be managed, like most of the skills described in this skills package; it is a skill in managing a relationship.

WINDOW ON PRACTICE

For many years until 2012 the UK sporting public was hungry for success in tennis. Wimbledon annually stages the world's greatest tennis tournament and winning is the greatest achievement in a player's career, yet it was over seventy years since a British man had won the title. A young Scot, Andy Murray, had emerged as the great hope of UK tennis. Young, skilled and with a great competitive temperament, he had been coached by his mother, but needed a different coach to take him forward to international success, someone with international experience as well as personal authority, who could take the already acquired skill of this fiery young man and develop it, and him, to greater international achievement. Brad Gilbert was an experienced international coach. He took on the coaching of Andy Murray, whose accomplishments soon began to increase. Gilbert was not personally as good a player as Murray, but had a breadth of international experience and expertise that provided the right complement to Murray's youth, talent and temperament *at that time*. The two would soon part as Andy Murray would seek other mentors including the 50-year-old Ivan Lendl, who had won Wimbledon himself and guided his protégé to success and an Olympic gold medal at Wimbledon, building on what Gilbert and Mrs Murray had earlier achieved.

Coaching is a part of the job of every manager, but it is an approach being used increasingly in business circles to bring on the effectiveness of people at all levels. As long ago as 1994, Clutterbuck and Wynne (1994: 156) made a comment combining mentoring and coaching:

They represent an increasing trend towards helping the individual take charge of his or her own learning: the primary driver . . . becomes the employee; the coach or mentor is available to give guidance, insight and encouragement.

Currently there is great enthusiasm for coaching to be seen as a central feature of the managerial role so that every manager is expected to act as a coach to those for whom the manager has direct line responsibility. The manager concentrates on developing the skills and capacities of the individual members of the team, enabling them to perform rather than directing their performance. This nice distinction takes account of changes in the types of jobs people have and the moves towards flexible rather than hierarchical organisation structures. It is rarely so clear cut, as managers have to combine coaching with direction. Not all managers like the coaching role. Carroll and Gillen (2001) identified various barriers to line manager acceptance of a teaching or coaching role, including lack of interpersonal competence, lack of time, performance pressures, a feeling that the teaching role was not valued and should be done by the HR department. Their article also provides material on what makes an effective coach.

Other members of the business may be involved in coaching on particular aspects of the learner's work. Janice Caplan identifies the elements of coaching as:

> to enable, encourage and facilitate so that staff have a stronger sense of control over their own work and their own time, and so that they identify their own options and solutions to problems. . . . The manager also needs to act as a role model of the desired . . . behaviours. Nonetheless, there may be times when the manager will still need to be more directive. (Caplan 2003: 20)

Before considering the appropriate qualities of a coach, we note the important concept of the career anchor, identified by Edgar H. Schein, one of the founding fathers of organisational psychology during his 30 years as Sloan Fellows Professor of Management at Massachusetts Institute of Technology. The career anchor is something so important to a person's self-confidence that it will be abandoned only reluctantly, and then only if it can be replaced by something else equally rewarding. Schein described career anchors as much broader than motivation, and as including the following:

- self-perceived talents and abilities;
- self-perceived motives and needs;
- self-perceived attitudes and values.

Our perception of ourselves in these areas comes from direct experiences of work, from successes, from self-diagnoses and from feedback. The conclusions that we draw both drive and constrain future career development. Career anchors can identify a source of personal stability in the person which has determined past choices and will probably determine future choices.

The problematic aspect of career anchors is the accuracy of the individual's self-perceptions, and the question of what happens in mid-career to those who feel their attitudes and values are changing. Schein (2004) acknowledges that career anchors are learnt rather than reflecting latent abilities and are the sorts of things that people are reluctant to abandon. Not only do we all need to identify and understand what our anchors are in order to make sure we are doing the right thing, but we also need to appreciate that there are things that we shall continue to need even if we make a career change.

The qualities of the coach

Coaching is usually a one-to-one activity, for which the coach needs various qualities:

1 **Trust.** Often the coach will need to deal with what are usually very private aspects of someone's life, so it is first necessary that the learner has absolute trust in the coach's integrity and commitment to the coaching. The interpersonal chemistry has to be

completely correct between the two of them, even though they will probably argue and may not speak to each other for days. If learners, for instance, are highly skilled performers with a shrewd knowledge of their job and a fair understanding of what they can and cannot do, a coach needing to challenge some part of that self-confidence will then be threatening something that seems to be removing one of the things that the learner has previously relied on, a career anchor. There will be a disagreement and it will not be easy for a learner to abandon something that has previously been an anchor; it will probably not happen unless there is a grounded belief in the coach's trustworthiness.

2 **Respect.** Closely allied to trust and the next requirement of expertise is *mutual* respect. The learner needs to feel that the coach is worthy of respect because he or she is trustworthy, is expert in the job of the learner, is proficient at the job of coaching, has a great deal of broader experience, is good at explaining things and explaining the right things. These 'things' have to be strong enough to overwhelm other possible thoughts about the coach, such as 'has-been', 'past-it', 'couldn't hack it at the sharp end', 'the job is not like it was in his day'. Coaches are nearly always older than learners, so there may be a temptation for ambitious learners to have such thoughts. Equally the coach must have respect for the learner: no condescension or patronising behaviour, but a real respect for the learner's skill, accomplishments and ambitions.

3 **Job expertise.** The coach needs to *know how* to do the learner's job at least as well as the learner; this is not the same as *being able* to do the job as well as the learner. The person training the novice usually has to be expert at actually doing the job of the learner; the coach enhancing the skill of someone who is proficient does not need that particular level of ability, as long as there is the understanding. It is often important that the coach is *not* as practically skilled, otherwise coaching may become 'watch me; do this' instead of 'listen to what I say and then work out how to do better'.

4 **Listening.** Coaches have to be very sensitive and conscientious listeners. The coaching relationship has many similarities with performance appraisal, in that the coach can only work to improve what the learner is able to acknowledge and understand. There will be a lot of explanation and even simple instruction, but the starting point will usually be in the learner's head. The learner will ask questions, express frustrations or describe a problem that the coach may believe to be the wrong problem. All the time the coach listens with close attention and works on understanding the questions, what lies behind the frustrations and why the wrong problem has been identified. What makes the coach so sure it is the wrong problem anyway?

School teachers sometimes say that gifted teachers are able to develop children's understanding almost entirely by getting them to ask the right questions. Coaches who can do this with adults are on the way to being outstanding, although the method has to be rather more subtle and not manipulative. We have already identified some of the basic skills required in this type of listening, especially reflection and reflecting and summarising.

5 **Evaluating.** The coach listens to the learner, listens to what other people say and can probably study aspects of the learner's performance, so that there is a collection of information to process. The coach needs to be able to evaluate all of this data dispassionately but effectively, having the advantage of a degree of objectivity which the learner cannot hope to have, and assembling it in a way that will make a constructive contribution to the coaching process.

6 **Challenging.** However true it may be that talking a problem through should enable a learner to solve whatever the career block may be, it is also true that few of us can do this with everything. We tend to construe a situation in a way that puts us in the right. There will be times when the coach simply has to confront the learner with a different interpretation of what is going on and challenge the learner to accept the validity of criticism. Some coaches who are not the direct line manager say that it is not their role to do this, and that challenging should be left to the manager, but that is just shirking the responsibility. A coach cannot just do the nice, agreeing things with lots of understanding smiles and sympathetic nods of support. The coach is in a privileged position, being trusted by the learner to provide help, including guidance on what is wrong, however reluctant the learner may be to hear it.

7 **Practical help.** A part of the coaching relationship will be to provide straightforward practical suggestions: 'Have you thought of . . . ?', 'Have you spoken to . . . ?', 'Would it help if I went through it with you . . . ?', 'No, that simply won't work'.

Ideally all of these great qualities would be found in any competent manager, so that the learner automatically has the line manager as coach. However, not all managers have all these qualities particularly well developed, and there are advantages in the coach being outside the line. The act of talking with a 'supportive outsider' can be a help to managers in unravelling and evaluating the mixed messages they are hearing in the workplace, where custom and practice are lagging behind policy, which appears to be out of line with organisational culture. However, a line manager may well be suspicious of supportive outsiders who appear to be giving messages that contradict what the manager is saying. After all, coaching is not quite the same as counselling, where an outsider has a better justification.

The solution to this dilemma seems to be to acknowledge that all managers need to adopt a coaching mode of working with individual members of their department, but that other supportive *insiders* could be called upon to act as individual mentors, where there is a good working relationship or prior familiarity between prospective coach and prospective learner. Clutterbuck and Gover (2004) suggest there are seven stages in the coaching process:

1 Identify the need.
2 Gather evidence.
3 Motivate and set targets.
4 Plan how to achieve.
5 Create opportunities to practise.
6 Observe and give feedback.
7 Support through the setbacks.

A further twist is that there are two different ways of focusing on coaching: pre-coaching and post-coaching. Pre-coaching is the main emphasis as you are preparing someone for the event they are about to handle, so lines of questioning may be: 'What difficulties do you anticipate?', 'How will you handle that?', 'What will you do if . . . ?'. All of these look forward. Post-coaching is equally valuable, but has a different nature after the event has happened. There is less intense focus, less adrenaline; much more reflective and analytical. It could include questions like 'How did it go?,' 'What happened that you didn't expect?', 'What can you learn from this experience?', and so on. The first focus is on motivation; the second is on learning and embedding the lessons learnt.

SUMMARY PROPOSITIONS

IV.1 Coaching is a way in which one person (the coach) enhances the working performance of another (the protégé) regardless of the level of job skill that the two have and regardless of the hierarchical relationship between them.

IV.2 Essential qualities in a coaching relationship are for there to be mutual trust and respect between the parties.

IV.3 Required qualities of a coach are: expertise in the job of the protégé, skilled listening, skill in evaluating information, an ability to challenge and a willingness to provide practical help.

IV.4 Coaching takes place that is pre-, looking forward and motivating, or post-, looking back to embed lessons learnt.

GENERAL DISCUSSION TOPIC

1 How would you rank (from 1 to 3) the relative importance of the coach being (a) expert in the protégé's job, (b) older than the protégé and (c) the direct line manager?

THEORY INTO PRACTICE

Sometimes a friend or relative will introduce a topic of conversation that is an implicit seeking of help in dealing with a problem, although it may be phrased in a different way. Ask yourself the question, 'Does the person just want to express exasperation or annoyance in order "to get it out"?' If you think the person will find a solution having got it out, then you need do little apart from nodding and listening sympathetically. If, however, your assessment is of someone still unsure of what to do, and if you think you have the right sort of relationship with your friend, then try a coaching approach, as outlined in the previous pages.

FURTHER READING

Schein, E.H. (1990) *Career Anchors*. San Diego, CA: University Associates.

Schein, E.H. (2004) *Organizational Culture and Leadership*, 3rd edn. New York: Wiley.
The 1990 book by Ed Schein is now not easy to obtain, although it contains the most thorough explanation of the career anchor concept. The 2004 third edition of his classic text contains a perfectly adequate treatment of the topic.

Hawkins, P. and Schwenk, G. (2006) *Coaching Supervision: Maximising the potential of coaching, a change agenda*. London: CIPD.

Jarvis, J. and Lane, D. (2006) *The Case for Coaching: Making evidence-based decisions on coaching*. London: CIPD.
Both these publications include solid research evidence to produce a thorough assessment of current practice, including examples of good practice and guidelines for managers.

REFERENCES

Caplan, J. (2003) *Coaching for the Future*. London: CIPD.
Carroll, S. and Gillen, D. (2001) 'Exploring the teaching function of the managerial role', *Journal of Management Development*, Vol. 21, No. 5, pp. 330–42.
Clutterbuck, D. and Gover, S. (2004) *The Effective Coach Manual*. Burnham: Clutterbuck Associates.
Clutterbuck, D. and Wynne, B. (1994) 'Mentoring and coaching', in A. Mumford (ed.), *Handbook of Management Development*, 4th edn. Epping: Gower.
Schein, E.H. (2004) *Organizational Culture and Leadership*, 3rd edn. New York: Wiley.

V Presentation

The skill of presentation is required to inform and explain. HR people constantly have to make presentations on such matters as explaining a change of policy, clarifying details of new procedures and HR systems or setting out the implications of a change of employment legislation. There may be presentations on career prospects in the business at careers conventions, pitching to a senior management group for an improvement in the budget, 'selling' the advantages of a new performance-related pay scheme, or explaining to a small group of job applicants the details of the post for which they have applied.

Objectives

As with almost every aspect of management, the starting point is the objective. What are you aiming to achieve? What do you want the listeners to do, to think or to feel? Note that the question is not 'What do you want to say?'. The objective is in the response of the listeners. That starting point begins the whole process with a focus on results and pay-off, turning attention away from ego. It also determines tone. If your objective is to inform, you will emphasise facts. If you aim to persuade, you will try to appeal to emotion as well as to reason.

The material

What is to be said or, more accurately, what should members of the audience take away having understood and remembered?

Organise your material with an introduction that previews, a body that develops, and a conclusion that reviews. When you organise the body of your presentation, start with the theme, a planning device that holds together the various ideas you want to discuss. If the theme of your presentation is informative, then the body should provide facts. If the theme is persuasive, the body should develop persuasive arguments. (Fandt 1994: 159)

In the introduction the speaker establishes rapport with the audience. Apart from gaining their attention, include here an answer to the unspoken questions: 'Is it going to be worth our while listening? Is this person worth listening to?'. The person worth listening to is someone who looks at the audience and looks friendly, knowledgeable and, above all, enthusiastic. A useful format for the introduction is to explain what the members of the audience will know or be able to do at the end. It is also helpful to sketch out the framework of what is to come, so that people can follow it more readily. But stick to what you promise. If you say there are going to be five points, the audience will listen for five to make sure that they have not missed one.

Having secured the attention of the listeners, you now have them waiting not just for what you say next, but with a framework in their heads of what they will hear, so they will be able to locate their understanding within that framework. The main body of the presentation is the message that is to be conveyed, the development of the argument and the buildup of what it is that the audience should take away having understood and remembered.

The main body needs effective organisation. This not only helps listeners to maintain attention, but also disciplines the speaker to avoid rambling, distracting irrelevance or forgetting. The most common methods are:

- *Chronological sequence*, dealing with issues by taking the audience through a series of events. A presentation to an employment tribunal often follows this pattern.

- *Known to unknown, or simple to complex*, where the speaker starts with a brief review of what the audience already know or can easily understand and then develops to what they do not yet know or cannot yet understand. The logic of this method is to ground the audience in something they can handle so that they can make sense of the unfamiliar. This is the standard method of organising teaching sessions.

- *Problem to solution*, which is almost the exact opposite of simple to complex. A problem is presented and a solution follows. The audience are again grounded, but this time grounded in an anxiety that the speaker is about to relieve.

- *Comparison*, a method which compares one account with another. Selling usually follows this path, as the new is compared with the old.

Whatever the method of organising the material, the main body always contains a number of key thoughts or ideas. This is what the speaker is trying to plant in the minds of the audience: not just facts, which are inert, but the ideas which facts may well illustrate and clarify. The idea that inflation is dangerously high is only illustrated by the fact that it is at a particular figure in a particular month.

The ideas in a presentation can be helpfully linked together by a device that will help the audience to remember them and to grasp their interdependence. One method is to enshrine the ideas in a story. If the story is recalled, the thoughts are recalled with it, as they are integral to the structure. Another method is to use key words to identify the points that are being made, especially if they have an alliterative or mnemonic feature, such as 'People Produce Prosperity'. In a lecture it is common to provide a framework for ideas by using a drawing or system model to show the interconnection of points.

Facts, by giving impact, keep together the framework of ideas that the speaker has assembled. They clarify and give dimension to what is being said. The danger is to use too many, so that the audience are overwhelmed by facts and figures which begin to bemuse them. If the presentation is to be accompanied by a handout, facts may be usefully contained in that, so that they can be referred to later, without the audience having to remember them.

Humour is the most dangerous of all aids. If the audience laugh at a funny story, the speaker will be encouraged and may feel under less tension, but how tempting to try again and end up 'playing for laughs'. Laughter is a most seductive human reaction, but too many laughs are even more dangerous than too many facts. What will the audience remember: the joke, or what the joke was intended to illustrate? Attempted humour is also dangerous for the ineffective comedian. If you tell what you think is a funny story and no one laughs, you have made a fool of yourself (at least in your own eyes) and risk floundering.

Very few people speak effectively without notes. Although there is a tendency to marvel at those who can, relying solely on memory risks missing something out, getting a fact wrong or drying up completely. Notes follow the pattern of organisation you have established, providing discipline and limiting the tendency to ramble. It is both irritating and unhelpful for an audience to cope with a speaker wandering off down a blind alley. When an amusing anecdote pops up in your brain, it can be almost irresistible to share it.

There are two basic kinds of notes: headlines or a script. Headlines are probably the most common, with main points underlined and facts listed beneath. Sometimes there will also be a marginal note about an anecdote or other type of illustration. The alternative, the script, enables the speaker to try out the exact wording, phrases and pauses to achieve the greatest effect. The script will benefit from some marking or arrangement that will help you to find your place again as your eyes constantly flick from the page to the audience and back again. This can be underlining or using a highlighter. When using a script it is important not to make the reading too obvious. Head down, with no eye contact and little light and shade, is a sure-fire way of turning off the attention of the audience. Public figures increasingly use electronic prompters which project the script progressively onto a glass screen some way in front of the speaker. By this means the script can be spoken with little break in eye contact with the audience. This will be too ambitious for most HR people, but the words should **always** be *spoken* rather than *read*.

There are many variations of these basic methods of organising the material, so that one approach is to use varying line length, while another is to use rows of dots to indicate pause or emphasis. Some people like to have their notes on small cards, so that they are unobtrusive, but this is difficult if the notes are more than headlines. Standard A4 paper should present no problem, if the notes are not stapled, are well laid out and can be handled discreetly. Never forget to number the pages or cards, as the next time you speak they may slip off your lap moments before you are due to begin, and they do not land on the floor in the same order that they were on your lap.

Most presentations benefit from using visual aids. You may use a model, a sample or even a person ('Here is our trainee of the month'), but mostly you will use visual images. Blackboards still exist and whiteboards are fairly common. Flip charts and overhead projector acetates are widely used, and especially images from a computer, projected onto a screen, usually using a PowerPoint package. This is so good that it can be dangerous because of its relative sophistication technically. It has to be operated by someone who knows what they are doing and has confidence in being able to manage the computer rather than being managed by it. Every reader will have had experience of a presenter being baffled by a technical glitch that held up the presentation and knocked the presenter's confidence sideways. If the computer is being managed by someone other than the presenter, there is the potential difficulty of presenter and operator not always being coordinated.

WINDOW ON PRACTICE

In 2006 a newly appointed vice chancellor of a UK university was giving his first major address to a large audience, using a PowerPoint presentation which he controlled with a remote, although technical staff at the side of the hall had overall control. At one point he went back to a previous page, then went forward to the wrong page without realising it. Technical staff corrected the mistake at the same time as he noticed it. He then corrected it without realising they had spotted it. Confusion and uncertainty persisted for several minutes. At the subsequent lunch the muddle was discussed more extensively than the content of the address.

The rationale for visual aids is that we remember what we see for longer than we remember what we are told, and we can sometimes understand what we see better than we can understand what we hear. Too much displayed material can obscure rather than illuminate what is being said. Television news provides a good example of how much can be used. The dominant theme is always the talking head with frequently intercut pieces of film. Very seldom do words appear on the screen and then usually as extracts from a speech or report, where a short sentence or passage is regarded as being especially meaningful. The other situation in which words and numbers appear is when facts are needed to illustrate an idea, so that ideas such as football scores or a change in the level of inflation almost always show the figures to clarify and illustrate. Seldom, however, will more than two or three numbers be displayed at the same time. Speakers need to remember the size of what they are displaying as well as its complexity. Material has to be big enough for people to read and simple enough for them to follow. Material also has to be timed to coincide with what is being said.

PowerPoint is a most seductive toy for the presenter. The box of tricks is enormous and too many people give a show, with clever figures dancing across the screen as well as other distractions. Always remember what the purpose of the presentation is; clever or spectacular forms of display can become what people remember rather than the message that is to be conveyed.

SUMMARY PROPOSITIONS

V.1 Presentation is the main method used to convey information and understanding to a group of listeners.

V.2 Alternative methods of constructing a presentation are (a) chronological sequence, (b) known to unknown or simple to complex, (c) problem to solution, (d) comparison.

V.3 A presentation is spoken, not read. Visual aids illustrate but do not distract.

GENERAL DISCUSSION TOPICS

1 There is an old saying, 'What I hear I forget, what I see I can understand and what I do I know.' What is the relevance of this to presentation?

2 Why do students attend lectures where information is presented to them, rather than reading that information presented in a book?

THEORY INTO PRACTICE

1 The next time you attend a lecture or presentation, study the arrangement of the room and note the changes you would make if you were the speaker.

2 Borrow from the library a book or CD containing speeches by an effective orator, such as Winston Churchill, Martin Luther King or Barack Obama, and make notes of the plan of the material.

3 Prepare a five-minute speech on one of:

   (a) Walking

   (b) Gardening

   (c) Your favourite sport or hobby.

4 After careful preparation deliver the speech in an empty room and record it. Play it back several times, making critical notes of energy level, voice, pace, timing, etc., following the points in the chapter, then deliver the speech again, with recording, and consider these points:

   (a) How was it better?

   (b) In what ways was it not so good?

   (c) What have you learnt about how you speak?

   (d) What can you still improve?

FURTHER READING

Fandt, P.M. (1994) *Management Skills: Practice and experience*. St Paul, MN: West Publishing.

Quinn, R.E., Faerman, S.R., Thompson, M.P. and McGrath, M.R. (2002) *Becoming a Master Manager*. New York: Wiley.
Material on management skills is everywhere, but in this context the above works are especially helpful.

Yate, M. and Sander, P. (2003) *The Ultimate Business Presentations Book*. London: Kogan Page.
Presentation is also preached very widely. This excellent text from the USA covers the ground thoroughly and readably.

REFERENCE

Fandt, P.M. (1994) *Management Skills: Practice and experience*. St Paul, MN: West Publishing.

VI Mediation

Mediation is resolving a disagreement, a misunderstanding or the breakdown of a relationship between two parties with the assistance of a third, the third party acting as honest broker. Sometimes it is a straight alternative to negotiation in industrial relations. The parties are sufficiently estranged that they will not be able to resolve their difficulties on their own, so a mediator is asked to chair joint meetings, partly to clarify the differences and partly to suggest ways forward. This is slightly different from arbitration, which is where the arbitrator proposes a solution rather than a way for the parties to move forward to find their own.

Similar in process, but different in nature, are disagreement and relationship breakdown between individuals, most dramatically seen in divorce but also to be found in employment situations. If colleagues need to work closely together but have a row or begin to suspect the others' motives, then mediation may be helpful.

WINDOW ON PRACTICE

Since the head designer had left suddenly, Barry had been asked to stand in pending a permanent appointment being made. Interviews were held among internal applicants, including Barry, who was surprised and bitterly disappointed when Julia was appointed head designer. As Barry put it to the HR Manager, 'a relative newcomer of 28 with less experience and far too big for her boots'. When Julia had been offered the job she had said, 'Barry won't like it, but it really would be a good idea if he moved on. He's good at the detail, but very old-fashioned.' The divisional director believed Barry was essential to the smooth running of the department and asked the HR manager to mediate. The HR manager followed the general plan described below.

The format outlined here will sound more formal and rigid than that in most situations in normal working life. Often mediation will occur spontaneously or the need will come at a very difficult time when two people have just had a flaming row and the mediator is inadvertently thrust into a mediator role. Sometimes it will be more like the Barry/Julia situation, but setting it out in this way illustrates a pattern which usually works, despite the need to modify it to suit specific situations.

Mediator briefing

The mediator finds out as much as possible about the problem beforehand, for example: Who has said what? To whom? What are the real points of contention? This will mainly be hearsay.

Introductory remarks

The mediator will wait until both parties are present and then make introductions. The physical setting will be controlled so that no party feels threatened. The mediator then gives an opening statement that outlines the role of the participants and demonstrates the mediator's neutrality. Some mediators will make comments about what they see as the issue and confirm the case data if briefs have been pre-submitted. Next, the mediator defines protocol and sets the timeframe for the process. Then the mediator will briefly recap what it is that he or she has heard as the issues.

The opening statement during the introductory remarks will set out the ground-rules for the mediation. These are what help the mediation move along smoothly. The mediator will usually ask that if lawyers are present, they can confer, but the clients should speak for themselves. Parties should not interrupt each other; the mediator will give each party the opportunity to share fully their side of the story.

Statement of the problem by the parties

After the opening statement, the mediator will give each side the opportunity to tell their story uninterrupted. Most often, the person who requested the mediation session will go first. The statement is not necessarily a recital of the facts, but it is to give the parties an opportunity to frame issues in their own minds, and to give the mediator more information on the emotional state of each party. The rationale behind the statement of the problem is not a search for the truth; it is just a way to help solve the problem.

Information gathering

The mediator will ask the parties open-ended questions to get to the emotional undercurrents. The mediator may repeat key ideas back to the parties, and will summarise often. This helps the mediator build rapport between the parties, especially when a facilitative style is used.

Problem identification

This might also be part of other segments. The mediator tries to find common goals between the parties while figuring out which issues are going to be able to settle or those that will settle first.

Bargaining and generating options/reaching an agreement

Once the participants are committed to achieving a settlement, the mediator will begin a brainstorming session to explore potential solutions. This can lead to a final agreement, which diffuses the conflict and provides a new basis for future relations.

The mediator may decide to hold private sessions with both parties in order to move things along. The goal is to find some common ground by exploring lots of options, and to bring about possible solutions for the parties to think about. The parties can also entertain alternative solutions to their problems without committing themselves to offer the solutions as concessions.

SUMMARY PROPOSITIONS

VI.1 Mediation is trying to resolve a damaging disagreement between colleagues by the intervention of a third person, whose neutrality is accepted by the parties.

VI.2 The intervention is to find a way forward that enables the parties to find their own solution. It is different from arbitration, where the arbitrator has the power to impose a solution.

GENERAL DISCUSSION TOPICS

1 Select a news report about a disagreement between parties, about which people in the group have at least a superficial knowledge. What would be a fruitful approach to settlement for a mediator to adopt?

2 Think of a situation in your own life where you tried to help settle an argument by acting as honest broker. What would you now do differently?

FURTHER READING

Whatling, T. (2012) *Mediation Skills and Strategies*. London: Jessica Kingsley.
This is particularly suitable for mediation between individuals, with examples drawn from a variety of situations.

Lewis, C. (2012) *Workplace Mediation and Managing Conflict at Work*. London: Globis.
This is similar, but with more discussion about collective issues; written by a consultant.

VII The disciplinary or grievance interview

If the appraisal interview is the hardest aspect of management for any manager to undertake, disciplinary interviewing is certainly the least popular: talking to people when things have gone wrong and have to be sorted out. At some point this involves a meeting between a dissatisfied manager and an employee who is seen as the cause of that dissatisfaction, or between a dissatisfied employee and a manager representing the employing organisation that is seen as the cause of the dissatisfaction. Procedures can do no more than force meetings to take place: it is the meetings themselves that produce answers. Material here assumes a familiarity with that on discipline and grievance presented earlier (see Chapter 20).

Our aim here is to formulate an approach to the interview that achieves an adjustment in attitude, with the changed attitude being confirmed by subsequent experience. Either the manager believes that the employee's subsequent working behaviour will be satisfactory, or the employee believes that his or her subsequent experience in employment will be satisfactory. The conflict of interest between the parties is resolved and the interview only succeeds when there is that confirmation.

The nature of grievance and disciplinary interviewing

Many grievance or discipline interviews are simple, that is giving information, explaining work requirements and delivering rebukes, but from time to time every manager will need to use a problem-solving approach, involving sympathy, perception, empathy and the essential further feature that some managers provide only with reluctance: time. The method is analytical and constructive, not only for the interviews built into the grievance and discipline procedure, but also for interviews that avoid the rigid formality of procedure. Such interviews are one of the means towards self-discipline and autonomy of employees, reducing the need for supervision. The sequence we advocate has discipline and grievance intertwined for much of the process but diverging in the interview itself (see Figure VII.1).

As mentioned earlier (see Chapter 20), grievance may be expressed only in manifest form, requiring interviewing to understand its latent content so that appropriate action is taken to remove the underlying dissatisfaction. Discipline problems will have underlying reasons for the unsatisfactory behaviour which need to be discovered before solutions to the problems can be found.

The discipline and grievance sequence

Preparation

Check the procedural position to ensure that the impending interview is appropriate. In a grievance situation, for instance, is the employee pre-empting the procedure by taking the matter to the wrong person or to the wrong point in the procedure? This is most common when the front-line supervisor is being bypassed, either because the employee or the representative feels that it would be a waste of time, or perhaps because

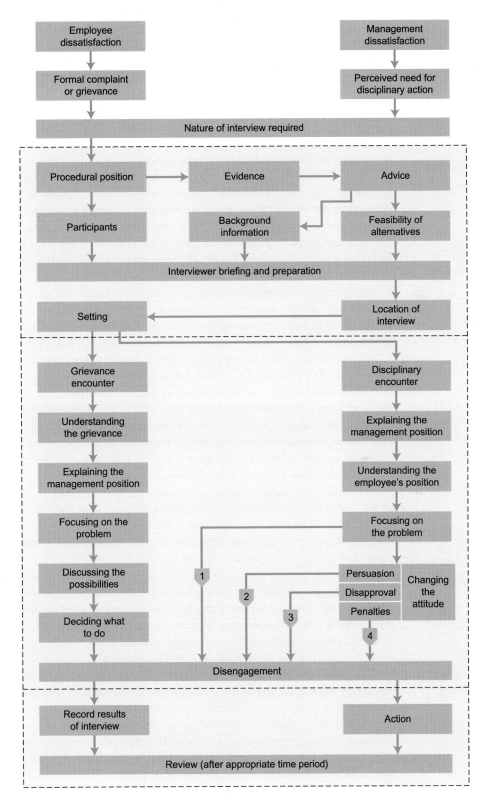

Figure VII.1
The grievance and disciplinary interviews

the supervisor is unsure of the appropriate action and is conniving at the side-stepping of the procedure.

In disciplinary matters even more care is needed about the procedural step, as the likelihood of penalties may already have been set up by warnings, thus reducing the scope for doing anything else in the impending interview apart from imposing a further penalty. In most cases interviews precede procedure, so the parties to the interview are less constrained by procedural rules. The manager will be at pains to explain that the interview is informal and without procedural implications. Alternatively the interview may be one where the likelihood of a move into procedure is so remote that the manager will be at pains to avoid any such reference, for fear of the complainant taking fright.

Who will be there? Here there are similar procedural considerations. In procedure there is the likelihood of employee representation; out of procedure that is less likely, even though the employee may feel anxious and threatened without it. If the manager is accompanied in the interview, the employee may feel even more insecure, and it is doubtful how much can be achieved informally unless the employee feels reasonably secure and able to speak frankly.

What are the facts that the interviewer needs to know? In grievance it will be the subject of the grievance and how it has arisen. This type of information will have been filtered through the management hierarchy and perhaps modified in the process, so it needs careful consideration and any additional background information collected.

Disciplinary interviews always start at the behest of the management so the manager will again collect evidence and consider how it may have been interpreted by intermediaries. This will include some basic details about the interviewee, but mainly information about why the working performance is unsatisfactory. Too often this information exists only in opinions that have been offered and prejudices that are held. This provides a poor basis for a constructive interview, so the manager needs to ferret out details, with as much factual corroboration as possible.

It is almost inevitable that the interviewee will start defensively, expecting to be blamed for something and therefore ready to refute any allegations, probably deflecting blame elsewhere. The manager needs to be prepared to deal with the reaction as well as with facts that have been collected. Unless the interview is at an early, informal stage, the manager also needs to know about earlier warnings, cautions or penalties that have been invoked.

For both types of interview more general information is required, not just the facts of the particular grievance or disciplinary situation, but knowledge to give a general understanding of the working arrangements and relationships. Other relevant data may be the employee's length of service, type of training, previous experience and so forth.

Most managers will benefit from advice before starting, particularly for anyone who is in procedure to check the position before starting, as management ability to sustain any action will largely depend on maintaining consistency with what the management has done with other employees previously. The manager may also have certain ideas of what could be done in terms of retraining, transfer or assistance with a domestic problem, and needs to verify the feasibility of such actions before broaching them.

Where is the interview to take place? However trivial this question may seem, it is included, because there may be an advantage in choosing an unusually informal situation, or an unusually formal location, according to the manager's assessment. A discussion over a pie and a pint in the local pub may be a more appropriate setting for some approaches to grievance and disciplinary problems, although they are seldom appropriate if the matter has reached procedure. Also employees frequently mistrust such settings, feeling that they are being manipulated or that the discussion 'does not count' because it is out of hours or off limits. If, however, one is trying to avoid procedural overtones, this can be a way of doing it.

Unusual formality can be appropriate in the later stages of procedure, especially in disciplinary matters, when proceedings take on a strongly judicial air. An employee is not likely to take seriously a final warning prior to probable dismissal if it is delivered over a pint in a pub. The large, impressive offices of senior managers can provide appropriate settings for the final stages of procedure.

ACTIVITY VII.1

What incidents have you experienced or heard about where the location of the interview was clearly unsuitable for the nature of the encounter?

The grievance interview

First clarify what the grievance is; a simple way of doing this is to state the *subject* of the grievance and get confirmation from the employee that it is correct. This is important because the manager will probably have a different perspective on the affair from the employee, particularly if it has got beyond the preliminary stage. A supervisor may report to a superior that Mr X has a grievance and 'will not take instructions from me', but when the interview begins Mr X may state his grievance as being that he is unwilling to work on Saturday mornings. In other situations it might be the other way round, with the supervisor reporting that Mr X will not work Saturday mornings and Mr X saying in the interview that he finds the style of his supervisor objectionable. Even where there is no such confusion, an opening statement and confirmation of the subject demonstrate that the two parties are talking about the same thing.

The manager then invites the employee to state the case, explaining the nature and reasons for the dissatisfaction. This enables the employee to explain, citing examples, providing further information and saying not just 'what' but also 'why'. Seldom will this be done well. The presentation of a case is not an easy task for the inexperienced, and few aggrieved employees are experienced at making a case of this type. Furthermore, there is the inhibition of questioning the wisdom of those in power and some apprehension about the outcome. The manager will need to ask questions in order to fill in any gaps and to clarify some points that were obscure in the first telling. It is better to have an episode of questioning after the case has been made, rather than to interrupt on each point that is difficult. Interruptions make a poorly argued case even more difficult to sustain. There may, however, be disguised pleas for assistance providing good opportunities for questioning to clarify: 'I'm not very good with words, but do you see what I'm getting at?', 'Do you see what I mean?' or 'Am I making myself clear?'. Among the strategies the manager needs at this stage could be the method of *reflection* that was mentioned briefly in our introduction to face-to-face skills.

After all the necessary clarification the manager restates the employee's grievance, and gives an outline of the case that has been presented, asking the employee to agree with the summary or to correct it. This is confirming and showing an understanding of the grievance and why it has been brought.

This phase of the interview can be summarised as follows:

Manager	Employee
1 States subject of grievance	
	2 Agrees with statement
	3 States case
4 Questions for clarification	
5 Restates grievance	
	6 Agrees or corrects

- **The grievance is now understood**

The next phase is to set out the management position on the grievance. This is not the action *to be taken* but the action that *has been taken*, with the reasons for the action. This may include an explanation of company policy, safety rules, previous grievances, supervisory problems, administrative methods and anything else which is needed to make clear why the management position has been what it has been. The manager will then invite the employee to question and comment on the management position and its justifications for them to be understood, even if they are not accepted.

- **The management position is now understood**

Setting out the two opposed positions will reveal a deal of common ground, agreement on some things, though disagreement on others. The points on which they agree can be ignored, as the need now is to find the outer limits.

- **Points of disagreement are now in focus**

As a preliminary to taking action in the matter under discussion, various possibilities can be put up for consideration. It is logical that the employee's suggestions are put first. Probably this has already been done either explicitly or implicitly in the development of the case. If, however, specific suggestions are invited at this stage they may be different ones, as the aggrieved employee now understands the management position and is seeing the whole matter clearly following the focusing that has just taken place. Then the manager can put forward alternatives or modifications, and these may include, or be limited to, the suggestion that the grievance is mischievous and unfounded so that no action should be taken. Nevertheless, in most cases there will be some scope for accommodation even if it is quite different from the employee's expectation. Once the alternative suggestions for action are set out, there is time for the advantages and disadvantages of both sets to be discussed.

- **Alternatives have now been considered**

The action is to be taken by the manager alone; it is not a joint decision even though the manager will look for a decision that all parties find acceptable. In bringing a grievance the employee is challenging a management decision and that decision will now be confirmed or it will be modified, but it remains a management decision.

Before making the decision the manager may deploy a range of behaviours to ensure that the decision is correct. There may be an adjournment for a while to seek further advice or to give the employee time to reflect further, but the manager has to decide and then explain the decision, not simply deciding and announcing, but supporting the decision with explanation and justification in the same way that the employee developed the case for the grievance at the beginning. There may be questions from the employee, and the employee may want time to think, but eventually the management decision will have to be accepted, unless there is some further procedural step available.

- **Management action is now clear and understood**

The disciplinary interview

Discipline arises from management dissatisfaction rather than employee dissatisfaction, so the opening move is a statement of what the dissatisfaction is, dealing with the *facts* of the situation rather than managerial feelings of outrage about them. This shows that the manager sees the interview as a way of dealing with a problem of the working situation and not (at least not yet) as a way of dealing with a malicious or indolent employee. If an employee has been persistently late for a week, it would be unwise for a manager to open the disciplinary interview by saying 'Your lateness this week has been deplorable', as the reason might turn out to be that the employee has a seriously ill child needing constant attendance through the night. Then the manager would be embarrassed and the potential for a constructive settlement of the matter jeopardised. An opening factual statement of the problem, 'You have been at least twenty minutes late each day this week', does not prejudge the reasons and is reasonably precise about the scale of the problem. It also circumscribes management dissatisfaction by implying that there is no other cause for dissatisfaction; if there is, it should be mentioned.

Now the manager asks the employee to say what the reasons for the problem are, perhaps also asking for comments on the seriousness of the problem itself, which the employee may regard as trivial but the manager regards as serious. Getting the employee's reaction is usually straightforward, but the manager needs to be prepared for one of two difficulties. Either there may be a need to probe because the employee is reluctant to open up, or there may be angry defiance. Disciplinary situations are at least disconcerting for employees and frequently very worrying, surrounded by feelings of hostility and mistrust, so it is to be expected that some ill feeling will be pent up and waiting for the opportunity to be vented.

First possible move to disengagement

If the employee sees something of the management view of the problem and if the manager understands the reasons for the problem, the next step is to seek a solution. It is as likely to be solved by management action as by employee action. If the problem is lateness, one solution would be for the employee to catch an earlier bus, but another might be for the management to alter the working shift to which the employee is assigned. If the employee is disobeying orders, one solution would be to start obeying them, but another might be for the employee to be moved to a different job where orders are received from someone else. Some people regard such thinking as unreasonable, as the contract of employment places obligations on individual employees that they should meet despite personal inconvenience. However, the point is not how people *should* behave, but how they do. Can the contract of employment be enforced on an unwilling employee? Not if one is seeking such attitudes as enthusiasm and cooperation, or behaviour such as diligence and carefulness. The disenchanted employee can always meet the bare letter rather than the spirit of the contract.

Many disciplinary problems require some action from both parties, some require action by the employee only and a small proportion require management action only. The problem-solving session may quickly produce the possibility for further action and open up the possibility of closing the interview.

This simple, logical approach outlined so far may not be enough, due to the unwillingness of employees to respond to disciplinary expectations. They may not want to be punctual or to do as they are instructed, or whatever the particular problem is. There is now a test of the power behind management authority. Three further steps can be taken, one after the other, although there will be occasions when it is necessary to move directly to considering penalties.

Second possible move to disengagement: persuasion

A first strategy is to demonstrate to employees that they will not achieve what they want, if their behaviour does not change:

> You won't keep your earnings up if you don't meet targets.
> It will be difficult to get your appointment confirmed when the probationary period is over if . . .

By such means employees may see the advantages of changing their attitude and behaviour. If convinced, there is a strong incentive for them to alter, because they believe it to be in their own interests.

Third possible move to disengagement: disapproval

Another strategy is to suggest that continuing the behaviour will displease those whose goodwill the employee wishes to keep:

> The Management Development Panel are rather disappointed . . .
> Some of the other people in the department feel that you are not pulling your weight.

A manager using this method needs to be sure that what is said is both true and relevant. Also the manager may be seen as shirking the issue, so it may be appropriate to use a version of 'I think this is deplorable and expect you to do better'.

We asked for a restraint from judgement in the early stages of the interview, until the nature of the problem is clear. The time for judgement has now come, with the proper deployment of the rebuke or the caution.

Fourth possible move to disengagement: penalties

When all else fails or is clearly inappropriate, as with serious offences about which there is no doubt, penalties have to be invoked. Usually the first penalty will be a formal warning as a preliminary to possible dismissal. In serious situations summary dismissal is both appropriate and possible within the legal framework.

Disengagement

After one of the four possibilities listed we come to a stage that is common to both grievance and discipline as a way of describing the process, although the nature of disengagement will obviously differ. The manager now needs to think of the working situation that will follow. In a grievance situation can the employee now accept the decision that has been made? Are there faces to be saved or reputations to be restored? What administrative action is to be taken? In closing a disciplinary interview, the manager will aim for the flavour of disengagement to be as positive as possible so that all concerned put the disciplinary problem behind them. Where the outcome of the interview is to impose or confirm a dismissal, then the manager will be exclusively concerned with the fairness and accuracy with which it is done, so that the possibility of tribunal hearings is reduced, if not prevented. It can never be appropriate to close an interview of either type leaving the employee humbled and demoralised.

WINDOW ON PRACTICE

The American Eric Harvey (1987) reduced what he calls 'positive discipline' to three simple steps:

1 Warn the employee orally.

2 Warn the employee in writing.

3 If steps 1 and 2 fail to resolve the problem, give the employee a day off, with pay.

A similar, very positive, approach was outlined in a seminal paper by Huberman in 1967.

SUMMARY PROPOSITIONS

VII.1 Grievance and disciplinary interviews are central to the process of sorting things out when there is a management/employee problem, but most managers dislike such interviews intensely.

VII.2 The steps in conducting a grievance interview are first to understand the nature of the grievance, to explain the management position, to focus on the problem, to discuss possibilities and then to decide what to do.

VII.3 The disciplinary interview starts the other way around, first explaining the management position, then understanding the employee's position and focusing on the problem. If that does not produce a satisfactory result, the manager may have to move through three more steps: persuasion, showing disapproval or invoking penalties.

GENERAL DISCUSSION TOPICS

1 Do individual grievance and disciplinary procedures weaken trade union organisation in a workplace by enabling the management to deal with employees individually rather than having to face the potential strength of collective action and representation?

2 In 1791 Edmund Burke, a British statesman, said, 'He that wrestles with us strengthens our nerves, and sharpens our skill. Our antagonist is our helper.' Do trade union officials help HR managers by strengthening their nerves and sharpening their skill?

3 How would your boss establish a gap between your actual performance and what is expected of you?

4 Are those lowest in the organisational hierarchy accused of poor performance because it is easier to establish a gap that is clearly the responsibility of the person being accused?

THEORY INTO PRACTICE

1 In the managerial folklore about discipline there is a type of stereotypically problematic employee which one consultant described as the professional weeper. In other words, some people respond to any dissatisfaction being pointed out by an acceptance that they never have been any good at anything or that what is expected is in some way impossible for them to achieve and appeal to the manager for enough compassion to let them just carry on as before, but trying really hard. A second stereotype is the counter-attacker who either flatly denies the allegation or produces vigorous counter-arguments to undermine the management's dissatisfaction. The idea that the counter-attacker actually has a problem that needs to be dealt with is simply not accepted.

How would you deal with both of these stereotypes?

2 Two different people have complained that the chairs they have are bad for their backs, so could they have better chairs? The supervisor, Barry Jones, who has a better chair, says that they must just get on with it. The matter has been referred to you. You suspect that part of Barry's problem is that he regards his chair as a tangible sign of his status. You also know that one of those complaining (Margaret) does have a bad back and has returned to work after childbirth slightly earlier than her doctor recommended. Apart from the other person who complained (John), everyone else in the office is happy with their chairs.

Margaret has still two weeks of unexpired maternity leave so you suggest that she should take those weeks off and then try again. She refuses, claiming that she cannot afford to be 'out of the loop' for any longer and that it is reasonable for her to have a chair 'like that idle slob Barry'.

How would you deal with (a) her request, (b) Barry and (c) John?

FURTHER READING

Hook, C.M., Rollinson, D.J., Foot, M. and Handley, J. (1996) 'Supervisor and manager styles in handling discipline and grievance', *Personnel Review*, Vol. 25, No. 3, pp. 20–34.
These studies provide further background and discussion of the place of interviewing in employment relations processes.

Borg, J. (2004) *Persuasion: The art of influencing people*. Harlow: Pearson Education.
This is a rather different book, popular in style but with solid content on this particular aspect of discipline and grievance handling.

The further reading and references for discipline and grievance (as in Chapter 20) are also relevant here.

REFERENCES

Harvey, E.L. (1987) 'Discipline versus punishment', *Management Review*, March, pp. 25–9.
Huberman, J.C. (1967) 'Discipline without punishment', *Harvard Business Review*, May, pp. 62–8.

VIII Report writing

Reports are written for both reading and action by the reader. What the writer wants to say is not as important as what the reader needs to know and then do. Action by the reader is the constant objective of the writer. Reports should be as brief as possible, but proposed action has to be thoroughly justified.

Content of report

Often the report has an appended *executive summary*. Most readers do not really want to read your report at all; what they want is a quick summary of the main points. This may annoy you as you have spent sleepless hours perfecting your arguments and analysing your data, but the executive summary may lead the reader to refer to your main report for further explanation of recommendations or for the justification of a puzzling conclusion. It is, of course, a summary of the report that you have already written, not the other way round. You do not write some brief notes in summary and then expand them with more information for the full report. The summary requires thorough analysis and succinct explanation, with clear references to the relevant sections and page numbers of the full report.

Appendices may be used to remove detailed data from the report which are illustrative of points made in the report, but not essential to understanding. Reference to the extra information in an appendix may help to convince a reader of an argument that is presented in the report with enough evidence to convince most readers, but not enough to persuade the sceptical.

Some reports may require a note of *sources*, if some of the readers may need to refer to published material which you have relied on. You may not need full bibliographical details, but always sufficient information for the reader to locate the material you have used.

Writing procedure

Before the writing begins you need to *assemble and organise your material*. Chucking a pile of papers on the back seat of your car may be a form of assembling, but certainly not organising. A simple method is to divide the papers into several piles of different categories like raw data, interview responses, external comparisons, suggestions, implications and probably not needed. Leaving out the 'probably not needed' for the time being, the next stage is to review the content of each pile for three reasons. First, you are recalling everything and beginning to see where you want to go. Second, you are probably moving some more material to that which is probably not needed. Third, as you begin to see where you want to go, you see what material you need to add: checks on the Internet, visits to the library, telephone calls, finding *and marking* pages where you may need to refer to that book on the shelf behind you. If you now have a clear idea of what you want to achieve with your report, and can see the logical way of getting there, you can proceed to the next stage. If not you may find the technique of mind-mapping helpful (Buzan 2009).

Structure

You now need a *framework* to give a logical sequence to the writing and avoid risks of duplication, as well as to ensure that you present material early in the report that will be needed to justify points made later. Ways of doing this vary. One popular writer of fiction, Harold Robbins, worked with just a diagram above his typewriter showing how each of his characters was connected. An equally popular writer of much better fiction, John Grisham, works out a comprehensive and detailed structure for each book before he starts writing. You have to employ the method that works for you. The framework comes from analysing the message that is to be sent in terms of the action expected and then subdividing the components of that message to be logically grouped. The framework may be modified during the writing until the writer is convinced that it is satisfactory.

You are likely to need a structure that has the following features:

Terms of reference

Who commissioned the report

Who has written it

Sources/methods used

A list of acronyms

Executive summary at front (as well as normal summary at end)

Contents list

Recommendations

Date

This is not necessarily the order in which they should appear, as you will want to draw the reader into the body of the report as soon as possible.

The logical grouping of the material takes the form of *sections*, each dealing with a distinct aspect of the report material. This arrangement emphasises the logic of the way that the material is grouped, but it is also part of the communication to the reader, because the sections have titles, like headlines in a newspaper, which sum up what the section contains. Titles should not tease or muddle the reader. 'Which way now?', for example, is an unhelpful title as it poses a question without giving any clue to the answer.

The *paragraph* is a unit of thought in the writing, dealing with a single topic or idea, and good paragraphing will ensure the material is read. It also reassures the reader that there will be occasional breathing spaces rather than a long solid block of text to be ploughed through.

The appropriate length of paragraph varies with the material being written. Textbooks usually average 100–200 words, popular novels 60–75 and popular newspapers 30–40. Short paragraphs are easier for the reader, but reports will sometimes require detailed argument involving greater length. It is wise to keep the average under 120, if possible.

The *sentence* is the bit of writing between full stops, which makes sense and usually has a subject and a verb. The main difficulties in writing sentences are that either they are too long or they set up expectations that are not realised. Writing sentences that are too long comes through adding extra clauses and qualifications. Setting up expectations that are not realised comes from inferring what is to come in the sentence, but then changing tack or emphasis without returning to the original thought.

Punctuation is important in making your meaning clear. There are great subtleties of punctuation that can be deployed by pedants, but the basics are simple.

PUNCTUATION

A *comma* makes a logical division within a sentence:

1 to separate the subject from descriptive words or phrases, 'Charles, Prince of Wales, plays polo.'

2 to separate clauses, 'If he scores, the crowd will cheer.'

3 to separate items on a list, 'Her parents, husband and children came to watch.'

A *semi-colon* links two sentences so closely related that a full stop would make too great a break: 'He didn't score; Jones did.'

A *colon* separates an announcement from what is announced, 'the order of play is as follows: . . .'.

An *apostrophe* indicates either a possessive, 'the team's performance', or a missing syllable in contractions, 'it's time for tea'. There is so much uncertainty about the apostrophe that one often sees the quite unnecessary and misleading use of an apostrophe in a simple plural. On the side of a delivery van, 'Laptops and PC's'; in a newspaper, 'The 1960's were the best time ever for popular music.'

Inverted commas can be quite confusing. Basically they are to identify in a sentence something that is being quoted, as in the above examples. They are sometimes used to highlight the use of a phrase which you know is not quite right, but which you are too idle to express properly: the fans are 'not best pleased' with the manager's performance.

Emphasis can be shown in various ways, by means of *italics*, <u>underlining</u>, **emboldening**, CAPITAL LETTERS or !!!!!!!!. The important thing is to use your chosen style for emphasis consistently and sparingly. Using styles for emphasis is quite different from using styles to differentiate headings, marking stages in the development of your argument and signalling what is coming next. In this text headings are given different weights, with emboldened capitals being for the biggest sections, followed perhaps by italics for sections within a bigger section and so on. For simple emphasis the best method is in the choice of words. In popular media there is a tendency to rely on extravagant language; in a reality TV programme a singer is described by successive judges as 'fantastic', 'absolutely fantastic' and 'truly amazing'. Much more effective are words and phrases which provide emphasis by describing what has happened accurately and meaningfully.

The following box provides a useful checklist for writers of reports.

A CHECKLIST FOR REPORT WRITERS

1 Before writing

(a) What action do you expect from this report?

(b) Who will read it?

(c) How short can it be?

2 Outline

(a) What precisely is the topic of the report?

(b) How many components are there?

(c) How can those best be grouped?

(d) How are the components brought into sections?

(e) Do the titles inform the reader?

Will the report, as outlined, produce the action specified in 1(a) above?

3 Writing the report

(a) Is the average paragraph length less than 100 words?

(b) Have you used more words than are needed?

(c) Have you used words that are precise and concrete rather than words that are vague and abstract?

(d) Have you any superfluous adverbs, adjectives and roundabout phrases?

(e) Have you shown the source of any facts quoted?

(f) Are any of the sentences too long?

4 Revising the report

(a) Will the report, as written, produce the action specified in 1(a) above?

(b) Is anything missing?

(c) Are all calculations accurate?

(d) Are the recommendations clear and justified?

(e) Is the choice between alternatives clear?

(f) Is any part of the report likely to cause offence to anyone? If so, can that be avoided?

(g) What objections do you expect to the recommendations, and how will you deal with them?

(h) Can any of the possible objections be prevented by rewriting part of the report?

5 Final presentation

(a) Is the typing perfect and without spelling mistakes?

(b) Are all the pages numbered?

(c) Are abbreviations and symbols used consistently throughout?

(d) Does the general appearance of the report encourage the reader to read it?

(e) Is there a single-page summary of proposals?

(f) Is the report being distributed to all the appropriate people?

(g) If the report is confidential, is that indicated on the report and ensured by the method of distribution?

SUMMARY PROPOSITIONS

VIII.1   Reports are written to be read and acted upon, not to show how clever the writer is.

VIII.2   A short executive summary is often added to the main report, both to summarise the main points and to guide the reader to particular sections for fuller explanation and evidence.

VIII.3 Appendices are often used to remove detailed evidence or illustration from the main report, while retaining it for reference by those who need it. One appendix might be necessary to give details of sources used.

VIII.4 Any report is planned with a framework, within which are sections so that the argument and recommendations can be written logically and appropriately for the reader.

VIII.5 Punctuation can alter the meaning of a phrase or sentence.

VIII.6 Some of the problems to be aware of in report writing are cant or cliché, inappropriate jargon, *non sequitors*, syllepsis and tautology.

THEORY INTO PRACTICE

This is not a topic that is suitable for general discussion, but refer back to our unit on presentation, at the end of which there was a suggestion that you should prepare a short speech on walking, gardening or your favourite hobby. Using the approach outlined here rewrite it as a report for people thinking about taking up the pastime.

FURTHER READING

Eats, Shoots and Leaves by Lynne Truss was first published in 2003. Although she has received some criticism, it is a popular and helpful book available in various editions. The original English edition as well as a special edition for Indian readers are published by Profile Books in London. Gotham Books of New York publish an American edition.

For German readers there is a similar book: Bastian Sick (2004) *Der Dativ ist dem Genitiv sein Tod* (Cologne: Kiepenhauer and Witsch).

So far we have said little about writing style. The classic guide is Burchfield, R.W. (2004) *Fowler's Modern English Usage*, rev. 3rd edn (Oxford: Oxford University Press). This is an updated version of the original 1926 book by Henry Watson Fowler. Oxford University Press republished the original in 2009, with an introduction and notes by David Crystal. A more compact guide is *The Elements of Style* by two Americans, William Strunk and E.B. White. It was first published in 1959 but a fourth edition (2000) is obtainable in the UK from Allyn and Bacon (a Pearson Education company).

REFERENCE

Buzan, T. (2009) *The Mind Map Book*. London: BBC.

IX Presentation at tribunal

When employment tribunals were first established in the UK in 1964 and remodelled in 1971 they were called industrial tribunals and intended to resemble traditional courts in terms of their function and power, but with more informality in their style of operation. In particular it was envisaged that the parties should represent themselves, professional lawyers only being present in unusually difficult cases. Since then things have changed. As the amount of employment law has grown and become more complex, both claimants and respondents have tended increasingly to brief lawyers to advocate their cases and to undertake a proportion of the preparatory work. Employment law has become a major source of earnings for some solicitors and barristers, firms of specialist consultants also being established to carry out this line of work. The rise of no-win–no-fee agreements has opened up the possibility of affordable, professional representation to employees and former employees as well as the employers with whom they are in dispute.

Nonetheless anyone is permitted to represent anyone else in the employment tribunal and it is common for claimants either to represent themselves or to be represented by a trade union official, and for respondents to be represented by an HR manager. Employment judges are accustomed to managing such situations by taking a more active role than when the parties are professionally represented. They are also well practised in the art of providing balanced chairmanship when one party is represented by a confident, knowledgeable lawyer and the other is not and requires some help in presenting their case effectively. Representing your organisation in the tribunal can be challenging and daunting, even where a case is relatively straightforward. But if you prepare thoroughly there is no reason why you cannot do a very effective job and save a lot of money otherwise spent on legal fees.

The key to effective representation is unquestionably very thorough preparation. The person advocating the case must be absolutely on top of all the facts of the case and, more importantly still, must fully understand the relevant law and how it is applied by the courts. You need clear understanding of the strengths and weaknesses of your case, what points you need to persuade the tribunal to accept, precisely what you are trying to prove and how you can do so in practice. This level of preparation is necessary not only in the tribunal room once a hearing has commenced, but also in the weeks and months beforehand as documents are collated, witness statements prepared and negotiations for a possible out-of-court settlement undertaken.

Settlements

A majority of cases lodged at a tribunal office are settled prior to a formal hearing, often quite late in the day. The number varies from year to year, but quite recent statistics issued by the tribunal service (Employment Tribunal and EAT Statistics (GB) 1 April 2008 to 31 March 2009) stated that 65% of claims were either 'withdrawn' (that could be because they are settled or because the claimant decided not to fight on with a weak case) or settled via ACAS. It is not at all unusual for the parties to settle cases 'on the steps of the courtroom' a few minutes before a hearing is due to start. Sometimes the parties even agree the terms of a settlement after a hearing has commenced and may well be urged in that direction by the judge.

In the months leading up to the hearing the parties or their representatives are often, though not always, contacted by an ACAS conciliation officer, whose role is to explore the possibility of an agreement and to facilitate the drawing up of a full and final, legally binding settlement. Conciliation officers are always keen to advocate a settlement and this is very helpful if your side's case has significant weaknesses and could well be lost if a full hearing goes ahead. However, when your case is strong and you are genuinely confident of a likely, ultimate victory on the key points, it is important to resist the blandishments of ACAS and to reject any suggested settlement which is more generous to your opponent than the tribunal is likely to be. In such circumstances you should be resolute when talking to the conciliation officer, stressing the strengths of your case and turning down any suggested offer politely but firmly.

When negotiating a settlement either through the services of ACAS or directly with the claimant's representative it is vital to be fully aware of what a tribunal would award by way of compensation were your side to lose the case. It is helpful to calculate a worst case scenario and also to work out the most likely outcome. This will enable you to negotiate credibly by demonstrating to the claimant that you are not going to pay him or her off with an over-inflated sum simply in order to dispose of the matter quickly. Paying a large sum is often tempting and can be justified as a means of reducing the costs which your organisation will have to shoulder if it goes ahead and fights the case in the tribunal room. But it sends out a bad message to other would-be litigants. An employer which is known to settle at pretty well any price to avoid tribunal hearings will inevitably attract speculative claims in the future.

Preparing for the hearing

The best advice is to start by preparing your closing statement. This is the statement that the representative of each side makes at the end of proceedings after all the evidence has been presented. It is your opportunity to set out your case clearly, to remind the panel of the main facts of the case as you see them and to explain how you think the law should be applied to the facts when the ruling is made. Representatives also use closing statements to draw the panel's attention to any case law that is relevant to the case and helpful to their arguments. Lawyers extemporise their closing statements and take considerable pride in their ability to do so well, often without recourse to even a few notes. This is not advisable for an inexperienced representative. It is much better to read out a carefully prepared closing statement, even if it is one that has to be adjusted to take account of unexpected developments during the hearing.

Writing a comprehensive, legally credible and clear closing statement is thus an essential stage in the preparation of a successful case. Take plenty of time to get it right and produce several drafts if necessary. Having completed it, you can then use it as your guide when preparing everything else. You need to be able to prove every fact in your closing statement and to be sure of your interpretation of each point of law you make. Facts are proved either with reference to documents in the bundle which is presented to the panel at the start of proceedings, or with reference to the evidence given by witnesses as a hearing proceeds. So you need to make sure, as far as you can, that each fact in the statement is provable with reference to one, the other or both. Points of law are made with reference to the wording of statutes and to published reports of previous cases dealing with the same legal principles. Tribunals are bound to follow precedents on points of law which have already been determined in the appeal courts, so you need to be aware of these and in a position to present copies of case reports to the panel when you start reading out your closing statement.

Your closing statement guides you when thinking about which documents you need to include in the bundle and also when taking statements from your witnesses. At the hearing your witnesses will take it in turn to enter the witness box (actually they just sit behind a table in most tribunal rooms), take their oath and read out their witness statements. This evidence will constitute the core of your case, so it is important that all points on which you want to rely are included in the statements and that they are structured clearly.

The final stage is to prepare your cross-examinations and examinations-in-chief. A week or two before the hearing you will exchange witness statements with your opponents. This needs to happen at the same time (or at least on the same day) so as to ensure that neither side can adjust their statements having had sight of the other's. At the hearing after your opponent's witnesses have read out their statements you will have the opportunity to question them about their evidence. This is known as cross-examination. Your aim is to push them into admitting points that weaken their case and to confirm agreed facts that serve to strengthen yours. A good cross-examination is courteous in style, but persistent. Do not give up a line of questioning if you do not get quite the answers you are hoping for. Instead try another way of asking the same question or putting the same points. By the same token, though, it is important to know when to stop a line of questioning that is having the effect of strengthening your opponent's case or weakening yours. If you get into a hole when cross-examining, stop digging! Sometimes you need to accuse a witness of failing to tell the whole truth or to have lied when giving evidence. This is not easy to do, but is often a necessary feature of an effective cross-examination. The key is to do this in a relatively polite way, avoiding aggression. A good approach involves asking the question with a degree of apparent regret, as in:

I'm afraid I have to put it to you that that statement is untrue.

Or to ask directly about a conflict in the evidence that has been presented, as in:

You stated in evidence that you were not formally warned about your poor performance before you were dismissed. Yet the letter sent to you on 1st April clearly contains a formal warning. Your witness statement was inaccurate, wasn't it?

The stage in proceedings known as examination-in-chief is your opportunity to put questions to your own witnesses after they have read out their witness statements. No new evidence can be presented at this stage, but witnesses can be asked to expand on points or to clarify exactly what they meant by words used in their statement. The most important task, however, is to give your witnesses an opportunity to comment on something, or to contradict a point which has been made in the claimant's witness statement or in that of one of the other witnesses appearing to support the claimant's case.

Remedies

As the respondent employer's representative you will always be anticipating that you are going to win your case on all points and that there will be no need for the tribunal to address the question of the remedy. However well prepared you are, and however strong your case, you can never be sure that you are going to win. Litigation always carries some risks. So you will need to prepare for the possibility that the tribunal will find against you and turn its attention at the end of the hearing to determining appropriate compensation. Sometimes claimants are not looking for compensation, wanting reinstatement for example, or a straightforward declaration that they have been treated unlawfully. Either way you need to be in a position to argue that the remedy the claimant is seeking is overly generous or inappropriate. Here too you will be guided by published precedents and by guidance set out in statutes.

Prior to the hearing the claimant will usually have sent you a copy of the 'Schedule of Loss'. This document sets out what is being sought by the claimant in terms of compensation. In practice, it is rare for victorious claimants to receive every penny they are seeking by way of compensation, but this can only happen if you, as the respondent's representative, argue strongly that a lower sum is appropriate. Here too, thorough preparation is necessary. You may, for example, in an unfair dismissal case be able to argue that the claimant was in part responsible for his or her own dismissal and that compensation should be reduced to take account of that. Alternatively you could argue that the claimant has not mitigated his or her losses adequately by seeking alternative employment and that compensation should be reduced on that account. In a redundancy case you can argue that while the matter was handled unlawfully in terms of procedure, it is likely that the claimant would have been selected and dismissed even if a lawful procedure had been followed. This should be reflected in the compensation. In discrimination cases there is usually an opportunity to argue that what is being sought by way of damages for 'injury to feelings' is too high and out of line with awards in similar cases decided in the past.

THEORY INTO PRACTICE

Knight and Latrelle (2001) reported the results of research they carried out into 'gender effects' in unfair dismissal cases dealt with in UK employment tribunals. Some of their findings were surprising:

- 69% of unfair dismissal cases are brought by men;
- 71% of cases that reach a full hearing are brought by men;
- women are considerably more likely to be offered a settlement by their employers prior to the tribunal hearing;
- 51% of cases brought by women resulted in a settlement, compared with only 44% in the case of male claimants;
- 49% of the women won their cases, only 37% of men won their cases;
- men represented themselves at the hearing in 34% of cases, for women the figure was only 19%;
- women won 57% of cases in which they represented themselves, the figure for men was 36%.

Questions

1 Why are men more likely than women to bring unfair dismissal cases to the tribunal?

2 What could explain the apparent success of women claimants relative to men?

FURTHER READING

Aside from thoroughly familiarising yourself with the facts of the case and the relevant law, there are a number of good sources of information which are helpful when preparing a case for the first time:

- The Legal Action Group (LAG) publishes a number of very user-friendly guides aimed at non-lawyers presenting cases in the employment tribunal, such as Jeremy McMullen, Rebecca Tuck and Betsan Criddle (2004) *Employment Tribunal Procedure: A user's guide to tribunals and appeals* and Naomi Cunningham and Michael Reed (2009) *Employment Tribunal Claims: Tactics and precedents*.

- The Law Society publishes a practical guide by Isobel Manley and Elaine Heslop (2008) *Employment Tribunals* along with a series of books about the major areas of employment law which put a particular focus on tribunal issues such as compensation and key precedents. An excellent practical guide is *Employment Tribunals Handbook: Practice, procedure and strategies for success* (Payne and Waite 2011).

- Each year Oxford University Press publishes a new edition of *Blackstone's Employment Law Practice* (Brown *et al.* 2013). This is a vast book edited by a team of leading lawyers who specialise in the field. It includes a detailed guide to the employment tribunal system, different types of hearings and all manner of procedural issues. It also contains copies of all the major employment statutes.

REFERENCES

Brown, D., Forshaw, S., Korn, A. and Palca, J. (2013) *Blackstone's Employment Law Practice 2013*, 8th edn. Oxford: Oxford University Press.

Cunningham, N. and Reed, M. (2009) *Employment Tribunal Claims: Tactics and precedents*. London: Legal Action Group.

Knight, K.G. and Latreille, P.L. (2001) 'Gender effects in British unfair dismissal hearings', *Industrial and Labour Relations Review*, Vol. 54, No .4, p. 816.

Manley, I. and Heslop, E. (2008) *Employment Tribunals: A practical guide*. London: The Law Society.

McMullen, J., Tuck, R. and Criddle, B. (2004) *Employment Tribunal Procedure: A user's guide to tribunals and appeals*. London: Legal Action Group.

Payne, A.R. and Waite, J.-P. (2011) *Employment Tribunals Handbook: Practice, procedure and strategies for success*. London: Bloomsbury.

X Dealing with bullying and harassment at work

Defining bullying and harassment

Bullying and harassment are increasingly common in the modern workplace and research suggests that around 20% of employees have experienced it in one form or another (Pate and Beaumont 2010). The consequences can be serious: it has been demonstrated to have a negative impact on employee well-being (Vartia 2001), there are potential legal consequences and one estimate puts the associated costs at around £2 billion a year (Tehrani 2005). Clearly it is an important issue. We first define bullying and harassment, demonstrating that a wide range of behaviours can be classified under this heading. We then consider both employer and employee perspectives on the issue and the skills required to deal with them.

The terms 'harassment' and 'bullying' are used interchangeably by many people but ACAS provides the following definitions:

Harassment, in general terms, is unwanted conduct affecting the dignity of men and women in the workplace. It may be related to age, sex, race, disability, religion, sexual orientation, nationality or any personal characteristic of the individual, and may be persistent or an isolated incident. The key is that the actions or comments are viewed as demeaning and unacceptable to the recipient. (ACAS 2009a: 2)

Bullying may be characterised as offensive, intimidating, malicious or insulting behaviour, an abuse or misuse of power through means intended to undermine, humiliate, denigrate or injure the recipient. (ACAS 2009b: 2)

These broad definitions are intended as guidance to both managers and employees about the types of conduct that are unwelcome in the workplace. In practice, examples of what constitute bullying are actions such as gossip, unwelcome jokes, exclusion from social or work groups, or items such as posters and graffiti. Managers misusing power, setting impossible deadlines or blocking promotions may also be classed as bullying employees. Tehrani (2005) presents very detailed examples of bullying behaviours in the workplace that the reader may find useful in establishing what can be classed as bullying. We list two examples in the excerpts in the Window on practice below. D'Cruz and Noronha (2010) also present a fascinating study of bullying in Indian call centres from an employee perspective, demonstrating that bullying and harassment are an issue that has relevance internationally.

WINDOW ON PRACTICE

A secretary joined a media organisation to work for a senior manager. Within a few days, she found that he was behaving very badly towards her. He would criticise her work, pointing out errors in front of visitors. He would become angry whenever he was kept waiting. The secretary then found out that he had behaved in the same way with all his secretaries and that no one stayed with him long.

Two research scientists had been working on a project and when one of the researchers made a breakthrough, he wrote a paper that failed to recognise the work undertaken by his colleague. From that time, the two men would not work together and continually undermined each other. The situation got so bad that they were moved to different locations.

Source: Excerpts from Tehrani (2005).

While the legal definitions of these terms are more precise than the definitions and examples given earlier (see Chapter 20), it can be seen that the parameters of bullying and harassment in the workplace are broadly drawn. Additionally, it is the individual's *perception* of being bullied that is the defining factor in establishing whether bullying has taken place. One employee may, for example, take exception to a joke that another finds inoffensive. This can make dealing with bullying and harassment complex and the CIPD (2007) has, therefore, devised useful self-assessment checklists for assessing and analysing organisational culture to determine whether it is likely to support or suppress bullying. Bullying and harassment may be hard to identify but employers have a legal and moral duty to tackle them. We consider in the following section the means through which employers can do this.

Policies to deal with bullying and harassment

In order to deal effectively with bullying and harassment, employers must have appropriate policies and procedures and ensure that they are enacted. Over 80% of employers in a survey suggest that they do have a policy as a mechanism for tackling these issues (Tehrani 2005). This is likely to be easier for large employers with appropriate resources than for small firms. ACAS (2009a), however, presents a detailed guide to employers on the subject and a helpful checklist (p. 6) on what should be included in a policy to deal with bullying and harassment. In the box below, we present a similar checklist on the topic from the CIPD (2009).

CHECKLIST FOR A POLICY ON BULLYING AND HARASSMENT

- Give examples of what constitutes harassment, bullying and intimidating behaviour including cyber-bullying, work-related events and harassment by third parties.
- Explain the damaging effects and why bullying and harassment will not be tolerated.
- State that bullying and harassment will be treated as a disciplinary offence.
- Clarify the legal implications and outline the costs associated with personal liability.

- Describe how to get help and make a complaint, formally and informally.
- Promise that allegations will be treated speedily, seriously and confidentially and that you prevent victimisation.
- Clarify the accountability of all managers, and the role of union or employee representatives.
- Require supervisors/managers to implement policy and ensure it is understood.
- Emphasise that every employee carries responsibility for their behaviour.

Source: Adapted from CIPD (2012) *Factsheet: Harassment and bullying at work*. Reproduced with the permission of the publisher, the Chartered Institute of Personnel and Development, London (**www.cipd.co.uk**).

It is important that a policy in some way covers all these steps and also that it is supported, and seen to be supported, by senior management who act in accordance with the policy. It is advisable to deal with issues informally where possible, to prevent escalation of the situation. If this fails, or if the matter is serious, it will be necessary to deal with a complaint formally. Some organisations have procedures specific to the bullying and harassment policy but many simply rely on their usual grievance procedures, as we outlined earlier (see Chapter 20). Depending on the outcome of the investigation, disciplinary action may be taken against the perpetrator of the bullying, as we also covered earlier in describing these procedures (see Chapter 20).

Where policies are robustly drawn and effectively implemented, they can have great effect, as we outline in the Window on practice below.

WINDOW ON PRACTICE

Pate and Beaumont (2010) present a case study which outlines the actions taken by one public-sector organisation to tackle bullying and harassment. In response to attitude surveys which identified bullying as an increasing problem, a new CEO launched a Dignity at Work policy which adopted a two-pronged approach to the problem. First, reported cases of bullying and harassment were vigorously pursued and this led to the dismissal of a number of employees, some of whom were at a senior level. Second,

compulsory training for all employees was rolled out. A further attitude survey demonstrated that there was a significant reduction in employee perceptions of bullying and harassment in the organisation. Indeed, those perceiving bullying to be problematic declined from a half to a quarter of employees in a three-year period. Trust in senior management overall, however, was not enhanced. Tackling bullying is not, it seems, a panacea for all ills.

Source: Adapted from Pate, J. and Beaumont, P. (2010) 'Bullying and harassment: A case of success?', *Employee Relations*, Vol. 32, No. 2, pp. 171–83.

Employee perspectives on bullying and harassment

The role of the organisation is critical in influencing employees' responses to bullying and harassment. It is, as noted above, important to have an effective policy but there is a danger that this may not be communicated to or believed by employees who may avoid the issue or resign rather than tackle it (D'Cruz and Noronha 2010). In the Window on practice below we illustrate how difficult it can be for employees to assimilate the fact that they are being bullied.

WINDOW ON PRACTICE

It never struck me what was happening. Work pressures are so high and TLs [team leaders] are also caught up with them – they yell and scream abuse to get the work done. So how can one dream that this is harassment. It is only after repeatedly experiencing it and carefully observing that it was only me who was getting the worst, the most frequent, the lousiest

treatment from him that I realised what was happening. It just took me off guard because I was a top performer, always at the top of the team . . . so there is no reason for this. Merit, objectivity . . . these are all jargons used to describe the organisation – they are so empty. But at that time, they deceived me well.

Source: Excerpt from: D'Cruz, P. and Noronha, E. (2010) 'The exit coping response to work place bullying', *Employee Relations*, Vol. 32, No. 2, pp. 102–20.

Vartia (2001), however, notes that it is not only the targets of bullying and harassment who suffer, but bystanders also, and that it is the problem of the entire work unit, not just the person targeted. The CIPD (2009) and ACAS (2009b) advocate certain actions for the organisation to ensure that bullying and harassment policies are implemented and taken seriously. For example, employees should be introduced to policies at induction and made aware of their rights and personal responsibilities. There should then be continuous communication of and training in policies and employees should have a point of contact to whom they can turn for advice and information. Many organisations appoint 'champions' as a source of advice for employees with concerns about bullying. Employees should also be made aware of the mechanisms for taking a complaint forward.

While much of the focus is, rightly, on those who suffer bullying and harassment, the impact on those instigating it should not be overlooked. There has recently been a high-profile example of a senior public figure found guilty of bullying. The case involved a Metropolitan Police Commander, convicted and ultimately jailed for serious offences of this nature. Although one may consider the individual involved to be the author of his own misfortune in engaging in this behaviour, a working environment that condones such behaviour protects all parties, not just the victims of it.

ACTIVITY X.1

Look at an organisation's policy on bullying and harassment, for example the University of Bradford's (2007) policy (**www.brad.ac.uk/admin/equalopp/policies/ HarassmentandBullyingPolicy07.pdf**) or one from an organisation with which you are familiar.

1 What are key aspects of the policy?

2 To what extent do you think it is likely to be successful in tackling bullying and harassment?

Tackling bullying and harassment

Recent research about the dynamics of relationships in management responses to claims of bullying has found that HR people are seen as typically supporting the manager and being suspicious of the employee making the complaint as they are anxious to maintain the goodwill of managers (Harrington *et al.* 2012). In this book we have already made the point that HR is inescapably a part of management, but this does not mean being automatically supportive of an individual manager.

As we suggest above, many organisations tackle bullying and harassment using their grievance policies and we discuss the skills appropriate to this above. In brief, the key aspects of dealing with bullying and harassment are:

- To address the issue as quickly as possible. It is often advised that grievances are best resolved informally, but this may not be appropriate for allegations of bullying and harassment. Where the allegations are of a serious or sensitive nature, the formal procedure should be instigated without delay.

- To provide a confidential and supportive environment for both the person who feels bullied and the person accused of bullying. The allegations may or may not be substantiated and both need to be dealt with fairly during the course of the investigations.

- The face-to-face and communication skills we deal with throughout this chapter are vital in what can be sensitive investigations and discussions.

- An open, transparent and fair investigation is essential, as are appropriate feedback mechanisms once the investigation is complete.
- Both parties are likely to need support once the process is completed, unless the outcome leads to dismissal. The provision of counselling can be invaluable in maintaining positive employment relations.

SUMMARY PROPOSITIONS

X.1 Bullying and harassment are common and problematic for both employers and employees.

X.2 Employers need to decide how to respond to these issues and are advised to do so using policies and procedures which require senior management support.

X.3 Employee responses to bullying and harassment often include avoidance and resignation. They need to understand the policy clearly and how to use it if it is to be successful in reducing bullying and harassment.

X.4 Dealing with allegations of bullying and harassment can be very sensitive and a wide range of skills must be deployed.

X.5 Bullying damages the person, it damages the bully and it damages the organisation within which bullying takes place, especially if it is a way of suppressing dissent from what some people see as examples of sustaining misguided management practice.

GENERAL DISCUSSION TOPICS

1 To what extent do you believe that setting challenging deadlines can be considered to be bullying?

2 'A robust policy on bullying and harassment will be effective in reducing employee perceptions that these behaviours are tolerated in the organisation.' Discuss this statement.

3 What actions can be taken to prevent employees resigning as a result of bullying and harassment?

THEORY INTO PRACTICE

The main emphasis in this chapter and most of recent academic and general discussion on this topic has been about the effect on the bullied individual and on the bully, but there is the associated impact on the effectiveness of the business. This was dramatically illustrated by the report of a public inquiry into failings at a Staffordshire Hospital (**www.midstaffspublicinquiry.com**) in 2013, where an unusually high death rate caused distress, complaint and outrage. The inquiry produced many explanations, among which was:

> *appalling care flourished because managers put corporate self-interest and cost control ahead of patients and their safety.*

One salient feature of this was a culture of management disregarding staff complaints and concerns about patient care because of an inward-looking focus on financial targets and the need for 'efficiency' improvements so that the hospital could achieve the objective of becoming a Foundation Trust. Staff members who raised other concerns felt bullied into compliance in 'a climate of fear'. As a business the hospital failed to meet its financial and efficiency objectives because it failed to meet its fundamental and overriding purpose of caring effectively for patients. A month after the report was published the financial situation was so serious that the hospital was put into administration. Although this was a public-sector body with unusual and drastic results of its failure, the same criterion applies to every organisation which is always essentially a business. There is always a 'customer', whose needs have to be met. A culture putting other objectives ahead of that imperative *and fosters an atmosphere of harassing or bullying staff members who raise other concerns* is in danger; bullying is damaging to the bullied person, but it also damages the business that fosters or tolerates bullying behaviour.

Questions

1 In what ways is a bully damaged by bullying?

2 Discussion topic 2 above invited you to discuss the proposition 'A robust policy on bullying and harassment will be effective in reducing employee perceptions that these behaviours are tolerated in the organisation.' Would that have been sufficient to deal with the hospital situation in this case?

3 It is quite common that senior or specialist personnel are required to sign agreements that they will not disclose sensitive information about the business if they leave. The reason is to maintain secrecy about matters that would assist a competitor. Can such agreements be reasonable where the information that might be disclosed indicates wrongdoing?

FURTHER READING

ACAS (2009a) *Bullying and Harassment at Work: A guide for employers and managers*, available at **www.acas.org.uk/index.aspx?articleid=797** (accessed 6 February 2010).

ACAS (2009b) *Guidance for Employees: Bullying and harassment at work*, available at **www.acas.org.uk/index.aspx?articleid=794** (accessed 6 February 2010).

ACAS has produced these two comprehensive and user-friendly guides to explain both employer and employee responsibilities on how to deal with bullying and harassment. The employer guide offers advice on how to establish policies and procedures and the employee guide advises employees on how to manage a workplace situation in which they are being bullied.

CIPD (2007) *Tool: Tackling bullying at work – a good practice framework*. London: CIPD.
The CIPD presents a tool that employers can adopt in analysing their workplace culture and establishing an action plan to eradicate workplace bullying.

Frost, R. (2013) *Mid Staffordshire NHS Foundation Trust Public Inquiry*. London: The Stationery Office.
Although this report was produced for general public information and was making recommendations mainly for government action, it is ideal reading for HR people, pointing out how easily major errors can develop from misguided management action, which is usually well intentioned. Written by a lawyer, it has perspectives and uses language that are slightly different from normal management speak and therefore fresh to management ears.

REFERENCES

ACAS (2009a) *Bullying and Harassment at Work: A guide for employers and managers*, available at **www.acas.org.uk/index.aspx?articleid=797** (accessed 6 February 2010).

ACAS (2009b) *Guidance for Employees: Bullying and harassment at work*, available at **www.acas. org.uk/index.aspx?articleid=794** (accessed 6 February 2010).

CIPD (2007) *Tool: Tackling bullying at work – a good practice framework*. London: CIPD.

CIPD (2009) *Factsheet: Harassment and bullying at work*, available at **www.cipd.co.uk/subjects/ dvsequl/harassmt/harrass.htm?IsSrchRes=1** (accessed February 2010).

D'Cruz, P. and Noronha, E. (2010) 'The exit coping response to work place bullying', *Employee Relations*, Vol. 32, No. 2, pp. 102–20.

Harrington, S., Rayner, C. and Warren, S. (2012) 'Too hot to handle? Trust and HR practitioners' implementation of anti-bullying policy', *Human Resource Management Journal*, Vol. 22, No. 4, pp. 392–408.

Pate, J. and Beaumont, P. (2010) 'Bullying and harassment: A case of success?', *Employee Relations*, Vol. 32, No. 2, pp. 171–83.

Tehrani, N. (2005) *Bullying at Work: Beyond policies to a culture of respect*. London: CIPD.

University of Bradford (2007) *Personal Harassment and Bullying Policy and Procedures*, available at **www.brad.ac.uk/admin/equalopp/policies/HarassmentandBullyingPolicy07.pdf** (accessed 6 February 2010).

Vartia, M. (2001) 'Consequences of workplace bullying with respect to the well-being of its targets and the observers of bullying', *Scandinavian Journal of Work and Environmental Health*, Vol. 27, No. 1, pp. 63–9.

Chapter 29

SKILLS SET 2: SKILLS FOR ANALYSIS AND DECISION MAKING

Now we have a short group of skills that are quite disparate. Using statistical techniques is an almost universal practice in management, even if it is quickly calculating a percentage on the back of an envelope. A number of our earlier chapters include statistics and refer to specific measures, but here are a range of techniques that have wide applicability for data analysis and to inform decision making.

Designing procedures aids decision making in a quite different way, by working out logical sequences of actions to be taken by people to reach a specified objective. These can be as varied as running down a manufacturing plant before the Christmas break, authorising travel expenses, dealing with grievances and so on. Careful thought and planning can produce a template for effective action.

We are all familiar with questionnaires, and equally familiar with the frustration of trying to answer questions that do not make sense. Skilful design will not only elicit constructive participation by the questionnaire recipient, but also help accurate analysis of the answers.

Perhaps you had never thought of using consultants as being a skill. Surely you are simply paying them to use *their skills* on your behalf? Not at all. The skill with which you specify what needs to be done, and then identifying the people capable of doing it, will enable the consultants to use their skills on your behalf in the way you need. Without this even the most conscientious consultants will do what they think you need, and that will be what they find easiest to do. It may be just right, but that would be simple luck rather than good judgement; it is also rare.

XI Using and interpreting statistics

The objective of this section is to help you interpret the meaning and value of statistics presented in a report or article, and to guide you in choosing the appropriate statistics to use when presenting numerical data. We focus on basic statistics with most relevance for business and HR management, and we have been very selective.

Descriptive statistics are used to organise and summarise data in order to communicate it more clearly. They are used when we have data for the whole population we are aiming to describe, for example all employees within an organisation. Some government statistics also cover the whole of the relevant population, such as unemployment statistics and the National Census.

Descriptive statistics can also be used to describe the findings of a sample, for example a sample survey sent to HR managers, each responding on behalf of a different multinational company (MNC), but it must be remembered that the results apply to the sample only. If we wish to say something about the total population from which the sample is drawn (i.e. all MNCs) we would need to use 'inferential statistics', which are more complex.

Our constant message throughout is one of caution. Statistics are factual pieces of information, designed to give the message that the producer of the statistics wants to put across. As Benjamin Disraeli, a British Prime Minister in the nineteenth century, said, 'there are lies, damned lies, and statistics'.

Frequency distributions

These distributions are often used in business generally and in HRM. For example, we could break down the workforce by gender, or by highest qualification, or days of absence.

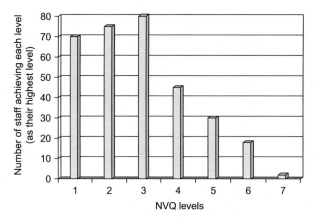

Figure XI.1
A bar chart of
qualification
levels

Figure XI.1 shows how the workforce may be broken down by highest NVQ equivalent qualification displayed as a bar chart, and in table form it would look like Table XI.1.

To present ages or salaries in a bar chart or frequency table it would be sensible to divide them into groups or bands, otherwise the figure or table would be far too big and fairly meaningless. Frequencies are often displayed as pie charts using the relevant percentages or frequencies, which are excellent for visual presentation. The most popular category is the **mode**, and in this case it is the NVQ level 3. The mode is the **most frequently occurring**, or most numerous category. Frequency tables and the mode are particularly useful for categorical measures. Another example of the use of these measures is to analyse stated reasons for leaving an organisation.

Table XI.1
Frequency table
of qualification
levels

NVQ level	Number of employees who have this as their highest qualification	Percentage of employees who have this as their highest qualification
1	70	22
2	75	23
3	80	25
4	45	14
5	30	9
6	18	6
7	2	1

Employee total number = 320.

WINDOW ON PRACTICE

Some simple definitions

A categorical (sometimes called discrete) measure is just that, a category, such as gender, highest qualification, job type, reason for leaving. These measures are usually labelled by means of a word.

Some measures are ordinal measures such as in the NVQ example in that they are ranked numerically in order of difficulty; however, the rankings are not necessarily evenly spaced, and do not have a true zero. Therefore the numbers do not have any arithmetic relationship, so we cannot say that NVQ4 is twice as hard as NVQ2 or an NVQ1 plus an NVQ5 adds up to an NVQ6.

Continuous numeric measures, which have a true zero, such as length of service, salary and age, all have arithmetic properties, so a person with four years' service has twice as much service as a person with two years' service.

Measures of central tendency

If you are not familiar with statistics you may find the idea of 'central tendency' somewhat impenetrable but it is fairly straightforward if you think of the word 'average', and apply this to, say, the average annual salary in your organisation. You add up the salaries of everyone in the organisation and divide by the number of people receiving a salary. 'Average' is not strictly a statistical term, the correct term is the **arithmetic mean**. This is a useful measure of central tendency but it has limitations. For example, let us consider Entrepreneur Co, which employs ten people including the owner manager (who earns £80,000 p.a. – the accountant has not been very creative). A full list of all the salaries is:

£80,000 (owner manager)	£14,000
£29,000	£13,000
£17,000	£13,000
£15,000	£13,000
£14,000	£13,000

The mean salary would be £22,100 calculated by adding all salaries together and dividing by 10 (number of employees). However, there is no indication here that eight employees earned less than the mean and only two employees were above, nor that one salary is at least £50,000 more than any other.

WINDOW ON PRACTICE

The clipped mean

Sometimes the clipped, or cropped, mean is used to remove the effects of outliers, such as the £80,000 in the example above. This would be done by removing the top 5% and the bottom 5% of all salaries.

WINDOW ON PRACTICE

Some more about different types of measures

The mean can only be calculated for continuous measures like salary, age and years of post-qualification experience. If we try and work out a mean for discrete measures the answer just does not make sense. For example, we cannot find an average for gender of racial groups or area of functional expertise.

Using the example above we either have an NVQ3 or an NVQ2, not an NVQ2.85, which would be the mean if we calculated it! The mean is not appropriate as we are dealing with ordinal data with no evidence that the NVQ levels are equally spaced and no true zero.

However, if we worked out the mean age of the workforce in our company it might work out at 32.25 years. This makes sense because age moves continuously, and a specific person could be 32.25 years old. This works because we are dealing with continuous numeric data with a true zero.

The same mean salary figure could have been reached in Cooperative Co, round the corner, where the salary list looks very different, and is based solely on length of service:

£22,850	£22,100
£22,850	£21,600
£22,600	£21,600
£22,600	£21,600
£22,100	£21,000

Someone comparing the wages paid in these two organisations on the basis of mean salary only would have no idea how different they were.

If on the other hand we took another measure of central tendency, the **median**, this would be £13,500 in Entrepreneur Co, a very different figure from the mean, as this represents the mid-point after everyone has been ranked according to their salary. The mid-point means that there are equal numbers of people above this salary and below it in the ranking. In Entrepreneur Co there is an even number of employees so the median is calculated by taking the middle two measures, which are £14,000 and £13,000, and taking the mid-point of these, which is £13,500.

This figure does distinguish the two organisations, as in Cooperative Co the median salary would be £ 22,100 (again based on taking the two middle salary points, which in this case turn out to be exactly the same). However, while the median may differentiate Entrepreneur Co from Cooperative Co, it is also a limited measure unless the end points of the range are disclosed. Tony Smith, on completing his degree and keen to pay off his student loan as fast as possible, might, on the basis of mean salaries, have no idea which was the best place to apply for a job. However, Tony gets more information from the median, which suggests that he might receive a better starting salary from Cooperative Co. However, even this information is insufficient, as it does not tell Tony anything about the range of salaries. We know that they are tightly bunched in Cooperative Co, but salaries in another company could be spread more widely and still have the same median. We look at spread in the following section.

All this shows that it is unwise to take statistics at face value, and organisations can use statistics very cleverly and selectively in order to support their message. In looking at a statistic three key questions to ask are:

1 What exactly can this statistic tell me?

2 What is it unable to tell me?

3 What more information do I need?

ACTIVITY XI.1

Gather some organisational HR statistics and look carefully at the information you are given. Absence statistics could be good ones to look at here or turnover statistics. Ask yourself the above three questions. When you have answered them check out your understanding with someone else, preferably the person who produced the statistics.

Measures of dispersion

Dispersion explains how the measures are spread out, and there are two well-used measures of spread which can be used in addition to the mean and the median, and which give us more information. The **range** is determined from the highest and the lowest points. So, in Entrepreneur Co salaries go from £80,000 down to £13,000, giving a range of 67,000; and in Cooperative Co they go from £22,850 down to £21,000, giving a range of 1,850. The range is useful and simple to identify, but its limitation is that it is very affected by 'outliers', measures at the extremes which are disconnected to the majority of measures. The owner manager's salary of £80,000 is an outlier at Entrepreneur Co. As another example we might say the age range in our organisation is from 18 to 66, but while there are many employees between 18 and 51, there is only one employee older than 51 and that person is 66. So while the range is a useful piece of information it only gives us limited knowledge about spread.

WINDOW ON PRACTICE

The interquartile range

As the range can be greatly affected by outliers, sometimes the interquartile range is used to counteract this effect. This uses the same principle as the median: if you remember, the median is the point at which half the results are above this point and half

below. Imagine the results being divided into quarters rather than just halves. So the top point of the interquartile range is where one-quarter of the results are above this point and three-quarters are below it. And the bottom point of the interquartile range is where three-quarters of the results are above this point and one-quarter below it. Subtracting the lower point from the higher point gives the interquartile range.

The other well-used measure of spread is the **standard deviation** and this statistic expresses the average deviation from the mean. In other words, having worked out the mean we now work out how much each measure, such as salary in the above example, differs from that mean, and then average all those differences. If everyone in an organisation earned exactly the same amount of money the standard deviation would be zero. It would not matter what the actual salary is – it could be £20,000 or £50,000; as long as everyone earns the same and there is no spread, the standard deviation is zero. The larger the standard deviation, the larger the spread it represents, and we would expect that the standard deviation for Entrepreneur Co would be greater than for Cooperative Co.

WINDOW ON PRACTICE

Let us compare the standard deviation at Entrepreneur Co and Cooperative Co:

The standard deviation from the mean at Entrepreneur Co is 20,934
The standard deviation from the mean at Cooperative Co is 631

So you can see that they are quite different.

The standard deviation is affected by outliers just like the mean and the range, so it is useful to express this statistic together with the median and with the mean. In some calculations there is a method for removing outliers and it is worth asking if this has been done when you are given a standard deviation.

Describing relationships or association

There are many times when we would like to see how measures within our organisation are connected, and these often focus on performance measures of some kind or other. We might like to find out how days of absence are related to age, or how absence is related to length of service. One way we can look at relationships is to do this visually in a scatterplot, and a further method is to use a statistical technique called correlation.

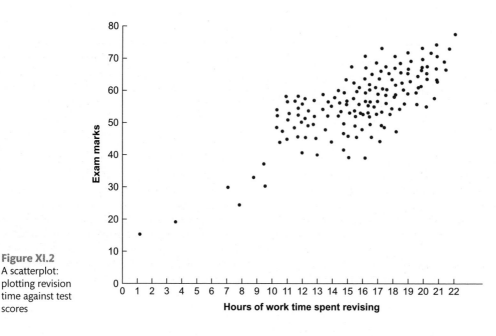

Figure XI.2
A scatterplot: plotting revision time against test scores

Scatterplots

These are fairly simple to draw up and just require that for every person we have the two measures that we are investigating. For example, what is the relationship between the amount of work time devoted to test revision and the scores of trainees in the test? First we draw a plot with test scores on the vertical axis and hours of work time devoted to revision on the horizontal axis, and then plot all the individuals on that according to their score and the time they were allowed for revision by their manager. In the example in Figure XI.2 we can see how a greater number of work hours devoted to revising appear to be associated with higher test scores, which is generally what we would expect.

Correlation

Correlation is a more sophisticated approach, often applied when relating the selection scores of individuals to eventual performance levels in the organisation. The selection processes are generally intended to give us sufficient information to enable us to predict who we think will perform best in our organisation. In our example we are going to relate the results that candidates achieved at an assessment centre to their performance two years later to see whether there is any relationship between them. To do this we rank the candidates who have been successful at the assessment centre and then rank their performance in two years' time. So, for example, we may be appointing fifty graduates to the company, all of whom have been through the assessment centre; we rank these from 1 to 50 according to their overall score at the centre. Two years later we look at the performance of each of the individuals and again rank them from 1 to 50. The individuals will now have a rank from the assessment centre and a rank for their performance and it is these ranks that will be analysed in the correlation. The sorts of results we might get are shown in the following Window on practice.

WINDOW ON PRACTICE

There are different statistics that can be used for correlation based on the nature of the data, but the results of a correlation are always between 1 and −1 and are expressed as a correlation coefficient (r).

In our example, if the assessment centre ranks perfectly matched the performance ranks, this would mean that Joe, who was ranked 6th in the assessment centre, would also be ranked 6th for performance, and Penny, who was ranked 49th in the assessment centre, would also be ranked 49th for performance, and so on for each graduate.

In this case of perfect correlation, r = 1. If there were such an assessment tool it would be very popular!

If the relationship was completely random (imagine the scatterplot with dots all over the place and no pattern whatsoever) then r = 0. The assessment tool results do not appear to be able to relate to performance.

Somewhere nearer the middle, which is where most assessment tools are, would be something like r = 0.3, in which case the tool shows some relationship with performance but not a great deal. Occasionally, higher associations have been found but they do not generally exceed r = 0.7.

If the relationship between assessment centre ranking and performance ranking produces a negative correlation, for example r = −0.6, then there is some evidence that higher assessment centre scores are related to lower performance scores and vice versa.

The statistic to use here would be a Spearman correlation coefficient as this is the appropriate one for ranked data.

One of the reasons that the results from selection tools do not appear to be highly related to performance measures may be that the performance measures are not well thought through. They could of course be anything from scores on performance assessment reports to days of absence, level of promotion, assessment of potential and so on.

When any statistics are presented it is always wise to ask how the measures have been developed, before being impressed by the statistics that are produced.

Treating statistics with caution

We have indicated throughout this section how easy it is to misinterpret statistics and how important it is to question them. So here are a series of questions to ask when presented with statistics:

1 If you are given a statistic which you have not met before, ask 'What can this statistic tell me and what can it not tell?' This should prevent you from making any assumptions.

2 Ask for the number of people that percentages are based on, as percentages can sound impressive but mean nothing if you do not know the numbers they are representing.

WINDOW ON PRACTICE

One of the authors was listening to student presentations on the psychological contract. One particular group contrasted the psychological contract in two organisations by comparing their answers with a range of questions. They produced wonderful histograms and pie charts and there were some

impressive differences in the percentages, but they never mentioned how many responses the percentages were based on. It turned out that there were twenty responses from one organisation and six from the other! The students explained that all six were from one department and that, had they gone to another department, they think the answers to the questions might have been quite different!

3 Ask how the sample was chosen, as responses from employees in one department do not represent the organisation as a whole. Responses from managers do not represent responses from employees.

4 If you are presented with a measure which is ambiguous, such as 'Performance', ask how that measure has been compiled.

5 Survey results purport to reflect the responses of all members of the organisation. For example, if an employee engagement survey has been sent to all employees it is important to ask about response rate. Did all employees reply? If not, what percentage of employees did reply? Also, what patterns are there in relation to responses and non-responses?

6 When presented with the results of a questionnaire always ask for a copy of the questionnaire as the way in which questions are asked can prompt different sorts of responses.

7 Ask yourself what further data you require to understand fully the information you are looking at.

ACTIVITY XI.3

Have a look at the results of an organisational survey, for example an employee engagement survey or something similar. Go through the above seven questions. Check out your interpretation with someone else, preferably the compiler of the survey.

XII Job analysis

Job analysis underpins a wide range of HR activities, particularly recruitment and selection, but also performance management, development, organisation development and design, and job evaluation for pay and equal opportunities. It can be used in organisations which need to restructure or downsize to identify redundant or replicated tasks and ineffective organisation of jobs. In mergers and alliances job analysis can provide a picture of how each organisation works and how jobs can be combined to avoid replication of tasks.

Job analysis collects and analyses information about the tasks, responsibilities and the context of jobs and collates this into some form of job description. As organisations change so quickly it needs constant updating if it is to be a useful tool. In this section we take a practical approach to the information to be collected, and explain two methods of collecting this.

The information to be collected

While the exact data will be affected by the specific purpose of job analysis, in general the following data needs to be collected:

1 **Job identification data**: Job title and location; department; division; company name.

2 **Purpose of job**: Overall purpose such as to 'ensure an effective marketing package is up and running as soon as product is licensed or delivered'.

3 **Job content/tasks**: Actual tasks or duties such as level of responsibility for tasks; importance of tasks; and how often they are performed.

4 **Performance standards/objectives**: These can be either for the job as a whole or specific tasks. They can be expressed in quantitative terms such as amount of output or sales, budgets or time limits to meet; or in qualitative terms such as maintaining group cohesiveness.

5 **Relationships with others**: This includes reporting relationships, supervisory relationships, liaison with others and coordinating relationships.

6 **Working conditions**: This includes the physical environment, such as heat, noise, light, accident and health risks, hours of work and any unusual times of work; pay and benefits; opportunity for flexibility in working hours or place of work; whether working in a group or alone.

7 **Human requirements**: The physical and psychological characteristics of the individual who could fulfil the demands of the job, for example (potential) strength and stamina requirements for a physical job such as greenkeeper, builder's labourer or walk leader. Psychological requirements may be tolerance of tight deadlines; calmness and confidence in a constantly busy environment or in the face of angry customers, such as in an airport.

Methods of collecting the data

There is a wide range of methods that may be used, as we explained earlier (see Chapter 6), and it is often a good idea to use more than one as a cross-check. Here are two methods in more detail.

Work diaries

This method requires the job participant to fill in a structured log of his or her daily activities over a period, the period being determined by the nature of the job. It would be no good asking a shop assistant to log the tasks for Monday to Wednesday if deliveries take place only on Thursdays and Saturdays. Similarly, asking an administrative assistant to make a log for a two-week period at the beginning of the month is of no use when there are end-of-month tasks that this does not cover. Asking a greenkeeper to log tasks for a month over the summer, when winter tasks are completely different, will be of little help. Professional jobs are usually even more varied and unpredictable. So some assessment of the nature of the job needs to take place before deciding whether work diaries will be a good method to analyse a job. Table XII.1 shows a structure that might be used for a work diary.

Table XII.1
An example of the structure of a work diary

Start time	End time	Task purpose	Task actions	Who else is involved	Means of communicating with others involved	Importance of task rate 1 to 10	Urgency of task rate 1 to 10	Who is responsible for decisions made	Other information
9.30	10.40	Agree structure of new induction programme for research staff	Act as chair of meeting + take notes	2 staff who report to me in the dept. + rep from HR	Face to face	7	10	I sign it off	

This structure is useful as it allows the job holder to note everything done at the time, rather than trying to remember it all, probably badly, at the end of the day. It is like an eating diary, if a person wants to lose weight, so that when it is analysed at the end of the week a picture will emerge that the person is probably not aware of, as they are so immersed in the day-to-day or minute-to-minute nature of their lives and eating. Thus trends and patterns emerge that the individual is not aware of. For example, 'I can see that in the mornings I eat a healthy breakfast and snack on fruit; I usually eat a healthy lunch and nothing in the afternoon; in the evening I eat crisps/nuts before my meal and will often eat two or three puddings and maybe more crisps'. Or, in another case, 'I can see that I spend half my time in meetings with employees from other departments and my role is usually to persuade others of the type of marketing strategy I think appropriate; and I spend 20% of my time on the phone answering queries about marketing material'. In other words, the job holders could not have expressed the nature of their job as accurately without this attention to detail over a period.

ACTIVITY XII.1

Try to keep a work diary for a week using the format suggested, or adapt this to better meet your needs.

1 What have you learnt about your job?

2 What other questions do you wish you had included in the work diary format?

3 Explain your experience of filling out a work diary. Would you recommend it as a method of job analysis? Justify your view.

However, this mass of information requires vast amounts of time to be analysed, and time costs money. Another problem with this approach is that the individuals completing the diaries will get bored and adopt a slapdash approach. Or they may become fretful that yet another task has been added to their already overloaded day.

Individual interviews

These are a fast and holistic means of collecting job data, and can be conducted with job holders, supervisors and perhaps peers and subordinates. Semi-structured interviews are probably most useful so that a range of topics and questions can be designed in advance, but there is still the opportunity to probe for details and follow up on unexpected information. An HR specialist is usually the most appropriate person to do this. The disadvantage with interviews is that processed data rather than raw data is collected as with work diaries. In other words, we find out what the job holders *think* they do rather than what they actually do. Some sample interview questions are given in the Window on practice below. You would need to adapt these questions so that they are relevant to the level and type of job which you are analysing.

WINDOW ON PRACTICE

Some basic questions for the job holder:

1 What is your job title and location in the organisation structure?

2 Where physically do you work? What/who determines this?

3 What hours of work do you do and what/who determines this?

4 Who do you report to directly, and who reports directly to you?

5 What is the overall purpose of your job?

6 How do you know when this purpose is achieved; and/or what standards are applied to the achievement of this purpose?

7 What tasks do you have to carry out to achieve this?

8 How frequently do these tasks need to be carried out?

9 Which are the most important/critical tasks, and what makes them so important?

10 Who do you have to liaise or work with to achieve your job tasks and purpose?

11 For what tasks do you have decision-making authority?

12 What tasks do you carry out which do not relate to the achievement of your purpose?

13 What do these tasks achieve, and what would happen if you did not do them?

14 What other things about your job have we not covered?

XIII Designing procedures

Procedures get things done. Splendid ideas and bold decisions are valueless without precise and efficient procedures to translate intention into action. Among the many types of administrative procedure designed by HR people are:

Signing on new employees

Terminating an employee's contract

Filling a vacancy

Running appraisals

Running courses

Implementing new legal obligations

Health and safety routines

Induction

Authorising expenses

Pay increases

Accidents/illness

These procedures have four main benefits. First, they reduce the need for decisions in the future. When the solution to a problem has been worked out once, the procedure provides a model for dealing with the same problem when it recurs. The procedure is a recipe, and the necessary action can be taken more quickly and by more people in an identical way than if it had to be worked out afresh every time.

Second, procedures produce consistency of action. If things are always done in the same way, those who are involved become practised in their dealings. Retail outlets develop similar procedures for dealing with customers, so that a customer will frequently need to ask only one question, 'Do you serve yourself or does someone serve you?', before being able to move smoothly through the purchasing routine. Employees become accustomed to procedural drills and can work together swiftly and harmoniously as long as methods are unaltered.

Third, procedures provide a form of control for management. Managers know that the system will keep things working correctly and smoothly, so they can turn their attention to future challenges and current problems without being distracted by constant requests for guidance and information. Whenever there is a human-made disaster, like the abuse and death of a child who should have been cared for, or a train crash, or an industrial accident, the appropriate authorities some time later announce that 'procedures have been reviewed'. It sounds hollow, but is usually the correct response.

Finally, there is the benefit of freedom from supervision. Learner drivers are under constant supervision during their first lesson, but as they learn the procedures of driving, supervision becomes less overbearing. A good administrative procedure gives staff members information and authority so that they know what to do and how to do it, with scope to interpret the rules in unexpected situations. In this way, the benefits of management control are accompanied by the advantages of individual autonomy.

Unfortunately procedures are dull, so few managers like to invest the time needed to get them right. Other problems can be that procedures inhibit change by providing a secure and familiar routine that people are reluctant to abandon. There is sometimes a problem of duplication, where one department has a procedure for its own stage in a process which is repeated by the next department in sequence. In producing a standard way of doing things, procedures may be interpreted as the only way of doing things and bring problems of rigidity. When procedural rigidity confronts managerial enthusiasm or employee discontent, enthusiasm undermines by 'cutting through the red tape' and discontent overcomes rigidity by 'short-circuiting the system'. The procedure will then collapse or become obsolete.

Procedures apply logic to common sense and understanding. Here is a **checklist** of principles:

1 What are *all* the objectives you want to achieve?

2 Are any of these not really needed because there is already a satisfactory method, or because procedure is not the right answer to the problem?

3 What are the starting and finishing points of the procedure?

4 What are the interim steps to be? They should be:

  (a) few as possible

  (b) as simple as possible

  (c) clear and logical

  (d) as complete as possible.

5 Pilot the procedure in circumstances that are as realistic as possible.

6 Modify the procedure in the light of the pilot. Retest.

7 Implement and monitor for effectiveness.

A simple way of moving forward from the checklist is the **flowchart**, a method originally developed by Frank Gilbreth in the early twentieth century to represent a process, showing the steps as boxes of various kinds, with their sequence being shown by connecting arrows. This was first used in industrial engineering and later in writing computer programs, but the method is equally valid for working out administrative procedures.

The chart is sketched out using symbols for each part of the process, either a box or an arrow. A box is an event or something being done. Arrows show what is called 'flow of control' in computer science. Figure XIII.1 shows a simplified procedure for buying a house. Most readers will regard this as ridiculously over-simplified, but it is merely to illustrate the method.

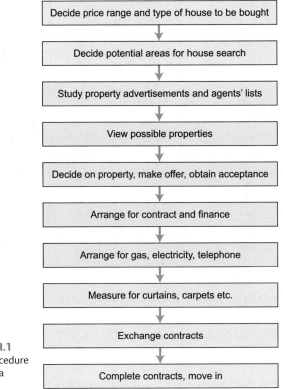

Figure XIII.1
Simple procedure for buying a house

This simple sketch is a basis for various developments:

1 Spotting omissions.

2 Working out ways to consolidate or take out steps that are not essential.

3 Identifying activities which are shown as being sequential, but could be carried out in parallel to save time.

4 Reviewing the logic of the flow to find other improvements and begin the process of understanding how the introduction of the procedure can be communicated to those who have to operate it.

The procedure might be changed, first by identifying actions that do not have to proceed in sequence, but can be done in parallel. (In HR procedures this is often a great way of expediting progress, which is often missed in procedure development.)

When the procedure seems perfect, you have two more steps to take: writing it out and testing it. You *write it out* because it has to be understood, used and believed in by other people. They may not be keen on the idea, so flaws will be found in your perfection. They may not understand it, they may not believe that it will work, they may not trust you not to have some hidden agenda. So you write it out, keeping in mind the people who have to use it, as they will either make it work or help it to fail. Go through it with one or two people who will be actively involved in its use, answering their questions, listening to their suggestions and asking them to spot flaws. After rethinking and rewriting, *test it*. Run it through once or twice and work on whatever further problems appear. If it is going to fail, let it fail in its test. Turn your write-up into an insert in the procedure manual, especially its online version, which is more likely to be up to date than the hard copy that is stuffed away somewhere with lots of coffee stains on the cover.

Then *train* everyone who will be affected in operating the procedure.

SUMMARY PROPOSITIONS

XIII.1 Administrative procedures (a) reduce the need for decisions in the future, (b) produce consistency of action, (c) provide a form of management control over what is going on, and (d) enable people to work free from close supervision.

XIII.2 The main problem is that they are dull.

XIII.3 Designing procedures requires (a) objectives, (b) a check that all objectives are needed and do not duplicate pre-existing arrangements, (c) that they have a clear and correct start and finish point, and (d) interim steps that are full, simple, clear and complete.

XIII.4 A standard method is to use a flowchart.

XIII.5 After working out the flowchart it should be written out as a procedure. This procedure should be used as a basis for consultation (to seek to improve it), for testing and training before implementation.

FURTHER READING

For a general understanding of flowcharting, see a sound article in Wikipedia, **www.wikipedia.org**. There is also coverage of an associated method, the Critical Path Method, which is useful for finding the most efficient route through a maze of different, interdependent activities.

ACTIVITY XIII.1

Use the checklist shown, together with the flowcharting steps, to do one or more of the following:

1 Getting ready to go on holiday.

2 Organising a stag or hen party.

3 Find someone else in your organisation who has to implement a policy decision and work out how you would put appropriate procedures in place. Then compare the other person's procedure plan with your own.

What have you learnt about designing procedures?

XIV Designing questionnaires

In HR, questionnaires are used in different ways, often to test attitudes among employees towards some draft policy initiative, although some organisations use them instead of exit interviews to establish reasons for leaving. Other examples are post-course assessments, views on aspects of current working practice, checking understanding of a new payment scheme, or testing the value of a house newspaper.

The questionnaire is a method of finding out, but very different from the finding out that is deployed in the selection interview that we considered earlier: it is more like the finding out that is used in application forms. The source of information, however, is not a sole individual where there is the need to shape the enquiry to the respondent as the interview proceeds. The questionnaire is intended to produce aggregate information from a group of people. Precise questions have to be prepared in advance with great care so that all respondents will understand them in the same way and provide an inflexible pattern of focused responses. In other words, the questionnaire must be designed to elicit responses that are answers to exactly the question presented and not to a similar but different question that the questionnaire has not asked.

ACTIVITY XIV.1

For which of the following would an attitude survey be an appropriate method of finding out the information required:

1 the sales prospects of a new line in cutlery;

2 the most popular dates for a company close-down at Christmas;

3 suggestions for improving company management;

4 the value of team briefing in a company;

5 identifying prospective volunteers for voluntary redundancy?

One of the preconditions for accurate responses is that the respondent should feel confident in the neutrality of the inquiry and in his or her anonymity, so that answers will be truthful and informative, rather than answers that sound right but are misleading. We discovered one survey in XYZ Ltd, a light engineering company, where every sixth question was, 'Is XYZ a great place to work?', so it was hardly neutral.

Preparing a questionnaire

In deciding what the survey is to discover, we begin by considering what this form of enquiry can discover. There are two basic requirements:

1 Respondents must have sufficient common vocabulary for it to be possible to formulate questions which will have the same meaning to all respondents.

2 The questions must be unambiguous so that all respondents understand what information is sought.

Careful pilot investigations, development and pre-testing will provide a final schedule of questions that meets these requirements. For the enquiry to be successful the respondents must, therefore, be a population with sufficient in common to fulfil the expectations. Also, the information sought must be of the type that can be reduced to precise units of response to standard questions. Here is a checklist:

1 What will be the reaction of respondents to the subject of the survey? Responses to questions about payment arrangements are likely to be more guarded than responses on the (slightly) less sensitive topic of catering facilities.

2 How can the subject be presented to respondents to achieve a high degree of useful responses? In-company investigations are less likely to have problems with response rate than those conducted among the public at large, as the respondents are almost a captive population, but the requirement of anonymity makes it possible that you will get some blank or spoilt responses if the initial reaction to the survey is not positive. The presentation of the questionnaire needs not only to make clear its subject and purpose, but also to explain what is expected from the respondent and what will be done with the aggregated information being collected.

3 What is the best order in which to introduce topics? The early questions need to be easy for respondents to understand and reply to accurately, as well as getting them 'on the wavelength' of the enquiry before proceeding to more complex questions.

4 What wording of questions will produce precise data? Spend as much time as possible on writing them out, improving them and trying them out on people. Here you need to take into account vocabulary and semantics; you need to use words that are unequivocal, where the meaning is not likely to 'drift' with the respondent. Another consideration is the distinction between questions to obtain facts and questions to seek opinion. There is more on this topic later.

5 How long will the questionnaire take to complete? The need to know has to be balanced with the ability and willingness of the respondent to reply. Some respondents will have difficulty in maintaining concentration and others will have much more to say than the questionnaire provides for. It is not much use if the questionnaire is fully completed only by the conscientious and enthusiastic. Some people will be fed up after 10–15 minutes, others will still be happily answering after 30.

6 What is the best layout of the survey forms? To some extent this depends on the make-up of the respondent population, but the layout must be clear and easy to follow, with a short explanatory introduction answering the questions 'What is it for?', 'Why me?', 'Is it in my interests to respond?', 'How long will it take?', 'What do I have to do?'. Each section of the form needs to have a short introduction indicating what the respondent is to expect, using phrases such as 'Now we turn to . . .', 'Now we have a slightly different type of question . . .'.

Types of question

In our discussion on face-to-face situations, we made a distinction between closed and open-ended questions (see Chapter 28). It is similar in a questionnaire. There will be some *closed questions* which ask for specific, factual information, like length of service. If the need of the questionnaire is for a precise number of years, it is best done with a box in which the four digits of a year can be written, but if a more general distribution will suffice, there could be a set of choices with a box to tick. For example:

How long have you been with the company? Please tick the appropriate box:

Less than 1 year	☐
1–5 years	☐
6–10 years	☐
More than 10 years	☐

This is easy and more anonymous, giving you the sort of general indication that you need.

Opinion-seeking questions are harder. Face to face you can ask a question like 'What do you think about . . . ?', and gradually shape and focus answers to clarify what the person means. In a questionnaire you have only one chance, so one method is the *forced choice* approach by asking respondents to pick which one of several statements most closely reflects their personal opinion. For example:

1 I understand the new pay arrangements and believe they represent a good way forward.

2 I don't yet fully understand the new pay arrangements, but they seem all right.

3 I don't understand the new pay arrangements and do not see the need to change.

4 I understand the new pay arrangements, but think they need improvement.

5 I understand the new pay arrangements and don't like them at all.

6 I will go along with whatever is suggested.

A different type of forced choice question is where the respondent is asked to rank a series of statements by writing a digit between 1 and 5, 1 and 9 or whatever number of statements is presented, with 1 being closest to the respondent's personal view and so on. There is a need to point out that each digit is used only once.

An alternative type of question is one that asks, 'To what extent do you agree with . . . ?', with a scale of 1–5, 1–7, 1–10 or even 1–3 being provided for the respondent to tick the appropriate box. The end points of such a scale may be labelled 'Disagree completely' or 'Agree completely' or with other more appropriate wording. Some questions may be of the simple Yes/No variety. They are closed because there are only two options, but the options must be precise and clear cut.

Questions such as these save the respondent from needing to find a suitable form of words to express an opinion and to make the process easy. The difficulty is finding a range of statements that reflects reliably the attitudes that are likely to prevail among the people completing the questionnaire. Devising these statements begins the process of classifying the answers.

Another method of seeking opinions is simply to ask respondents to put in writing their opinion on a question, but this is difficult. Some will not have an opinion at all, some will have a vague idea only, some will write clearly and succinctly while others will express themselves poorly on paper. Classifying the answers is a nightmare. One modification is to provide after a forced choice question a box in which the respondent may add further comments. By now you have forced a focus on the respondent's thinking, so *you may* get some additional useful ideas, but do not count on it, and do not be seduced into thinking that one interesting statement is representative of all respondents.

Data analysis

When all the forms are complete and gathered together, analysis of the data begins. This is basically counting the numbers in each category in each section and making sense of those numbers. This will first be done by compiling simple totals of answers, for example those saying 'Yes' and those saying 'No' or whatever the question asked. There may then be a stage of collating the numbers for different groups and perhaps deploying some of the statistical interpretations, such as moving averages or the standard deviation, described earlier in this skills package. Whatever is done is for the sole purpose of answering the classic question 'So what?' Analysis is not just for fun, nor to show how clever you are, but to provide a justification for some form of action to be taken, abandoned or changed.

Report writing

Having processed all the numbers, you now need to write a report to show what the facts mean and how they are related. The information has to be understood and then explained in the report by means of a theory which makes sense of the data. The final, and crucial, stage of the report is producing some conclusions about future action which the interpretation of the facts illuminates.

FURTHER READING

Wilson, N. and Maclean, S. (1994) *Questionnaire Design: A practical introduction*. Newtonabbey: University of Ulster.

Oppenheim, A.N. (2012) *Questionnaire Design, Interviewing and Attitude Measurement*. London, Continuum International.

XV Using consultants

Arnold Weinstock was a leading industrialist in the 1980s and is reported to have said:

Consultants are invariably a waste of money. There has been the occasional instance when a useful idea has come up, but the input we have received has usually been banal and unoriginal, wrapped up in impressive sounding but irrelevant rhetoric. (Caulkin 1997)

The amount of money spent on consultants by the UK government and its agencies has recently been increasing at a rapid rate, and this has been widely criticised by political opponents and by media correspondents expressing great scepticism about the value for money that has been achieved. Unflattering views of consultants persist, whether justified or unjustified, but the problem can be as much with those who employ them as with the consultancies themselves. Too often the reason for calling in consultants is inappropriate or not properly thought through. Some of the reasons are these (although they are rarely expressed this way):

I really don't know how to handle this, so I'll give the job to a consultant.

We're short-staffed since we had our budget cut, so I'll farm it out.

This is going to be really unpopular, so I'll bring in consultants; they can take the blame.

The MD plays golf with X and thinks he would be really useful to us in a consultancy role. I wonder how long it will be before he gets my job?

I think I will bring in a consultant to do some of this difficult stuff. If they mess things up it will prove that those upstairs should never have introduced this crazy idea in the first place – as I told them.

Consultants can rarely produce useful results if the project is simply parcelled up and given to them to get on with, particularly if it is given to them with the grudging or negative attitude expressed above. They may undertake jobs that others do not have the time or skill to do, but their input must always be monitored closely and built in to the rest of what has to be done so that the benefits of their work can be maximised and used in the future, after they have left. Here is an approach to using consultants in HR work.

Describe the problem. What is the issue on which you are thinking of obtaining outside assistance? This is not as obvious as it might seem. If, for example, the marketing director leaves abruptly, the immediate 'problem' presents itself as being to find a replacement, but worrying away at that issue might suggest that the real problem is to find out why the marketing director left so abruptly, especially if the current deputy does not fancy the promotion. You might then reshape your description of the problem as: 'work out why the position of marketing director is untenable'. Be honest. If your motivation is like one of the last three examples quoted above, you are heading for trouble. You must be able to present a consultant with a clear and realistic brief, otherwise you are in trouble.

Work out how to do it without using consultants. Consultants are expensive and they take time because they have to find out exactly how your business works, the structure, the ethos and the personalities of the key players, as well as its policies and products. Time and expense could both be saved if you could find an easier way of dealing effectively with your problem. Perhaps a recently retired senior executive from the organisation could come and spend a few days wandering round and chatting to people to give you a different perspective on the issue, or to show that you are dead right? Have one or two people to lunch to talk it over: say, people from your local CIPD branch or from a nearby business school, provided that you know them and have confidence in them. Talk to the marketing director's deputy to find out what makes the obvious promotion unattractive. You now already have the answers to the first questions that a consultant would ask and can work out how to tackle the problem without turning to a consultant. If you can convince yourself that it is a sound answer, and if you can sell it to your key colleagues and organisational superiors, then the job is done. If you are unsure, or cannot get backing, then move to the next step.

Approach consultants. Provided that you have identified and understood the problem accurately, and provided that you can describe it clearly to someone who has never been inside your business, then you can brief one or more outside suppliers of expertise and invite them to bid for the business. Do not start until you can pass all the tests in that sentence!

Keep control of the project at this stage. Beware of the suggestion that they will come and carry out a preliminary study at your expense before they formulate their approach. Any consultancy will want to work within the framework of their own expertise, but also of their own *experience*. You may not necessarily need some well-practised approach that has worked elsewhere, but in situations that are markedly different from your own. Successful experience elsewhere is invaluable but is limited in value if the organisational context or the business situation is dissimilar. Even large and well-regarded consultancies can be unsuitable. Their breadth of experience in all sorts of different situations may gradually generate an excellent standard product, which they may be reluctant to adapt, or even abandon, if they encounter the unfamiliar.

You have to produce a brief that will be the basis of your dealings with them. You should have the basis after going through the steps suggested above, but the brief needs to be reworked so as to make unequivocal sense to outsiders and to form a framework from which they cannot deviate.

WINDOW ON DUBIOUS PRACTICE

There is a story about a very long-established firm of consultants, which will remain anonymous for obvious reasons, that had a practice of responding to a call for help from a company by flying in a team of three to carry out a free preliminary investigation that would take up to five days. The story goes that their mission was to locate a possible crisis in the business and to estimate what the company would be able to pay to solve the problem. The team would then prepare to leave before reporting to the chief executive that the 'real' problem was both different and more serious than they 'had been led to believe'. They would finalise their conversation in one of two ways. If they had decided that the business would be able to pay a significant amount, then they would offer to brief other colleagues about the crisis when they returned who could prepare a fully costed proposal for the chief executive's consideration. If they had decided that the company was in a bad way, they would simply leave with apologies.

Like all apocryphal stories there is probably a great deal of exaggeration in this one and the practice is extremely rare nowadays, but it is wise to be wary. One of the people who told a version of how he might have been misled by such a report explained that there had been a problem that the consultants had spotted and that he had missed, but it certainly was not a crisis; he solved it quite easily and quickly, so he had no regrets.

Decide between alternatives. You now have to decide whether to continue with the consultants or to pursue your own rough-cut strategy. If the consultants can produce the most desirable outcome, can you afford it? Have you the resources to implement your own plan? How much time do you have?

Own the solution. If you do decide to continue with the consultants, your objective must be to control the next phase and to follow implementation closely, creating a situation in which local ownership of the solution is achieved as quickly as possible. Only when the new arrangements are working well and owned by your own people will the implantation be complete.

SUMMARY PROPOSITIONS

XV.1   Using consultants can often fail because there is insufficient clarity in briefing them and a reluctance to work closely with them on the project.

XV.2   Suggested steps in using consultants are (a) describe the problem, (b) work out how to solve the problem without consultants, (c) approach consultants, (d) decide between the alternatives and (e) own the solution.

GENERAL DISCUSSION TOPICS

1   Earlier we quoted, 'This is going to be really unpopular, so I'll bring in consultants; they can take the blame.' Is this a manager avoiding unfairly and unrealistically a proper responsibility, or is it a sensible way of dealing with a problem on the grounds that management is weakened by making itself unpopular?

2   What aspects of HR work do you think are most suitable for using consultants?

THEORY INTO PRACTICE

You have recently been appointed to replace the HR director in an organisation where members of the board felt that HR practice had become over-preoccupied with fashionable ideas and was not meeting the needs of the business and the people who worked there. They have asked you to review the ways in which HRM is being conducted across the entire business, within the line as well as by the HR specialists.

On investigation you find:

1 A scheme of employee involvement in management decision making has foundered because of resistance from two unions with members in the organisation, whose representatives were excluded from discussions about the proposals; and by reservations held by a number of senior managers, who felt that the scheme had not been properly thought through and that it was too radical.

2 The concept of performance management has been introduced at the same time as moves to empower line managers. Many line managers feel that empowerment means no more than their taking the blame for things that go wrong, and many of their subordinates feel that they are now cut off from the centralised, expert services of the HR function.

3 Members of the HR function say that they have lost credibility and job satisfaction by a series of grandiose schemes that were not fully developed and which could not be fully implemented in a short time.

4 Reporting to you are three people:

   – Charles is the long-serving Training Officer, whose opening comment to you was, 'In training I try to see it as establishing a learning community that is separate from the hurly burly of commercial operations.'

   – Henry is the Employee Relations Manager, currently on holiday.

   – Susan is the Personnel Manager, a recent appointee of your predecessor with the task of coordinating and developing the HR operation. Your first conversation with her begins with her saying, 'I hope you don't mind if I speak frankly, but I am totally frustrated. Catherine [your predecessor] was off the wall. It was all about changing everything, but she had no grasp of the practicalities of running a business and knew nothing of HR. They hired her because she had a PhD in marketing, but she was hopeless. Henry is all right, up to a point. He certainly has his finger on the pulse on the shop floor, but he has problems with women in positions of authority. He copes with me but Catherine was another matter. She insisted on an employee involvement scheme that was radical to an extreme, and she refused any consultation with the unions. Henry did not simply disagree with her scheme (quite rightly in my view) but it also confirmed his prejudice about women.'

You are now six months into the job and things are going well. Charles has left in order to take a job as a lecturer in a further education college in charge of a group of apprentices. Henry is changing his view of women and is now working very well after you had a long discussion with him about his understanding of Catherine's employee involvement proposals. He is working on a modification to that plan, which he believes will deliver what the members of the board will encourage and of which he thinks he can get shop floor acceptance. He is due to discuss it with you next week. Susan has calmed down and clearly has a lot to offer.

Exercises

1 You need to replace Charles.

   (a) Referring back to Chapter 7 and to Skill III in the previous chapter, how would you rate, from 1 to 7, the following in their importance in identifying the most appropriate candidate – and why?

Experience	Qualifications	Aptitude testing
Personality testing	Trainability testing	General intelligence testing
Competencies		

   (b) Assume you have fifty applications, of which you decide twenty are worth interviewing. What statistical analysis, if any, would you use at any further stage in the selection process?

   (c) Who should interview the candidates, and how (e.g. you, Henry and Susan individually; you and a board member together; you, Henry, Susan and a board member together; or some other arrangement)?

   (d) In the light of your answer to (a) above, what other means of assessment would you use when the candidates come for interview, and why?

2 Henry was not making his full contribution because of a poor relationship with Catherine, based on his attitude towards working with women. It is now apparent to you that there are other long-serving employees who share this attitude. Referring to Chapters 16, 19, 21 and Skills III and IV in the previous chapter, what sort of initiatives will you consider to deal with this problem?

3 Surf the Internet for news stories about cases of alleged bullying at work. Which of the methods in Skill X in the previous chapter would you regard as especially appropriate to forestall such incidents?

4 Think of a situation in your experience where a number of people have been working together in one place. It might be a workplace where you were employed, a sports team or a course on which you were a member, a voluntary body you joined, or anything similar.

   (a) Identify a topic on which you would like to canvas opinion among the people involved, preferably one that is not too simple!

   (b) Prepare a questionnaire for use, following recommendations in Skill XIV above.

   (c) What methods will you use to analyse your data?

   EITHER:

   (d) Explain your answers to questions (a) to (c) above to a small group of friends or fellow students and discuss their criticisms.

   OR:

   (e) Test and then administer the questionnaire, analysing the results.

   (f) What have you learnt from this exercise?

FURTHER READING

Two books of general interest on the subject from a US perspective are:

Lewis, H. (2008) *Choosing and Using Consultants and Advisers*. London: Kogan Page.

Zahn, D. (2004) *The Quintessential Guide to Using Consultants*. New York: HRD Press.

WEB LINKS

Finding and Using Consultants, available at **www.cim.co.uk**.

Using Consultants in Your Business, available at **www.yoursmallbusiness.co.uk**.

REFERENCE

Caulkin, S. (1997) 'The great consultancy cop-out', *Management Today*, February, pp. 32–8.

Glossary

The terms in this glossary have been taken selectively from the text. Rather than repeating definitions we have already given, we have chosen terms which are neologisms that may not appear in a dictionary, or are invented words, like presenteeism, which do not yet appear in a dictionary. We also include terms, like bureaucracy, which can benefit from more interpretation than we have provided in the text.

Absence/attendance. Until quite recently attendance at work was universally accepted as a duty and absence had to be justified by external verification, such as by a medical note or a call to undertake jury service. Without such independent evidence, some sort of punishment was usual. As social attitudes have changed and rights to time off have increased, so the managerial emphasis has changed, requiring managers to manage attendance, by paying attention to reasons for avoidable absence. This has a degree of altruistic concern for employee well-being, where some aspect of the work required from employees is a contributory cause of, for instance, an inability to return to work. There is also an emphasis on trying to minimise disruption to working patterns and persuading people not to be unreasonable. Stress has become a major absence factor since it has become more socially acceptable. Usually it is a perfectly valid feature of a person's working or personal life and can perhaps be alleviated by managerial initiatives. In some other situations it is manipulated by people who place their own interpretation on a right to sick leave. A recent visit to an engineering drawing office in March was surprising as more than half the staff were missing. The drawing office manager explained that the absentees were 'getting in their sick leave' before the end of the leave year. A management attempt to make allowance for understandable sickness absence had been mismanaged in allowing it to become gradually accepted as an additional leave entitlement. In a different, current situation a school teacher has recently shown such unwillingness to implement new professional requirements that there is a risk of the school implementing capability procedure with the response, 'if they do that I will simply go off with stress'.

Apprenticeship. The typical idea of an apprentice is of a male who left school as soon as possible and then trained on the job in a manual trade like plumbing or as an electrician, possibly continuing education part time at a local college. Since a university degree has gradually become the must-have qualification for many fields of employment, the number of apprentices has dwindled: certainly not a prelude to a 'nice job'. Currently they are seeing a renaissance, as skills shortages are seen as an impediment to economic growth, but not necessarily for young males. In 2013 more than half of those pursuing an apprenticeship were over 25.

Benchmarking. Originally a benchmark was a mark on a work bench that could be used to measure off a standard size. This idea of comparative measurement is used in HRM to describe the process of checking some aspect of work in one's own business against an external standard, like the average number of days lost through absence across the working population as a whole, or in a particular industry, by age, occupation, gender and so forth. It is slightly different from 'yardstick', which is literally a measuring stick a yard long. This is sometimes used as a rough-and-ready measure for some aspect of management effectiveness, but it lacks the dimension of external comparison.

Best fit/fit. In many fields of human endeavour there is an aim to find and implement the one best way, or the right way, of doing things. An alternative is to work out the best way of doing things in this or that situation. There is no single approach or method that is always right.

Bottom line. A term derived from accountancy, where it is the final total in a profit and loss statement or other financial document. In management generally it is used as the ultimate criterion or most important factor: financial viability.

Brand. A term taken from marketing to describe a company or product name that is very distinctive and powerful. Examples are Coca-Cola, Microsoft, Rolls-Royce or Virgin. It was illustrated by the retail director of a fashion chain who said, 'If I buy a ready meal from X and I don't like it, I take it back. If I buy it from Marks & Spencer, either I haven't followed the instructions or there is something wrong with my cooker.' To HR people the company brand can be very important in matters of commitment and recruitment.

Bureaucracy. This has become almost a term of abuse, describing rigidity, lack of responsiveness by staff, lack of willingness to take responsibility and too much emphasis on the rules. It is, however, a time-honoured method of making any large organisation work. In contemporary business usage it describes a type of centralised social order that makes things happen by having guidelines of policy, procedure and precedent to empower role holders to do their jobs, conferring appropriate authority for action as well as limiting the scope for individual whim or prejudice. It is therefore both more acceptable and more practical as a method of organisation for any large undertaking than relying on the autocratic alternative of everything being decided by a small number of people at the centre, while everyone else waits and grumbles. HR managers are occasionally derided by some of their colleagues in other

functions for their apparent preoccupation with the 'rules' of procedure and employment law. These colleagues are, of course, wrong, but bureaucracy has a serious inherent flaw in that it always grows, requiring frequent pruning and review.

Career. The idea of a career involving moving from job to job is relatively recent. For most people a career was an occupation, like nursing or teaching or carpentry or bricklaying. It was only in bureaucracies that people looked for a promotional ladder. In most of the long-standing professions a career was a lifetime of doing the same job, although perhaps introducing a change of emphasis. A clergyman was a clergyman, even though a few might become deans or bishops. A writer was a writer, although there might be moves from writing poetry to writing novels. An architect is an architect, a dentist is a dentist, a driver is a driver. In some areas the idea of moving 'up' has been created artificially by inventing new pay grades and titles. Until the 1970s nursing in the UK had three levels: nurse, sister and matron. In order to provide a career structure, new jobs were introduced: nursing officer, senior nursing officer and principal nursing officer. The flattening of hierarchies is changing the emphasis. There is now a greater number of sideways, cross-functional moves than vertical moves, thus the increasing trend for careers to involve changes in occupation.

Casual work is work where someone is employed on a temporary and probably irregular basis without any obligation on either party to further employment when a spell is complete.

Change initiatives are often regarded as invariably desirable, particularly by consultants trying to sell you something. Although constantly advocated in HRM, they have to be balanced against other issues such as stability and security. Furthermore, few changes in HR practice can be made quickly and easily. The ideas are usually easy or obvious. Getting them accepted and making them work requires a great deal of hard work, which means that changes have to be worth the trouble and not just some transitory idea that will have been overtaken by something else in six months' time. 'Initiative fatigue' is a term used to describe the experience of some people who have scarcely got used to one new initiative before another is imposed that contradicts the first.

Clocking on (or in) is a term still in common usage, although the practice is not now widespread. In the heyday of large-scale production businesses, manual employees registered their arrival for work by operating an automatic time-recording machine, usually by punching a hole in a personal card. Sometimes they clocked out as well as on. This gave a reliable record of hours worked and enabled pay calculations to be made. Although initially seen as a way to be fair, it eventually became a symbol of close, overbearing control – 'the tyranny of clocking on'. It has become less common although variants are used by, for example, security staff who clock their arrival at various parts of the premises at regular times during the night, or by managers of motorway service stations to demonstrate that they have recently checked the cleanliness of the toilets. A refinement and extension of clocking is the tachograph in road-haulage vehicles.

Coach/mentor/protégé. A coach is someone who gives specialised training and guidance as well as general support and encouragement. This may be to an individual, like a tennis player, or to a team, as in cricket. A mentor gives the same sort of service to an individual in what is often a very close personal relationship, requiring from the protégé a high degree of trust in the integrity and goodwill of the mentor. A protégé is someone who is guided by a mentor, acknowledging a need for that person's greater standing and expertise. Novak Djokovic is the world's most successful tennis player, but still needs a coach: he is not the coach's protégé. One of the most ghastly bits of management jargon is the word 'mentee', presumably invented by someone who could not cope with three syllables, as an alternative to protégé.

Commitment is widely used in contemporary HR to describe the quality of being dedicated to the cause, and various methods are used (see Chapter 9, for example) to develop this quality among the members of the workforce in their dedication to the cause of company success. Some may be committed to a career or to the employment security that is associated with the success of the business, while others are committed to the success of their career perhaps at the expense of the business, and others have no commitment at all. In these circumstances the value of the brand may be important.

Competitive advantage. Any business has to be competitive,

no matter how much many of its members may not like the idea. A school has to be seen by parents to be at least as good as other schools, otherwise parents will remove their children and the pupils will not have self-respect. Commercial organisations seek competitive advantage for more immediate reasons of survival, but schools, hospitals, charities and churches will all decline and may close if they do not meet the current needs and expectations of their 'clients', although they will quite rightly cavil at the terms 'customers' or 'clients'.

Contingency is a word much used in sociology and organisation theory. Apart from its normal usage of describing a possible future event that cannot be predicted with certainty, in management it is used to differentiate from the absolute. Solutions to problems are seldom invariably right: it depends on the particular circumstances of the event.

Contract/consideration. In this book the use of material about contract is mainly about legal agreements, although there is also the reference to psychological contracts. The fundamental principle of a legal contract is that there must be consideration. A contract is a spoken or written agreement that is intended to be enforceable at law, but the offer of agreement by one party only becomes legally enforceable when there is consideration from the other party, that is an undertaking of some sort, to do something or to stop doing something or to abandon a claim. An offer of employment, for instance, is not legally binding on the employer making the offer until and unless the prospective

employee accepts the offer and agrees to provide the work (consideration) that the employer is offering. This same sense of reciprocity is equally fundamental to the psychological contract: there must be an agreed exchange. Contracting out (from a pension scheme, for instance) involves withdrawing from an agreement and thereby relinquishing the benefits that would otherwise have been received.

Culture/organisational culture. In management circles interest in culture is an attempt to grasp the realities of collective life in a department or organisation that cannot be easily seen and described with such identifiers as job titles, departments and organisation charts. It is an aspect of the hard/soft distinction. Recently it has been especially important in explaining the differences in management practice in various countries, but organisational culture refers to the beliefs, conventions and general patterns of behaviour that characterise a particular organisation.

Delayering is a method of downsizing that reduces the number of people in a hierarchy by removing a tier in the organisation structure.

Demographics describe statistical data relating to the age and gender structure of the population. They are an important element in understanding the labour market.

Diversity is subtly different from equality and refers principally to the value to management of making the most of employees from two distinct groups, women and those from ethnic minorities, rather than assuming that core employees are white and male. Although these two groups have been the main focus of debate and action, greater attention has recently been paid to other groups, such as those who are potentially discriminated against on the grounds of age or disability.

Downsizing describes an approach to increasing organisational efficiency by reducing the number of people employed in the business and therefore reducing the costs associated with their employment. The main methods are delayering and outplacement/outsourcing.

Employee relations/industrial relations are not simply different terms for the same activities; they denote a significant change of emphasis. Concern with industrial relations developed when the emphasis was on collective relationships within an industry, such as engineering, agriculture or teaching. Each business within the ambit of that industry observed the terms and conditions agreed between employers' representatives and unions, which bound every employer. Employee relations have little regard for industry criteria and focus on collective arrangements within an individual business.

Employee voice is a term that has only come into use during the twenty-first century, largely as a result of the globalisation issue (see Chapter 2). It refers to a wide variety of processes and structures which enable people to contribute to decision making in the place where they work and perhaps to influence decision making in other places that affect the place where they work.

Environment. We typically think nowadays of the physical environment in which we live and the environmental issues that are of concern: pollution, greenhouse gases, GM crops, vulnerable species and so forth. In HRM it is more likely to refer to the social, political and legal environment of the business.

Flexibility is something managers try hard to achieve and trade unions and the legal system try to limit. The flexible workforce makes managerial life easier by giving more scope to managers to manipulate the labour supply, as do flexible hours arrangements. Flexibility agreements with unions reduce rigidity in work practices. All these practices reduce the problems of bureaucracy but the advantages for employees may be more mixed. Flexible hours are probably the most attractive, but there are always disadvantages for employees with flexibility initiatives that at least slightly erode their personal security.

Globalisation/internationalization are both terms coined recently to describe two slightly different aspects of modern business. Many companies work internationally, importing materials and resources and exporting products and services. If their business expands they may appoint agents in overseas countries to represent their interests, or they may establish overseas subsidiaries. The company remains with a distinctive national head office and branding. Globalisation represents a distinctive further step as the company operates major businesses in different countries and regions. Its national identity is submerged beneath its global identity and branding. As these businesses grow larger and therefore more powerful, some commentators and pressure groups grow very concerned that their commercial interests can destabilise and harm the economies of individual countries, especially smaller countries in the developing world.

Grievance/discipline. Everyone who is employed has a contract in two parts. The first part is the wage/work bargain. One party to the contract pays money and provides benefits to the other party, who provides work in exchange. The second part of the contract is the psychological contract, referred to throughout this book, where what is exchanged between the two parties is a less tangible – but no less important – form of satisfaction. Both parts of the contract are maintained through the mutual satisfaction of the parties. When something happens to reduce the level of satisfaction of either party, HRM uses the terms 'grievance' or 'discipline' to describe the processes whereby satisfaction may be restored.

Hard/soft. Hard data is precise and can be accurately measured by numbers and statistical calculation. Soft data is less precise but may be more important in planning. It includes judgement, assessment and informed guesswork.

Hierarchy is the system of organisation which ranks all the people according to their status or authority. This is used for all manner of purposes, ranging from the trivial, like who has the biggest office and who is allowed to travel first class, to the identification of who is empowered to do what, as the hierarchical system includes titles or labels to make sense of the jobs that people do. In the UK the growth of hierarchy received a boost when an early management theorist, E.F.L. Brech, advanced his theory of the span of control, saying that no manager should supervise directly the work of four or five subordinates *whose work interlocks*. Many people accepted the theory but conveniently forgot the last three words.

Human capital. Economists, rather reluctantly, conceded that any economic analysis of an organisation or an economy needed to include the concept of a value or cost assigned to skills, knowledge or experience of the population. It has proved a more acceptable and useful concept than the sterile accountancy technique of human asset accounting. Its main value to HR practitioners is the idea that human capital requires investment.

The Human Relations School. A school of thought that developed in the 1930s as a reaction against the perceived mechanical thinking of scientific management. It aimed to develop high productivity by concentrating on the well-being of the individual worker and the surrounding social relationships in the workplace, with an emphasis on adapting the task to the worker rather than adapting the worker to the task.

Marketplace/labour market. The importance of both these concepts (taken from economics) in HRM is to emphasise that people management can never be entirely inward in focus. The business has to operate in a context in which there is a market for its products or service, and the business has to survive in that market no matter how inconvenient it may be for the

people inside the business. Equally there is an external market for labour and skills, which cannot be ignored. Even employees totally loyal to the business will be aware of prevailing conditions elsewhere, not only how much people are paid but also conditions of work, hours and fringe benefits.

Matrix is a term that has recently come into popular currency because of film and television programmes using it in a very specialised way. In management it has long been used to describe a particular form of organisation in which levels of specialisation, accountability and responsibility are set out in vertical columns crossed by horizontal lines, with points of intersection identifying individual people who have a line of communication in one direction (line management) as well as a distinct accountability to someone else. An office manager, for instance, might be responsible for most things to the immediate superior, but accountable to the HR manager for health and safety issues. 'The line' is often mentioned in this book and refers to the vertical line of accountability.

Meta-analysis is an analysis which combines a number of existing analyses already carried out by others into one summary analysis. 'Meta' is a scientific term indicating a change in condition, such as in metamorphosis. In social sciences it denotes something beyond, of a higher-order kind.

Mission/aims/objectives/targets. These are all terms used quite loosely in management jargon and are in a rough hierarchy from the broad to the specific. Mission comes from religion and is used in a

business to describe what the organisation is for, what its purpose is. A mission statement is typically vague and general, but can be useful in developing commitment. Aims and objectives describe the more specific purposes of individual functions, departments, teams or individuals within the mission framework. Targets are very specific and usually short term as stages on the way for teams and individuals to achieve longer-term objectives. Recently we have seen examples of how targets can be a dangerous distraction from mission, as when some hospitals concentrated so hard on a target of reducing a financial deficit that they lost focus on their clear mission to care for the sick.

Occupational health. Many businesses describe their medical departments as 'Occupational Health' departments, regardless of the skills possessed by the people who work in them, but it is worth bearing in mind that occupational medicine is a defined specialism, not general practice in an occupational setting. Both doctors and nurses can acquire qualifications in occupational medicine, but they are most likely to be needed in a business with specific hazards, like radiation or toxic materials.

Organisation. Few words have attracted so much attention in so many different areas of human enquiry, fascinating administrators, anthropologists, archaeologists, biologists, economists, military strategists, political activists and theorists, psychologists, sociologists, trade unionists and many more. This plethora of perspectives can be confusing or even bewildering when trying to define a management perspective that comes within the

649

purview of this book, especially for those whose education has included a thorough grounding in such widely taught subjects as economics, psychology or sociology. Basically our interest is in two meanings of the word, organisation as an arena in which human activity takes place (an **entity**) and organisation as a way of getting things done in such an arena (a **process**). To most academics the first is of much greater interest than the second; to most managers the second is of more interest than the first.

HR managers need to understand first the contexts within which their organisation or entity operates. There is the political context which provides a legal and broad administrative framework of benefits and limitations. The social context includes the availability of prospective employees, the educational situation and the prevailing ethical standards that govern attitudes and behaviour. Every organisational entity exists within a market, or series of markets. If there is not sufficient demand for the products and services that are offered, the entity will eventually wither and die. This is not only true of commercial activities. In 1780 Robert Raikes started a Sunday School for the children of chimney sweeps in the appropriately named Sooty Alley in the centre of Gloucester. This was the first time that education of any type apart from the memorising of catechisms had been provided for working-class children and adults. Sunday Schools spread rapidly, so that four years later there were nearly 2,000 pupils in Manchester and Salford and in Leeds. They continued to flourish for a century until their function was taken over

by the secular authorities. Sunday Schools steadily declined as centres for general education until the middle of the twentieth century before they finally relinquished that function.

Organisation behaviour, organisational development, organisational psychology all focus on the micro-entity of the individual business or businesses. Organisational psychology, for instance, studies the interaction between working people and their employing organisational entity and the resultant behaviour of those people.

Outplacement/outsourcing. There is a small difference between these two terms. Outplacement describes taking a complete activity and shifting it to a supplier, while outsourcing describes looking outside the business for human resources without the responsibility of being the legal employer.

Peers is an equivocal term in the UK because it has two meanings. One is to describe members of the aristocracy: earls, baronets, dukes, marquesses and viscounts. In this book, and in more general usage, it describes people of the same age, status, ability or qualification as oneself. A peer group is therefore a group of one's equals, not one's superiors.

Performance. Everyone wants effective performance. The individual wants the satisfaction of achievement and results, managers want individuals to be effectively coordinated and productive, customers want a good product and good service at the right price, governments want efficient

businesses in a growing economy. Achieving performance is complicated. It is not simply paying people lots of money, although not paying people enough money may well inhibit performance. It is not simply being nice to people and releasing them from supervision, as without supervision they may do the wrong things. Achieving effective performance also varies according to the work done. A symphony orchestra requires members of great expertise at different instruments, yet all must work to an identical score under the strict leadership of the conductor, with very little scope for individual flair. The jazz quartet is more loosely coordinated, with many individual riffs. Those working for a courier firm or in the operating theatre of a hospital can only perform well by following a tight schedule arranged by someone else. Those working in an advertising agency have a much looser rein in order to encourage their creativity.

Portfolio is a collection of items that represent a person's work. Very familiar for people whose work can best be demonstrated by examples, like painters or cartoonists, it is also now much used by all classes of worker to demonstrate their skills and accomplishments, thereby justifying a qualification to practise.

Presenteeism. Absenteeism is defined in the dictionary as regularly staying away from work without good reason, but is scarcely used in this book. It is included here simply to give point to its antonym 'presenteeism', a term recently coined to describe the practice of people coming to work when they should not, as when unwell, for instance. Some people feel they may lose their job or a promotion opportunity if they are away.

Reactive/proactive. This distinction is important in HRM because there is a natural emphasis in people matters to await developments and deal with them (reactive). Many HR people report that they spend much of their time putting right problems created by the impetuosity or thoughtlessness of their colleagues in other functions. There is also a need, however, to create opportunities for growth and change and to think ahead of issues so that problems can be averted. A well-rounded HR/personnel function is able to maintain a balance between both types of approach, vigorously and calmly sorting out problems or disasters but also taking matters forward in a creative way when the problems are all under control.

Recruitment/selection. Recruitment is the process whereby a business seeks applicants either generally or for particular vacancies. Potential applicants are interested but there is no mutual obligation. Selection is the process whereby not only does the employer choose between two or more interested applicants, but applicants also select, deciding how much further they wish to pursue their original enquiry. The end of the process is a legally binding agreement.

Resourcing. This term has only recently come into common usage and means simply providing the needed resources. For HR people this is providing the human resources that are needed, although some pedantic academics (like at least one of your authors) dislike the term 'employee resourcing' as it is

the employing organisation that is being provided with resources, not the employees. Also employees are not the only source of human resources for the business. Consultants or subcontractors are alternative sources.

Ritual is a series of actions or a type of behaviour that is invariably followed, in accordance with a convention. Developed originally to help people feel secure in the mysteries of religious practices, rituals are widespread in contemporary society (the ritual of going to the pub on Friday after work, the ritual of the pre-match huddle, the ritual of Prime Minister's Question Time). All provide the benefit of enabling people to feel comfortable and accepted in a social situation, and are therefore important in many employment situations where there is a felt need to conform to existing conventions. The selection interview is the most obvious. Other examples are the 'leaving do', collections before a marriage, negotiations, and the office party.

Scenario. A method of envisaging the future is to bring together various bits of evidence, both hard and soft, and fit them together in a way that describes a reliable version of the future in X years' time.

Scientific management. The first modern theory of management, formulated by F.W. Taylor and using the principles of industrial engineering to raise productivity by adapting the worker to the machine or the process. It relied heavily on adjusting the worker's earnings to the level of individual output. The basic ideas remain in place and are at the root of many payment

systems, but most management academics and commentators throughout the last three-quarters of the twentieth century disparaged and deplored the 'mechanistic and inhuman' practices spawned by scientific management.

Sex/gender. The word sex is pretty clear in its meaning as describing either a range of interesting activities, or to describe the biological distinction between male and female. Until recently gender was a grammatical term to distinguish between classes of noun or pronoun in some languages, loosely based on natural distinctions of sex: masculine, feminine or neuter. It is now also used to refer to social and cultural differences between the sexes.

SMEs. Small and Medium-sized Enterprises in full. The European Commission has defined SMEs as either micro-entities with less than 10 employees, small businesses with less than 50 and medium-sized businesses having less than 250. Their significance is that they outnumber larger businesses by some distance and they are seen as an engine for innovation and economic growth. In the Preface we mentioned the example of a small business with thirteen employees that had been bought for £1 billion.

Statutory rights. Rights of the individual citizen or citizens that derive explicitly from a statute or Act of Parliament.

Stress presents managers with two problems. An employee may be absent from work suffering from stress, but this is a condition that is easy to fake and not easy to diagnose. How does a manager detect malingering and take appropriate action? More significantly, a manager may exacerbate or cause stress in someone. How can this be avoided and what remedies are available to employees? A further complication is that stress is not necessarily undesirable. Any football fan will suffer periods of intense stress when the wrong team is winning a match, but this only makes sweeter the euphoria when the right team wins. Stress can be stimulating as well as harmful and some jobs are best done and most enjoyed where there is frequent stress followed by achievement (journalists' deadlines and surgical crises being two examples).

Tells. 'I love you' is a statement by one person to another that is normally accompanied by certain actions and behaviours that demonstrate to the recipient how sincere the feeling is. Sometimes, however, we say things that we do not believe, or of which we are unsure. Then the listener may try to guess what we really mean, not just what the words say. We give clues to our uncertainty or our truthfulness by what we do, especially what we cannot help doing. These are tells. Blushing shows we are embarrassed, many people put their hands to their mouths when they feel guilty. HR managers need to learn what tells to look for in situations like selection, where not all candidates are strictly accurate in what they say, or in appraisal, where people may be very guarded in what they say.

Tribunal in this book refers almost exclusively to the three-person panel that makes up the employment tribunal that decides matters of employment law, although it can be any sort of body used to settle disputes. It is not always made up of three people, but it is normal to have an odd number to avoid deadlock.

Unitarist/pluralist. For HRM these terms come from industrial relations analysis. A unitarist thinker believes that all authority and all responsibility are centred in one place or person, so that senior management can, and must, decide on all key issues, while other people involved simply have to accept the consequences. The pluralist says that is both unacceptable and impractical. Employees have a legitimate interest in the business that cannot be disregarded; the local community is another important stakeholder.

Index